L.A. Marathon

The First Ten Years

LOS ANGELES TIMES SYNDICATE

AND

THE CITY OF LOS ANGELES MARATHON

Los Angeles, California

ON THE COVER: *Julie Isphording of Cincinnati wins the women's open at the 1990 L.A. Marathon.*
Photo: Thomas Kelsey, Los Angeles Times

Editor's Note: Valuable assistance in compiling this book was provided by a number of persons associated with the City of Los Angeles Marathon.
Thanks especially to Bill Burke, President; Marie Patrick, Vice President; Amy Jonesco, Press Manager; Brooks Roddan,
Roddan and Paolucci Advertising and Public Relations; and Howard L. Bingham, photographer.
Special thanks to the writers and photographers of the Los Angeles Times, whose work is reproduced in many of these pages.
Finally, thanks to the thousands of runners whose participation in the L.A. Marathon made this book possible.

Los Angeles Times Syndicate

Jesse Levine, President and CEO

Project Director: Don Michel
Editor: Noel Greenwood

Produced by: Bill Dorich, I.P.A. Graphics Management, Inc.
Book Design: Patricia Moritz

Library of Congress Catalog Card Number: 95-76143
ISBN 1-883792-08-8
Copyright © 1995, Los Angeles Times Syndicate

Times Mirror Square 90053
Los Angeles, California

First Printing April 1995
Printed and bound in Hong Kong

Contents

Foreword

ROD DIXON, A 22-YEAR CAREER RUNNER, WAS BRONZE MEDALIST IN THE 1972 OLYMPICS AND WINNER OF THE 1983 NEW YORK MARATHON. HE HELPED ORGANIZE THE L.A. MARATHON AND RAN THE FIRST THREE YEARS. HE RESIDES IN HIS NATIVE NEW ZEALAND.

Dixon (foreground, in white) runs L.A. in 1987.

Ten years after it began, the L.A. Marathon clearly ranks in the first tier of the world's great marathons, along with New York, Boston and London.

That's an incredible accomplishment for a city so reliant on the automobile.

Years ago, the attitude among runners was that you came into L.A., did what you had to do, and then headed East to the more serious running communities. It was a bit scary to run in Los Angeles. Motorists would try to run you over or throw things at you or yell abuse at you. It was an automobiles-only city with too much traffic, too many intersections, and not too many sidewalks.

Now, if you're in running gear, motorists stop to let you go through—even if they have the green light. People root for you when they see you out running. That didn't happen 20 years ago.

■

My feelings about Los Angeles changed when I ran in the 1984 Olympic marathon here. The city's enthusiasm was so great that I thought L.A. might be ready for its own marathon. Two years later, Bill Burke and Marie Patrick invited me to help them organize the first City of Los Angeles Marathon.

Bill had a vision. He knew what he wanted to achieve. First and foremost, it was to be a people's race. If this marathon was going to succeed, everyday people had to embrace it.

That meant everybody had to be treated the same, from the first person to the last. Because somebody runs faster, it is not a good enough reason to care less about everyone else. I have a lot of respect for the people who are out there for 5 hours. They've got to be looked after a little better, to be sure the water's there when they come through, to know there is medical help available. At some other marathons, I had heard runners say, "Nobody cared about me." We didn't want to hear that in Los Angeles.

■

The proof of L.A.'s success is in the number of people who continue to participate. When 20,000 or so runners show up each year, someone likes it. And everybody gets something a little different out of it. I think that's why people still talk about the event days after. Nobody gets tired of talking about it or hearing about it.

The fans are different from when we started. They're more knowledgeable, more educated as to what the marathon's about.

And they give the runners a real lift. Runners come up to get their cups of water, and they get encouragement. All along the course, they get encouragement. If you stop to do your shoelaces up or catch your wind, people call out, "Come on, go for it…You're looking great."

■

Runners today have the advantage of better footwear, more knowledge of how the body works, the importance of fluids and carbohydrates and all that. But the marathon is no easier than it was 200 years ago. It's still 26 miles and 385 yards to the end.

I like to think that anyone who finishes has achieved a dream. I don't care if you are the first or the last across the finish line. You challenged yourself, set your own agenda and beat the odds. You did it for yourself, by yourself.

It's a great accomplishment, a personal triumph. That's why everyone who finishes in L.A. gets a medal. In a very real way, everyone's a winner. This book is a celebration of that spirit.

"It's more than a marathon, it's a happening."

—Radio broadcaster at 1987 race

nybody studying the history of marathons in Los Angeles would have bet against the success of the City of Los Angeles Marathon when it was first proposed.

There had been at least four previous attempts at staging such events, all with disappointing results. At one race in the early 1980s, the course was so badly marked that many runners lost their way after the first mile. A magazine for runners declared Los Angeles to be the "Bermuda Triangle for marathons."

Then Bill Burke and business partner Marie Patrick staged the first running of the City of Los Angeles Marathon in 1986—and turned marathon history upside down.

On its 10th anniversary, the L.A. Marathon—as it's come to be know—is the third largest in the world, attracting more than 19,000 runners and 1 million-plus spectators each year. Many more watch the live TV coverage in the U.S. and overseas.

One running expert has called the Los Angeles race "the best-marketed, slickest, most modern...of the world's major marathons."

■

The field of competitors is amazingly varied. Elite runners from around the world chase the big prize money and merchandise, including new automobiles. So-called stunt runners dressed in animal costumes or flipping pancakes or impersonating Elvis Presley provide comic relief. Wheelchair racers impress with their speed and strength. An array of physically challenged runners—with artificial limbs, or on crutches, or

Introduction

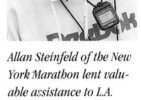

Allan Steinfeld of the New York Marathon lent valuable assistance to L.A. Marathon organizers.

The Los Angeles Marathon, founded in 1986, is the youngest of the major American marathons.

Boston, the granddaddy of them all, was launched in 1897, just one year after the first modern Olympic Games. New York came along in 1972, sparked by the 70s jogging craze.

But L.A. got off to a faster start than most. The first New York marathon drew 127 entrants. The opening race in L.A. attracted 10,787.

fighting life-threatening illnesses like cancer—inspire with their courage.

And tens of thousands of ordinary people—high school students, nuns, weekend joggers, fathers and sons, moms pushing children in strollers, seniors in their 70s and 80s, entire families—take to the course determined to go the distance. As a Running Times writer covering the 1992 race noted: "Ordinary people named Chet and Jane kiss family members goodbye, swallow their fears, confront them again, persevere and stagger across the finish line."

A touch of celebrity glitz tops it off—Hollywood, after all, is the halfway point in the race.

Heavyweight boxing great Muhammad Ali has become a regular on the starting platform, waving the runners on their way each year. Actors like Corbin Bernsen ("L.A. Law"), Brian Patrick Clark ("General Hospital"), Tim Matheson ("Animal House") and Jack Scalia ("Dallas") have run the race and finished in credible times.

Many more celebrities have given their active support to various marathon activities over the years, including actors Beau Bridges, Cesar Romero and Jack Klugman; Olympic medalists Rafer Johnson, Bob Seagren and Grace Jackson; and former pro football star Roosevelt Grier.

Headline writers have likened the L.A. Marathon to a "a 26-mile-long block party"—in tribute to the festive atmosphere surrounding the event.

The party really begins before the race. Upwards of 100,000 running enthusiasts visit the Quality of Life Expo, a three-day display of health, fitness and related products leading up to race day. On the eve of the marathon, 5,000 or so runners stoke up on pasta, potatoes and other energy food at the traditional Carbo Load Dinner.

On race day, runners leave the starting line to the spirited sounds of Randy Newman's "I Love L.A." Out on the course, entertainment centers keep spirits high with everything from folk dancers and gospel singers to mariachis and rock bands. Friends and relatives crowd sidewalks to shout encouragement at individual runners and wave signs with hand-drawn messages like "You Can Do It!". After the race, 250,000-plus spectators and competitors mingle at the Finish Line Festival.

Spectator George McGee of Los Angeles may have described it best: "The L.A. Marathon is something that everyone can get involved in—no matter what color you are, or how much money you have. It's one of the best events in L.A.—a real bright spot."

In fact, community involvement has been an essential ingredient in the event from the start.

More than 16,000 volunteers—the largest such contingent at any marathon—show up each year to provide medical care, staff water stations and otherwise make the event run smoothly.

Corporate donors, community groups and runners with pledges from the public have raised $6 million-plus in cash and in-kind contributions for more than 200 charitable organizations under a program launched in 1988 by marathon organizers.

Even the course route is a symbol of community involvement. It is a proud reflection of the diversity of Los Angeles: from Exposition Park through Downtown;

An enterprising vendor hawks his products amid festival atmosphere of race day.

past Olvera Street (the city's birthplace), Little Tokyo and Chinatown; up Sunset Boulevard to Hollywood; then through Koreatown, the upscale Hancock Park district and the heart of the city's Central American community before heading to the finish at the historic Los Angeles Coliseum.

■

In a very real sense, the L.A. Marathon owes its existence to the success of the 1984 Olympic Games in Los Angeles.

The games were run like a business and actually turned a profit, thanks to the corporate-sponsorship approach of Peter Ueberroth, who led the city's Olympic organizing committee. Ueberroth's strategy impressed Bill Burke, who was tennis commissioner for the games. Burke was also mindful of the euphoria that swept the city while the games were underway. It was not hard to imagine that some of that enthusiasm might rub off on a marathon.

City officials had similar thoughts, and invited proposals for an officially sanctioned marathon—to be staged, like the Olympics, at no cost to taxpayers.

Burke and his Los Angeles Marathon, Inc. submitted the winning proposal. Now his company had the exclusive right to own and operate the marathon, in return for which it would pay the city a fee. But success did not come easily.

"In the beginning, it was easier to sell the dream than the real event," Burke recalls.

"I heard a lot of statements like, 'Don't do it; it'll fail. There aren't enough runners to support a marathon,'" remembers Marie Patrick. "Yet I drove up and down the streets and saw thousands of people running every day."

In the end, Burke and Patrick made it work, thanks to saavy marketing and creative salesmanship —and the wisdom to seek help from people who knew something about running. Rod Dixon, the prominent New Zealand marathoner, took charge of designing the course and recruiting runners. Allan Steinfeld, then race coordinator for the New York City Marathon, gave valuable technical assistance. The late Fred LeBow, then director of the New York Marathon, dropped by to look things over.

They had barely a year to prepare for the first race. "You need 18 months to put on a marathon," Dixon told an interviewer. "It was inside 12 months before we got started. But it's going to happen."

And it did, on March 9, 1986, when 10,787 runners lined up for the first staging of the City of Los Angeles Marathon. Afterwards, Nancy Ditz, winner of the women's race, said all that needed to be said: "At last, Los Angeles has a marathon. It's about time." ●

A partial list of what it takes to stage the L.A. Marathon:

- 1 field hospital and 10 medical stations

- 1,940 medical volunteers, including doctors, nurses and paramedics.

- 8,700 adhesive bandages

- 170 pounds of petroleum jelly

- 400 ham radio operators to provide communications.

- 3,750 volunteers to hand paper cups of water to the runners.

- 1,300,000 paper cups.

- 102 rakes to clean up the paper cups.

- 60,000 half-liter bottles of spring water.

- 120 Gatorade mixing cans, each holding 40 gallons.

- 3,000 Mylar blankets to keep runners from cooling down too quickly.

- 5,000 pounds of pasta and sauce for pre-race dinner.

- 2,000 trash cans.

*Burke and
Patrick on
race day.*

Only at the L.A. Marathon would an earthquake be cause for an award.

After the Jan. 17, 1994, Northridge earthquake rumbled across the region, marathon organizers announced a "Rock 'n' Roll Award" for the next running of the race on March 6.

The first male and female runners to finish after an aftershock of 3.0 or more on the Richter Scale would win free airline tickets to Memphis, Tenn., to visit Elvis Presley's Graceland.

"This award says that this is L.A., this is Hollywood, and we can survive anything," declared Bill Burke, marathon president.

Mother Nature, though, failed to cooperate. Race day came and went without the requisite aftershock.

They Make It Happen

Bill Burke and Marie Patrick first worked together at the 1984 Olympic Games in Los Angeles. He was tennis commissioner and she was sports manager for tennis. After the games, they co-founded a special events firm and then launched the Los Angeles Marathon as a business venture.

Burke, a successful entrepreneur, is the marathon's president. Patrick, an experienced manager of professional tennis and other sporting events, is vice president. Their bold gamble has turned into a multi-million dollar enterprise.

"All along, I expected the event to succeed," says Burke. "But never in my wildest dreams did I ever expect the kind of sponsorship and community support we have received."

Adds Patrick: "I told myself if we can make this happen three years in a row, it's something. Now it's a solid business. I'm extremely proud of that. And it touches so many lives. You have 19,000 runners and 19,000 stories."

Although neither came from the running world, both can rightly say they understand the marathon experience: Burke and Patrick each ran the 1988 New York Marathon, and he competed in the London Marathon in 1991 as well.

Now, a Word From Our Sponsors...

When Runner's World magazine asked L.A. Marathon boss Bill Burke for his advice on starting up a marathon, the answer came quickly: "Sponsorship. Get some money."

Indeed, corporate sponsorship—an idea lifted from the 1984 Olympic Games in Los Angeles—is what made the L.A. Marathon different from the very start. Burke's success at underwriting the event with fees paid by some of America's biggest companies inspired one headline writer to call it "The Selling of the Marathon."

But Burke makes no apologies for his approach. "If an event is not economically viable, it will not endure," he says. "We showed the running world that big business and sports have a natural bond."

Partner Marie Patrick agrees. "Without your sponsors, you're nothing," she says. "Each runner pays us $35 to run, but it costs us about $180 per runner to stage the race. The sponsors make up the difference."

Mercedes-Benz of North America, Packard Bell, Shell Oil Co., American Airlines and PacificCare Health Systems are just a few of the big names taking part. Burke limits the number of sponsors to 10 each year (fees are in the mid-six figures or higher, paid in cash and/or in-kind contributions).

In exchange, the sponsors get total identification with the event. Their company logos appear in virtually every marathon promotion, including race literature, banners and ads. The marathon marketing staff, in turn, helps the companies develop special promotions for their products.

The marathon also licenses an unlimited number of companies to use the event for promotional purposes and to advertise their association with the race. The licensees, including names like Gatorade and Naya Spring Water, pay substantially smaller fees.

The marathon sells its name to licensees and suppliers, who donate everything from fruit and water to the official salted snack and the official hair-growth product. This banner identifies—what else—the official carbohydrate of the 1991 marathon.

Left: Mercedes-Benz, primary sponsor of the L.A. Marathon for the first ten years, awarded new automobiles to the top male and female finishers.

"This is part of what Los Angeles is all about. I'm so very proud of it."

—Los Angeles Mayor Richard Riordan,
at the L.A. Marathon's 10th anniversary

ON A RAINY DAY IN L.A., A MILESTONE IS REACHED

It was the wettest marathon in the city's history. Among spectators and runners alike, the most visible fashion statements were umbrellas, bright ponchos and plastic garbage bags converted into makeshift raincoats. But the day-long downpour couldn't obscure the fact that a milestone had been reached: it was Sunday, March 5, 1995, and this was the 10th anniversary running of the L.A. Marathon.

Thousands of bicycle enthusiasts kicked off the special day at dawn by riding in the first-ever bike tour of the race course. Later, more than 500 runners who had finished all nine previous marathons were cheered as they set out to conquer No. 10.

Although the foul weather cut into spectator attendance, it didn't seem to discourage the runners. Seventy-eight percent of the 19,442 entrants finished the grueling run, equal to the second highest completion rate in the event's history. That level of determination seemed especially appropriate on this particular day. As Bill Burke, marathon president, put it: "I would have liked to have a California Chamber of Commerce day of weather for the 10th anniversary, but you've got to take what you get."

Amby Burfoot, executive editor of Runner's World magazine, recalled the reaction in 1985 when plans were first announced for an L.A. Marathon. "At first, we were skeptical. We thought it would be more of a media event than a running event…We thought, 'Who are these people?'" said Burfoot. "Now at 10 years, it's a good time to give credit for all that they have accomplished. You have to give them credit for hanging in and growing in stature."

By day's end, thoughts were turning to the next decade of the L.A. Marathon, and the changes that might be in store. Organizers were studying the pros and cons of altering the marathon route to encourage faster times and ease traffic disruption in some neighborhoods. Also under study were proposals to approximately double the number of runners by the year 2000 and incorporate still more sports into the eclectic lineup of race-affiliated events. A major sponsorship change was announced: starting in 1996, American Honda Motor Co. will become the marathon's primary sponsor.

Meanwhile, the afterglow of the event's 10th staging promised to linger for many days to come. As cyclist Lia Watters of Newport Beach, Calif., said: "We were all one today. I felt there were no boundaries. The rich, the poor, we were all out there." ●

Only once before—in 1990—did rain fall on the L.A. Marathon. But it was nothing like the steady downpour in 1995 that sent runners and spectators in search of creative ways to keep dry.

About 12,000 cyclists registered for the first annual bike tour of the marathon course. Rain and fog made for slippery conditions at the 6:30 a.m. start—two hours before runners took to the streets. One biker with a flat tire got repair help from onlookers and a traffic officer. Spectators especially admired a reproduction of an 1880s bicycle, built and ridden by David Moore of Rosemead, Calif. Another rider, Los Angeles city firefighter Matt Johnson, explained the event's attraction: "It's real pretty to see the city when it's quiet…to go when there's nobody around, so you can enjoy it."

Meet the 'Tenners'

These runners know the race course better than any others. They are the "Tenners"—the 518 competitors who finished all 10 runnings of the L.A. Marathon. One of them wore the same shoes in every race, another the same T-shirt. Doug Hibbard of Corona, Calif., always showed up in his Chicago Cubs baseball cap. "My wife thinks marathoning and being a Cubs fan naturally go together, both requiring the ability to withstand long durations of pain," he explained. Having a sense of humor seemed important.

Said Cliff Housego of Agoura, Calif.: "At Mile 1, I think, 'Wow, I made it again.' At Mile 20, I think, 'Why do I do this?'" And, of course, optimism helped. Who else but a Tenner like David Brittain of Pacific Palisades, Calif., would have declared on a rainy and blustery Sunday morning in 1995, "It feels great. It's perfect weather for running!"

Above: The 540 runners eligible to become "Tenners" gather at the Los Angeles Memorial Coliseum where they were honored prior to the 1995 marathon.
Left: On race day, these two veterans went into the record books as the oldest and the youngest runners to complete all 10 marathons. Felix Saldumbide, 76, of Alhambra, Calif., covered the course in 6:58:40; Aimee Wyatt, 25, of Glendale, Calif., clocked in at 4:56:20.

THE 10 YEAR FINISHERS

Ahmed Abdul-Bari, L.A., CA	Maria Beltran, L.A., CA
Paul Ablett, Costa Mesa, CA	Weldon Bennett, Gardena, CA
Paul Aguirre, Montclair, CA	Rick Bingham, Norco, CA
Francis Akahoshi, Mission Viejo, CA	Flavio Bisignano, Torrance, CA
Ted Alarcon, Reno, NV	Rick Blakely, Albuquerque, NM
Luis Alatorre, Claremont, CA	Robert Blakemore, Covina, CA
Jeff Allan, Torrance, CA	Jim Blanck, Simi Valley, CA,
Albert Allen, Inglewood, CA	Stephen Bland, L.A., CA
John Allen, L.A., CA	Javier Bobadilla, Alhambra, CA
Aaron Alvarado, L.A.	Dennis Bock, Palmdale, CA
Daniel Alvarez, L.A., CA	Matthew Boyd, Seal Bch, CA
Ray Andrzejewski, Crestline, CA	James Brandt, Danville, CA
Larry Anners, Watsonville, CA	Charles Braun, Barstow, CA
John Araujo, West Covina, CA	Marygail Brauner, S. Monica, CA
Carlos Arellanes, Pomona, CA	Paul Brestyanszky, H'ngtn Bch, CA
Joe Armstrong, Laguna Beach, CA	Curtiss Briggs, L.A., CA
Kevin Armstrong, Bellflower, CA	Lou Briones, L.A., CA
Edward Arnold, Coto De Caza, CA	David Brittain, Pacific Palisades, CA
Stephen Auth, Manhattan Bch, CA	Thomas Brown, Downey, CA
Bobby Avery, Riverside, CA	Claude Bruni, L.A., CA
Marshall Avila, Colton, CA	Rick Brush, Camarillo, CA
Porfirio Ayala, Riverside, CA	Joseph Bugbee, Huntington Bch, CA
Vladimir Babichev, L.A., CA,	Richard Burd, Redondo Bch, CA
John R. Backman, Encinitas, CA	Robert Burdick, Huntington Bch, CA
Ronald Badie, Flintridge, CA	John Butcher, L.A., CA
Mary Baker, L.A., CA	Fred Butler, Hawthorne, CA
Michael Bare, Valencia, CA	Jose Cadenas, Winnetka, CA
Joanne Barker, Camarillo, CA	Michael Calvert, Downey, CA
Don Barton, Riverside, CA	Terry Cammack, West Covina, CA
Thomas Baughman, S. Monica, CA	Frank Campbell, Coronado, CA
Cy Baumann, Irvine, CA	Vincent Campbell, L.A., CA
Jon Bechtel, Rowland Heights, CA	Faustino Campos, Glendale, CA

John Carey, L.A., CA
Alan Carlisle, Upland, CA
Chris Carlson, Santa Monica, CA
Len Carlson, Sherman Oaks, CA
Ruth Carter, Rowland Heights, CA
Juan Castaneda, South Gate, CA
Laura Castaneda, South Gate, CA
Alfonso Castillo, Montebello, CA
Marcos Cedillo Jr, Newhall, CA
Carlos Celiz, Norwalk, CA
Caesar Cepeda, Monrovia, CA
Pete Cerda, L.A., CA
Craig Chambers, Santa Monica, CA
John Chin, San Gabriel, CA
Jean Chromoy, L.A., CA
T. C. Chung, Monterey Park, CA
Chuck Church, San Dimas, CA
Kevin Cimarusti, Long Bch, CA
Marilyn Clark, Marina Del Rey, CA
Red Clark, Long Bch, CA
Walter Clarke, San Bernadino, CA
Steven Clemons, Washington, DC
Scott Cline, Monterey Park, CA
William Colangelo, Reseda, CA
Lou Colletta, Fullerton, CA
Terry Collier, Moreno Valley, CA
Stephen Collins, Pomona, CA
Jack Conrad, Alta Loma, CA
John Contreraz, Sylmar, CA
Joe Cordova, La Puente, CA
Ralph Cripe, Carlsbad, CA
Juan Cueva, L.A., CA
Charles Cutting, Loma Linda, CA
Jane Cutting, Loma Linda, CA
Michael Daly, Manhattan Bch, CA
Craig Davidson, Phoenix, AZ
James Davis, Sylmar, CA
Thomas Davis, Huntington Bch, CA
Omar De Leon, Gardena, CA
Rudy De Leon, Torrance, CA
Patricia De Vita, Granada Hills, CA
Lyle Deem, Riverside, CA
Danny Demercado, Helendale, CA
Neal Dempsey, Monte Sereno, CA
Timothy Denardo, Dana Point, CA
Bill Deom, San Dimas, CA
Mickey Depalo, Burbank, CA
Raumond Deschenes, L.A., CA
Edward Deto, Manhattan Bch, CA
Patrick Devine, Rancho P.V., CA
Anthony Di Bari, Northridge, CA
Vincent Di Franco, P.V. P'sula, CA
Rene Diaz, Redondo Bch, CA
Robin Dickinson, Vancouver BC
Steve Doering, Carlsbad, CA
Thomas Dolan, Irvine, CA
John Dominguez, Acton, CA
Low Dong, Lomita, CA
Thomas Dorosky, Anaheim, CA
Gene Doss, Diamond Bar, CA
Frankie Dowey, Hawthorne, CA
Ariel Drachenberg, Tujunga, CA
Timothy Droke, Van Nuys, CA
May Du Bois, L.A., CA
Manuel Duarte, L.A., CA
Robert Dubarr, Riverside, CA
Jim Dudley, Lancaster, CA
Mary Dugan, Huntington Bch, CA
Robert Duitsman, Culver City, CA
Jim Dunleavy, Anaheim, CA
Alnita Dunn, L.A., CA
Yoshio Dupree, San Gabriel, CA
George Durr, Camarillo, CA
Diane Eastman, Los Alamitos, CA
Roger Edelson, L.A., CA
Thomas Edwards, Pasadena, CA
Howard Einberg, L.A., CA
Ed Ely, Redondo Bch, CA
Rich Endo, Gardena, CA
Miguel Enriquez, Fontana, CA
Roger Enriquez, Cudahy, CA
Sanford Erickson, Playa Del Rey, CA
Ronald Exley, L.A., CA
Louis Fernandez, Hacienda Hts., CA
Arlene Fichman, L.A., CA
Tomas Fierro, Riverside, CA
Rosalio Figueroa, Highland, CA
Marshall Fisher, Corona Del Mar, CA
Diane Fitzhugh, R'ndo Bch, CA
Tim Fitzhugh, Rodondo Bch, CA
Carlos Flores, San Diego, CA
Eleazar Flores, Calexico, CA
David Follett, P.V. Peninsula, CA
Wayne Fong, Chatsworth, CA
Herbert Fragosa, Venice, CA
Richard Franco, Canoga Park, CA,
Lloyd Fukuda, Culver City, CA
Mario Gaitan, L.A., CA
Luis Gallardo, Whittier, CA
Rob Gandin, Encino, CA
Rafael Garay, Whittier, CA
Manny Garcia, Monterey Park, CA
Tom Garcia, Fountain Valley, CA
Samuel Gardner Jr, L.A., CA,
James Garren, Torrance, CA
Albert Gaskin, Culver City, CA
Stuart Gater, Long Bch, CA
Robert Gay, Trabuco Canyon, CA
Sam Gee, Monterey Park, CA
Dana Gemme, Lakewood, CA
Frank Genco, Covina, CA
Bruce Gietzen, L.A., CA,
Andrew Gillespie, Pac. P'sades, CA
Don Gillman, Pasadena, CA
Sara Gilmore, P.V. Peninsula, CA
Frank Glavan, Glendora, CA
Jan Glavan, Glendora, CA
Gary Goldman, L.A., CA
Michael Goldman, Long Bch, CA
Greg Goltz, Brea, CA
Alfred Gonzales, Chino, CA
Marco Gonzales, Glendora, CA
Pete Gonzalez, Long Bch, CA
George Good, L.A., CA
Steve Gooselaw, Garden Grove, CA
David Gracia, Upland, CA,
George Gradias, Whittier, CA
Rick Graf, Saugus, CA
Chester Graine III, Gardena, CA
James Graves, Burbank, CA
Jon Graves, Burbank, CA
Jerry Guritzky, Santa Monica, CA
Rick Gutman, R. Cucamonga, CA
Mary Hack, Redondo Bch, CA
Jussi Hamalainen, Agoura Hills, CA
Brian Hamblin, Torrance, CA
Richard Hammervold, Torrance, CA
Ronald Hancock Sr, Buena Park, CA
Marga Hanks, Camarillo, CA
Jack Hanna, Laguna Hills, CA
Lisa Harris, Gardnerville, NV
Lonnie Harris, Carson, CA
Michael Harris, Glendale, CA
Carlos Hassey, Trabuco Canyon, CA
Bryan Hayward, West Covina, CA
Dougg Healy, L.A., CA
Redge Heislitz, San Ramon, CA
Mick Hemp, Anaheim, CA
Daniel Henderson III, Anaheim, CA
Steve Henrich, Lancaster, CA
Elaine Herfert, West Covina, CA
Steve Herfert, West Covina, CA
Cruz Hernandez, Mission Hills, CA
Eduardo Hernandez, Simi Valley, CA
Frank Hernandez, Lynwood, CA
Juvenal Herrera, Santa Ana, CA
Dale Hershey, Encinitas, CA
Douglas Hibbard, Corona, CA
Gregory Hickey, Venice, CA
Bill Higgins, Huntington Bch, CA
Masako Higuchi, L.A., CA
Louis Hill, San Pedro, CA
Mary Sean Hodges, San Gabriel, CA
Jay Hoffman, P.V. Peninsula, CA
Rob Hogan, Mission Viejo, CA
Bob Holguin, Whittier, CA
Gordon Hopkins, Palmdale, CA
Jack Horvath, La Palma, CA
Cliff Housego, Agoura Hills, CA
Dennis Huffman, La Habra, CA
Don Hughes, Agua Dulce, CA
Clarence Hunter Jr, L.A., CA
Van Hutchins, L.A., CA
Herbie Inglove, Santa Monica, CA
Joe Iseri, Gardena, CA
Stanley Ito, San Diego, CA
Tom Jackman, L.A., CA
Bruce Jaffe, Manhattan Bch, CA
Jay Jahanmir, Tucson, AZ
Johnnie Jameson, Inglewood, CA
Kan Jew, L.A., CA
Edward Jimenez, Whittier, CA
Jerry Johnson, Moreno Valley, CA
Calvin Jones, Carson, CA
Gary Jones, San Dimas, CA
Danny Kalantarian, Whittier, CA
Juri Kalviste, Redondo Bch, CA
Douglas Kaylor, Needles, CA
Sean Kelly, Irvine, CA
Morris Kelly Sr, Lynwood, CA
Joseph Kendall, Beverly Hills, CA
Debra Kenneybrew, L.A., CA
Sharon Kerson, Culver City, CA
Howard Kieffer, Temple City, CA
Leroy Kim, Redondo Bch, CA
Robert Kimmell, La Canada
Flintridge, CA
Larry King, Burbank, CA
Douglas Kinzle, Redlands, CA
Kathy Kirchner, Helendale, CA
Bill Kissell, Covina, CA
Rick Kissler, Santa Monica, CA
Edwin Kitchen, Thousand Oaks, CA
Brad Knoernschild, Long Bch, CA
Steve Kohler, Woodland Hills, CA
Robert Krause, Carlsbad, CA
Willard Krick, El Segundo, CA
Gary Kunkler, Downey, CA
Kenneth Lacy, L.A., CA
Susan Lahr, Laguna Niguel, CA
Thomas Lakin, Thousand Oaks, CA
Manouch Lankarani, Crestline, CA
Paul Lapierre, Van Nuys, CA
Calvin Lau, L.A., CA
Ken Lawlor, Hermosa Bch, CA
James Lee, L.A., CA
John Lee, Van Nuys, CA
Stephen Lee, Beverly Hills, CA
Karma Leeds, Lakewood, CA
Richard Lem, L.A., CA,
Barry Leonard, Panorama City, CA
Howard Leupp, Carpinteria, CA
Ernest Limon, Whittier, CA
Charles Lindsey, Canyon Country, CA
Stan Lisiewicz, Glendale, CA
Thomas Loffarelli, Studio City, CA
Laurie Loon, L.A., CA
Mike Loperfido, Huntington Bch, CA,
Irma Lopez, L.A., CA
Rene Lopez, Rialto, CA
Robert Lopez, Fullerton, CA
Yolanda Lopez, Moorpark, CA
James Ludgood, L.A., CA
Antonio Luisoni, Granada Hills, CA
Edward Lujan, Bakersfield, CA
Juventino Luna, Norwalk, CA
Steve Mager, Hermosa Bch, CA
Brad Malamud, L.A., CA
Victor Mansour, Northridge, CA
Rosa Marin, Alhambra, CA
Ignacio Mariscal, L.A., CA
John Marshall, El Segundo, CA
Ursula Marti, Sebastopol, CA
Alfred Martinez, Oxnard, CA
Brian Matthews, Santa Ana, CA
Odell McCormick, L.A., CA
Dale McCree, Compton, CA
Ron McDaniel, Tucson, AZ
Benjamin McDonnell, S.J. Cap., CA
Kevin Mcgrade, Covina, CA
Jon McIntosh, Montebello, CA
William McLain, Van Nuys, CA
Michael McLaughlin, S.J. Cap., CA
Vincent McMillen, El Monte, CA
Alex Meade, Woodland Hills, CA
Albert Medrano, Wilmington, CA
Jahangir Mehrkhodavandi, Simi
Valley, CA
Ruben Mejia, La Puente, CA
Jacques Meyer, Sun Valley, CA
Jose Meza, L.A., CA
John Michaels, Hacienda Hts., CA
Melvin Miles, Ridgecrest, CA
Gary Miller, Van Nuys, CA
Peter Mireles, Hacienda Heights, CA
Wayne Mitchell, Modjeska Cyn., CA
Ernest Molina, Inglewood, CA
Alonzo Monk, P.V. Peninsula, CA
Alvin Moore, Newhall, CA
Dennis Moore, Simi Valley, CA
Ernie Morales, Hacienda Hts., CA
Donald Morse, Playa Del Rey, CA
Brian Muldoon, North Hollywood, CA
Warren Mullisen, Culver City, CA
Ric Munoz, West Hollywood, CA
Christopher Murphy, Pomona, CA
Elaine Murphy, Arcadia, CA
Michael Murphy, Lancaster, CA
Pamela Nagami, Covina, CA
Mikio Nagato, West Hollywood, CA
Glen Nakano, Torrance, CA
Gunnar Nelson, L.A., CA
John Nevins, Redondo Bch, CA
Don Newman, Northridge, CA
Claudia Newsom, San Pedro, CA
Alfredo Neyra, South Pasadena, CA
Tak Nikaido, La Palma, CA
Gordon Niva, Laguna Niguel, CA,
Bob Norton, Huntington Bch, CA
Jack Nosco, Newbury Park, CA
Myron Oakes, Altadena, CA
Donald Ocana, Placentia, CA
John Odell, Glendora, CA
Richard Olmeda, Ontario, CA
Carlos Orosco, Covina, CA
Ken Orphey, Inglewood, CA
Jaime Urtiz, Cudahy, CA
Thomas Ouimet, Granada Hills, CA
Gene Overmyer, El Segundo, CA
David Padilla, Las Vegas, NV
William Parker, Gardena, CA
Francisco Pedraza, Bell, CA,
Raymond Penkert, El Cajon, CA
William Peplow, Glendale, CA
Freddie Perez, Sylmar, CA
David Perkins, Torrance, CA
Perry Petschar, L.A., CA
Wayne Phillips, Huntington Bch, CA
William Phillips, Glendale, CA
Thomas Philo, Santa Monica, CA
James Picker, Glendale, CA
Steve Pinkney, L.A., CA
Frank Pitts, L.A., CA
Jim Pool, San Marcos, CA
Carlos Prieto, R. Cucamonga, CA
Albert Pugliese, Sun City, AZ
Richard Radford, El Segundo, CA
Edward Rasky, West Hills, CA
Robert Rauch, Rolling Hills Est, CA
Francisco Raul-Rivera, L.A., CA
Paul Redoble, Castaic, CA
Larry Reeves, Lompoc, CA
Leslie Rehak, Oxnard, CA
Barbara Reukema, Temple City, CA
Keith Reynolds, Lake Forest, CA
Jerry Rican, Cypress, CA
Leonard Riccio, Anaheim, CA
Wade Richmond, Fullerton, CA
Rosemarie Rieger, Claremont, CA
Richard Ringwald, Simi Valley, CA
Ron Rissler, Carlsbad, CA
Gary Roberts, Pacific Palisades, CA
Michael Roberts, M'hattan Bch, CA
Jerry Robinson, L.A., CA
Michael Robinson, L.A., CA
Alonso Robles, Pasadena, CA
Trini Robles, Placentia, CA
Gaylon Rodin, Saugus, CA
Roberta Rodin, San Pedro, CA
Robert Rodriguez, Fresno, CA
Jack Rohde-Moe, Fullerton, CA
Thomas Rohrer, Carlsbad, NM
Edward Roman, Paramount, CA
Marcelino Roman Jr, Duarte, CA
Alan Romansky, L.A., CA
Mary Romo, Northridge, CA
Ruben Rosales, Woodland Hills, CA
Robert Rose, Dallas, TX
Fred Rosenfelt, L.A., CA
Francisco Rubio, Paramount, CA
Daniel Rupp, Lancaster, CA
John Rusling, San Marino, CA
William Russell, Glendale, CA
Frank Russo, Dana Point, CA
Anne Ryan, Long Bch, CA
Van Ryujin, Orange, CA
Rick Salas, Pico Rivera, CA,
Ed Saldivar, Encino, CA
Felix Saldumbide, Alhambra, CA
Miguel Sanchez, Miami, FL
David Sanders, Venice, CA
Chris Sato, Montebello, CA
Bill Sauser, Upland, CA
Jude Schreiner, San Pedro, CA
Edward Schuppe, Van Nuys, CA
John Scribner, Hesperia, CA
Jose Segura, Santa Monica, CA
Ralph Semprevio, Aliso Viejo, CA
Randy Senn, Costa Mesa, CA
Harry Shabazian, L.A., CA
Michael Sheehan, L.A., CA
Dan Sheeran, Orange, CA
Kevin Sheu, Carmel, CA
James Shrader, Woodland Hills, CA
Christa Sidles, Santa Clarita, CA
Russell Sidles, Santa Clarita, CA
August Simien Jr, Shadow Hills, CA
Steven Simons, Santa Monica, CA
Francesco Siqueiros, L.A., CA
Linda Siqueiros, Glendale, CA
Andrei Slezak, Long Bch, CA
Alan Smith, Redondo Bch, CA
Dennis Smith, Manhattan Bch, CA
Garry Smith, Chicago, IL
James Smith, Orange, CA
Johnnie Smith, Diamond Bar, CA
Samuel Smith, L.A., CA
Dale Snowberger, Manhattan Bch, CA
Kie Soohoo, Anaheim, CA
David Sowers, San Pedro, CA
Lincoln Spurgeon, Orange, CA
John Squires Sr, Santa Maria, CA
Christopher Staudle, S. Monica, CA
John Stearns, Marina Del Rey, CA
Kevin Steele, Malibu, CA
Marie Stevenson, Thousand Oaks, CA
Kim Stocksdale, Marina Del Rey, CA
Mike Stone, San Pedro, CA
Paul Straub, Rolling Hills, CA
Milton Strief, Fullerton, CA
Anthony Sylvester, San Francisco, CA
Tyler Tabor, Santa Monica, CA
Ann Tack, Westminster, CA
Roy Tanaka, Cerritos, CA
John Thomas, San Fernando, CA
Mary Thompson, San Diego, CA
John Thvedt, Ephrata, PA
Andy Tomenchuk, Downey, CA
Ray Tomlinson, L.A., CA
Salvador Torres, Arleta, CA
Sylvia Toste-Rodgers, Rancho
Cucamonga, CA
William Traub, La Palma, CA
Reinhold Ullrich, Rolling Hills, CA
Cesar Vasquez, L.A., CA
Joseph Vega, L.A., CA
Rigoberto Vega, L.A., CA
Jose Vidauri, Riverside, CA
Earl Vinson, Covina, CA
Dave Vint, Newbury Park, CA
Richard Viramontes, Corrales, NM
Peter Von Kleist, Alta Loma, CA
Donald Vulich, Sylmar, CA
Ted Wada, Rosemead, CA
James Walker, Thousand Oaks, CA
Jerone Walker, Northridge, CA
Rick Wallace, Malibu, CA
Robert Wallen, Van Nuys, CA
Jim Walling, Banning, CA
Stephen Walsh, Redondo Bch, CA
Steve Waltner, Tustin, CA
Steve Watts, San Clemente, CA
Big Foot Wells, Thousand Oaks, CA
Jerry Weyer, Santa Monica, CA
Ralph Whittington, Riverside, CA
Joseph Wiger, Glendora, CA
Wayne Wightman, P.V., CA
Scott Wilbur, Venice, CA
Doug Wilde, Van Nuys, CA
Adell Williams, Inglewood, CA
Daniel Williams, Corona, CA
Irvin Williams, Culver City, CA
Gregory Willis, P.V. Estates, CA
Everett Wilson, Altadena, CA
Wayne Wirth, Avalon, CA
Daniel Witt, Reseda, CA
Joseph Wojcik, Claremont, CA
Jerry Woods, L.A., CA
Michael Woods, Balboa, CA
Jerry Wothe, Tucson, AZ
Raymond Wright, Corona, CA
Aimee Wyatt, Glendale, CA
Michael Yeomans, Goleta, CA
Joseluis Zepeda, Rowland Heights, CA
Ivan Zetina, Long Bch, CA

A POTHOLE LEAVES THIS RABBIT FRUSTRATED, OUT OF THE RACE

Pilkington (far left) starts to fade.

Such is life for a racing rabbit. One year, you're a hero. The next, you're Harvey.

The most famous runner in the 1995 Los Angeles Marathon was also the most invisible after Paul Pilkington slipped into a pothole on a downtown street. By the time the race was 30 minutes old, he was limping back toward his hotel. "Just a hole in the street," he said with a sigh. "So frustrating."

The accident occurred just after the three-mile marker. He said he attempted to keep running, but his twisted left ankle tightened. At four miles, he slowed and told fellow runner Arturo Barrios that somebody else was going to have to play the rabbit. And with that, he was gone.

"There were a lot of runners yelling at me, all of them saying, 'What happened?'" Pilkington said. "This is really, really disappointing."

You could look at it that way, considering Pilkington, of Roy, Utah, was the main pre-race attraction. He captured international attention in 1994 when he won the marathon even though he was paid to set a 15-mile pace and then get out of the way. "This year, I was going for it again," he said. "I was in great shape, p.r. [personal record] shape. That's what makes it so tough."

Or, you could look at it like his agent, Bob Wood. "Hey, last year he ran twice as far as he was supposed to," Wood said. "So this year, he runs half as long."

If you have a truly amazing good sense of humor, you could look at it like Bill Burke, marathon president. After paying $3,000 in fees to ensure Pilkington's appearance in 1994, Burke was forced to more than triple that figure this time. Pilkington's $10,000 contract was possibly the richest in rabbit history. On Sunday, that worked out to $2,500 a mile. "I'm going to bill the Department of Public Works," Burke said with a smile.

Wood was afraid that Burke was going to bill Pilkington. After all, he did not set the pace for the necessary 13 miles. But Burke, not wanting to get skewered for mistreating everyone's favorite bunny, said money would not be a problem. "Paul is a great guy, he tried, he did his best, I'm going to pay him," Burke said. "That's just what happens sometimes in this business."

Judging by the reaction of fans and other runners Sunday, Pilkington is worth at least part of it. Nobody received louder cheers before the race. While warming up, he was greeted by dozens of upraised fists and shouts of "Do it again!" Said Pilkington: "The reaction here really did surprise me. Everybody was cheering for me. It's really too bad." ●

—From a March 6, 1995 report by Bill Plaschke of the Los Angeles Times.

Runners burst across starting line at 10th anniversary marathon.

No major event records were set at the 1995 L.A. Marathon, but several runners did earn positions for the first time in various "best performance" listings.

- Three competitors set course records for runners in their age groups:
  Men 35-39, Martin Pitayo, Mexico, 2:12:49.
  Women 35-39, Lyobov Klochko, Ukraine, 2:33:31.
  Women 60-64, Wen-Shi Yu, New York, 3:51:03.
- Three men turned in times that put them among the 20 fastest male runners in L.A. Marathon history: Rolando Vera of Ecuador, ranked 7th; Bob Kempainen of Minnesota, ranked 9th; and Martin Pitayo of Mexico, ranked 17th.
- Women who broke into the top 20 female listings were: Nadia Prasad of France, ranked 7th; Anna Rybicka of Poland, ranked 12th; Lyobov Klochko of Ukraine, ranked 15th; and Aniela Nikiel of Poland, ranked 20th.
- A woman racewalker finished with a time that placed her among the five fastest to ever compete in L.A.: Brenda MacIsaac of Costa Mesa, Calif., ranked 3rd.
- Jean Driscoll of Champaign, Ill., became the 6th ranked finisher in the women's wheelchair division.

"Maybe it was the bands playing everything from rock 'n' roll to Japanese drums. Or the people of various sizes, ages and colors handing us water, cheering us on, urging us to take one more step regardless of who we were. Or the little kids giving everyone who'd take the time a high five. For once this city that seemed so divided along ethnic and economic lines felt like a place where even if you didn't know everyone, you wanted to."

—Runner Aaron D. Heinrich of Arcadia, Calif.

A Sign Becomes a Memorial

Steve Herfert carries the "L" and Elaine Herfert hoists the "II" at 1987 race. A friend, Ed Arevalo, holds the "A." The Herferts have run every L.A. Marathon with their 7-foot-tall letters.

Ever wonder about that big "L. A." sign carried by a group of runners during the first quarter mile of each race? It is a tradition begun by Elaine Herfert and her son Stephen, of West Covina, Calif. The sign was originally devised so that Elaine's ailing husband, Robert, could spot the two of them on television. He died after the second race, but the family continued the tradition as a memorial. The signs, once cut from cardboard, now are built of Styrofoam, with plastic piping for support. Trickiest of all was the sign for 1993. There were so many letters — "L.A. VIII" — that the Herferts had to tow them to the race in a trailer. Friends help the Herferts carry the letters each year. "We have a good corps of runners," says Mrs. Herfert. "Everybody wants to get in front of it because of the cameras."

On a Sunday in 1987, Los Angeles Went Big Time

"Fifteen thousand people ran themselves silly on our city streets Sunday. Now the streets are back to normal,

clogged with cars. The 15,000 runners are back to normal, or as normal as people who do this kind of thing get.

"But the city will never be the same. Sunday, Los Angeles went big time.

"'Sure, you've got a decent little sports town here,' people used to say, 'but where's your marathon?' Sunday, Los

Angeles showed 'em. The 1987 City of Los Angeles Marathon was short on superstars but long on everything else you look

for in a great marathon, including a man running with a dummy on his shoulders, a one-legged roller skater and a mysteri-

ous Mr. Slo-mo, who should hit the finish line by early October.

"'This is a lot more fun,' said women's winner Nancy Ditz, comparing the City of L.A. Marathon to the world's other

marathons of note. 'This is like the people's marathon. Marathoning is not a life and death proposition. The participants

here were ready to have fun.'

"In only its second running, the City of Los Angeles also emerged as an event with a personality and style that sets it

apart from other marathons. 'It's more than a marathon, it's a happening,' one radio broadcaster gushed. And a TV guy

referred to it as the 'athletic Woodstock,' even though nobody got naked and flashed peace signs, and the only bad acid

trips Sunday were on lactic acid.

"The reward for the runners was a handsome medal on a ribbon, free water, and the sheer joy and personal satisfac-

tion that comes of beating your body until it screams in pain and breaks out in throbbing blisters and searing cramps. In

other words, Sunday was party time."

—Columnist Scott Ostler in the *Los Angeles Times*, the day after the 1987 race

Runners on 6th Street,
downtown.

A BLEND OF SPORT AND CELEBRATION

One year, there were Indian tribal dancers near the Coliseum, kimono dancers in Little Tokyo, firecrackers and fan dancing in Chinatown, a mariachi band at Olvera Street, Israeli folk guitarists on Sunset Boulevard, Playboy bunnies along Hollywood Boulevard, a rock 'n' roll band in front of Mann's Chinese Theater, a gospel choir in central Los Angeles, and clowns at the finish line.

Vendors peddled everything from foot futons to "therapeutic magnetic jewelry." You could sign up to join the Rainforest Action Network or get a free spinal screening. The menu items at food stands ranged from hot dogs to steamed fish, their ethnic flavor changing neighborhood by neighborhood along the route of the marathon.

As the runners crested a hill on Wilshire Boulevard heading to Koreatown, Kim Eun Soo stood happily clapping her hands. "Jal han da!" she said, again and again. Her neighbor explained that in Korean it means, "Very good!"

In Hancock Park, residents held brunches and sipped champagne and Bloody Marys on their front lawns, all the while cheering the runners on.

In Silver Lake, a 6-year-old stuck his hand out for a "high five" slap from the runners. "Energy slaps," one marathoner shouted as he passed by.

"We love it," said mail carrier Ralph Fajardo, a volunteer at one of the water stations. "People bring their families, their kids."

The L.A. Marathon has become a genuine civic festival, blending sport with celebration and community pride. Giant freeway murals capture its excitement. Hundreds of thousands of spectators crowd along the marathon route, to be entertained and inspired. In 1995, thousands of bicycle riders toured the 26.2 mile course at dawn on race day.

"This is exciting because people are up for it," said one spectator. "They are friendly. In L.A., how many times do you find people talking to people they don't know?"

There's always a touch of Hollywood, of course. One year, instead of the usual starting gun, a technician pulled the cord on a cannon that once appeared on the television show "Magnum P.I."

Celebrities pop up everywhere—at the entertainment sites, during race ceremonies, even in the race itself. Often, they are there to help charities raise money, as when actors Cesar Romero, Iron Eyes Cody and Norman Fell took part in a three-mile walkathon. Cracked Fell: "This must be a really big event. It's the only one I know of that can get people in Los Angeles to walk."

The marathon's charity program is the serious side of the festival. Marathon Sunday has come to be known as the "Million Dollar Morning"—a reflection of the large amounts of money that runners and community groups raise each year for charities.

"In our first year we were trying to survive, and all of Los Angeles helped us," explained L.A. Marathon President Bill Burke. "Now we're doing better, so we are trying to give something back and help others if we can."

Welcome to the festival.●

THE PEOPLE

FRIENDS, FAMILIES

AND THOUSANDS OF RACE FANS

SPEND THE DAY

SHOUTING ENCOURAGEMENT

FROM THE SIDELINES.

"THE SPECTATOR SUPPORT

AT LOS ANGELES

IS TREMENDOUS,"

SAID ONE RUNNING COACH.

*Spectator's high five gives
runner a lift.*

Seen on the Street

One runner stopped in a neighborhood of neatly manicured lawns, took off his wet, dirty socks and turned to a woman watching the race from her front yard. "Would you please throw these out for me?" he asked politely, before donning another pair and scampering off. She did.

Michael P. Woronieki of Grand Rapids, Mich., looked over the starting line crowd with disapproval. "You Are Headed for Hell," read the 10-foot-high sign that he carried. He was there, he said, because the runners were wasting "all that energy." Declared Woronieki: "I'm a party-pooper for Jesus."

Friends and family members bring homemade signs to encourage runners.

In Chinatown, runners and spectators were greeted with the ear-splitting sound of 20,000 Chinese firecrackers. Spectators covered their ears, but the runners did not flinch. "It brings them good luck," noted a somber Bill Hong, a Chinatown restaurant manager, who lit the wick.

■

Churches and temples along the route of the marathon often lose parishioners on race day because of street closures and traffic congestion. Faced with that problem one year, Bishop Satoru R. Kawai came up with a compromise. He cancelled Sunday morning services at Jodo Shuy Buddhist Temple, and instead invited "anyone who wants" to an interfaith prayer service at the start of the race. ●

The marathon course is a study in contrasts as it winds through Los Angeles. Racewalkers have a view of the downtown skyline (upper left) while runners are greeted with fireworks in Chinatown. Opposite page: apartment dwellers in immigrant district of Echo Park watch race from their balconies while residents of Hancock Park set up folding chairs and canvas shelters on front lawns. The youngest spectators, meanwhile, climb trees for a better view of finish—or doze off.

Heard on the Street

"I love the variety of neighborhoods in this marathon. We got cheered at in more languages here than we did in the Frankfurt [Germany] marathon."

– Ingrid Hainline of Ventura, Calif., pausing at mile 13.

■

"This is the crisis point—where the runners start overheating and getting thirsty and tired. This is where a lot of them will either quit the race or get a boost of energy. It's real important for the crowd to cheer them on at this point."

– Steve Salazar of Los Angeles, volunteer at mile 22 water station.

■

"This is equal opportunity in action. Look at this! Every color. It's like a big rainbow, a human rainbow."

– Adelaide Martinez, a teacher from Panorama City, Calif., marveling at diverse field of runners.

The marathon goes over three freeways as it winds through the city.

"Pump it up! All the way! Come on! Over the hill!"

– Jerry Johnson of Los Angeles, curbside after realizing the marathon she was watching on TV was right outside her door.

■

"This neighborhood is very insular, but look at this! I think this is the most people I've seen on this street before. Even the dogs are out."

– Laurel Martin in Hancock Park district of Los Angeles, with a silver tray of bananas at her side for hungry runners.

■

"I need help. I don't have the strength."

– Plea from wheelchair racer with damaged wheel after he took a spill. Bystanders bent the wheel back into shape; he rolled on.

■

"It gives me a great feeling just to cheer them on. I've been bringing my son here since he was a baby. I tell him, 'Look at those runners; maybe someday you could try it too.'"

– Rachel Rodriguez of Echo Park district in Los Angeles, with 4-year-old son Francisco at her side.

"I have made more money this morning than I usually get standing here for the entire day."

– Pancho Jones of Los Angeles, after panhandling $11 from spectators.

■

"Now to me, this is the interesting part. You see the ordinary people, the people you work with, the people who bag your groceries, the guy who lives down the street."

– Alfred Egervari of Los Angeles, as middle-of-the-pack runners approach his vantage point.

■

"It makes them feel good about themselves. It makes them feel it's worth it."

– Seventh-grader Johnathon Briggs of Los Angeles, leading cheers a mile from the finish line.

■

"I didn't know there were that many healthy people."

– Young street person watching from a Hollywood curb.

Ten entertainment centers provide music, dance and song all day long. In addition, about 120 other entertainment groups, from gospel singers to jazz combos, are stationed along the course. Homeowners and businesses on the marathon route provide staging space and electricity for the sound systems and instruments.

THE ENTERTAINERS

RACE DAY ENTERTAINMENT

IS AS DIVERSE AS THE CITY.

YOU CAN HEAR MARIACHIS,

GOSPEL SINGERS,

HEAVY METAL BANDS,

JAPANESE DRUM GROUPS,

A JAMES BROWN LOOK-ALIKE

AND THE REAL FABIAN

ALL IN ONE DAY.

The Raiderettes, a fixture at Los Angeles Raiders football games, help raise spirits in the start-finish line area.

Marching bands from high schools and colleges are part of the show.

Aztec dance group is one of the most colorful to appear.

Retired teacher Ed Rasky of Los Angeles, a marathon regular, is one of the best at raising charitable dollars while he runs—an astounding $53,000 in ten years. Most of his pledge money has gone to a camp for children with cancer, where the kids call him "Big Ed, the Marathon Man." In 1995 alone, he generated $8,000 by touring the course in 5 hours, 30 minutes—at age 69. "It's very rewarding even to finish a marathon," he says, "but it's even more rewarding to do this for the kids."

GOOD DEEDS

THE L.A. MARATHON'S

CHARITY PROGRAM

HAS RAISED $6 MILLION-

PLUS IN CASH

AND IN-KIND SERVICES,

INCLUDING A RECORD $1,088,038 IN 1992.

THE FUNDS HAVE GONE

TO MORE THAN 200

CHARITABLE ORGANIZATIONS

THROUGHOUT

SOUTHERN CALIFORNIA.

At the 1992 marathon, enthusiastic volunteers for the Red Cross, an official charity that year, prepare to cheer runners on. The charities raise funds by enlisting corporate sponsors, staging marathon-related events and recruiting runners who collect cash pledges for every mile they complete.

Former pro football star Roosevelt Grier promoted the retinitis pigmentosa cause at 1989 marathon. Other celebrities lending support to marathon charities have included Olympic medalists Grace Jackson, Rafer Johnson and Bob Seagren; actors Jack Klugman, Jack Scalia, Brian Patrick Clark, Tim Matheson, Garrett Morris and Beau Bridges; actresses Erin Grey, Susan Walters and Jo Ann Willette; and TV weatherman Fritz Coleman.

IT'S SHOWTIME

CELEBRITIES?

BUT OF COURSE.

THIS IS HOLLYWOOD, AFTER ALL.

MOST MAKE APPEARANCES

IN SUPPORT OF

MARATHON-RELATED ACTIVITIES,

ESPECIALLY THE CHARITY PROGRAM.

BUT OTHERS COME TO RUN.

A DAYTIME TELEVISION SOAP STAR

IS THE BEST OF THE CELEBRITY ATHLETES.

Film stars can be spotted at pre-marathon events or the race itself. From left, Ed Asner, Karl Malden, Danny Glover, Cliff Robertson and Cicely Tyson.

On stage at the start line to perform National Anthem: singer Al Jarreau in 1988 and actress Jasmine Guy ("Different World") in 1991.

Former heavyweight champion Muhammed Ali with entertainer Sinbad at pre-race party.

World class track stars show up to encourage the runners. From left, Rafer Johnson, Carl Lewis and Florence Joyner-Kersee.

John Tesh of "Entertainment Tonight"
makes music at pre-race exposition.

Celebrity Moments

- *Actor Garrett Morris of "Saturday Night Live" fame, who completed the 1993 L.A. Marathon at age 56, joked: "I'm so slow, I've been passed up by pregnant women."*

- *Corbin Bernsen ("L.A. Law"), a three-time finisher, never intended to go the distance when he entered his first L.A. Marathon in 1987 to raise money for the Red Cross. But, reported Runner's World magazine, Bernsen got "caught up in the excitement," made it to the end in 4 hours, 40 minutes, and was "so thrilled that he leapt up and slapped the time clock."*

- *Singer-actress Susan Anton and swimsuit supermodel Kim Alexis both completed the 1991 race. Anchorwoman Mary Hart of "Entertainment Tonight" ran part of the 1988 race. Actor Julian Sands ("Room With a View") clocked in at 3:58:15 in 1995.*

- *Charlie Robinson ("Night Court" and "Love and War") entered his first L.A. Marathon in 1992 at the age of 46—and finished in just under 5 hours. He also went all the way in 1994.*

- *TV weatherman Fritz Coleman, who jogged a portion of the 1989 race for charity, is also a stand-up comic. In a pre-race interview, he explained how easy it was to spot a comedian-marathoner: "You can't miss us. We have that pasty pallor, most of our equipment is borrowed, and we squint in direct sunlight."*

Actresses Susan Walters ("Nightingales"), left, and Jo Ann Willette ("Just the 10 of Us") completed two L.A. Marathons, touring the course in 4 plus hours. The 1988 race was especially memorable for Walters: "My dad and I ran the first 16 together, then my mom jumped in and we finished together. It was beautiful. I was bawling at the finish line."

They have been Hollywood's most frequent — and fastest—entrants in the L.A. Marathon. From left, Jack Scalia ("Dallas"), Tim Matheson ("Animal House") and Brian Patrick Clarke ("General Hospital"). Clarke holds the celebrity record—2:58:45 in 1988. Best times for the others: Scalia, 3:07:48; Matheson, 3:52:23.

Fred LeBow, founder of the New York Marathon, pitched his running book at the Expo one year. LeBow, a valued adviser to the L.A. Marathon in its early years, died of brain cancer in 1994.

IT'S PARTYTIME

THE QUALITY OF LIFE EXPO

KICKS OFF MARATHON WEEK,

FOLLOWED BY

THE CARBO LOAD DINNER

THE NIGHT BEFORE THE RACE,

AND THE FINISH LINE FESTIVAL

WHEN IT'S ALL OVER.

It's called the Circulator, which is what it does to anyone curious enough to climb inside and go for a spin. Hundreds of sports, health and lifestyle products are on display at the Expo, which attracts 100,000 or so visitors.

On the night before the marathon, some 5,000 runners and their guests sit down at what must be the world's largest carbohydrate banquet. The aptly named Carbo Load Dinner, held at the Hollywood Paladium, is heavy on pasta, rice and potatoes. It's energy food for race day.

SNAPSHOTS

The menu for a Carbo Load Dinner:

Green salad and dressing
Cold pasta salad
Bananas, yogurt, raisins, apples
Chips and dips, rolls
Two kinds of pasta, three sauces
Tuna and rice
Potatoes
Butter, parmesan cheese
Ice cream, granola bars

Soft drinks, non-alcoholic beer, Gatorade, milk, bottled water, coffee

At the Finish Line Festival, where nearly 100 exhibit booths and live bands compete for attention, these clowns also entertain. Bottom, from left: Gary Geise, Mark Ellmaker, Troy Peace. Standing: Bob Williams, Liana Salinas, Ginger Geise, Bob Keeler.

Power in Slow Motion

The marathoners loom larger than life alongside the San Diego Freeway near Los Angeles International Airport, seemingly poised to sprint through the 12 lanes of traffic below.

The painted figures, up to 18 feet tall, are the work of famed muralist Kent Twitchell, who describes his creation as "having the feeling of people being very powerful beings, but it's almost in slow motion and completely in silence, so the power is held in check."

This is a view of his mural as it neared completion. Twitchell used 147 gallons of paint and acrylic to complete the first figure, 1988 San Diego Marathon winner Chantal Best (in L.A. Marathon T-shirt). Most celebrated runner on the wall is Rod Dixon, 1983 New York Marathon winner (second from right).

The mural, completed in 1991 with 26 runners in all, was commissioned by the City of Los Angeles Marathon Foundation as the first in a series intended to encircle the city. A second work, painted in 1994 by artist Ramiro Fauve on a Santa Monica Freeway wall, is a futuristic vision of marathoners striding through Los Angeles in the year 2026.

Recipes are always fun to experiment with, but marathoners in search of a faster food fix can fill up on bananas and other healthy treats in the finish line area.

THE RECIPES

THESE CARBOHYDRATE-LADEN RECIPES

ARE SPECIAL. THEY WERE ALL COLLECTED

BY FOOD WRITER ROSE DOSTI

OF THE LOS ANGELES TIMES

TO CELEBRATE THE 1987 L.A. MARATHON.

THE RECIPES WERE OFFERED UP BY FIVE

RESTAURANTS ALONG THE RACE ROUTE:

PERINO'S, THE BILTMORE (WHOSE CHEF,

ROGER PIGOZZI, WAS A RACE ENTRANT),

L.A. NICOLA, LES FRERES TAIX AND

THE HOLLYWOOD ROOSEVELT HOTEL.

PERINO'S SPAGHETTI LIDO

3 cloves garlic
Oil
10 ounces swordfish, diced
5 ounces dry white wine
1 medium eggplant, diced
2 pounds ripe tomatoes, peeled and diced
5 to 6 leaves basil, chopped
4 to 5 leaves mint, chopped
Salt, pepper
1 pound spaghetti
2 tablespoons rock salt
2 to 3 tablespoons virgin olive oil

In large skillet, saute garlic in 2 to 3 tablespoons cooking oil until light brown in color. Add diced swordfish and wine. Cook over medium heat 2 to 3 minutes, stirring occasionally. Add eggplant, tomatoes, basil and mint. Season to taste with salt and pepper. Cook 3 minutes longer, stirring occasionally.

Meanwhile, cook spaghetti in rapidly boiling rock-salted water 5 minutes or until al dente. Drain and pour over sauce in skillet. (If sauce is too thick, add ½ cup of water in which spaghetti cooked.) Mix lightly but thoroughly over heat. Turn off burner, then add virgin olive oil.

L.A. NICOLA'S TABBOULEH SALAD

1 ½ cups finely chopped parsley
4 green onions, chopped
I large tomato, chopped
6 sprigs mint, chopped
¼ cup bulgur wheat, soaked in cold water for ½ hour
Juice of 2 lemons
¼ cup oil
Salt

Mix parsley and green onions, tomato, mint and bulgur wheat with hands or 2 forks. Add lemon juice, oil and season to taste with salt. Mix well. Makes 4 servings.

BILTMORE ANGEL HAIR PASTA WITH TOMATO BASIL SAUCE

(Roger Pigozzi)

1 pound angel hair pasta
Salt, white pepper
½ cup olive oil
4 to 6 cloves garlic, pureed
6 large tomatoes, peeled or unpeeled and diced
2 tablespoons chopped sweet basil
1 teaspoon chopped parsley
½ cup grated Parmesan cheese
¾ cup toasted pine nuts (optional)

Cook pasta in boiling salted water until firm to bite. Drain and rinse in warm water. Season lightly with salt and white pepper. Add 1 tablespoon olive oil. Pasta can be covered and refrigerated up to 3 days at this point.

Heat ¼ cup olive oil in skillet or saucepan. Add half the garlic and cook 1 minute. Add tomatoes and basil. Bring to boil, reduce heat and let simmer 30 to 45 minutes or until sauce begins to thicken.

In separate pan, heat remaining olive oil and add garlic. Cook 1 minute. Add pasta and toss over high heat until heated through. Sprinkle with most of parsley and Parmesan cheese and toss lightly. Transfer to hot serving platter. Top with tomato sauce. Garnish with remaining parsley and pine nuts. Makes 6 servings.

TAIX POTATO SALAD

(Pete Santana and Mike Taix)

4 medium red potatoes, boiled to cut into ½ inch pieces
½ cup minced celery
¼ cup green onions
¼ cup chopped dill pickle
¼ cup chopped hard-cooked egg
Dijon Mustard Dressing

Combine potatoes, celery, onions, dill pickle and hard-cooked egg in bowl. Pour Dijon Mustard Dressing over salad and mix well. Season to taste with salt and pepper. Makes 4 servings.

To make Dijon Mustard Dressing:

¼ cup French dressing (oil and vinegar)
2 tablespoons mayonnaise
1 tablespoon Dijon mustard
3 drops hot pepper sauce
3 drops Worcestershire sauce
Salt, pepper

Blend together dressing, mayonnaise, mustard, hot pepper and Worcestershire sauces. Season to taste with salt and pepper.

BILTMORE DARK BLUEBERRY BRAN MUFFINS

(Roger Pigozzi)

2 cups flour
1 teaspoon salt
2 teaspoons soda
2 cups bran
6 tablespoons margarine
2 eggs, beaten
2 ½ cups milk
1 cup dark molasses
2 cups berries

Sift together flour, salt and baking soda. Add bran and blend well. Cream together margarine, eggs, milk and molasses. Combine flour mixture with egg mixture until dry ingredients are absorbed. Do not overmix. Fold in berries. Pour batter into large, well-greased muffin pans, filling ⅔ full. Bake at 350 degrees 20 minutes. Makes 1½ dozen.

PINE NUT TART HOLLYWOOD ROOSEVELT HOTEL

(Kathleen Venezia)

6 egg yolks
½ cup water
2 cups sugar
1 pound cream cheese, at room temperature
10 amaretti cookies
Tart Shell
2 ounces shelled pine nuts or more

Beat egg yolks to blend in bowl and set aside. Bring water and sugar to boil. Boil 2 to 3 minutes. Slowly pour into yolks, whisking constantly and quickly. Place sugar-yolk mixture and cream cheese in food processor or blender container and process until smooth. There should be no lumps.

Crumble amaretti cookies until fairly fine and sprinkle in bottom of partially baked Tart Shell. Pour cream cheese mixture in Tart Shell over crumbs and sprinkle evenly with pine nuts. Bake at 350 degrees 15 to 20 minutes for 10-inch pie, 20 to 30 minutes for 9-inch pie or until lightly browned. Cool before cutting into wedges or squares. Makes 8 to 12 servings.

To make the Tart Shell:

6 ounces melted butter
2 cups flour
¼ cup sugar

Mix butter with flour and sugar. Press into 9-inch round or rectangular tart pan with removable bottom. Bake in 9- or 10-inch pie shell at 350 degrees until pale brown, about 10 to 15 minutes. Remove and set aside to cool.

HOLLYWOOD ROOSEVELT HOTEL TUNA AND EGGPLANT SANDWICH

(Joe Venezia)

1 large eggplant, cut into 12 thin slices
Salt, pepper
Olive oil
2 red peppers
Rosemary leaves
1 long French baguette, cut in half
1 large clove garlic
12 ounces ahi tuna or salmon, thinly sliced
2 tablespoons butter or margarine

Season eggplant slices to taste with salt and pepper. Heat ¼ cup oil in large skillet. Add eggplant slices and char on both sides.

Place red peppers on broiler rack 2 inches from source of heat and broil until skins are charred and blistered on all sides. Place peppers in paper bag, close for 10 minutes to soften and cool. Remove blistered skins under running water. Slice red peppers into strips, discarding seeds and membrane. Mix eggplant and pepper slices in small amount of additional olive oil and sprinkle with rosemary. Let stand 10 minutes to marinate.

Meanwhile, grill or toast bread and rub toasted sides with garlic and brush with olive oil. Cut each half into 4 sandwich-size portions. Season tuna to taste with salt and pepper. Grill, broil or saute in butter until medium rare. Place tuna on sandwich halves, cover with eggplant and red pepper.

Cover with remaining bread slices. Makes about 4 sandwiches.

"*The runners came in all ages and in nearly every physical condition, in every get-up from slick running gear to bunny ears, midriff tops and what looked like an armadillo suit…For many, the day was a chance to simply see if they could run, walk or hobble to the finish line. But for the elite runners—who came from all corners of the world to compete—it was a serious athletic event.*"

—From a *Los Angeles Times* report

With 19,000 or more entrants each year, the marathon course has to be wide enough at all points to accomodate large clusters of runners like these. When the course was first designed, the route underwent several adjustments to avoid potential bottlenecks.

*Before the race, runners have their own favorite ways of
loosening up. Sometimes it requires help from a friend.*

SNAPSHOTS

**Who runs in the L.A. Marathon?
Here are some interesting facts:**

• There are more men than women. The ratio generally
runs about 75% male, 25% female.

• At least 113 nations have been represented in the
marathon. After the U.S., the countries with the great-
est presence have been, in order: Mexico, Canada,
Japan, Great Britain, Guatemala, El Salvador, West
Germany and France.

• Competitors come from every state in the union. After
California, the states with the strongest representation
have been, in order: Arizona, New York, Texas,
Colorado, Illinois, New Jersey, Washington, New
Mexico, Florida, Oregon, Nevada, Minnesota and Ohio.

• In the 10-year history of the event, the percentage of
runners competing in their first marathon has ranged
from 34% to 50%.

• Fifty-eight per cent of the runners are 30 to 50 years
old. Another 30% are in the 18- to 29-year-old group,
and 10% are 50- to 70-years old.

• The percentage of entrants who are college educated
has ranged from 48% to 67%. depending on the year.

*The high point of the marathon's start is
the appearance of boxing legend
Muhammad Ali, whose presence has
become a race tradition. From his vantage
point on the starter's stand, the former
champion gestures the runners on their
way. Arms waving in return, they chant
"Ali! Ali! Ali!" as they stride by.*

Racewalkers have been a part of the L.A. Marathon since it began. The division draws about 200 entries each year, almost evenly divided between men and women. Here are the first-place finishers and their times:

MEN'S DIVISION

1986 – Federico Valerio, USA, 3:45:50
1987 – Aristeo Cortez, USA, 3:51:09
1988 – Rene Haarpainter, USA, 2:54:18
1989 – Gary Null, USA, 4:05:20
1990 – Wayne Wurzburger, USA, 4:26:13
1991 – Norman Frable, USA, 4:22:42
1992 – Ronald L. Baers, USA, 3:30:47
1993 – Raul Hector Nunez Macias, Mexico, 3:53:57
1994 – Bill Neder, USA, 4:38:33
1995 – Enrique Camarena, USA, 4:16:40

WOMEN'S DIVISION

1986 – Susan Travellin, USA, 5:16:20
1987 – Susan Henricks, USA, 4:43:35
1988 – Wendy Harp, USA, 4:55:18
1989 – Patricia Carroll, USA, 4:20:22
1990 – Jill Latham, USA, 4:47:18
1991 – Daniela Hairabedian, USA, 4:42:27
1992 – Lorraine A. Miller, USA, 4:47:40
1993 – Margery A. Kraus, USA, 5:00:29
1994 – Margaret Govea, USA, 4:34:35
1995 – Brenda MacIsaac, USA, 4:41:17

Note: New watches were awarded to winners in 1993, 1994 and 1995.

Raul M. Nuñez, a racewalker from Southern California, on his way to third place finish in 1992.

The distinctive gait of the racewalker is evident in this glimpse of the 1991 competition. Finishing times for the winners have ranged widely in the marathon's history, from about 3 to $4^{1}/_{2}$ hours for the men, usually a bit slower for the women.

Runners in the 1991 5K sprint into the Los Angeles Memorial Coliseum, where the race ends.

While some 19,000 runners are out on the marathon course, another 4,000 or so are opting for the 5K that is staged in conjunction with the L.A. Marathon. The 3.1-mile race was first held in 1990. World-class athletes set the pace, but many recreational runners also take part. The 5K winners, their times and prize money:

MEN'S DIVISION

1990 – Jesus Herrera, Mexico, 14:48*
1991 – Mauricio Gonzalez, Mexico, 13:43, $3,500
1992 – Khalid Skah, Morocco, 13:28, $3,500
1993 – Phillimon Hanneck, Zimbabwe, 13:27, $3,500
1994 – Eric Mastalir, USA, 15:02*
1995 – Robert Nelson, USA, 14:28*

WOMEN'S DIVISION

1990 – Chris McNamara, USA, 16:12*
1991 – Shelly Steely, USA, 15:22, $3,500
1992 – Sonia O'Sullivan, Ireland, 15:24, $3,500
1993 – Yvonne Murray, Scotland, 15:22, $3,500
1994 – Priscilla Welch, USA, 18:03*
1995 – Laurie Chapman, USA, 17:21*

* prize money not awarded

Marathoners who are 40 or older compete in the masters division. Here are the champion master runners of the L.A. Marathon, with their times and winnings:

MEN'S DIVISION

1986 – Kjell-Erik Stahl, Sweden, 2:19:20, $1,200
1987 – Victor Mora Garcia, Columbia, 2:19:44, $1,500
1988 – Bob Schlau, USA, 2:19:27, $1,500 + camera gear
1989 – John Campbell, New Zealand, 2:17:51, $2,000
1990 – John Campbell, New Zealand, 2:20:15, $2,000 + watch
1991 – John Campbell, New Zealand, 2:14:33, $2,000 + watch
1992 – Manuel Garcia Perez, Mexico, 2:25:35 *
1993 – Angel Lara, USA, 2:42:10, watch
1994 – Gregg Horner, USA, 2:34:20, watch
1995 – John Bednarski, USA, 2:36:40, watch

WOMEN'S DIVISION

1986 – Harolene Walters, USA, 2:57:26, $1,200
1987 – Barbara Filutze, USA, 2:47:21, $1,500
1988 – Harolene Walters, USA, 2:54:18, $1,500 + camera gear
1989 – Carol Mather, USA, 3:02:57, $2,000
1990 – Graziela Striuli, Italy, 2:36:48, $2,000 + watch
1991 – Priscilla Welch, Great Britain, 2:40:20, $2,000 + watch
1992 – Sandra Marshall, USA, 3:02:47 *
1993 – Candy Dodge, USA, 3:03:10, watch
1994 – Emma Scaunich, Italy, 2:37:05, watch
1995 – Alfreda Iglehart, USA, 3:13:29, watch

* no prizes awarded

Two legendary American marathoners competed in the 1988 masters division in Los Angeles, Frank Shorter (shown here, finishing) and Bill Rogers. Shorter, whose 1972 Olympics victory in Munich is credited with starting the marathon boom in the U.S., ran well off the pace. Rogers, winner of the Boston and New York marathons four times each, finished a close second.

THE RACE THAT OLGA WANTED TO WIN

OLGA APPELL WON THE WOMEN'S OPEN AT THE 1994 LOS ANGELES MARATHON. SHE WAS A NATIVE OF MEXICO WHO BECAME AN AMERICAN CITIZEN ONLY WEEKS BEFORE THE RACE. WHEN SHE WAS INTRODUCED FOR THE FIRST TIME AS A U.S. RUNNER, ONLOOKERS CHEERED. "SHE WAS REALLY AFFECTED BY THAT," SAID HER HUSBAND, BRIAN, WHO IS ALSO HER COACH. IN THIS Q AND A, OLGA RECALLS THE EXCITEMENT OF WINNING IN LOS ANGELES AND TALKS ABOUT HER LIFE AS AN ELITE DISTANCE RUNNER:

Q: What do you remember about the 1994 race?

A: It was a special time for me. I knew there was a huge Latino population in Los Angeles, and I wanted them to see me run and win the race. They made me feel like a young runner in my hometown. It was also special because it was my first race as an American citizen. That made it very special.

Q: Did the fans live up to your expectations?

A: The fans along the course were great, very supportive. They made a big difference, encouraging me.

Q: There is a photograph of you after breaking the tape and your face is filled with emotion. It must have been an intense moment.

A: When I won, I was just so happy because I had accomplished what I wanted. I had always wanted to run this marathon and win it. And then finally I got the opportunity to do it. I had set a goal and accomplished the goal that I set.

Q: When did you start running?

A: I didn't get into running until I was 23 years old. I had given birth to my daughter, and I wanted to lose weight. Later on, I got more into it. I joined a running club. I found that I was really attracted to long distance running. I liked going long, long distances.

Q: And when did you get into marathons?

A: In 1990, I said I'm going to run marathons. I was 27 years old when I ran my first marathon, in Minnesota. It was a good experience. I learned a big lesson. I started too fast, and hit the wall very badly. I was in good shape, I was prepared for the race, but I didn't have a strong finish. I learned about pacing myself, good pacing. I finished in ninth place, in 2:40:08.

Q: Most marathoners are men. Did you ever run into hostility or skepticism when you began running because you were a woman?

A: No, I didn't encounter any of those things. Most people were very supportive. I think women runners today are taken as seriously as the men.

Q: What would you tell young women who think they might like to become marathoners?

A: It will take dedication, a long term goal, persistence. It's a combination of natural ability and desire. A school track team is the best way to start.

Q: Can they be marathoners and have a normal life?

A: Oh, yes! Also, they will come to know many fellow runners. It's great.

Q: Is there an ideal age to begin?

A: I think 18 years old is a good age to start, to seriously compete. If you're younger, you can do it but it should just be for fun, for the enjoyment. I have seen young people who start too early, I mean training very hard, but their bodies are not ready for it, they're not fully grown up.

Q: Any other thoughts for the serious beginner?

A: It's good to have guidance, to have a coach, someone who knows you as a runner, who can see what is good for you, who can be there for all your important workouts.

Q: Is it easy to overtrain?

A: A lot of runners tend to overtrain. It's very easy to do because you think, if I do more I'm going to be better. The results are burnout later on. The desire is not going to be there.

Olga Appell crosses finish line.

Q: Other than a chance to collect prize money, what are the rewards of running for an elite competitor like yourself?

A: There is a lot of traveling involved, exposure to all the cultures. You make many new friends. There is a sense of community among marathoners. And when you run and do well, it makes you feel good because you achieved what you set out to do. You feel good about yourself. I think it's the best thing.

Q: Once you know you're going to enter a marathon, how do you prepare?

A: I start training about two to three months before the race. I run every day. I start fairly easily, maybe running an hour to an hour and a half, and then it becomes more demanding. I eat very balanced meals.

Q: Does there come a time when you know you are ready?

A: Oh, yes, I can feel it in the training, that I'm peaking. It's a good feeling, it gives you a lot of confidence. You can feel the power, you are ready.

Q: Are you ever nervous before a race?

A: A little bit. Three or four days before the race, you are ready to go. I think it's normal. But once you start the race, it's just fine. ●

ORDINARY PEOPLE

THEY ARE FAMILIES, NEWLYWEDS, OLD FRIENDS,

LONERS, RUNNING BUDDIES—

THE THOUSANDS OF

RECREATIONAL RUNNERS WHO MAKE UP

THE BULK OF THE PACK

AT EVERY L.A. MARATHON.

THEY KEEP COMING BACK,

DESPITE THE PAIN AND AGONY

THAT MANY EXPERIENCE.

SAID ONE WEARY RUNNER,

SPRAWLED OUT NEAR THE FINISH LINE

WITH ICE PACKS ON BOTH HIS KNEES:

"I HAVEN'T FELT THIS GOOD IN A LONG TIME."

Clara and Manuel Scruggs (in T-shirts and sweat pants) of Los Angeles are a mother and son running team. Here, they are on their way to a 7 1/2 hour finish in the 1991 L.A. Marathon. Mrs. Scruggs, 46, agreed that Manuel, 26, could have clipped a few hours off that time, but he wasn't about to finish without her. "At the end," she said, "you feel exhausted. Everything hurts. But when my son hugs me, it feels good."

In the 1990 race, an energetic marathoner pushes a baby stroller.

Four buddies from Santa Maria, Calif., dubbed themselves the "Wild Dogs" after a Grand Canyon run, then ran together in the 1991 L.A. Marathon. From left, David Book, Quentin Sims, Luis Escobar and Gary Silva.

Together Again

Some snapshots of families and friends in the L.A. Marathon:

• Six California brothers who entered the 1987 race dubbed themselves the "Bartel Runners." The oldest, 56-year-old Erv Bartel of Glendale, explained: "It's an opportunity for a reunion."

• A finish line scene: Marine Lt. Thomas Torpy proclaimed that he and his buddy, John Rice, felt "absolutely wonderful." Rice, however, was less sanguine. "This was my first one," he groaned, doubling over and taking a deep breath. "I was just happy to finish."

• Talk about togetherness: The Guerra family of Helendale, Calif., crossed the finish line shoulder-to-shoulder in 1992. Jerman Guerra, 43, and his three sons, Ivan, 10, Fabian, 11, and Jordan, 13, clocked in at 3 hours, 31 minutes.

• John Cleveland, 30, and his wife, Genevieve, 29, of Fullerton, Calif., had an unusual reason for entering the 1987 event. They were there to celebrate their wedding anniversary.

Marathoners come in all sizes and shapes—and occupations. Almost 11% of them are students. The other occupational groups most often represented are, in order: administrators/managers, teachers/educators, engineers, attorneys, accountants, salespeople, business owners, physicians and nurses.

Espresso at 16 Miles

This is an unusual marathon tradition—a reunion on foot, you might say. Each year, Ellen Pearlman of Los Angeles and five or so of her women friends enter the L.A. Marathon together. They spend the day getting caught up on events in each other's lives.

"We get to talk to each other for 6½ hours," explained Pearlman, 45, a child development specialist at Cedars-Sinai Medical Center. "We finish stories that we started a long time ago and never got the chance to finish."

They do it with style and sophistication: "At 10 miles, I get a chilled double espresso. At 16 miles, a friend brings us chocolate and tepid coffee."

The tradition began after Pearlman walked the marathon by herself one year and found the experience "exhilarating." She invited a companion the next year, and her sister joined the following year. Recalls Pearlman: "It was better than a long distance phone call."

The group grew a couple more times. Now, she says, "Sometimes it feels like the six of us are the only ones in the race."

Ellen Pearlman and friends at 1994 race. Front, from left, Linnea Burnette, Laura Perloff. Rear: Marilyn Howard, Pearlman, Joan Miller, Laurel Sgro.

TWO RUNNERS THE QUAKE COULDN'T STOP

ON JAN. 17, 1994, THE NORTHRIDGE EARTHQUAKE CAUSED WIDE-SPREAD DAMAGE THROUGHOUT LOS ANGELES. IT DISRUPTED THE LIVES OF HUNDREDS OF ATHLETES PREPARING FOR THE NINTH L.A. MARATHON, LESS THAN TWO MONTHS AWAY. HERE ARE THE EXPERI-ENCES OF TWO OF THOSE RUNNERS, EXCERPTED FROM A PRE-RACE COLUMN BY BILL PLASCHKE OF THE LOS ANGELES TIMES:

Dave Callahan and Juanesta Holmes were pounding toward a single vision when the dark rumblings of Jan. 17 nearly stole everything. It took their walls. Their furniture. Their memories. Their composure.

But upon sifting through the rubble, they each realized the Northridge earthquake had left something behind: their running shoes.

Sunday morning, Callahan is going to fulfill his pledge to run in the L.A. Marathon even though he hasn't run much since the morning of Jan. 17. That is when he sprinted from the window of his Northridge apartment and directly onto a parking lot that used to be 15 feet below.

Holmes vowed to run her first marathon when she turned 30, and she's been 30 for five months, so she's not quitting either. She never dreamed she would be running without a home address or phone.

Their friends say they are foolish. Their sensibilities tell them to think about it. Their bodies cry for more time.

But for them, a race which once was frivolity has become necessity. They need the L.A. Marathon to convince them of what nobody else can.

That life goes on.

When asked if they had considered dropping out, their answers were polite, but short. Typical was the response of Callahan. He needed three words:

"No, no, no."

■

Callahan, a dialysis technician, thinks about control every time he climbs into his rented Chevrolet. His own car, a 1987 royal blue Camaro he treated like a child, remains crushed under the rubble of his apartment building.

Considering that he lived across the parking lot from the deadly Northridge Meadows apartment complex, where several persons died, he considers himself lucky.

But considering that he stopped all training for a month after the earthquake while searching for a place to live, and now runs only two to three miles a day, he knows there are more aches in his future.

"This marathon is going to be painful for me," Callahan said. "About halfway through the race, I'm really going to start hurting. This is going to take me more than six hours, I am sure."

Callahan, 35, might have made the decision to remain in the marathon while riding his bike through damaged streets on the morning of the quake.

He came upon a section of the street that had cracked and burst into flames. Sitting on that crack was the burned-out shell of a car. "I thought to myself, 'Man, I'm alive,'" Callahan said. "And now I'm going to live out my commitment."

■

Juanesta Holmes knew her life had been disrupted the moment she looked up from behind her bed in Northridge on the morning of Jan. 17. Instead of a bedroom wall, she saw a parking lot.

Holmes had planned to get up in an hour and drive to Venice Beach for her usual run. She didn't make that drive for another 12 days.

"Running is a mental game, and with all that was happening, I just couldn't bring myself to go out there," she said. "I was just a nervous wreck."

She is still living in three places. The only way to reach her is via electronic voice mail. There are times she still doesn't want to be alone.

But she will have plenty of company Sunday. Not merely from the thousands of runners and spectators, but also the hopes of thousands of earthquake victims still searching for ways to cope.

"When I'm done with this, I'm still not going to have a place to live," she said, pausing. "But I will have accomplished something."

The tone in her voice made it clear which she considered more important. ●

(Juanesta Holmes finished the 1994 L.A. Marathon in 5 hours, 15 minutes. Dave Callahan, walking the final 10 miles, completed the race in 7 hours, 26 minutes.)

Always a Happy Ending

A marathon can be a romantic experience. Just ask these couples:

• Jack Slater and Bonnie Wells, both of Hampton, Ill., had met through a running club. When they decided to marry, they wanted an appropriate wedding. So they ran the 1988 L.A. Marathon together (Bonnie with a bridal veil in her hair), then headed for the awards stage—where they were married by an accomodating judge. Bonnie said she had to smile when she heard a spectator shout: "Gee, my wife would never have run that far for me."

• Horacio Pino, 23, and Valerie French, 27, crossed the finish line of the 1990 marathon together, in 4 hours, 26 minutes. Minutes later, Pino, a Marine sergeant stationed at Camp Pendleton, Calif., proposed to her. She accepted.

• Two California runners, Peter Elkin and Lorin Johnson, met each other for the first time at the finish line in 1990. Two years later, they returned to run again, but with a twist: at mile 13, they stopped to exchange wedding vows. The bride wore a white wedding skirt. The groom wore a tuxedo top and shorts. The judge wore a Reebok jacket. Then the newlyweds scampered off to finish the marathon.

• In 1995, two couples had marathon weddings. Rosa Lia and David Descargar were married before the race began. Jill Hickey and Gary Brigandi wed at the ten mile mark.

Peter and Lorin Elkin after wedding at mile 13.

One woman went her own way on 6th Street, seemingly unconcerned about all those people running past her in the 1991 marathon.

Runners in the back of the pack can take as long as seven minutes to get across the start line. Once on the course, the race is more physically grueling for them than the faster elite runners, many agree. Back-of-the-pack runners "are in pain from the first mile. We (elite runners) are hurting only from about the last four or five miles," said a respectful Mark Plaatjes, who won the 1991 L.A. Marathon. "I've always told people, 'If you could take the minds of the six-hour runners and put them in the bodies of the elite runners, you'd have a champion.'" Gerald Lazansky of Palm Desert, a back-of-the-pack runner in 1992, elaborated: "It becomes a mental game. I had shin splints the whole time. You have to fight through all that. The thing is, we're out there so long. When you're at the two-hour mark, you still have three hours to go."

LET'S HEAR IT FOR THE BACK OF THE PACK

Contrary to what you may have heard, the longest day wasn't in Normandy on June 6, 1944. For some, it was in L.A. on Sunday, March 1, 1987.

"My feet were all blistered, my left toenail was coming off," Modena MacFarlane recalled. "Even my eyeballs were aching."

So would yours if you had just spent more than seven hours navigating city streets with other back-of-the-pack runners in the second annual City of Los Angeles Marathon.

This one's for you, Modena, and the others who didn't come anywhere near Art Boileau's winning time of 2:13:08 or Nancy Ditz's time of 2:35:24. Here's a toast to those who only missed by about five hours. Some of you wanted to run in the worst way — and that is what happened.

Of the 14,937 entrants, 10,881 finished. MacFarlane, 63, a retired analyst from Riverside, Calif., was No. 10,863.

"The officials at the finish line were ready to pack up," she recalled. "The race had started at 9 a.m., and here it was around 4 p.m. But my husband, Otis, had walked down the street where he knew I was due. He yelled to them that I was getting near."

Of necessity, since the streets along the marathon route can't be closed for the entire day, the late finishers must take to the sidewalks.

Every runner finishing the race receives a medal. They are designed by John Stearns, a marathon commissioner.

"That means you wait for the stoplights," MacFarlane said. "It does give you a chance to pause. But it also means that there are curbs, and my feet were so sore that I had to ease down on them like a very old person.

"After the finish (7 hours and 8 minutes later), I couldn't even talk. But I refused to collapse until I got into the car. When I got home, I soaked in a bathtub of hot water for 45 minutes."

Robert Morris, a 45-year-old insurance agent from Altadena, Calif., persevered for 7 hours and 4 minutes, finishing No. 10,852.

"For about eight miles, I was just a couple steps ahead of the mechanical street sweeper following everybody," Morris remembered. "Sometimes I got accidentally sprayed."

Ahmad Cook of Los Angeles, who checked in at 7 hours, 7 minutes and finished No. 10,858, was running his first marathon.

By the halfway point, the 18-year-old auto repairman said, "I had hit the wall…I hadn't done any training and my legs started knotting up on me. Another runner I had never met before was near me, and we began pacing each other. If I was going too fast, he'd tell me to slow down, and vice versa.

"People were shouting, 'Hurry up—they're still waiting for you at the finish.'"

William Satz, 53, an auto parts supplier from Canoga Park, Calif., was finisher No. 10,849, in 7 hours and 3 minutes, and better stand back if you plan to joke about it.

Previously, he had run 11 other marathons, all in respectable times. But in September of 1986, he had to undergo knee surgery. His doctor told him to pass up the next L.A. Marathon. He entered anyway.

"After about seven miles, my knee (the one operated on) locked up. I couldn't even bend it," Satz recalled. "I limped over to what looked like a M.A.S.H. unit and saw about 50 people sitting on the ground. I said to myself, never mind, keep going.

"I pretty much walked the rest of the way in. My leg would lock and unlock. From time to time, I had to stop and shake it."

Finally, for sheer determination, consider Bill Taylor of Hesperia, Calif. Taylor, a teacher, was sick with flu the week before the race "and I wasn't able to get in any running. All I was able to do was stretching exercises at home."

And then the marathon began. "In the beginning, your adrenaline is working overtime," Taylor explained. "You feel so good, it carries you along. I felt relaxed and strong until about four miles—then I began to feel heavy. It seemed as if my whole body was heavy.

"I had made the mistake of attaching a Walkman radio to my shorts. I thought the music would give me rhythm for running. But right before I got to Olvera Street, that radio felt like two tons."

He tried holding the radio in his hands, but that didn't help. So he handed it to a puzzled but grateful youngster on the sidelines.

Then his knees began hurting.

"Somewhere in Hollywood, my right knee gave out and I collapsed right in the middle of the street. I rolled out of the way of everybody, and over to the curb. A nice lady came over and asked if I needed a medic. I said no, I'll run. I lay there about 25 minutes, and every five minutes or so she would come over and bring me a cup of water.

"When I continued, I had to hop on my left leg all the rest of the way—about 12 miles. Every so often, I had to stop."

Taylor did finish and did get his medal, completing the course in 6 hours, 58 minutes, placing No. 10,837. But his ordeal wasn't quite over. "My right leg still hurt, and I had to drive all the way home with my left foot on the accelerator. Try that sometime." ●

—Excerpted from a Los Angeles Times report on the 1987 L.A. Marathon.

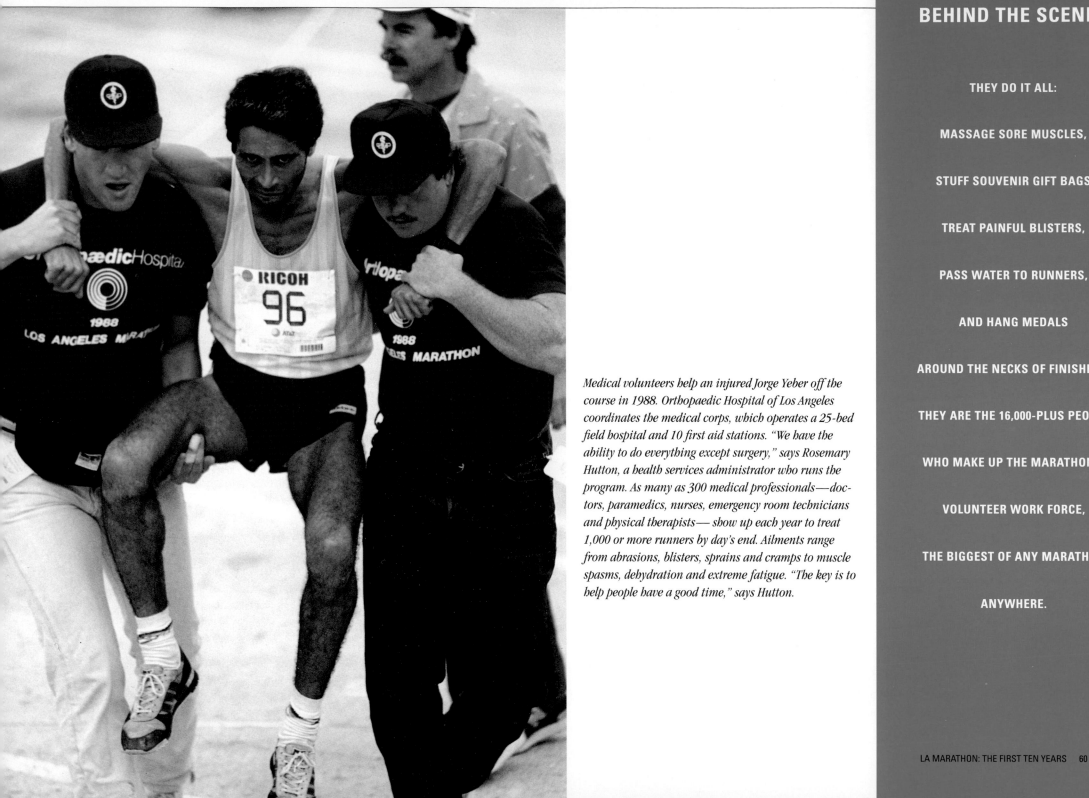

Medical volunteers help an injured Jorge Yeber off the course in 1988. Orthopaedic Hospital of Los Angeles coordinates the medical corps, which operates a 25-bed field hospital and 10 first aid stations. "We have the ability to do everything except surgery," says Rosemary Hutton, a health services administrator who runs the program. As many as 300 medical professionals—doctors, paramedics, nurses, emergency room technicians and physical therapists— show up each year to treat 1,000 or more runners by day's end. Ailments range from abrasions, blisters, sprains and cramps to muscle spasms, dehydration and extreme fatigue. "The key is to help people have a good time," says Hutton.

BEHIND THE SCENES

THEY DO IT ALL:

MASSAGE SORE MUSCLES,

STUFF SOUVENIR GIFT BAGS,

TREAT PAINFUL BLISTERS,

PASS WATER TO RUNNERS,

AND HANG MEDALS

AROUND THE NECKS OF FINISHERS.

THEY ARE THE 16,000-PLUS PEOPLE

WHO MAKE UP THE MARATHON'S

VOLUNTEER WORK FORCE,

THE BIGGEST OF ANY MARATHON

ANYWHERE.

The volunteer staff is busy on race day. At top, Edna Milner is ready to hand out souvenir posters. Below, from left, a volunteer posts race times in press room, some of her colleagues take time out for a light-hearted bow, and another volunteer brings medals to runners as they finish.

More than 1,300 runners seek treatment from a volunteer team of 105 massage therapists. Some come for a pre-race rubdown. But most hobble in later. "We get busiest between 1 and 4 p.m. and the most common complaints are sore muscles and cramps," says UCLA sports medicine researcher Steve Jackson, who has directed the effort since the L.A. Marathon began. "We can usually fix them up and send them on their way in less than 15 minutes." Jackson's volunteers come from throughout Southern California. They work a long day: some arrive as early as 3:30 a.m. to set up the facility, and the last are on the job until past 7 p.m.

DOING IT THE HARD WAY

DR. STEVEN SIMONS IS THE MARATHON'S MEDICAL COMMISSIONER, IN CHARGE OF ALL MEDICAL CARE. HE HAS HELPED THOUSANDS OF RUNNERS TRAIN FOR THE EVENT, AND HAS RUN ALL 10 RACES HIMSELF. TODAY, SIMONS IS A SAVVY VETERAN OF DISTANCE RUNNING, BUT HE WAS A LESS-THAN-WELL-PREPARED NOVICE WHEN HE ENTERED THE FIRST L.A. MARATHON IN 1986 AT THE AGE OF 37. HERE IS HOW HE REMEMBERS THE EXPERIENCE.

I never really intended to enter the marathon. It was all the result of an impulsive answer I gave during a TV interview about exercise physiology three months before the first L.A. Marathon. In the middle of my most animated explanation, the reporter asked: "Of course, you're going to run the marathon, aren't you?" Without the slightest hesitation, I heard myself reply, "Of course!"

I had been a casual runner for 15 years, but I had never participated in a marathon, and I wasn't running steadily at the time. Still, I couldn't very well back out.

So I began training and gradually reached the point where I was able to complete several long runs. I felt as prepared as I would ever be, considering a history of really being non-athletic all my life.

Because of my schedule, most of my training runs had to start around 4:30 or 5 a.m. One morning, about a quarter to five, still pitch black, I ran head-on into a runner coming from the opposite direction on San Vicente Blvd. We both went down. We were the only two people within miles—and we found each other. That was the low point of my training.

The night before the race, I overdid it on pasta, so I didn't feel very well. And there was a lot of anxiety about the race. I got up three or four times during the night, changing my mind about which T-shirt and shoes to wear, and rearranging my gear.

■

Before the race, in the Sports Arena, the hallways were full of runners going through their various ceremonial stretches and exercises, tying and retying their shoes in all kinds of funny ways, and so on. So I tried to do whatever I saw anybody else doing, figuring that would be the appropriate way to prepare.

Finally, as race time approached, I drank four cups of coffee because I had read that coffee improved performance. Then, waiting for the start, in the middle of all these runners—I realized I had to go to the bathroom. Now I was trying to figure out what to do, in this mass of humanity.

The starting gun went off, and it took almost four minutes to cross the starting line. As we ran past the Hilton Hotel, I was in the middle of the pack, and looking for my wife, Doni. She had walked over to the Hilton and was going to wave to me as I ran by. So she was somewhere up there waving, looking for me, and I was waving, and of course there was no way—we never saw each other.

■

The coffee, of course, was my predominant problem, especially when I discovered that there were no portable toilets early in the race. But fortunately, several other people felt the same way I did, and we quickly learned—about a mile down the road—that during the race you're not so concerned about what you do where.

■

Somewhere around three miles, we started into a series of turns. I quickly learned that you don't want to be on the inside of a turn. If you're near a curb, you get forced onto the curb by the other runners who are all turning the corner. So after the second turn, I learned to stay in the middle or on the lateral edge of the large pack of runners.

■

Miles 8 thru 10 were along Sunset Blvd., a slight downhill, very smooth sailing. I remember feeling very good. We were all just having a good time. There were people talking to each other, beginning to encourage each other. There was a feeling, at least at that point in the race, that we were not competing against each other. Our goal was just to finish.

A while later, I had this twinge in my calf, a mild cramp. It would get worse.

■

A Survival Guide

Here are helpful hints for marathoners from Dr. Steven Simons, medical commissioner of the L.A. Marathon:

1 *YOUR TRAINING PROGRAM SHOULD BEGIN AT LEAST FOUR MONTHS PRIOR TO THE RACE, even earlier if you don't run regularly. If you are 40-plus or older, you should check with your doctor first, and undergo a treadmill test if deemed necessary.*

2 *DURING TRAINING, FOLLOW A DIET HIGH IN CARBOHYDRATES AND LOW IN FAT. Run five to six days per week, slowly building up to 40 to 50 miles weekly. Include one long run each week. Four weeks before the race, complete at least one 22-mile run. Two such runs would be ideal. But remember: it is not necessary to complete a marathon-length run during training.*

3 *THREE WEEKS PRIOR TO THE RACE, BEGIN TAPERING OFF SO THAT YOUR MUSCLES CAN HAVE TIME TO RECOVER. Limit yourself to a total of 30 miles two weeks before the race. Cut that to 10 miles or less in the final week. During the last three days before the race, run minimally or not at all.*

4 *BEGIN CARBO LOADING TWO TO THREE DAYS PRIOR TO THE RACE. The day before is not enough.*

5 *GET ADEQUATE SLEEP, especially during the two or three nights leading up to the race. Nerves may hinder sleep the night before the race. Also, you will be getting up very early on race day to get to the starting line on time.*

6 *USE PROPER SHOES. Don't think that in order to run fast, you must have the lightest pair of shoes. If you make that mistake, you will not have the support and cushioning you need. Always choose adequate support and cushioning over the lightest weight gear. Whatever you do, don't run in new shoes. The experience will be awful.*

7 *KNOW THE COURSE. Be familiar with the route and the elevations. That way, you can anticipate areas of difficulty.*

8 *PREPARE YOURSELF MENTALLY. Be motivated! Visualize, think positively, be confident that you're going to finish. And remember: in a marathon, the real race begins with the last six miles of the course.*

9 *DRESS APPROPRIATELY. It may be cool at the start of a race but quite warm only a few hours later. So dressing with disposable outer layers —things you can throw away—is a good idea. Recommended: a big inverted garbage bag with holes cut in it for arms and head.*

10 *DRINK ENOUGH LIQUIDS. Most runners underestimate their needs for fluids. Before and during the race, make sure you get enough water or whichever sports drink you choose. Most importantly, don't pass any of the water stations without getting a drink. For extra protection against dehydration, carry your own lightweight water container.*

11 *START THE RACE SLOWLY. Resist the temptation of a big start. You can always increase your speed as the race progresses.*

12 *AFTER THE RACE, IMMEDIATELY REFRESH YOURSELF. Stop at the food and water tables at the finish line area to replace those carbohydrates and liquids that you lost. Intake of adequate carbohydrates during the first three hours after running will greatly speed up your recovery.*

Young volunteer signals runners who need Vaseline. One year, some ate it.

In Hollywood, I saw volunteers from Orthopaedic Hospital handing out Vaseline on tongue depressors. It was to prevent chafing of the skin. But a lot of the runners were eating it. I couldn't believe what I was seeing. I guess when they saw the tongue depressor, they figured it must go in the mouth because that's where tongue depressors go.

Near Vine St. I saw a sports medicine specialist I knew leave the pack and run into a McDonald's. I was starting to get nauseous at that point, and I thought he must be going in for a drink. About a mile later, he passed me, eating a hamburger and french fries, loaded with ketchup. I was just trying to keep going, feeling a little queasy, and here he was offering me those greasy french fries. That was difficult.

■

Around mile 16 or 17, I got another sharp cramp in that same calf. I stopped for a while, and stretched with my heel on the curb, trying to work it out. I was beginning to feel very tired.

■

Going through a very upscale residential area, I saw people having champagne parties on their front lawns while they watched the runners. It made me think of people watching Roman gladiators.

■

Right around 18 miles, out of nowhere, my right calf cramped up so badly that I fell on my face. The other runners nearly ran over me. My emotions were so intense that I could feel tears on my face. Someone tried to direct me to a bus back to the start, but I refused. I was committed to finishing the race. I shuffled along for a while. I started to become confused. When we got to mile 19, I said, "No, we passed that already. It's got to be mile 20." A little later, I wanted to use a portable toilet, but had to walk around it three times before I could find the door.

Around mile 21, I was doing my intermittent walks and passing runners who were just lying down by the side of the road. Again, I couldn't control my emotions; my eyes teared up.

At mile 22, my gaze was fixed on the back of the runner in front of me who was shuffling about as much as I was. All of a sudden, I saw his knee bend the wrong way, out to the side, and I knew that he had done major damage. But he just kept going.

■

Running through a poor residential area, I took an orange slice offered by a child who looked like he could use the food more than I could. I was really touched.

■

Along Exposition Blvd., people on the sides of the street were really cheering us on. And then I began to encounter people who had already finished the race running back-along the course to meet someone else and run them in. Here I was just trying to make the last two miles, my legs were killing me —and these people looked as fresh as if they had just started the day. Amazing.

■

At mile 26, I realized that I was actually going to finish the race, so I tried to sprint, thinking the finish line was just a few yards ahead. Well, it wasn't. But I sprinted maybe 30 steps anyhow.

All of a sudden, the calf went again. I started limping but trying to smile and look real good with all these spectators lined up on both sides, cheering.

I ended up shuffling over the finish line, but with a sense of triumph that couldn't have been exceeded even if I had won the race. It was unlike anything I had ever experienced, a feeling of monumental accomplishment. ●

ROADRUNNERS: A SUCCESS STORY

NOT MANY TRAINING PROGRAMS CAN BOAST A 99% SUCCESS RATE, BUT THAT HAS BECOME THE STANDARD FOR GRADUATES OF L.A. ROADRUNNERS, THE OFFICIAL TRAINING PROGRAM OF THE LOS ANGELES MARATHON. VIRTUALLY EVERYONE WHO COMPLETES THE 30-WEEK COURSE (FROM AUGUST TO MARCH) GOES ON TO FINISH THE RACE. ORTHOPAEDIC HOSPITAL OF LOS ANGELES HAS SPONSORED ROADRUNNERS SINCE ITS FOUNDING IN THE LATE 1980S. THE FEE IS A MODEST $50 AND ENROLLMENT NOW TOTALS ABOUT 1,600 A YEAR. PAT CONNELLY, A VETERAN COACH AND ACCOMPLISHED DISTANCE RUNNER HIMSELF, IS IN CHARGE. ENROLLEES JOIN HIM FOR WEEKEND TRAINING SESSIONS ALONG THE COAST, AND WORK OUT ON THEIR OWN DURING THE WEEK. HERE, CONNELLY TALKS ABOUT THE PROGRAM'S DESIGN AND GOALS.

The class of 1995 gathers a few months before the race.

*W*e try to provide a program for everyone, especially the novice who would normally never think of taking on a goal such as running 26 miles through the streets of Los Angeles.

The mix of people who enroll is tremendous. The ages can run from 17 to 80, probably evenly split between male and female. Most of them have never run a marathon. In fact, many of them have not experienced athletics in their life. It's amazing how many are in their 40s and their 50s. Even a man 80 trying to run his first marathon.

We divide the program into three sections: the beginner, someone who has maybe done some light running, some physical fitness; the intermediate runner, a little more accomplished, maybe trains throughout the year; and the advanced runner, a competitor who trains all year round.

I start out in August to develop a foundation of strength that we can build on: easy running, anywhere from a 20-minute jog to a half hour. Gradually, they get to the point where they can run an hour to an hour and a half.

*Pat Connelly coaches
the Roadrunners.*

Once we reach that stage, I add other ingredients, such as track interval training or hill training. Finally, they are ready for those 15 or 20 mile runs, five or six of them through the months of January and February, and then tapering off for the race itself.

What do you need to complete the program? Patience, motivation and desire. You want to get the job done. Anyone, unless they have a crippling injury, can complete a marathon. They have to set the appropriate goal but those who want to do it will do it.

To a non-runner, it may look overwhelming. But these people are taking it a step at a time, over a six-month period. So each step they take is a new excitement, a new goal. And then we move to the next step and pretty soon I hear, "Coach, today I went 15 miles. I've never gone 15 miles before." That's when the light goes on: "I'm going to complete this marathon. It's not just a dream. I know I can do it."

I've competed in every level of running myself —from high school to college, on up through club running, the United States Track and Field Team— but there's nothing more rewarding than to see these people blossom and develop. To see the discipline, the courage, the wellness that the experience provides them.

They come to Roadrunners just to put one foot in front of the other. And so their successes deserve great respect. When they leave, they are new and different people. ●

*Former Los Angeles Mayor Tom Bradley helped
Orthopaedic Hospital get its message to would-be
marathoners on this billboard. The hospital sponsors the
L.A. Roadrunners training program.*

JUNIORS, SENIORS

AGE BARRIERS ARE

CHALLENGED FROM BOTH

DIRECTIONS

AT THE L.A. MARATHON.

HUNDREDS OF STUDENTS —

SOME STILL IN

ELEMENTARY SCHOOL —

SHARE THE COURSE WITH

RUNNERS IN THEIR

60S, 70S AND 80S.

STUDENTS RUN L.A.:
HOW HARRY DID IT

Harry Shabazian (right) had a modest idea that blossomed into Students Run L.A. With him are two other Los Angeles high school teachers who were pioneers in the effort, Paul Trapani (left) and Eric Spears.

THE MARATHON'S FLAGSHIP PROGRAM FOR YOUNG RUNNERS IS CALLED STUDENTS RUN L.A., A HUGELY SUCCESSFUL EFFORT BEGUN IN 1987 BY HIGH SCHOOL TEACHER HARRY SHABAZIAN. HERE IS AN ACCOUNT OF HOW IT CAME ABOUT, CONDENSED FROM A 1993 COLUMN BY JIM MURRAY OF THE LOS ANGELES TIMES.

When Harry Shabazian came up with his proposal, most people thought it was the worst idea they had ever heard. It was about disaffected kids. But Harry wasn't proposing to take them to the beach or the mountains or a picnic.

His idea was going up to them and asking innocently, "How would you like to run 26 miles, 385 yards a few times a year and about 10 miles twenty or thirty other times, get tired, sore and out of breath most of the time?" This was supposed to beat hanging around with the gang, breaking up the dances, cruising the mean streets in a stolen car? Gidoudda here!

But Harry Shabazian, who had emigrated from Bulgaria, is a liquid-eyed idealist who doesn't give up easily and has the unsullied view of America's youth problem only a teacher in the barrio could acquire.

Harry got his inspiration in 1986 when he ran the first L.A. Marathon. At mile 14, he hit his wall of pain.

"I sat down and said to myself, 'You're crazy. You're never going to finish this thing. Your legs are cramping, your calves ache, you can't breathe.' But I got up and I crossed the finish line. There's no feeling like it. You have beaten yourself.

"Then I thought I really had to share this with my students. I wanted them to share this emotion."

A marathon was a hard sell, though. Eighty-five per cent of Harry's students came from single-family homes and their only purpose in life seemed to be to get into gangs so they could take out their frustrations on society.

"At first, the kids looked at me peculiarly. 'Why would I get into something this tough just to get a T-shirt?' they would ask me," Harry recalls.

He managed to put together a small track club of five boys and two girls, and he worked them hard.

The problem was not so much to beef up their lung capacity as their self-esteem. Harry taught in a school district unit euphemistically called a "continuation" school. It was more like a "discontinuation" school, the educational equivalent of a last-chance station before entering a trackless waste of a life.

Harry coached his team by running with them. He wasn't "Coach" or even "Mr." They called him Harry.

Six of the seven finished the L.A. Marathon that year. One of them, Andrew Duran, a tattooed and mustachioed one-time classroom terrorist, ran the race in 2:45 and, a month later, was to take a razor blade and bottle of rubbing alcohol and scrape the gang tattoos off himself.

Harry's little band didn't know it, but their suc-

cess was to seed a program that not only became progressively bigger but national in scope. The following year, 12 came out and all 12 finished. And their athletic success carried over to academics.

One girl, Carmen Mendoza, who had had a two-pack-a-day cigarette habit and no-show policy toward classes, became the valedictorian of her graduating class. A 320-pound budding dropout, Rene Mendoza (no relation), ended up not only doing the marathon but the equivalent of two years' academics in a year.

Word of the program reached Roberta Weintraub, a school board member, who promptly got the L.A. Unified School District involved and a city-wide project known as "Students Run L.A." was formed. Last year, 651 kids entered the marathon from all over the city and 625 finished. Better than finishing the marathon, though, was finishing school: Harry reports almost all graduated.

"This is by no means the solution," Shabazian acknowledges. "But it is a solution. The continuation school had a 70% dropout rate. Only 30% graduated. Of those involved in the marathon program, over 90% graduated.

"I know running is an addiction," he concludes. "But it's a better addiction than pot, crack cocaine, cigarettes and alcohol. Kids need something to come home to, besides watching video games on TV or waiting for the gangs to gather." ●

Above: These enthusiastic youngsters were part of the Students Run L.A. delegation in 1994. By then, some 1,100 were enrolled in the L.A. Marathon-affiliated program, coached by 70 teachers or administrators from 48 different schools. On race day, their efforts paid off: an impressive 98% finished.

Left: Burbank, Calif. teacher Deborah J. Gal in 1992 marathon with fifth-graders Steve Reyes (left), Raul Beltran and Heather Brown. The youngsters were members of a racewalking club, part of the Students Run L.A. program.

Fourteen-year-old Jessica Wendrick of Los Angeles made it to mile 18 in the 1993 marathon before exhaustion forced her out. Even so, her appearance was a victory of sorts. She had trained for the race while homeless, at times living in a car with her mother and three sisters. Her pre-marathon workouts included this 10K.

SNAPSHOTS

- Seven-year-old Carlos Santana of Los Angeles may be the youngest ever to run an L.A. Marathon. He cruised through the 1991 race in 4 hours, 29 minutes. His dad, Jose, ran about an hour behind him.

- Carrie Garritson of Fullerton, Calif., age 11, crossed the 1988 finish line in 2 hours, 49 minutes. Carrie, competing in her first marathon, actually led the women's race for a time.

- Salvador Campos of Pasadena, Calif., age 14, finished in 3 hours, 43 minutes his first time out in 1992. Two years later, his 13-year-old brother, Martin, got into the act, clocking in at 4 hours, 15 minutes. Their running mentor was 40-year-old engineer Roy Wiseman, a tutor at their school.

Manny Wein of Los Angeles was 89 when he went out on this training run for the 1992 L.A. Marathon. Wein is the oldest man to ever compete in the race. Blisters forced him off the course in 1992 after 19 miles. His best time was 9 hours, 30 minutes in 1988 — when he was a mere 85.

Ignore the Aches and Pains

Words of wisdom from the L.A. Marathon's senior ranks:

- *Don't break your training, advised Manny Wein after he was felled by dehydration at mile 13 of the 1991 race. Wein, 88 at the time, said he made the "foolish and disconcerting" mistake of dancing late into the night at the pre-race Carbo Load Dinner. His normal training routine: a strict vegetarian diet, stretching exercises, swimming, gym workouts and short runs. "I absolutely love to run," he declared.*

- *"I think many older people are nervous or embarrassed to exercise publicly," said Antonie Urba, 79, of Los Angeles as she trained for her fifth L.A. Marathon in 1994. "But I outlasted the sneers by younger people and earned respect. I encourage seniors to get out and do it." Her training routine includes mountain climbing.*

- *"I get aches and pains, but I don't pay attention to them," said Lois Lieberman, 70, of Simi Valley, Calif., after her 6 hour, 11 minute finish in 1992. "In the morning I start out sometimes limping a little bit. But I just work through it. Whatever it is—in life, too—you work it. That's my philosophy."*

Mavis Lindgren, 86, on her way to a 7 hour, 35 minute finish in the 1994 race. Lindgren, from Orleans, Calif., is the oldest woman to ever run the L.A. Marathon. In 1992, she set the fastest-ever pace for any entrant over 80 by finishing in 6 hours, 14 minutes. Her companion here is Tetsuya Hanada, 22, of Los Angeles.

One of the most energetic of the senior runners is Los Angeles personality Gypsy Boots. A health food devotee, he has made several marathon appearances, including this one in 1992 when he was 81.

William Kuester, 84, relaxes after 8 hour, 5 minute finish in the 1993 race. He said he resorted to a running monologue with his sore feet to keep them moving: "You can't quit, keep going, let's go. We're going to make it regardless of anything." The retired minister from Thousand Oaks, Calif., is an L.A. Marathon regular.

STUNT RUNNERS

EVERY L.A. MARATHON HAS ITS STUNT RUNNERS,

A ZANY LOT WHO PROVIDE COMIC RELIEF

FOR SPECTATORS AND COMPETITORS ALIKE.

WHO COULD FORGET PENNY MAN, IN A SUIT MADE OF

STRUNG-TOGETHER PENNIES;

COW MAN, WITH THE STUFFED HEAD OF

A BUFFALO ON TOP OF HIS OWN;

OR PANCAKE MAN, CARRYING A SKILLET

AND FLIPPING PANCAKES.

OTHER STUNT RUNNERS JUGGLE,

SKIP, DANCE OR BALANCE TRAYS WITH DRINKS.

A Stunt Runner Sampler

- *Albert Lucas of Las Vegas, who ran while juggling three balls in the air, said he wanted to win respect for jugglers. "Juggling isn't taken seriously here, but it is in Europe," he said. "Hockey and basketball players in the Soviet Union are taught to juggle to increase their hand-to-eye coordination."*

- *Five Orange County, Calif., runners were dressed as Elvis in white jumpsuits, wraparound sunglasses and pompadours. They finished in 5½ hours, but said they would have done better if they had not stopped to hand out scarves to "Priscillas" along the way.*

- *Thomas Rohrer handed out red roses from a hat as he ran.*

- *Ventriloquist Ronn Lucas toured the course with Buffalo Billy, his dummy, perched on his shoulder.*

- *Joey Hamp gave new meaning to the term "marathon dancer" by halting her run every four miles to dance for spectators.*

- *When Jerry Dunn of Indianapolis showed up for the 1994 race, he got*

Mark Millington, 34, of London ran the 1994 race in just over five hours—inside a 30-pound rubber rhinoceros suit. He said he wasn't doing it for laughs, but for Save the Rhino International, a group trying to stop rhino poaching worldwide.

attention simply by telling people how many marathons he had run the year before: a record 104.

- Costumed runners have come dressed as Spider-Man, Superman (complete with cape), Kermit the Frog (he hopped part way), Mardis Gras celebrants, Robin the Clown (in orange hair and floppy shoes), and hockey great Wayne Gretzky (wearing a copy of Gretzky's L.A. Kings uniform).

- Gary Fanelli of Hawaii, best known for his Blues Brothers outfit (sharkskin suit, skinny tie, hat and sunglasses), explained stunt running this way: "I'm an entertainer. I wear costumes for the people, so they can loosen up and not be stuffed shirts. It's an uptight world, and this is one way to relax. Races are like a parade of humanity."

- Sol Wroclawsky of Long Beach, Calif., pulled what looked like an instrument of torture in the 1994 race. Actually, he was promoting an invention of his called "the Rickshaw Runner." The device is marketed to runners for resistance training. Wroclawsky and his contraption covered the course in 5 hours, 40 minutes.

Dennis Marsella of Ft. Lauderdale, Fla., known as the Coat Man, runs marathons in a winter coat and wingtip shoes. He has covered the L.A. course in 4 hours, 26 minutes, and insists there is a purpose to it: "The appeal is in the absurdity of the situation…It's comedy, It's an athletic feat, it's an art…I work it all together; I see myself as an artist."

French bistro manager Roger Bourban was immortalized in the Guinness Book of World Records for his ability to go the distance while carrying a tray and champagne bottle. Here he is in the 1987 race.

Flip and Run

It's not easy being the Pancake Man. First, there is the 1 pound, 8 ounce pan to carry. Then there is the pancake to flip, 300 to 400 times per mile.

Not to worry, says Dominic (Mike) Cuzzacrea, a postal carrier from Lockport, N.Y., who has become a regular at the L.A. Marathon after first appearing in 1991:

"I switch arms every few miles. You get used to it; you do every trick you can in your mind…you lie to your body."

Cuzzacrea, who likes to run for charities, hit on the pancakes as a gimmick that might attract bigger pledges. One thing led to another, and before long he was in the Guinness Book of World Records for running a 3:06:22 marathon while flipping a pancake all the way.

The Guinness people had to approve his recipe: two pancakes held together with plastic wrap and weather stripping. A bit of water in the pan solves any sticking problems.

A CENTIPEDE WITH 40 LEGS AND ARMS

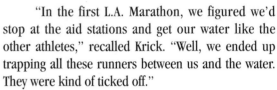

Think about the hazards of running in a centipede. Willard Krick, lead runner in the L.A. Marathon's official centipede for several years, knows them all. He even remembers the time one runner blacked out only yards from the finish line and was nearly trampled by his teammates.

The runners, connected by a continuous fabric with openings for their heads, must step to the same cadence and listen for the lead runner's shouted warnings of potholes or other hazards ahead. Their view of the roadway is virtually nil.

Substitute runners trail alongside to replace anyone who is injured or must make a pit stop. They also provide water.

The Pancake Man flips his way through 1991 L.A. Marathon in 3 hours, 22 minutes.

"In the first L.A. Marathon, we figured we'd stop at the aid stations and get our water like the other athletes," recalled Krick. "Well, we ended up trapping all these runners between us and the water. They were kind of ticked off."

Frank Worman, a Hughes Aircraft executive in the South Bay region of Los Angeles, came up with the idea of a marathon centipede in 1985 after seeing a prototype at a shorter race. The next year, he and seven others from a running club at Hughes entered the first L.A. Marathon with their odd creation.

The centipede doubled in length the next year and then stretched an amazing 140 feet to accomodate 20 runners in the third year—the most ever. Along the way, it picked up a sponsor, Nike, and became a crowd favorite at the L.A. race.

"Our best time was 3:31:20, in 1987," said Krick, a manager at Hughes. "That was with 16 runners inside the costume all the way to the finish."

As lead runner, Krick was tied into the fabric. Other runners could duck in and out at will.

The centipede suspended its racing career in 1993, an unintended victim of the aerospace industry shakeup. Krick said too many runners were transferred away from their South Bay jobs or had to move away from the area. ●

The L.A. Marathon Centipede on the course in 1992.

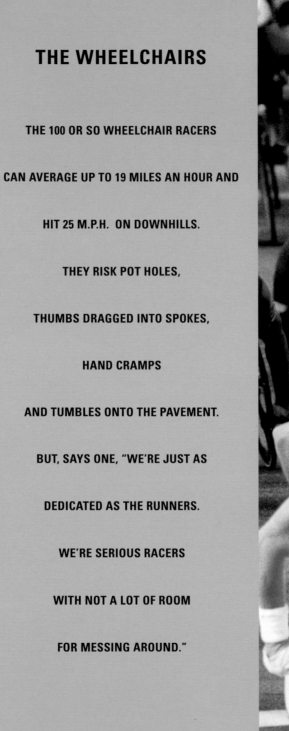

THE WHEELCHAIRS

THE 100 OR SO WHEELCHAIR RACERS

CAN AVERAGE UP TO 19 MILES AN HOUR AND

HIT 25 M.P.H. ON DOWNHILLS.

THEY RISK POT HOLES,

THUMBS DRAGGED INTO SPOKES,

HAND CRAMPS

AND TUMBLES ONTO THE PAVEMENT.

BUT, SAYS ONE, "WE'RE JUST AS

DEDICATED AS THE RUNNERS.

WE'RE SERIOUS RACERS

WITH NOT A LOT OF ROOM

FOR MESSING AROUND."

Knaub Likes to Win

Jim Knaub reached out for water at the 20-mile mark of the wheelchair race, and instead got congratulatory handshakes from spectators.

"All I wanted was water, and people wanted to shake my hand," he said later, "but I had to get going because guys were coming up on me."

Not fast enough, though. Knaub, a 35-year-old speedster from Long Beach, Calif., won the event in record setting time.

The year was 1991. Two years before, Knaub had also finished first. And a year later, he would do it again— and set another course record. That made the former Cal State Long Beach pole vaulter the winningest male wheelchair racer in L.A. Marathon history.

Knaub was an Olympic trials finalist in the pole vault in 1976. In 1978, he was struck by a car while sitting on his motorcycle at a stoplight. Though disabled by his injuries, he never lost his love of sports.

Soon, wheelchair racing was on his agenda. "I'm not on the same level as Magic Johnson, but I have put so much into it over the last 12 years, particularly the past two years," he said after the 1991 win. "It's the last thing on your mind when your head hits the pillow."

Knaub after record runs in 1992 (top) and 1991.

SNAPSHOTS

It was a bet that got Peter Lassen of Los Angeles into wheelchair racing.

"I was sitting in a bar with a buddy in a wheelchair and we bet each other that we could do it," said the 53-year-old architect at his eighth marathon, in 1993.

Lassen, a Vietnam veteran, lost the use of his legs after a land mine explosion.

"I'm not one of those guys with shoulders out to here," he said modestly. "I just love doing it."

The winner of the 1995 women's wheelchair race, Jean Driscoll of Champaign, Ill., has an unusual training method. She rolls around the farm roads near her home and tries to outrace dogs.

"It's a pretty good training motivation," she says. "The dogs come at me from all over the place...One time I even outran a German shepherd."

Driscoll came into the L.A. race after winning the last five Boston Marathons—and setting world records each time.

Connie Hansen of Denmark, wearing victory garland after 1992 women's wheelchair race, has won the event four times— and set a course record every time. Before Hansen went on her winning spree, the race had been dominated by Candace Cable-Brookes of Lake Tahoe, Calif., champion for the first four years.

In the 1994 men's wheelchair race, Philippe Couprie (left in photo) and Paul Wiggins were close to the finish line, with the pack far behind. "Do you want to finish this together?" Wiggins asked. "Fine, let's do it," Couprie said. And they did, to the cheers of the crowd as they wheeled across the line. Couprie, of France, and Wiggins, of Tasmania, belong to the same racing team. They had spent most of the day alternating in the lead position, an energy-conserving tactic. The unusual finish was a first for the L.A. Marathon, and the 30-year-old teammates were obviously pleased. "Either one of us could have won it," said Wiggins, "but so what?...This isn't only about winning." In 1995, he returned to Los Angeles—and won the race on his own.

First place finishers in wheelchair racing, with their times and winnings:

MEN'S DIVISION

1986 – Bob Molinatti, USA, 2:16:36 *
1987 – Ted Vance, Canada, 1:54:06, $5,000
1988 – Bob Molinatti, USA, 1:56:35, camera gear
1989 – Jim Knaub, USA, 1:46:52, $1,500
1990 – Moustapha Badid, France, 1:45:40, $4,000
1991 – Jim Knaub, USA, 1:40:53, $7,300 **
1992 – Jim Knaub, USA, 1:33:47, $10,660 **
1993 – Jan Mattern, USA, 1:32:15, $7,500 + watch **
1994 – tie, Phillipe Couprie, France, and Paul Wiggins,
　　　　Australia, 1:34:52, each awarded $3,100 + watch
1995 – Paul Wiggins, USA, 1:36:06, $5,000 + watch

WOMEN'S DIVISION

1986 – Candace Cable-Brookes, USA, 2:23:10 *
1987 – Candace Cable-Brookes, USA, 2:05:45, $5,000
1988 – Candace Cable-Brookes, USA, 2:19:38, camera gear
1989 – Candace Cable-Brookes, USA, 2:07:03, $1,500
1990 – Ann Cody-Morris, USA, 2:03:49, $4,000
1991 – Connie Hansen, Denmark, 1:57:11, $7,300 **
1992 – Connie Hansen, Denmark, 1:56:17, $8,740 **
1993 – Connie Hansen, Denmark, 1:51:26, $7,500 + watch **
1994 – Connie Hansen, Denmark, 1:48:58, $7,500 + watch **
1995 – Jean Driscoll, USA, 1:52:51, $5,000 + watch

MEN'S QUAD

1988 – John Brewer, USA, 2:22:54 *
1989 – John Brewer, USA, 2:18:28, $100
1991 – Christoph Etzlstorfer, Austria, 2:10:00, $1,000
1992 – Christoph Etzlstorfer, Austria, 2:01:22, $1,700 **

WOMEN'S QUAD

1988 – Mary Thompson, USA, 2:51:39 *
1989 – Mary Thompson, USA, 2:56:52, $225
1991 – Mary Thompson, USA, 2:56:43, $1,000
1992 – Mary Thompson, USA, 2:52:57, $520

MEN AND WOMEN'S COMBINED QUAD

1993 – Clayton Gerein, Canada, 2:05:10, $2,000 + watch
1994 – Greg Smith, Australia, 2:06:12, $2,000 + watch
1995 – Christoph Etzlatorfer, Austria, 2:14:46, $2,000 + watch

* 　No prizes awarded.
** 　Winnings include course record or other bonuses.
　Note: Separate quad divisions not staged every year.

TRUE GRIT

THE HISTORY OF THE L.A. MARATHON

IS FILLED WITH REMARKABLE ACCOUNTS

OF INDIVIDUAL COURAGE

AND ACCOMPLISHMENT.

SOME RUNNERS HAVE OVERCOME

PHYSICAL BARRIERS

THAT SEEM INSURMOUNTABLE.

OTHERS HAVE MADE THE MARATHON

ALMOST A HEALING EXPERIENCE.

HERE ARE SOME OF THEIR STORIES.

Antoinette Noel, a 31-year-old social worker from West Covina, Calif., in training for 1992 L.A. Marathon. She toured the course in just under 8 hours. Noel, born without arms, said she was physically active from childhood: "I wanted to be normal, so I attempted everything everyone else was doing." At work, she uses artificial arms.

Legless Vietnam veteran Bob Wieland, 41, of Arcadia, Calif., crosses the finish line at 1987 race. Wieland, who competes by swinging his torso along with his powerful arms, started the race earlier in the week, covering six or seven miles a day and sleeping for a few hours at a time. On Marathon Sunday, as he slowly came into view, the emotional cheers from finish line spectators built into a roar. Wieland, a former medic who lost his legs to a land mine, declared it "the most intense time of my life, outside of Vietnam."

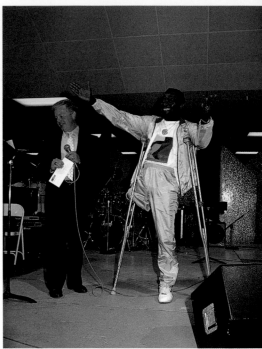

Jesse Al-uqdah of Los Angeles, being honored at a pre-race dinner, is a familiar face at the marathon. Completing the race on crutches requires unusual stamina: in 1992, at age 67, he was out on the course for 12 hours, 26 minutes.

WHEN THE RUNNING GETS TOUGH...

These marathoners know the meaning of willpower:

■ Recovering cancer patient Raymond Derrick of Los Angeles, 63, uses a modified walker to move along the course. Derrick said he wants to recruit "five to ten elderly people in walkers to run with me and demonstrate that we still have what it takes."

■ Margo Apostolos, 39, director of dance at USC, broke into tears of triumph when she crossed the finish line of the 1988 race. Months earlier, she had undergone a partial mastectomy. Against her doctor's advice, she entered and ran her first marathon. After the race, she explained: "What all of it did was help me overcome the psychological aspects of the illness…It was a test of internal strength and will."

■ Scott Wagner, 37, of Miami, was living in a Florida institution, afflicted with Down's syndrome and physically unable to run 100 yards. But not incapable. After intensive training with runner psychologist David Nathanson, Wagner began to enter road races. In 1988, he came to L.A. and ran the marathon in just over six hours. Said Nathanson: "The perception has always been that these people (with Down's syndrome) could not run distance at all, and that was bothersome to me."

■ Moti Gurbaxani, an electronics engineer from Diamond Bar, Calif., started running while recovering from triple heart bypass surgery in 1979. Within a few years, he was entering marathons. Recalled Gurbaxani: "The doctor said, 'If you can control yourself and not run too fast, you've got my blessings. Don't try to beat the 18- or 25-year-olds;

you could kill yourself doing that.'" He ran his first L.A. Marathon in 1986 at the age of 54, and has come back several times since then.

■ Jim MacLaren of Greenwich, Conn., running with an artificial leg, finished the 1993 race in 3 hours, 26 minutes. No big deal, said MacLaren, an ex-college football player who lost his leg in a motorcycle accident in 1985. He had already competed in eight marathons and five triathlons before coming to L.A. ●

Above: The 77-year-old man in the oversized stroller is Mack Robinson, brother of baseball great Jackie Robinson and once a world-class athlete himself. At the 1936 Olympics in Berlin, Mack Robinson won a silver medal by finishing second behind the legendary Jesse Owens in the 200-meter run. In a touching tribute to Robinson's athletic past, his son William (in red trunks) brought the now-disabled track star to the 1992 L.A. Marathon and pushed him 18 miles along the course, to the delight of everyone. William fashioned the stroller by combining parts from two wheelchairs. The elder Robinson lives in Pasadena, Calif., where he and his baseball star brother grew up.

Left: Blind runner Sharlene Wills, 40, of Los Angeles and her guide dog, Sheba, in their first marathon, the 1988 L.A. race. Wills later became a marathon regular, walking or running several events in California and elsewhere, and twice finishing under 5 hours. Sheba kept the pair on track, recalled Wills: "She always knew when we were in a race." The dog died in 1990, and Wills now races with a sighted person as a guide (the two are connected by a rope with handles at each end).

'She Taught Us How to Live'

Patsy Choco of Highland, Calif., always dreamed of running the L.A. marathon.

While training in 1990 for what she hoped would be her first race, she was stricken with breast cancer. Her race plans were set aside, and she underwent surgery.

A year later, in training for the 1992 race, she was diagnosed with lung cancer. Again, she would be unable to run. Several months later, after undergoing a bone marrow transplant and chemotherapy, her condition appeared hopeless.

A determined Choco then wrote this request to marathon officials: "I have entered the L.A. Marathon for 1993 as a walker…I am not sure how far I will be able to go…I am petitioning to you, that if I am unable towards the end of the marathon to finish walking it, that I be allowed to finish in a wheelchair."

Marathon officials gave her the necessary waiver, but it wasn't needed: Patsy Choco, 37, with terminal cancer, went the distance, finishing on her feet in slightly over 7 hours, her dream complete.

She died just over a year later.

Her husband, Alan, best described her accomplishment: "She taught us how to live each day with courage, and for that her daughters, myself and thousands of others will always be grateful."

Patsy Choco at press
conference.

WORKING THE WATER STATIONS

Volunteer workers at this water station in 1993 showed good form. The runner, Delmir Dos Santos of Brazil, maintained his full stride even as he took cup extended to him from sidelines.

Julie Hofstedt of Los Angeles was a volunteer worker at the Mile 2 water station in 1994, an experience she will never forget: "You're standing there, 10,000 people running at you all at once, all of them wanting water…It's really something."

During every marathon, more than a million paper cups with water are handed to the runners for drinking and dousing. Without liquids, marathoners quickly become dehydrated, leading to dizziness, headaches and fainting.

Like relay racers handing off a baton, there is a fine art to slipping a cup into the grip of a runner who is sailing by at 12 m.p.h.

At pre-race training sessions, water station volunteers learn the tricks of the trade. "Grab the top of the cup with your thumb and middle finger," a veteran worker explains. "There has to be enough area for the runner to grab onto it. Hold it out for the runner to take it from you. Try to move with him."

Experienced runners attest to the value of well-trained water battalions. "It definitely helps," said Maria Trujillo, an Olympian who ran the 1987 L.A. Marathon. "When you have to slow down and grab water for yourself, runners can't keep their pace."

Said one volunteer, Mary Page of Los Angeles: "Sometimes, they yell at you if you're not holding it the right way. Or they yell, 'Too full!'"

A runner can get soaked at a water station without even trying. This happens when the runner ahead of him takes a mouthful of water and then spits it out.

"You get downwind of some of those guys and you get drenched," said one L.A. marathoner. "But you know, depending on what kind of day it is, that's all right."

Over the years, the L.A. Marathon has been a leader in water distribution methods. It was the first marathon in America to offer water at every mile, for example. The older Boston and New York races, which used to start handing out water at Mile 5, now also space stations every mile along the course.

The most difficult water day was March 7, 1993 —the hottest L.A. Marathon in history. The temperature was 71 when the race began at 9 a.m., and peaked at 87 by early afternoon.

As the race wore on, runners consumed so much water that stations toward the end of the course started to run dry. Race officials used flatbed trucks to resupply those stations with unused water from earlier points on the course.

Finally, at the request of race officials, then-Mayor Tom Bradley ordered several street hydrants opened. That gave race volunteers a back-up supply of water. A sympathetic Fred Lebow, director of the New York Marathon and an entrant in the L.A. Marathon's 5K that year, summed up: "You can prepare for everything, but you can't prepare for the sun." ●

Wet pavement and a carpet of discarded paper cups are sure signs of a water station. Here, volunteers in 1992 race extend drinks to parched runners along Hollywood Boulevard.

Traffic officer Norman Kellems and his squirt bottle of "liquid ice" provided temporary relief for dozens of aching or cramped leg muscles during the 1993 race. The Los Angeles policeman, a veteran of marathon patrol duty, said he hit on the idea after seeing a number of runners in distress. A marathon aid station gave him a supply of the soothing liquid formula, and he quickly put it to good use (right). "Pretty soon, all these runners were coming up to me and I kept going back to the aid station to get more," he said. "I did it until they ran out."

SHARED MEMORIES

WHEN THE L.A. MARATHON

INVITED COMMENTS FROM RUNNERS

WHO HAD FINISHED EVERY YEAR,

THE RESPONSE WAS ENTHUSIASTIC.

MANY TOLD HOW

THE RACE HAD CHANGED

SOME ASPECT OF THEIR LIVES.

OTHERS EXPRESSED THE PURE

ENJOYMENT OF FINISHING

OR SHARED AMUSING MOMENTS.

HERE ARE EXCERPTS

FROM WHAT THEY HAD TO SAY:

One year just as I crossed under the 25-mile sign, plodding along to an unremarkable 4 hours-plus finish, I looked to my right and noticed another runner approximately my same age, size and weight. He looked over at me and said, "If we kick it, we can come in under 4 hours."

My body was one big hurt. My carbohydrates long gone, I was burning muscle tissue for fuel. The finish line seemed way too far away to think about going any faster. I knew this guy was in the same condition I was, because he looked just like I felt.

Even though I felt like I'd rather walk it on in, I heard myself say, "OK, let's do it!" It was tough to pick up the pace, but soon we started passing everyone around us. Then my new friend started falling behind. I urged him on, saying, "Come on, you can do it. This was your idea anyway!"

He smiled and pulled up to me and we both ran together like a couple of puffing locomotives charging down the tracks. For about half a mile we both held the pace. Then I started losing it. He yelled, "Reach down! Way down! Under 4, we can do it!"

I did reach down, way down, with a final kick into the Coliseum finish area. The cheers of the crowd, the music and the voice from the PA system seemed a hundred miles away. All I could hear was my own ragged deep breathing and my heart pounding like thunder in my chest. We crossed the finish line together in 3:58:40.

After the race, we introduced ourselves, talked a little and then went our separate ways. What would have been an unremarkable finish had turned into a finish that he and I will never forget.

—Tom Jackman, Los Angeles

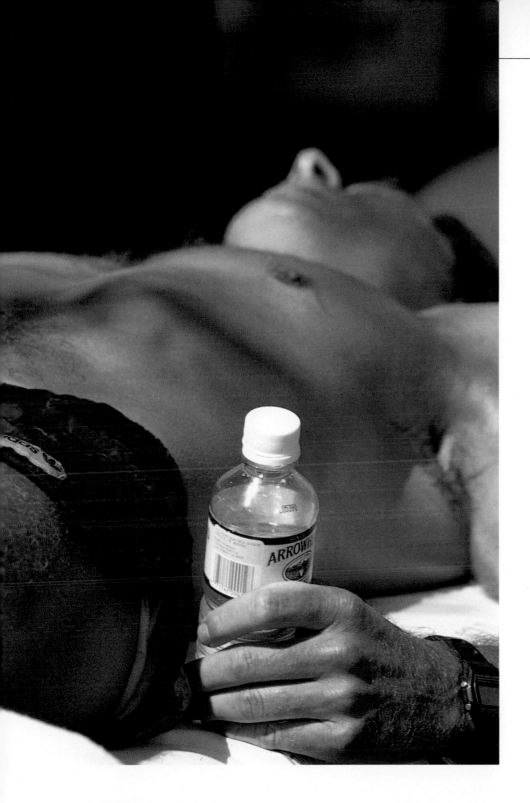

I used to be a fairly normal person until I was struck down with Mid-Life Crisis. I needed a mission in life.

I'd always been told that young ladies did not perspire, and so a hotly contested game of chess was the nearest I ever came to contact sports. However, I decided to buy a pair of fuchsia running shoes and take up long distance running. "Long distance" turned out to be a quarter of a mile.

Perhaps fuchsia shoe laces would improve my performance? They did. I managed an extra 20 yards the next day. What about adding matching shorts, T-shirt, hat and wrist bands? Being color coordinated did the trick and I was up to half a mile and, more importantly, I was hooked.

Fast forward 18 months to 4 a.m. on a cold March morning. The City of Los Angeles was hosting its first marathon. I was too nervous to drive, so I kicked my complaining family out of bed and demanded chauffeur service. "Why are you doing this, Mom?" my older son inquired. "Because I have a mission," I snapped.

The race didn't start until 9 a.m. I went out at my usual pace for a 10-mile race. This was fine for the first 10 miles, but then I was exhausted and I hadn't even reached the halfway mark. The rest of the race was an experience in different levels of agony. After 20 miles, every part of my body was screaming with pain, and my feet were blistered and bleeding.

But all good things must come to an end, and I still remember turning the last corner and seeing the finish line. My thoroughly bored family greeted me with cries of, "Why are you running so slowly?" and "You look like a duck with sore feet."

Four Advil and 20 Bandaids later, we went for a celebration meal. I literally fell asleep in the middle of my dessert. They propped me up in a corner and wiped the lemon meringue pie off my face.

"Why are you doing this, Mom?" my younger son inquired. "Because I have a mission," I mumbled wearily. "What's the mission?" he persisted. "To see how much I can embarrass you guys." "You're doing a great job there, Mom."

—Barbara Reukema, Temple City, Calif.

I thought it was time to exercise when I turned 30. And this was one way of doing just that. The 1986 L.A. Marathon was my very first road race. After finishing the 1992 marathon, my twin sisters, Sharon Martin and Lynda Arnold, asked if they would be able to finish a marathon. I said, "Sure, I'll coach you." We've been running together in the L.A. Marathon ever since.

—Edward Arnold, Coto de Caza, Calif.

The L.A. Marathon has become a permanent part of my life—it's no longer optional. It's over-the-top, a true challenge that is personal and very emotionally rewarding.

—Steven Clemons, Los Angeles

With so many people at the start, my goal is to get through the first mile without getting tripped! The ultimate is to look good at the finish line so that the picture you receive will look good, and that others may think that you have not worked too hard out there on the course. What they don't know won't hurt them.

—Craig Davidson, Phoenix, Ariz.

I never planned on completing all 10 L.A. Marathons. The first one I did on a complete dare from my co-workers. I nearly killed myself, but I limped across that finish line. I feel like the L.A. Marathon was meant for people like me: an ordinary person with a pair of running shoes and a strong will to finish what I start.

—Marco Gonzales, Glendora, Calif.

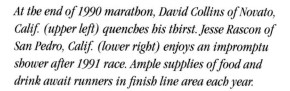

At the end of 1990 marathon, David Collins of Novato, Calif. (upper left) quenches his thirst. Jesse Rascon of San Pedro, Calif. (lower right) enjoys an impromptu shower after 1991 race. Ample supplies of food and drink await runners in finish line area each year.

Running the marathon is more than just a self-esteem booster. A successful marathoner is someone who can decide on a goal, set a pace, and complete a mission regardless of the pain or adversity he or she faces along the way. The physical accomplishment of completing a marathon is terrific, and I do enjoy that part, but the mental toughness that I have proven to myself and demonstrated to others is much more important to me.

—Douglas Hibbard, Corona, Calif.

I like the big running pack, the bands, the hoopla, the super fans along the course. I like the incredible energy and excitement. I like the feeling of unity that all the athletes share and is a very strong presence—there's nothing in the world like it.

—Bill Higgins, Huntington Beach, Calif.

My running is really not about time, it's more about how it mimics life. Along the 26 miles of the course, quitting is a thought that often crosses my mind. But the important part of running a marathon is about crossing the finish line. Someone once told me, "Running is lonely." But I run for those who cheer me on during the races, and for those who support me—my children and my husband.

—Masako Higuchi, Los Angeles

I've finished every marathon I've started. I'm never going to win a car, but that's not what it's all about. Run within yourself.

—Bob Holguin, Whittier, Calif.

Weary after completing their runs, these marathoners drape themselves with lightweight Mylar blankets to ward off chills.

Runners in the middle of the pack are a blur in this overhead view of the route through downtown Los Angeles.

It is a great, fun-filled day that you never forget. Every marathon gives you a chance to reaffirm your beliefs in yourself and what you as a person are capable of accomplishing.

— Harry Shabazian, Long Beach, Calif.

■

I'm not very fast by wheelchair standards; my P.R. is 2:32. But finishing first isn't what's important to me. My goal is just to finish no matter what it takes. In 1990, I had three flat tires. At mile 12, my left rear tire blew. I was carrying a spare, so I replaced it. At mile 16, my right rear tire blew. I only had the one spare, so I continued the race with the right tire flat. Then, about half a mile from the finish line, my left front tire blew. Finally, after three hours, fifty-eight minutes, I rolled across the finish line. I was sore and I was tired but I completed the race.

— Richard Radford, El Segundo, Calif.

■

I was out of shape and overweight when I first started. The Los Angeles Marathon changed me a lot, not only physically but my character too. My tenth marathon is a prized possession in my life that nobody can ever take away.

— Paul Redoble, Castaic, Calif.

■

Each L.A. Marathon marks a milestone in my life. All of them are good, except some years are just faster than others. The key to successful long term running is tenacity and perseverance. It's not the race that is so difficult, it's the day-to-day training that is the real challenge. The marathon itself is simply the celebration of that training.

— Gregory B. Willis, Palos Verdes Estates, Calif.

Nuns, priests and seminarians who run for the Catholic Archdiocese of Los Angeles get encouragement from Cardinal Roger Mahoney before taking to the course. The team uses the marathon to advertise the need for more religious vocations. Spectators at seven Catholic parishes along the race route cheer them on.

I used two of Dr. Kay Porter's imagery concepts and I think I took 12 minutes off the time I anticipated (a 3:18). One was to imagine Golden Bolts of energy coming out of the ground into your feet. Another is that when your legs are tired, imagine Giant Skyhooks lifting at your knees with each step. For those who scoff, it is effective. Marathoners need something to focus on in the last few anaeobic miles, especially when you can barely add two plus two and simple division in your head is out of the question.

— Wayne Wightman, Palos Verdes Estates, Calif.

■

At mile 25, I concentrate on keeping my form. I know if I can keep my form and head up for the next mile or so, I will finish in good shape and maintain my time. Also, fewer people will say, "Keep it up, oldtimer, you're just about done." I hate that (the oldtimer part).

— Jerry Wothe, Tucson, Ariz.

Many of the runners were bedecked in red, white and blue costumes—sometimes in unusual places.

A GRAND OLD FLAG

PATRIOTIC COLORS WERE EVERYWHERE

IN THE 1991 RACE, INSPIRED BY

THE SUCCESSFUL CONCLUSION

OF THE GULF WAR ONLY DAYS EARLIER.

AT THE STARTING LINE,

RUNNERS STOOD UNDER A GIANT YELLOW

RIBBON AND SANG THE NATIONAL ANTHEM.

ON THE COURSE,

SPECTATORS WAVED FLAGS AND CHEERED.

"IT'S A WAY OF SUPPORTING THE RUNNERS

AND THE TROOPS,"

SAID ONLOOKER MARI GARCIA.

"IT'S A DOUBLE CELEBRATION."

Flags were attached to shorts, eyeglasses and— in this case—to a cap.

Salvador Gutierrez, 26, of Reseda, Calif., was one of several runners who carried the colors.

BEFORE THE START

1 The last 10 or 15 minutes before the race is a time of contemplation and quiet, very little conversation. You are gathering your energies and focusing on the task at hand.

OFF AND RUNNING

2 Most marathons don't have as nice a start as L.A. It's a flat, straight shot for almost 2½ miles, and the street is very wide. I use that first stretch to get into a rhythm, get my stride nice and relaxed, and see where everybody is. I check my first mile split and my second mile split, and decide if I'm comfortable at that pace. If I feel like it's too easy, I'll pick it up. If I feel like it's too fast, I'll slow it down.

INTO THE TURNS

3 From 2½ miles through 6 miles there's a lot of turns. You have to slow down a bit to get into them. They're pretty sharp. But that's the thing I like about L.A. You can get into a good rhythm in the first 2½ miles and then slow down slightly in the turns. I concentrate on relaxing and feeling good in those first 6 miles.

TESTING, TESTING

4 There's one steep hill on College Street in Chinatown. It's pretty short, but it's a nice climb. I like to test the pace on that hill, just pick it up a little bit and see how the other runners respond. I want to know what they are interested in

doing…whether they close the gap easily or not.

ON BROADWAY

5 That nice long stretch along North Broadway is a good place to relax until you get to the next hill.

GOING UP

6 For me, the real race starts here. The first mile up Sunset is a very significant hill, the biggest in the course. That's where the race breaks up. You might have a lead pack of, say, 15 runners up to that point and then at 7 miles all of a sudden it's down to 3 or 4 or 5. Why? Because up until then, the course has been relatively flat. A lot of people are feeling good but in reality they have been running over their heads. Now comes Sunset hill. You have to maintain a 5-minute pace running up this hill if you want to stay with the leaders. That's when a lot of runners decide, uh uh, this is not the right pace for me—and they start dropping back. People just get sorted out here.

REST OF SUNSET

7 Sunset keeps going up and down from mile 6 to about 9½ miles…maybe three more hills. The lead group is

reduced to a few runners and I'm more comfortable with that. I kind of get antsy when there are too many people around me. This is my favorite part of the course; it sorts out the pretenders from the serious contenders.

This is also a great section to run because there are lots of spectators on this part of the course. They are shouting and giving you support, and it really helps. Also, you're using different muscles because you're going up and down…it's not just flat.

RELIEF IN SIGHT

8 There's a very nice section starting at about 10 miles and continuing along Hollywood Blvd. where the course is slightly-down-to-flat. It's a good time to just open up your legs and get into a rhythm again.

MILE 13

9 At the halfway point, I really start focusing on how I'm feeling—my breathing, any tightness in my legs. Am I on pace, am I struggling to maintain pace? I don't like to race a marathon from start to finish. I try to relax for as long as I can. So I like to get through the first half feeling relatively comfortable. That

gives me the confidence that I can do another half at the same pace or even a bit quicker. Thirteen miles is a long way, and if you underpace and you are still feeling good, you have lots of time to make up any ground that you may have lost in the first half.

I also want to know about the runners around me. How do they look and how are they responding to changes in the pace? Sometimes it is difficult to know how other people are doing. You can look at a runner one minute and he's looking good, pushing the pace—and half a mile later, he's out the back door. It's hard to predict. A marathon is very tough, very difficult. A lot of things can accumulate over that period of time, and then go wrong.

Some runners like to hang back in the early stages and then come on pretty strong. It can be an effective strategy in a marathon because people in the front tend to die from about mile 18 onwards. So if you really have the confidence that you can pick it up, then you can pick off a lot of people. For myself, I don't like to do that. I try to run my splits even.

When I won in 1991, I ran 65:19 and 65:10. I try to run a marathon as even as possible. So if you employ that come-from-behind tactic and I'm in the lead, you're not going to catch me.

LOOSEN THE LEGS

10 After mile 14, when you turn onto Vine and you get into Rossmore, that's a nice stretch. There are a few places in L.A. that I like to loosen my legs and pick the pace up a bit, and this is one of them, to about mile 16½. The road is wide and open, a gradual downhill, and there is always good spectator support. I'm working hard here.

THE TURN ONTO WILSHIRE

11 This is where it starts getting difficult. You have gradual undulations again in the roadway—short little rises—and there's quite a few turns coming up. From mile 18 to mile 20, you need to concentrate, be economical, just maintain.

MAKING UP TIME

12 The course is quite significantly downhill from about mile 20½ to mile 23. I try to pick it up here. You can make up a lot of time along this stretch.

TURNING TOWARD HOME

13 From mile 23 to the finish seems to be ever-so-slightly uphill. Maybe it's because you have just finished a stretch of great downhill and all of a sudden you hit the flat. Maybe it just feels like uphill. But I think it actually is. Whatever, it's a very, very difficult piece of real estate because it comes at the wrong time. It comes when your energies are drained. The only thing that keeps you going is the knowledge that you are only 3 and a bit miles from the finish.

GO FOR IT

14 This is where I lay it on the line. In a marathon, I hate to leave it to the finish. I think it's the worst possible feeling in the world to be in the lead for 26 miles and then get out-sprinted at the end. So I try and get the race over with in this stretch, from mile 23 to the finish. If anybody is with me, I will use everything I have left to dispose of him.

AN ENERGY LIFT

15 Spectators are packed along the course from mile 23 to the finish, cheering us on, and they make a difference for me, absolutely they do. I'm not able to acknowl-

Plaatjes awaits the start.

Mark Plaatjes won the world marathon championship in August of 1993, three weeks after becoming an American citizen. The former South African, a physical therapist, now lives in Boulder, Colo., with his wife and three daughters. He knows the L.A. Marathon well, having competed five times and won once. Here, he narrates the course map as only an elite runner could.

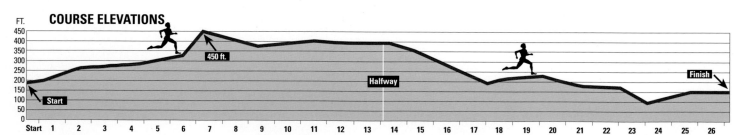

COURSE ELEVATIONS

FT.
450
400
350
300
250
200
150
100
50
0

Start 450 ft. Halfway Finish

Start 1 2 3 4 5 6 7 8 9 10 11 12 13 14 15 16 17 18 19 20 21 22 23 24 25 26

edge them, but it really does give me energy when they are shouting and encouraging. I don't know why, but it does.

THE FINISH

16 Coming down to the finish, it's absolutely a wonderful feeling for everybody, whether you are the winner or a 5-hour runner. The road is lined five-people-deep, everyone is clapping and shouting, there's music playing at the end, the finish line banner is in sight—and you know you've completed a marathon. It's a feeling of accomplishment, a wonderful sense of giving everything you've got. Because, really, that's what the marathon is all about, trying to spread everything you have over 26 miles.

"*This race takes a lot of mental preparation, as well as physical. You have to convince yourself that nothing will stop you from finishing.*"

–Alfonso Hernandez of Los Angeles, waiting to make the 1989 run.

"We thought we were pretty macho playing football, but this makes football seem like a (sissy) sport."

–Brian Patrick Clarke, after twice completing the L.A. Marathon.

LA I

MARCH 9, 1986

Division	Winners and Times	Prizes
Men's Open	Ric Sayre, USA, 2:12:59	$10,000 + new car
Women's Open	Nancy Ditz, USA, 2:36:27	$10,000 + new car

Conditions: Cool and cloudy at start, becoming sunny and mild. High, 65 degrees.

Total entrants: 10,787

Percent finishing: 70%

Total prize pool: $106,200

1986

Sayre Does It His Way

When 32-year-old Ric Sayre won the Long Beach Marathon in February and blithely announced he would run five weeks later in the first City of Los Angeles Marathon, jaws dropped. It's not unheard of, but it is rare that a runner would attempt two marathons so close to each other. Sayre, though, made it look easy. In Los Angeles, he surged to the front after four-plus miles and led the rest of the way, beating back a challenge from Tanzania's Gidamis Shahanga to win by 28 seconds.

Sayre takes a new car home.

"I tend to do well when I race a lot," Sayre explained later. "When I ran well in Boston in '83, it was my third marathon in 60 days. I tend to recover well between marathons."

Sayre, of Ashland, Ore., made his move just before the hilly part of the course and, to his delight, no one came with him. "I was a little surprised," he admitted. "I went out and tried to set as comfortable a pace as I could. I didn't want to expend too much energy early; that's where the hills were and I didn't want to get thrashed."

Third place finisher Rod Dixon of New Zealand praised Sayre's performance: "I think a lot of the runners treated the course with too much respect. I think Ric Sayre was the only guy who said, 'I'm going to run my own race.'"

Sayre's time of 2:12:59 was his personal best.

A Coming Out for Ditz

She was everybody's favorite to win, but Nancy Ditz was upstaged much of the way by an "illegal" runner—a mystery woman who had never officially entered the race. The woman led Ditz for the first 19 miles, then dropped out.

At first, Ditz didn't know what to make of the situation. "I could see her at five miles. I was beginning to get very anxious about her. But people kept telling me that she was unregistered, so I relaxed." Ditz went on to win the race 10 seconds ahead of Christa Vahlensieck of West Germany.

It was a coming out party of sorts for the 31-year-old from Woodside, Calif., who got everyone's attention by winning the California International Marathon three months earlier in 2:31:36. That time was good enough to make her America's second fastest woman marathoner, behind Olympic champion Joan Benoit Samuelson. So she came into Los Angeles a heavy favorite —and didn't disappoint.

The mystery woman? She turned out to be a well-known local runner, 19-year-old Sylvia Mosqueda. Her coach said she was running only for a workout, and never intended to finish.

An elated Ditz hits the tape.

LA II

MARCH 1, 1987

Division	Winners and Times	Prizes
Men's Open	Art Boileau, Canada, 2:12:08	$15,000 + camera gear + new car
Women's Open	Nancy Ditz, USA, 2:35:24	$15,000 + camera gear + new car

Conditions: Mild at start, then hazy and warmer. High, 68 degrees.

Total entrants: 14,937

Percent finishing: 71%

Total prize pool: $176,000

1987

Shaking Off the Nightmare

Art Boileau had unpleasant memories of Los Angeles. He had come to the city in 1984 to run the Olympics marathon, but was bothered by the heat and finished 44th. "The Olympics was kind of a nightmare," said Boileau three years later. "That's kind of why I wanted to come back —to redeem myself, in a way."

The two-time Canadian champion did just that, leaving a pack of three runners behind in the 15th mile and then holding off a late challenge from defending champion Ric Sayre to win by a 30-second margin.

Boileau, 29, won despite running what he described as a "pretty stupid" race. He ran the first 16 miles at a sub-five-minute-mile pace, then slowed considerably while hanging on until the finish.

"I didn't know if I was cutting my own throat or what," he said. "Running five-minute miles was maybe a little too aggressive. I kind of wanted to get off and run my own race—sort of separate myself—but I paid for it in the last eight miles or so."

Sayre, 33, closed fast, but Boileau's lead was too much to overcome, especially under the warm weather conditions. "It wasn't overwhelming, but it took the edge off," Sayre said of the heat.

Boileau at the finish.

Ditz and Mosqueda, Together Again

Nancy Ditz won the women's title for the second straight year—in a race that was eerily similar to the previous year's run.

Ditz trailed Los Angeles college sophomore Sylvia Mosqueda until the 24th mile. Then, "it all caved in" for an exhausted Mosqueda, and Ditz pushed ahead to win by a two-minute-plus margin.

A year earlier, Mosqueda was the "mystery woman" who ran unofficially without a number and led Ditz through the first 19 miles before dropping out. Mosqueda said later she was only running for a workout.

This time, she was a legal entrant—but the outcome was the same.

The 32-year-old Ditz, from Woodside, Calif., said she was never worried. "Nothing's certain, but I was confident," she told reporters.

She said she went into the race assuming that the 20-year-old Mosqueda would go the distance. At one point, Ditz estimated, she was trailing by about two minutes. But after 19 miles, Mosqueda "came back to me very quickly."

Mosqueda said her vision became blurred and she was reduced to "practically jogging…I was really delirious out there."

She hung on to finish second, just nine seconds ahead of Maria Trujillo of Mexico.

Ditz after her second win.

Doing What She Wanted

Less than 24 hours before the start of the L.A. Marathon, Sylvia Mosqueda was competing in a track meet for Cal State L.A., winning the 800 meters and setting a school record while winning the 1,500 meters.

Not the way most runners would prepare for a marathon, but pretty much in character for the free-spirited 20-year-old. Mosqueda, her coach said, "is going to do what she wants to do."

While Mosqueda had to settle for second place behind Nancy Ditz, that seemed to be satisfaction enough.

In a post-marathon interview, she explained: "I don't really like running that far. The only reason I wanted to finish in L.A. was to accomplish something from last year. I didn't want to hear people say, 'Oh, she dropped out again.'

"My idea wasn't to win, and I'm glad it wasn't because if you go out and try to win, it's a lot of pressure."

LA III

MARCH 6, 1988

Division	Winners and Times	Prizes
Men's Open	Martin Mondragon, Mexico, 2:10:19	$25,000 + $5,000 course record bonus + new car + camera gear
Women's Open	Blanca Jaime, Mexico, 2:36:11	$25,000 + new car + camera gear

Conditions: Mild, skies overcast. High, 64 degrees.

Total entrants: 17,040

Percent finishing: 75%

Total prize pool: $191,573

1988

A Duel to the Last Mile

As marathons go, this one was a real nail-biter. South African exile Mark Plaatjes, the pre-race favorite, dueled with Martin Mondragon of Mexico mile after mile. Then, at the 25-mile mark, Mondragon pulled into the lead, and went on to win in record-breaking time.

"In the last mile, my legs gave," Plaatjes said later. "He ran the exact race I like to run. He was steady and constant. He ran very, very well."

Mondragon, 34, was not the most highly regarded member of his delegation: 10 Mexican runners had better times than he. And he had only turned to running at age 30 after giving up hope of becoming a professional soccer player.

Mondragon broke out of the lead pack at about mile 20, with Plaatjes right on his shoulder. Mondragon tried to rid himself of his irritating and dangerous shadow by surging ahead in short bursts, settling in for a time, then surging again. It was energy-sapping, but for Plaatjes, "I had no choice but to go with him."

Mondragon took clear control in the last mile, and finished 22 seconds ahead of Plaatjes. Plaatjes, in turn, was nipped by one second at the tape—by Jesus Herrera of Mexico—and had to settle for third.

Gianni Poli of Italy, two-time winner of the New York Marathon, outran the field for the first 10 miles. But a hamstring injury later slowed him down and he finished seventh.

Mexico's big day:
Mondragon and Jaime.

Outrunning
Two Veterans

A 22-year-old secretary from Mexico City made it a clean sweep for her country by running a steady race that wore out the early leaders.

Blanca Jaime came into Los Angeles with only three years experience as a marathoner. And in the early going, it appeared the honors would go to one of two marathon veterans, Christa Vahlensieck of West Germany and Magda Ilands of Belgium.

The two led most of the way. But neither would win. First, Vahlensieck fell off the pace. Jaime passed her. Then Ilands, the mother of an 18-year-old, began to lose ground. She ended up second, and Vahlensieck finished fourth.

Plaatjes (left)
and Mondragon
fight it out.

An Orange Peel at Twenty Paces

At mile 20, which marathoners sometimes refer to as "The Wall" because of the physical and mental exhaustion that often sets in, two large banners were set up.

A target with a bullseye was attached to each, giving runners something to throw their orange peels and paper cups at. Race organizers thought it might be a good way to vent frustrations, and perhaps pick up spirits.

Most of the time-conscious early runners ignored the target. But by early afternoon, many runners were walking—and throwing whatever was handy at the target. The vast majority missed.

Finally, a 40ish man with red hair hit the bullseye dead center with an orange peel from 15 feet away in a dazzling display of marksmanship.

The crowd cheered. The runner's mouth turned up into a smile, his fists rose in the air, and he sped away.

LA IV

MAR 5 · CALIFORNIA · 1989

LA26PT.2

The City of Los Angeles Marathon IV

MARCH 5, 1989

Division	Winners and Times	Prizes
Men's Open	Art Boileau, Canada, 2:13:01	$26,385 + new car + watch
Women's Open	Zoya Ivanova, USSR, 2:34:42	$26,385 + new car + watch

Conditions: Mild at start, becoming sunny and warm. High, 73 degrees.

Total entrants: 18,917

Percent finishing: 72%

Total prize pool: $215,220

1989

A Second Win for Canada's Boileau

Art Boileau had won in Los Angeles two years earlier, but this time it looked like he would finish out of the money. "I was running pretty conservative," the 31-year-old Canadian agreed later. "I was in 10th place with (Taisuka) Kodama (of Japan). We were helping each other. I was just nailing the guys who would fall behind." Turned out Boileau nailed everyone as a fast early pace and the heat gradually took their toll.

Late in the race, virtually unnoticed, he began to close on the frontrunners. "I knew I had a little more gas in the tank," he said later. With a mile remaining, he passed second-place Pedro Ortiz of Colombia and then overtook the fading Gidamis Shahanga of Tanzania, who had led most of the way.

"The heat just got to me," said Shahanga, who stopped briefly and then resumed at a shuffle pace. "I missed the water stations at 23 and 24 miles. I think that affected my performance. I felt so very tired that I had to walk." Also left behind was former South African Mark Plaatjes, who was running with Ortiz and Shahanga until blistered feet forced him out at the 18.5 mile mark.

Boileau finished a comfortable 27 seconds ahead of runner up Ortiz.

Ivanova, the Taxi Driver

All eyes were on Rosa Mota of Portugal, the marathon champion of the 1988 Olympics. Could she repeat in Los Angeles a year later?

It was not to be. An on-again, off-again nerve injury flared up, and the 5-foot-1 inch runner had to settle for second place behind Zoya Ivanova of the Soviet Union. "I was not…running well by the half marathon," Mota said after the race. "I didn't feel very good in the legs."

Mota ran much of the race amid a pack of male runners who virtually surrounded her. Ivanova went solo; running at first behind them, then slightly in front of Mota, but never side by side. After 20 miles, Ivanova began to put distance between herself and Mota. She finished 45 seconds ahead of the Portuguese runner. "I just can't catch," said Mota. "It was a bad day for me."

But it was a big day for Ivanova. The 37-year-old Soviet was a cross-country skier until she switched to long distance running in 1981, and had only one marathon victory before winning in Los Angeles. Ivanova, used to getting around on city buses or trollies in the Soviet Union, promptly chose a white Mercedes as her prize. "My (3 year old) daughter likes to go by taxi," a delighted Ivanova said. "Now I am her taxi driver."

Boileau and Ivanova: two winners overwhelmed by emotion.

The four Soviet runners arrived in Los Angeles with no shoes or toothbrushes after an airline lost their luggage. It meant they might have to run in new shoes, something one observer noted "you don't want to do unless you want to develop blisters that look like water beds."

Portugal's Rosa Mota offered to lend a pair of well-worn shoes to Soviet runner Zoya Ivanova, but they were too small.

The luggage finally arrived four days late but in time for the race. Equipped with her own shoes, Ivanova ignored the disruption and won the women's open in record time.

In an interview, Mota recalled what it was like to be a pioneer female runner in her country: "I started training in 1972. It was very difficult because the men didn't like me to be in the street, running. They would tell me a woman should be at home. When I was training, they say, 'Go home, woman. You should be at home.'"

Mota still upbeat after "bad day."

Shahanga, in lead at mile 22, looks for the rest of the field. Three miles later, after missing two water stations, he becomes so tired that he is forced to stop and walk.

19

How About Doing Another Take?

"The start [in 1989] was nearly a catastrophe. Big races have chronic problems with exhibitionists—or dreamers—who sprint to the front in the first 200 meters in order to get their pictures in the papers before disappearing into the maw of the real runners.

"Here, despite the best starting line security I've ever seen, one of these misfits somehow got on the front line...[He] apparently wasn't familiar with what a starting gun sounds like. A few minutes before the scheduled start, a balloon popped and the guy took off, followed by the front edge of a human tidal wave.

"Amazingly, the race officials were able to stop the horde and bring them back—which says something about the show-biz character of this event. Where else but in Hollywood can they stop a stampede in the middle and do another take?"

—Ed Ayres in *Running Times* magazine

89

LA V

THE WORLD RETURNS

THE CITY OF
LOS ANGELES
MARATHON

MARCH 4, 1990

MARCH 4, 1990

Division	Winners and Times	Prizes
Men's Open	Pedro Ortiz, Colombia, 2:11:54	$26,385 + new car + watch
Women's Open	Julie Isphording, USA, 2:32:25	$26,385 + new car + watch

Conditions: Cloudy and humid with occasional light rain. High, 62 degrees.

Total entrants: 19,201

Percent finishing: 75%

Total prize pool: $272,520

A Sprint Decides It

Ortiz, intense after his win.

It was an uncommon sight this late in a marathon. About a mile from the finish, three runners were bunched tightly together: Pedro Ortiz of Colombia, Antoni Niemczak of Poland and Peter Fonseca of Canada. What happened next was downright rare.

Ortiz broke into a sprint and, after a beat, Niemczak responded. Fonseca, 23 and running his first marathon, kept his own pace. "I was real apprehensive to go with these guys," he said later. "I thought if I died I would look like an idiot. I decided to hang back and just play the game."

It was no game to Ortiz, who had finished second the previous year and was eager to win this time. "I wanted to be in control of the race," he said afterwards. "If anyone was going to go, I wanted to go with him."

Only Niemczak could go with Ortiz. The two men had the advantage of experience: they were each a decade older than the rookie Fonseca, and had run scores of marathons. Niemczak had placed second in his last four marathons since returning from a drug suspension.

But it was Ortiz who flashed across the finish line first, 11 seconds ahead of the Pole, who later commented wryly: "I am always a runner up."

Mark Plaatjes, the former South African, finished fourth behind Fonseca. He had stayed with the leaders until the 21st mile, but could not maintain their pace.

The victors: Isphording, Ortiz.

Second Chance for Julie

Julie Isphording of Cincinnati flashed a wide smile as she crossed the finish line in record breaking time. She had every reason to. Doctors had told her she might never walk again, never mind run, after back surgery for a ruptured disc three years earlier.

But after a four-month layoff, she began running again. A year later, she was back in marathons.

"Surgery just made me appreciate running more," she said. "When something's taken away from you, you learn not to take it for granted."

Isphording, 28, ran a patient race, watching early leader Sylvia Mosqueda of Los Angeles fade at the 11th mile and staying on the heels of Sirje Eichelmann of the Soviet Union until mile 22.5. Then Isphording overtook the Soviet runner: "I passed her coming down a hill and I never looked back...I could hear the crowd cheering me. It just got really good."

Isphording shaved more than two minutes off the old record.

The victory was especially sweet considering her ordeal in the 1984 Olympics. Running a similar course in the Los Angeles games, Isphording suffered a torn tendon in her right foot and withdrew after 11 miles. "I did get my second chance out here," she said after her win. "This race means a lot for me to win for that reason."

Isphording trims two minutes off the women's record.

A LOOK AND A BUMP

Frontrunner Pedro Ortiz did not give ground willingly in the men's open. Some runners said he even used his elbows and hips if necessary to keep them at bay. Said third-place finisher Peter Fonseca of Canada: "Ortiz would get a little mad and give you a look or a bump and I'd go, 'Whoa, dude.'"

Carlos Pilo Godoy, the La Crescenta, Calif. businessman who trained Ortiz, told a reporter that it was time to recognize Colombia for something other than drug dealing. "We would like to see you put big headlines that a Colombian has won the L.A. Marathon," he declared. "Put very big headlines in your newspaper to tell everybody not all Colombians are bad news."

BEFORE THE CRUNCH: *Well past the halfway mark, the showdown is about to begin. Ortiz (8) and Plaatjes (3) are in front; Niemczak (4) is in the middle of the pack, with Fonseca (27) directly behind him.*

NOW IT'S A FOURSOME: *With everyone else left behind, Ortiz, Plaatjes, Fonseca and Niemczak match each other stride for stride. Plaatjes will be the first to give ground, at about mile 21.*

MAKING THEIR MOVE: *Fonseca is still close to the two leaders after Plaatjes slips off the pace. But Ortiz and Niemczak are about to "blast off" (as Fonseca later described their finishing sprint), and that will be too much for the Canadian rookie.*

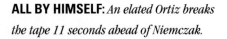

ALL BY HIMSELF: *An elated Ortiz breaks the tape 11 seconds ahead of Niemczak.*

DOWN TO THE WIRE: *The two veterans, Ortiz and Niemczak, duel to the finish. "If anyone was going to go, I wanted to go with him," Ortiz said afterwards.*

LA VI

WHERE EVERY RUNNER IS A STAR · THE CITY OF LOS ANGELES MARATHON · MARCH 3, 1991

MARCH 3, 1991

Division	Winners and Times	Prizes
Men's Open	Mark Plaatjes, USA, 2:10:29`	$50,000 + new car + watch
Women's Open	Cathy O'Brien, USA, 2:29:38	$50,000 + $10,000 course record bonus + new car + watch

Conditions: Mild and partly cloudy at start, occasional sunshine later. High, 73 degrees.

Total entrants: 18,830

Percent finishing: 78%

Total prize pool: $378,000

1991

"Run and Win!"

Three times before, Mark Plaatjes had run the Los Angeles Marathon. In 1988, he was nipped at the tape and finished third; in 1989, his shoes filled with blood from blisters and he dropped out at 18½ miles; in 1990, he mis-timed his training and finished fourth. Los Angeles seemed to be the race that would always break his heart—until his decision this year to try once more.

The 29-year-old Plaatjes took the lead after six miles. From that point on, he churned along unchallenged, laughing to himself when he heard a television announcer tell his audience that Plaatjes had made a serious error in taking the lead, and could not hope to hold it. His winning time was only 10 seconds off the course record.

It was a fitting climax to an agonizing struggle that began in 1988, when he renounced his South African citizenship and was granted political asylum in the United States. For a time, he was the running world's "man without a country," not allowed to compete for South Africa because of international sanctions and not yet a U.S. citizen. "I'm from South Africa, and they don't want to touch me," he said glumly of race organizers. But the Los Angeles Marathon quickly welcomed him and he ran his first race as an exile.

He had not planned to run in Los Angeles in 1991, but changed his mind 10 days before the race after an anguished phone call from his older brother in South Africa. The brother had just been diagnosed with terminal cancer. "Run and win!" he urged Plaatjes. The victorious runner later used a portion of his winnings to bring his ailing brother to the U.S. for a visit.

Four miles from finish, Plaatjes has the lead all to himself.

The Secret Is Relaxing

Boltz a happy second.

Cathy O'Brien, a five foot 102 pound speedster from New Hampshire, did all the work in winning the women's open: she set the pace and led nearly the entire race. And broke the course record in the process.

All told, it was a fine day for the 23-year-old runner who was sixth in the 1984 Olympic Trials at age 16 and made the team in 1988. She finished nearly three minutes ahead of the runner up, Marcia Narloch of Brazil, and shaved seven seconds off the old record established the year before by Julie Isphording of Cincinnati.

O'Brien was especially proud of breaking the critical 2:30 barrier for the first time. How did she do it? By relaxing and not putting pressure on herself, she said in a post-race interview.

Three other runners went into the race with personal best times faster than Isphording's course record: Maria Trujillo of Mexico, who had won in Mexico City, San Francisco and Columbus; Anne Audain, a four-time Olympian from New Zealand; and Priscilla Welch of England, winner of the New York Marathon in 1987 at the age of 42.

But none of them could stay with O'Brien on this Sunday. Audain finished fifth, about five minutes off the pace, and Trujillo came in sixth, about a minute later. Welch did not make it into the top ten, but did win the master's division.

A victory tip of the hat from O'Brien.

Daniel Boltz, the Swiss runner who finished second to Mark Plaatjes, trained for the race in snow. Boltz usually avoids the wet stuff by working out in Australia. But this time he gambled on a warming trend in Bern, and lost the gamble. "I couldn't do much speed training," he said. "I was just tramping snow." Boltz ran for two hours at a time through the snowy countryside; his biggest worry was slipping and breaking a bone on the icy roads.

What can 10 seconds cost you in the Los Angeles Marathon? If you're Mark Plaatjes, the answer is $10,000. That is the bonus that the former South African failed to collect when he missed setting a course record by 10 seconds.

A year earlier, Pedro Ortiz of Colombia and Julie Isphording of the United States were the big winners at the Los Angeles Marathon. This year, neither was able to compete. Isphording was sidelined by a stress fracture and Ortiz dropped out also because of an injury.

LA VII

MARCH 1, 1992

Division	Winners and Times	Prizes
Men's Open	John Treacy, Ireland, 2:12:29	$20,000 + new car + watch + $10,000 special bonus
Women's Open	Madina Biktagirova, CIS, 2:26:23	$20,000 + new car + watch + $10,000 course record bonus + $35,000 special bonus

Conditions: Mild, cloudy. High, 71 degrees.

Total entrants: 19,530

Percent finishing: 78%

Total prize pool: $426,740

1992

Treacy Changes His Luck

John Treacy of Ireland had fond memories of Los Angeles ever since winning a silver medal in the 1984 Olympics marathon, his first race ever at that distance. He returned to the city in later years to run indoors and in various road races, always doing well enough.

But he seemed to have bad luck in other races in other cities, and his confidence gradually waned. His wife, Fionnuala, suggested that the best tonic might be another marathon in Los Angeles. "I told him, 'You've had success in L.A., why not try it there?'" It was good advice.

Treacy, 34, returned in 1992, determined to change his luck. He broke quickly, left the pack behind at the seventh mile, and then struggled through the last three miles to finish first—just 25 seconds ahead of Brazil's Joseildo Rochas, who put on a late surge.

Treacy explained his strategy in a post-race interview: "I'm a very strong uphill runner and I kind of wanted to intimidate everyone there. So I made a move (at mile 7). I knew I'd probably suffer for it later in the race, but if you don't hurt and you're not in great pain..."

Treacy working hard for his win.

He cut it close. By the 23rd mile Treacy was fading fast, fighting cramps and a painful hamstring—and losing ground to Rocha with every stride. It was then that he decided to get mental. "I told myself, 'OK, I got 10 more minutes of running.'" At the finish line, he told his wife triumphantly: "I stuck in there."

Champions Treacy and Biktagirova.

"It's Fantastic, Unbelievable"

Big time runners usually feign nonchalance at earning thousands of dollars at one pop. Not Madina Biktagirova of Belarus.

In Los Angeles, she collected more money in one day than she had earned in her entire running career: $20,000 and a Mercedes for finishing first, a $10,000 bonus for breaking the course record and $35,000 for breaking 2:27.

The newly minted capitalist fairly shrieked when handed the keys to her new automobile, undaunted by the fact that she had no license and didn't know how to drive. As for the money, Biktagirova said through an interpreter: "It's fantastic. It's unbelievable to me."

An extra bonus for Biktagirova was making the Olympic team for the Commonwealth of Independent States. Seven women from the former Soviet Union had set up a training camp for six weeks in Florida, with the knowledge that only the top three would qualify for the Olympic team. That incentive made the women's race the fastest and most competitive in Los Angeles Marathon history. The top four finishers ran under 2:30, the benchmark for elite women marathoners.

The pace was fast even for Biktagirova, who shaved more than six minutes from her previous best. Still, the 27-year-old ran steadily, often glancing at her watch, adjusting her glasses and modestly waving to the crowd.

At the finish line, a beaming Biktagirova draped the tape around her neck and declared: "I'm looking forward to coming back next year."

Biktagirova likes what she sees—a record time.

SNAPSHOTS

John Treacy's punishing finish in the last few miles of the men's open was too nerve wracking for his wife, Fionnuala, who finally turned away from a TV monitor displaying the race. "I was a wreck," she said "I couldn't watch the last two miles, I was so nervous."

Every marathoner is familiar with the pecking order at the starting line. Elite runners go first, then the rest of the pack, with faster runners toward the front and slower runners toward the rear. "Corrals" are used to hold back large groups of runners until it is safe to release them onto the course. The last of the pack requires about seven minutes to get across the starting line. The Marines provide starting line security.

In the early stages of the marathon, conditions are crowded. This is a view of runners in the middle of the pack, getting through the first mile of the race along Figueroa Street.

LA VIII

Division	Winners and Times	Prizes
Men's Open	Joseildo Rocha, Brazil, 2:14:29	New car + watch + $2,500 bonus
Women's Open	Lyubov Klochko, Ukraine, 2:39:49	New car + watch

Conditions: Sunny and hot. High, 87 degrees.

Total entrants: 19,122

Percent finishing: 76%

Total prize pool: $169,490

1993

A Brazilian Beats the Heat

One year earlier, fighting for the lead in the Los Angeles Marathon, Brazil's Joseildo Rocha had trouble gauging his position and ended up settling for second place. Afterwards, he vowed: "I will not let it happen again. I will be in the lead." Rocha lived up to his promise in 1993, outrunning fellow Brazilian Jose Santana late in the race to win.

Unseasonable heat—the high was 87 degrees —produced some of the slowest times in the marathon's history. The race was still unfolding at the halfway point, and the most experienced runners were reassessing their condition at each mile. Tactics were crucial on a day like this.

Rocha's strategy was to stay back and conserve energy. Like other elite runners, he ignored the race's two rabbits, who set a blistering early pace. "The pace in the beginning was too fast," said Rocha. "I waited. I knew I would have a lot left in the second half."

Peter Renner of New Zealand, third the year before, had a tenuous grip on the lead until Mile 20, when he began to cramp. Rocha and Santana sensed Renner's distress and pounced. The two Brazilians, who trained together, matched stride for stride for three miles. Then they began racing in earnest, and Rocha pulled away to win by 29 seconds.

Said Rocha later: "The biggest enemy was the heat."

Rocha in front, with Santana on his heels.

Klochko, flanked by male runners, at mid-course.

She Makes Running A 'Womanly Pursuit'

Lubov Klochko of Ukraine had a score to settle with the Los Angeles Marathon. A year earlier, she had to drop out with back pain after 13 miles. It was an especially frustrating decision because the race served as an Olympic qualifying trial for the runners from the Commonwealth of Independent States.

That frustration festered while Klochko trained in the snowy mountains of Ukraine, thinking of her teammates who ran at the Barcelona Olympics, one of whom won the gold medal in the marathon. Klochko's will to win in Los Angeles was further strengthened at home, where her brother ridiculed her choice of professions. "Running is not a womanly pursuit," he told her.

Klochko could only laugh after this year's race, which she led wire to wire. As she twirled the keys to her new Mercedes, someone asked what would her brother say to her now? "He would say, 'You must give me the keys to your car. I want it,'" Klochko said. Then, with a smile, she added: "He will never get it."

Klochko's race strategy, as she put it, was: "Run with everyone in the first part, then it depends." She finished ahead of her nearest competitor, Carole Rouillard of Canada, by nearly a minute and a half.

Peter Tshikila of South Africa, the fourth place finisher in the men's open, came into the race still recovering from a back injury. The cause of the 30-year-old's injury? Worn out running shoes, according to his agent.

'We Are Here to Stay'

As the running of the 1993 marathon approached, Los Angeles was still feeling the aftermath of rioting only months earlier—a TV-screen horror seen nationwide. Marathon organizers faced some tough questions. Would runners come to the still-tense city? Should the race be rerouted to avoid central city neighborhoods hard-hit by the riots?

"We wondered…if there would be an L.A. Marathon in 1993," said race president William A. Burke.

That the event survived intact was largely the result of a dogged marketing campaign by Burke and his staff. After weighing the route decision for weeks, he decided that abandoning the old course would be "the wrong message" to send to an anguished city. Instead, marathon officials prepared an intensive promotional campaign that confronted the city's embattled reputation but also made the case for supporting the race. Additional security measures were put in place. Race organizers sent delegates to other marathons to drum up interest and reassure runners. "We are here to stay," Burke declared.

On race day, it all paid off. Entries topped the 19,000 mark, and spectators numbered in the hundreds of thousands. Los Angeles had remembered how to smile. An ebullient Mayor Tom Bradley summed up: "It's always an event that pulls the city together. Some idiotic people wanted to change the race (route), but people know better. This is still a city of harmony."

After rioting in Los Angeles, marathon officials scrapped the traditional race motto—"The L.A. Marathon, Where Every Runner's a Star"—and substituted a slogan that seemed more meaningful: "Together We Win."

Residents along the marathon route in 1993 used garden hoses to help runners cool off. Temperatures were the highest ever—about 20 degrees above normal.

How hot was it? About 30 degrees higher than marathoners prefer. Here is how temperatures soared at the hottest Los Angeles Marathon of all:

9 a.m.: 71 degrees
10 a.m.: 77 degrees
11 a.m.: 81 degrees
noon: 84 degrees
1 p.m.: 87 degrees
2 p.m.: 85 degrees
3 p.m.: 84 degrees

Source: National Weather Service

John Treacy of Ireland, winner of the men's open the year before, was unprepared for the heat. "It really saps you," he said after finishing fifth, "and there's nothing that can be done once you are in the race. That last two miles…the only way I would sum them up would be, they are murder."

Carole Rouillard of Canada, the 32-year-old runner-up in the women's open, said that when the day dawned hot, she abandoned any thoughts of a fast time. "I decided to run carefully," she said after the race. "I knew at a certain point that she (front runner Lubov Klochko) was ahead of me by almost three minutes. I thought to just run for second. Then later, people were telling me, 'She's dying.' I thought to myself, 'I'm dying, too.'"

LA IX

MARCH 6, 1994

Division	Winners and Times	Prizes
Men's Open	Paul Pilkington, USA, 2:12:13	$15,000 + $12,000 title bonus + car + watch
Women's Open	Olga Appell, USA, 2:28:12	$15,000 + car + watch

Conditions: Cool and cloudy. High, 67 degrees.

Total entrants: 19,033

Percent finishing: 79%

Total prize pool: $132,500

1994

The Year of the Rabbit

Utah's Paul Pilkington was hired to be the "rabbit"—to set a fast pace for the best runners before dropping out himself. Somebody else was supposed to win.

Pilkington knew the drill: he had been a rabbit in at least five previous marathons, including twice in New York. But on this Sunday in Los Angeles, the 35-year-old high school teacher from Utah surprised everyone.

With nearly a two-minute lead and 10 miles remaining, Pilkington decided to go the distance. "After I did my job by getting out fast, nobody came after me," he said later. "I figured as long as I was out there and feeling good, why stop?"

He finished first, 39 seconds ahead of runner-up Luca Barzaghi of Italy, the pre-race favorite.

Barzaghi had fallen so far behind Pilkington that he could no longer see him. He figured Pilkington had dropped out of the race—as promised, according to Barzaghi—so he slowed. "I thought the rabbit had dropped out; nobody told me he was still running. I thought I won," Barzaghi said angrily through an interpreter. "I was keeping my own pace. I was not running against him."

But Pilkington, whose rabbit fee was $3,000, said he never promised to quit. Anyhow, he added, the rabbit always has the option of staying in the race. "It doesn't happen very much, but it's always possible," said he.

He couldn't have timed it better. Because this race for the first time was considered the U.S. Track and Field men's marathon championship, Pilkington collected a $12,000 bonus for winning the national title.

A dizzy day in marathon history.

Salah trails Salvador Garcia of Mexico.

'I Will Be Different'

This marathon, said Olga Appell, would be "very, very special"—her first race as an American. The Mexican-born runner had taken her oath of citizenship in Albuquerque, where she lived, only a week before heading to Los Angeles.

In a pre-race interview, she said proudly: "I will wear the same running clothes as always, I will be the same runner. But I will be different."

An emotional Appell, spurred on by chants of "Go U.S.A.," won with ease—and in her best personal time. Overnight, Mexico's fastest female marathoner had become America's fastest female marathoner.

Her only problem was coping with enthusiastic Latino runners, who surrounded her early in the race. They wanted to give her encouragement. Worse, they wanted to break marathon rules and give her a drink of water. "I had to tell them to please back off, that I needed to run," said Appell. "I understand that they wanted to help, but I needed more room."

By the second half of the race, she was far ahead. Then, "I heard somebody say I was headed for a 2:30 finish. I wanted to do better than that, so I got it going." She finished nine minutes ahead of the runner-up, Emma Scaunich of Italy.

Appell after victory.

SNAPSHOTS

Ahmed Salah, an army lieutenant from the African republic of Djibouti, came into Los Angeles with the fastest previous time of anyone entered—2:07:07. But at age 37, his best days seemed to be behind him. He challenged Pilkington for five miles before dropping off the pace and finishing 13th, struggling with severe cramps at the finish.

The 1994 Los Angeles Marathon marked the first time in nine years that the men's and women's winners in one of the big three marathons—New York, Boston, Los Angeles were U.S. citizens at the time of the race.

Paul Pilkington wore a white glove on his left hand as he ran, but it was not a fashion statement. Pilkington, an asthma sufferer, stored his inhaler inside the glove.

A 5-Carrot Performance

"The use of a rabbit is a widespread if questionable part of track. These are kind of the sport's version of stunt men. They are not really part of the race, just decoys of a sort. Meet promoters habitually hire them in order to set up world records for the mega-stars. They are like the guys who set themselves on fire or leap off a cliff into a torrent below or crash cars for the film's leading men.

"Paul Pilkington was practically the Easter Bunny of the craft. He had rabbitted at the New York City Marathon, as well as those in Cleveland and Tokyo.

"Traditionally, the rabbit is supposed to run an unrealistic pace until he has pulled the race along behind him and set it up for the serious runners. Then, he is meant to step off the track.

"This is what Pilkington had been hired to do in Los Angeles. But, along about the step-off time, the 16th mile or so, he found himself so alone in the race, he decided to keep running, at least until they caught up to him.

"They never did.

"It was rabbitry's finest hour. Bugs Bunny at the finish line chomping on a carrot and grinning, 'What's up, doc?'"

—Columnist Jim Murray in the *Los Angeles Times*

A QUICK START: *As expected, Paul Pilkington takes the early lead. But he isn't expected to remain in the race.*

ALL ALONE: *Approaching the halfway point in the race, Pilkington has the course all to himself. A few miles later, he decides to go the distance.*

A WRONG ASSUMPTION: *Italy's Luca Barzaghi, meanwhile, has lost sight of Pilkington and assumes he has quit. With Ahmed Salah close behind, Barzaghi looks back at the field to see who else is still with him.*

RABBIT RUNS FIRST: *Pilkington, with a broad smile, hits the tape. He couldn't understand what all the fuss was about, he said later.*

SORRY, BUT NO: *Barzaghi crosses the finish line 39 seconds later, thinking he has won. He reacts angrily when told that Pilkington has already arrived.*

LA X

MARCH 5, 1995

Division	Winners and Times	Prizes
Men's Open	Rolando Vera, Ecuador, 2:11:39	$15,000 + car + watch
Women's Open	Nadia Prasad, France, 2:29:48	$15,000 + car + watch

Conditions: Rain, heavy at times. Windy and cold. High, 62 degrees.

Total entrants: 19,442

Percent finishing: 78%

Total prize pool: $136,900

A Tactical Race On a Soggy Day

"The main goal for everyone is to run under 2:10," said reigning world champion Mark Plaatjes before the race. "It's the 10th anniversary, and we'd like to see a fast time." Indeed, at least four of the men—including Plaatjes—had run faster than the L.A. record of 2:10:19. But at the end of a blustery day, the record still stood.

"Too much rain and too much water," summed up winner Rolando Vera, 29, of Ecuador. He hung back until the late stages, then overtook frontrunner Bob Kempainen, a 30-year-old Minnesota medical student who went into the race as America's fastest (2:08:47) marathoner ever.

A trio of U.S. men—Plaatjes, Kempainen and Arturo Barrios—took turns leading an 11-member pack in the early going. But by mile 20, the race was between Vera and Kempainen. Vera, small and slightly built, stayed on Kempainen's heels, letting the taller and heavier American runner block the wind. Just past mile 22, Vera made his move, and it was all over.

Later, Kempainen described his dilemma: "It came down to being a real tactical race...Unfortunately, he hung really tough and I got into the situation where I was leading into the wind and he was stronger at the end."

Said Vera: "I am very happy to win this race."

A happy Vera.

Prasad Gets 'The Big One'

Nadia Prasad, a 27-year-old from the French territory of New Caledonia, prepared for the L.A. race by working out in Boulder, Colo., with veteran runner Mark Plaatjes. As the rain came down before race time, she observed: "I trained in the very cold weather in Boulder, I trained in the very hot weather in New Caledonia. So I'm ready for anything."

She certainly was. Prasad went out front at the start, staying in lockstep with Lyobov Klochko, 35, of Ukraine for the first six miles. Then she pulled into a commanding lead and ran unchallenged to the finish, a full 3 minutes and 11 seconds ahead of runner-up Anna Rybicka, 31, of Poland. Klochko finished third.

"At the end, it was getting very cold," Prasad said afterwards. "The rain wasn't bothering me very much, but it was the wind. It makes it cold." She declared herself "very proud" of her victory, adding: "It's a big one for me."

Prasad wasn't exaggerating. The victory revived her marathon career, which had begun to dim after she failed to finish the 1994 Boston and New York marathons. A few days before the L.A. race, she had vowed: "No matter what happens, I will finish this race. Even if I am on my knees, I will finish." She not only finished, she did it in her best personal time ever—2:29:48.

Prasad in front.

Marathon organizers put more than $500,000 on the line to encourage fast times by the male elite runners. In addition to so-called appearance fees, performance bonuses were set to kick in for men who finished at 2:10 and below. The high stakes helped lure the strongest field of elite men in the history of the race, but times were not fast enough to trigger the bonuses.

How does it feel to be known as a rabbit? No problem, says Paul Pilkington, the surprise winner in L.A. in 1994 and a veteran at setting the pace for pay. "I'm the rabbit that won," he said in an interview. "I don't mind that. I don't mind the term *rabbit*. It's what I do."

Bob Kempainen, second in the men's race, is looking forward to 1996. That is the year he hopes to complete his medical studies and run in the Atlanta Olympic Games. And then it will be strictly Dr. Kempainen, retired marathoner, perhaps specializing in internal medicine—but not sports medicine. "It just doesn't appeal to me," he said.

A Mystery Man Who Just Wanted to Help

The scene was puzzling: a male runner with one leg covered in black tights, striding with Nadia Prasad mile after mile, like a bodyguard. He passed paper cups of water to her. At times, he ran in front of her to block the wind. He became such a fixture at her side that television viewers phoned in to ask who was this mystery helper.

Two miles from the finish, Prasad sprinted ahead to win the women's race. Her male companion, she agreed, had been helpful—but she had no idea who he was. "I don't even know this person," she told a news conference.

The mystery was solved when reporters tracked down 28-year-old Jorge Marquez, a teacher's assistant from Hermosa Beach, Calif., who explained: "All I wanted to do was help. This was a training run for me. A bigger deal for her. We're all in this together."

Marquez, who stayed with Prasad for 24 miles before falling behind, finished in a very respectable 2 hours and 32 minutes. He said he was preparing for the upcoming inaugural Disneyland Marathon.

Marquez offered so much assistance that Prasad's race might have violated distance running rules, except no other women runners protested. He told reporters that he recognized her from a newspaper photograph, and volunteered to help. Said Marquez: "She had no idea who I am. Still doesn't. But this sort of thing, it happens all the time."

Marquez with Prasad.

AN ARGUMENT OVER STRATEGY

They had a deal, Mark Plaatjes said, and Rolando Vera didn't keep up his end of it. Instead, he let others do the work while taking home the $15,000 winner's check. That was the gist of a post-race dispute over Vera's hang-back strategy in the men's race.

Runners in the elite pack were slowed by windy conditions—except for Vera, who decided to let somebody else block the breeze, much to the chagrin of those getting it in their faces. As Plaatjes later explained it, the elites had met the day before to establish a pace for race rabbit Paul Pilkington. "But we said that if something happens to the rabbit, it was up to us to keep up the pace," said Plaatjes.

Pilkington stepped into a pothole and left the race early. "I dropped back and said, 'The rabbit is gone,'" Plaatjes explained. "I think that all of us felt obligated to take a lead. After that, each of us took a turn in front, except [Vera]."

Bob Kempainen, who ran two critical miles with Vera close behind, admitted to feeling frustrated: "I think anyone who has ever been in that situation can tell you, when you're hammering the pace up front and the guy's right there every time you take a look over your shoulder, it is frustrating. You want to take a swat [said with a smile]. But at the same time, he ran a smart race. I mean, it's totally within running etiquette to run that [kind of race]. I could have slowed down if I wanted to, but I thought eventually I'd be able to break him."

Kempainen at times tried to shake Vera by zig-zagging, but Vera zig-zagged with him. A bit after mile 22, the Ecuadorian runner took the lead from Kempainen and went on to win. His timing, said Kempainen, was perfect: "It seemed as soon as he took the lead, we turned a corner and there was a tailwind."

Vera's version of events? "I was waiting for that last three miles," he told reporters. "It really helped me to run behind [Kempainen]." Asked why he did not take a turn leading the pack, he said: "I wasn't feeling good at that time and I want to apologize. I was just trying to win the race." ●

Vera (5) hangs back in early going, then stays on the heels of Kempainen (2) before pulling away for win.

the agony...

Yasu Yuki Sakakibara of Japan rests dejectedly at 20-miles after blistered feet forced him out in 1989.

"It's going pretty bad. I'm in a lot of pain. (But) I'm going to finish. I have to."

– PHILLIP PARK, 33, as he stopped to massage an ankle at 17-mile mark in 1994.

"I'm dehydrated. I'm dizzy. This isn't my proudest moment."

– Anonymous runner sidelined by heat in 1993.

"I feel like a dog."

– MARK PLAATJES, former South African runner, after foot blisters forced him out in 1989.

"It was like someone took a sledge hammer to the bottoms of my feet."

– KEN ERNST, 28, of Los Angeles after going the distance in 1990.
It was his first marathon.

"I couldn't even really stand. I felt awful. It took me a good 45 minutes to recuperate and become myself again. I felt like I was a zombie or something."

–SYLVIA MOSQUEDA, 20, of Los Angeles after finishing second in 1987 women's open.

"I am in extreme pain and will probably be this way for a few days."

– SUE HOWARD, 31, of Irvine, Calif., after completing 1989 run.

Josef Slozeblemski, a 35-year-old mechanic from Poland, completed the 1990 marathon in 6 hours, 39 minutes, on crutches and an artificial leg.

One runner finishes despite apparent cramps; another is so exhausted that medical volunteers must carry her from the course.

...the ecstasy

Moustapha Badid of France, former world record holder, after he won the 1990 wheelchair race.

"...You feel great afterwards, you feel alive! There's a sense of accomplishment, a private thing. Something that's yours."

— Actress JO ANN WILLETTE, 25, a two-time finisher in L.A. Marathon.

"I've had such great memories of L.A. Things go well for me here. Now, it's my town!"

— Irish runner JOHN TREACY after winning the men's open in 1992

"Mom, I can't believe it. I wish you could have been here. It was so intense."

–JULIE ISPHORDING on the phone to her mother after winning women's open in 1990.

"It was my dream to run in America."

– Ukraine runner VLADIMIR KRIVOY, 41, at 1991 marathon.

"It was the strangest sensation—
agony, happiness, ecstasy.
...The next day at the studio
I was telling everyone,
'Guess what, I ran the marathon.'"

–"L.A. Law" actor CORBIN BERNSEN after his first L.A. Marathon in 1987.

"...A tremendous event...It was a hell of
a way to celebrate my 60th birthday!"

–KEITH TAYLOR of Chula Vista, Calif., after finishing 1990 race.

Christina Lightfoot, 26, of Woodland Hills, Calif., is delighted with her 3 hour, 21 minute finish in 1991.

An elated Peter Kim, 38, of La Canada, Calif., after 1994 run. "It's indescribable," says Kim. "You have to run a marathon to understand it."

Mexico's Martin Mondragon moments after his win in 1988.

L.A. MARATHON COURSE RECORDS

Date	Set	Time	Name/Country
OPEN DIVISION:			
3/6/88	Men	2:10:19	Martin Mondragon/Mexico
3/1/92	Women	2:26:23	Madina Biktagirova/C.I.S.
MASTERS DIVISION:			
3/3/91	Men	2:14:33	John Campbell/New Zealand
3/4/91	Women	2:36:48	Graziela Striuli/Italy
RACEWALKING DIVISION:			
3/6/92	Men	3:30:47	Ronald Baers/USA
3/5/89	Women	4:20:22	Patricia Carroll/USA
WHEELCHAIR OPEN DIVISION:			
3/7/93	Men	1:32:1	Jan Mattern/USA
3/6/94	Women	1:48:58	Connie Hansen/Denmark
WHEELCHAIR QUAD DIVISION:			
3/1/92	Men	2:01:22	Christoph Etzlstorfer/Austria
3/6/88	Women	2:51:3	Mary Thompson/USA

AGE GROUP COURSE RECORDS:

Age Group	Time	Name/Country	Year
Men under 17	2:50:27	Enrique Villagrana/USA	1992
Men 18-24	2:12:08	Peter Fonseca/Canada	1990
Men 25-29	2:10:29	Mark Plaatjes/USA	1991
Men 30-34	2:10:19	Martin Mondragon/Mexico	1988
Men 35-39	2:12:49	Martin Pitayo/Mexico	1995
Men 40-44	2:14:33	John Campbell/New Zealand	1991
Men 45-49	2:30:25	Robert Abbott/USA	1987
Men 50-54	2:28:26	Eloy Lozada/Mexico	1990
Men 55-59	2:39:42	Ruben Cordon/USA	1991
Men 60-64	2:52:13	Jim O'Neill/USA	1986
Men 65-69	3:14:00	Alex Ratelle/USA	1990
Men 70-74	3:40:56	Eddie Lewin/USA	1987
Men 75-79	4:02:29	Chick Dahlsten/USA	1986
Men 80+	5:12:11	Balmukund Sharma/India	1988
Women under 18	2:49:19	Carrie Garritson/USA	1988
Women 18-24	2:29:38	Cathy O'Brien/USA	1991
Women 25-29	2:26:23	Madina Biktagirova/CIS	1992
Women 30-34	2:28:12	Ramilia Burangulova/CIS	1992
Women 35-39	2:33:31	Lyobov Klochko/Ukraine	1995
Women 40-44	2:36:48	Graziella Striuli/Italy	1990
Women 45-49	2:40:20	Priscilla Welch/Great Britain	1991
Women 50-54	3:12:38	Carolyn Boyum/USA	1990
Women 55-59	3:22:30	Wen-Shi Yu/USA	1990
Women 60-64	3:51:03	Wen-Shi Yu/USA	1995
Women 65-69	4:09:01	Vostile Goodrich/USA	1992
Women 70-74	4:31:22	Margret Lee/USA	1990
Women 75-79	5:39:32	Bess James/USA	1986
Women 80+	5:43:07	Mavis Lindgren/USA	1988

L.A. MARATHON BEST PERFORMANCES

MEN'S OPEN DIVISION:

Time	Name/Country	Place	Year
2:10:19	Martin Mondragon/Mexico	(1)	1988
2:10:29	Mark Plaatjes/USA	(1)	1991
2:10:40	Jesus Herrera/Mexico	(2)	1988
2:10:41	Plaatjes	(3)	1988
2:11:10	Daniel Boltz/Switzerland	(2)	1991
2:11:30	Carlos Retiz/Mexico	(4)	1988
2:11:39	Rolando Vera/Ecuador	(1)	1995
2:11:54	Pedro Ortiz/Columbia	(1)	1990
2:11:59	Bob Kempainen/USA	(2)	1995
2:12:06	Antoni Niemczak/Poland	(2)	1990
2:12:08	Peter Fonseca/Canada	(3)	1990
2:12:13	Paul Pilkington/USA	(1)	1994
2:12:29	John Treacy/Ireland	(1)	1992
2:12:52	Luca Barzaghi/Italy	(2)	1994
2:12:54	Joseildo Rocha/Brazil	(4)	1992
2:12:59	Ric Sayre/USA	(1)	1986
2:12:59	Martin Pitayo/Mexico	(3)	1995
2:13:01	Art Boileau/Canada	(1)	1989
2:13:08	Boileau	(1)	1987
2:13:12	Manuel Vera/Mexico	(5)	1988

WOMEN'S OPEN DIVISION:

Time	Name/Country	Place	Year
2:26:23	Madina Biktagirova/CIS	(1)	1992
2:28:12	Olga Appell/USA	(1)	1994
2:28:12	Ramilia Burangulova/CIS	(2)	1992
2:29:38	Cathy O'Brien/USA	(1)	1991
2:29:40	Kerstin Pressler/Germany	(3)	1992
2:29:41	Valentina Egorova/CIS	(4)	1992
2:29:48	Nadia Prasad/France	(1)	1995
2:31:24	Lizanne Bussiers/Canada	(5)	1992
2:32:25	Julie Isphording/USA	(1)	1990
2:32:42	Marcia Narloch/Brazil	(2)	1991
2:32:56	Narloch/Brazil	(6)	1992
2:32:59	Anna Rybicka/Poland	(2)	1995
2:33:17	Tatiana Zuyeva/CIS	(7)	1992
2:33:27	Olga Markova/USSR	(3)	1991
2:33:31	Lyobov Klochko/Ukraine	(3)	1995
2:33:44	Alevtina Naumova/USSR	(4)	1991
2:33:44	Lizanne Bussieres/Canada	(2)	1990
2:34:37	Anne Audain/New Zealand	(5)	1991
2:34:42	Zoya Ivanova/USSR	(1)	1989
2:34:51	Aniela Nikiel/Poland	(4)	1995

MEN'S MASTERS DIVISION:

Time	Name/Country	Place	Year
2:14:33	John Campbell/New Zealand	(4)	1991
2:17:46	Artemio Navarro/Mexico	(11)	1991
2:17:51	Campbell	(9)	1989
2:19:20	Kjell-Erik Stahl/Sweden	(7)	1986
2:19:27	Bob Schlau/USA	(18)	1988
2:19:44	Victor Mora Garcia/Colombia	(11)	1987
2:20:15	Campbell	(14)	1990
2:20:30	Bill Rodgers/USA	(21)	1988

WOMEN'S MASTERS DIVISION:

Time	Name/Country	Place	Year
2:36:48	Graziela Striuli/Italy	(4)	1990
2:37:05	Emma Scaunich/Italy	(2)	1994
2:40:20	Priscilla Welch/Great Britain	(11)	1991
2:47:21	Barbara Filutze/USA	(7)	1987
2:51:23	Harolene Walters/USA	(13)	1987
2:54:18	Walters	(19)	1988
2:57:05	Cindy Dalrymple/USA	(25)	1988
2:57:26	Walters	(11)	1986
2:59:10	Claudia Ciavarella/USA	(28)	1986

MEN'S RACEWALKING DIVISION:

Time	Name/Country	Place	Year
3:30:47	Ronald Baers/USA	(1)	1992
3:41:16	Rene Haarpainter/USA	(1)	1988
3:43:15	Jose Lopez/USA	(2)	1992
3:44:53	Alfredo Perez Carmona/Mexico	(2)	1988
3:45:50	Frederico Valerio/USA	(1)	1986
3:49:57	Patrick Kelly/USA	(3)	1988
3:51:09	Aristeo Cortez/USA	(1)	1987
3:53:57	Raul Nunez Macias/Mexico	(1)	1993

WOMEN'S RACEWALKING DIVISION:

Time	Name/Country	Place	Year
4:20:22	Patricia Carroll/USA	(1)	1989
4:34:35	Margaret Gorea/USA	(1)	1994
4:41:17	Brenda MacIsaac/USA	(1)	1995
4:42:27	Daniela Hairabedian/USA	(1)	1991
4:43:35	Susan Henricks/USA	(1)	1987
4:47:18	Jill Latham/Great Britain	(1)	1990
4:47:40	Lorraine Miller/USA	(1)	1992
4:48:19	Latham	(2)	1991
4:54:26	Latham/USA	(2)	1992
4:54:35	Judy Heller/USA	(3)	1992
4:55:18	Wendy Harp/USA	(1)	1988
4:58:23	Lorraine Miller/USA	(3)	1991
4:58:44	Latham	(2)	1988
4:58:59	Henricks	(2)	1989
4:58:44	Latham	(2)	1988

MEN'S WHEELCHAIR OPEN DIVISION:

Time	Name/Country	Place	Year
1:32:15	Jan Mattern/USA	(1)	1993
1:33:47	Jim Knaub/USA	(1)	1992
1:34:47	Craig Blanchette/USA	(2)	1993
1:34:52	Philippe Couprie/France	(1)	1994
1:34:52	Paul R. Wiggins/Australia	(1)	1994
1:34:52	Scot Hollonbeck/USA	(4)	1993
1:34:57	Andre Viger/Canada	(5)	1993
1:35:35	Jorge Luna/USA	(6)	1993
1:36:06	Wiggins	(1)	1995
1:36:16	Claude Issorat/France	(1)	1992
1:36:26	James A. Briggs/USA	(3)	1994
1:37:45	Jan Mattern/USA	(4)	1994
1:38:26	Moustapha Badid/France	(5)	1994
1:38:27	Scot A. Hollonbeck/USA	(6)	1994
1:38:27	Eric T. Neitzel/USA	(7)	1994

WOMEN'S WHEELCHAIR OPEN DIVISION:

Time	Name/Country	Place	Year
1:48:58	Connie Hansen/Denmark	(1)	1994
1:51:26	Hansen	(1)	1993
1:51:49	Lily Anngreny/Germany	(2)	1993
1:51:51	Jeanette Jansen/Netherlands	(3)	1993
1:52:30	Louise Sauvage/Australia	(4)	1993
1:52:51	Jean Driscoll/USA	(1)	1995
1:54:02	Deanna Sodoma/USA	(5)	1993
1:54:38	Louise Sauvuge/Australia	(2)	1994
1:54:40	Tanni Grey/Great Britain	(3)	1994
1:56:17	Connie Hansen/Denmark	(1)	1992
1:57:11	Hansen	(1)	1991
1:57:18	Ann Cody-Morris/USA	(2)	1991
1:57:18	Cody-Morris	(1)	1990
1:57:32	Sodoma	(2)	1992
2:00:48	Sauvage	(2)	1995

MALE COURSE RECORD::			FEMALE COURSE RECORD:		
Martin Mondragon, Mexico			Madina Biktagirova		
2:10:19 (March 6, 1988)			2:26:23 (March 1, 1992)		
Elapsed Time			**Elapsed Time**		
Mile 1	4:58	9:14:58 a.m.	Mile 1	5:35	9:15:35 a.m.
Mile 2	9:56	9:19:56	Mile 2	11:10	9:21:10
Mile 3	14:54	9:24:54	Mile 3	16:45	9:26:45
Mile 4	19:52	9:29:52	Mile 4	22:20	9:32:20
Mile 5	24:50	9:34:50	Mile 5	27:55	9:37:55
Mile 6	29:48	9:39:48	Mile 6	33:30	9:43:30
Mile 7	34:46	9:44:46	Mile 7	39:05	9:49:05
Mile 8	39:44	9:49:44	Mile 8	44:40	9:54:40
Mile 9	44:42	9:54:42	Mile 9	50:15	10:00:15
Mile 10	49:40	9:59:40	Mile 10	55:50	10:05:50
Mile 11	54:38	10:04:38	Mile 11	1:01:25	10:11:25
Mile 12	59:36	10:09:36	Mile 12	1:07:00	10:17:00
Mile 13	1:04:34	10:14:34	Mile 13	1:12:35	10:22:35
Mile 14	1:09:32	10:19:32	Mile 14	1:18:10	10:28:10
Mile 15	1:14:30	10:24:30	Mile 15	1:23:45	10:33:45
Mile 16	1:19:28	10:29:28	Mile 16	1:29:20	10:39:20
Mile 17	1:24:26	10:34:26	Mile 17	1:34:55	10:44:55
Mile 18	1:29:24	10:39:24	Mile 18	1:40:30	10:50:30
Mile 19	1:34:22	10:44:22	Mile 19	1:46:05	10:56:05
Mile 20	1:39:20	10:49:20	Mile 20	1:51:40	11:01:40
Mile 21	1:44:18	10:54:18	Mile 21	1:57:15	11:07:15
Mile 22	1:49:16	10:59:16	Mile 22	2:02:50	11:12:50
Mile 23	1:54:14	11:04:14	Mile 23	2:08:25	11:18:25
Mile 24	1:59:12	11:09:12	Mile 24	2:14:00	11:24:00
Mile 25	2:04:10	11:14:10	Mile 25	2:19:35	11:29:35
Mile 26	2:09:08	11:19:08	Mile 26	2:25:20	11:35:10
Finish	2:10:19	11:20:19	Finish	2:26:23	11:36:23

RACE RESULTS: 1986–1995

L.A. I–MARCH 9, 1986

MEN'S OPEN DIVISION:

Name/Country	Time	Prize
1. Ric Sayre/USA	2:12:59	$10,000 + car + camera
2. Gidimas Shahanga/Tanzania	2:13:27	7,000
3. Rod Dixon/New Zealand	2:14:48	3,000
4. Eberhard Weyel/West Germany	2:18:00	2,000
5. Gary Tuttle/USA	2:18:05	1,000
6. Doug Kurtis/USA	2:19:04	800
7. Kjell-Erik Stahl/Sweden	2:19:20	600
8. Chris Schallert/USA	2:19:42	400
9. Victor Mora Garcia/Colombia	2:20:46	200
10. Luis Pinon/USA	2:22:02	100

WOMEN'S OPEN DIVISION

Name/Country	Time	Prize
1. Nancy Ditz/USA	2:36:27	$10,000 + car
2. Christa Vahlensieck/W. Germany	2:36:37	7,000
3. Magda Ilands/Belgium	2:38:25	3,000
4. Mariela Hurtado-Fuentes/Mexico	2:42:10	2,000
5. Laurie Madison/USA	2:51:01	1,000
6. Josita Bear/USA	2:51:54	800
7. Araceli Salas/USA	2:51:54	600
8. Michelle Tiff/USA	2:54:30	400
9. Pamela Morris/USA	2:54:50	200
10. Kathy Thomas/USA	2:54:56	100

MEN'S MASTERS DIVISION:

Name/Country	Time	Prize
1. Kjell-Erik Stahl/Sweden	2:19:20	$ 1,200
2. Victor Mora Garcia/Colombia	2:20:46	800
3. Patrick Murphy/USA	2:22:50	600
4. David Oropeza/USA	2:28:24	300
5. John Loeschorn/USA	2:28:27	100

WOMEN'S MASTERS DIVISION:

Name/Country	Time	Prize
1. Harolene Walters/USA	2:57:26	$ 1,200
2. Sheila Hasham/USA	3:17:33	800
3. Wendy Watson/USA	3:17:50	600
4. Lillian Mahoney/USA	3:18:03	300
5. Mattie Wilkes/USA	3:19:22	100

AGE GROUP WINNERS:

Group	Name/Country	Age	Time
Men 18-24	Luis Pinon/USA	21	2:22:02
Men 25-29	Gidimas Shahanga/Tanzania	27	2:13:27
Men 30-34	Ric Sayre/USA	32	2:12:59
Men 35-39	Rod Dixon/New Zealand	35	2:14:48
Men 40-44	Kjell-Erik Stahl/Sweden	40	2:19:20
Men 45-49	Robert Abbott/USA	45	2:36:43
Men 50-54	Severino Venzor/Mexico	54	2:43:14
Men 55-59	Patrick Devino/USA	57	2:50:03
Men 60-64	Jim O'Neill/USA	60	2:52:13
Men 65-69	Paul Reese/USA	68	3:18:50
Men 70-99	Jon Baldwin/USA	70	3:52:19
Women 18-24	Araceli Salas/USA	21	2:51:54
Women 25-29	Mariela Hurtado-Fuentes/Mexico	26	2:42:10
Women 30-34	Nancy Ditz/USA	31	2:36:28
Women 35-39	Christa Vahlensieck/W. Germany	36	2:36:37
Women 40-44	Harolene Walters/USA	43	2:57:26
Women 45-49	Mattie Wilkes/USA	46	3:19:22
Women 50-54	Marjorie Gilmore/USA	51	3:51:40
Women 55-59	Ruth Bloland/USA	57	3:57:00
Women 60-64	Virginia Hastings/USA	61	4:23:11
Women 65-69	Norma Bernardi/USA	66	4:21:48
Women 70-99	Bess James/USA	76	5:39:52

MEN'S RACEWALKING DIVISION:

Name/Country	Time
1. Federico Valerio/USA	3:45:50
2. Alan Jacobson/USA	4:14:04
3. Gary Null/USA	4:20:32
4. Fred Dong/USA	4:21:43
5. Mark Hartzell/USA	4:27:00

WOMEN'S RACEWALKING DIVISION:

Name/Country	Time
1. Susan Travellin/USA	5:16:20
2. Ana Oliva/USA	6:00:57
3. Jill Latham/Great Britain	6:17:10
4. Gretchen Ambrose/USA	6:18:25
5. Bernadine Ward Kallon/USA	6:59:28

MEN'S WHEELCHAIR DIVISION:

Name/Country	Time
1. Bob Molinatti/USA	2:16:36
2. Peter Brookes/USA	2:19:55
3. Randy Snow/USA	2:20:00
4. Rafael Ibarra/USA	2:20:02
5. Kie Soo Hoo/USA	2:23:07

WOMEN'S WHEELCHAIR DIVISION:

Name/Country	Time
1. Candace Cable-Brookes/USA	2:23:10
2. Mary Thompson/USA	3:17:23
3. Mary Jones/USA	4:40:31
(only competitors)	

L.A. II–MARCH 1, 1987

MEN'S OPEN DIVISION:

Name/Country	Time	Prize
1. Art Boileau/Canada	2:13:08	$15,000 +car + camera
2. Ric Sayre/USA	2:13:38	8,000 +camera gear
3. Jose Gomez/Mexico	2:14:31	5,000 +camera gear
4. Artemio Navarro/Mexico	2:14:46	4,000
5. Ivo Rodriguez/Brazil	2:14:48	3,000
6. Domingo Tibaduiza/Columbia	2:17:20	2,500
7. Joel Hernandez/Mexico	2:18:05	2,000
8. Geoffrey Koech/Kenya	2:19:17	1,500
9. Yasuhiko Mori/Japan	2:19:34	1,000
10. Mark Sheehan/USA	2:19:38	500

WOMEN'S OPEN DIVISION:

Name/Country	Time	Prize
1. Nancy Ditz/USA	2:35:24	$15,000 + car + camera
2. Sylvia Mosqueda/USA	2:37:40	8,000 + camera gear
3. Maria Trujillo/Mexico	2:37:49	5,000 + camera gear
4. Christa Vahlensieck/FDR	2:40:11	4,000
5. Magda Ilands/Belgium	2:40:45	3,000
6. Michelle Aubuchon/USA	2:42:57	2,500
7. tie, Margarita Galuez/USA, Barbara Filutze/USA	2:47:21	3,500 share
9. Deborah Sharp/USA	2:48:44	1,000
10. Mary Tracey/USA	2:49:22	500

MEN'S MASTERS DIVISION:

Name/Country	Time	Prize
1. Victor Mora Garcia/Columbia	2:19:44	$ 1,500
2. John Loeschorn/USA	2:26:32	1,000
3. Patrick Murphy/USA	2:28:16	800
4. Robert Abbott/USA	2:30:25	500
5. Jussi Haimalainen/USA	2:34:40	200

WOMEN'S MASTERS DIVISION:

Name/Country	Time	Prize
1. Barbara Filutze/USA	2:47:21	$ 1,500
2. Harolene Walters/USA	2:51:23	1,000
3. Georgia Gustafson/USA	3:05:01	800
4. Molly Thayer/USA	3:09:18	500
5. Mary Campbell/USA	3:11:58	200

AGE GROUP WINNERS:

Group	Name/Country	Age	Time
Men 18-24	Joel Hernandez/Mexico	22	2:18:05
Men 25-29	Art Boileau/Canada	29	2:13:08
Men 30-34	Ric Sayre/USA	33	2:13:38
Men 35-39	Artemio Navarro/Mexico	37	2:14:46
Men 40-44	Victor Mora-Garcia/Columbia	42	2:19:44
Men 45-49	Robert Abbott/USA	46	2:30:25
Men 50-54	Andre Tocco/USA	51	2:44:22
Men 55-59	Patrick Devine/USA	58	2:55:51
Men 60-64	John Keston/USA	62	2:52:38
Men 65-69	Harold Daughters/USA	65	2:23:41
Men 70-99	Eddie Lewin/USA	70	3:40:56

Women 18-24	Sylvia Mosqueda/USA	20	2:37:46
Women 25-29	Maria Trujillo/Mexico	27	2:37:50
Women 30-34	Nancy Ditz/USA	32	2:35:24
Women 35-39	Christa Vahlensieck/FDR	37	2:40:11
Women 40-44	Barbara Filutze/USA	40	2:47:21
Women 45-49	Nancy Mustard/USA	45	3:27:02
Women 50-54	Sandra Kiddy/USA	50	3:14:09
Women 55-59	Evelyn Dabritz/USA	56	3:57:56
Women 60-64	Joanne Schmitz/USA	61	3:59:23
Women 65-69	Norma Bernardi/USA	67	4:20:46
Women 70-99	Lucile Adney/USA	83	6:23:52

MEN'S RACEWALKING DIVISION:

Name/Country	Time
1. Aristeo Cortez/USA	3:51:09
2. Eliseo Salgado/USA	4:02:24
3. Enrique Camarena/USA	4:03:43
4. Dale Sutton/USA	4:23:27
5. Richard Oliver/USA	4:26:52

WOMEN'S RACEWALKING DIVISION:

Name/Country	Time
1. Susan Henricks/USA	4:43:35
2. Jill Latham/Great Britain	5:13:00
3. Annie Mance/USA	5:23:04
4. Kathy Blackmer/USA	5:23:41
5. Vanessa George-Goulden/USA	5:32:14

MEN'S WHEELCHAIR DIVISION

Name/Country	Time	Prize
1. Ted Vance/Canada	1:54:06	$ 5,000
2. Mike Postell/USA	1:54:06	2,500
3. Marc Quessy/Canada	1:55:07	1,500
4. Jim Martinson/USA	1:56:57	1,000
5. Rafael Ibarra/USA	1:58:58	500

WOMEN'S WHEELCHAIR DIVISION:

Name/Country	Time	Prize
1. Candace Cable-Brookes/USA	2:05:45	$ 5,000
2. Angela Ieriti/Canada	2:15:42	2,500
3. Karin Baumohl/USA	3:01:09	1,500
4. Mary Thompson/USA	3:05:22	1,000
5. Mary Jones/USA	3:13:01	500

Note: special awards valued at $2,250 were distributed to other wheelchair competitors.

L.A. III–MARCH 6, 1988

MEN'S OPEN DIVISION:

Name/Country	Time	Prize
1. Martin Mondragon/Mexico	2:10:19	$30,000 +car + camera
2. Jesus Herrera/Mexico	2:10:40	8,000 +camera
3. Mark Plaatjes/ex-South Africa	2:10:41	5,000 +camera
4. Carlos Retiz/Mexico	2:11:30	4,000
5. Manuel Vera Canelo/Mexico	2:13:12	3,000
6. Alejandro Cruz/Mexico	2:13:14	2,500
7. Gianni Poli/Italy	2:13:55	2,000
8. Filemon Lopez/Mexico	2:15:00	1,500
9. Jorge Gonzales/Puerto Rico	2:15:04	1,000
10. Pedro Ortiz/Colombia	2:15:23	500

WOMEN'S OPEN DIVISION:

Name/Country	Time	Prize
1. Blanca Jaime/Mexico	2:36:11	$25,000 +car + camera
2. Magda Ilands/Belgium	2:37:03	8,000 + camera gear
3. Jillian Costly/New Zealand	2:37:12	5,000 + camera gear
4. Christa Vahlensieck/W. Germany	2:39:29	4,000
5. Sharon Higgins/New Zealand	2:41:51	3,000
6. Bernie Portenski/New Zealand	2:42:40	2,500
7. Gillian Horovitz/Great Britain	2:43:22	2,000
8. Margarita Galicia/Mexico	2:43:24	1,500
9. Maria Elena Reyna/Mexico	2:43:37	1,000
10. Janis Klecker/USA	2:43:38	500

MEN'S MASTERS DIVISION

Name/Country	Time	Prize
1. Bob Schlau/USA	2:19:27	$ 1,500 + camera gear
2. Bill Rodgers/USA	2:20:30	1,000
3. Murray James Hunt/New Zealand	2:22:02	800

4. Jussi Hamalainen/USA   2:32:13   500
5. Barry Brown/USA   2:32:26   200

WOMEN'S MASTERS DIVISION:

Name/Country	Time	Prize
1. Harolene Walters/USA	2:54:18	$ 1,500 + camera gear
2. Cindy Dalrymple/USA	2:57:05	1,000
3. Sally Edwards/USA	2:59:54	800
4. Charlene Groet/USA	3:02:07	500
5. Betty Ferguson/USA	3:07:00	200

AGE GROUP WINNERS:

Group	Name/Country	Age	Time
Men 18-24	Alejandro Cruz/Mexico	20	2:13:14
Men 25-29	Jesus Herrera/Mexico	25	2:10:40
Men 30-34	Martin Mondragon/Mexico	34	2:10:19
Men 35-39	Manuel Vera Canelo/Mexico	36	2:13:12
Men 40-44	Bob Schlau/USA	40	2:19:27
Men 45-49	Bob Abbott/USA	47	2:36:17
Men 50-54	Andre Tocco/USA	52	2:47:42
Men 55-59	Jack Cagot/USA	55	2:51:59
Men 60-64	Otis McKinney/USA	60	3:02:11
Men 65-69	William Norris/USA	67	3:37:19
Men 70-99	Walther Troger/W. Germany	71	3:53:40
Women under 18	Carrie Garritson/USA	11	2:49:19
Women 18-24	Blanca Jaime/Mexico	22	2:36:11
Women 25-29	Jillian Costly/New Zealand	27	2:37:12
Women 30-34	Gillian Horovitz/Great Britain	32	2:43:22
Women 35-39	Magda Ilands/Belgium	38	2:37:03
Women 40-44	Sally Edwards/USA	40	2:59:54
Women 45-49	Harolene Walters/USA	45	2:54:18
Women 50-54	Marianna McMullen/USA	50	3:32:25
Women 55-59	Esther Milich/USA	56	4:24:17
Women 60-64	Beverly Smith/USA	61	4:38:26
Women 65-69	Margaret Lee/USA	68	4:41:45
Women 70-99	Mavis Lindgren/USA	80	5:43:08

MEN'S RACEWALKING DIVISION:

Name/Country	Time
1. Rene Haarpainter/USA	3:41:16
2. Alfredo Perez Carmona/Mexico	3:44:53
3. Art Cortez/USA	4:06:36
4. Richard Oliver/USA	4:27:19
5. Enrique Camarena/USA	4:33:14

WOMEN'S RACEWALKING DIVISION:

Name/Country	Time
1. Wendy Harp/USA	4:55:18
2. Jill Latham/Great Britain	4:58:44
3. Anne Long/Great Britain	5:13:01
4. Inez Phillips/USA	5:22:15
5. Leona Davis/USA	5:30:17

MEN'S WHEELCHAIR DIVISION:

Name/Country	Time	Prize
1. Bob Molinatti/USA	1:56:35	camera gear
2. Tim O'Connell/USA	1:59:07	
3. Danny Westley/Canada	1:59:09	
4. Junior Rice/USA	1:59:49	
5. Phil Carpenter/USA	1:59:51	

WOMEN'S WHEELCHAIR DIVISION:

Name/Country	Time	Prize
1. Candace Cable-Brookes/USA	2:19:38	camera gear
2. Sherry Ramsey/USA	2:22:08	
3. Sharon Frenette/USA	2:35:30	
4. Tami Oothoudt/USA	2:36:04	
5. Ingrid Lauridsen/Denmark	2:43:26	

MEN'S WHEELCHAIR QUAD DIVISION:

Name/Country	Time
1. John Brewer/USA	2:22:54

WOMEN'S WHEELCHAIR QUAD DIVISION:

Name/Country	Time
1. Mary Thompson/USA	2:51:39

L.A. IV—MARCH 5, 1989

MEN'S OPEN DIVISION:

Name/Country	Time	Prize
1. Art Boileau/Canada	2:13:01	$26,385 + car + watch
2. Pedro Ortiz/Colombia	2:13:28	$10,000 + watch
3. Ernest Tjela/Lesotho	2:14:30	4,000 + watch
4. Gidimas Shahanga/Tanzania	2:15:32	3,500 + watch
5. Greg Meyer/USA	2:16:46	3,000 + watch
6. Taisuke Kodama/Japan	2:17:14	2,500 + watch
7. Tom Birnie/New Zealand	2:17:30	2,000 + watch
8. Isidro Rico/Mexico	2:17:51	1,500 + watch
9. John Campbell/New Zealand	2:17:51	1,000 + watch
10. Filemon Lopez/Mexico	2:17:57	500 + watch

WOMEN'S OPEN DIVISION:

Name/Country	Time	Prize
1. Zoya Ivanova/USSR	2:34:42	$26,385 + car + watch
2. Rosa Mota/Portugal	2:35:27	$10,000 + watch
3. Olga Dourinina/USSR	2:40:25	4,000
4. Gretchen Lohr-Cruz/USA	2:41:41	3,500
5. Marie Ellena Reyna/Mexico	2:42:49	3,000
6. Gail Hall/USA	2:44:08	2,500
7. Sirje Eichelmann/USSR	2:44:42	2,000
8. Kerryn Hindmarsh/Australia	2:45:17	1,500
9. Beatrix Peralta/Mexico	2:45:25	1,000
10. Cindy James/USA	2:45:47	500

MEN'S MASTERS DIVISION:

Name/Country	Time	Prize
1. John Campbell/New Zealand	2:17:51	$ 2,000
2. Bill Rodgers/USA	2:22:24	1,250
3. Miguel Mendez/Mexico	2:31:34	750
4. Jussi Hamalainen/USA	2:31:51	
5. Javier Jardines Ortiz/Mexico	2:38:37	

WOMEN'S MASTERS DIVISION:

Name/Country	Time	Prize
1. Carol Mather/USA	3:02:57	$ 2,000
2. Odette Osantowski/USA	3:05:26	1,250
3. Nina Bovio/USA	3:10:31	750
4. Marygail Brauner/USA	3:11:34	
5. Harolene Walters/USA	3:11:40	

AGE GROUP WINNERS:

Group	Name/Country	Age	Time
Men 18-24	Jose Carlo Santana Silva/Brazil	21	2:18:56
Men 25-29	Isidro Rico/Mexico	27	2:17:51
Men 30-34	Art Boileau/Canada	31	2:13:01
Men 35-39	Tom Birnie/New Zealand	36	2:17:30
Men 40-44	John Campbell/New Zealand	40	2:17:51
Men 45-49	Julian Barrera/USA	46	2:39:43
Men 50-54	Ron Navarrette/USA	50	2:53:08
Men 55-59	Jack Cagot/USA	56	3:00:37
Men 60-64	Patrick Devine/USA	60	2:58:52
Men 65-69	Jack Pennington/USA	66	3:37:28
Men 70-74	Eddie Lewin/USA	72	4:10:09
Men 75-79	John Zentmyer/USA	77	4:51:39
Men 80-99	Manning Wein/USA	87	10:31:19
Women 18-24	Olga Dourinina/USSR	24	2:40:25
Women 25-29	Gretchen Lohr-Cruz/USA	29	2:41:41
Women 30-34	Rosa Mota/Portugal	30	2:35:27
Women 35-39	Zoya Ivanova/USSR	36	2:34:42
Women 40-44	Carol Mather/USA	40	3:02:57
Women 45-49	Harolene Walters/USA	46	3:11:40
Women 50-54	Wen-Shi Yu/USA	54	3:32:43
Women 55-59	Hisae Reichel/USA	55	4:06:58
Women 60-64	Peggy Ewing/USA	61	4:52:10
Women 65-69	Margaret Lee/USA	69	4:39:42
Women 70-74	Althea Jureidini/USA	70	5:57:30
Women 75-79	Bess James/USA	79	5:51:07
Women 80-99	Mavis Lindgren/USA	81	6:09:33

MEN'S RACEWALKING DIVISION:

Name/Country	Time
1. Gary Null/USA	4:05:20
2. Franco Pantoni/USA	4:21:30
3. Enrique Camarena/USA	4:30:51
4. Clyde Hatfield/USA	4:35:09
5. Carl Acosta/USA	4:42:18

WOMEN'S RACEWALKING DIVISION:

Name/Country	Time
1. Patricia Carroll/USA	4:20:22
2. Susan Henricks/USA	4:58:59
3. Veda Roubideaux/USA	5:12:02
4. Anne Barrick/USA	5:12:18
5. Susan Hoch/USA	5:15:43

MEN'S WHEELCHAIR DIVISION:

Name/Country	Time	Prize
1. Jim Knaub/USA	1:46:52	$ 1,500
2. Bob Molinatti/USA	1:46:55	1,000
3. Ray Stewart/USA	1:54:32	500
4. Wolfgang Petersen/W. Germany	1:54:33	
5. Chris Hallam/Great Britain	1:54:37	

MEN'S WHEELCHAIR QUAD DIVISION:

Name/Country	Time	Prize
1. John Brewer/USA	2:18:28	$ 100
2. Russell Monroe/USA	2:29:48	75
3. Richard Nolen/USA	2:40:55	50

WOMEN'S WHEELCHAIR DIVISION:

Name/Country	Time	Prize
1. Candace Cable-Brookes/USA	2:07:03	$ 1,500
2. Mary Jones/USA	2:49:51	1,000
3. Mary Thompson/USA	2:56:52	500
4. Nanci Cotton/USA	3:11:59	
(only finishers)		

WOMEN'S WHEELCHAIR QUAD DIVISION:

Name/Country	Time	Prize
1. Mary Thompson/USA	2:56:52	$ 225
(only reported finisher)		

L.A. V—MARCH 4, 1990

MEN'S OPEN DIVISION:

Name/Country	Time	Prize
1. Pedro Ortiz/Colombia	2:11:54	$26,385 + car + watch
2. Antoni Niemczak/Poland	2:12:05	$15,000 + watch
3. Peter Fonseca/Canada	2:12:07	9,000 + watch
4. Mark Plaatjes/USA	2:13:44	7,000 + watch
5. Art Boileau/Canada	2:14:36	6,000 + watch
6. Mohamed Salmi/Algeria	2:15:35	5,000 + watch
7. Merv Johnstone/Australia	2:16:13	4,000 + watch
8. Sam Ngatia/Kenya	2:17:02	3,500
9. Guido Genicco/Italy	2:18:19	3,000
10. Steve McCormack/USA	2:18:50	2,500

WOMEN'S OPEN DIVISION:

Name/Country	Time	Prize
1. Julie Isphording/USA	2:32:25	$26,385 + car + watch
2. Lizanne Bussieres/Canada	2:33:44	$15,000 + watch
3. Helen Moros/New Zealand	2:36:44	9,000 + watch
4. Graziella Striuli/Italy	2:36:48	7,000 + watch
5. Lorraine Hochella/USA	2:37:23	6,000 + watch
6. Ellen Rochefort/Canada	2:37:59	5,000 + watch
7. Blanca Jaime, Mexico	2:38:20	4,000 + watch
8. Flora Moreno/Mexico	2:38:21	3,500
9. Rosalva Bonilla/USA	2:40:38	3,000
10. Martha Jimenze/Mexico	2:41:14	2,500

MEN'S MASTERS DIVISION:

Name/Country	Time	Prize
1. John Campbell/New Zealand	2:20:15	$ 2,000 + watch
2. Artemio Navarro/Mexico	2:20:57	1,250
3. Ryszard Marczak/Poland	2:22:00	750

WOMEN'S MASTERS DIVISION:

Name/Country	Time	Prize
1. Graziela Striuli/Italy	2:36:48	$ 2,000 + watch
2. Odette Osantowski/USA	3:03:32	1,250
3. Harolene Walters/USA	3:11:00	750

AGE GROUP WINNERS:

Group	Name/Country	Age	Time
Men 17 & Under	Jesus Ortiz, Jr./USA	17	3:04:59
Men 18-24	Peter Fonseca/Canada	23	2:12:07
Men 25-29	Mark Plaatjes/USA	27	2:13:44
Men 30-34	Pedro Ortiz/Columbia	32	2:11:54
Men 35-39	Bill McDermott/USA	38	2:27:40
Men 40-44	John Campbell/New Zealand	41	2:20:15
Men 45-49	Robert Nelson/USA	49	2:34:30
Men 50-54	Eloy Lozada/USA	50	2:28:26
Men 55-59	Jack Cagot/USA	57	3:01:28
Men 60-64	Patrick Devine/USA	61	3:05:46
Men 65-69	Alex Ratelle/USA	65	3:14:00
Men 70-74	Eddie Lewin/USA	73	3:41:20
Men 75-79	Dutch Benedetti/USA	75	4:11:49
Men 80-98	William Kuester/USA	81	7:37:45
Women 17 & Under	Denise Castellanos/USA	15	3:17:54
Women 18-24	Helen Moros/New Zealand	22	2:36:44
Women 25-29	Julie Isphording/USA	28	2:32:25
Women 30-34	Sirje Eichelmann/USSR	34	2:33:36
Women 35-39	Ellen Rochefort/Canada	35	2:37:59
Women 40-44	Graziella Striuli/Italy	41	2:36:48
Women 45-49	Harolene Walters/USA	47	3:11:12
Women 50-54	Carolyn Boyum/USA	53	3:12:38
Women 55-59	Wen-Shi Yu/USA	55	3:22:30
Women 60-64	Maeann Garty/USA	62	4:09:42
Women 65-69	Judy Golding/USA	69	5:03:26
Women 70-74	Margaret Lee/USA	70	4:31:22
Women 75-79	Lucile Adney/USA	76	7:18:49
Women 80-98	Mavis Lindgren/USA	82	6:25:26

MEN'S RACEWALKING DIVISION:

Name/Country	Time
1. Wayne Wurzburger/USA	4:26:13
2. Stephen Collins/USA	4:34:07
3. John Stowers/USA	4:36:25
4. Bill Neder/USA	4:37:15
5. Robert Mimm/USA	4:38:35

WOMEN'S RACEWALKING DIVISION:

Name/Country	Time
1. Jill Latham/USA	4:47:18
2. Karen Helms/USA	5:12:00
3. Susan Wientjes/USA	5:23:04
4. Trudy Patrick/USA	5:23:06
5. D. Murray/USA	5:29:53

MEN'S WHEELCHAIR DIVISION:

Name/Country	Time	Prize
1. Moustapha Badid/France	1:45:40	$ 4,000
2. Andre Viger/Canada	1:52:14	2,000
3. Wolfgang Petersen/W. Germany	1:52:15	1,000

WOMEN'S WHEELCHAIR DIVISION:

Name/Country	Time	Prize
1. Ann Cody-Morris/USA	2:03:49	$ 4,000
2. Connie Hansen/Denmark	2:03:50	2,000
3. Daniela Jutzler/Switzerland	2:15:39	1,000

L.A. VI—MARCH 3, 1991

MEN'S OPEN DIVISION:

Name/Country	Time	Prize
1. Mark Plaatjes/USA	2:10:29	$ 50,000 +car + watch
2. Daniel Boltz/Switzerland	2:11:10	25,000 + watch
3. Eddy Hellebuyck/Belgium	2:14:14	20,000 + watch
4. John Campbell/N. Zealand	2:14:33	15,000 + watch
5. Juan Juarez/Argentina	2:15:20	10,000 + watch
6. Rafael Zepeda/Mexico	2:15:51	9,000 + watch
7. Ivo Rodriguez/USA	2:16:15	8,000 + watch
8. Michael Heilmann/Germany	2:16:26	7,000
9. Francesco Fauci/Italy	2:16:38	6,000
10. Ivan Huff/USA	2:17:25	5,000

WOMEN'S OPEN DIVISION:

Name/Country	Time	Prize
1. Cathy O'Brien/USA	2:29:38	$ 50,000 +car + watch
2. Marcia Narloch/Brazil	2:32:42	25,000 + watch
3. Olga Markova/USSR	2:33:27	20,000 + watch
4. Alevtina Naumova/USSR	2:33:44	15,000 + watch

Name/Country	Time	
5. Anne Audain/New Zealand	2:34:37	10,000 + watch
6. Maria Trujillo/USA	2:35:52	9,000 + watch
7. Irino Bogacheva/USSR	2:36:31	8,000 + watch
8. Mary Alico/USA	2:37:19	7,000
9. Laura Konantz/Canada	2:39:57	6,000
10. Heather Tolford, USA	2:40:14	5,000

MEN'S MASTERS DIVISION:

Name/Country	Time	Prize
1. John Campbell/New Zealand	2:14:33	$ 2,000 + watch
2. Artemio Navarro/Mexico	2:17:46	1,250
3. Rodolfo Gomez/Mexico	2:24:21	750

WOMEN'S MASTERS DIVISION:

Name/Country	Time	Prize
1. Priscilla Welch/Great Britain	2:40:20	$ 2,000 + watch
2. Claudia Ciavarelli/USA	2:59:10	1,250
3. Alfreda Iglehart/USA	3:05:26	750

AGE GROUP WINNERS:

Age Group	Name/Country	Age	Time
Men 17 & Under	George K. Chen/USA	17	3:09:31
Men 18-24	Sergio Jimenez/Mexico	24	2:21:47
Men 25-29	Mark Plaatjes/USA	29	2:10:29
Men 30-34	Eddy Hellebuyck/Belgium	30	2:14:14
Men 35-39	Alejandro Vazquez/Mexico	35	2:20:19
Men 40-44	John Campbell/New Zealand	42	2:14:33
Men 45-49	Phil Grant/USA	45	2:39:29
Men 50-54	David G. Whitten/USA	53	2:50:26
Men 55-59	Ruben Cordon/USA	56	2:39:42
Men 60-64	Jack P. Horne/USA	63	3:02:58
Men 65-69	Raymond W. Penkert/USA	66	3:31:01
Men 70-74	Antonio Tejada/Mexico	70	3:55:10
Men 75-79	Dutch Benedetti/USA	76	4:32:53
Men 80-98	William E. Kuester/USA	82	7:52:59
Women 17 & Under	Stephanie L. Norberg/USA	14	3:37:19
Women 18-24	Cathy O'Brien/USA	23	2:29:38
Women 25-29	Irino Bogacheva/USSR	29	2:36:31
Women 30-34	Alevtina Naumova/USSR	30	2:33:44
Women 35-39	Anne Audain/New Zealand	35	2:34:37
Women 40-44	Claudia Ciavarelli/USA	42	2:59:10
Women 45-49	Priscilla Welch/Great Britain	46	2:40:20
Women 50-54	Zofia Turosz/USA	52	3:13:35
Women 55-59	Wen-Shi Yu/USA	56	3:23:48
Women 60-64	Aslaug G. Tomas/USA	64	4:42:39
Women 65-69	Lois N. Lieberman/USA	69	6:20:18
Women 70-74	Elizabeth D. Vainerman/USA	72	8:59:34
Women 75-79	no finishers		
Women 80-98	Mavis Lindgren/USA	83	6:45:55

MEN'S RACEWALKING DIVISION:

Name/Country	Time
1. Norman Frable/USA	4:22:42
2. Art Grant/USA	4:25:48
3. Gerald Bocci/USA	4:29:10
4. Shaul Ladany/Israel	4:30:48
5. Bill Neder/USA	4:39:10

WOMEN'S RACEWALKING DIVISION:

Name/Country	Time
1. Daniela Hairabedian/USA	4:42:27
2. Jill Latham/USA	4:48:19
3. Lorraine Miller/USA	4:58:23
4. Lisa Rhode/USA	5:03:11
5. Nora Flynn/USA	5:03:26

MEN'S WHEELCHAIR DIVISION:

Name/Country	Time	Prize
1. Jim Knaub/USA	1:40:53	$ 7,300
2. Moustapha Badid/France	1:42:21	2,250
3. Farid Amarouche/France	1:42:22	1,000

WOMEN'S WHEELCHAIR DIVISION:

Name/Country	Time	Prize
1. Connie Hansen/Denmark	1:57:11	$ 7,300
2. Ann Cody-Morris/USA	1:57:18	2,250
3. Candace Cable/USA	2:04:09	1,000

MEN'S WHEELCHAIR QUAD DIVISION:

Name/Country	Time	Prize
1. Christoph Etzlstorfer/AUS	2:10:00	$ 1,000
T2. Bert Berns/USA	2:10:55	188
T2. John Brewer/USA	2:10:55	187

WOMEN'S WHEELCHAIR QUAD DIVISION:

Name/Country	Time	Prize
1. Mary Thompson/USA	2:56:43	$ 1,000

L.A. VII—MARCH 1, 1992

MEN'S OPEN DIVISION:

Name/Country	Time	Prize
1. John Treacy/Ireland	2:12:29	$ 30,000 + car + watch
2. Joseildo Rocha/Brazil	2:12:54	25,000 + watch
3. Peter Renner/New Zealand	2:14:13	12,500 + watch
4. Jose Santana/Brazil	2:14:26	7,500
5. Dacha Driss/Morocco	2:14:44	5,000
6. Marco Ochoa/Mexico	2:16:34	
7. Alvaro Sanchez/Mexico	2:17:02	
8. Luciano Flores/Mexico	2:17:06	
9. Alfredo Vigueras/USA	2:17:32	
10. Agapius Masong, Tanzania	2:18:32	

WOMEN'S OPEN DIVISION:

Name/Country	Time	Prize
1. Madina Biktagirova/CIS	2:26:23	$ 65,000 + car + watch
2. Ramilia Burangulova/CIS	2:28:12	40,000 + watch
3. Kerstin Pressler/Germany	2:29:40	25,000 + watch
4. Valentina Egorova/CIS	2:29:41	20,000
5. Lizanne Bussieres/Canada	2:31:24	7,500
6. Marcia Narloch/Brazil	2:32:56	2,600
7. Tatiana Zuyova/CIS	2:33:17	
8. Erin Baker/New Zealand	2:35:49	
9. Lucia Rendon/Mexico	2:38:11	
10. Paola Cabrera Palafo/Mexico	2:41:14	

MEN'S MASTERS DIVISION:

Name/Country	Time
1. Manuel Garcia Perez/Mexico	2:25:35
2. Fred Schaffstein/USA	2:33:37
3. Jussi Hamalainen/USA	2:34:59

WOMEN'S MASTERS DIVISION:

Name/Country	Time
1. Sandra Marshall/USA	3:02:47
2. Candy Dodge/USA	3:03:08
3. Odette Osantowski/USA	3:12:41

AGE GROUP WINNERS:

Age Group	Name/Country	Age	Time
Men 17 & Under	Enrique Villagrana/USA	17	2:50:27
Men 18-24	Anteimo De La Luzva/USA	19	2:20:30
Men 25-29	Luciano Flores/Mexico	28	2:17:06
Men 30-34	Cayetano De La Luz/USA	31	2:22:40
Men 35-39	Ernesto G. Perez Ernes/Mexico	35	2:25:59
Men 40-44	Fred Schaffstein/USA	43	2:33:37
Men 45-49	Jussi Hamalainen/USA	45	2:34:59
Men 50-54	Angel Lara-Escudero/USA	52	2:44:18
Men 55-59	Andre Tucco/USA	57	3:05:57
Men 60-64	Patrick Devine/USA	63	3:10:50
Men 65-69	Donald Thomson/Canada	67	3:40:34
Men 70-74	Antonio Tejada Vergara/Mexico	70	3:47:37
Men 75-79	Dutch Benedetti/USA	77	4:28:29
Men 80-98	Moriyoshi Yagi/Japan	80	5:12:37
Women 17 & Under	Stephanie Norberg/USA	15	3:33:17
Women 18-24	Christy Grimsley/USA	23	3:04:53
Women 25-29	Krisia Lorenu Garcia de Galan/El Salvador	28	2:56:41
Women 30-34	Jackie Zawertailo/Canada	34	2:47:25
Women 35-39	Jennifer Rabinowitch/USA	38	3:08:36
Women 40-44	Sandra Marshall/USA	44	3:02:47
Women 45-49	Gloria McCoy/USA	46	3:28:45
Women 50-54	Mae Palm/Canada	52	3:37:43
Women 55-59	Wen-Shi Yu/USA	57	3:33:43
Women 60-64	Thelma Wilson/USA	60	4:07:16
Women 65-69	Vostile Goodrich/USA	69	4:09:01
Women 70-74	Mareva Fulcher/USA	73	5:45:27
Women 75-79	Lucile Adney/USA	78	8:04:11
Women 80-98	Mavis Lindgren/USA	84	6:14:23

MEN'S RACEWALKING DIVISION:

Name/Country	Time
1. Ronald L. Baers/USA	3:30:47
2. Jose L. Lopez/USA	3:43:15
3. Raul M. Nunez/USA	4:07:50
4. Fidel S. Martinez/USA	4:13:12
5. Christoph Dreher/USA	4:18:53

WOMEN'S RACEWALKING DIVISION:

Name/Country	Time
1. Lorraine A. Miller/USA	4:47:40
2. Jill Latham/USA	4:54:26
3. Judy Heller/USA	4:54:35
4. Julie Gebron/USA	4:58:20
5. Helen Hoover/USA	5:01:54

MEN'S WHEELCHAIR DIVISION:

Name/Country	Time	Prize
1. Jim Knaub/USA	1:33:7	$10,660
2. Claude Issorat/France	1:36:6	7,590
3. Douglas Kennedy/USA	1:37:47	500

WOMEN'S WHEELCHAIR DIVISION:

Name/Country	Time	Prize
1. Connie Hansen/Denmark	1:56:17	$ 8,740
2. De Anna M. Sodoma/USA	1:57:32	4,710
3. Candace Cable/USA	2:00:46	1,460

MEN'S WHEELCHAIR QUAD DIVISION:

Name/Country	Time	Prize
1. Christoph Etzlstorfer/Austria	2:01:22	$ 1,700
2. Willey Clark/USA	2:02:13	1,450

WOMEN'S WHEELCHAIR QUAD DIVISION:

Name/Country	Time	Prize
1. Mary H. Thompson/USA	2:52:57	$ 520
2. Helga McKay/Canada	3:19:54	150

L.A. VIII – MARCH 7, 1993

MEN'S OPEN DIVISION:

Name/Country	Time	Prize
1. Joseildo Rocha/Brazil	2:14:29	$ 2,500 + car + watch
2. Jose Santana/Brazil	2:15:00	15,000 + watch
3. Gumercindo Olmedo/Mexico City	2:15:40	10,000 + watch
4. Peter Tshikila/South Africa	2:17:22	5,000 + watch
5. John Treacy/Ireland	2:17:28	2,500 + watch
6. Brad Hudson/USA	2:20:00	
7. Rustam Shagiev/Moscow	2:23:18	
8. Peter Renner/New Zealand	2:25:19	
9. Sam Rotich/USA	2:26:37	
10. Joe Gilboy/USA	2:28:14	

WOMEN'S OPEN DIVISION:

Name/Country	Time	Prize
1. Lyubov Klochko/Ukraine	2:39:49	car + watch
2. Carole Rouillard/Canada	2:41:09	$15,000 + watch
3. Lutsia Belaeva/Russia	2:44:26	10,000 + watch
4. Maddie Tormoen/USA	2:53:13	5,000 + watch
5. Judy A. Mercon/USA	2:55:01	2,500 + watch
6. Mary J. Button/USA	2:57:24	
7. Candy Dodge/USA	3:03:10	
8. Marina Jones/USA	3:04:07	
9. Jondelina D. Buckley/USA	3:04:17	
10. Stefania Oggiano/USA	3:06:29	

MEN'S MASTERS DIVISION:

Name/Country	Time	Prize
1. Angel Lara/USA	2:42:10	watch
2. Ismael Martinez/Mexico	2:45:45	watch
3. Julian Barrera/El Salvador	2:46:11	watch

WOMEN'S MASTERS DIVISION:

Name/Country	Time	Prize
1. Candy Dodge/USA	3:03:10	watch
2. Marina Jones/USA	3:04:07	watch
3. Leslie King/USA	3:25:13	watch

AGE GROUP WINNERS:

	Name/Country	Age	Time
Men 17 & Under	Jose Padilla/USA	16	3:05:53
Men 18-24	Joshua Breslow/USA	24	2:30:03
Men 25-29	Joseildo Rocha/Brazil	28	2:14:29
Men 30-34	Gumercindo Olmedo/Mexico	30	2:15:40
Men 35-39	John Treacy/USA	35	2:17:28
Men 40-44	Ismael Martinez/Mexico	40	2:45:45
Men 45-49	Dennis Bock/USA	45	2:36:32
Men 50-54	Angel Lara/USA	53	2:42:10
Men 55-59	Paul Redoble/USA	56	2:58:08
Men 60-64	Patrick Devine/USA	64	3:15:52
Men 65-69	Ruben Vigil/USA	65	3:49:37
Men 70-74	Milton Bassett/USA	70	4:09:56
Men 75-79	Eddie Lewin/USA	76	4:58:13
Men 80-98	Bill Kuester/USA	84	8:05:12
Women 17 & Under	Megan Ericson/USA	16	3:50:45
Women 18-24	Liliana Valdez/Colombia	23	3:09:50
Women 25-29	Jondelina Buckley/USA	28	3:04:17
Women 30-34	Lyubov Klochko/Ukraine	33	2:39:49
Women 35-39	Lutsia Belaeva/Russia	35	2:44:26
Women 40-44	Candy Dodge/USA	43	3:03:10
Women 45-49	Kathleen Slinger/USA	45	3:38:11
Women 50-54	Diane Eastman/USA	50	3:17:34
Women 55-59	Wen-Shi Yu/USA	58	3:48:26
Women 60-64	Norma Surmon/USA	62	4:20:03
Women 65-69	Inez Phillip/USA	65	5:58:07
Women 70-74	Luci Byers/USA	70	5:04:09
Women 75-79	Toni Vrba/USA	78	7:47:39

MEN'S RACEWALKING DIVISION:

Name/Country	Time	Prize
1. Raul Hector Nunez Macias/Mexico	3:53:57	watch
2. Amitai Lavon/USA	4:29:54	watch
3. Christoph Dreher/USA	4:31:39	watch
4. Robert M. Nagtegaal/Netherlands	4:38:44	
5. Robert F. Minn/USA	4:47:54	

WOMEN'S RACEWALKING DIVISION:

Name/Country	Time	Prize
1. Margery A. Kraus/USA	5:00:29	watch
2. Lorraine A. Miller/USA	5:01:32	watch
3. Laurie Kahn/USA	5:04:33	watch
4. Cathy L. Chung/USA	5:04:56	
5. Sheila Galinsky/USA	5:11:11	

MEN'S WHEELCHAIR DIVISION:

Name/Country	Time	Prize
1. Jan Mattern/USA	1:32:15	$ 7,500 + watch
2. Craig Blanchette/USA	1:34:47	1,500 + watch
3. Phillippe Couprie/France	1:34:47	600 + watch

WOMEN'S WHEELCHAIR DIVISION:

Name/Country	Time	Prize
1. Connie Hansen/Denmark	1:51:26	$ 7,500 + watch
2. Lily Anngreny/Germany	1:51:49	1,500 + watch
3. Jeanette Jansen/Netherlands	1:51:51	600 + watch

MEN'S & WOMEN'S COMBINED QUAD WHEELCHAIR DIVISION:

Name/Country	Time	Prize
1. Clayton Gerein/Canada	2:05:10	$ 2,000 + watch
2. Christoph Etzlstorfer/Austria	2:06:36	600 + watch
3. Jan-Owe Mattsson/Sweden	2:15:01	500 + watch

L.A. IX – MARCH 6, 1994

MEN'S OPEN DIVISION:

Name/Country	Time	Prize
1. Paul Pilkington/USA	2:12:13	$27,000 + car
2. Luca Barzaghi/Italy	2:12:52	10,000 + watch
3. Andrzej Krzyscin/Poland	2:13:21	7,500 + watch
4. Marnix Goegebeur/Belgium	2:13:23	3,500 + watch
5. Gumercindo Olmedo/Mexico	2:13:33	1,500 + watch
6. Marcelino Crisanto/Mexico	2:13:38	
7. Katsuya Natsume/Japan	2:14:19	
8. Ernesto Eberstadt/Mexico	2:14:33	
9. Juan Torres Ruiz/Spain	2:14:40	
10. Diamantino Dos Santos/Brazil	2:14:41	

WOMEN'S OPEN DIVISION:

Name/Country	Time	Prize
1. Olga Appell/USA	2:28:12	$15,000 + car + watch
2. Emma Scaunich/Italy	2:37:05	10,000 + watch
3. Silvia Mosqueda/USA	2:40:12	Disqualified
4. Olga Youdenkova/Belarussia	2:40:24	3,500 + watch
5. Olga Mitchourina/Russia	2:46:01	1,500 + watch
6. Marina Jones/USA	2:50:19	
7. Lilia Pina/Mexico	2:51:55	
8. Stefania Oggiano/USA	2:53:05	
9. Lisa Dorfman/USA	2:53:49	
10. Alice McGrew/USA	2:56:44	

USA TRACK & FIELD MEN'S NATIONAL CHAMPIONSHIP:

Name/Country	Time	Prize
1. Paul Pilkington	2:12:13	$12,000
2. Danny Gonzales	2:14:42	6,000
3. Darrell General	2:18:47	4,000
4. Joshua Breslow	2:25:24	2,000
5. Kevin Broady	2:27:48	1,000

MEN'S MASTERS DIVISION:

Name/Country	Time	Prize
1. Gregg Horner/USA	2:34:20	watch
2. Rafael Parra/Columbia	2:35:07	watch
3. Angel Lara/Mexico	2:36:13	watch

WOMEN'S MASTERS DIVISION:

Name/Country	Time	Prize
1. Emma Scaunich/Italy	2:37:05	watch
2. Marina Jones/USA	2:50:19	watch
3. Diane Eastman/USA	3:14:17	watch

AGE GROUP WINNERS:

Age Group	Name/Country	Age	Time
Men 18-24	Luis Pinon/USA	21	2:22:02
Men 25-29	Gidimas Shahanga/Tanzania	27	2:13:27
Men 30-34	Ric Sayre/USA	32	2:12:59
Men 35-39	Rod Dixon/New Zealand	35	2:14:48
Men 40-44	Kjell-Erik Stahl/Sweden	40	2:19:20
Men 45-49	Robert Abbott/USA	45	2:36:43
Men 50-54	Severino Venzor/Mexico	54	2:43:14
Men 55-59	Patrick Devine/USA	57	2:50:03
Men 60-64	Jim O'Neill/USA	60	2:52:13
Men 65-69	Paul Reese/USA	68	3:18:50
Men 70-99	Jon Baldwin/USA	70	3:52:19
Women 18-24	Araceli Salas/USA	21	2:51:54
Women 25-29	Mariela Hurtado-Fuentes/Mexico	26	2:42:10
Women 30-34	Nancy Ditz/USA	31	2:36:28
Women 35-39	Christa Vahlensieck/W. Germany	36	2:36:37
Women 40-44	Harolene Walters/USA	43	2:57:26
Women 45-49	Mattie Wilkes/USA	46	3:19:22
Women 50-54	Marjorie Gilmore/USA	51	3:51:40
Women 55-59	Ruth Bloland/USA	57	3:57:00
Women 60-64	Virginia Hastings/USA	61	4:23:11
Women 65-69	Norma Bernardi/USA	66	4:21:48
Women 70-99	Bess James/USA	76	5:39:52

MEN'S RACEWALKING DIVISION:

Name/Country	Time	Prize
1. Bill Neder/USA	4:38:33	watch
2. Charles A. Cutting/USA	4:40:43	watch
3. Arvid Rolle/USA	4:50:19	watch
4. David Wormwald/USA	4:53:50	watch
5. Clyde Hatfield/USA	4:55:12	watch

WOMEN'S RACEWALKING DIVISION:

Name/Country	Time	Prize
1. Margaret Govea/USA	4:34:35	watch
2. Laurie E. Kahn/USA	4:53:33	watch
3. Cathy L. Chung/USA	5:00:23	watch
4. Lanora A. Dodson/USA	5:19:55	watch
5. Sheila L. Galinsky/USA	5:23:53	watch

MEN'S WHEELCHAIR DIVISION:

Name/Country	Time	Prize
1. Phillipe Couprie/France	1:34:52	$ 1,550 + watch
Paul R. Wiggins/Australia	1:34:52	1,550 + watch
3. James Briggs/USA	1:36:26	750 + watch

WOMEN'S WHEELCHAIR DIVISION:

Name/Country	Time	Prize
1. Connie A. Hansen/Denmark	1:48:58	$ 7,500 + watch
2. Louise Sauvage/Australia	1:54:38	1,200
3. Tanni Grey/Great Britain	1:54:40	750

MEN'S AND WOMEN'S COMBINED QUAD WHEELCHAIR DIVISION:

Name/Country	Time	Prize
1. Greg Smith/Australia	2:06:12	$ 2,000 + watch
2. Clayton R. Gerein/Canada	2:08:03	700 + watch
3. John C. Brewer/USA	2:15:47	600 + watch

L.A. X—MARCH 5, 1995

MEN'S OPEN DIVISION:

Name/Country	Time	Prize
1. Rolando Vera/Ecuador	2:11:39	$15,000 + car + watch
2. Bob Kempainen/USA	2:11:59	10,000 + watch
3. Martin Pitayo/Mexico	2:12:59	7,500 + watch
4. Arturo Barrios/USA	2:14:42	3,500 + watch
5. Mark Plaatjes/USA	2:15:41	1,500 + watch
6. Jose Santana/Brazil	2:18:01	
7. Danny Ree/USA	2:21:06	
8. Daniel Martinez/USA	2:21:35	
9. Hiroyuki Ito/Japan	2:23:33	
10. Katsuya Natsume/Japan	2:23:54	

WOMEN'S OPEN DIVISION:

Name/Country	Time	Prize
1. Nadia Prasad/France	2:29:48	$15,000 + car + watch
2. Anna Rybicka/Poland	2:32:59	10,000 + watch
3. Lyobov Klochko/Ukraine	2:33:31	7,500 + watch
4. Aniela Nikiel/Poland	2:34:51	3,500 + watch
5. Kirsi Rauta/Finland	2:41:46	1,500 + watch
6. Olia Kopsolapova/Ukraine	2:44:49	
7. Yuki Ando/Japan	2:45:42	
8. Judy Mercon/USA	2:55:57	
9. Stephanie J. Wossoll/USA	3:02:09	
10. Keena L. Carstensen/USA	3:02:10	

MEN'S MASTERS DIVISION:

Name/Country	Time	Prize
1. John Bednarski/USA	2:36:40	watch
2. Ronald Coleman/USA	2:41:18	watch
3. Carlos Vallel/USA	2:52:48	watch

WOMEN'S MASTERS DIVISION:

Name/Country	Time	Prize
1. Alfreda Iglehart/USA	3:13:29	watch
2. Patricia Brumbalow/USA	3:24:34	watch
3. Kathleen Slinger/USA	3:27:16	watch

AGE GROUP WINNERS:

Age Group	Name/Country	Age	Time
Men 17 and under	Andrew Hori/USA	17	3:02:27
Men 18-24	Marcos Juarez/Guatemala	21	2:26:03
Men 25-29	Rolando Vera/Ecuador	29	2:11:39
Men 30-34	Arturo Barrios/USA	32	2:14:47
Men 35-39	Martin Pitayo/Mexico	35	2:12:49
Men 40-44	Ronald Coleman/USA	43	2:41:18
Men 45-49	John Bednarski/USA	45	2:36:40
Men 50-54	Wayne Mitchell/USA	50	2:56:15
Men 55-59	Carlos Vallel/USA	59	2:52:48
Men 60-64	Epifanio Morales Tellez/USA	60	2:54:05
Men 65-69	Richard Roodberg/USA	66	3:17:24
Men 70-74	Fred Nagelschmidt/USA	70	3:47:28
Men 75-79	John Rodriguez/USA	75	5:42:17
Men 80-98	Ernest Van Leeuwen/USA	82	5:38:17
Women 17 and under	Gabriela Arriaga/USA	17	3:29:47
Women 18-24	Yuki Ando/Japan	24	2:45:42
Women 25-29	Nadia Prasad/France	27	2:29:40
Women 30-34	Anna Rybicka/Poland	31	2:32:59
Women 35-39	Lyobov Klochko/Ukraine	35	2:33:31
Women 40-44	Alfreda Iglehart/USA	44	3:13:29
Women 45-49	Kathleen Slinger/USA	47	3:27:16
Women 50-54	Patricia Brumbalow/USA	53	3:24:34
Women 55-59	Mary Baker/USA	55	3:28:37
Women 60-64	Wen-Shi Yu/USA	60	3:51:03
Women 65-69	Anna Hollenberg/USA	65	4:16:51
Women 70-74	Evelyn Riel/USA	70	5:12:32
Women 75-79	Sarah London/USA	76	5:55:43
Women 80-98	Mavis Lindgren/USA	87	7:50:21

MEN'S RACEWALKING DIVISION:

Name/Country	Time	Prize
1. Enrique Camarena/USA	4:16:40	watch
2. Mark W. Ericson/USA	4:18:12	watch
3. Christoph Dreher/USA	4:23:28	watch
4. John W. Loeschhorn/USA	4:43:05	watch
5. Charles A. Cutting/USA	4:48:09	watch

WOMEN'S RACEWALKING DIVISION:

Name/Country	Time	Prize
1. Brenda MacIsaac/USA	4:41:17	watch
2. Laura G. Urish/USA	5:14:12	watch
3. Dianne Dalbey/USA	5:15:22	watch
4. Brierly P. Reybine/USA	5:16:28	watch
5. Cathy L. Chung/USA	5:24:36	watch

MEN'S WHEELCHAIR DIVISION:

Name/Country	Time	Prize
1. Paul R. Wiggins/USA	1:36:06	$5,000 + watch
2. Thomas P. Sellers/USA	1:40:11	1,200 + watch
3. Claude Issorat/Guadeloupe	1:41:22	750 + watch

WOMEN'S WHEELCHAIR DIVISION:

Name/Country	Time	Prize
1. Jean Driscoll/USA	1:52:51	$5,000 + watch
2. Louise A. Sauvage/Australia	2:00:48	1,200 + watch
3. Deanna M. Sodoma/USA	2:00:49	750 + watch

MEN'S & WOMEN'S COMBINED QUAD WHEELCHAIR DIVISION:

Name/Country	Time	Prize
1. Christoph Etzlstorfer/Austria	2:14:46	$2,000 + watch
2. Bradley M. Romage/USA	2:14:51	700 + watch
3. Brent McMahon/USA	2:16:16	600 + watch

THE CITY OF LOS ANGELES MARATHON X
MARCH 5, 1995
DIVISION RESULTS

MEN 17 & UNDER

1. Andrew Hori (270) 03:02:27
2. Heriberto Cruz (384) 03:07:46
3. Matt Swarts (437) 03:09:38
4. Gabriel Valdovinos (683) 03:17:34
5. Edgar Reyes (708) 03:18:29
6. Juan Garcia (1017) 03:25:56
7. Jesus Zaragoza (1037) 03:26:19
8. Gary Garay (1067) 03:27:07
9. Jared Christoffersen (1068) 03:27:08
10. Oscar Zuniga (1070) 03:27:10
11. Raymundo Delgado (1103) 03:27:40
12. Samir Patel (1114) 03:27:52
13. Jeremiah Mcminn (1135) 03:28:15
14. Gustavo Ramos (1192) 03:29:21
15. Daniel Parra (1269) 03:30:51
16. David Galvez (1270) 03:30:52
17. Bobby James (1462) 03:34:48
18. Chris Hsu (1482) 03:35:05
19. Hugo Lemus (1510) 03:35:35
20. Jesse Montes (1561) 03:36:31
21. Nelson Chavarria (1615) 03:37:25
22. Humberto Vargas (1621) 03:37:37
23. Eleazar Roman (1660) 03:38:15
24. Jose Lorenzo (1729) 03:39:32
25. Blas Lechuga (1745) 03:39:45
26. Cesar Suchite (1801) 03:40:41
27. Josh Stiles (1969) 03:43:19
28. Leonel Pineda (2066) 03:44:42
29. Kevin Beaudine (2113) 03:45:19
30. Alvaro Ferreira (2146) 03:45:51
31. Oliver Gonzalez (2235) 03:47:14
32. Joel Mendoza (2247) 03:47:24
33. Jorge Corzo (2327) 03:48:30
34. Brent Miller (2365) 03:49:00
35. Eric Benzant-Feldra (2526) 03:51:08
36. Chad Clements (2565) 03:51:38
37. Jaavier Antonio (2575) 03:51:49
38. Elvis Navarro (2586) 03:51:57
39. Naim Ruiz (2674) 03:53:06
40. Javier Villalobos (2721) 03:53:41
41. Ramiro Marchena (2793) 03:54:31
42. Gerado Saavedra (2865) 03:55:24
43. Roberto Campos (3102) 03:57:52
44. Heladio Arzate (3127) 03:58:07
45. Aldo Hernandez (3214) 03:59:09
46. Felix Robles (3244) 03:59:33
47. Joel Valenzuela (3325) 04:00:17
48. Yohni Martinez (3366) 04:00:54
49. Roberto Romero (3414) 04:01:28
50. Edwin Anzora (3438) 04:01:46
51. Oscar Castillo (3455) 04:02:01
52. Daniel Oliva (3470) 04:02:15
53. Eddie Olivo (3488) 04:02:30
54. Octavio Bonilla (3532) 04:03:09
55. Leo Howard (3589) 04:04:03
56. Oscar Juarez (3599) 04:04:11
57. Bicford Nava (3621) 04:04:23
58. Jonathan Pedroza (3670) 04:04:52
59. Eric Bruce Gonzalez (3705) 04:05:15
60. Oscar Carrillo (3724) 04:05:34
61. Erick Bernal (3741) 04:05:51
62. James Ochoa (3760) 04:06:04
63. Arnold Newman (3769) 04:06:11
64. Jason Martinez (3801) 04:06:37
65. Vicente Gutierrez (3828) 04:06:57
66. Alex Lemus (3852) 04:07:09
67. Eyal Allweil (3945) 04:08:22
68. Ben Arden (3946) 04:08:22
69. Elias Santos (3977) 04:08:47
70. Jose Cardenas (3978) 04:08:47
71. Eric Mendoza (4009) 04:09:13
72. Jose Diaz (4018) 04:09:20
73. Heliodoro Camilo (4068) 04:10:00
74. John Torres (4071) 04:10:01
75. Danilo Antonio (4086) 04:10:14
76. Armando Sanchez (4098) 04:10:25
77. Oscar Madrogal (4137) 04:10:53
78. Gonzalo Balderas (4149) 04:10:58
79. Manuel Santiago (4150) 04:10:59
80. Xavier Alaniz (4198) 04:11:37
81. Zachary Aaron (4275) 04:12:36
82. Mauricio Piceno (4279) 04:12:41
83. Andy Santa Maria (4305) 04:13:01
84. David Montes (4365) 04:13:51
85. Randy Montanez (4369) 04:13:53
86. Ramon Rosales (4376) 04:13:56
87. Rivera Pascual (4426) 04:14:27
88. Alexander Nittka (4458) 04:14:44
89. Eloy Reyes (4480) 04:14:53
90. Mario Colombini (4487) 04:14:58
91. Sean Fargo (4489) 04:14:59
92. Edwin Martinez (4521) 04:15:29
93. Randy Reyes (4589) 04:16:05
94. Cesar Diaz (4609) 04:16:21
95. Carlos Soh (4628) 04:16:30
96. Jaime Guzman (4699) 04:17:28
97. David Reynolds (4782) 04:18:25
98. Ismael Beleche (4787) 04:18:30
99. Carlos Velazquez (4818) 04:18:46
100. Uriel Rivera (4825) 04:18:50
101. Marton Alfaro (4884) 04:19:22
102. Juan Linares (4887) 04:19:27
103. Jesus Rosas (4990) 04:20:52
104. Scott Alba (5002) 04:21:02
105. Steven Di Bene (5081) 04:21:53
106. Tom Starr (5082) 04:21:53
107. Isaiah Peterson (5084) 04:21:54
108. Francisco Calvillo (5088) 04:21:56
109. Israel Ortiz (5097) 04:22:03
110. Luis Rincon (5193) 04:23:09
111. Buenrostro Adan (5223) 04:23:28
112. Thomas Mitchell (5247) 04:23:46
113. David Montoya (5262) 04:24:07
114. Tony Quijada (5309) 04:24:36
115. Angel Gonzalez (5397) 04:25:32
116. Ricardo Flores (5444) 04:25:59
117. Salvador Alcaraz (5453) 04:26:04
118. Ernesto Mercado (5532) 04:27:09
119. Oscar Flores (5534) 04:27:09
120. Jose Hidalgo (5546) 04:27:17
121. Abraham Blas (5556) 04:27:22
122. Jeouanny Justo (5580) 04:27:34
123. Miguel Medel (5631) 04:28:05
124. Ramiro Mendoza (5694) 04:28:49
125. Tony Alfaro (5720) 04:29:04
126. Brian Loarca (5747) 04:29:20
127. Juan Marroquin (5807) 04:30:06
128. Omar Rodriguez (5818) 04:30:15
129. Jorge Arreola (5889) 04:30:52
130. Andy Quijano (6016) 04:32:26
131. Antonio Miranda (6052) 04:32:53
132. Jaime Vazquez (6088) 04:33:17
133. Justin Child (6167) 04:34:10
134. Scott Morse (6169) 04:34:11
135. Andy Hernandez (6232) 04:34:52
136. Jesus Lerma (6245) 04:35:01
137. Philip Cable (6258) 04:35:13
138. Jim Ercek (6276) 04:35:22
139. Cesar Reyes (6351) 04:36:10
140. Octavio Montano (6366) 04:36:18
141. Javier Corona (6421) 04:36:46
142. Israel Gonzales (6430) 04:36:54
143. Carlos Hernandez (6456) 04:37:21
144. Alex Hernandez (6458) 04:37:22
145. Alejandro Brizuela (6468) 04:37:26
146. Mike Johnson (6508) 04:37:46
147. Michael Drlik (6551) 04:38:14
148. Bob Kennedy (6639) 04:39:10
149. Joshua Gonzales (6643) 04:39:11
150. Mohammad Moussari (6780) 04:41:03
151. Jose Galindo (6794) 04:41:10
152. Javier Garcia (6803) 04:41:20
153. Alfonso Gutierrez (6814) 04:41:30
154. Carlos Herrera (6835) 04:41:45
155. Aldridon Siapno (6872) 04:42:08
156. Jose Hernandez (6944) 04:43:04
157. Rene Alfaro (6945) 04:43:05
158. David Camacho Jr (6948) 04:43:06
159. Yusef Beckles (6950) 04:43:08
160. Gilberto Solorio (6996) 04:43:35
161. Jorge Lam (7002) 04:43:38
162. Alex Solano (7014) 04:43:44
163. Sergio Mireles (7023) 04:43:53
164. Harold Pierce (7061) 04:44:20
165. John Ryu (7062) 04:44:21
166. David Reid (7188) 04:45:58
167. Hugo Urbina (7204) 04:46:10
168. Wilfredo Centeno (7207) 04:46:11
169. Cristian Enriquez (7208) 04:46:12
170. Carlo Martinez (7210) 04:46:12
171. Fredy Garcia (7218) 04:46:19
172. Enrique Camacho (7233) 04:46:31
173. Luis Leon (7247) 04:46:39
174. Harry Matundan (7259) 04:46:46
175. Victor Flores (7299) 04:47:13
176. Miguel Lopez (7321) 04:47:28
177. Miguel Ruiz (7379) 04:48:10
178. Edwin Corcamo (7384) 04:48:12
179. Luis Rojas (7390) 04:48:15
180. Patrick Anderson (7394) 04:48:17
181. Chris Hernandez (7407) 04:48:27
182. Luiz Quintanilla (7421) 04:48:37
183. Rogelio Castro (7436) 04:48:47
184. Milton Zamarripa (7440) 04:48:50
185. John Ercek (7490) 04:49:21
186. Stan Smith (7501) 04:49:24
187. Eric Bobadilla (7562) 04:50:07
188. Julio Quilla (7568) 04:50:13
189. Edward Galan (7641) 04:51:06
190. Jerome Hatathle (7660) 04:51:28
191. Ludwin Escobar (7677) 04:51:39
192. Reggie Dominguez (7727) 04:52:19
193. Jorge Lopez (7744) 04:52:32
194. Erik Perez (7806) 04:53:19
195. Igor Ibarra (7807) 04:53:20
196. Ruben Miranda (7825) 04:53:32
197. Gabriel Escobar (7833) 04:53:35
198. Hugo Zamudio (7834) 04:53:37
199. Dominique Zoida (7852) 04:53:50
200. Uri Hernandez (7858) 04:53:53
201. Ignacio Mendez (7863) 04:53:56
202. Juan Hernandez (7876) 04:54:05
203. Mario Aguilar (8013) 04:55:34
204. Jose Rodriguez (8017) 04:55:37
205. Kevin Diamond (8028) 04:55:47
206. Carlos Sanchez (8039) 04:55:52
207. Charles Canchola (8051) 04:56:05
208. Jesse Shapiro (8073) 04:56:19
209. Marlon Rosales (8102) 04:56:42
210. Byron Marroquin (8115) 04:56:48
211. Leo Hernandez (8120) 04:56:54
212. Omar Ortega (8143) 04:57:14
213. Francisco Corona (8167) 04:57:30
214. Jesus Marquez (8178) 04:57:39
215. Homero Pineda (8181) 04:57:40
216. Gabriel Hinojosa (8195) 04:57:51
217. Elisha Wiesenberg (8203) 04:57:57
218. Rafael Martinez (8208) 04:58:00
219. Bhavesh Patel (8219) 04:58:05
220. Leo Vargas (8282) 04:58:44
221. Armando Reyes (8310) 04:58:57
222. Jesus Serna (8331) 04:59:12
223. Jose Lopez (8416) 05:00:20
224. Joe Hernandez (8435) 05:00:41
225. Jason Razon (8437) 05:00:44
226. Samuel Joe (8457) 05:01:02
227. Ricardo Miranda (8484) 05:01:22
228. Kenneth Leichman (8588) 05:02:42
229. Henry Marmol (8628) 05:03:20
230. Rigoberto Cruz (8658) 05:03:49
231. Danilo Burgos (8686) 05:04:09
232. Marcus Lewis (8687) 05:04:10
233. Jacob Burgess (8712) 05:04:29
234. Abel Carrillo (8717) 05:04:32
235. Pariet Hernandez (8719) 05:04:34
236. Quog Droung (8731) 05:04:47
237. Jose Cueva (8734) 05:04:50
238. Kevin Krainman (8776) 05:05:35
239. Eduardo Salazar (8825) 05:06:29
240. Pedro Medrano (8829) 05:06:33
241. Ben Camacho (8885) 05:07:33
242. Jaime Hernandez (8919) 05:08:04
243. Bernie Solloa (8927) 05:08:09
244. Alan Narcho (8928) 05:08:11
245. Juan Muratalla (8957) 05:08:37
246. Ivan Osornio (8966) 05:08:41
247. Ramon Candejas (8967) 05:08:41
248. Carlos Florian (8972) 05:08:43
249. Richard Guevara (9032) 05:09:32
250. Elisha Peterson (9045) 05:09:45
251. Victor Sanchez (9067) 05:10:00
252. Ramon Figueroa (9093) 05:10:16
253. Robert Dela Torre (9094) 05:10:17
254. Brian Zark (9102) 05:10:20
255. Luis Robles (9119) 05:10:28
256. Julius Askew (9139) 05:10:51
257. Manuel Villegas (9146) 05:10:57
258. Alberto Ambriz (9157) 05:11:09
259. Joshua Stillwagon (9167) 05:11:25
260. Dagoberto Milendez (9170) 05:11:28
261. Mario Saldana (9190) 05:11:40
262. Robert Baldizon (9377) 05:14:17
263. Gerson Hernandez (9381) 05:14:21
264. Edward Motts (9388) 05:14:26
265. Gustavo Torres (9468) 05:16:01
266. Jorge Hernandez (9642) 05:18:35
267. William Spangenberg (9681) 05:19:07
268. Norwin Nava (9707) 05:19:32
269. Eduardo Saldivar (9708) 05:19:33
270. Jesus Castellanos (9735) 05:20:11
271. Jose Zatarain (9737) 05:20:13
272. Scott Cala (9783) 05:20:49
273. Manuel Meza (9795) 05:20:57
274. Jesse Galvez (9813) 05:21:13
275. Jacob Olid (9817) 05:21:17
276. Jose Orozco (9854) 05:21:49
277. Raul Garcia (9860) 05:21:55
278. Carlos Castillo (9861) 05:21:55
279. Baldomero Rodriguez (9863) 05:21:56
280. Jimmy Enriquez (9885) 05:22:14
281. Eric Josephbek (9974) 05:23:53
282. Hayden Wong (9990) 05:24:06
283. Enrique Nava (9992) 05:24:10
284. K Cardenas (10010) 05:24:28
285. Lorne Matundan (10026) 05:24:52
286. Luke Perez (10073) 05:25:42
287. Joel Rodriguez (10089) 05:25:53
288. Philip Borlin (10092) 05:25:56
289. Juan Corzo (10131) 05:26:37
290. Joaquin Mora (10132) 05:26:38
291. Matt Jasper (10140) 05:26:51
292. Eduardo Martinez (10146) 05:26:55
293. Brad Nilles (10150) 05:27:03
294. Ken Kirk (10173) 05:27:23
295. Enrique Loera (10177) 05:27:25
296. Ariel Arana (10178) 05:27:26
297. Luis Basulto (10217) 05:27:59
298. Donny Sanchez (10218) 05:27:59
299. Edgar Aleman (10259) 05:28:45
300. Jessie Flores (10260) 05:28:45
301. Edwardo Borja (10264) 05:28:47
302. Neil Virani (10288) 05:29:01
303. Matt Salmon (10353) 05:30:08
304. Jorge Recinos (10407) 05:30:51
305. Frank Hernandez (10442) 05:31:28
306. Carlos Ceja (10473) 05:31:51
307. Marco Molina (10484) 05:32:01
308. Julio Hernandez (10506) 05:32:24
309. Hoang Pham (10509) 05:32:33
310. Ivan Aguilar (10513) 05:32:39
311. Cesar Andrade (10547) 05:33:06
312. Armando Solis (10575) 05:33:33
313. Oscar Manjarres (10612) 05:33:58
314. Daniel Hernandez (10613) 05:33:58
315. Sean Heffrnan (10644) 05:34:30
316. Omar Serrato (10655) 05:34:41
317. Javier Galvez (10660) 05:34:43
318. David Avalos (10667) 05:34:45
319. Richard Mares (10707) 05:35:26
320. Dustin Smith (10708) 05:35:27
321. Julio Figueroa (10735) 05:35:52
322. Ramon Montiel (10802) 05:37:06
323. Jeff Ratlief (10806) 05:37:10
324. Miguel Aguilera (10840) 05:37:46
325. Chutintorn Jaroensook (10842) 05:37:51
326. Eric Mejia (10852) 05:38:04
327. Jimi Wang (10853) 05:38:05
328. Duong Luu (10874) 05:38:40
329. Rogaciano Baltazar (10876) 05:38:45
330. Ramon Barrientos (10912) 05:39:23
331. Guillermo Garcia (10924) 05:39:47
332. Glen Yamauchi (10961) 05:40:30
333. Kenfred Wong (10966) 05:40:36
334. Christian Fenton (10979) 05:41:05
335. Blanca Valenzuela (10997) 05:41:26
336. Wyn Ericson (11000) 05:41:28
337. Bryce Patrick (11037) 05:42:06
338. Phong Long (11040) 05:42:09
339. Fernando Suarez (11044) 05:42:12
340. Jesus Suarez (11045) 05:42:13
341. Bradley Dutkiewicz (11055) 05:42:19
342. Roney Gonzalez (11088) 05:42:46
343. Rodolfo Quiroz (11114) 05:43:14
344. Fernando Lopez (11115) 05:43:14
345. Nestor Nidome (11138) 05:43:41
346. Israel Gettinger (11158) 05:44:05
347. Jesse Castellanos (11169) 05:44:13
348. Christian De Luna (11170) 05:44:13
349. James Cruz (11227) 05:44:51
350. Cristobal Leon (11288) 05:46:01
351. Jesse Alcala (11289) 05:46:01
352. Brian Ingino (11302) 05:46:17
353. Don Sullivan (11352) 05:47:22
354. Uy Chan (11389) 05:48:37
355. Hector Munoz (11391) 05:48:38
356. Milton Membreno (11416) 05:49:13
357. Keigo Matsuda (11432) 05:49:30
358. Henry Servellon (11441) 05:49:37
359. Eric Doyle (11449) 05:49:44
360. Manuel Pulido (11483) 05:50:13
361. Mario Lopez (11492) 05:50:25
362. William Castro (11493) 05:50:25
363. Frank England (11506) 05:50:31
364. David Cruz (11510) 05:50:33
365. Randy Carrasco (11533) 05:50:55
366. Donald Gomez (11538) 05:51:01
367. Johnny Quiroa (11540) 05:51:06
368. Jairon Rivera (11562) 05:51:39
369. Christian Garcia (11565) 05:51:44
370. Hugo Jimenez (11570) 05:52:03
371. Juan Mejia (11573) 05:52:07
372. Ruben Mendoza (11601) 05:52:23
373. Kevin Williams (11602) 05:52:26
374. Edgar Monzon (11607) 05:52:38
375. Geovani Vega (11618) 05:52:58
376. Jose Martinez (11620) 05:52:58
377. Andres Rodriguez (11627) 05:53:00
378. Hector Palacios (11635) 05:53:04
379. Darren Kwok (11666) 05:53:38
380. Daniel Swid (11668) 05:53:40
381. Carlos Rosales (11728) 05:55:00
382. Jesse Zambrano (11757) 05:55:32
383. Jose Betancourt (11785) 05:56:12
384. Henry Bautista (11787) 05:56:13
385. Freddy Hidalgo (11789) 05:56:15
386. Roberto Garcia (11806) 05:56:45
387. Irving Garcia (11807) 05:56:45
388. Antonio Cortez (11815) 05:56:54
389. William Gomez (11816) 05:56:56
390. Narciso Velazco (11823) 05:57:10
391. George Patini Jr (11865) 05:58:10
392. Hang Long (11912) 05:58:55
393. Juan Flores (11913) 05:58:55
394. Josue Flores (11919) 05:59:08
395. Scot Britton (11922) 05:59:21
396. Robert Garcia (11930) 05:59:27
397. Dominic Nahas (11944) 05:59:47
398. Javier Ruiz (11950) 05:59:54
399. Jose Ramirez (11983) 06:00:33
400. Julio Aleman (11987) 06:00:51
401. Frederick Mabalot (12016) 06:01:43
402. Rodrigo Gonzalez (12079) 06:03:28
403. Roque Solis (12120) 06:04:39
404. Joaquin Sierra (12122) 06:04:40
405. Roy Snear (12134) 06:04:48
406. Cesar Mendoza (12142) 06:05:02
407. Mauricio Cortez (12184) 06:06:01
408. Julio Alvarez (12191) 06:06:16
409. Matthew Valdez (12192) 06:06:18
410. Gerardo Gomez (12200) 06:06:31
411. Christian Garcia (12222) 06:07:19
412. Josue Alvarado (12275) 06:08:41
413. Eduardo Sermeno (12276) 06:08:43
414. Raul Ortega (12282) 06:08:49
415. Marlon Servellon (12284) 06:08:51
416. Christopher Navarro (12311) 06:09:18
417. Cary Grant (12342) 06:10:10
418. Daniel Green (12345) 06:10:12
419. Abraham Calvasio (12365) 06:11:00
420. Seiyua Tang (12407) 06:11:54
421. Chris Iniguez (12416) 06:12:10
422. Oscar Buenrostro (12417) 06:12:11
423. Tomas Hernandez (12423) 06:12:21
424. Omar Gutierrez (12471) 06:13:39
425. David Lazaro (12479) 06:13:53
426. Jonathan Walker (12481) 06:13:57
427. Eldred Franklin (12483) 06:13:57
428. Jamien Arakawa (12509) 06:14:40
429. Chris Duenas (12522) 06:15:02
430. Jonathon Anderson (12567) 06:15:59
431. Isaac Mejia (12569) 06:16:05
432. Moses Mejia (12570) 06:16:07
433. Miguel Guerra (12580) 06:16:29
434. Rudy Morales (12601) 06:16:54
435. Bobby Rissolo (12629) 06:17:47
436. Dennis Chan (12654) 06:18:36
437. Edgar Perez (12671) 06:19:16
438. Joel Hernandez (12695) 06:20:00
439. Michael Allen (12712) 06:20:29
440. Luis Maldonado (12734) 06:21:24
441. Jason Kwan (12736) 06:21:26
442. Tom Johnson (12742) 06:21:34
443. Marvin Barrera (12801) 06:22:49
444. Saovona Bun (12810) 06:23:13
445. Jared Gutierrez (12846) 06:23:56
446. Ronaldo Manalo (12870) 06:24:43
447. Mike Quintana (12895) 06:25:46
448. Brian Salmon (12896) 06:25:46
449. Charles Kohli (12949) 06:27:16
450. Shannon Boyd (12954) 06:27:35
451. Jesus Mendoza (12966) 06:27:49
452. Vidal Pedro (12974) 06:27:58
453. Luke Adler (12975) 06:27:59
454. Kalief Washington (12984) 06:28:08
455. Hugo Garcia (12991) 06:28:27
456. Brandon Weldon (12992) 06:28:29
457. Andrew Martinez (13041) 06:30:05
458. Donald Nickel (13066) 06:30:53
459. Erick Ramirez (13075) 06:31:06
460. Alejandro Ponce (13076) 06:31:13
461. Abel Farias (13079) 06:31:17
462. Michael Weinstein (13102) 06:31:51
463. Javier Rodriguez (13137) 06:32:43
464. Luis Martinez (13163) 06:33:07
465. William Hernandez (13187) 06:34:09
466. Daniel Zauala (13188) 06:34:10
467. Robespierre Howard (13196) 06:34:24
468. Jose Reyes (13213) 06:34:47
469. Joey Hinzo (13227) 06:35:06
470. Tony Chen (13230) 06:35:13
471. Alejandro Dominguez (13235) 06:35:23
472. Andrew Coronado (13251) 06:35:52
473. Doug Eckhoff (13295) 06:37:09
474. Mike Lind (13323) 06:38:26
475. Kevin Patrick (13350) 06:39:11
476. Miguel Ramirez (13362) 06:39:34
477. Stephen Allard-Valdivieso (13393) 06:40:47
478. Eugene Williams (13411) 06:41:26
479. Jose Girron (13416) 06:41:36
480. Martin Johnstone (13454) 06:42:56
481. Jay Yoshizumi (13472) 06:43:48
482. Jonathan Nguyen (13479) 06:44:02
483. Juan Muniz (13523) 06:45:50
484. Junior Orantes (13538) 06:46:16
485. Jerome Mccuin (13558) 06:46:50
486. Joseph Chavez (13562) 06:46:54
487. Jose Cardenas (13571) 06:47:12
488. Daniel Ozuna (13604) 06:48:26
489. Hugo Pena (13606) 06:48:29
490. Asahel Rabadan (13607) 06:48:30
491. Miguel Aguilar (13616) 06:48:51
492. Tony Nguyen (13660) 06:50:06
493. Antwione Haywood (13663) 06:50:11
494. Paul Bucur (13667) 06:50:25
495. Michael Romero (13680) 06:50:35
496. Miguel Chavarria (13688) 06:50:43
497. Adam Coburn (13740) 06:52:43
498. Brian Mc Lafferty (13741) 06:52:44
499. Ian Feldman (13759) 06:53:59
500. Rene Cervantes (13765) 06:54:19
501. Walter Hernandez (13770) 06:54:31
502. Jason Espino (13773) 06:54:34
503. Ricky Valle (13783) 06:54:59
504. Danny Hinojonn (13792) 06:55:08
505. Ernesto Lopez (13798) 06:55:14
506. Mike Long (13800) 06:55:15
507. Bernie Jara (13835) 06:56:22
508. Oracio Gomez (13836) 06:56:23
509. Hayro Donado (13843) 06:56:44
510. Douglas Johnston (13868) 06:57:20
511. Carlos Privado (13883) 06:57:51
512. Ivan Arreola (13955) 07:00:02
513. Eddie Puc (14046) 07:03:06
514. Jim Rincan (14058) 07:03:42
515. Vinay Viswanathan (14066) 07:04:08
516. Gilbert Nieves (14096) 07:06:17
517. Miguel Mendoza (14104) 07:06:35
518. Tizoc Cruz-Gonzalez (14122) 07:07:27
519. Agustin Herrera (14137) 07:08:32
520. Rene Garcia (14150) 07:09:14
521. Mohamed Haroun (14167) 07:10:47
522. Art Casas (14205) 07:12:56
523. Jose Panaza (14210) 07:13:03
524. Gerardo Ruiz (14222) 07:14:00
525. Luis Aguillon (14235) 07:14:40
526. Waldo Gonzalez (14263) 07:15:50
527. Rene Garcia (14279) 07:16:36
528. Thomas Olaes (14320) 07:19:27
529. Vincent Alvarez (14356) 07:21:47
530. Rob Pilloud (14372) 07:22:44
531. Ludim Garcia (14382) 07:23:03
532. Jerry Yip (14384) 07:23:18
533. Darryl Briley (14449) 07:29:34
534. Donovan Peters (14452) 07:29:44
535. Marquette Howard (14481) 07:32:34
536. Sergio Varela (14491) 07:33:30
537. Daniel Gattas (14499) 07:34:00
538. Moises Cardoza (14514) 07:35:12
539. Jose Cabrera (14515) 07:35:13
540. Pramdeep Chase (14548) 07:37:05
541. Christian Quinones (14565) 07:38:38
542. Michael Mcclure (14566) 07:38:41
543. Carlos Rivera (14581) 07:39:44
544. Romulo Ayala (14582) 07:39:44
545. Leonardo Zamudio (14598) 07:40:57
546. Freddy Guevara (14599) 07:40:59
547. Cristian Teodscio (14601) 07:41:01
548. Joseph Martinez (14612) 07:41:59
549. Marquis Mcclure (14630) 07:44:09
550. Kevin Tisdale, Jr. (14660) 07:47:14
551. Marcelino Tinajero III (14682) 07:49:00
552. Israel Arroyo (14689) 07:49:47
553. Luis Elorreaga (14706) 07:51:37
554. Edgar Ovando (14715) 07:52:11
555. Richard Yoon (14747) 07:54:49
556. Juan Cano (14781) 07:57:26
557. Bryan Dodge (14802) 08:00:57
558. Gilbert Bravo (14806) 08:01:20
559. Gabriel Hernandez (14807) 08:01:26
560. Sait Marcos (14817) 08:01:38
561. Eliazar Bravo (14876) 08:11:39
562. Juan Fuentes (14902) 08:16:40
563. Johnathan Magana (14903) 08:16:41
564. Rudy Escobar (14904) 08:16:42
565. Christian Escobar (14905) 08:16:43
566. Michael Booker (14941) 08:21:04
567. Eduardo Hernandez (14967) 08:26:08
568. Richard Almaraz (14976) 08:28:27
569. Joey Ruiz (15015) 08:34:51
570. Angel Packaz (15016) 08:34:55
571. Jeremy Borlin (15021) 08:36:00
572. Steven Loarca (15098) 09:06:23
573. Irwin Salim (15100) 09:06:40
574. Phillip Sino-Cruz (15105) 09:10:25

WOMEN 17 & UNDER

1. Gabriela Arriaga (1224) 03:29:47
2. Alison Howard (2778) 03:54:24
3. Kellyn Wong (4627) 04:16:30
4. Jennifer Degeer (4788) 04:18:30
5. Lydia Mcdonald (5246) 04:23:45
6. Melissa Bonds (5996) 04:32:08
7. Jamie Montgomery (6044) 04:32:47
8. Boyden Rohner (6101) 04:33:26
9. Maria Vonkohler (6407) 04:36:38
10. Elizabeth Moore (6454) 04:37:20
11. Denise Johns (6884) 04:42:25
12. Rose Mendoza (7130) 04:45:13
13. Nancy Monterrosa (7131) 04:45:14
14. Michelle Hernandez (7149) 04:45:31
15. Sohyun Oh (7279) 04:46:59
16. Sofia Martos (7280) 04:47:00
17. Sarit Shwartz (7320) 04:47:27
18. Grace Shin (7348) 04:47:45
19. Rena Yamada (7574) 04:50:17
20. Crystal Nylander (7838) 04:53:39
21. Jennifer Corona (7891) 04:54:15
22. Patricia Robles (7989) 04:55:12
23. Maria Wynne (8036) 04:55:51
24. Heather Offenstein (8146) 04:57:16
25. Alma Robles (8380) 04:59:44
26. Teresa Holzbaugh (8604) 05:03:03
27. Norberta Moreno (8657) 05:03:49
28. Jessica Merino (8677) 05:04:01
29. Valori Book (8815) 05:06:21
30. Songhoa Cho (8924) 05:08:07
31. Jessica Lee (8977) 05:08:45
32. Brissa Sotelo (9006) 05:09:10
33. Elizabeth Cioffi (9182) 05:11:36
34. Basilia Huang (9212) 05:11:57
35. Lina Aldaz (9336) 05:13:45
36. Sonya Noriega (9394) 05:14:31
37. Ruth Chuquimia (9523) 05:16:47
38. Zhanna Pogosyan (9525) 05:16:49
39. Maria Osorio (9605) 05:17:58
40. Phong Tran (9610) 05:18:06
41. Teresa Pascual (9791) 05:20:53
42. Flor Piedrasanta (9893) 05:22:20
43. Ami Steward (9938) 05:23:18
44. Suzanne Hinds (10011) 05:24:29
45. Vilma Menendez (10147) 05:26:56
46. Margarita Valenzuela (10219) 05:27:59
47. Claudia Jarquin (10243) 05:28:30
48. Carol Mendoza (10483) 05:32:00
49. Karin Ragudo (10493) 05:32:11

50. MacAria Ison (10502) 05:32:20
51. Africa Faison (10503) 05:32:22
52. Marybell Castaneda (10622) 05:34:06
53. Kumi Vilahu (10639) 05:34:27
54. Mireya Islas (10680) 05:35:01
55. Sharon Febre (10747) 05:36:11
56. Genara Ventura (10786) 05:36:49
57. Nancy Dominguez (10873) 05:38:39
58. Carita Mcclain (10941) 05:40:07
59. Janell Mcclain (10942) 05:40:08
60. Amy El-Akabawi (10962) 05:40:30
61. Candy Penate (10984) 05:41:08
62. Issa Ventureno (10990) 05:41:16
63. Brenda Salgado (10991) 05:41:16
64. Sally Madera (11224) 05:44:49
65. Crystal Nguyen (11279) 05:45:54
66. Ann Harrie (11336) 05:46:56
67. Tara Olson (11353) 05:47:23
68. Melinda Gonzalez (11509) 05:50:32
69. Tieanna Jenkins (11525) 05:50:47
70. Brandy Adney (11564) 05:51:43
71. Gabriela Rojo (11670) 05:53:41
72. Stephanie Huang (11719) 05:54:47
73. Brenda Castaneda (11720) 05:54:48
74. Maria Castaneda (11737) 05:55:09
75. Danielle Lubeley (11811) 05:56:50
76. Jennifer Grboyan (11812) 05:56:50
77. Doris Gonzalez (11856) 05:58:00
78. Edith Gomez (11875) 05:58:24
79. Nahirohi Madrid (11876) 05:58:24
80. Alma Gomez (11877) 05:58:24
81. Margarita Gonzalez (11936) 05:59:39
82. Yanira Vargas (11947) 05:59:52
83. Trish Villegas (12040) 06:02:19
84. Maricela Cortez (12049) 06:02:30
85. Sarah Boaz (12108) 06:04:28
86. Elvia Valdes (12113) 06:04:33
87. Stacy Sullivan (12193) 06:06:20
88. Octavia Askew (12209) 06:06:55
89. Laura Soto (12259) 06:08:19
90. Thania Garcia (12270) 06:08:37
91. Hoa Huynh (12313) 06:09:24
92. Irene Valencia (12371) 06:11:04
93. Elia Hernandez (12379) 06:11:16
94. Sandra Herrera (12418) 06:12:11
95. Arlian Cruz (12466) 06:13:33
96. Ryan Poe (12534) 06:15:17
97. Arpi Abraham (12551) 06:15:39
98. Alejandra Olano (12574) 06:16:16
99. Carolina Ramirez (12599) 06:16:52
100. Suzanne Armstrong (12606) 06:16:56
101. Marleen Rodriguez (12645) 06:18:25
102. Alice Kiselyuk (12676) 06:19:27
103. Dora Hernandez (12688) 06:19:46
104. Mikeya Banks (12790) 06:22:35
105. Carolyn Smith (12797) 06:22:45
106. Perla Cisneros (12805) 06:23:03
107. Evelyn Popolu (12806) 06:23:03
108. Tania Morales (12807) 06:23:04
109. Annie Rosales (12814) 06:23:20
110. Maribel Cortez (12855) 06:24:10
111. Jennifer Neal (12874) 06:24:53
112. Pilar Sanchez (12900) 06:25:40
113. Dessa Keesee (12929) 06:26:34
114. Karla Quezada (12995) 06:28:33
115. Minerva Ramos (13004) 06:28:46
116. Reyna Robles (13005) 06:28:46
117. Abby Figueroa (13040) 06:30:03
118. Lorraine Gordon (13068) 06:30:57
119. Maritza Arevalo (13089) 06:31:32
120. Alishia Zimmerman (13096) 06:31:44
121. Cecilia Montanez (13110) 06:32:03
122. Marie Ly (13119) 06:32:27
123. Annie Wu (13129) 06:32:37
124. Naomi Fink (13130) 06:32:37
125. Elsy Galdamez (13144) 06:32:46
126. Aolibama Solis (13200) 06:34:30
127. Erika Valladares (13241) 06:35:34
128. Deana Brunson (13254) 06:35:56
129. Jamie Arakawa (13255) 06:35:59
130. Charlena Ware (13280) 06:36:33
131. Annmarie Juliano (13300) 06:37:30
132. Margarita Verduzco (13342) 06:39:02
133. Dolores Mcbride (13349) 06:39:10
134. Cinthia Mejia (13357) 06:39:29
135. Sara Burchfiel (13368) 06:39:44
136. Christina Loya (13383) 06:40:34
137. Chrishaun Collins (13419) 06:41:49
138. Kristal Tureaud (13420) 06:41:52
139. Ivelise Arguello (13431) 06:42:11
140. Ceci Canales (13458) 06:43:00
141. Edna Valdes (13461) 06:43:10
142. Karla Gonzalez (13464) 06:43:20
143. Roxanne Huertas (13495) 06:44:45
144. Teresa Camilo (13497) 06:44:48
145. Chandra Semien (13507) 06:45:13
146. Ixche Cruz-Gonzalez (13512) 06:45:18
147. Sarah Churchill (13547) 06:46:24
148. Angelica Garcia (13576) 06:47:30
149. Yesenia Verduzco (13580) 06:47:32
150. Belinda Lee (13592) 06:48:08
151. Sarah Castillo (13599) 06:48:17
152. Debbie Wong (13605) 06:48:29
153. Leticia Del Rio (13614) 06:48:40
154. Astrid Silva (13615) 06:48:43
155. Alice Vu (13645) 06:49:55
156. Nicole Balderrama (13647) 06:49:58
157. Teresa Beaudine (13650) 06:50:00
158. Bertha Ochoa (13659) 06:50:06
159. Priscilla De La Torre (13668) 06:50:26
160. Aisha Rahman (13673) 06:50:28
161. Silvia Ledesma (13693) 06:50:50
162. Melissa Flores (13695) 06:50:53
163. Juanita Middleton (13698) 06:51:02
164. Ulyana Wms-Kohlmeyer (13703) 06:51:07
165. Mabel Monarrez (13737) 06:52:40
166. Sonia Raygoza (13742) 06:52:45
167. Elyse Velasco (13752) 06:53:40
168. Jeannette Chavez (13761) 06:54:04
169. Adrianna Valencia (13827) 06:56:00
170. Lizarraga Joann (13864) 06:57:15
171. Yvette Ribancos (13867) 06:57:18
172. Laurna Wong (13869) 06:57:20
173. Monique Gaznick (13886) 06:57:56
174. Margaret Gabikyan (13887) 06:57:58
175. Laura Sullivan (13902) 06:58:27
176. Daisy Antee (13945) 06:59:42
177. Leslie Lima (13948) 06:59:54
178. Yeni Anaya (13949) 06:59:54
179. Leticia Alvarado (13950) 06:59:55
180. Janeth Jaimes (13959) 07:00:11
181. Maria Turcios (13960) 07:00:14
182. Kristiana Spajio (13974) 07:00:39
183. Zoe Tasou (13998) 07:01:09
184. Michelle Whang (13999) 07:01:10
185. Adriana Rangel (14007) 07:01:36
186. Dwana Sankey (14027) 07:02:12
187. Avygail Sanchez (14079) 07:04:57
188. Evelyn Colindres (14082) 07:04:58
189. Ceci Contreras (14098) 07:06:18
190. Elizabeth Padilla (14102) 07:06:30
191. Guillermina Munoz (14105) 07:06:36
192. Monica Aleman (14110) 07:06:47
193. Kathy Palacios (14112) 07:07:01
194. Lakeshi Germany (14133) 07:08:23
195. Isabel Alvarado (14165) 07:10:45
196. Mari Nakashima (14166) 07:10:45
197. Yadira Pineda (14181) 07:11:42
198. Victoria Browder (14194) 07:12:35
199. Alma Murillo (14204) 07:12:55
200. Michelle Torres (14220) 07:13:53
201. Nancy Ho (14228) 07:14:36
202. Shnelka Tulloss (14232) 07:14:39
203. Vanessa Mayer (14234) 07:14:40
204. Angeline Medina (14242) 07:14:52
205. Carmen Bautista (14357) 07:21:48
206. Elizabeth Alvarez (14358) 07:21:48
207. Guadalupe Zambrano (14360) 07:22:05
208. Stephanie Garcia (14366) 07:22:35
209. Delia Gonzalez (14371) 07:22:37
210. Courtney Drake (14374) 07:22:58
211. Ebony Lawson (14375) 07:22:58
212. Jenelle Pitt (14376) 07:22:59
213. Natashia Wright (14377) 07:22:59
214. Stephanie Vargas (14386) 07:23:53
215. Adriana Magana (14411) 07:26:10
216. Hermillia Bustamante (14415) 07:26:21
217. Cynthia Garcia (14416) 07:26:21
218. Joanna Sosa (14457) 07:30:07
219. Ariadna Arreola (14468) 07:30:40
220. Marina Castellanos (14469) 07:30:40
221. Olure Awolava (14492) 07:33:32
222. Lisa Thomas (14522) 07:35:43
223. Wendy Rivera (14523) 07:35:44
224. Dania Chavez (14524) 07:35:51
225. Christine Muratori (14527) 07:36:00
226. Mara Altman (14543) 07:36:57
227. Jenny Mazariego (14545) 07:37:04
228. Melissa Astete (14546) 07:37:04
229. Kim Myers (14550) 07:37:09
230. Nancy Gutierrez (14583) 07:39:56
231. Victoria Tamayo (14584) 07:39:57
232. Mayra Guiterrez (14593) 07:40:36
233. Elba Lozano (14594) 07:40:37
234. Carol Ruelas (14627) 07:43:25
235. Brittany Cotton (14638) 07:44:57
236. Sandra Mejia (14639) 07:44:59
237. Ethel Rodriguez (14640) 07:45:00
238. Aideet Pineda (14684) 07:49:22
239. Elsa Cobian (14717) 07:52:18
240. Jannet Quinones (14722) 07:52:28
241. Juliet Polintan (14741) 07:54:20
242. Sherrie Faylona (14742) 07:54:21
243. Jennifer Lamb (14743) 07:54:22
244. Megan Stark (14774) 07:56:46
245. Monica Arellano (14809) 08:01:28
246. Nochilt Garcia (14820) 08:01:55
247. Bridgette Freeman (14829) 08:02:33
248. Kimberly Tanaka (14841) 08:03:46
249. Rose Santilena (14849) 08:05:53
250. Patty Rodriguez (14852) 08:06:59
251. Maritza Hernandez (14875) 08:11:38
252. Veronica Zatarain (14877) 08:11:42
253. Kelly Finn (14879) 08:11:45
254. Elizabeth Ferretti (14892) 08:14:52
255. Ilana Kozlenko (14973) 08:27:59
256. Iris Sornellon (14980) 08:28:39
257. Yazmin Romero (15020) 08:35:36
258. Maribel Ramos (15023) 08:36:24
259. Michelle Churchill (15036) 08:40:08
260. Yanina Bazemore (15048) 08:45:57
261. Candice Valdez (15078) 08:55:21
262. Krystle Dennis (15080) 08:55:22
263. Shalonna Mcroy (15094) 09:00:43
264. Brandi Mathews (15095) 09:00:43
265. Jasmine Houston (15099) 09:06:40
266. Natasha Bowman (15101) 09:06:40
267. Veronica Rocha (15102) 09:08:00
268. Leslie Sino-Cruz (15106) 09:10:25
269. Gina Lutcher (15125) 09:29:00
270. Mayra Delgado (15126) 09:29:00
271. Sujey Aispuro (15127) 09:29:40
272. Caroline Sommers (15131) 09:31:02
273. Alicia Villa (15134) 09:32:55
274. Kris Kissinger (15138) 09:36:38
275. Liza Sino-Cruz (15157) 09:58:33
276. Maria Huizar (15160) 10:01:36
277. Raquel Zepeda (15161) 10:02:36
278. Roxana Flores (15162) 10:02:36
279. Dierra Morrow (15165) 10:07:10
280. April Jameson (15166) 10:07:10
281. Lucy Le (15168) 10:08:54
282. Tiffany Jeffrey (15169) 10:08:54
283. Arlela Haro (15170) 10:08:54

MEN 18 TO 24

1. Marcos Juarez (13) 02:26:03
2. Curtis McLaurin (66) 02:47:45
3. Santos Per Mich (94) 02:49:50
4. Jose Acuchi (98) 02:50:10
5. Scott Phillips (112) 02:52:00
6. Miguel Juarez (116) 02:52:18
7. Wilfried Kerau (117) 02:52:23
8. Cesar Guerrero (144) 02:53:59
9. Michael Plechocki (147) 02:54:08
10. Armando Torres (158) 02:55:33
11. Miguel Mendoza (160) 02:55:40
12. Yasuhara Kanto (179) 02:56:55
13. Marco Martinez (183) 02:57:09
14. Ernesto Sanchez (185) 02:57:19
15. Mike Neill (195) 02:57:54
16. David Medina (198) 02:58:04
17. Benjamin Williams (207) 02:58:33
18. Miguel Daniel (235) 03:00:32
19. Mark Rothery (252) 03:01:17
20. Julio Felix (253) 03:01:19
21. Adolfo Moratalla Folghr (254) 03:01:19
22. Cesar Mata (257) 03:01:37
23. David Giangrande (271) 03:02:29
24. Rene Cuahonte (284) 03:03:02
25. Jose Roberto Flores Mariscal (289) 03:03:13
26. Dan Pineda (301) 03:03:44
27. Jay Wohlgemuth (318) 03:04:43
28. Paul Ishimine (348) 03:06:22
29. Oscar Velazco (368) 03:07:20
30. Juan Pablo Garcia Garcia (407) 03:08:34
31. Louis Guillermo (413) 03:08:50
32. Robert Sandoval (436) 03:09:37
33. Chris Giangrande (468) 03:10:43
34. Mark Culbertson (470) 03:10:50
35. Arturo Arreola (489) 03:11:29
36. Lucas Ramirez (501) 03:12:13
37. Melges Scott (523) 03:12:59
38. Jose Ramirez (529) 03:13:09
39. Michael Thaxton (532) 03:13:15
40. Daniel McDonald (552) 03:13:45
41. Javier Avila (562) 03:13:54
42. Brett Peterson (577) 03:14:25
43. Tony Sanchez (587) 03:14:41
44. Roger Forest (609) 03:15:29
45. Amalio Menor (626) 03:16:14
46. Roderick Brown (630) 03:16:20
47. Jose Valencia (635) 03:16:29
48. Miguel Tello (658) 03:17:05
49. Abisai Gonzales (669) 03:17:20
50. Jose Rivera (718) 03:18:48
51. Raul Corter (722) 03:18:55
52. Erick Quiej (746) 03:19:31
53. Sabino Beltran (757) 03:19:48
54. Enrico Krause (777) 03:20:22
55. Carlk Vause (780) 03:20:25
56. Eladio Ramirez (783) 03:20:30
57. Mark Proden (789) 03:20:41
58. Manuel Ceja (790) 03:20:42
59. Robert Lopez Jr (794) 03:20:46
60. Art Ayala (801) 03:21:10
61. George Espinoza (813) 03:21:28
62. Robert Leach (834) 03:21:47
63. Ricardo Verboomen (842) 03:22:02
64. Tim Foy (858) 03:22:24
65. Carlos Mayen-Solorzano (863) 03:22:28
66. Brian Treeful (888) 03:23:00
67. Cecilio Martinez (889) 03:23:02
68. Jeffrey Butler (906) 03:23:25
69. Bruce Inosencio (933) 03:24:00
70. Daniel Carrillo (952) 03:24:24
71. Matthew Sanderson (966) 03:24:38
72. Tony Buenrostro (968) 03:24:44
73. Paul Baker (976) 03:24:54
74. Omar Alfaro (991) 03:25:15
75. Hector Castellon (992) 03:25:16
76. John Swing (999) 03:25:27
77. Andres Lopez (1033) 03:26:15
78. Pedro Chavez Jr (1041) 03:26:29
79. Arturo Gomez (1042) 03:26:31
80. Ozzie Ruiz (1088) 03:27:29
81. Michael Kirst (1093) 03:27:32
82. Sam Warren (1096) 03:27:34
83. Jason Schrage (1101) 03:27:38
84. Damian Horstman (1129) 03:28:07
85. Joseph Swimmer (1134) 03:28:14
86. Juan Duarte (1139) 03:28:17
87. Don Sevesind (1177) 03:29:03
88. Jeffrey Bennett (1182) 03:29:09
89. Scott Nichols (1210) 03:29:37
90. Martin Martinez (1230) 03:29:58
91. Matthew Woods (1254) 03:30:27
92. Craig Huxley (1299) 03:31:24
93. Mickey Mckay (1301) 03:31:25
94. Carlos Gonzalez (1325) 03:31:45
95. Robert Reinhart (1340) 03:32:02
96. Sai Natarajan (1396) 03:33:07
97. Alexander Bunn (1399) 03:33:10
98. Andrew Wartenburg (1420) 03:33:50
99. Armando Conde (1421) 03:33:52
100. Charlie Smith (1439) 03:34:09
101. Osmin Rodriguez (1469) 03:34:52
102. Leeland Turner (1473) 03:34:55
103. Francisco Brizuela (1489) 03:35:11
104. Chris Pisano (1514) 03:35:43
105. Tomi Saarnio (1519) 03:35:45
106. Brett Leake (1534) 03:35:58
107. David Polidori (1536) 03:36:00
108. David Chahua (1583) 03:36:56
109. Rigoberto Reyes (1589) 03:37:00
110. Jonah Borris (1595) 03:37:06
111. Jose Aguirre (1608) 03:37:19
112. Reinhard Koelbl (1657) 03:38:13
113. Enrique Jauregui (1664) 03:38:18
114. Phillip Stewart (1668) 03:38:20
115. Rogelio Acevedo (1669) 03:38:20
116. Carlos Szaiankiewicz (1687) 03:38:45
117. Emile MacAire (1694) 03:38:51
118. Antonio Guillermo (1711) 03:39:09
119. Lang Lee (1715) 03:39:12
120. Luis Raygoza (1746) 03:39:47
121. Imre Szombathy (1756) 03:40:01
122. Curtis Bixler (1759) 03:40:04
123. Eric Marsh (1765) 03:40:12
124. Cedric Westphal (1769) 03:40:15
125. Gregory Pound (1775) 03:40:19
126. Carlos Sian Choc (1792) 03:40:31
127. Ruben Covarrubias (1799) 03:40:38
128. Alejandro Tinajero (1800) 03:40:40
129. Jose Briseno (1823) 03:41:02
130. Melvin Campos (1827) 03:41:04
131. Rodrigo Duran (1845) 03:41:16
132. Morten Haastrup (1847) 03:41:16
133. Dexter Mahaffey (1871) 03:41:36
134. Jose Fernandez (1902) 03:41:59
135. David Ramirez (1918) 03:42:18
136. Eric Klingsporn (1926) 03:42:27
137. Rick De Leon (1927) 03:42:28
138. Jerome Hohman (1929) 03:42:31
139. Omar Menendez (1954) 03:43:08
140. Michael Mazza (1973) 03:43:25
141. Aniceto Espinoza (1993) 03:43:45
142. Jeff McCann (2007) 03:43:59
143. Brian Moore (2010) 03:44:01
144. Aaron Bennett (2016) 03:44:03
145. Daniel Yaroslaski (2044) 03:44:24
146. Joe Traba (2054) 03:44:34
147. Orlando Prado (2075) 03:44:50
148. Blakely Hume (2096) 03:45:06
149. Keith Epperson (2100) 03:45:09
150. Brad Ayres (2114) 03:45:19
151. Han Cho (2121) 03:45:27
152. Everardo Zamora (2142) 03:45:47
153. Rutger De Vink (2152) 03:45:54
154. Peter Griego Jr (2172) 03:46:12
155. Ibrahim Khamis (2173) 03:46:13
156. Jacob Heck (2178) 03:46:19
157. Ralph Duarte (2187) 03:46:26
158. Brett Ensor (2199) 03:46:43
159. Gary Willis (2203) 03:46:48
160. Masahito Kobayashi (2214) 03:46:56
161. Justin Mofo (2229) 03:47:10
162. Brent Saxwold (2233) 03:47:14
163. Eric Benson (2241) 03:47:19
164. Mark Etter (2258) 03:47:33
165. Jason Middleton (2259) 03:47:33
166. Stephen Thomas (2271) 03:47:43
167. Jeffrey Miller (2279) 03:47:50
168. Scott Wichmann (2283) 03:47:54
169. Jeff Schulte (2287) 03:47:59
170. Thomas Donovan (2324) 03:48:28
171. Salvador Siordia (2335) 03:48:34
172. Saul Pena (2338) 03:48:36
173. Dan Whitecotton (2343) 03:48:37
174. Yasunori Saito (2350) 03:48:44
175. Juventino Rosas (2352) 03:48:46
176. Juan Reyna (2368) 03:49:03
177. Jason Gondek (2378) 03:49:08
178. Dumitru Popa Jr (2381) 03:49:09
179. Akira Iwase (2384) 03:49:12
180. Horacio Cervantes (2401) 03:49:23
181. David Sides (2407) 03:49:30
182. Walter Montano (2417) 03:49:39
183. Thom Vertotic (2418) 03:49:39
184. Eduardo Juarez Romero (2420) 03:49:41
185. Julio Moreno (2427) 03:49:45
186. Ricardo Aguilar (2430) 03:49:40
187. Robert Jones (2433) 03:49:49
188. Paul Andrews (2440) 03:49:56
189. Wade Cochran (2455) 03:50:10
190. Paul Hamilton (2459) 03:50:14
191. Victor Suarez (2472) 03:50:25
192. Osbaldo Gutierrez (2483) 03:50:33
193. Bret Edgar (2511) 03:50:54
194. Glenn Johnson (2524) 03:51:06
195. Kevin Callahan (2539) 03:51:23
196. Luis Torres (2543) 03:51:26
197. Shin Ogasawara (2548) 03:51:28
198. Griffith Lee (2557) 03:51:35
199. Patrick Wuebben (2567) 03:51:40
200. Brad Jones (2572) 03:51:46
201. Lucas Beebe (2590) 03:51:59
202. Leon Lo (2604) 03:52:15
203. Samir Garg (2632) 03:52:36
204. Greg Ahmann (2641) 03:52:44
205. Art Ruiz (2666) 03:52:59
206. Michael Lauruhn (2678) 03:53:09
207. William Abbott (2688) 03:53:17
208. Marc Smith (2695) 03:53:20
209. Jose Corral (2700) 03:53:25
210. Paul Wang (2703) 03:53:26
211. Brian Mitchell (2706) 03:53:27
212. Alejandro Sanchez (2722) 03:53:42
213. Juan Reyes (2727) 03:53:45
214. Thomas Rollinger (2734) 03:53:50
215. Dan Jung (2759) 03:54:12
216. Armen Mitilian (2777) 03:54:24
217. Edgardo Flores (2794) 03:54:32
218. Jose Vargas (2797) 03:54:33
219. Manuel Uribe (2825) 03:54:51
220. Steve Porter (2863) 03:55:23
221. Rod Barbosa (2875) 03:55:27
222. Katsusuke Itayama (2887) 03:55:32
223. Tony Iniguez (2891) 03:55:33
224. Dwayne Tschoepe (2896) 03:55:41
225. Michael Medrano (2920) 03:55:58
226. James Chambers (2936) 03:56:09
227. Ravish Patwardhan (2943) 03:56:13
228. Jose Ramon (2945) 03:56:14
229. Michael Quezada (2990) 03:56:46
230. Todd Lund (2991) 03:56:46
231. Rudy Paz (3015) 03:56:57
232. David O'Toole (3035) 03:57:06
233. K. Blackson (3074) 03:57:32
234. Richard Schmidt (3113) 03:57:56
235. Rafael Deojuan (3116) 03:57:59
236. Terrel Reyes (3118) 03:58:01
237. Matthew Ryan (3130) 03:58:10
238. Gregory Hann (3146) 03:58:23
239. Saluador Ramos (3147) 03:58:24
240. Eric Westendorf (3218) 03:59:13
241. Edgar Hernandez (3221) 03:59:16
242. Heath Sims (3232) 03:59:24
243. Tom Coates (3242) 03:59:31
244. Luis Ignacio Gascon Lopez (3247) 03:59:36
245. Carlos Aguilar (3251) 03:59:38
246. Bennett Brookstein (3268) 03:59:46
247. Tony Sola (3298) 04:00:01
248. Lynn Allen (3301) 04:00:02
249. Gustavo Chavez (3307) 04:00:05
250. Brian Wilkening (3313) 04:00:09
251. Albert Avalos (3319) 04:00:15
252. Mario Hernandez (3322) 04:00:16
253. Juan Perez (3323) 04:00:17
254. Teodoro Rayo (3404) 04:01:19
255. Alan Friedl (3426) 04:01:33
256. Raul Ramirez (3430) 04:01:41
257. Caesar Castaneda (3440) 04:01:48
258. Nicholas Haley (3445) 04:01:55
259. Mark Clingan (3472) 04:02:17
260. Chris Clark (3474) 04:02:17
261. David Carper (3475) 04:02:17
262. Gabriel Cuevas (3494) 04:02:37
263. Craig Sherrod (3507) 04:02:48
264. Ismael Ortega (3518) 04:02:57
265. Tyler Vachon (3519) 04:02:58
266. Isaac Villarreal (3520) 04:02:59
267. Santiago Gomez (3594) 04:04:09
268. Richard Bolster (3603) 04:04:13
269. Brian Jensen (3617) 04:04:21
270. Jose Prado (3665) 04:04:48
271. Mateo Jimenez (3692) 04:05:08
272. Shannon Michaels (3694) 04:05:08
273. Ben Seuplveda (3714) 04:05:29
274. Suchir Batra (3729) 04:05:38
275. Allan Potter (3732) 04:05:42
276. Marcos Ayala (3737) 04:05:48
277. Demetrio Hernandez (3738) 04:05:49
278. V Adam Carter (3743) 04:05:52
279. Antonio Ballesteros (3750) 04:06:03
280. David Fox (3763) 04:06:06
281. Tim Kao (3774) 04:06:15
282. Trevor Kirk (3833) 04:06:59
283. Bill Cao (3841) 04:07:03
284. Bob Cao (3842) 04:07:04
285. Marcus Dawson (3848) 04:07:06
286. Rodolfo Suarez (3850) 04:07:07
287. Jeremy Plager (3854) 04:07:09
288. Sergio Herrera (3857) 04:07:15
289. Hugo Zepedo Quinones (3875) 04:07:30
290. Chris Baird (3896) 04:07:41
291. Noe Rodriguez (3933) 04:08:15
292. Javier Garcia (3937) 04:08:17
293. Juan Pineda (3958) 04:08:27
294. Jason Goldberg (3960) 04:08:29
295. Daniel Philips (3993) 04:09:01
296. Richard DeAngelo (4030) 04:09:26
297. David Hale (4037) 04:09:33
298. Douglas Rosenberg (4078) 04:10:09
299. Lester Pataki (4081) 04:10:10
300. Javier Benitez (4091) 04:10:15
301. James Stafford (4100) 04:10:27
302. Martin Rosales Rico (4106) 04:10:31
303. Jeffery Williams (4156) 04:11:02
304. Felipe Hernandez (4177) 04:11:16
305. Victor Ruiz (4183) 04:11:21
306. Michael Rivera (4189) 04:11:27
307. Nai Saelee (4196) 04:11:34
308. Ernesto Vega (4204) 04:11:40
309. Brian Timmerman (4242) 04:12:13
310. Joseph Lechner (4247) 04:12:16
311. Jose Rodriguez (4251) 04:12:19
312. Ralf Almonte (4254) 04:12:21
313. Jeffery Sammons (4258) 04:12:24
314. Vanz Steimle (4268) 04:12:30
315. Jorge Mendez (4269) 04:12:31
316. Takatsugu Terachi (4306) 04:13:02
317. Maceo Esquivel (4311) 04:13:06
318. Tony Mariscal (4327) 04:13:15
319. Phil Ditty (4347) 04:13:32
320. Dagoberto Antunez (4350) 04:13:35
321. Eric Mozilo (4362) 04:13:49
322. Jeffrey Fulfer (4371) 04:13:54
323. Gustavo Cruz (4388) 04:14:03
324. Rene Rosa (4398) 04:14:09
325. Brandon Miller (4408) 04:14:19
326. Brett Holt (4423) 04:14:26
327. Jorge Ruiz (4442) 04:14:37
328. Tyler Cabot (4448) 04:14:39
329. Gerardo Hernandez (4454) 04:14:42
330. Martin Ortega (4530) 04:15:32
331. Daniel Kelley (4547) 04:15:40
332. Nelson Morales (4549) 04:15:41
333. Maurice Kuiper (4562) 04:15:49
334. Joshua Cascade (4565) 04:15:50
335. Stephen Sides (4567) 04:15:51
336. Salvador Roman (4570) 04:15:53
337. Yoshihiro Takada (4574) 04:15:56
338. Dan Blaine (4585) 04:16:03
339. Nick Martin (4597) 04:16:11
340. Matt Herr (4611) 04:16:23
341. Joe Mariles (4620) 04:16:20
342. Frances Jordan (4667) 04:17:00
343. Isidro Zavala (4694) 04:17:25
344. Louis Gossett (4701) 04:17:29
345. Steve Laguana (4711) 04:17:37
346. Joshua Mathiesen (4739) 04:17:56
347. Joseph Seymour (4774) 04:18:21
348. Mike Hardy (4783) 04:18:26
349. Ted Huber (4793) 04:18:32
350. Charles Yun (4823) 04:18:50
351. Joe Hogan (4875) 04:19:17
352. David Vazquez (4888) 04:19:27
353. Didier Ushijima (4897) 04:19:35
354. Fred Anderson (4903) 04:19:38
355. Kenneth Bailey (4918) 04:19:49
356. Mike Kindle (4939) 04:20:02
357. Derek Van Camp (4954) 04:20:15
358. Jeffrey Freedberg (4955) 04:20:16
359. Hugo Valencia (4961) 04:20:23
360. Murray Dubow (4975) 04:20:35
361. Naoya Nakamura (4983) 04:20:41
362. Fernando Ibarra Maldonado (4995) 04:20:56
363. Ernesto Sandoval (4996) 04:20:57
364. Igor Lukashin (5043) 04:21:30
365. Jon Viele (5090) 04:21:57
366. Arturo Echeverria (5092) 04:21:58
367. Aaron Butcher (5105) 04:22:06
368. Marc Apkarian (5155) 04:22:42
369. Ronald Harvey (5163) 04:22:46
370. Mayorvy Cordova (5172) 04:22:53
371. Christopher Degroof (5191) 04:23:08
372. Bolivar Sanchez (5219) 04:23:23
373. Donal Soto (5229) 04:23:33
374. Jose Rivera (5242) 04:23:39
375. Michael Bogdan (5244) 04:23:42
376. Sean Murray (5271) 04:24:12
377. Joshua Paez (5297) 04:24:31
378. Andre Crouch (5308) 04:24:35
379. Andy Kim (5323) 04:24:49
380. Robert Telles (5330) 04:24:54
381. Wenceslao Hernandez (5337) 04:24:58
382. Darin Reid (5347) 04:25:06
383. Enry Sanchez (5376) 04:25:22
384. Scott Neubauer (5382) 04:25:24
385. Paul Kollee (5384) 04:25:25
386. Stephen Kwo (5410) 04:25:40
387. Juan Rivera Bautista (5435) 04:25:55
388. Jose Aguirre (5446) 04:26:00
389. Patrick Flood (5448) 04:26:03
390. Alex Galvez (5496) 04:26:37
391. Earnest Jackson (5525) 04:27:03
392. Ross Genovese (5544) 04:27:15
393. Michael Hen (5582) 04:27:36
394. Michael Anderson (5612) 04:27:56
395. Chris Fowler (5635) 04:28:09
396. Parker Lake (5643) 04:28:14
397. Miguel Rodriguez (5675) 04:28:37
398. Eric Nelson (5679) 04:28:38
399. Ricardo Figueroa (5680) 04:28:39
400. Mario Tapia (5722) 04:29:05

401. Moises Jacobo (5725) 04:29:05
402. Stephen Rianda (5727) 04:29:06
403. Derek Hansen (5737) 04:29:16
404. Orlando Martinez (5744) 04:29:19
405. Atanacio Haro (5771) 04:29:38
406. Michael Mayo (5776) 04:29:40
407. George Carlos (5780) 04:29:43
408. Juan Rodriguez (5817) 04:30:14
409. Cesar Rodriguez (5862) 04:30:37
410. Mark Bachand (5863) 04:30:37
411. Louie Sanchez (5879) 04:30:44
412. David Veloz (5937) 04:31:26
413. Michael Michaud (5938) 04:31:26
414. Rigoberto Luna (5940) 04:31:27
415. Joshua Ellison (5948) 04:31:31
416. Stephen Banta (5950) 04:31:32
417. Juan Flores (5957) 04:31:40
418. Sergio Colon (5987) 04:32:01
419. Brian Kessler (5988) 04:32:02
420. Mark Snow (5989) 04:32:03
421. Lawson Bartell (6004) 04:32:19
422. Margarito Solano (6009) 04:32:21
423. Tom Jankowski (6010) 04:32:22
424. Steven Smither (6011) 04:32:22
425. Raul Romero (6030) 04:32:42
426. Michael Keith (6032) 04:32:43
427. Edmundo Quijada (6039) 04:32:45
428. Christopher Noyes (6046) 04:32:48
429. Edwin Escobar (6051) 04:32:53
430. Jesus Olivas (6071) 04:33:04
431. Jerry Weitzman (6077) 04:33:08
432. Mauricio Jovel Reyes (6097) 04:33:22
433. Humberto Ochoa (6134) 04:33:46
434. Jose Flores (6168) 04:34:11
435. Paul Sandoral (6174) 04:34:14
436. Alex Romero (6192) 04:34:26
437. Alex Montes (6197) 04:34:29
438. Daniel Mccarthy (6201) 04:34:32
439. Alex Flores (6209) 04:34:39
440. Mark Siddall (6233) 04:34:53
441. Domingo Carranza (6239) 04:34:58
442. Mauro Zamora (6240) 04:34:59
443. Vincent Walden (6246) 04:35:02
444. Louis Bednar (6247) 04:35:04
445. Magdaleno Garcia (6286) 04:35:27
446. Dave Kreider (6296) 04:35:35
447. Jeffrey Jacobs (6299) 04:35:37
448. John Childs (6312) 04:35:45
449. Bradley Ter Keurst (6359) 04:36:14
450. James Morales (6367) 04:36:19
451. Gaku Okusada (6377) 04:36:23
452. Bani Vasquez (6394) 04:36:30
453. John Ament (6404) 04:36:36
454. Corey Ebbin (6412) 04:36:39
455. Jose Gutierrez (6432) 04:36:56
456. Mark Robinson (6433) 04:36:58
457. Endhit Esteban (6447) 04:37:12
458. Carlos Molina (6467) 04:37:26
459. Rafael Huerta (6472) 04:37:28
460. Roberto Bautista (6473) 04:37:29
461. Juan Rios (6475) 04:37:30
462. Pablo Castro (6491) 04:37:38
463. Devin Mc Mahan (6492) 04:37:38
464. Stephen Jacoby (6504) 04:37:45
465. Napoleon Diaz De Leon (6512) 04:37:48
466. Oscar Sierra (6515) 04:37:50
467. James Ozenne (6542) 04:38:09
468. Terry Woods (6550) 04:38:14
469. Naotaka Suzuki (6553) 04:38:14
470. Adan Roesner (6557) 04:38:16
471. Joseph Liu (6567) 04:38:24
472. Timothy Crane (6578) 04:38:32
473. Bob Kim (6579) 04:38:32
474. David Oh (6580) 04:38:33
475. Talia Acosta (6583) 04:38:33
476. Tyler Harrison (6612) 04:38:50
477. A Peter Kuperman (6635) 04:39:05
478. Lester Gregory (6641) 04:39:10
479. Nicholas Harris (6642) 04:39:11
480. Jeremy Haas (6644) 04:39:11
481. Straughan Petrie (6660) 04:39:28
482. William Becher III (6662) 04:39:28
483. Efrain Vergara (6666) 04:39:31
484. Paxson Chia (6673) 04:39:38
485. Derek Meyer (6687) 04:39:45
486. Paul Gilden (6690) 04:39:45
487. Anthony Amado (6732) 04:40:21
488. Demetrio Hernandez (6743) 04:40:33
489. John Middlebrook (6764) 04:40:50
490. Matthew Berg (6773) 04:40:58
491. Victor Liu (6812) 04:41:28
492. Kevin Carolan (6813) 04:41:29
493. Jongkuk Oh (6822) 04:41:35
494. Jacob Guzman (6864) 04:42:04
495. Ricardo Garcia (6865) 04:42:04
496. Agustin Tabares (6882) 04:42:23
497. Adam Symson (6896) 04:42:33
498. Gerhard Figueroa (6899) 04:42:35
499. Jose Ruelas (6920) 04:42:49
500. Horacio Falcon (6924) 04:42:51
501. Garrett Maze (6937) 04:43:01
502. Antonio Angurano (6949) 04:43:08
503. Kevin Armstrong (6988) 04:43:30
504. Ricardo Rodriguez (6994) 04:43:34
505. Polo Molina (7015) 04:43:44
506. Bill Moore (7026) 04:43:54
507. Hector Bejar (7038) 04:44:01
508. William Glennan (7042) 04:44:03
509. Cameron Carter (7043) 04:44:04
510. Brian Spangler (7064) 04:44:21
511. Gerardo Aguilera (7081) 04:44:39
512. Christopher Garcia (7126) 04:45:11
513. Richard Rios (7128) 04:45:12
514. Roy Ahn (7134) 04:45:15
515. Isaias Hernandez (7167) 04:45:42
516. Ronald Seley (7169) 04:45:43
517. Julius Caesar Baradas (7190) 04:45:59
518. Jose Ramos (7192) 04:46:00
519. Robert Castaneda (7213) 04:46:14
520. Robert Edmonds (7234) 04:46:31
521. Kenneth Koo (7269) 04:46:55
522. Shawn Bond (7275) 04:46:57
523. Frank Romero (7284) 04:47:02
524. Hugo Guillermo (7310) 04:47:22
525. Dung Pham (7319) 04:47:27
526. John Cramer (7359) 04:47:57
527. Mark D'avila (7367) 04:48:03
528. Lawrence Juarez (7381) 04:48:11
529. Dat Ngo (7397) 04:48:19
530. Jaime Perez (7406) 04:48:26
531. Alex Allen (7409) 04:48:27
532. Sarabjit Bhalla (7410) 04:48:29
533. Jack Baun (7413) 04:48:30
534. Richard Smits (7414) 04:48:30
535. Stuart Wiffen (7451) 04:48:58
536. Fernando Hernandez (7478) 04:49:13
537. Takahiro Hiramaki (7480) 04:49:14
538. Jose Matildes (7486) 04:49:19
539. Kyo Lee (7489) 04:49:20
540. Julio Gurrola (7508) 04:49:29
541. Rodolfo Vazqez (7510) 04:49:29
542. Cesar Romero (7520) 04:49:34
543. Phillip Williams (7527) 04:49:38
544. Jose Contrars (7540) 04:49:51
545. Antonio Varela (7553) 04:49:59
546. Akira Asano (7653) 04:51:22
547. Daniel Cummings (7682) 04:51:40
548. Stephen Nebel (7685) 04:51:41
549. Daniel Moreno (7703) 04:52:00
550. Mynor Marquez (7710) 04:52:06
551. Ernesto Martinez (7712) 04:52:07
552. Jose Rodriguez (7717) 04:52:10
553. Julio Cruz (7724) 04:52:16
554. Sean Griffith (7745) 04:52:35
555. Angel Alba (7771) 04:52:53
556. Chad Williamson (7778) 04:52:58
557. Johnny Pellot (7793) 04:53:11
558. Dan Garcia (7836) 04:53:38
559. Samuel Minyard (7851) 04:53:49
560. Jesus Hernandez Jr (7888) 04:54:13
561. Barry Dorris Lee (7890) 04:54:15
562. Adam Melcher (7894) 04:54:17
563. Louie Rizo (7895) 04:54:18
564. Angel Munoz (7922) 04:54:31
565. Mike Ziemienski (7946) 04:54:41
566. Elias Vallecino (7956) 04:54:46
567. Eduard Zubo (7967) 04:54:50
568. Manuel Martinez (7968) 04:54:50
569. Isidro Ramirez (7975) 04:55:01
570. Loren Leigh (7979) 04:55:07
571. Ever Hernandez (8008) 04:55:30
572. Tony Arias (8010) 04:55:33
573. Efrain Gomez (8049) 04:56:01
574. Andrees Mota (8061) 04:56:11
575. Oscar Ayala (8078) 04:56:23
576. Dominique Pham (8096) 04:56:36
577. Trinh Nguyen (8097) 04:56:36
578. Sal Solis (8108) 04:56:45
579. Felix Jacobo (8109) 04:56:45
580. Julio Torres (8123) 04:56:57
581. Scott Mc Kay (8130) 04:57:03
582. Scott Booker (8145) 04:57:15
583. Concepcion Camacho (8147) 04:57:17
584. Quillermo Jimenez (8185) 04:57:45
585. Luis Romero (8191) 04:57:49
586. Francisco Ceja (8194) 04:57:51
587. Erik Priedkalns (8243) 04:58:17
588. Moises Aviles (8250) 04:58:20
589. Ricardo Vazquez (8252) 04:58:21
590. Apraham Gogus (8259) 04:58:27
591. Andres Irlando (8260) 04:58:28
592. Chris Scott (8280) 04:58:43
593. Rajinder Marula (8286) 04:58:48
594. Damian Bradlwy (8300) 04:58:54
595. Phillip Freeman Jr (8313) 04:59:01
596. Laurence Alvidrez (8325) 04:59:08
597. Pablo Zermeno (8332) 04:59:13
598. Richard Rizo (8361) 04:59:35
599. Todd Watson (8402) 05:00:05
600. Patrick Chu (8404) 05:00:09
601. Randy Wong (8422) 05:00:23
602. Fidencio Chavez (8434) 05:00:41
603. Fernando Ramirez (8454) 05:01:00
604. Gerardo Leal (8460) 05:01:03
605. Carlos Parodi (8470) 05:01:09
606. Gerardo Ponce (8490) 05:01:24
607. George Morris (8495) 05:01:28
608. Jonathan Robertson (8499) 05:01:31
609. Bill Jones (8515) 05:01:41
610. Juan Gamez (8535) 05:01:51
611. Harjinder Singh (8541) 05:01:59
612. David Prodian (8555) 05:02:10
613. Marcus Bertilsson (8560) 05:02:14
614. Justin McGivney (8616) 05:03:10
615. Alexis Cremieux (8633) 05:03:22
616. Howard Hsieh (8646) 05:03:38
617. Jose Garcia (8649) 05:03:42
618. Hector Vega (8656) 05:03:49
619. Patrick Lopez (8659) 05:03:50
620. Ferris Pacheco (8673) 05:03:59
621. Rodney Chadderton (8683) 05:04:07
622. Eddie Escobar (8729) 05:04:46
623. Natnael Israel (8740) 05:04:58
624. Miguel Cisneros (8751) 05:05:14
625. Raymond Bush (8759) 05:05:23
626. Alan Phan (8764) 05:05:27
627. David Castillo (8780) 05:05:40
628. Jeremy McKenzie (8784) 05:05:46
629. Kolt Killman (8790) 05:05:52
630. Rolando Tzua (8794) 05:05:56
631. Darren Rusk (8808) 05:06:08
632. Ray Valerio (8844) 05:06:51
633. Mike Price (8851) 05:06:58
634. David Grajaler (8897) 05:07:46
635. Fabian Guerreri (8915) 05:08:01
636. William Ihrke (8999) 05:09:07
637. Patrick George (9014) 05:09:18
638. Ramon Parra (9027) 05:09:27
639. Ramon Hernandez (9031) 05:09:30
640. German Ortiz (9038) 05:09:43
641. David Calderon (9065) 05:09:59
642. Phil Phan (9068) 05:10:00
643. Diego Ramirez (9080) 05:10:11
644. Christopher Marchese (9083) 05:10:12
645. Hechtor Alanza (9113) 05:10:25
646. Jose Macias (9114) 05:10:25
647. Freddy Hernandez (9128) 05:10:40
648. Jorge Tirado (9156) 05:11:07
649. Francisco Djohan (9165) 05:11:24
650. Roy Cushing (9200) 05:11:48
651. Justin Haller (9202) 05:11:49
652. Marc Decol (9208) 05:11:55
653. Michael Martinez (9231) 05:12:23
654. Armando Lopez (9251) 05:12:40
655. Mario Bencivenga (9275) 05:13:05
656. Steve Loh (9291) 05:13:18
657. Jason Reid (9294) 05:13:20
658. Sammy Ciaramilaro (9295) 05:13:21
659. David Hardt (9308) 05:13:29
660. Thomas MacDougall (9315) 05:13:33
661. Barak Raviv (9323) 05:13:37
662. Daniel Long (9326) 05:13:38
663. Michael Cramer (9339) 05:13:47
664. Johnny Pedroza (9346) 05:13:53
665. Jerry Bryant (9347) 05:13:53
666. Fernando Millan (9348) 05:13:54
667. Damon Moss (9364) 05:14:07
668. Simon Kim (9401) 05:14:43
669. Masato Nakazawa (9406) 05:14:49
670. Greg Scuderi (9413) 05:14:58
671. Benjamin Eaton (9427) 05:15:17
672. Gary Guluzza (9431) 05:15:19
673. Andrew Nicdao (9453) 05:15:49
674. Eddie Villegas (9456) 05:15:53
675. William Hutton (9472) 05:16:08
676. Alejandro Reyes (9477) 05:16:13
677. Takeshi Tsushima (9490) 05:16:22
678. Alberto Alfaro (9506) 05:16:35
679. Manuel Perez (9514) 05:16:39
680. Kenneth Pedersen (9532) 05:17:00
681. Ruben Castro (9554) 05:17:12
682. Jesse Olivas (9584) 05:17:36
683. Roberto Bolonos (9599) 05:17:50
684. Sam Reynolds III (9606) 05:17:58
685. Tom Shimada (9609) 05:18:04
686. Kambiz Ghandeharizadeh (9636) 05:18:30
687. Matthew Schmutzier (9652) 05:18:41
688. Jesse Williamson (9659) 05:18:48
689. Akos Gulyas (9680) 05:19:06
690. Bart Ney (9744) 05:20:21
691. Arnoldo Centeno (9746) 05:20:21
692. Hiroomi Ishitsuka (9753) 05:20:29
693. Hoa Diep (9774) 05:20:42
694. Fernando Ortiz (9779) 05:20:46
695. Ed Rodriguez (9807) 05:21:10
696. Mark Walter (9825) 05:21:31
697. Robert Perez (9843) 05:21:44
698. Marco Zambrano (9858) 05:21:54
699. Matthew August (9873) 05:22:04
700. Michael Jacobo (9884) 05:22:13
701. Eduardo Casillas (9911) 05:22:45
702. Salvador Velez (9924) 05:22:55
703. Jose Uribe (9936) 05:23:17
704. Songho Cho (9939) 05:23:19
705. Saul Rodas (9946) 05:23:24
706. Greg Tolbert (9949) 05:23:28
707. David Kwon (9953) 05:23:31
708. Sung Hong (9969) 05:23:46
709. Mario Elias (9972) 05:23:53
710. Edson Ponraj (9995) 05:24:13
711. Alfredo Vargas (10015) 05:24:32
712. Masaki Kato (10016) 05:24:36
713. David Ludwig (10021) 05:24:45
714. Eli Sanchez (10039) 05:25:03
715. Bruce Weimer (10066) 05:25:38
716. Satoru Mimura (10070) 05:25:40
717. Marco Martinez (10085) 05:25:49
718. Kevin Campbell (10097) 05:26:04
719. Keith Pugh (10115) 05:26:18
720. Rudy Bracamonte (10116) 05:26:19
721. Leo Kato (10119) 05:26:25
722. Angel Vasquez (10142) 05:26:52
723. Richard Machado (10157) 05:27:09
724. Jesse Morales (10181) 05:27:28
725. Filemon Carrillo Jr (10196) 05:27:38
726. John Marlette (10213) 05:27:56
727. Mon Takada (10216) 05:27:59
728. Oscar Torres (10222) 05:28:02
729. John White (10229) 05:28:08
730. Karl Ting (10256) 05:28:43
731. Duke Nguyen (10278) 05:28:54
732. Keith Hartigan (10339) 05:29:53
733. Mike Nguyen (10405) 05:30:50
734. Shinji Suzuki (10425) 05:31:17
735. Marcos Rosales (10444) 05:31:29
736. Eddie Dunne (10455) 05:31:39
737. Phillip Vasquez (10456) 05:31:39
738. Bryan Weimer (10464) 05:31:48
739. John Brown (10465) 05:31:48
740. Victor Perez (10474) 05:31:51
741. Christopher Lay (10488) 05:32:05
742. Sergio Martinez (10508) 05:32:32
743. Noe Guerrero (10524) 05:32:51
744. Isaias Cruz (10525) 05:32:52
745. Abraham Cruz (10526) 05:32:52
746. Marco Hernandez (10551) 05:33:13
747. Rodney Corey (10563) 05:33:26
748. Jeremy Rivera (10566) 05:33:27
749. Bernard Chen (10616) 05:34:03
750. Jose Millan (10642) 05:34:29
751. Matt Gee (10693) 05:35:18
752. Timothy Mcnees (10717) 05:35:35
753. Naotaka Kishida (10749) 05:36:12
754. Tjin Hok Kho (10760) 05:36:23
755. Alfredo Mayen (10762) 05:36:26
756. Carlos Leiva (10764) 05:36:27
757. Robyn Oke (10768) 05:36:35
758. Jerry Merayo (10769) 05:36:35
759. Florentino Munoz (10784) 05:36:48
760. Alex Miramontes (10793) 05:36:59
761. Jaz Wray (10797) 05:37:02
762. Carlos Torres (10839) 05:37:46
763. Manuel Perez (10843) 05:37:51
764. Ciro Cruz (10889) 05:38:54
765. Cesar Moreno (10905) 05:39:16
766. John Stroud (10937) 05:39:59
767. Jacob Stein III (10944) 05:40:11
768. Orlando Pobre (10963) 05:40:32
769. Laty Banks (11009) 05:41:38
770. Julio Villagomez (11014) 05:41:42
771. Koji Morimoto (11018) 05:41:45
772. Matthew Slaven (11020) 05:41:46
773. Jeffery Bengoit (11031) 05:42:00
774. Albert Pina (11038) 05:42:07
775. Jeremy Kahn (11039) 05:42:09
776. Tung Han Wan (11052) 05:42:18
777. Ian Tarrant (11065) 05:42:27
778. Joel Baez (11092) 05:42:53
779. Boon Mikko Ang (11130) 05:43:34
780. Nima Rabiee (11133) 05:43:36
781. Amildo Rodriguez (11156) 05:44:04
782. Michael Palanca (11189) 05:44:22
783. Jason Mills (11197) 05:44:29
784. Makoto Hirayama (11246) 05:45:12
785. Derek Meyer (11313) 05:46:35
786. Juan Basilio (11329) 05:46:49
787. Jonathan Williams (11337) 05:46:57
788. Kedame Mekonen (11347) 05:47:18
789. Marvin Vargas (11362) 05:47:40
790. Alan Tan (11367) 05:47:50
791. Rene Santos (11371) 05:47:53
792. Allan Diaz (11382) 05:48:24
793. John Fruttero (11394) 05:48:51
794. Bernardo Munoz (11448) 05:49:43
795. Noe Servellon (11470) 05:50:00
796. William Hernandez (11498) 05:50:27
797. Tony Nguyen (11536) 05:50:58
798. Miguel Villegas (11539) 05:51:05
799. Milton Bonilla (11560) 05:51:39
800. George Hernondez (11569) 05:51:57
801. Don Mc Namara (11574) 05:52:08
802. Mario Mario (11579) 05:52:10
803. Dan Coe (11597) 05:52:21
804. Michael Proctor (11598) 05:52:21
805. David Coscia (11605) 05:52:35
806. Amado Perez (11631) 05:53:01
807. Garry Naval (11637) 05:53:08
808. Daniel Torres (11640) 05:53:10
809. Glenn Purcell (11675) 05:53:46
810. Gerry Ruiz (11680) 05:53:52
811. Jorge Garcia (11688) 05:53:57
812. Rodolfo Perez (11693) 05:54:03
813. Joshua Cohen (11696) 05:54:08
814. Victor Rosales (11726) 05:54:58
815. Matthew Denson (11730) 05:55:03
816. Eriberto Montaya (11735) 05:55:09
817. Ben Kaniut (11743) 05:55:18
818. Victor Nanongkhai (11766) 05:55:45
819. Rex Ledesma (11790) 05:56:21
820. Paulo Kang (11792) 05:56:28
821. Marcos Kang (11793) 05:56:29
822. Roger Bain (11794) 05:56:29
823. Michael Nili (11801) 05:56:41
824. Herman Novello (11814) 05:56:54
825. Omar Diaz (11832) 05:57:19
826. Luis Tejeda (11840) 05:57:34
827. Moises Mata (11844) 05:57:40
828. Tim Murray (11862) 05:58:07
829. Ricardo Vazquez (11866) 05:58:12
830. Jose Salazar (11871) 05:58:20
831. Jorge Castaneda (11896) 05:58:36
832. Noel Claude (11897) 05:58:37
833. Noriyuki Nakamura (11972) 06:00:23
834. Michael Rodriguez (11978) 06:00:29
835. Michael Chio (11988) 06:00:51
836. Tyron Hetherington (11991) 06:00:55
837. Rudy Cuevas (12017) 06:01:44
838. Fernando Vargas (12043) 06:02:21
839. Jimmy Soga (12046) 06:02:23
840. Alejandro Zapata (12097) 06:03:56
841. Jose Perez (12099) 06:04:03
842. Bernard Ojeda (12115) 06:04:18
843. Roger Moreno (12125) 06:04:42
844. Pedro Arroyo (12126) 06:04:42
845. Masanobu Shintani (12139) 06:04:57
846. Shanond Hill (12146) 06:05:05
847. Alex Berger (12155) 06:05:20
848. Dionne Calhoun (12160) 06:05:25
849. Keith Delacroix (12172) 06:05:40
850. Tommy Salcido (12173) 06:05:41
851. Kenneth Abrong (12175) 06:05:44
852. Kota Onouchi (12177) 06:05:49
853. Romel Chavez (12189) 06:06:13
854. Paul Panza (12215) 06:07:09
855. Roel Arambulo (12217) 06:07:15
856. Parker Workman (12221) 06:07:19
857. Gerald Low (12230) 06:07:26
858. Christopher Low (12231) 06:07:26
859. Robert Panza (12247) 06:07:45
860. Jorge Delgado (12286) 06:08:52
861. Ignacio Torres (12292) 06:08:59
862. Delbert Carillo (12304) 06:09:09
863. Ernie Gonzalez (12305) 06:09:10
864. Carlos Ibarra (12310) 06:09:17
865. Phil Okamoto (12321) 06:09:42
866. Robert Vasquez (12322) 06:09:43
867. Felipe Rosas (12352) 06:10:32
868. Larry Olivares (12368) 06:11:02
869. Narongchai Nimitbunanan (12387) 06:11:23
870. John Barragan (12392) 06:11:33
871. Jesse King (12396) 06:11:38
872. Ron Laughton (12401) 06:11:48
873. Charles Sotomayor (12414) 06:12:07
874. Willliam Perea (12488) 06:14:02
875. John Choi (12502) 06:14:23
876. John Gee (12519) 06:14:52
877. Ronnie Thomas (12521) 06:14:56
878. Ricardo Gutierrez (12550) 06:15:38
879. Ismael Gudino (12600) 06:16:52
880. Hung Tran (12604) 06:16:56
881. Patricia Hernandez (12605) 06:16:56
882. Jose Manzo (12610) 06:17:02
883. Jose Mendoza (12617) 06:17:21
884. Eduardo Modesto (12627) 06:17:39
885. Juan Olivo (12634) 06:18:06
886. Eric Van Der Heide (12656) 06:18:43
887. Guillermo Verdin (12658) 06:18:54
888. William Kwon (12724) 06:20:52
889. Robert Taylor (12727) 06:21:04
890. Nicolas Thacker (12733) 06:21:23
891. Michael Schlaifer (12741) 06:21:32
892. Fabio Castillo (12785) 06:22:23
893. Alain Camou (12792) 06:22:38
894. Chris Synnes (12799) 06:22:46
895. Jose Lopez (12804) 06:23:01
896. Luis Perez (12811) 06:23:14
897. John Packer (12817) 06:23:25
898. Anthony Montes (12841) 06:23:50
899. Enrique Nieto (12852) 06:24:09
900. Rob Sanders (12879) 06:25:08
901. Jim Coronado (12897) 06:25:47
902. Roberto Villegas (12903) 06:25:52
903. Hirotsugu Kobayashi (12914) 06:26:14
904. Kenneth Fraser (12950) 06:27:18
905. Jesse Reneria (12968) 06:27:50
906. Edwin Sato (12982) 06:28:05
907. Rin Takada (13001) 06:28:37
908. De Andre Martin (13003) 06:28:41
909. Carlos Aleman (13063) 06:30:45
910. Mike Wilson (13086) 06:31:22
911. Daniel Villanueva (13104) 06:31:58
912. Xavier Estacio (13108) 06:32:01
913. James Oldenburg (13111) 06:32:08
914. Osada Mitsumasa (13120) 06:32:29
915. Jose Gomez (13122) 06:32:30
916. Douglas Nichols (13132) 06:32:38
917. Jason Crow (13138) 06:32:44
918. Michael Gill (13166) 06:33:17
919. Phillip Rodriguez (13178) 06:33:47
920. Julio Orellana (13197) 06:34:25
921. Ryan Alcantara (13244) 06:35:38
922. Ed Kiernan Jr (13268) 06:36:17
923. Armando Gonzales (13281) 06:36:40
924. Trinidad Contreras (13341) 06:39:01
925. Eli Morales (13343) 06:39:03
926. Steven Oh (13361) 06:39:33
927. Naoki Nio (13367) 06:39:43
928. Horacio Alvarado (13391) 06:40:46
929. Fernando Perez (13392) 06:40:47
930. Gio Villanueva (13395) 06:40:56
931. Maveicio De La Torre (13451) 06:42:44
932. Jesus Alba (13490) 06:44:24
933. Henry Paz (13548) 06:46:25
934. Yusaku Takaoka (13549) 06:46:26
935. Bud Soetrisno (13550) 06:46:31
936. Johnny Mora (13577) 06:47:31
937. Michael Lou (13584) 06:47:48
938. Alfonso Navarro (13589) 06:47:50
939. Kazuya Hatakeyama (13629) 06:49:15
940. Corey Felder (13677) 06:50:33
941. Jerry Guerrero (13679) 06:50:34
942. Bobby Parker (13699) 06:51:03
943. Tad Oki (13717) 06:51:47
944. Tom Chen (13722) 06:51:50
945. Jorge Montes (13729) 06:52:06
946. Ken Ichinose (13745) 06:53:12
947. Richard Arias (13764) 06:54:12
948. Sergio Castellanos (13769) 06:54:25
949. Mario Lugo (13788) 06:55:05
950. Steve Reaves (13819) 06:55:51
951. Takahiro Otomo (13852) 06:56:55
952. Allen Oh (13905) 06:58:32
953. Dung Tran (13927) 06:59:03
954. Jose Sanchez (13934) 06:59:07
955. Leonard Sanchez (13953) 06:59:58
956. Shintaro Okuzawa (13958) 07:00:11
957. Valdis Pukite (13970) 07:00:32
958. Sean Corbett (13971) 07:00:33
959. Ryan Oleary (13972) 07:00:34
960. Blake Parsons (13973) 07:00:36
961. Gerardo Coronado (14023) 07:02:09
962. Gamaliel Solis (14095) 07:06:15
963. Noel Rojas (14171) 07:11:06
964. Victor Duron (14187) 07:12:10
965. Jon Kritzer (14188) 07:12:10
966. Willing Wong (14230) 07:14:38
967. Hamid Sabet (14246) 07:15:08
968. Gene Oliveros (14264) 07:15:51
969. Alex Mendoza (14270) 07:16:13
970. Kaoru Koshimizu (14275) 07:16:23
971. Hiroaki Ohara (14305) 07:18:29
972. Tsuruta Kazuhiro (14312) 07:19:00
973. Sergio Alvarado (14345) 07:21:01
974. Robert Lee (14393) 07:24:21
975. John Robles (14428) 07:27:08
976. Hiroto Uehara (14467) 07:30:34
977. Juan Arias (14480) 07:31:42
978. Hector Perez (14493) 07:33:32
979. Juan Shimabukuro (14517) 07:35:33
980. John Li (14520) 07:35:38
981. Jesus Rodriguez (14533) 07:36:15
982. Paul Nagakura (14571) 07:38:58
983. Miguel Lopez (14573) 07:39:01
984. Stephen Rinos (14576) 07:39:27
985. Jesse Fleiss (14603) 07:41:24
986. Juan Cerda (14644) 07:45:45
987. Takanobu Nishiyama (14673) 07:48:20
988. Julio Alfaro (14692) 07:49:53
989. Michael Williamson (14704) 07:51:07
990. Sal Urzua (14719) 07:52:23
991. Allen Rowe (14758) 07:55:34
992. Raul Rodriguez (14762) 07:55:44
993. John Arnold (14765) 07:56:04
994. Anthony Berryman (14792) 07:59:55
995. Carlos Nogen (14805) 08:01:09
996. Rene Dorantes (14808) 08:01:27
997. Edwin Buenaventura (14835) 08:03:26
998. Hung Du (14843) 08:04:28
999. George Parra (14884) 08:12:43
1000. Paul Aguilar (14885) 08:12:49
1001. Ismael Rueda (14908) 08:16:52
1002. Sammy Lara (14909) 08:17:14
1003. Onnie Thomas (14914) 08:17:38
1004. Ronald Sino-Cruz (15104) 09:10:25
1005. Anthony Tang (15133) 09:32:04

WOMEN 18 TO 24

1. Yuki Ando (78) 02:45:42
2. Nicole Logan (503) 03:12:17
3. Chrystee Perkins (598) 03:15:03
4. Allison Page (675) 03:17:23
5. Maria Wodraska (734) 03:19:18
6. Jill Penman (829) 03:21:43
7. Erin Noonan (844) 03:22:08
8. Stephanie Norberg (1118) 03:27:55
9. Christine Hicklin (1273) 03:30:55
10. Jennifer Sticksel (1284) 03:30:59
11. Laura Flynn (1302) 03:31:25
12. Alison Hunt (1393) 03:33:04
13. Sita Jones (1406) 03:33:25
14. Jolene Rowe (1412) 03:33:37
15. Tamaki Myers (1426) 03:33:59
16. Carrie Miller (1487) 03:35:08
17. Judith Di Giacomo (1749) 03:39:52
18. Alisha Portnoy (1813) 03:40:53
19. Amy Hanlon (1834) 03:41:07
20. Vicki Lamberis (1836) 03:41:08
21. Evelyn Hamdorff (1843) 03:41:15
22. Jennifer Allen (1848) 03:41:17
23. Julie Neumann (1937) 03:42:40
24. Gloria Rios (1971) 03:43:20
25. Heidi Jo Peterson (2067) 03:44:43
26. Sarah Beane (2087) 03:45:00
27. Jacqueline Sahara (2125) 03:45:28
28. Carmen Orellana (2141) 03:45:47
29. Kristin Schweizer (2185) 03:46:25

30. Bridget Flynn (2282) 03:47:53
31. Olga Korobova (2297) 03:48:05
32. Tricia Mathiesen (2358) 03:48:53
33. Nora Szabo (2370) 03:49:04
34. Heather Wolf (2408) 03:49:31
35. Shauna Traub (2462) 03:50:17
36. Loretta Sullivan (2490) 03:50:37
37. Tricia La Bonta (2492) 03:50:39
38. Jennifer Weems (2503) 03:50:50
39. Sandy Zinkowski (2531) 03:51:13
40. Kristen Tiberg (2551) 03:51:29
41. Pam Smith (2588) 03:51:57
42. Holly Alegre (2654) 03:52:49
43. Lori Montoya (2684) 03:53:15
44. Jennifer Kornacker (2773) 03:54:23
45. Sara Conant (2783) 03:54:25
46. Darlene Arvizu (2832) 03:54:56
47. Renae Bartolone (2840) 03:55:05
48. Melissa Haynes (2846) 03:55:09
49. Laura Goodman (2938) 03:56:10
50. Vanessa Hernandez (3026) 03:57:02
51. Sophia Briseno (3090) 03:57:45
52. Angie Torres (3108) 03:57:55
53. Malia Kaizuka (3137) 03:58:17
54. Karen Daniher (3236) 03:59:27
55. Ana Tapia (3269) 03:59:47
56. Laurie Schellenberg (3327) 04:00:18
57. Maria Roque (3352) 04:00:41
58. Magdalena Martinez (3371) 04:00:57
59. Kelly Murphy (3398) 04:01:15
60. Maya Skubatch (3411) 04:01:24
61. Julie Basaraba (3421) 04:01:32
62. Kelly Ruff (3428) 04:01:38
63. Kathryn Buchan (3620) 04:04:23
64. Amy Gavel (3659) 04:04:45
65. Kimberly Gavel (3661) 04:04:46
66. Dawn Gray (3688) 04:05:04
67. Lynn Corcoran (3752) 04:06:01
68. Elizabeth Green (3872) 04:07:28
69. Kerry Kelleher (3920) 04:08:03
70. Lainie Kartoon (3929) 04:08:12
71. Juliana Adair (3991) 04:08:59
72. Nicole Simmerok (4095) 04:10:20
73. Heather Collins (4099) 04:10:25
74. Norma Jean Eiche (4111) 04:10:34
75. Mary Lambert (4129) 04:10:48
76. Kathleen Domille (4131) 04:10:50
77. Jeannine Pera (4157) 04:11:02
78. Jennifer Lu (4175) 04:11:15
79. Jennifer Gaspar (4276) 04:12:38
80. Crystal Sherman (4290) 04:12:50
81. Catherine Wedding (4302) 04:12:59
82. Karen Castelblanco (4329) 04:13:18
83. Lindsay Sedgwick (4407) 04:14:19
84. Lydia Welton (4409) 04:14:20
85. Emily Drucker (4514) 04:15:23
86. Kelly Wheeler (4515) 04:15:24
87. Stephonie Burns (4517) 04:15:26
88. Nga Do (4518) 04:15:26
89. Sophia Lizarraga (4532) 04:15:33
90. Teresa Haggerty (4533) 04:15:33
91. Lana Schumacher (4568) 04:15:51
92. Dawn Bushnaq (4569) 04:15:52
93. Mayra Martinez (4612) 04:16:24
94. Kelli Hoinly (4641) 04:16:38
95. Erinn Nava (4657) 04:16:54
96. Kelli Dobbs (4688) 04:17:17
97. Andrea Ching (4754) 04:18:07
98. Essie Kim (4756) 04:18:09
99. Deena Schwary (4764) 04:18:12
100. Kristen Baker (4784) 04:18:29
101. Laura Melendez (4800) 04:18:38
102. Kathleen Page (4921) 04:19:50
103. Rachel Suojanen (5086) 04:21:54
104. Silvia Arroyo (5103) 04:22:05
105. Mary Jane Mullen (5121) 04:22:15
106. Jennifer Quiniero (5151) 04:22:38
107. Michelle Galligan (5195) 04:23:10
108. Karina Anderson (5203) 04:23:14
109. Vicky Wood (5204) 04:23:15
110. Kellie Lane (5224) 04:23:29
111. Roeline Hansen (5294) 04:24:29
112. Kirsten Fischer (5310) 04:24:36
113. Kimberly Seibert (5366) 04:25:16
114. Imani Bakari (5368) 04:25:17
115. Meredith Gordon (5405) 04:25:39
116. Julie Roos (5408) 04:25:39
117. Krista Huerta (5434) 04:25:54
118. Keri Randels (5470) 04:26:19
119. Megan Newman (5639) 04:28:12
120. Jody Ehlers (5641) 04:28:13
121. Tracy Williams (5673) 04:28:35
122. Phuong Nguyen (5682) 04:28:40
123. Rimmel Goh (5721) 04:29:04
124. Janette Knowlton (5730) 04:29:11
125. Lara Swann (5782) 04:29:45
126. Jana David (5826) 04:30:23
127. Joanna Parsons (5833) 04:30:26
128. Lorin Dytell (5848) 04:30:33
129. Lorena Zurita (5858) 04:30:35
130. Liliana Rameriz (5975) 04:31:53
131. Gigi Maaliki (6037) 04:32:45
132. Gwen Wist (6075) 04:33:07
133. Marisa Mueller (6125) 04:33:41
134. Cherie Conrad (6161) 04:34:09
135. Holly Peterson (6214) 04:34:42
136. Nicole Young (6217) 04:34:43
137. Elicia Garske (6219) 04:34:43
138. Lisa Liguori (6230) 04:34:51
139. Celina Sedillo (6336) 04:35:56
140. Jennifer Stern (6355) 04:36:12
141. Cami Obrecht (6356) 04:36:12
142. Michelle Majers (6361) 04:36:15
143. Erin Thomsen (6390) 04:36:27
144. Suzanne Chittick (6431) 04:36:55
145. Joyce Cruz (6482) 04:37:33
146. Rosa Melendez (6509) 04:37:47
147. Joylene Lotero (6590) 04:38:40
148. Gila Cocos (6615) 04:38:53
149. Eleen Straw (6628) 04:38:59
150. Marni Matsumoto (6681) 04:39:42
151. Carmen Diaz (6737) 04:40:25
152. Jennifer McMahon (6745) 04:40:34
153. Ana Mata (6793) 04:41:09
154. Barbara Letzt (6866) 04:42:05
155. Melissa Hamblin (6875) 04:42:12
156. Katie Kolb (6905) 04:42:40
157. Kristin Olsen (6906) 04:42:41
158. Eileen Morelos-Gutierrez (6911) 04:42:46
159. Liz Bui (6958) 04:43:15
160. Ana Flores (6960) 04:43:16
161. Karen Wright (6961) 04:43:17
162. Paige Dunn (6971) 04:43:22
163. Cari Hightower (6973) 04:43:22
164. Melissa Sanchez (7034) 04:43:59
165. Kara Rehwoldt (7047) 04:44:10
166. Christine Guadagnini (7063) 04:44:21
167. Elizabeth Cornejo (7157) 04:45:39
168. Jennifer Grammes (7161) 04:45:40
169. Rachel Kuipers (7221) 04:46:23
170. Jackie Day (7243) 04:46:36
171. Ina Shum (7270) 04:46:55
172. Alison Nguyen (7302) 04:47:16
173. Michelle Marks (7355) 04:47:53
174. Dixie Duncan (7381) 04:47:58
175. Erin Rosenwald (7382) 04:48:11
176. Mary Grounds (7432) 04:48:46
177. Claudia Hernandez (7439) 04:48:50
178. Laura Livingston (7528) 04:49:41
179. Tracy Huang (7533) 04:49:46
180. Debbie Newell (7542) 04:49:52
181. Viva Vinson (7648) 04:51:15
182. Lisa Riehn (7673) 04:51:38
183. Claudia Lopez (7706) 04:52:03
184. Sara Rende (7713) 04:52:07
185. Annette Delaney (7728) 04:52:19
186. Robin Schroador (7812) 04:53:25
187. Deborah Garcia (7837) 04:53:39
188. Sherri Kim (7845) 04:53:44
189. Anne Marie O'Donnell (7940) 04:54:38
190. Angelica Muratalla (7953) 04:54:45
191. Julie Devries (7958) 04:54:46
192. Malitzin Flores (7982) 04:55:08
193. Michelle Rojas (8058) 04:56:09
194. Deborah Spaulding (8062) 04:56:12
195. Cynthia Vidaurre (8125) 04:57:00
196. Maria Duschletta (8148) 04:57:17
197. Miriam Bradley (8158) 04:57:25
198. Diane Pratt (8209) 04:58:00
199. Julie Busek (8210) 04:58:00
200. Suzanne Schafer (8225) 04:58:07
201. Rebecca Mc Alexander (8247) 04:58:18
202. Jennifer Weingarden (8265) 04:58:31
203. Courtney Adams (8324) 04:59:08
204. Lynette Meinecke (8354) 04:59:30
205. Kimberly Hayford (8364) 04:59:37
206. Denise Noyer (8504) 05:01:34
207. Amy Wegman (8565) 05:02:18
208. Mersedeh Ahrabzou (8595) 05:02:48
209. Alyssa Cardenas (8619) 05:03:12
210. Tammie Watson (8640) 05:03:31
211. Jennifer Thompson (8691) 05:04:13
212. Hilary Reichmann (8745) 05:05:08
213. Kelli Ketring (8768) 05:05:31
214. Jennifer Niswander (8805) 05:06:07
215. Tiffany South (8848) 05:06:56
216. Kristen Lowry (8888) 05:07:35
217. Christina Misegadis (8930) 05:08:12
218. Kristen Soltis (8932) 05:08:12
219. Billeye Gladen (8945) 05:08:29
220. Karyn Thomas (8947) 05:08:30
221. Marta Rivas (8956) 05:08:36
222. Christine Hilow (8960) 05:08:38
223. Tricia Londelius (8964) 05:08:40
224. Aya Hori (8998) 05:09:07
225. Heather Anderson (9019) 05:09:22
226. Kiera Goodman (9079) 05:10:10
227. Jude Daricek (9082) 05:10:12
228. Melissa Martinez (9087) 05:10:14
229. Candace Thompson (9105) 05:10:21
230. Marcela Tovar (9134) 05:10:45
231. Jennifer Worley (9166) 05:11:24
232. Jennifer Glantz (9206) 05:11:53
233. Rufina Zarate (9253) 05:12:48
234. Veronica Garcia (9278) 05:13:09
235. Jessica Rios (9307) 05:13:29
236. Eren Piceno (9309) 05:13:29
237. Eileen Toloza (9317) 05:13:34
238. Rocio Alvarado (9370) 05:14:09
239. Tamara Walton (9375) 05:14:15
240. Yvonne Huffman (9392) 05:14:28
241. Monika Zech (9420) 05:15:11
242. Robin Caine (9422) 05:15:12
243. Dora Daniels (9504) 05:16:34
244. Bea Barajas (9507) 05:16:36
245. Pamela Gillis (9531) 05:17:00
246. Myrella Huizar (9593) 05:17:47
247. Sonia Urquilla (9612) 05:18:00
248. Nimfa Santos (9623) 05:18:22
249. Maricar Bernardo (9626) 05:18:26
250. Elizabeth Martin (9640) 05:18:34
251. Juliana Gonzalez (9700) 05:19:24
252. Autumn Burke (9710) 05:19:37
253. Dynela Garcia (9754) 05:20:30
254. Kelly Jones (9801) 05:21:03
255. Ana Pleitez (9857) 05:21:53
256. Stacy Dushey (9874) 05:22:06
257. Bethanne Doles (9878) 05:22:09
258. Julie Hibbaro (9883) 05:22:13
259. Marvlin Ceballos (9940) 05:23:20
260. Maria Sosa (9945) 05:23:24
261. Lisa Felzien (9994) 05:24:11
262. Lupe Aguilar (10054) 05:25:29
263. Viorela Ghitea (10153) 05:27:05
264. Tuey Kay Jew (10158) 05:27:09
265. Erica Lawson (10211) 05:27:55
266. Josefina Esquivias (10223) 05:28:03
267. Dominique Hitchcock (10226) 05:28:08
268. Karena Gibbs (10228) 05:28:08
269. Jennifer Rice (10235) 05:28:11
270. Jenni Birxen (10244) 05:28:20
271. Rebecca Weer (10246) 05:28:35
272. Amber Hogges (10270) 05:28:50
273. Anita Bennett (10279) 05:28:55
274. Sherry Menor (10291) 05:29:06
275. Yohantus Noisette (10292) 05:29:07
276. Krista Anderson (10314) 05:29:18
277. Hideki Takahashi (10327) 05:29:36
278. Ikuko Ohmura (10357) 05:30:11
279. Beverly Walters (10360) 05:30:14
280. Karen Wilkening (10361) 05:30:16
281. Bonnie MacLeod (10362) 05:30:16
282. Hanh Dao (10369) 05:30:20
283. Evalene Okasaki (10392) 05:30:38
284. Rebecca Botello (10440) 05:31:27
285. Janet Pimentel (10477) 05:31:52
286. Gabriella Schneider (10527) 05:32:53
287. Shauna Donfeld (10528) 05:32:53
288. Katja Lubina (10529) 05:32:53
289. Marisa Rodgriquez (10597) 05:33:49
290. Alma Fregoso (10623) 05:34:06
291. Yanet Pineda (10625) 05:34:07
292. Amber Martin (10648) 05:34:34
293. Sara Villalta (10694) 05:35:19
294. Kim Bengelsdorf (10724) 05:35:42
295. Sarah Lee (10795) 05:37:00
296. Suzanne Garner (10798) 05:37:03
297. Analaura Benitez (10846) 05:37:57
298. Kim Miller (10860) 05:38:11
299. Kellye George (10864) 05:38:16
300. Miriam Deojuan (10897) 05:39:00
301. Aya Hamaguchi (10920) 05:39:40
302. Gabriela Lopez (10955) 05:40:23
303. Shannon Martinez (10959) 05:40:26
304. Angela Martinez (10960) 05:40:27
305. Shelley Hartfield (10989) 05:41:15
306. Brynja Kohler (10998) 05:41:27
307. Ida Kim (11069) 05:42:30
308. Monica Ayala (11081) 05:42:41
309. Mollie Anderson (11141) 05:43:44
310. Lafleche Laporte (11151) 05:43:59
311. Haydee Cortez (11157) 05:44:05
312. Angelica Lopez (11161) 05:44:08
313. Aimee Cook (11166) 05:44:12
314. Michelle Bonner (11171) 05:44:14
315. Kelly Petriccione (11172) 05:44:14
316. Jennifer Schulz (11173) 05:44:14
317. Hilda Cabrera (11181) 05:44:18
318. Susanna Esquivias (11208) 05:44:35
319. Jane Kramer (11280) 05:45:54
320. Jennifer Korinko (11300) 05:46:16
321. Laurie Ingino (11301) 05:46:16
322. Aura Solorzano (11368) 05:47:51
323. Nicole Policicchio (11369) 05:47:51
324. Julia Greenberg (11395) 05:48:52
325. Lucy Mendoza (11417) 05:49:14
326. Allison Bruhn (11445) 05:49:40
327. Trevi Hibsman (11451) 05:49:44
328. Anna Su (11460) 05:49:49
329. Kim Wittkopf (11472) 05:50:04
330. Karen McComas (11473) 05:50:05
331. Sheri Sanders (11474) 05:50:05
332. Ana Garcia (11477) 05:50:07
333. Shoko Kasajima (11523) 05:50:46
334. Luisa Cardenas (11543) 05:51:10
335. Katie Morrison (11557) 05:51:36
336. Amy Morrison (11561) 05:51:39
337. Nicole Daigneault (11575) 05:52:08
338. Kerry Olin (11576) 05:52:09
339. Mari Gomez (11603) 05:52:29
340. Teresa Araiza (11665) 05:53:37
341. Elizabeth Sanchez (11702) 05:54:26
342. Lenay Herndon (11744) 05:55:19
343. Reyna Casas (11770) 05:55:48
344. Angela McCauley (11805) 05:56:44
345. Adrienne Fleming (11809) 05:56:49
346. Magdalena Fausto (11838) 05:57:28
347. Rosa Gonzalez (11850) 05:57:52
348. Catherine Oh (11878) 05:58:26
349. Nicole Daddona (11901) 05:58:43
350. Sarah Biddle (11938) 05:59:39
351. Theresa Van Niekerk (11997) 06:01:04
352. Norma Nunez (12022) 06:01:51
353. Terra Hess (12024) 06:01:54
354. Lizette Zermeno (12048) 06:02:25
355. Amy Berg (12051) 06:02:33
356. Heather South (12053) 06:02:36
357. Megan Hanson (12061) 06:02:46
358. Kerri Morigaki (12101) 06:04:08
359. Wendy Fox (12168) 06:05:33
360. Sara Pellegrino (12195) 06:00:22
361. Mercedes Bertagna (12212) 06:07:04
362. Michelle German (12220) 06:07:18
363. Lupe Juarez (12267) 06:08:27
364. Laura Moran (12273) 06:08:40
365. Angelique Dominguez (12406) 06:11:54
366. Mario Marquez (12409) 06:11:55
367. Monica Walshin (12426) 06:12:25
368. Elizabeth Rossi (12446) 06:13:03
369. Jody-Marie Cosgrove (12447) 06:13:04
370. Karen Wurtemberg (12487) 06:14:01
371. Gloria Garcia (12490) 06:14:03
372. Mirna Garcia (12491) 06:14:06
373. Alma Alaniz (12493) 06:14:13
374. Maria Romo (12494) 06:14:14
375. Dina Coronado (12532) 06:15:17
376. Gloria Del Cid (12555) 06:15:44
377. Dina Helm (12578) 06:16:26
378. Ellie Avina (12621) 06:17:36
379. Ana Murcia (12624) 06:17:37
380. Hiromi Kudo (12666) 06:19:10
381. Shefali Choksi (12670) 06:19:16
382. Sarah Miklaski (12697) 06:20:06
383. Stacy Georgilas (12698) 06:20:07
384. Nancy Gracia (12717) 06:20:37
385. Jennifer De Jesus (12738) 06:21:28
386. Cheyenne Alejandro (12739) 06:21:31
387. Sylvia Padilla (12783) 06:22:17
388. Amber Edwards (12819) 06:23:26
389. Consuelo Garcia (12862) 06:24:18
390. Monique Faison (12877) 06:25:02
391. Susan Kim (12901) 06:25:51
392. Magee Kundrat (12915) 06:26:16
393. Terry Casillas (12933) 06:26:37
394. Leslie Garcia (12934) 06:26:38
395. Sheila Williams (12970) 06:27:55
396. Jennifer Canillas (12981) 06:28:05
397. Maria Rivera (13031) 06:29:37
398. Michele Scolaro (13045) 06:30:09
399. Norma Stang (13081) 06:31:19
400. Tamara Piatkiewicz (13091) 06:31:33
401. Mika Tsuruta (13094) 06:31:40
402. Maricela Ojeda (13097) 06:31:48
403. Mitzi Imperial (13109) 06:32:02
404. Perla Hernandez (13135) 06:32:42
405. Lori Lilly (13146) 06:32:48
406. Ana Maria Morales (13164) 06:33:11
407. Jung Hee Oh (13169) 06:33:24
408. Lesvia Pena (13195) 06:34:17
409. Marisol Delgado (13201) 06:34:31
410. Nadya Senftleben (13245) 06:35:41
411. Claudia Padilla (13284) 06:36:51
412. Katie Boudreau (13306) 06:37:38
413. Jennifer Boudreau (13307) 06:37:43
414. Abelia Sloey (13308) 06:37:48
415. Allison Pilmer (13319) 06:38:17
416. Adriane Ullrich (13335) 06:38:50
417. Martha Navarro (13344) 06:39:03
418. Anjali Pandya (13345) 06:39:05
419. Angie Minton (13371) 06:39:54
420. Diana Cordero (13380) 06:40:26
421. Randelyn Clarke (13382) 06:40:33
422. Angela Wamsher (13443) 06:42:32
423. Michelle Ramirez (13446) 06:42:36
424. Christine Wong (13456) 06:42:59
425. Katrina Williams (13468) 06:43:26
426. Adriana Andaluz (13469) 06:43:28
427. Ana Caceres (13470) 06:43:28
428. Xochitl Leyva (13496) 06:44:47
429. Malaka Saied (13500) 06:44:54
430. Serbrina Macias (13518) 06:45:32
431. Anita Zulkarnain (13535) 06:46:10
432. Janelle Ann D'Anna (13559) 06:46:52
433. Denise Combes (13562) 06:47:44
434. Kath Cheely (13583) 06:47:44
435. Samantha Underwood (13595) 06:48:00
436. Akane Handa (13633) 06:49:23
437. Heather Lamb (13651) 06:50:00
438. Erin Marston (13674) 06:50:29
439. Brenda Comstock (13736) 06:52:40
440. Jennifer Park (13749) 06:53:18
441. Monica Rez (13753) 06:53:42
442. Dinna Farahmand (13754) 06:53:45
443. Danielle Sandoval (13760) 06:54:02
444. Jessie Morales (13771) 06:54:31
445. Jennifer Dyer (13779) 06:54:49
446. Sonia Ayala (13787) 06:55:04
447. Darcy Long (13801) 06:55:15
448. Mihoko Ito (13833) 06:56:20
449. Belinda Contreras (13839) 06:56:34
450. Jennifer Wright (13851) 06:56:54
451. Debora Ochoa (13874) 06:57:30
452. Melinda Mah (13870) 06:57:44
453. Socorro Fosado (13884) 06:57:55
454. Maribel Osorio (13888) 06:58:01
455. Carla Pinto (13901) 06:58:26
456. Lynda Daniel (13923) 06:58:57
457. Ekehe Udeoji (13946) 06:59:42
458. Nicole Gentempo (13954) 07:00:01
459. Sloan Hamilton (13964) 07:00:27
460. Cherie Parungo (13967) 07:00:31
461. Susan Taylor (13968) 07:00:32
462. Lakisha Simpson (14026) 07:02:11
463. Yumi Hirota (14037) 07:02:39
464. Keiko Mori (14038) 07:02:40
465. Chiaki Hamajima (14039) 07:02:40
466. Vanessa Merlino (14050) 07:02:59
467. Christine Rossi (14056) 07:03:41
468. Rosanne Sanchez (14061) 07:03:56
469. Iwata Maki (14068) 07:04:11
470. Buster Olmos (14094) 07:05:52
471. Mildred Moh (14146) 07:09:08
472. Marian Estonilo (14176) 07:11:11
473. Martha Castillo (14186) 07:11:58
474. Maureen Madsen (14203) 07:12:54
475. Bita Fahiman (14208) 07:13:02
476. Lisa Northrup (14223) 07:14:00
477. Janean Weekly (14225) 07:14:14
478. Karin Barkley (14260) 07:15:40
479. Rikae Ohara (14277) 07:16:34
480. Lorena Guillien (14299) 07:17:56
481. Sandra Murillo (14324) 07:19:37
482. Raquel Espinoza (14397) 07:24:37
483. Amber Nichols (14402) 07:24:55
484. Kymberly Perez (14409) 07:26:05
485. Naoko Tanaka (14437) 07:28:18
486. Monica Ochoa (14494) 07:33:33
487. Mara Calderon (14506) 07:34:59
488. Maricela Gracia (14507) 07:35:00
489. Maria Aguilar (14508) 07:35:01
490. Mariana Ramos (14521) 07:35:41
491. Angelica Pimente (14553) 07:37:18
492. Ivonne Diaz (14619) 07:42:47
493. Tishana Gibbs (14645) 07:45:45
494. Nanako Ono (14669) 07:47:52
495. Amanda Price (14687) 07:49:37
496. Areli Lucatero (14696) 07:50:16
497. Ana Landaverde (14718) 07:52:19
498. Elena Martinez (14731) 07:53:32
499. Alma Lopez (14766) 07:56:04
500. Janel Acosta (14836) 08:03:26
501. Farrah Sarkissian (14881) 08:12:30
502. Melanie Long (14918) 08:18:42
503. Noelia Monarrez (14925) 08:19:24
504. Barbara Parsons (14933) 08:20:19
505. Maria Heredia (14948) 08:21:42
506. Martina Heredia (14949) 08:21:54
507. Delia Morales (14997) 08:31:43
508. Lori Turner (15064) 08:51:22
509. Janya Mercado (15069) 08:53:06
510. Sandra Ochoa (15073) 08:53:48
511. Debbi Kahn (15096) 09:01:46
512. Mayra Alas (15108) 09:11:00
513. Corinna Kao (15118) 09:25:34
514. Monica Guerrero (15128) 09:30:11

MEN 25 TO 29

1. Rolando Vera (1) 02:11:39
2. Bob Kempainen (2) 02:11:59
3. Hiroyuki Ito (9) 02:23:33
4. Katsuya Natsume (10) 02:23:54
5. Hector Lopez (11) 02:25:47
6. Michael Alexander (12) 02:25:58
7. Joshua Breslow (19) 02:29:08
8. Abdriaz Drayer (22) 02:29:52
9. Dagoberto Perez (23) 02:29:56
10. Chuck Mullane (25) 02:30:56
11. Jorge Marquez (26) 02:32:00
12. Refugio Servin (33) 02:35:20
13. Darryl Wagner (35) 02:35:48
14. Rafael Ramos (36) 02:35:57
15. David Serina (43) 02:37:46
16. Jose Zavala (45) 02:39:25
17. Jerry Spears (47) 02:39:53
18. Pedro Gutierrez (40) 02:40:29
19. Emigdio Zarazua (51) 02:41:09
20. Michael Latham (59) 02:42:49
21. Hugo Vargas (70) 02:44:49
22. Brian King (72) 02:45:01
23. Armando Onofre (79) 02:45:43
24. Hynn Kang (81) 02:46:49
25. Barry Steinwand (84) 02:47:29
26. Michael Littmann (87) 02:47:52
27. Brad Alexander (101) 02:50:36
28. Ricardo Sarabia (102) 02:50:47
29. Norberto Romero (103) 02:50:52
30. Rick Herr (108) 02:51:30
31. Alvaro Morales (109) 02:51:34
32. Samuel Morales Cabello (121) 02:52:31
33. Mateo Villalobos (123) 02:52:34
34. Steve Sharp (124) 02:52:40
35. Alvaro Solares (143) 02:53:57
36. Xavier Estrada (155) 02:55:05
37. Gabriel Flores (157) 02:55:16
38. Gumby Anderson (159) 02:55:34
39. Holger Beckmann (163) 02:55:54
40. Lorenzo Marangoni (178) 02:56:51
41. James Kelly (190) 02:57:31
42. Steve Goin (197) 02:57:59
43. Daniel Ifcher (209) 02:58:34
44. Buster McCoy (210) 02:58:43
45. Robert Brauneisen (213) 02:58:56
46. Julian Navarrete (226) 02:59:47
47. Lee Rosen (229) 02:59:55
48. Jimmy Honda (230) 02:59:57
49. Enrique Carranza (232) 03:00:00
50. Benito Alvarado (234) 03:00:28
51. Joaquin Hartman (240) 03:00:36
52. Byron Monterroso (259) 03:01:45
53. Alexander Juarez (264) 03:02:12
54. Mario Hernandez (272) 03:02:31
55. Wilfrido Garcia (275) 03:02:44
56. Enrique Camacho (278) 03:02:51
57. Ricky Quintana (282) 03:03:00
58. Aristides Perez (288) 03:03:12
59. Jorge Pacheco (292) 03:03:17
60. Nicolas Vargas (297) 03:03:36
61. Cecilio Hernandez (326) 03:05:14
62. Randall Little (328) 03:05:22
63. Cuauhtemoc Quezada (330) 03:05:34
64. Jacques Zaimeddine (340) 03:05:56
65. Michael Gutierrez (346) 03:06:15
66. Chip Logan (350) 03:06:26
67. Patrick Brown (352) 03:06:28
68. Sam Mejia (359) 03:06:50
69. Robert Gutierrez (360) 03:06:59
70. Alexander Kostich (363) 03:07:04
71. Jason Wolf (379) 03:07:40
72. Karl-Heinz Evers (382) 03:07:45
73. Brian King (385) 03:07:49
74. Harry Browne (399) 03:08:18
75. Martin Garcia (403) 03:08:21
76. Jose Martinez (412) 03:08:48
77. Charles Eckel (418) 03:08:58
78. Francisco Hamm (423) 03:09:12
79. Fernando Hernandez (427) 03:09:21
80. Robert Benz (433) 03:09:33
81. Dan Powers (443) 03:09:45
82. Agustin Moran Jimenez (445) 03:09:48
83. Steffen Brost (447) 03:09:52
84. Ben Crouch (455) 03:10:04
85. Ekkehard Gerndt (472) 03:10:55
86. Reginald Love III (474) 03:11:00
87. Gerardo Yanez (481) 03:11:11
88. William Conn (482) 03:11:12
89. Martin Hernandez (484) 03:11:17
90. David Matern (486) 03:11:20
91. Bonfilio Aguilera Orozco (488) 03:11:27
92. Jonathon Vakneln (490) 03:11:36
93. Michael Ramirez (497) 03:12:05
94. Gerald Wallace (509) 03:12:23
95. Jose Rivas (512) 03:12:35
96. Juan Torrealba (518) 03:12:47
97. Dave McKissick (519) 03:12:47
98. Nimbus Couzin (521) 03:12:52
99. Juan Villarreal (522) 03:12:58
100. Tyrone Williams (536) 03:13:19
101. Michael Hardesty (544) 03:13:34
102. Scott Smith (547) 03:13:41
103. Gary Eigen (548) 03:13:41
104. Raul Gonzalez (553) 03:13:45
105. Dino Pelliano (559) 03:13:53
106. Jose Hernandez (561) 03:13:54
107. Osnaldo Santos (566) 03:14:06
108. Chris Kyle (573) 03:14:19
109. Scott Ulik (575) 03:14:20
110. Elmer Martinez (580) 03:14:28
111. POLIN BELISLE (591) 03:14:46
112. Jose Alonso Monzon Aguilar (600) 03:15:08
113. Pablo Castells (602) 03:15:14
114. Javior Quinones (611) 03:15:35
115. Erio Prosswimmer (614) 03:15:39
116. Juan Pacheco (618) 03:15:49
117. David Lippes (637) 03:16:38
118. Thomas Lavender (640) 03:16:43
119. Mario Ochoa Crdi (643) 03:16:46
120. Gregory Smith (647) 03:16:48
121. Wilfred Solano (649) 03:16:51
122. Theodore Leonard (656) 03:17:00
123. Jesus Montoya (663) 03:17:10
124. Rodrigue Desmorat (682) 03:17:33
125. James Bergmann (684) 03:17:36
126. Jose Lopez (690) 03:17:54
127. Joubine Dustzadeh (712) 03:18:41
128. David Chickering (714) 03:18:42
129. Jose Escobedo (716) 03:18:44
130. Michael Wills (720) 03:18:52
131. Bernardo Chona (723) 03:18:57
132. Morikawa Hiroya (728) 03:19:09
133. Felipe Olivar (730) 03:19:12
134. Michael Valdez (738) 03:19:22
135. Lorenzo Hernandez (741) 03:19:24
136. David Elder (748) 03:19:34
137. Jorge Tellez Romero (750) 03:19:37
138. Kevin Hawn (761) 03:19:54
139. Jose Rodriguez (769) 03:20:09
140. Jason Emmons (770) 03:20:10
141. Peter Tommasi (805) 03:21:16
142. James Gaffney (807) 03:21:18
143. Kent Lawrence (809) 03:21:21
144. David Loud (810) 03:21:21
145. Pedro Martinez (814) 03:21:28
146. Dago Perez (818) 03:21:30
147. Angel Gallefos (837) 03:21:59
148. Stefan Schweizer (850) 03:22:14
149. Matt Garcia (853) 03:22:19

150. John Joire (861) ... 03:22:27
151. Hector Reyes Quezada (867) ... 03:22:32
152. Erwin Lynch (868) ... 03:22:34
153. Rocelio Erazo (872) ... 03:22:41
154. Juan Mora (874) ... 03:22:42
155. Kerry Ward (885) ... 03:22:55
156. Steven Hunt (890) ... 03:23:02
157. Thomas Motherway (891) ... 03:23:08
158. Jose Campos (892) ... 03:23:08
159. Poul Johansen (893) ... 03:23:09
160. Jay Biles (895) ... 03:23:10
161. Freddie Piro (904) ... 03:23:23
162. Victor Navarrete (907) ... 03:23:26
163. Carlos Ayala (917) ... 03:23:40
164. Rodolfo Arellano (920) ... 03:23:44
165. Fidel Hurtado (921) ... 03:23:45
166. Christopher Cota (932) ... 03:23:59
167. Ron Lambke (939) ... 03:24:06
168. James Galante (949) ... 03:24:20
169. Gregg Falk (950) ... 03:24:22
170. Jun Onuma (959) ... 03:24:32
171. Brandon Groller (967) ... 03:24:42
172. Joseph Rista (971) ... 03:24:49
173. Scott Mattoon (973) ... 03:24:51
174. Armando Gracian (981) ... 03:25:01
175. Michael Bert (982) ... 03:25:02
176. Nigel Chalk (986) ... 03:25:09
177. Tim Sullivan (989) ... 03:25:12
178. Francisco Gonzalez (996) ... 03:25:24
179. Scott Hanifan (1002) ... 03:25:31
180. Jeff Gann (1009) ... 03:25:39
181. Mauricio Escobar (1012) ... 03:25:40
182. John Nash (1023) ... 03:26:04
183. Josef Kiechler (1032) ... 03:26:14
184. R Ted Arnold (1035) ... 03:26:16
185. Damon Collier (1036) ... 03:26:19
186. Werner Kauer (1044) ... 03:26:35
187. Ray Hu (1062) ... 03:27:01
188. Francisco Esparza (1073) ... 03:27:14
189. Craig Manning (1089) ... 03:27:30
190. Mark Nolte (1098) ... 03:27:36
191. Alfredo Munoz (1110) ... 03:27:47
192. Lewis Gersh (1119) ... 03:27:57
193. Terence Young (1127) ... 03:28:06
194. Ross McCabe (1141) ... 03:28:20
195. Felix Rodriguez (1148) ... 03:28:28
196. Jeffrey Roy (1149) ... 03:28:28
197. Ravenal Pamparo (1165) ... 03:28:50
198. Ed Diffendal (1173) ... 03:29:00
199. Efrain Sosa (1176) ... 03:29:01
200. Michael Sansoucy (1179) ... 03:29:07
201. Eugene Hallinan (1184) ... 03:29:16
202. Thomas Freer (1186) ... 03:29:17
203. Erich Van Stralen (1195) ... 03:29:23
204. Patrick Aragon (1208) ... 03:29:35
205. Travis Schweizer (1217) ... 03:29:41
206. Arturo Olvera (1220) ... 03:29:45
207. Marc Greenwald (1225) ... 03:29:50
208. Scott Bauer (1234) ... 03:30:02
209. Ignacio Fonseca (1237) ... 03:30:09
210. William Bowers (1242) ... 03:30:15
211. Santiago Resendiz (1256) ... 03:30:30
212. Paul Martinez (1259) ... 03:30:32
213. Hjortur Gretarsson (1263) ... 03:30:39
214. Bert Diola (1266) ... 03:30:46
215. Mauricio Rojas (1275) ... 03:30:55
216. Jose Garlin (1277) ... 03:30:56
217. David Beutel (1280) ... 03:30:57
218. Fermin Duarte Coria (1286) ... 03:31:02
219. Alvaro Jimenez (1310) ... 03:31:32
220. Felipe Melendez (1330) ... 03:31:50
221. Ricardo Garcia (1334) ... 03:31:54
222. Brad Mumbrue (1345) ... 03:32:09
223. Thomas Ludwig (1350) ... 03:32:16
224. Benjamin Palomares (1353) ... 03:32:18
225. James Foster (1357) ... 03:32:20
226. Scott Pollack (1359) ... 03:32:22
227. Jose Garcia Raul (1370) ... 03:32:41
228. Peter Naschak (1374) ... 03:32:45
229. Andres Rios (1375) ... 03:32:46
230. Brenda Sullivan (1384) ... 03:32:53
231. Steven Phillips (1401) ... 03:33:18
232. Stephen Sharp (1404) ... 03:33:23
233. Rene Kirchoefer (1407) ... 03:33:26
234. Michael Lowe (1435) ... 03:34:05
235. Ignacio Lopez (1442) ... 03:34:12
236. Marc Vermill (1458) ... 03:34:47
237. Mark Williamson (1461) ... 03:34:48
238. Armando Brideno (1463) ... 03:34:48
239. Louis Bond (1468) ... 03:34:52
240. Douglas Morash (1476) ... 03:35:00
241. Kevin Kayl (1479) ... 03:35:02
242. Michael Smith (1484) ... 03:35:07
243. Jaime Avila (1492) ... 03:35:14
244. Paul Mussenden (1496) ... 03:35:17
245. Patrick McGinnis (1507) ... 03:35:33
246. Jean Paul Masson (1509) ... 03:35:34
247. Andrew Petranek (1515) ... 03:35:40
248. Ruben Gonzalez (1516) ... 03:35:41
249. Nery Soto (1522) ... 03:35:46
250. David Allen (1526) ... 03:35:48
251. Arend Westra (1527) ... 03:35:49
252. Mario Robles (1529) ... 03:35:51
253. Jose Garcia (1554) ... 03:36:20
254. Lance Raisanen (1558) ... 03:36:28
255. Jon Miller (1569) ... 03:36:43
256. Martin Rodriguez (1570) ... 03:36:43
257. Kelly Nix (1573) ... 03:36:44
258. Nohe Mendieta (1581) ... 03:36:55
259. Miguel Rodriguez (1582) ... 03:36:55
260. David Wolf (1588) ... 03:37:00
261. Guillermo Cuevas (1590) ... 03:37:02
262. Jeffrey Sylvia (1609) ... 03:37:20
263. Bryan Barbosa (1619) ... 03:37:32
264. Joe Tieso (1626) ... 03:37:45
265. James Espinoza (1628) ... 03:37:47
266. Oscar Mazariegos (1638) ... 03:37:56
267. Michael McCaffrey (1649) ... 03:38:08
268. Patrick Tighe (1655) ... 03:38:11
269. Rogelio Haro (1659) ... 03:38:14
270. David Guillory (1671) ... 03:38:30
271. Charles Lewis (1672) ... 03:38:31
272. Guillermo Morelos (1673) ... 03:38:34
273. Francisco Santos (1683) ... 03:38:44
274. William Phillips (1688) ... 03:38:46
275. William McSwain (1691) ... 03:38:48
276. Vance Ryan (1700) ... 03:38:57
277. Matthew Barba (1720) ... 03:39:20
278. Scott Lawrence (1728) ... 03:39:29
279. Armando Dominguez (1736) ... 03:39:39
280. Jonathan Duarte (1740) ... 03:39:42
281. Douglas Ritenour (1744) ... 03:39:44
282. Richard Arvizu (1758) ... 03:40:02
283. Eric Espinal (1802) ... 03:40:42
284. John Bush (1803) ... 03:40:43
285. Sean Clemens (1821) ... 03:40:59
286. Jose Gutierrez (1826) ... 03:41:03
287. Walter Santucci (1828) ... 03:41:04
288. Wendell Eaton (1835) ... 03:41:07
289. Vincent Wicker (1846) ... 03:41:16
290. Tsutomu Kawanobe (1850) ... 03:41:19
291. Anthony Sindelir (1852) ... 03:41:21
292. Jon Rubenstein (1886) ... 03:41:46
293. David Varela (1905) ... 03:42:02
294. Charles Unger (1915) ... 03:42:16
295. Prisciliano Quechotl (1928) ... 03:42:30
296. Scott Brewer (1930) ... 03:42:31
297. Alberto Cristo (1933) ... 03:42:34
298. Santos Gutierrez (1939) ... 03:42:47
299. Jay Ackerman (1943) ... 03:42:54
300. Christopher Szczech (1944) ... 03:42:56
301. Jose Perez (1947) ... 03:42:59
302. Robert Briggs (1965) ... 03:43:14
303. Paul Cummings (1972) ... 03:43:24
304. Jesus Rojas (1977) ... 03:43:29
305. John Henry (1980) ... 03:43:31
306. Roger Galbraith (1991) ... 03:43:43
307. Jeff Hogan (1992) ... 03:43:44
308. Chris Coscino (1994) ... 03:43:47
309. Robert Reyna Jr (2002) ... 03:43:55
310. Martin Horner (2004) ... 03:43:56
311. Michael Buckingham (2009) ... 03:44:00
312. Keith Egly (2014) ... 03:44:02
313. Juan Rios (2032) ... 03:44:17
314. Keith Brace (2034) ... 03:44:19
315. Angel Hurtado (2035) ... 03:44:19
316. Stephen Sorensen (2053) ... 03:44:34
317. Carlos Levario Jr (2057) ... 03:44:35
318. Garth Olson (2072) ... 03:44:45
319. Sean Cluse (2073) ... 03:44:46
320. Michael Connor (2107) ... 03:45:15
321. Jose Alvarez (2123) ... 03:45:27
322. Abel Martinez (2127) ... 03:45:31
323. Thomas Cooper (2131) ... 03:45:38
324. Bernie Ramirez (2134) ... 03:45:41
325. Dana Sanders (2139) ... 03:45:45
326. Benjamin Piper (2147) ... 03:45:52
327. G. Guzman Morales (2177) ... 03:46:19
328. David Noles (2183) ... 03:46:23
329. Timothy Tyndorf (2186) ... 03:46:25
330. Echo Edmonson (2196) ... 03:46:40
331. Charles Kaplan (2215) ... 03:46:57
332. Brian Porter (2216) ... 03:46:58
333. Alfredo Aguilera (2236) ... 03:47:15
334. David Duke (2255) ... 03:47:30
335. Scott Zerga (2265) ... 03:47:41
336. Christopher Clauss (2290) ... 03:48:00
337. John Yu (2300) ... 03:48:07
338. Facundo Castaneda (2316) ... 03:48:17
339. Jorge Torres (2328) ... 03:48:30
340. Mark Watson (2351) ... 03:48:45
341. Kenneth Lindemann (2354) ... 03:48:48
342. Manuel Ayala (2360) ... 03:48:55
343. Adrian Hendricks (2366) ... 03:49:02
344. Darren Gill (2369) ... 03:49:04
345. Dan Thompson (2374) ... 03:49:07
346. Michael Bell (2397) ... 03:49:21
347. Eric Erenstoft (2410) ... 03:49:32
348. Akihiko Koda (2415) ... 03:49:37
349. Charles Mazza (2416) ... 03:49:38
350. Jim Lockert (2422) ... 03:49:41
351. Jose Delgadillo (2435) ... 03:49:52
352. James Schilder (2439) ... 03:49:56
353. Brian Green (2453) ... 03:50:08
354. Micheal Alacon (2460) ... 03:50:14
355. Bruce Greenspon (2474) ... 03:50:26
356. Paul Maletich (2476) ... 03:50:27
357. Christopher Wright (2477) ... 03:50:27
358. Jose Puebla Rojas (2498) ... 03:50:43
359. Victor Valentino (2499) ... 03:50:45
360. Paul McNeil (2500) ... 03:50:45
361. Eduardo Santos (2506) ... 03:50:51
362. Miguel Garcia (2508) ... 03:50:54
363. Henry Call (2509) ... 03:50:54
364. Tom Rude (2517) ... 03:51:00
365. Dan Roper (2540) ... 03:51:23
366. Michael Matt (2566) ... 03:51:39
367. Wayne Churyk (2568) ... 03:51:41
368. Michael Romero (2579) ... 03:51:51
369. Jake Cunningham (2589) ... 03:51:58
370. Marcial Caceres (2593) ... 03:52:00
371. Antonio Flores (2595) ... 03:52:05
372. Robert Quigley (2597) ... 03:52:08
373. Steve Tuszywski (2603) ... 03:52:15
374. Erick Mazariegos (2609) ... 03:52:18
375. Patrick Doran (2617) ... 03:52:22
376. Frank La Plante (2619) ... 03:52:23
377. Jimmy Gillespie (2626) ... 03:52:30
378. James Plouffe (2639) ... 03:52:43
379. Larry Forcey (2686) ... 03:53:16
380. Victor Rabadan (2698) ... 03:53:22
381. Bryan Jew (2710) ... 03:53:30
382. Felipe Galarza Gonzalez (2712) ... 03:53:34
383. Forrest Moore (2714) ... 03:53:35
384. Ray Alcantar (2730) ... 03:53:48
385. Jim Givens (2754) ... 03:54:09
386. Randolph Hicks (2762) ... 03:54:14
387. Rich Hathaway (2763) ... 03:54:14
388. Leonardo Zendejas (2768) ... 03:54:16
389. Richard Lawson (2788) ... 03:54:28
390. Sam Hayes (2805) ... 03:54:39
391. John Donnelly (2810) ... 03:54:42
392. Chris Wille (2812) ... 03:54:43
393. Cesar Yanes (2813) ... 03:54:44
394. Juergen Schulze (2815) ... 03:54:45
395. Jonathan Webber (2821) ... 03:54:48
396. Marshall Nord (2843) ... 03:55:06
397. Robert Del Ghiaccio (2851) ... 03:55:12
398. David Schnur (2852) ... 03:55:13
399. Agustin Antonio (2861) ... 03:55:21
400. Rodney Moulton (2867) ... 03:55:24
401. Erik Smith (2897) ... 03:55:41
402. John Mason (2902) ... 03:55:47
403. Anthony Sambrano (2903) ... 03:55:47
404. Mario Sanchez (2907) ... 03:55:52
405. Andrew Radden (2919) ... 03:55:57
406. Neil Parsons (2925) ... 03:55:59
407. Chris Williams (2931) ... 03:56:06
408. Spencer King (2937) ... 03:56:09
409. Darren Hollis (2956) ... 03:56:21
410. Matt Byers (2966) ... 03:56:30
411. John Bowlin (2969) ... 03:56:35
412. Don Sabino (2970) ... 03:56:35
413. Joseph Burke (2971) ... 03:56:36
414. Todd Garrett (2982) ... 03:56:44
415. Rob Ho (2999) ... 03:56:49
416. Brian Moorhouse (3010) ... 03:56:54
417. Lance Fenton (3022) ... 03:57:00
418. Andrew Miller (3041) ... 03:57:09
419. Juan Ferreira (3043) ... 03:57:11
420. Bruce Bair (3057) ... 03:57:21
421. Paul Goode (3068) ... 03:57:29
422. Jaime Romo (3071) ... 03:57:30
423. Padriac Reddington (3072) ... 03:57:31
424. Albert Trevisan Jr (3077) ... 03:57:34
425. Miguel Isaza (3109) ... 03:57:55
426. Douglas Fye (3119) ... 03:58:01
427. Michael Ascher (3135) ... 03:58:16
428. Vincent Luna (3136) ... 03:58:17
429. Wilfred Gonzalez (3149) ... 03:58:25
430. James Stathas (3152) ... 03:58:27
431. Jean-Luc Tenot (3161) ... 03:58:35
432. Kevin Laird (3162) ... 03:58:35
433. Marc Cryer (3170) ... 03:58:39
434. Dan Morris (3181) ... 03:58:50
435. Michael Wiley (3193) ... 03:58:55
436. Jose Delcarmen (3205) ... 03:59:04
437. Luis Guevara (3208) ... 03:59:05
438. Franklin Hilton (3228) ... 03:59:21
439. York Valderrama (3234) ... 03:59:26
440. Timothy Vallez (3237) ... 03:59:28
441. David Weber (3252) ... 03:59:39
442. Tony Calhoun (3270) ... 03:59:47
443. Robert Kacer (3273) ... 03:59:49
444. Michael Blair (3292) ... 03:59:57
445. Damian Morales (3295) ... 03:59:58
446. Tom Triggs (3304) ... 04:00:04
447. Dale Smith (3314) ... 04:00:11
448. Bernardino Lopez (3317) ... 04:00:14
449. Andy Voggenthaler (3331) ... 04:00:22
450. Bernabe Roman (3362) ... 04:00:52
451. Suk-Kyu Koh (3364) ... 04:00:53
452. Robert Zuniga (3369) ... 04:00:55
453. Felix Gonzalez (3380) ... 04:01:02
454. Mark Michaelian (3384) ... 04:01:04
455. Vaughn Smider (3389) ... 04:01:09
456. James Saunders (3395) ... 04:01:14
457. Garo Mansourian (3397) ... 04:01:14
458. Peter Hayes (3402) ... 04:01:16
459. Ishii Hiroyuki (3409) ... 04:01:23
460. Carlos Altamirano Jr (3423) ... 04:01:33
461. Hirofumi Shoji (3448) ... 04:01:56
462. Keith Allen (3454) ... 04:02:00
463. Jose Briseno (3456) ... 04:02:02
464. Bryan Zickefoose (3461) ... 04:02:06
465. Jimmy Jimenez Jr (3465) ... 04:02:11
466. Mark Barrera (3469) ... 04:02:14
467. Al Kim (3476) ... 04:02:18
468. Kelly Fuchino (3477) ... 04:02:18
469. Matsutaro Ueto (3490) ... 04:02:33
470. Steve Harrison (3492) ... 04:02:36
471. Ryan Heritage (3493) ... 04:02:37
472. Daniel Prado (3512) ... 04:02:52
473. John Merna (3514) ... 04:02:54
474. Terry Davis (3521) ... 04:03:00
475. Richard Culp (3539) ... 04:03:15
476. Scott Baur (3540) ... 04:03:18
477. James Bender Jr (3553) ... 04:03:29
478. Richard Mullis (3554) ... 04:03:30
479. Joaquin Gonzalez (3556) ... 04:03:33
480. Nathan Dixon (3557) ... 04:03:33
481. Raul Albavera (3565) ... 04:03:37
482. Alonso Robles (3566) ... 04:03:40
483. Sean Sullivan (3574) ... 04:03:48
484. Michael Johnston (3575) ... 04:03:51
485. Kenny Rudolph (3586) ... 04:04:00
486. Kenneth Watkins (3601) ... 04:04:12
487. Bobby Bostic (3604) ... 04:04:13
488. David Feldman (3613) ... 04:04:19
489. Cesar Cruz (3625) ... 04:04:26
490. Brian Kelly (3630) ... 04:04:30
491. Atsuya Urano (3645) ... 04:04:36
492. Toby Tortorilla (3675) ... 04:04:57
493. Adam Silver (3676) ... 04:04:57
494. Glenn Zoller (3693) ... 04:05:08
495. Daniel Chou (3698) ... 04:05:10
496. Carl Castelblanco (3718) ... 04:05:31
497. Stefan Bien (3721) ... 04:05:33
498. Edward Keating (3726) ... 04:05:36
499. Carlos Santana (3754) ... 04:06:02
500. Richard Cluff (3761) ... 04:06:05
501. John Kramber (3788) ... 04:06:28
502. Aaron Aviles (3824) ... 04:06:53
503. Michael Dimkich (3836) ... 04:07:02
504. Robert Remington (3856) ... 04:07:10
505. Christopher Means (3868) ... 04:07:23
506. Fabio Flagiello (3879) ... 04:07:32
507. Matt Dell (3886) ... 04:07:36
508. Uvaldo Madrigal (3890) ... 04:07:38
509. Manuel Garcia (3901) ... 04:07:45
510. Howard Huckins (3902) ... 04:07:46
511. Brian McKenna (3909) ... 04:07:49
512. Louis Fernandez (3919) ... 04:08:02
513. Eddy Maillot (3921) ... 04:08:06
514. David Rabow (3934) ... 04:08:15
515. Ricardo Ortega (3940) ... 04:08:17
516. John Hendra (3967) ... 04:08:40
517. Jack Rohbach (3974) ... 04:08:45
518. Ted Smirley (3976) ... 04:08:46
519. Yader Jarquin (3986) ... 04:08:54
520. Milton Lopez (3996) ... 04:09:03
521. Stephen Labonge (3998) ... 04:09:04
522. Anhlinh Tang (4001) ... 04:09:07
523. Tory Wiese (4022) ... 04:09:22
524. Glenn Hamburger (4027) ... 04:09:24
525. Richard Woodroof (4036) ... 04:09:32
526. John Smith (4059) ... 04:09:54
527. Peter Bollenbecker (4061) ... 04:09:56
528. Lloyd Chang (4062) ... 04:09:56
529. Steve Nelson (4085) ... 04:10:14
530. Juan Carlos Alcala (4130) ... 04:10:49
531. Richard Chow (4155) ... 04:11:02
532. Jeffrey Kligman (4158) ... 04:11:03
533. Mark Theberge (4159) ... 04:11:03
534. Dominic Albo (4162) ... 04:11:05
535. Thomas George (4164) ... 04:11:06
536. Michael Barella (4170) ... 04:11:11
537. T Kevin Powells (4188) ... 04:11:26
538. Juan Luis Gonzalez (4215) ... 04:11:53
539. Porfirio Lopez Sanchez (4229) ... 04:12:01
540. Jose Muratalla (4230) ... 04:12:02
541. David Kocipak (4245) ... 04:12:14
542. Juan Avila (4280) ... 04:12:42
543. Mark Jolley (4294) ... 04:12:54
544. Richard Gayle (4313) ... 04:13:07
545. David Bowen (4322) ... 04:13:10
546. Douglas Osborne (4324) ... 04:13:11
547. Dana Jarvis (4333) ... 04:13:21
548. Todd Priebe (4336) ... 04:13:22
549. Donald Sharp (4356) ... 04:13:43
550. Robert Crosswhite (4373) ... 04:13:55
551. Armando Murillo (4377) ... 04:13:57
552. Charles Ybarra (4397) ... 04:14:08
553. Robert Papp (4415) ... 04:14:21
554. Javier Haldonado (4417) ... 04:14:22
555. Christopher George (4418) ... 04:14:22
556. John Maanum (4435) ... 04:14:33
557. Mark Scanlon (4439) ... 04:14:35
558. Dan Robin (4440) ... 04:14:35
559. Cesar Perez (4467) ... 04:14:48
560. Brad Jarvinen (4470) ... 04:14:48
561. Christopher Olson (4478) ... 04:14:52
562. Joel Kirshman (4501) ... 04:15:09
563. Sang Kim (4505) ... 04:15:14
564. Al Walsh (4516) ... 04:15:25
565. Eric Richardson (4519) ... 04:15:28
566. Chris Bayz (4542) ... 04:15:37
567. Bruce Leibovitch (4543) ... 04:15:37
568. Ishtar Khan (4546) ... 04:15:39
569. Carlos Olmos (4573) ... 04:15:54
570. Kenya Kura (4587) ... 04:16:03
571. Don Gray (4603) ... 04:16:18
572. Armando Ortuno Davila (4640) ... 04:16:38
573. George Garcia (4643) ... 04:16:40
574. Thomas Seeburger (4644) ... 04:16:40
575. Ricky Perez (4658) ... 04:16:55
576. Ray Haynes (4663) ... 04:16:57
577. Luis Tielemans (4666) ... 04:17:00
578. Steve Singer (4669) ... 04:17:02
579. Elmer Lara (4671) ... 04:17:04
580. Dirk Craft (4680) ... 04:17:11
581. Randall Goddard (4681) ... 04:17:12
582. Gustavo Bulgach (4682) ... 04:17:13
583. Pete Choi (4698) ... 04:17:28
584. Jongho Oh (4700) ... 04:17:29
585. Enrique Matamoros (4702) ... 04:17:29
586. Benjamin Kunde (4710) ... 04:17:36
587. Alejandro Herrera (4721) ... 04:17:48
588. Andrew Radovan (4725) ... 04:17:50
589. Armando Berriz (4736) ... 04:17:55
590. Phil Nelson (4745) ... 04:18:00
591. Paul Marrietti (4752) ... 04:18:06
592. Anthony Flores (4757) ... 04:18:09
593. Steve Garcia (4765) ... 04:18:13
594. Ross Linstrom (4775) ... 04:18:21
595. Abel Orozco (4801) ... 04:18:38
596. Alfredo Urrutia (4804) ... 04:18:39
597. Raul Morales (4826) ... 04:18:51
598. Carlos Gallegos (4827) ... 04:18:52
599. Marc Susac (4839) ... 04:18:58
600. Christopher Brewer (4840) ... 04:18:58
601. Ryan Noto (4849) ... 04:19:02
602. Derrick Jacobson (4860) ... 04:19:09
603. Masahiko Kinoshita (4865) ... 04:19:12
604. Anthony Morrison (4868) ... 04:19:14
605. Sergio Estrada (4871) ... 04:19:15
606. Brian Nobe (4892) ... 04:19:30
607. Jerfi Cicin (4907) ... 04:19:40
608. John Kitayama (4917) ... 04:19:47
609. Peter Stamos (4919) ... 04:19:49
610. Joe Gutierrez (4929) ... 04:19:56
611. Blas Marquez (4959) ... 04:20:20
612. Vincent Brigham (4962) ... 04:20:24
613. James Hover (4965) ... 04:20:26
614. Robert Hellebrand (4993) ... 04:20:55
615. Timothy Flood (5012) ... 04:21:16
616. Clayton Becker (5020) ... 04:21:18
617. Jon Swanson (5022) ... 04:21:19
618. Darrell Vigil (5024) ... 04:21:21
619. Mark Jardino (5030) ... 04:21:24
620. Brian Green (5032) ... 04:21:29
621. Scott Gruber (5033) ... 04:21:30
622. David Domash (5046) ... 04:21:37
623. Craig Broderick (5050) ... 04:21:39
624. Daniel Martinez (5053) ... 04:21:40
625. Alfredo Elizondo (5060) ... 04:21:44
626. Josh Oman (5078) ... 04:21:53
627. Gustavo Gonzalez (5079) ... 04:21:53
628. Paul Durant (5085) ... 04:21:54
629. Tom Gonzales (5095) ... 04:22:01
630. Mario De Jesus (5099) ... 04:22:03
631. Maxx Garris (5104) ... 04:22:06
632. Craig Arceneaux (5107) ... 04:22:07
633. Raul Chavez (5111) ... 04:22:08
634. Jose Fuentes (5116) ... 04:22:10
635. Alain Rousseau (5118) ... 04:22:13
636. Sergey Lototsky (5119) ... 04:22:13
637. Pablo Rodriguez (5120) ... 04:22:13
638. Kevin McClellan (5122) ... 04:22:17
639. Scott Reeves (5125) ... 04:22:18
640. Matt Strittmatter (5131) ... 04:22:22
641. Brian Anderson (5133) ... 04:22:24
642. Steve Paek (5168) ... 04:22:51
643. Robert Vasquez (5169) ... 04:22:51
644. Joe Marando (5183) ... 04:23:00
645. Baron Wolt (5189) ... 04:23:06
646. Douglas Miller (5205) ... 04:23:15
647. Harold Isaac (5213) ... 04:23:19
648. Jason Terry (5233) ... 04:23:35
649. Enrique Rosete Sosa (5236) ... 04:23:36
650. Robert Martin (5253) ... 04:23:53
651. Keith Greteman (5269) ... 04:24:11
652. Adam Saltzman (5274) ... 04:24:15
653. Ramon Guzman (5280) ... 04:24:20
654. David Wood (5316) ... 04:24:40
655. Mat Talag (5353) ... 04:25:10
656. Craig Storey (5354) ... 04:25:11
657. Riccardo Graddick (5357) ... 04:25:14
658. Ricardo Lasso (5359) ... 04:25:15
659. Ivan Pierra (5360) ... 04:25:15
660. Armando Tiscareno (5361) ... 04:25:15
661. Andrew Kunde (5362) ... 04:25:15
662. Paul Ablett (5389) ... 04:25:27
663. Verle Inman (5392) ... 04:25:29
664. Bryan Roos (5406) ... 04:25:39
665. David Alexander (5418) ... 04:25:45
666. Anthony Estrada (5419) ... 04:25:46
667. Alejandro Lopez (5438) ... 04:25:58
668. Jun San Antonio (5442) ... 04:25:59
669. Henry Sanin (5461) ... 04:26:11
670. Jaime Flores (5468) ... 04:26:16
671. Leo Evans (5471) ... 04:26:19
672. Jeffrey Kirkpatrick (5489) ... 04:26:31
673. Blake Beltram (5508) ... 04:26:50
674. Eric Welch (5509) ... 04:26:51
675. Ollie Ocampo (5514) ... 04:26:53
676. Kevin Dobbert (5521) ... 04:26:58
677. David Dolphin (5524) ... 04:27:02
678. Troy Leonard (5529) ... 04:27:06
679. Gilbert Turrietta (5542) ... 04:27:13
680. Victor Escobar (5564) ... 04:27:28
681. Rod Swan (5566) ... 04:27:29
682. Ronald Hawkins (5568) ... 04:27:30
683. Jeff Timmerman (5575) ... 04:27:32
684. Carl Arnold (5592) ... 04:27:41
685. Kirk Foster (5607) ... 04:27:54
686. Scott Van Horn (5627) ... 04:28:04
687. Paul Rudman (5629) ... 04:28:05
688. John Davidson (5638) ... 04:28:11
689. Eric Sagerman (5640) ... 04:28:13
690. Bernard Sweeny (5649) ... 04:28:18
691. Luis Wong (5652) ... 04:28:20
692. Warren Vasquez (5668) ... 04:28:32
693. Phillip Jimenez (5671) ... 04:28:34
694. Steve Schneider (5674) ... 04:28:36
695. Jack Zernik (5678) ... 04:28:38
696. Robert Alejo (5708) ... 04:28:59
697. Michael Fowler (5710) ... 04:29:01
698. Antonio Flores (5715) ... 04:29:02
699. Scott Thompson (5738) ... 04:29:16
700. Eric Osmonson (5752) ... 04:29:26
701. Joseph Thomas (5758) ... 04:29:30
702. Joseph Zazzu (5761) ... 04:29:32
703. David Snyder (5764) ... 04:29:33
704. Jeffrey Yap (5790) ... 04:29:52
705. Aaron Furlong (5791) ... 04:29:53
706. Martin Cadenas (5796) ... 04:29:58
707. Prashanth Banuru (5803) ... 04:30:03
708. David Baker (5809) ... 04:30:08
709. John Kramer (5814) ... 04:30:13
710. John Babcock (5822) ... 04:30:18
711. Jess Vizcaino (5828) ... 04:30:25
712. Phil Jauregui (5830) ... 04:30:25
713. Richard Stout (5844) ... 04:30:31
714. Joseph Osbron (5869) ... 04:30:41
715. Marcelino Pedroza (5870) ... 04:30:41
716. Gregory Borchard (5891) ... 04:30:54
717. Darren Statt (5902) ... 04:31:03
718. Robert Burnett (5904) ... 04:31:04
719. Roy Corona (5905) ... 04:31:04
720. Enrique Pita (5916) ... 04:31:09
721. Ricardo Rauda (5919) ... 04:31:13
722. Marco Morales (5925) ... 04:31:18
723. Edgar Solorzano (5934) ... 04:31:25
724. David Cusiter (5944) ... 04:31:29
725. Michael Banta (5949) ... 04:31:32
726. Nick Ruiz (5951) ... 04:31:33
727. Edward Jew (5962) ... 04:31:44
728. John Cressey (5973) ... 04:31:53
729. Rich Katz (5976) ... 04:31:54
730. Thomas Nunez (5980) ... 04:31:57
731. David Cash (5984) ... 04:32:00
732. Todd Pam (6005) ... 04:32:19
733. Jeff Pohlig (6007) ... 04:32:20
734. Koji Fujiki (6025) ... 04:32:32
735. Myrna Salmeron (6036) ... 04:32:45
736. Petyr Beck (6049) ... 04:32:51
737. Benjamin Almeida (6055) ... 04:32:54
738. Rafael Serrano (6057) ... 04:32:57
739. Tylan Hannan (6106) ... 04:33:28
740. Ron Spyker (6114) ... 04:33:33
741. Greg Ching (6132) ... 04:33:45
742. Hiroshi Takimoto (6142) ... 04:33:53
743. Chris Mandery (6190) ... 04:34:25
744. Anders Johnsson (6191) ... 04:34:26
745. Shannon Driscoll (6194) ... 04:34:28
746. Amado Cervantes (6203) ... 04:34:35
747. Delpino Morales (6206) ... 04:34:38
748. Casey O'Brien (6216) ... 04:34:43
749. Giancarlo Graneto (6222) ... 04:34:45
750. Ray Salcepuedes (6223) ... 04:34:45
751. Eric Smith (6228) ... 04:34:50
752. Ray Morris (6259) ... 04:35:13
753. Herb Marroquin (6260) ... 04:35:14
754. Ted Mackey (6263) ... 04:35:15
755. Steven Kraft (6268) ... 04:35:18
756. Manuel Esquivel (6279) ... 04:35:24
757. Kjell Lenngren (6284) ... 04:35:26
758. Ricky Baker (6285) ... 04:35:26
759. Rick Cervantes (6287) ... 04:35:27
760. Michael Thompson (6311) ... 04:35:43
761. David Miller (6314) ... 04:35:45
762. David Holland (6319) ... 04:35:49
763. John Gaither (6321) ... 04:35:50
764. Balentin Aguilar (6331) ... 04:35:55
765. Tim Hull (6379) ... 04:36:24
766. Sam Banuelos (6386) ... 04:36:26
767. John Riordan (6406) ... 04:36:36
768. Jose Gonzalez (6428) ... 04:36:52
769. Rodrigo Vargas (6436) ... 04:37:02
770. Ronald Schultz (6439) ... 04:37:05
771. Anthony Suarato (6440) ... 04:37:05
772. Frank Bellamy (6446) ... 04:37:11
773. Enrique Robles (6460) ... 04:37:23
774. Marcelo Fortunato (6471) ... 04:37:28
775. Fabio Fortunato (6476) ... 04:37:30
776. Scott Wilbur (6494) ... 04:37:39
777. Kolja Spoeri (6500) ... 04:37:43
778. Michael Soliz (6510) ... 04:37:48
779. Gary Shawn (6511) ... 04:37:48
780. Marshall Taylor (6528) ... 04:38:00
781. Charles Rueda (6548) ... 04:38:12
782. Lorenzo Ben (6566) ... 04:38:23
783. Bruce Amman (6588) ... 04:38:38
784. Steve Dark (6589) ... 04:38:39
785. Manuel Cortez (6598) ... 04:38:42
786. Robert Magnusson (6616) ... 04:38:53

787. Hal Berman (6618) 04:38:54
788. Modesto Salgado (6620) 04:38:56
789. Ben Gonzalez (6625) 04:38:58
790. Daniel Jose Hernandez (6631) 04:39:00
791. Edgar Whitmore III (6636) 04:39:08
792. Robert Chagolla (6685) 04:39:44
793. Paul Gianetto (6705) 04:39:57
794. Marcos Marin (6714) 04:40:04
795. Peter Peru (6724) 04:40:15
796. Timothy Kincaid (6726) 04:40:18
797. Edward MacKenzie (6744) 04:40:34
798. Ramon Fabian (6759) 04:40:42
799. David Gonzalez (6766) 04:40:53
800. Robert Hall (6768) 04:40:55
801. Chuck Filliettaz (6772) 04:40:58
802. Hector Morales (6779) 04:41:03
803. John Golob (6798) 04:41:13
804. Angel Arias (6805) 04:41:21
805. John Castro (6818) 04:41:33
806. Arthur Renteria (6826) 04:41:37
807. Raul Quezada (6831) 04:41:41
808. David Stewart (6840) 04:41:49
809. William Ibarra (6841) 04:41:49
810. Luis Moreno (6846) 04:41:51
811. Hernan Galvez (6860) 04:42:01
812. Javier Lopez (6890) 04:42:28
813. John McGoogan (6922) 04:42:49
814. Yoshimitsu Watanabe (6923) 04:42:50
815. John Cordero (6932) 04:42:57
816. Redentor Magpayo (6962) 04:43:17
817. Minh Bui (6966) 04:43:19
818. Adrian Silva (6974) 04:43:22
819. Mike Choi (6984) 04:43:28
820. Kenny Gibbs (6989) 04:43:30
821. Makoto Waki (6998) 04:43:37
822. Yann Lefievre (7000) 04:43:38
823. Agustin Armienta (7036) 04:44:00
824. Emilio Cienfuegos (7052) 04:44:16
825. Juan Villalobos (7056) 04:44:17
826. Jeffrey Candido (7057) 04:44:18
827. Bud Birch (7073) 04:44:33
828. Peter Demieri (7097) 04:44:53
829. Dion Hatch (7113) 04:45:02
830. George Huang (7124) 04:45:08
831. Emanuel Sanchez (7150) 04:45:35
832. Victor Leyva (7165) 04:45:41
833. Charles Bolanos (7177) 04:45:49
834. Jose Varela (7181) 04:45:53
835. Leovardo Villanueva (7197) 04:46:06
836. Roberto Madrid (7200) 04:46:08
837. Jason Kartalian (7248) 04:46:40
838. David Berman (7258) 04:46:46
839. Dennis Lapid (7260) 04:46:47
840. Renard Paras (7267) 04:46:54
841. Ronald Santoro (7272) 04:46:56
842. Elan Segura (7283) 04:47:01
843. Charles King (7292) 04:47:09
844. Jesus Limon (7307) 04:47:19
845. John Ogata (7309) 04:47:22
846. Robert Calixto (7333) 04:47:35
847. Steve Loop (7343) 04:47:42
848. Juan Cardenas (7347) 04:47:45
849. Dylan Wakasa (7352) 04:47:50
850. Kevin Murphy (7358) 04:47:56
851. Ernesto Ramos (7362) 04:47:59
852. Gregory Monteilh (7383) 04:48:12
853. Nick Vestal (7388) 04:48:14
854. Patrick O'Malley (7391) 04:48:16
855. Scott Carichner (7405) 04:48:25
856. Mark Davis (7422) 04:48:38
857. Joaquin Havens (7434) 04:48:47
858. Rich Robin (7443) 04:40:51
859. Scott Abramson (7444) 04:48:52
860. Jb Kalani (7445) 04:48:53
861. James Flynn (7448) 04:48:55
862. Tony Oshiro (7468) 04:49:07
863. David Navarro (7469) 04:49:08
864. Bud Wurth (7472) 04:49:09
865. Jahangir Mehrkhodavandi (7487) 04:49:20
866. Mitchell Hamerman (7505) 04:49:27
867. John Miranda (7512) 04:49:30
868. Kevin Rautenstrauch (7514) 04:49:31
869. Douglas Barker (7526) 04:49:38
870. David Greathouse (7529) 04:49:41
871. Margarito Lopez (7554) 04:50:00
872. John Torgerson (7581) 04:50:21
873. Dan Colvin (7590) 04:50:32
874. Jose Gutierrez (7602) 04:50:41
875. Kevin Davey (7616) 04:50:49
876. John Kim (7617) 04:50:49
877. Kyle Deshay (7629) 04:50:58
878. Mark Jen (7631) 04:50:59
879. Juan Parra (7632) 04:50:59
880. Don Hughes II (7661) 04:51:31
881. Garry Wang (7687) 04:51:44
882. Michael Jimenez (7704) 04:52:00
883. Jose Moline (7714) 04:52:07
884. Fabio Minervini (7718) 04:52:11
885. Todd Shanholtzer (7741) 04:52:30
886. Joey Ramirez (7769) 04:52:52
887. Robert Gerald (7779) 04:52:58
888. Carlos Hernandez (7791) 04:53:08
889. Joe Newell (7796) 04:53:14
890. William Howard (7797) 04:53:14
891. Pete Contreras (7799) 04:53:16
892. Jason Anderson (7815) 04:53:26
893. Gary Jimenez (7856) 04:53:52
894. Rey Arguello (7865) 04:53:57
895. Mario Perez (7874) 04:54:04
896. Steve Sheffield (7917) 04:54:29
897. Michael Johanson (7927) 04:54:33
898. Romo Sangoluisa (7937) 04:54:36
899. Joseph Meehan (7959) 04:54:47
900. Jon Umeda (7969) 04:54:51
901. Apolonio Santos (7973) 04:54:56
902. Flavio Vargas (7983) 04:55:09
903. David Reynaldo (7990) 04:55:13
904. Arturo Gonaalez (7999) 04:55:22
905. Nestor Michelena (8056) 04:56:08
906. William Gode-Von Aesch (8076) 04:56:21
907. Maximino Garcia Gutierrez (8084) 04:56:30
908. Joseph Fessenden (8106) 04:56:44
909. Brian Selem (8116) 04:56:48
910. Eric Guefew (8134) 04:57:07
911. Troy West (8157) 04:57:24
912. Michael Moore (8164) 04:57:27
913. Gary Bogdasarian (8200) 04:57:55
914. David Gracia (8211) 04:58:00
915. Jeffrey Nicholson (8217) 04:58:03
916. Steven Slaughter (8227) 04:58:08
917. Aram Yeghiazarian (8237) 04:58:15
918. Chris Conte (8266) 04:58:31
919. Hector Aguilar (8269) 04:58:33
920. Germand Jesus Diaz Marcos (8270) 04:58:34
921. Derwin Tate (8291) 04:58:50
922. Derrick Carbon (8292) 04:58:50
923. Juan Naranjo (8299) 04:58:53
924. Jose Guerrero (8326) 04:59:08
925. Shawn Bjorklund (8338) 04:59:16
926. Jose Arteaga (8341) 04:59:17
927. Jose Mejia (8342) 04:59:19
928. David Denunzio (8352) 04:59:29
929. Yuji Tanaka (8378) 04:59:41
930. Diego Alferez (8381) 04:59:45
931. Koji Chikatani (8389) 04:59:49
932. John Rizzi (8391) 04:59:52
933. Ignacio Delahoya (8401) 05:00:05
934. Keith Gissel (8403) 05:00:07
935. Daniel Ponce (8412) 05:00:16
936. Orlando Canton Jr (8415) 05:00:20
937. Pedro Ramos (8419) 05:00:22
938. Herbert Carranza (8439) 05:00:48
939. Dan Hernandez (8445) 05:00:53
940. Tien Nguyen (8492) 05:01:27
941. Henry Ouyang (8503) 05:01:33
942. Fernando Fernandez (8505) 05:01:34
943. Carlos Tobar (8507) 05:01:34
944. Samuel Francis (8521) 05:01:43
945. Stewart Jesse (8527) 05:01:47
946. John Chominsky (8534) 05:01:51
947. David Cox (8543) 05:02:01
948. Takashi Ota (8547) 05:02:04
949. Adrian Feben (8559) 05:02:12
950. Roberto Mendez (8571) 05:02:22
951. Bill Lansford (8574) 05:02:24
952. David Gracia (8577) 05:02:25
953. Juan Rivera (8578) 05:02:25
954. James Jolicoeur (8593) 05:02:47
955. Rolando Miranda (8610) 05:03:07
956. Luis Hernandez Jr (8613) 05:03:08
957. Benito Mejia (8618) 05:03:11
958. Brad Gordon (8622) 05:03:14
959. Bill Wilson (8626) 05:03:16
960. Bartholomew Zimmermann (8631) 05:03:22
961. Clemente Banuelos (8647) 05:03:38
962. Octavio Aldana (8663) 05:03:53
963. Magin Calderon (8669) 05:03:57
964. Jonathan Sopher (8682) 05:04:06
965. Clement Tabe (8685) 05:04:09
966. Rod Palomino (8694) 05:04:17
967. Scott McAlister (8708) 05:04:24
968. John McKinney (8711) 05:04:28
969. Dan Dieffenbach (8713) 05:04:29
970. Mario Lara (8733) 05:04:49
971. Andrew Duran (8736) 05:04:52
972. Fernando Miranda (8741) 05:05:00
973. Jose Roberto Mora Montero (8748) 05:05:12
974. Rick Martinez (8760) 05:05:23
975. Carl Williams (8765) 05:05:28
976. Robert Keating (8796) 05:05:57
977. David Wiley (8855) 05:06:59
978. Damian Mendoza (8863) 05:07:09
979. Chee Quan Lim (8869) 05:07:11
980. Daniel Shay (8874) 05:07:14
981. Jluis Villalobos (8880) 05:07:30
982. Moises Estrada (8887) 05:07:35
983. Jose Reyna (8893) 05:07:41
984. Laurent Buffi (8903) 05:07:49
985. Abez Gomez (8904) 05:07:55
986. Bernard Magat (8912) 05:07:57
987. Andres Razo (8917) 05:08:01
988. Sergio Nava (8923) 05:08:07
989. Uriel Ocampo (8936) 05:08:21
990. Les Butler (8937) 05:08:22
991. Joseph Marquez (8951) 05:08:33
992. Larry Krieger (8955) 05:08:36
993. Tomoyoshi Hirakawa (8979) 05:08:48
994. Marciel Salgado (8982) 05:08:53
995. Thomas Delgado (8989) 05:09:02
996. David Weiner (8996) 05:09:06
997. Vicente Escalante (9016) 05:09:20
998. Rick Quintero (9022) 05:09:24
999. Eric Montag (9036) 05:09:41
1000. Irving Flores (9041) 05:09:44
1001. Dale Hoth (9050) 05:09:49
1002. Ed Kho (9071) 05:10:02
1003. Angel Chavez (9074) 05:10:05
1004. Ed Rios (9076) 05:10:08
1005. Aung Maung (9078) 05:10:10
1006. Albert Flores (9089) 05:10:15
1007. Howard Stern (9099) 05:10:19
1008. Kenneth Donovan (9100) 05:10:19
1009. Luis Vasquez (9103) 05:10:21
1010. Sabas Gonzalez (9109) 05:10:23
1011. Victor Clescerl (9112) 05:10:25
1012. Angelica Sandoval (9116) 05:10:26
1013. Adam Krajchir (9125) 05:10:31
1014. Kenneth Harris (9126) 05:10:38
1015. Yoshiki Fuyama (9131) 05:10:43
1016. Daniel Covarrubias (9162) 05:11:19
1017. Thomas Messner (9185) 05:11:38
1018. Jose Mena (9194) 05:11:44
1019. Keith Abbott (9229) 05:12:21
1020. Alexander Aguirre (9230) 05:12:22
1021. Roger Ruaboro (9232) 05:12:23
1022. Danny Tate (9241) 05:12:31
1023. Steven Scott (9263) 05:12:53
1024. Alexx Guevara (9268) 05:12:56
1025. Carlos Ponce (9272) 05:13:03
1026. David Rockwer (9276) 05:13:07
1027. Andy Bishop (9312) 05:13:31
1028. Alexander Faulkner (9335) 05:13:43
1029. Thomas Vargas (9341) 05:13:48
1030. Edward Garcia (9355) 05:13:56
1031. Francisco Morales (9357) 05:13:59
1032. Scott Hammond (9359) 05:14:02
1033. Vernon Boros (9360) 05:14:07
1034. Kevin Webb (9372) 05:14:09
1035. Stacey Evans (9379) 05:14:19
1036. Kary Golden (9414) 05:14:58
1037. Jon Talberg (9425) 05:15:14
1038. Jim Morris (9435) 05:15:23
1039. Rudy Velasquez (9446) 05:15:37
1040. Robert Sullivan (9451) 05:15:47
1041. Jorge Guzman (9460) 05:15:56
1042. Michael Lawrence (9479) 05:16:15
1043. Aarre Laakso (9482) 05:16:17
1044. Jimmy Morin (9485) 05:16:18
1045. Tim Mc Lellan (9488) 05:16:19
1046. Okamoto Noboru (9499) 05:16:31
1047. Benjamin Limo (9502) 05:16:33
1048. Scott Bell (9535) 05:17:01
1049. Fernando Aguilar (9542) 05:17:04
1050. Steven Johnson (9555) 05:17:12
1051. Mario Dirnberger (9558) 05:17:14
1052. Troy Huckle (9560) 05:17:17
1053. Art Gonzalez (9569) 05:17:24
1054. Rusty Oshita (9570) 05:17:24
1055. Robert Cosner (9571) 05:17:25
1056. Manuel Garcia (9579) 05:17:32
1057. Gerry Kwan (9582) 05:17:33
1058. John Cornett (9585) 05:17:37
1059. Wyatt Johnson III (9611) 05:18:08
1060. Edmundo Murrugarra (9618) 05:18:16
1061. Hector Zeballos Jr (9621) 05:18:19
1062. Jess Juarez (9635) 05:18:30
1063. David Neville (9637) 05:18:32
1064. Anthony Parada (9666) 05:18:57
1065. Victor Luna (9671) 05:19:01
1066. Casey Clyce (9678) 05:19:05
1067. Fred Cedro (9692) 05:19:15
1068. Lucky Gold (9703) 05:19:26
1069. Don Pad (9714) 05:19:44
1070. Paul Arceri (9725) 05:20:00
1071. Mike Gin (9728) 05:20:05
1072. Antonio Bugarin (9730) 05:20:07
1073. Andrew Morrison (9739) 05:20:14
1074. Steven White (9747) 05:20:22
1075. Maurice Vanegas (9752) 05:20:29
1076. Vincent Mecca (9775) 05:20:42
1077. Jaisen Brown (9781) 05:20:48
1078. Shuji Tokumaru (9785) 05:20:50
1079. Katsuhide Arakaki (9789) 05:20:51
1080. Aaron McIlvain (9796) 05:20:58
1081. Dennis Hoth (9800) 05:21:02
1082. Phil Gutierrez (9802) 05:21:05
1083. Sergio Bonilla (9805) 05:21:07
1084. Hugo Reyes (9808) 05:21:11
1085. James Marbas (9824) 05:21:28
1086. Saul Avellaneda (9831) 05:21:37
1087. Christopher Harris (9839) 05:21:40
1088. Norberto Chavez (9840) 05:21:41
1089. Deyow Reid (9852) 05:21:48
1090. Darren Kavinoky (9880) 05:22:11
1091. George Bradshaw (9888) 05:22:17
1092. Peter Rankin (9896) 05:22:26
1093. Gerardo Rubio (9925) 05:22:57
1094. Anthony Zuniga (9931) 05:23:11
1095. Antonio Licea (9964) 05:23:42
1096. Steve Economos (9970) 05:23:47
1097. Clark Yogi (9983) 05:24:03
1098. Robert Padilla (10028) 05:24:54
1099. Richard Arreola (10038) 05:25:02
1100. Rogelio Hernandez (10048) 05:25:16
1101. Raaymond Fierro (10050) 05:25:25
1102. Michael Jester (10058) 05:25:33
1103. Jae Kim (10059) 05:25:34
1104. Daniel Massey (10062) 05:25:36
1105. Jaime Smith (10065) 05:25:38
1106. Douglas Zee (10078) 05:25:46
1107. Saburo Hora (10098) 05:26:05
1108. James McLain (10101) 05:26:07
1109. Javier Murillo (10109) 05:26:13
1110. Mike Doan (10125) 05:26:34
1111. Michael Ferrara (10128) 05:26:36
1112. Manuel Rivera (10137) 05:26:48
1113. Tomita Hiromichi (10141) 05:26:52
1114. Frank Zaragoza (10144) 05:26:54
1115. David Rivera (10163) 05:27:14
1116. Milthon Galindo (10170) 05:27:21
1117. Wilson Luo (10180) 05:27:27
1118. Anthony Engeron III (10100) 05:27:33
1119. David Pesko Jr (10194) 05:27:37
1120. Rod Trujillo (10208) 05:27:49
1121. Todd Hebert (10224) 05:28:04
1122. Noe Cordero (10234) 05:28:10
1123. David Lim (10237) 05:28:12
1124. Walter Sawczuk Gulino (10251) 05:28:38
1125. Todd McGowan (10267) 05:28:49
1126. Shawn Davis (10271) 05:28:50
1127. Rogelio Rocha (10289) 05:29:02
1128. Jimnel De Pano (10299) 05:29:13
1129. Chris Fernandez (10300) 05:29:14
1130. Takahiro Jimbo (10301) 05:29:14
1131. Oswaldo Gonzalez (10316) 05:29:20
1132. David Blen (10336) 05:29:51
1133. Fernando Rivera (10350) 05:30:00
1134. Jonathan Fiske (10372) 05:30:24
1135. Cris Stevens (10376) 05:30:27
1136. Marisa Lopez (10380) 05:30:31
1137. Aram Kenyon (10390) 05:30:37
1138. Hugo Nuno (10415) 05:31:06
1139. Andy Temesvary (10472) 05:31:50
1140. Gary Fernandez (10545) 05:33:04
1141. David Gomez (10557) 05:33:24
1142. Milan Jurovich (10559) 05:33:25
1143. Jaime Naranjo (10560) 05:33:25
1144. Kevin Deutsch (10598) 05:33:50
1145. John Mooers (10608) 05:33:55
1146. Jose Luis Lopez (10624) 05:34:07
1147. Vincent Cabral (10640) 05:34:27
1148. Sal Diosdado (10658) 05:34:42
1149. Melvin Santos (10679) 05:35:01
1150. Yen Seng Chee (10687) 05:35:09
1151. Aurelio Molina (10690) 05:35:10
1152. Akihiko Hirano (10728) 05:35:48
1153. Benjamin Gayatin (10729) 05:35:49
1154. Tharon Daniels (10737) 05:35:55
1155. Ricky Harris (10758) 05:36:19
1156. Robby Stenzel (10791) 05:36:54
1157. Carlos Perez (10805) 05:37:09
1158. John Chan (10822) 05:37:28
1159. Samuel Sato (10823) 05:37:29
1160. Daniel Olmeda (10862) 05:38:13
1161. Robert Furr (10884) 05:38:50
1162. Jose Useche (10898) 05:39:01
1163. Stephen Bollinger (10900) 05:39:10
1164. Mark Salcido (10907) 05:39:18
1165. Ernest Trejo (10909) 05:39:19
1166. Isao Uruma (10914) 05:39:25
1167. Kenten Wang (10923) 05:39:45
1168. Juan Carlos Ramirex (10927) 05:39:48
1169. James Hereth (10934) 05:39:55
1170. Gerardo Ferraris (10943) 05:40:10
1171. Takuya Inoue (10968) 05:40:41
1172. Paul Gibson (10978) 05:41:03
1173. Carlos Caceres Samayoa (10988) 05:41:14
1174. Haim Azerad (10992) 05:41:17
1175. Rob Parsons (10995) 05:41:22
1176. Toshiyuki Ishige (10999) 05:41:28
1177. Gonzalo Vincent (11004) 05:41:33
1178. Thom Hinde (11013) 05:41:42
1179. Kenneth Scudder (11021) 05:41:49
1180. Kyu Rhee (11030) 05:41:59
1181. Garabet Sakatvan (11033) 05:42:02
1182. Timothy Bingaman (11057) 05:42:20
1183. Jose Hernandez (11110) 05:43:10
1184. Ernie Ramirez (11120) 05:43:25
1185. Walter Garciacano (11154) 05:44:01
1186. David Orozco Santos (11155) 05:44:03
1187. Luis Martinez (11179) 05:44:16
1188. Scott Ostlund (11225) 05:44:50
1189. Duo Pham (11252) 05:45:19
1190. Aaron Rosenberg (11253) 05:45:21
1191. Dave Young (11267) 05:45:30
1192. Diego Robles (11298) 05:46:14
1193. Rich Howard (11315) 05:46:37
1194. Seth Streeter (11320) 05:46:40
1195. Thomas Carrillo (11321) 05:46:40
1196. M Jawad Pashmi (11346) 05:47:16
1197. Miguel Godinez (11350) 05:47:21
1198. Sikun Lan (11351) 05:47:22
1199. Rudy Martinez (11356) 05:47:27
1200. Guuillermo Perez (11373) 05:48:02
1201. Leo Ramirez (11386) 05:48:28
1202. Joel Henson (11388) 05:48:34
1203. Minas Khodagolian (11407) 05:49:02
1204. Phu Au (11411) 05:49:07
1205. Craig Smith (11418) 05:49:15
1206. Leopoldo Casco (11439) 05:49:34
1207. Yoshinori Takeichi (11443) 05:50:00
1208. Richard Tetreault (11459) 05:50:40
1209. Nobuhiro Maeda (11476) 05:50:05
1210. Robert Scothorn (11508) 05:50:32
1211. Premnath Maharaj (11511) 05:50:35
1212. Eric Putzi (11524) 05:50:47
1213. David Hall (11547) 05:51:17
1214. Ruben Verdin (11582) 05:52:11
1215. Stephan Sandoval (11583) 05:52:11
1216. Arthur Vasenius (11596) 05:52:20
1217. Mark Rodriguez (11615) 05:52:53
1218. Michael Donahue (11628) 05:53:00
1219. Jason Schneider (11643) 05:53:15
1220. Ferdie Pulido (11653) 05:53:22
1221. Leonard Martinez (11669) 05:53:40
1222. Jaime Marmol (11681) 05:53:52
1223. Ramon Carreon Jr (11701) 05:54:20
1224. Eric Andre Weiss (11703) 05:54:28
1225. Antonio Saragosa (11734) 05:55:07
1226. Timothy Darr (11754) 05:55:26
1227. Ralph Maestas (11759) 05:55:36
1228. John Jaramillo (11763) 05:55:41
1229. Christopher Beltran (11776) 05:55:59
1230. Jay Jackson (11783) 05:56:06
1231. Steve Del Rio (11784) 05:56:11
1232. Jorge Espinoza (11808) 05:56:47
1233. Michael Smith (11821) 05:57:04
1234. Alfonso Espinosa (11826) 05:57:13
1235. Edward Casillas (11828) 05:57:16
1236. Daniel Granados (11836) 05:57:25
1237. Matthew Nagle (11882) 05:58:26
1238. Hugo Lopez (11883) 05:58:26
1239. Omkar Bhide (11910) 05:58:54
1240. Baltazar Fedalizo (11926) 05:59:23
1241. Alex Saucedo (11927) 05:59:24
1242. Joel Ross (11941) 05:59:44
1243. Nicholas Rodriguez (11953) 05:59:56
1244. Cal Wong (11956) 05:59:57
1245. Elmer Tancinco (11975) 06:00:27
1246. Michael Muchin (12002) 06:01:16
1247. Bobby Oh (12005) 06:01:21
1248. Christopher Brun (12014) 06:01:42
1249. Alexander Hess (12025) 06:01:54
1250. Oscar Garcia (12065) 06:02:55
1251. Armando Murillo (12073) 06:03:11
1252. Ramon Aguilar (12078) 06:03:27
1253. John Hagberg (12119) 06:04:38
1254. Ronald Cherry (12133) 06:04:47
1255. Yasuo Aoki (12138) 06:04:56
1256. Darrin Prescott (12145) 06:05:04
1257. Luis Cabrera (12152) 06:05:15
1258. Rudy Alpers (12196) 06:06:23
1259. Miguel Garcia (12208) 06:06:54
1260. Ronnie Watkins (12253) 06:08:14
1261. Michael McGlynn (12263) 06:08:21
1262. John Shulda (12268) 06:08:27
1263. Keith Lee (12278) 06:08:47
1264. Akihiro Koakutsu (12299) 06:09:03
1265. Sandro Albert (12324) 06:09:45
1266. Daniel Bain (12325) 06:09:46
1267. Anthony Arreola (12340) 06:10:02
1268. Kimihiro Inagawa (12353) 06:10:32
1269. Rommy Williams (12362) 06:10:58
1270. Daisaku Takaoka (12386) 06:11:23
1271. Todd Holmes (12394) 06:11:36
1272. Kevin Baker (12395) 06:11:37
1273. Paul Grazulis (12404) 06:11:52
1274. Ventura Nandi (12405) 06:11:53
1275. Romulo Gutierrez (12412) 06:12:04
1276. Marcel Terlouw (12413) 06:12:07
1277. Dante Hall (12424) 06:12:24
1278. Jonathan Kelley (12425) 06:12:25
1279. Albert Melena (12436) 06:12:45
1280. Pat Ignacio (12437) 06:12:45
1281. Thomas Clauer (12444) 06:13:01
1282. Scott Gordon (12452) 06:13:10
1283. Blair Browne (12462) 06:13:30
1284. Sidney McCoy (12469) 06:13:37
1285. Roland Ortiz (12472) 06:13:41
1286. Jack Gale (12495) 06:14:15
1287. Rolando Ochoa (12514) 06:14:49
1288. Michael Proud (12515) 06:14:50
1289. Patrick Williams (12526) 06:15:10
1290. Jessie Ramirez (12529) 06:15:14
1291. Don Pitts (12533) 06:15:17
1292. Walter Sample (12540) 06:15:26
1293. Fernando Hernandez (12552) 06:15:39
1294. Richard Moreno Jr (12553) 06:15:40
1295. Ahmad Cook (12556) 06:15:46
1296. David Kim (12557) 06:15:48
1297. Salvadore Velasquez (12558) 06:15:52
1298. Steven Yam (12587) 06:16:41
1299. Bradley Harriss (12609) 06:17:01
1300. Leo Torres (12628) 06:17:46
1301. Motomichi Shibata (12649) 06:18:29
1302. Belbert White (12679) 06:19:34
1303. Eric Fehrmann (12689) 06:19:46
1304. David Duenas (12713) 06:20:30
1305. George Goldstone (12748) 06:21:36
1306. Anthony Cardillo (12766) 06:21:56
1307. Jeff Harris (12789) 06:22:32
1308. James Lopez (12826) 06:23:37
1309. Thomas Lapidario (12827) 06:23:38
1310. Paul Elizalde (12836) 06:23:47
1311. Dan Stikkers (12838) 06:23:48
1312. John Valdez (12856) 06:24:13
1313. Mario Alvarez (12860) 06:24:17
1314. Stewart Ginsberg (12866) 06:24:22
1315. Choku Tanaka (12867) 06:24:35
1316. Hideaki Daigo (12912) 06:26:12
1317. Ernesto Perdomo (12924) 06:26:29
1318. Jose Salan (12926) 06:26:32
1319. James Feenstra (12980) 06:28:03
1320. Shawn Reeder (12988) 06:28:16
1321. Daniel Manalac (12999) 06:28:35
1322. David Salan (13030) 06:29:31
1323. Paul Caseley (13085) 06:31:21
1324. Dan Augustyn (13100) 06:31:49
1325. Charles Warner (13115) 06:32:20
1326. Enrique Cisneros (13126) 06:32:34
1327. Sandeep Hardas (13149) 06:32:53
1328. Ken Pak (13168) 06:33:24
1329. Jack Woods (13192) 06:34:13
1330. Saul Castro (13199) 06:34:29
1331. Patrick Hayashibara (13211) 06:34:45
1332. Rochon Starks (13212) 06:34:46
1333. Leon Jost (13304) 06:37:33
1334. Oscar Garza (13330) 06:38:38
1335. Keun Bae Cho (13348) 06:39:09
1336. James Cassel (13375) 06:40:08
1337. Kunihiko Nagasaki (13388) 06:40:42
1338. Darryl Adams (13435) 06:42:14
1339. David Marietti (13441) 06:42:23
1340. Albert Lara (13450) 06:42:44
1341. Guy Toubes (13478) 06:43:58
1342. D Medland (13488) 06:44:19
1343. Wasi Khursheed (13513) 06:45:18
1344. Kenneth Goss (13544) 06:46:21
1345. David Chavez (13568) 06:47:03
1346. Satoru Sugitani (13575) 06:47:30
1347. Mario Acosta (13591) 06:47:54
1348. Jan Rischawy (13601) 06:48:20
1349. Robert Madewell (13638) 06:49:39
1350. Richard Melillo (13697) 06:50:56
1351. William May (13707) 06:51:27
1352. Gabriel Munoz (13727) 06:52:05
1353. Manuel Villafuerte (13732) 06:52:19
1354. Jose Arevalo (13796) 06:55:12
1355. Takashi Ohno (13834) 06:56:21
1356. Angel Munibe (13866) 06:57:17
1357. David Nations (13871) 06:57:23
1358. Kelly Mayo (13877) 06:57:39
1359. Michael Cantila (13879) 06:57:44
1360. Johannes Hutauruk (13880) 06:57:47
1361. Fernando Sanchez (13900) 06:58:21
1362. Robin Sanders (13982) 07:00:53
1363. Glenn Bland (14006) 07:01:35
1364. Bryan Blankenship (14014) 07:01:56
1365. Froilan Barajas (14147) 07:09:09
1366. Karnel Chevry (14212) 07:13:15
1367. Noel Alumit (14280) 07:16:39
1368. Kojima Kazauki (14353) 07:21:34
1369. James Ngo (14383) 07:23:06
1370. David Boyle (14385) 07:23:40
1371. Tetsuya Shiota (14404) 07:25:04
1372. Greg Blodgett (14435) 07:27:51
1373. Chris Mason (14450) 07:29:38
1374. Larry Lui (14474) 07:31:09
1375. Gale Matteson (14477) 07:31:28
1376. Kevin Martis (14519) 07:35:36
1377. Mitsukuni Yoshida (14530) 07:36:11
1378. Spyridon Zapantis (14538) 07:36:40
1379. Daniel Dailo (14572) 07:38:59
1380. Mauricio Sanchez (14605) 07:41:32
1381. Mitsu Iwata (14670) 07:47:55
1382. Gil Goren (14714) 07:51:59
1383. Newton Darrell (14744) 07:54:27
1384. Jose Gomez (14759) 07:55:34
1385. Jacque Torres (14779) 07:57:00
1386. Ming Hsueh (14812) 08:01:33
1387. Ochavio Saracco (14814) 08:01:36
1388. Daniel Hernandez (14821) 08:02:08
1389. Dean Drummond (14924) 08:19:24
1390. Tony Navaro (14947) 08:21:41
1391. Michael Dingman (15011) 08:34:15
1392. David Jones (15012) 08:34:19
1393. Peter Chin (15060) 08:49:27
1394. Lawrence Dunn (15150) 09:53:11

WOMEN 25 TO 29

1. Nadia Prasad (21) 02:29:48
2. Aniela Nikiel (32) 02:34:51
3. Stephanie Wessell (263) 03:02:09
4. Isabel Tum Canto (354) 03:06:37
5. Carla Figueroa (414) 03:08:52
6. Rosalinda Garcia (453) 03:10:00
7. Marni Ryti (513) 03:12:38
8. Renee Covi (721) 03:18:53
9. Jennifer Austin (725) 03:19:02
10. Anne Spillane (792) 03:20:43
11. Robin Barrett (825) 03:21:41
12. Lora Logsdon (827) 03:21:41
13. Wendy Slay (887) 03:22:58
14. Katie Ferguson (922) 03:23:45
15. Sally Rogers (960) 03:24:32
16. Britta Jensen (1034) 03:26:16
17. Maria Gallardo (1109) 03:27:46
18. Esther Schindeler (1120) 03:28:00
19. Linda Favuzza (1151) 03:28:30
20. Anne Charron (1158) 03:28:45
21. Missy Mandery (1203) 03:29:33
22. Susan Nishiyama (1235) 03:30:07
23. Anne Mudie (1246) 03:30:20
24. Merce Sastre (1258) 03:30:32
25. Shelly Stevenson (1298) 03:31:23
26. Mirza Gallardo (1303) 03:31:26

27. Christine Carter (1305) 03:31:27
28. Alexandra Carey (1317) 03:31:38
29. Kelly Vandyke (1337) 03:31:57
30. Clare MacAulay (1347) 03:32:11
31. Galia Pistotnik (1372) 03:32:44
32. Debbie Jester (1385) 03:32:54
33. Erika O'Brien (1520) 03:35:45
34. Melissa Sutton (1542) 03:36:08
35. Rochelle Zolna (1586) 03:36:58
36. Bettina Ernst (1662) 03:38:16
37. Heather Holmes (1663) 03:38:17
38. Jacqueline Walsh (1674) 03:38:35
39. Theresa Coyle (1677) 03:38:40
40. Gina Lavender (1681) 03:38:42
41. Karen Parker (1698) 03:38:55
42. Julie Myatt (1714) 03:39:10
43. Tracey Leonard (1719) 03:39:18
44. Meredith Hollen (1737) 03:39:40
45. Britt Jung (1739) 03:39:41
46. Ann Pailes (1795) 03:40:35
47. Linda Kiely (1806) 03:40:45
48. Nai Kang (1837) 03:41:09
49. Joan MacAulay (1891) 03:41:51
50. Nidia Vargas (1922) 03:42:20
51. Nancy Scharf (1981) 03:43:32
52. Maria Filonczuk (1990) 03:43:43
53. Linda Rosenthal (2204) 03:46:50
54. Jacqueline Allen (2253) 03:47:29
55. Lisa Taylor (2276) 03:47:48
56. Miroslava Chavez (2291) 03:48:00
57. Molly Friel (2302) 03:48:08
58. Sheryl Fant (2314) 03:48:16
59. Peggy Caron (2320) 03:48:22
60. Kristin Webb (2325) 03:48:29
61. Denise Hendrickson (2336) 03:48:35
62. Yasuhara Kayo (2353) 03:48:47
63. Christina Ayrassian (2385) 03:49:14
64. Rocio Santana (2396) 03:49:20
65. Laura Maestre (2475) 03:50:26
66. Catherine Shields (2486) 03:50:36
67. Jackie Sepulveda (2493) 03:50:39
68. Diana Gray (2501) 03:50:47
69. Nancy Huffman (2515) 03:50:59
70. Angela Garrott (2550) 03:51:29
71. Lori Wagner (2563) 03:51:37
72. Ann Marie Reardon (2582) 03:51:52
73. Juli Hester (2624) 03:52:29
74. Kate Huston (2648) 03:52:47
75. Annette Johansson (2658) 03:52:52
76. Adrienne Hill (2685) 03:53:16
77. Amy Vander Kley (2772) 03:54:23
78. Rebecca Legg (2806) 03:54:40
79. Susie Sirak (2823) 03:54:49
80. Lori Heinselman-Craig (2841) 03:55:05
81. Jill Weckerly (2911) 03:55:54
82. Lisa Bollinger (2929) 03:56:04
83. Michelle Kusiek (2957) 03:56:21
84. Lauren Cepeda (3040) 03:57:09
85. Linda Bernier (3053) 03:57:18
86. Lea Kelley (3101) 03:57:51
87. Kirsten Moll (3165) 03:58:36
88. Tina Wilmott (3182) 03:58:50
89. Elizabeth German (3192) 03:58:55
90. Diva Cooper (3226) 03:59:20
91. Sina Werdi (3254) 03:59:40
92. Tara Ryan (3271) 03:59:48
93. Caroline Wallace (3315) 04:00:13
94. Becky Engel (3342) 04:00:31
95. Sandra Schmidt (3351) 04:00:40
96. Junko Wakaki (3378) 04:01:01
97. Amy Joseph (3407) 04:01:20
98. Theresa Uhrig (3412) 04:01:26
99. Valerie Crain (3434) 04:01:42
100. Annie Peterson (3457) 04:02:03
101. Nga Dang (3460) 04:02:06
102. Elsa Rojas (3502) 04:02:42
103. Megan Morey (3522) 04:03:01
104. Rochelle Lara (3537) 04:03:14
105. Julie Given (3578) 04:03:54
106. Dena Herman (3612) 04:04:18
107. Kim Hackbarth (3636) 04:04:32
108. Martha Van Orsdel-Atnip (3700) 04:05:11
109. Janet De La Vega (3727) 04:05:37
110. Maureen Showalter (3759) 04:06:04
111. Heather Bova (3767) 04:06:09
112. Stacy Schloetel (3795) 04:06:33
113. Kyra Chenoweth (3797) 04:06:34
114. Erin King (3808) 04:06:42
115. Christie Quigley (3864) 04:07:19
116. Stephanie Poole (3869) 04:07:23
117. May Ton (3873) 04:07:28
118. Lisa Laughlin (3885) 04:07:35
119. Catherine Riley (3904) 04:07:47
120. Linda Giunta (3966) 04:08:39
121. Anna Frolova (3970) 04:08:43
122. Amy Sheals (3982) 04:08:51
123. Pamela Hawley (3984) 04:08:52
124. Chrissy Choy (4007) 04:09:12
125. Vivian Ricaurte (4029) 04:09:26
126. Celeste Kirk (4064) 04:09:58
127. Whitney Karm (4066) 04:09:59
128. Julie Rupert (4072) 04:10:04
129. Krista Huntley (4089) 04:10:15
130. Lilia Gonzales (4109) 04:10:33
131. Michelle Lazorek (4118) 04:10:40
132. Christine Costley (4121) 04:10:43
133. Laura Brittain (4136) 04:10:52
134. Robyn Benincasa (4142) 04:10:55
135. Judy Komatsu (4209) 04:11:47
136. Cinnamon Mullin (4217) 04:11:55
137. Linda Pinkham (4231) 04:12:03
138. Lila Scarlato (4235) 04:12:05
139. Christina Jansson (4250) 04:12:18
140. Yvette Allori (4261) 04:12:26
141. Mojca Cater (4262) 04:12:27
142. Lani Matzelle (4264) 04:12:27
143. Brenda Katz (4271) 04:12:34
144. Diana Sparks (4285) 04:12:44
145. Sonja Lyubomirsky (4338) 04:13:23
146. Gina Polanco (4360) 04:13:47
147. Diane Demario (4391) 04:14:05
148. Katty Romero (4401) 04:14:13
149. Judy Williams (4445) 04:14:38
150. Julie Slayton (4452) 04:14:41
151. Stephanie Richardson (4457) 04:14:44
152. Lorena Hernandez (4475) 04:14:51
153. Lori Perino (4524) 04:15:30
154. Patricia Donmoyer (4525) 04:15:30
155. Jacqueline Navarrete (4557) 04:15:46
156. Kelly Mac Kenzie (4665) 04:16:59
157. Nicole Knight (4703) 04:17:30
158. Moya Samarzich (4719) 04:17:45
159. Lynair Groom (4729) 04:17:52
160. Kelly Hunziker (4742) 04:17:58
161. Molly Fitzgerald (4815) 04:18:44
162. Jamie Nichols (4819) 04:18:47
163. Michelle Fiore (4833) 04:18:54
164. Patti Cutler (4853) 04:19:03
165. Joann Frescas (4874) 04:19:16
166. Robin Roy (4877) 04:19:18
167. Jane Foster (4923) 04:19:50
168. Sue Shay (4944) 04:20:06
169. Mary Haliburton (4946) 04:20:07
170. Kristin Dantagnan (4953) 04:20:15
171. Carla Heilman (4964) 04:20:25
172. Mary Minicucci (4969) 04:20:30
173. Susan Petrie (5010) 04:21:14
174. Carolyn Silas (5074) 04:21:51
175. Carmen Herrera (5094) 04:22:00
176. Kelly Hopkins (5145) 04:22:36
177. Michelle Lee (5146) 04:22:36
178. Lorrie Chantry (5176) 04:22:56
179. Cheryl Essery (5254) 04:23:54
180. Carol Kutch (5256) 04:23:58
181. Jill Witter (5293) 04:24:28
182. Lynn Murphy (5379) 04:25:23
183. Amy Sheffield (5403) 04:25:37
184. Harriet Wagner (5443) 04:25:59
185. Elizabeth Bayard (5455) 04:26:04
186. Michelle Magazino (5456) 04:26:04
187. Shannon Wiens (5488) 04:26:31
188. Kristi Grall (5519) 04:26:57
189. Kathy Reeves (5579) 04:27:34
190. Stacey Hoffman (5585) 04:27:39
191. Melanie Reed (5591) 04:27:41
192. Kathy Zeiler (5657) 04:28:23
193. Katherine Aquavia (5661) 04:28:27
194. June Scherer (5666) 04:28:31
195. Amber Hanlin (5685) 04:28:41
196. Stephanie Saba (5686) 04:28:43
197. Amy McQuistion (5704) 04:28:57
198. Felicia Bastman (5729) 04:29:09
199. Gloria Ambriz (5740) 04:29:17
200. Ramora Adibi (5759) 04:29:30
201. Leslie Clayton (5763) 04:29:33
202. Kristen Brunson (5767) 04:29:35
203. Gretchen Fermenn (5781) 04:29:44
204. Barbra Orozco (5811) 04:30:09
205. Jill Morison (5859) 04:30:36
206. Karen Neal (5880) 04:30:44
207. Michele Herrera (5897) 04:30:58
208. Helene Higbee (5917) 04:31:10
209. Janyee Cox (5930) 04:31:22
210. Christina Riley (5941) 04:31:27
211. Kathleen Ryan (6050) 04:32:51
212. Leigh Huhn (6066) 04:33:02
213. Tami Carlson (6099) 04:33:23
214. Karen Zamos (6113) 04:33:33
215. Doreen Parker (6136) 04:33:48
216. Dawn Hecker (6140) 04:33:51
217. Lois Swanson (6146) 04:33:56
218. Nancy Sas (6153) 04:34:05
219. Cynthia Ruksenas (6155) 04:34:05
220. Amy Murray (6163) 04:34:09
221. Jocelyn Manullang (6176) 04:34:16
222. Elizabeth Stefanov (6195) 04:34:29
223. Mary Louth (6204) 04:34:36
224. Christina Booth (6213) 04:34:42
225. Melissa Fishman (6261) 04:35:14
226. Lisa Yen (6374) 04:36:22
227. Sarah Vallejo (6389) 04:36:27
228. Felicia Fraijo (6402) 04:36:34
229. Michelle Barker (6477) 04:37:31
230. Shelli Lohman (6483) 04:37:34
231. Adrienne Flores (6507) 04:37:46
232. Linda Lewis (6525) 04:37:59
233. Leah Pisano (6560) 04:38:17
234. Suzie Lipton-Moll (6572) 04:38:27
235. Treat Costi (6577) 04:38:31
236. Heidi Booker (6611) 04:38:50
237. January Ornellas (6645) 04:39:11
238. Tracy Johnson (6751) 04:40:36
239. Lily Yu (6753) 04:40:37
240. Kirsten Seiffert (6755) 04:40:40
241. Nicole Sanchez (6757) 04:40:41
242. Rachel Winograd-Bollenbecker (6774) 04:40:59
243. Candie Croyts (6775) 04:41:00
244. Lori Abosch (6776) 04:41:01
245. Margaret Erker (6856) 04:41:57
246. Patricia Velat (6870) 04:42:07
247. Jacqueline Mann (6894) 04:42:30
248. Sheila Stewart (6912) 04:42:46
249. Beverly Graves (6919) 04:42:49
250. Sherry Falcon (6928) 04:42:55
251. Laura Conte (6951) 04:43:08
252. Debbie Ball (6963) 04:43:18
253. Daphne Feng (7001) 04:43:38
254. Barb Cantu (7004) 04:43:39
255. Jacqueline Cohn (7092) 04:44:51
256. Lisa Garcia (7111) 04:45:01
257. Desiree Lesicko (7162) 04:45:40
258. Mary McNerney (7186) 04:45:57
259. Gretchen Krueger (7187) 04:45:58
260. Theresa Gerig (7224) 04:46:25
261. Carey Doust (7262) 04:46:50
262. Rachel Judson (7323) 04:47:28
263. Kimberly Howe (7338) 04:47:38
264. Beverly Bull (7346) 04:47:45
265. Maria Schupler (7370) 04:48:04
266. Marietta Hurwitz (7411) 04:48:29
267. Mary Kemp (7462) 04:49:04
268. Sonya Rohrs (7516) 04:49:32
269. Besh Barcega (7521) 04:49:34
270. Kelly Helstrom (7532) 04:49:46
271. Tania Foster (7536) 04:49:49
272. Salya Mohamedy (7543) 04:49:52
273. Dara Morgan (7552) 04:49:59
274. Susie Scheuble (7583) 04:50:24
275. Ana Rodriguez (7598) 04:50:38
276. Amy Buehrle (7599) 04:50:38
277. Sheryl Hamlin (7601) 04:50:40
278. Catherine Spong (7606) 04:50:43
279. Diana Levitt (7608) 04:50:44
280. Julie Lee (7657) 04:51:24
281. Carol McNerney (7679) 04:51:40
282. Melinda Rolfs (7684) 04:51:41
283. Wissal Swar (7735) 04:52:27
284. Francine Lemaster (7750) 04:52:39
285. Kimberly Walmer (7782) 04:53:00
286. Yumi Sueishi (7844) 04:53:43
287. Amy Downing (7846) 04:53:44
288. Shay Brown (7847) 04:53:44
289. Mary Eum-Irwin (7869) 04:54:00
290. Lily Salgado (7883) 04:54:09
291. Sharon Elm (7886) 04:54:10
292. Rachel Scheinman (7912) 04:54:26
293. Alcira Vasquez (7920) 04:54:31
294. Laurie Walter-Hadley (7945) 04:54:40
295. Mirna Cornejo (7957) 04:54:46
296. Lisa Salazar (7974) 04:54:58
297. Tamara Wright (7977) 04:55:05
298. Michelle Clancy (7994) 04:55:19
299. Gracie Saavedra (8005) 04:55:28
300. Isabelle Dejean (8027) 04:55:47
301. Gabrielle Kymbourne (8035) 04:55:50
302. Aimee Wyatt (8074) 04:56:20
303. Esther Delgado (8138) 04:57:12
304. Tammy Krueger (8215) 04:58:02
305. Mary Barnes (8295) 04:58:52
306. Holly Howard (8336) 04:59:15
307. Miyuki Ito (8343) 04:59:19
308. Sherry Thomas (8392) 04:59:53
309. Annette Thompson (8417) 05:00:21
310. Alicia Fernandez (8433) 05:00:40
311. Lizabeth Binnell (8438) 05:00:45
312. Hillary Crowe (8463) 05:01:05
313. Becky Youman (8469) 05:01:09
314. Kami Celano (8488) 05:01:23
315. Jocelyn Lumaban (8494) 05:01:27
316. Leann Standish (8511) 05:01:39
317. Maria Gutierrez (8514) 05:01:41
318. Temperance Evans (8540) 05:01:59
319. Mei Lin Kwan-Gett (8542) 05:01:59
320. Janet Leonard (8567) 05:02:19
321. Eva Rojes (8584) 05:02:38
322. Jeneva Galletti (8608) 05:03:06
323. Lisa Rosales (8621) 05:03:13
324. Natsuko Kawanaka (8670) 05:03:58
325. Yvonne Clemente (8692) 05:04:13
326. Siran Khatcherian (8754) 05:05:17
327. Kazuki Uema (8773) 05:05:34
328. Mary Hagerty (8798) 05:05:58
329. Iveta Zakovic (8818) 05:06:22
330. Leticia Posada (8857) 05:07:01
331. Connie Falfan (8901) 05:07:48
332. Kristen Delgado (8987) 05:09:00
333. Chie Nakamura (8992) 05:09:05
334. Laura Ramirez (9002) 05:09:08
335. Denise Morones (9058) 05:09:55
336. Cora Coomber (9061) 05:09:57
337. Miranda May (9075) 05:10:07
338. Laura Carlos (9092) 05:10:16
339. Allyson Lund (9140) 05:10:52
340. Valerie Prescott (9172) 05:11:29
341. Brenda White (9181) 05:11:35
342. Michelle Gyetvai (9209) 05:11:55
343. Lorena Hernandez (9226) 05:12:18
344. Sandra Mendoza (9233) 05:12:23
345. Gabriele Heidfeld (9239) 05:12:29
346. Jacquelyn Dylla (9240) 05:12:30
347. Lisa Saginian (9249) 05:12:38
348. Ingrid Barauskas (9265) 05:12:55
349. Tracy Steinberg (9281) 05:13:11
350. Sara Maradiaga (9361) 05:14:04
351. Deborah Siegel (9384) 05:14:24
352. Kelly Dunlap (9390) 05:14:28
353. Lori Lakin (9405) 05:14:48
354. Sandra Solorzano (9417) 05:15:08
355. Yvonne Torres (9418) 05:15:08
356. Joye Swan (9501) 05:16:32
357. Stephenie Rottenberg (9529) 05:16:57
358. Janel Coats (9534) 05:17:01
359. Connie Rodriguez (9540) 05:17:03
360. Jo Mowery (9545) 05:17:06
361. Kathryn Arceneaux (9550) 05:17:10
362. Heather Campbell (9562) 05:17:19
363. Maria Bautista (9563) 05:17:20
364. Renee Bontempo (9564) 05:17:21
365. Lisa Gamble (9578) 05:17:30
366. Linda Koga (9613) 05:18:09
367. Tina Lo (9643) 05:18:36
368. Stacey Wishner (9647) 05:18:38
369. Cheryl Bates (9649) 05:18:39
370. Joanne Silva (9653) 05:18:41
371. Ratina Burris (9679) 05:19:06
372. Lonna Donin (9685) 05:19:11
373. Erika Swenson (9705) 05:19:30
374. Kimberly Gode (9767) 05:20:38
375. Irma Garcia (9771) 05:20:40
376. Susan Smederovac-Wilcox (9772) 05:20:41
377. Emi Suzuki (9790) 05:20:52
378. Tristan Baker (9816) 05:21:17
379. Patricia Murillo (9818) 05:21:19
380. Kim Fodran (9837) 05:21:39
381. Janet Donaldson (9890) 05:22:18
382. Gabriela Luebeck (9892) 05:22:19
383. Melissa Keller (9934) 05:23:14
384. Heidi Armer (9944) 05:23:24
385. Yoomi Shou (9979) 05:23:57
386. Linda Baker-Samson (10036) 05:25:01
387. Julie Smith (10064) 05:25:37
388. Nicole Larkey (10069) 05:25:40
389. Jeanette Morimoto (10117) 05:26:23
390. Monica Haun (10149) 05:27:02
391. Kimberly Knowlton (10160) 05:27:11
392. Sheila Heacock (10162) 05:27:14
393. Julie Linden (10179) 05:27:27
394. Carmen Mares (10184) 05:27:29
395. Darcey Eldridge (10203) 05:27:47
396. Veronica Kistner (10215) 05:27:58
397. Danielle Perrin (10220) 05:28:00
398. Debra Carlisle (10254) 05:28:39
399. Stacey Powell (10268) 05:28:49
400. Ann Stasik (10281) 05:28:57
401. Sara Ancla Kelly (10284) 05:29:00
402. Angela Bates (10310) 05:29:16
403. Delia Escobar (10333) 05:29:48
404. Julie Drake (10340) 05:29:54
405. Emiko Kawahigashi (10367) 05:30:19
406. Kelly Thornton (10403) 05:30:48
407. Donna Kenney (10428) 05:31:19
408. Karen Keppler (10432) 05:31:24
409. Laura Birn (10434) 05:31:25
410. Holly Porter (10448) 05:31:33
411. Mary Torres (10450) 05:31:35
412. Lisa Dunne (10454) 05:31:38
413. Carolina Munoz (10480) 05:31:57
414. Harumi Kumagai (10481) 05:31:58
415. Rhonda Kruse (10491) 05:32:09
416. Francine Reed (10500) 05:32:18
417. Tricia McCarthy (10504) 05:32:23
418. Denise Wood (10543) 05:33:03
419. Suzanne Quance (10628) 05:34:08
420. Delia Cruz (10635) 05:34:24
421. Angela Dobson (10664) 05:34:44
422. Michale Samuels (10681) 05:35:02
423. Jeanne Anne Carriere (10688) 05:35:10
424. Kimberly Williams (10697) 05:35:21
425. Debra Balbo (10714) 05:35:29
426. Jill Carstensen (10715) 05:35:29
427. Sandra Kreuzberger (10721) 05:35:39
428. Stacy Parker (10759) 05:36:19
429. Casey Moss (10761) 05:36:25
430. Krista Forzley (10767) 05:36:34
431. Elisabeth Camaur (10778) 05:36:40
432. Teresa Perez (10816) 05:37:22
433. Stephanie Richards (10817) 05:37:23
434. Christine Sauter (10828) 05:37:34
435. Monica Sauter (10829) 05:37:34
436. Elizabeth Alfonso (10851) 05:38:03
437. Belinda Heck (10878) 05:38:47
438. Jodie Colebrooke (10891) 05:38:54
439. Christina Faapouli (10892) 05:38:55
440. Isabelle Turpin (10936) 05:39:58
441. Maryellen Mason (10956) 05:40:23
442. Martha Avila (10967) 05:40:38
443. Teresa Phung (10985) 05:41:08
444. Henrietta Vincent (11003) 05:41:32
445. Michelle Tamkin (11011) 05:41:41
446. Maybelle Gazmen (11041) 05:42:10
447. Lisa Conway (11053) 05:42:19
448. Berta Blen (11061) 05:42:24
449. Adriana Garcia (11078) 05:42:40
450. Anita Arvizu (11105) 05:43:04
451. Diane McEvers (11106) 05:43:04
452. Nancy Santos (11121) 05:43:26
453. Kelly Vogel (11153) 05:44:00
454. Robin Jacobs (11167) 05:44:12
455. Lisa Palma (11174) 05:44:15
456. Stacy Myer (11203) 05:44:32
457. Helene Zernik (11210) 05:44:36
458. Lisa Escoto (11229) 05:44:53
459. Kathy Tamashiro (11265) 05:45:36
460. Ayumi Kumagai (11266) 05:45:36
461. Maryum Ali (11339) 05:47:00
462. Tracy Gamble (11341) 05:47:06
463. Rosa Lopez (11355) 05:47:25
464. Karen Fish (11383) 05:48:25
465. Victoria Briggs (11404) 05:49:01
466. Karen Hubbard (11410) 05:49:06
467. Heidi Crowley (11415) 05:49:09
468. Leslee Neail (11424) 05:49:20
469. Martha Cerda (11447) 05:49:43
470. Veronica Hermansson (11458) 05:49:48
471. Julie Lui (11478) 05:50:09
472. Dawn Palmer (11480) 05:50:12
473. Patricia Foster (11519) 05:50:39
474. Joann Mc Donald (11604) 05:52:32
475. Frances Macguire (11606) 05:52:37
476. Ellen Morrison (11611) 05:52:46
477. Sheila Gee (11614) 05:52:51
478. Sonia Ladage (11658) 05:53:26
479. Sharon Gee (11659) 05:53:27
480. Amal Khalil (11674) 05:53:45
481. Anne Scibelli (11705) 05:54:29
482. Nancy Farrell (11732) 05:55:05
483. Lisa McCown (11736) 05:55:09
484. Elizabeth Flores (11738) 05:55:10
485. Lani Meltzer (11750) 05:55:22
486. Maria Cantv (11752) 05:55:24
487. Susie Rios (11762) 05:55:41
488. Rebecca Carlson (11788) 05:56:14
489. Celia Rodriguez (11817) 05:56:58
490. Annette Hricko (11818) 05:56:59
491. Robin Havekost (11837) 05:57:25
492. Veronique Despret (11873) 05:58:23
493. Jacqueline Martinez (11939) 05:59:40
494. Julie Anderson (11960) 06:00:03
495. Christine Ramirez (11961) 06:00:03
496. Nora Cendejas (11964) 06:00:13
497. Rita Mendoza (12000) 06:01:08
498. Rebecca Bahner (12042) 06:02:20
499. Laura McGuckin (12058) 06:02:45
500. Tevy Campos (12082) 06:03:32
501. Rosa Ronquillo (12083) 06:03:36
502. Laura Bresson (12093) 06:03:47
503. Susie Morales (12105) 06:04:18
504. Dawn Weekes-Glenn (12223) 06:07:19
505. Gloria Martinez (12225) 06:07:20
506. Cecilia Becerra (12240) 06:07:51
507. Gina Carasik-Lintz (12256) 06:08:18
508. Patty Hight (12287) 06:08:53
509. Sarah Covington-French (12289) 06:08:54
510. Jen Roper (12307) 06:09:13
511. Melissa Tabbaraia (12336) 06:09:59
512. Yolanda Avella (12339) 06:10:01
513. Carolyn Parry (12358) 06:10:47
514. Suzanne Robinson (12375) 06:11:07
515. Evelyn McCorckle (12389) 06:11:26
516. Krista Van Cott (12400) 06:11:48
517. Kimberly Katsaros (12429) 06:12:39
518. Pamela Markert (12458) 06:13:24
519. Carlotta Walters (12459) 06:13:24
520. Mia Inderbitzin (12484) 06:14:00
521. Lynda Wurtemberg (12486) 06:14:01
522. Tanya Shay (12559) 06:15:53
523. Joyce Wagner (12564) 06:15:57
524. Jennifer Lee (12586) 06:16:40
525. Isabel Peruyera (12616) 06:17:18
526. Yuriko Hirakawa (12641) 06:18:17
527. Elizabeth Kaplan (12646) 06:18:26
528. Theresa Jimenez (12660) 06:18:55
529. Ampy Go (12753) 06:21:43
530. Dolores Weatherbie (12776) 06:22:05
531. Jennifer Andrus (12821) 06:23:26
532. Susan Pilmer (12834) 06:23:46
533. Maria Cardenas (12847) 06:23:59
534. Maria Bautista (12859) 06:24:17
535. Sonia Hodgers (12878) 06:25:05
536. Angelita Noche (12907) 06:25:59
537. Tabea Keesee (12928) 06:26:34
538. Yolanda Byrd (12935) 06:26:40
539. Sharon Stewart (12976) 06:27:59
540. Mona Diedrich (12989) 06:28:20
541. Cynthia Hubbard (12994) 06:28:32
542. Kim Forster (13014) 06:29:04
543. Christen Alford (13028) 06:29:29
544. Ellen Harris (13053) 06:30:28
545. Christine Chavez (13056) 06:30:38
546. Karen Guzman (13078) 06:31:16
547. Joycelynne Palmer (13099) 06:31:48
548. Katya Fuentes (13106) 06:32:00
549. Rohannah Hutauruk (13112) 06:32:10
550. Mary Ann Cordova (13118) 06:32:25
551. Maricruz Beltran (13128) 06:32:36
552. Paula Jacob (13151) 06:32:58
553. Cheen Lin (13157) 06:33:01
554. Kimberly Wood (13186) 06:34:06
555. Elena Batarse (13218) 06:34:50
556. Kristi Ross (13219) 06:34:51
557. Tracy Adamson (13238) 06:35:27
558. Victoria Knafelc (13266) 06:36:15
559. Estela Morales (13269) 06:36:19
560. Rachel Messenger (13290) 06:37:06
561. Jamie Jun (13293) 06:37:08
562. Kellie Sandas (13314) 06:38:03
563. Dariel Miller (13318) 06:38:16
564. Paula Gudinho (13333) 06:38:39
565. Tomoko Yamamoto (13366) 06:39:42
566. Annaliza Apostol (13386) 06:40:39
567. Lita Papero (13389) 06:40:44
568. Christine Fax (13413) 06:41:27
569. Laura Koehler (13430) 06:42:08
570. Teresa Rivas-Adams (13434) 06:42:14
571. Angie Golden (13447) 06:42:37
572. Donna Waites (13465) 06:43:21
573. Lisa Thomas (13466) 06:43:25
574. Kathy Desautels (13467) 06:43:26
575. Michele Yoshikawa (13476) 06:43:53
576. Jayne Simon (13480) 06:44:06
577. Michele Szklarski (13492) 06:44:32
578. Nancy Wang (13503) 06:44:56
579. Rebecca Thorp (13519) 06:45:36
580. Lee Ann Schulz (13528) 06:45:56
581. Vilma Curiel (13567) 06:47:01
582. Carol Juneau (13570) 06:47:09
583. Noelle Pechar (13622) 06:49:00
584. Nada Saweeres (13623) 06:49:00
585. Sandra Auzene (13626) 06:49:04
586. Susan Wooton (13627) 06:49:08
587. Karen Wieden (13632) 06:49:22
588. Yvonne Gracia (13730) 06:52:11
589. Yamamoto Aiko (13744) 06:52:47
590. Judith Tobar (13747) 06:53:13
591. Angie Storm (13802) 06:55:16
592. Christina Magdaleno (13803) 06:55:16
593. Karen Bell (13832) 06:56:18
594. Amanda Lynch (13845) 06:56:45
595. Daphne Laraneta-Davis (13850) 06:56:51
596. Marlene Ramos (13856) 06:57:01
597. Kelly Mulry (13881) 06:57:49
598. Holly Whatley (13891) 06:58:03
599. Lulie Lara (13957) 07:00:10
600. Sandra Gallegos (13978) 07:00:46
601. Patricia Espinoza (14015) 07:01:57
602. Tammy Genna (14036) 07:02:38
603. Lori Juarez-Jacobus (14057) 07:03:42
604. Florrie Laurence (14063) 07:04:03
605. Sarah Dyer (14064) 07:04:03
606. Sarah Soriano (14109) 07:06:46
607. Gina Davis (14114) 07:07:02
608. Joyce Fung (14121) 07:07:26
609. Ann Magovern (14231) 07:14:39
610. Susan Tierney (14255) 07:15:37
611. Deborah Garcia (14274) 07:16:20
612. Kelly Aponno (14276) 07:16:33
613. Veronika Vandermarliere (14282) 07:16:43
614. Wendy Wang (14284) 07:16:53
615. Malena Neal (14333) 07:20:21
616. Frances Meier (14421) 07:26:50
617. Sandra Gray (14429) 07:27:27
618. Alyce Caro (14432) 07:27:38
619. Mary Ong (14445) 07:29:02
620. Doreen Daniels (14484) 07:32:52
621. Angela Arakaki (14518) 07:35:33
622. Julie Rosenfeld (14539) 07:36:41
623. Brooke Okelly (14574) 07:39:08
624. Sheri Emily (14578) 07:39:32
625. Stacy Neal (14585) 07:40:01
626. Sandra Kinsey (14615) 07:42:40
627. Angela Sherer (14616) 07:42:41
628. Sharon Smason (14641) 07:45:08
629. Cynthia San Miguel (14642) 07:45:16
630. Sylvia Ramos (14646) 07:45:46
631. Claudia Villalobos (14654) 07:46:23
632. Kandis Knox (14680) 07:48:50
633. Andrea Whittaker (14699) 07:50:53
634. Richerc Laporte (14776) 07:52:39
635. Rosa Ramos (14753) 07:55:04
636. Bernice Jackson (14780) 07:57:23
637. Jessica Van Leeuwen (14788) 07:59:25
638. Maria Russell (14799) 08:00:43
639. Virginia Correa (14816) 08:01:36
640. Angela Johns (14827) 08:02:32
641. Kelley Gillespie (14838) 08:03:29
642. Eva Vargus (14857) 08:08:17
643. Oubol Sou (14891) 08:14:50
644. Theresa Gutierrez (14950) 08:21:55
645. Denise Hyndman (14975) 08:28:19
646. Stephanie Chaisson (14978) 08:28:34
647. Damaris Munoz (15027) 08:36:32
648. Eleonore Koury (15029) 08:36:47
649. Shaunn MacDonald (15033) 08:37:02
650. Karen Frobish (15041) 08:44:35
651. Karen Schwarz (15050) 08:46:16
652. Anetta Stark (15056) 08:48:34
653. Canny Dang (15063) 08:51:07
654. Hanna Tran (15119) 09:25:34
655. Lauren Shaftow (15144) 09:45:58
656. Maria Duarte-Nguyen (15150) 09:50:42

1. Arturo Barrios (4) 02:14:47
2. Mark Plaatjes (5) 02:15:41
3. Jose Santana (6) 02:18:01
4. Danny Ree (7) 02:21:06
5. Daniel Martinez (8) 02:21:35
6. Gerard Kolbeck (14) 02:26:22
7. Richard Rono (15) 02:26:51
8. Jesus Vazquez (16) 02:27:03
9. Lazaro Vasquez Sosa (17) 02:28:14
10. Kevin Broady (20) 02:29:40
11. Gilberto Chicol (24) 02:30:41
12. Jose Luis Arriaga (27) 02:32:29
13. Dean Rinde (28) 02:32:31
14. Paulo Scherer (31) 02:34:46
15. Jaime Ortiz (44) 02:35:29
16. Steve Brunt (44) 02:38:18
17. Marco Antonio Aguilar Rodas (50) 02:41:05
18. Hans Gouwens (53) 02:41:19
19. Cesar Vasquez (54) 02:41:31
20. Rudy Son Gonzalez (55) 02:41:37
21. Ecequizl Hernandez (58) 02:42:36
22. Henry Fuentes Yerry (62) 02:43:15
23. Ramon Ramos (63) 02:43:26
24. Salvador Araujo (65) 02:43:40
25. Raymond Knerr (66) 02:43:44
26. Sergio Correa (67) 02:43:57
27. John Jericiau (68) 02:44:22
28. David Roberson (69) 02:44:40
29. Matt Barnard (74) 02:45:25
30. Jesus Garcia (76) 02:45:40
31. Michael Beichele (80) 02:46:32
32. Andrew Tuovinen (82) 02:47:02
33. Por Jamtelii (83) 02:47:28
34. Bill Carlson (85) 02:47:40
35. Chad Pratt (89) 02:48:22
36. Daniel Goldstein (91) 02:48:38
37. Hansjoerg Mueller (96) 02:50:02
38. Thom Yojacek (99) 02:50:14
39. Kenneth Cottrell (105) 02:50:55
40. Felipe Sanchez (118) 02:52:24
41. Carlos Navarro (119) 02:52:24
42. Pedro Avalos (122) 02:52:33
43. Felipe Avila (126) 02:52:51
44. Trinidid Campos (127) 02:52:44
45. Alberto Queredo (130) 02:52:56
46. Ricardo Carranza (134) 02:53:23
47. Charly Perje (137) 02:53:33
48. Book Cosenza (138) 02:53:38
49. Kenny Belisle (140) 02:53:47
50. Lance Davis (148) 02:54:12
51. Steve McMillin (149) 02:54:21
52. Genaro Diaz (152) 02:54:43
53. Al Bates (153) 02:54:55
54. Ruben Rodriguez (158) 02:55:07
55. Ralph Schadwill (166) 02:55:58
56. Leonel Estrada (175) 02:56:47
57. Luis Escobar (176) 02:56:49
58. Jose Gallardo (181) 02:57:04
59. Roberto Leonardo (188) 02:57:27
60. Rod Ieeple (191) 02:57:38
61. Roberto Camargo (190) 02:57:56
62. Terrell Worley (203) 02:58:34
63. Daniel Arteaga (208) 02:58:34
64. Kurt Bonnette (217) 02:59:19
65. Trini Robles (219) 02:59:27
66. Giacomo Ciabattini (220) 02:59:30
67. William Ayyad (222) 02:59:33
68. Arnulfo Zuniga (228) 02:59:54
69. Mark Schwochert (239) 03:00:35
70. Sean Smith (242) 03:00:39
71. David Filler (245) 03:00:52
72. Greg Bohdan (246) 03:00:54
73. Kirby Lee (247) 03:00:54
74. Tony Amos (248) 03:00:56
75. John Wallin (260) 03:01:58
76. Rod Barragan (266) 03:02:15
77. Bob Sola (273) 03:02:34
78. Nelson McCabe Jr (276) 03:02:47
79. Scott Stein (277) 03:02:48
80. Michael Hilbelink (285) 03:03:04
81. Paul Garcia (286) 03:03:07
82. Brian Scott (287) 03:03:09
83. Gerardo Vera (291) 03:03:15
84. Dana Taylor (293) 03:03:22
85. Ramon Estrada (294) 03:03:31
86. Scott Marrett (296) 03:03:33
87. Bill Whitman (298) 03:03:39
88. Jhonny Camacho (299) 03:03:39
89. Israel Ramirez (304) 03:04:00

90. Chris Morgeson (305) 03:04:03
91. Miguel Rodriguez (311) 03:04:23
92. Arthur Van Veen (315) 03:04:38
93. Oscar Campos (319) 03:04:57
94. Efren Guerra Palacios (334) 03:05:38
95. Tim Thomas (337) 03:05:49
96. Scott Fukunaga (338) 03:05:53
97. Zeferino Sanchez Gomez (345) 03:06:14
98. Marc Gallardo (351) 03:06:26
99. Mark Ezzo (358) 03:06:48
100. Hilaria Matinez (361) 03:07:02
101. Mike McAlister (365) 03:07:14
102. Frank Lopez (366) 03:07:15
103. David Flores (367) 03:07:17
104. Stig Nybo (370) 03:07:22
105. Mark Metcalfe (371) 03:07:23
106. Javier Regalado (372) 03:07:24
107. Bruce Walrath (374) 03:07:30
108. Nick Gomez (375) 03:07:33
109. Marc Bran (388) 03:07:57
110. Russell Shuirman (390) 03:08:01
111. Roberto Leonardo (392) 03:08:07
112. Terrance Jakubowski (404) 03:08:22
113. John Luddy II (410) 03:08:41
114. Angel Ibarra (430) 03:09:27
115. Melvin Alvarez (431) 03:09:27
116. Daryl Bibicoff (432) 03:09:29
117. Rick Hernandez (434) 03:09:34
118. Marco Arteaga (439) 03:09:41
119. Trip Switzer (446) 03:09:51
120. Gregory Schafer (450) 03:09:56
121. Jose Cuenca (456) 03:10:07
122. Angel Soto (465) 03:10:37
123. Jeffrey Nowacki (467) 03:10:40
124. Geoff Mutton (471) 03:10:52
125. Leonardo Almanza (479) 03:11:09
126. Jason Nixon (480) 03:11:10
127. Oscar Favela (487) 03:11:25
128. Herb Blodgett (491) 03:11:39
129. Mark Bell (505) 03:12:18
130. Drew Scoular (515) 03:12:41
131. Niels-Ole Pedersen (520) 03:12:48
132. Joseph Campbell (528) 03:13:07
133. Andreas Kiefer (557) 03:13:49
134. Martin Madrigal (563) 03:13:58
135. Henry Biggs (565) 03:14:06
136. James Marquez (567) 03:14:07
137. Daeon Butler (571) 03:14:14
138. Jeffrey Anderson (572) 03:14:16
139. Tatsushi Kanazawa (579) 03:14:27
140. Alfred Zinn (581) 03:14:29
141. Kenneth Sasaki (584) 03:14:39
142. Jose Espinoza (594) 03:14:51
143. Fred Garcia (603) 03:15:15
144. Mark Donaldson (615) 03:15:41
145. Eliseo Marquez (620) 03:15:57
146. Jorge Rodas (621) 03:16:01
147. Jimmy Vargas (624) 03:16:04
148. Charles Brown (637) 03:16:14
149. Jose Martinez Medina (639) 03:16:40
150. Jaime Mejia (642) 03:16:45
151. Tripp Wood (644) 03:16:46
152. Shan Work (645) 03:16:47
153. Charles Decker (648) 03:16:49
154. Larry Schmidlin (650) 03:16:51
155. Eric Bonwitt (652) 03:16:53
156. Antonio Davila (654) 03:16:55
157. Luis Diaz (661) 03:17:08
158. Nelson Abac (666) 03:17:16
159. Kenneth Drazan (672) 03:17:22
160. Acacio Mendoza (688) 03:17:47
161. Tim Bell (691) 03:17:55
162. Raul Cervantes (699) 03:18:10
163. Jose Magana (701) 03:18:12
164. David Dean (702) 03:18:16
165. Ted Wada (704) 03:18:19
166. Jim Tabb (710) 03:18:32
167. Ernesto Figueroa (732) 03:19:15
168. Sal Romero (733) 03:19:15
169. Randy Morales (739) 03:19:23
170. Abel Cruz (740) 03:19:24
171. Stephen Katz (743) 03:19:26
172. Mark Ludvik (749) 03:19:36
173. Donald White (751) 03:19:39
174. Ezequiel Cortes (753) 03:19:45
175. Juan Martinez Jose (764) 03:20:02
176. Danilo Perez (775) 03:20:15
177. Chris Brown (785) 03:20:34
178. Amarildo Quiej (786) 03:20:34
179. Jaime Rios (788) 03:20:40
180. Brian Bass (791) 03:20:43

181. Santos Rodriguez (804) 03:21:16
182. Dennis Bowden Jr (811) 03:21:23
183. Michael Canlas (812) 03:21:24
184. Michael Skotzko (819) 03:21:30
185. Robert Barrett (822) 03:21:38
186. Kevin Ashcraft (824) 03:21:40
187. Bhupinder Mudhar (828) 03:21:41
188. Anthony Villalobos (831) 03:21:43
189. Rutilo Contreras (832) 03:21:44
190. Len Kinzel (835) 03:21:54
191. Jack Nosco (838) 03:22:00
192. Jerry Davis (840) 03:22:01
193. David Greene (845) 03:22:10
194. James Goodrich (846) 03:22:12
195. Jose Venegas (848) 03:22:13
196. Charles Wells (849) 03:22:13
197. Marco Lopez (859) 03:22:26
198. James Hebbaz (879) 03:22:46
199. Hank King (875) 03:22:43
200. Marty O'Malley (880) 03:22:47
201. Daniel Trujillo (883) 03:22:51
202. Gregory Sporleder (884) 03:22:54
203. Jamie Phillips (896) 03:23:11
204. Gino Brunello (897) 03:23:11
205. Dennis Schmitz (900) 03:23:18
206. Jesse Duarte (905) 03:23:24
207. Javier Burciaga (909) 03:23:28
208. Roger Maier (919) 03:23:43
209. Niall Kearney (925) 03:23:48
210. Angel Montoya (926) 03:23:49
211. Jerry Norton (928) 03:23:52
212. Dean Ashimine (930) 03:23:55
213. Jose Garcia (936) 03:24:01
214. Timo Pikkarainen (944) 03:24:16
215. Miguel Huerta Rangel (948) 03:24:20
216. Atsushi Shiozawa (953) 03:24:25
217. Thierry Broucqsault (955) 03:24:36
218. Barry Mendel (965) 03:24:36
219. Jesus Gracian (972) 03:24:43
220. Scott Franklin (978) 03:24:57
221. Jorge Peñado (979) 03:24:58
222. Javier Fragoso (980) 03:24:58
223. Greg Sykes (987) 03:25:10
224. Patrick Matthes (993) 03:25:17
225. Mark Rule (995) 03:25:22
226. T Monterroso (1001) 03:25:29
227. Christopher Clardy (1010) 03:25:40
228. Juan Perez (1013) 03:25:44
229. Jesus Garcia (1016) 03:25:54
230. Conrado Alba (1020) 03:26:00
231. Alex Vaquerano (1024) 03:26:05
232. Richard Graves (1029) 03:26:11
233. Damian Stone (1031) 03:26:12
234. Wesley Foote (1048) 03:26:39
235. Jose Iniguez (1057) 03:26:52
236. Ignacio Maciel (1065) 03:27:06
237. Steve Epstein (1071) 03:27:11
238. Armando Flores (1077) 03:27:13
239. Dominic Cuzzacrea (1078) 03:27:18
240. Jeremy Oury (1079) 03:27:20
241. Anthony Maycock (1082) 03:27:22
242. Jay Grobeson (1107) 03:27:42
243. Anselmo Foliojono (1115) 03:27:53
244. Sven De Vos (1124) 03:28:04
245. Caesar Cepeda (1133) 03:28:13
246. Julio Villacorta (1142) 03:28:21
247. John Alan (1144) 03:28:23
248. Karl Guder (1146) 03:28:25
249. Ralph Grippo (1150) 03:28:31
250. Todd Moore (1156) 03:28:42
251. Robert Roza (1162) 03:28:47
252. Alfredo Korzenik (1166) 03:28:51
253. James Jones (1169) 03:28:53
254. Greg Fujimoto (1171) 03:28:58
255. Ashraf Ghattas (1172) 03:28:59
256. Alfredo Ortiz (1181) 03:29:09
257. Gary Abraham (1183) 03:29:16
258. Michael Greenfield (1185) 03:29:16
259. Nate Brady (1189) 03:29:18
260. Sean Richardson (1191) 03:29:23
261. Tommy Ruskowski (1196) 03:29:23
262. Frank Palpallatoc (1213) 03:29:38
263. Jim Mc Laughlin (1215) 03:29:40
264. Steve Gooselaw (1222) 03:29:46
265. Miguel Morales (1232) 03:30:00
266. Ken Common (1238) 03:30:16
267. Steve Engel (1251) 03:30:24
268. Matthew Radeski (1265) 03:30:42
269. John Hendrix (1271) 03:30:54
270. Steve Oliveira (1272) 03:30:55
271. Carlos Perez (1278) 03:30:56

272. Nhien Chau (1281) 03:30:58
273. Braulio Martinez (1285) 03:31:02
274. Erwin Perez (1289) 03:31:11
275. John Caro (1308) 03:31:29
276. Ricardo Amador Leon (1311) 03:31:34
277. Reyes Rodriguez (1315) 03:31:37
278. Christopher Rubalcava (1322) 03:31:40
279. Charles Lymos (1327) 03:31:46
280. Paul Silka (1328) 03:31:48
281. Joseph Moran (1332) 03:31:51
282. Eugene Romero (1333) 03:31:53
283. Bert Blanchette (1335) 03:31:54
284. Craig Glick (1336) 03:31:55
285. Gary Koba (1339) 03:31:59
286. Ray Schroeter (1348) 03:32:13
287. Greg Amano (1349) 03:32:13
288. Jeff Howard (1351) 03:32:17
289. Craig Steiner (1355) 03:32:19
290. Scott Bell (1371) 03:32:43
291. Allan Saadus (1387) 03:32:59
292. Bear Arellano (1389) 03:33:01
293. Robert Wong (1392) 03:33:04
294. Paul Cantin (1400) 03:33:11
295. Bruce Hill (1403) 03:33:21
296. Randy Batastini (1414) 03:33:44
297. Luis Hernandez (1441) 03:34:12
298. Chad Hughes (1450) 03:34:32
299. Ried Ku (1451) 03:34:33
300. Oliver Dorigo (1455) 03:34:42
301. Michael Darnold (1459) 03:34:47
302. Phillip Palacios (1460) 03:34:48
303. Larry Hadcock (1467) 03:34:51
304. Ed Luce (1471) 03:34:53
305. Darrin Neutz (1486) 03:35:08
306. John Bertolli (1488) 03:35:10
307. Vincent Ortego (1505) 03:35:33
308. John Spykerman (1506) 03:35:33
309. Francisco Linares (1512) 03:35:37
310. Jose Felix (1517) 03:35:41
311. Charles Wilber (1610) 03:35:44
312. Robert Bryant (1524) 03:35:48
313. Vincent Arbet-Engels (1525) 03:35:48
314. Lawrence Medina (1528) 03:35:49
315. Mark Becker (1530) 03:35:52
316. Ricardo Menjivar (1532) 03:35:55
317. Mauricio Zena (1535) 03:35:56
318. Michael McColligan (1541) 03:36:07
319. Jaime Escobar (1549) 03:36:15
320. John Burke (1559) 03:36:30
321. Arturo Enriquez (1560) 03:36:30
322. Adedayo Akintobi (1566) 03:36:39
323. Alex Mattheyssen (1574) 03:36:45
324. Hector Menchaca (1578) 03:36:47
325. Daniel Vigil (1580) 03:36:54
326. Brian Corrigan (1599) 03:37:13
327. Matt Harley (1601) 03:37:14
328. David Brittain (1605) 03:37:16
329. Tiburcio Aguilar (1607) 03:37:18
330. Jurentino Martinez (1619) 03:37:31
331. Thomas Roth (1624) 03:37:43
332. Gerald Hier (1627) 03:37:46
333. Manuel Garcia (1637) 03:37:55
334. Randy Burdick (1646) 03:38:04
335. Paul Weir (1652) 03:38:10
336. Edward Purcell IV (1661) 03:38:16
337. Mike Partlow (1665) 03:38:18
338. Rusty Robertson (1667) 03:38:19
339. Raul Castilleja (1676) 03:38:37
340. Dave Kobrine (1680) 03:38:41
341. James Husbands (1686) 03:38:45
342. Joseph Frankhouse (1689) 03:38:46
343. Javier Verdin (1695) 03:38:53
344. Robert Schneider (1699) 03:38:56
345. Manuel Nunez (1703) 03:39:03
346. Vincent Hernandez (1704) 03:39:03
347. Noe Mejia (1705) 03:39:03
348. John Dunn (1716) 03:39:13
349. Richard Reasons (1726) 03:39:28
350. Michael Monnahan (1727) 03:39:28
351. Ed Ely (1733) 03:39:34
352. Vic Aguirre (1757) 03:40:01
353. James Bresch (1761) 03:40:05
354. Matt MacLeod (1768) 03:40:14
355. Alberto Villanueva (1779) 03:40:21
356. Jerry Johnson (1780) 03:40:22
357. Michael Wysong (1781) 03:40:22
358. Daniel Cravens Jr (1789) 03:40:28
359. James Hogg (1790) 03:40:30
360. Jose Juarez (1791) 03:40:30
361. Scott Morgan (1804) 03:40:43
362. Lorenzo Rodriguez (1807) 03:40:47

363. Nunuz Gustano (1817) 03:40:56
364. Thomas Cheney (1818) 03:40:56
365. Chris Haasz (1819) 03:40:56
366. Kyle Lapalm (1825) 03:41:03
367. Ruben Flores (1863) 03:41:29
368. Eddie Campos (1866) 03:41:31
369. Tom Lassally (1869) 03:41:36
370. Paul Burke (1872) 03:41:36
371. Nathan Applewhite (1873) 03:41:37
372. Charles Belty (1878) 03:41:42
373. Patrick Quinlan (1880) 03:41:43
374. Rob Kobrine (1881) 03:41:43
375. Steve Kobrine (1882) 03:41:44
376. Bruce Markgraf (1887) 03:41:46
377. Stephen Priess (1901) 03:41:58
378. Axel Schlemm (1904) 03:42:02
379. Juan Ruiz (1912) 03:42:14
380. Lucio Rodriguez (1921) 03:42:20
381. Michael McCarthy (1924) 03:42:26
382. Hector Santos (1925) 03:42:27
383. Mike Hamson (1934) 03:42:36
384. Steven Fitch (1935) 03:42:40
385. Greg Slevcove (1945) 03:42:58
386. Christopher Sogge (1946) 03:42:59
387. Pablo Salinas (1956) 03:43:05
388. Kevan Chung (1960) 03:43:11
389. Douglas Sharitz (1961) 03:43:12
390. Brian Findley (1964) 03:43:14
391. Tyler Tabor (1966) 03:43:15
392. Jose Fco Cordon Jara (1967) 03:43:15
393. Obdulio Melgarejo (1970) 03:43:19
394. Miguel Medina (1975) 03:43:28
395. Gary Dagan (1976) 03:43:29
396. Mario Padilha (1985) 03:43:34
397. Frank Wiley (1986) 03:43:35
398. Joseph Bollinger (1987) 03:43:37
399. Guillermo Andrade (1989) 03:43:41
400. Robert Gwizdala (2012) 03:44:02
401. Rich Doingr (2021) 03:44:08
402. Dean Smith (2022) 03:44:08
403. Stephen Noble (2030) 03:44:15
404. Edward Herrera (2039) 03:44:23
405. Scott Costi (2040) 03:44:23
406. Jose Carmen Navarro (2042) 03:44:24
407. Bruce Talbot (2049) 03:44:31
408. Carlos Lopez (2050) 03:44:32
409. Daniel Whitaker (2051) 03:44:33
410. Michael Mesko (2060) 03:44:38
411. Maximo Vizcardo (2061) 03:44:39
412. Patrick Beagle (2062) 03:44:39
413. Robert Lyznick (2063) 03:44:40
414. Alan Lee (2068) 03:44:43
415. James Schondel (2069) 03:44:44
416. Kenneth Ott (2081) 03:44:57
417. Jeff Anderson (2082) 03:44:57
418. Alan Beatty (2092) 03:45:07
419. Donald Simkovich (2118) 03:45:20
420. Alfonso Lopez (2118) 03:45:20
421. Steve Montantes (2122) 03:45:27
422. Larry Marni (2129) 03:45:37
423. Timothy Droko (2130) 03:45:37
424. Omar Valerio-Jimonez (2132) 03:45:39
425. Jeffrey Jones (2138) 03:45:45
426. Guy Hallnck (2140) 03:45:45
427. Thomas Queally (2145) 03:45:51
428. Raul Villalobos (2149) 03:45:52
429. Anthony Brown (2151) 03:45:54
430. Mark Graham (2167) 03:46:08
431. Manuel Pichardo (2169) 03:46:10
432. Bill Mengert (2171) 03:46:12
433. John Cooney (2176) 03:46:15
434. Edward Arenberg (2179) 03:46:20
435. Steven Burstein (2193) 03:46:35
436. Robert Ruiz (2207) 03:46:52
437. Dennis Tuma (2217) 03:47:00
438. Brian Dobbin (2221) 03:47:02
439. Ralm Jung (2227) 03:47:08
440. Rob Beck (2232) 03:47:13
441. Todd Nathanson (2234) 03:47:14
442. Eric Baker (2248) 03:47:27
443. Rogelio Lopez (2257) 03:47:31
444. Claude Hemphill (2269) 03:47:43
445. Danny Kalantarian (2270) 03:47:43
446. Jorge Rodriguez (2288) 03:47:59
447. Manuel Cano (2293) 03:48:01
448. Jim Lewis (2298) 03:48:06
449. Steve Jezina (2306) 03:48:12
450. Mike Barrett (2310) 03:48:13
451. Matt Kugler (2319) 03:48:16
452. Stuart Sheffer (2322) 03:48:23
453. Mike Norman (2323) 03:48:23

454. Mario Garcia (2332) 03:48:33
455. Patrick McDonagh (2333) 03:48:34
456. Neal Kleinman (2340) 03:48:36
457. Charles Love (2345) 03:48:38
458. Ernesto Garcia (2346) 03:48:39
459. Michael Kaminski (2357) 03:48:53
460. James McGrade (2359) 03:48:54
461. Samuel Contreras (2364) 03:48:59
462. Steve Diaz (2380) 03:49:08
463. D Jesus Estrada (2386) 03:49:18
464. Jim Krueger (2393) 03:49:19
465. Paul Dechant (2398) 03:49:22
466. Stephen Sanchez (2399) 03:49:22
467. Kazuhiro Ikeda (2402) 03:49:23
468. Jeff Wilhite (2406) 03:49:31
469. Stephen Elder (2414) 03:49:37
470. Jose Gutierrez (2426) 03:49:45
471. David Sobel (2428) 03:49:45
472. Tom White (2431) 03:49:47
473. Guadalupe Escobedo (2432) 03:49:47
474. Abel Torres (2438) 03:49:59
475. Jerry Quinn (2448) 03:50:04
476. Kendall Nix (2458) 03:50:13
477. Jose Hernandez-Rojas (2473) 03:50:26
478. Kenneth Mortensen (2465) 03:50:21
479. Chris Geras (2482) 03:50:31
480. John Parodi Jr (2495) 03:50:41
481. Fernando Saavedra (2497) 03:50:43
482. Gunnar Nelson (2502) 03:50:49
483. John Turrubiartes (2504) 03:50:50
484. Armando Salas (2505) 03:50:51
485. David Araujo (2507) 03:50:53
486. Michael Knauer (2507) 03:50:53
487. John Hatch (2510) 03:50:54
488. Joel Miles (2523) 03:51:06
489. Ruben Ramirez (2525) 03:51:07
490. Michael Antone (2547) 03:51:28
491. Guillermo Morales (2556) 03:51:33
492. Luis Villalobos (2562) 03:51:37
493. Demo Diaz-Ifante (2564) 03:51:38
494. Andrew Panzo (2569) 03:51:41
495. Sal Pena Jr (2576) 03:51:49
496. Matthew Soper (2596) 03:52:07
497. Grant Snyder (2599) 03:52:12
498. Mikhail Mashhadsari (2605) 03:52:16
499. Bayardo Carvajal (2612) 03:52:21
500. Rainer Kurz (2616) 03:52:23
501. Cesar Augusto Santos Olayo (2625) 03:52:30
502. Alvin Tolosa (2637) 03:52:42
503. Charlie Adams (2638) 03:52:43
504. Mauro Santos (2640) 03:52:43
505. David Martinez (2642) 03:52:45
506. Domingo Hernandez (2645) 03:52:45
507. Christopher Marsh (2656) 03:52:50
508. David Currie (2660) 03:52:57
509. David Glasgow (2663) 03:52:57
510. Robert Luter (2664) 03:52:57
511. David Severance (2667) 03:52:59
512. Darren Hoab (2672) 03:53:06
513. Sean Hughes (2676) 03:53:15
514. Chang Kim (2689) 03:53:17
515. John Ramirez (2690) 03:53:18
516. Bruce Mori (2691) 03:53:18
517. Rogelio Cabrera (2697) 03:53:23
518. Felix Zuniga (2699) 03:53:23
519. Steve Aird (2705) 03:53:28
520. Roehl Caragao (2708) 03:53:28
521. Jeffrey Carl (2711) 03:53:31
522. Douglas Edwards (2713) 03:53:35
523. Rosalio Martinez (2720) 03:53:40
524. Patrick McCullough (2737) 03:53:52
525. Patrick Neary (2742) 03:53:56
526. David Penny (2744) 03:54:01
527. Craig Caster (2749) 03:54:05
528. Franco Espinosa (2752) 03:54:14
529. Shai Herzog (2764) 03:54:14
530. John Reynolds (2767) 03:54:19
531. Kevin McClelland (2781) 03:54:25
532. Raymond Molina (2792) 03:54:30
533. George Turner (2804) 03:54:37
534. Tracy Hergert (2808) 03:54:41
535. Gary Downs (2811) 03:54:47
536. Roderick McBride (2822) 03:54:49
537. Shan Thomas (2834) 03:55:02
538. Brian Sheps (2836) 03:55:02
539. William Bachicha (2853) 03:55:15
540. Jeffrey Bast (2855) 03:55:15
541. Sal Murillo (2876) 03:55:28
542. Caifan Viderreal (2883) 03:55:31
543. Allen Krone (2884) 03:55:31
544. Robert Schulte (2888) 03:55:32

545. Noel Hernandez (2889) 03:55:32
546. Galo Abril (2893) 03:55:39
547. Edward Morrison (2898) 03:55:48
548. Sonny Rodil (2905) 03:55:48
549. Joseph Heneghan (2912) 03:55:54
550. Billy Ray (2915) 03:55:55
551. Luis Alonso Melgar (2921) 03:55:58
552. Tony Girard (2922) 03:55:58
553. Jose Landivar (2923) 03:55:58
554. Hector Rendon (2926) 03:56:13
555. Mark Parish (2942) 03:56:13
556. Mike Garcia (2952) 03:56:28
557. Jeffrey Colegrave (2961) 03:56:28
558. Anton Bilchik (2968) 03:56:34
559. Rene Gallardo (2975) 03:56:39
560. David Gallup (2977) 03:56:39
561. Vic Bello (2989) 03:56:47
562. Jesse Saldana (2993) 03:56:47
563. Ed Foster (3002) 03:56:50
564. Greg Mastoras (3005) 03:56:51
565. Matthew Boyd (3014) 03:56:55
566. Raymond Meza (3017) 03:56:59
567. Glenn Smith (3019) 03:56:59
568. William Brockley (3021) 03:57:00
569. Mark Mozilo (3032) 03:57:03
570. Leon Hart (3038) 03:57:07
571. Akira Zamma (3044) 03:57:11
572. Manuel Ibarra (3047) 03:57:13
573. John Turrubiartes (3050) 03:57:17
574. Danny Real (3066) 03:57:29
575. Eladio Diaz (3069) 03:57:30
576. Jeff Vininn (3075) 03:57:32
577. Martin Benjarano (3080) 03:57:38
578. James Moss (3085) 03:57:42
579. Ramon Lopez (3086) 03:57:44
580. Luis Trejo (3088) 03:57:44
581. Andrew Kearney (3089) 03:57:45
582. Ricardo Gutierrez (3091) 03:57:46
583. Gerard Hekker (3120) 03:58:02
584. Ernesto Patino (3121) 03:58:03
585. Harley Jenkins (3124) 03:58:05
586. David Cerniglia (3128) 03:58:09
587. Brian Ring (3132) 03:58:12
588. Salvador Rosales (3133) 03:58:12
589. Stan Wilcox (3138) 03:58:19
590. Steven Clemons (3139) 03:58:20
591. Jae Hoon Chung (3143) 03:58:21
592. Roy Guillermo (3156) 03:58:31
593. Gabriel Kaplan (3160) 03:58:34
594. Morco Gomez (3180) 03:58:48
595. Heriberto Aparicio (3187) 03:58:52
596. Hector Gonzalez (3198) 03:58:58
597. Robert Dittmer (3201) 03:59:01
598. Timothy Rock (3210) 03:59:06
599. Peter Thorin (3212) 03:59:10
600. John Tuck (3216) 03:59:10
601. Chris Dyrek (3235) 03:59:22
602. Arturo Geronimo (3238) 03:59:28
603. Bill Bustos (3241) 03:59:31
604. James Flaherty (3245) 03:59:34
605. Raul Rivera Jr (3246) 03:59:35
606. David Bolko (3249) 03:59:38
607. Raymond Robles Jr (3259) 03:59:44
608. Dan Thompson (3265) 03:59:45
609. Mike Mc Cabe (3266) 03:59:45
610. Saul Arellano (3272) 03:59:45
611. Michael Wiser (3276) 03:59:51
612. Jerry Sniffin (3280) 03:59:54
613. Wayne Matayoshi (3285) 03:59:54
614. Paul Tenner (3289) 03:59:56
615. Miguel Sanchez (3291) 04:00:01
616. John Martins (3300) 04:00:01
617. Vic Canel Jr (3302) 04:00:03
618. Paul Witte (3306) 04:00:05
619. Paul Jacobs (3310) 04:00:09
620. James Daniel (3318) 04:00:14
621. Freddy Wilson (3328) 04:00:22
622. Arthur Bahadourian (3330) 04:00:22
623. Glenn Han (3334) 04:00:24
624. Brian League (3336) 04:00:27
625. Micheal Pechie (3339) 04:00:30
626. Michael Sheehan (3341) 04:00:30
627. Michael Engel (3343) 04:00:32
628. Jorge Garcia (3346) 04:00:35
629. Burton Smith (3353) 04:00:41
630. Alfredo Ramos (3355) 04:00:47
631. Ron Bourgault (3365) 04:00:53
632. Fred Murillo (3367) 04:00:54
633. Milton Drachenberg (3382) 04:01:03
634. Nick Alvarez (3392) 04:01:11
635. Jim Miller (3396) 04:01:14

636. David Bethany (3410) 04:01:23
637. Chuck Miranda (3413) 04:01:27
638. Stephen White (3419) 04:01:31
639. Manuel Galvan (3436) 04:01:44
640. Daniel Delaney (3437) 04:01:45
641. Efrain Bencomo (3444) 04:01:55
642. Anthony Carvajal (3463) 04:02:10
643. Thomas Buetemeister (3466) 04:02:11
644. Richard Sanchez (3471) 04:02:16
645. Jaime Noriega (3479) 04:02:20
646. Alvino Villegas (3495) 04:02:37
647. Esteban Agundez (3505) 04:02:46
648. Keith Chura (3506) 04:02:47
649. Scott Outtrim (3511) 04:02:50
650. Todd Thibodo (3515) 04:02:55
651. Russell Gaither (3535) 04:03:11
652. Tyrone Ganoe (3549) 04:03:27
653. Jesus Aguilar (3550) 04:03:28
654. Christopher Copper (3558) 04:03:34
655. Martin Richter (3560) 04:03:36
656. Edward Gonzales (3564) 04:03:37
657. Les Deal (3568) 04:03:41
658. Wayne Joness (3571) 04:03:44
659. Shinichi Ogata (3573) 04:03:47
660. Gary Hammerle (3576) 04:03:53
661. Robert Aparicio (3581) 04:03:56
662. Primo Baybayan (3584) 04:03:56
663. Gus Mariscal (3590) 04:04:04
664. Byron Kurt (3592) 04:04:08
665. Bryan Cochran (3600) 04:04:12
666. Frank Duda (3605) 04:04:14
667. Andy Garcia (3607) 04:04:14
668. Jose Ocelolt (3614) 04:04:19
669. Jeffory Wyscarver (3615) 04:04:20
670. Robby Perkins (3622) 04:04:24
671. Mark Emerson (3627) 04:04:27
672. Stephen Wadsworth (3629) 04:04:29
673. Ken Williams (3632) 04:04:31
674. Erasmo Sanchez (3634) 04:04:31
675. Geronimo Uribe (3641) 04:04:33
676. John Singer (3649) 04:04:39
677. Fernando Morales (3653) 04:04:41
678. Jose Luis Salas (3657) 04:04:45
679. Danny Drake (3667) 04:04:51
680. Frank Arroues (3678) 04:04:58
681. Kerry Wills (3680) 04:04:59
682. Steven Morrow (3683) 04:05:00
683. Juan Servin (3686) 04:05:03
684. Hector Curiel (3707) 04:05:20
685. Joseph D'amato (3709) 04:05:24
686. Mark Simmons (3711) 04:05:25
687. Genaro Magana (3713) 04:05:29
688. Juan Galarza (3715) 04:05:29
689. Gary Baskett (3716) 04:05:29
690. Allen Leblanc (3720) 04:05:32
691. Paul Beaudoin (3731) 04:05:41
692. Steve Wolf (3736) 04:05:47
693. Ross Ellis (3745) 04:05:54
694. Jeff Tepich (3747) 04:05:55
695. Maurio Deshay (3749) 04:05:56
696. Ignatio Verduzo (3751) 04:05:59
697. Amador Zamora (3753) 04:06:01
698. Mark Hedman (3755) 04:06:02
699. Steven Chamberlin (3764) 04:06:07
700. Simon Gee (3775) 04:06:17
701. Tom Tapparo (3784) 04:06:27
702. Franck Talpaert (3791) 04:06:30
703. Martin Heredia (3799) 04:06:36
704. David Kent (3809) 04:06:43
705. Steve Ivers (3815) 04:06:46
706. Steven Smith (3816) 04:06:48
707. John Fitzsimons (3823) 04:06:52
708. Eric Ostendorff (3835) 04:07:01
709. Thomas Tietjen (3843) 04:07:05
710. Steve Colucci (3849) 04:07:07
711. David Bond (3859) 04:07:16
712. Alejandro Jimenez (3860) 04:07:17
713. Jesus Castro (3861) 04:07:18
714. Steven Cancino (3884) 04:07:35
715. Guadalupe Murguia (3889) 04:07:37
716. Charles Ver Hoeve (3892) 04:07:39
717. Daniel Thompson (3893) 04:07:39
718. Hamid Kossarian (3906) 04:07:48
719. Ronald McClure (3907) 04:07:48
720. Arthur Mortell (3908) 04:07:49
721. David Gomez (3910) 04:07:49
722. Robert Krause (3911) 04:07:52
723. Mike Burke (3916) 04:07:58
724. Sean Leenaerts (3924) 04:08:10
725. Robert Bernstein (3928) 04:08:12
726. Carlos Alvaro Inocente (3936) 04:08:16
727. John Gerhart (3947) 04:08:22
728. Phil Brown (3962) 04:08:30
729. Richard Shea (3964) 04:08:37
730. Eric Fentem (3969) 04:08:42
731. Alistair Fyfe (3979) 04:08:48
732. Arturo Herrera (3981) 04:08:49
733. Lee Gagyi (3985) 04:08:54
734. Edwin Hovsepian (3987) 04:08:58
735. David Ide (3990) 04:08:59
736. Marco Pedemonte (3995) 04:09:02
737. Michael Daly (3997) 04:09:04
738. Kelvin Sampson (4013) 04:09:15
739. Akira Matsui (4015) 04:09:17
740. John Malagon (4016) 04:09:18
741. Al Valdez (4023) 04:09:23
742. Gary Crawford (4031) 04:09:28
743. Greg Hamson (4033) 04:09:31
744. Paul MacDonald (4038) 04:09:35
745. Allan Myles (4043) 04:09:39
746. Ambrose Calderon (4044) 04:09:39
747. Dennis Scott (4045) 04:09:40
748. Thomas Giordano (4047) 04:09:42
749. Michael Marks (4049) 04:09:47
750. Stuart Posnock (4053) 04:09:48
751. Daniel Zepeda (4055) 04:09:51
752. Robert Moody (4065) 04:09:58
753. David Gault (4070) 04:10:01
754. Refugio Sandoval (4074) 04:10:05
755. Michael Neal (4083) 04:10:12
756. Wayne Wu (4090) 04:10:15
757. Red Clark (4092) 04:10:16
758. Paul Kingsbury (4097) 04:10:23
759. David Rainey (4102) 04:10:29
760. Damon Kelliher (4103) 04:10:30
761. Jose Carbajal (4107) 04:10:31
762. Anthony Seferian (4110) 04:10:33
763. Hisatoshi Kato (4112) 04:10:36
764. William Mercer (4124) 04:10:45
765. Santos Reyes (4133) 04:10:51
766. Raul Martinez (4140) 04:10:54
767. Kazutaka Nukariya (4153) 04:11:01
768. Tim Catlin (4154) 04:11:01
769. Peter Jackson (4174) 04:11:13
770. Chris Thompson (4178) 04:11:17
771. Jose Galeas (4181) 04:11:19
772. Richard Gorham (4182) 04:11:21
773. Gerardo Canton (4184) 04:11:22
774. Kenneth Westlake (4186) 04:11:24
775. Thurston Watson (4187) 04:11:26
776. Clay Palmer (4190) 04:11:28
777. John Rauber (4193) 04:11:33
778. Sacha Marcroft (4195) 04:11:34
779. Mike Loftus (4202) 04:11:39
780. Mike Santoyo (4203) 04:11:40
781. Alvayo Herrera (4222) 04:11:58
782. Gary Dunn (4248) 04:12:16
783. Allan Anopol (4255) 04:12:22
784. Tim Graves (4263) 04:12:27
785. Barnaby Jackson (4270) 04:12:32
786. Anthony Chan (4272) 04:12:34
787. Richard Guerrero (4295) 04:12:55
788. William Brace (4308) 04:13:03
789. Eddis Marks (4310) 04:13:05
790. Alex Moreno (4312) 04:13:07
791. Adrian Cerda (4315) 04:13:08
792. Ken Hughey (4316) 04:13:09
793. Stephen Davoren (4317) 04:13:09
794. Rogelio Barrera (4321) 04:13:10
795. Alex Valdez (4332) 04:13:21
796. Merceo Mejia (4339) 04:13:24
797. Rolando Ayala (4343) 04:13:27
798. Jim Langford (4348) 04:13:32
799. Patrick Murphy (4349) 04:13:34
800. Duane Caster (4363) 04:13:49
801. Mike Hardy (4367) 04:13:52
802. David Allen (4372) 04:13:54
803. Jeff Appell (4389) 04:14:03
804. Mike Romero (4395) 04:14:08
805. Jorge Vazquez (4403) 04:14:15
806. Francisco Mayen (4412) 04:14:21
807. Jonathan Lustig (4434) 04:14:32
808. Michael Molinyawe (4436) 04:14:33
809. Russ Graves (4438) 04:14:34
810. David Wolter (4447) 04:14:39
811. Howard Jens (4451) 04:14:41
812. John Torrijos (4453) 04:14:42
813. Tanveer Akhtar (4456) 04:14:43
814. Hugo Olguin (4460) 04:14:44
815. Mark Duss (4462) 04:14:46
816. David Hutchison (4463) 04:14:46
817. Dave Ritchie (4472) 04:14:50
818. Cruz Hernandez (4477) 04:14:52
819. Jose Ortega (4479) 04:14:53
820. Richard Apodaca (4491) 04:15:00
821. Greg Sabala (4495) 04:15:03
822. Roberto Mena Bolanos (4500) 04:15:09
823. Charley Maorales (4504) 04:15:12
824. Heriberto Munoz (4510) 04:15:18
825. Harold Ring (4536) 04:15:34
826. Mark Eickhoff (4537) 04:15:35
827. Miguel Hernandez (4538) 04:15:35
828. Henry De Guevara (4551) 04:15:42
829. Tim Van Dixhorn (4552) 04:15:42
830. Bruce Dall (4560) 04:15:48
831. Al Taira (4578) 04:16:00
832. Brett Smith (4594) 04:16:08
833. Rod Zuniga (4598) 04:16:11
834. Thomas Grummitt (4601) 04:16:13
835. Stuart Rogers (4607) 04:16:20
836. Edgar Saenz (4610) 04:16:23
837. Gordon Chavis (4613) 04:16:24
838. Peter Watler (4621) 04:16:28
839. Bernardo Gomez Valdez (4623) 04:16:29
840. Jay Strojnowski (4655) 04:16:52
841. Steve Scott (4662) 04:16:57
842. Mark Jordan (4673) 04:17:05
843. Michael Tyler (4676) 04:17:08
844. Daniel Ramon (4693) 04:17:23
845. Ken Broderick (4696) 04:17:26
846. Andrew Carroll (4714) 04:17:39
847. Kevin Yaryan (4724) 04:17:50
848. Vittorio Miranda (4730) 04:17:52
849. John McDonald (4731) 04:17:53
850. Jim Shaw (4733) 04:17:54
851. Michael Hoffee (4753) 04:18:07
852. Eric Lagier (4755) 04:18:08
853. Edward Hayes (4758) 04:18:09
854. Noiel Fontaine (4761) 04:18:11
855. Brett Lawrence (4767) 04:18:14
856. Dan Kluzik (4794) 04:18:32
857. John Roberts (4799) 04:18:37
858. Kirt Kingzett (4805) 04:18:40
859. Kevin Drabinski (4808) 04:18:41
860. Brian Miller (4809) 04:18:41
861. Jose Vigil Chavez (4824) 04:18:50
862. Edward Mayeda (4829) 04:18:52
863. Marcellus Beaird (4831) 04:18:53
864. Robert Fiore (4834) 04:18:55
865. Oscar Escobar (4836) 04:18:56
866. Robert Colaizzi (4837) 04:18:57
867. Donald Lema (4843) 04:18:59
868. Hal Halladay (4855) 04:19:06
869. Paul Bolock (4856) 04:19:06
870. John Greaves (4873) 04:19:16
871. Robert Hughes (4885) 04:19:23
872. Jorge Ortega Perez (4893) 04:19:30
873. Carlos Porras Jr (4904) 04:19:39
874. Javier Ruiz (4905) 04:19:39
875. Harold Kempfer (4912) 04:19:43
876. Greg Minter (4957) 04:20:17
877. Jose Olmos (4958) 04:20:19
878. Humberto Sauri (4968) 04:20:30
879. James White (4972) 04:20:33
880. Yasukazu Hatakeyama (4974) 04:20:35
881. William Reeves (4985) 04:20:43
882. Steve Noble (4986) 04:20:44
883. James Smith (4992) 04:20:54
884. Ruben Rojes (5001) 04:21:01
885. Andy Vuncanon (5013) 04:21:17
886. Ravi Alagappan (5015) 04:21:17
887. Sean Housel (5036) 04:21:31
888. Ken Lee (5039) 04:21:32
889. Kenji Tatsugi (5051) 04:21:40
890. Lester Richardson (5058) 04:21:43
891. Vince Leano (5091) 04:21:58
892. Arthur McGovern (5093) 04:21:59
893. Salvador Montes De Oca (5096) 04:22:01
894. Gilbert Brenes (5102) 04:22:05
895. Dan Sowash (5109) 04:22:07
896. Jim Hoch (5115) 04:22:09
897. Richard Martin (5127) 04:22:19
898. Mark Blum (5132) 04:22:22
899. Ruben Gudino (5148) 04:22:36
900. Mark Sparks (5152) 04:22:38
901. Yoshiaki Kubota (5159) 04:22:45
902. Ray Renneker (5161) 04:22:46
903. Joseph Heneghan (5162) 04:22:46
904. Myron Talbert (5164) 04:22:48
905. Dwayne Burke (5167) 04:22:50
906. Tomas Roberto Valero Saldana (5181) 04:22:59
907. Jonathan Fish (5182) 04:23:00
908. Michael Hall (5197) 04:23:11
909. Paul Herrera (5212) 04:23:19
910. Robert Livengood (5215) 04:23:20
911. Aristides Orellana (5220) 04:23:26
912. Jimmy Spinelli (5225) 04:23:29
913. Alfred Mendoza (5240) 04:23:38
914. Sam Fibish (5245) 04:23:44
915. Steven Truesdale (5248) 04:23:47
916. Alfredo Gomez (5250) 04:23:51
917. Douglas Hochstadt (5263) 04:24:07
918. Richard Gillis (5264) 04:24:08
919. Michael Bacharach (5270) 04:24:11
920. Brian Hannemann (5273) 04:24:14
921. John Mochowski (5277) 04:24:17
922. Bob Shisler (5279) 04:24:19
923. Louis Wang (5282) 04:24:22
924. Brian Comer (5286) 04:24:25
925. Randy Case (5289) 04:24:27
926. Thomas Barrera (5298) 04:24:31
927. Bill McLaughlin (5299) 04:24:31
928. Rafael Herrera (5311) 04:24:37
929. Hector Melendez (5312) 04:24:37
930. Steven Crocker (5325) 04:24:50
931. Troy Haynes (5329) 04:24:54
932. Richard Larson (5332) 04:24:55
933. Ralph Terrazas (5335) 04:24:55
934. Floyd Spaulding (5336) 04:24:56
935. Wilfredo Quintanilla (5349) 04:25:08
936. Lonnie Sumrall (5393) 04:25:29
937. Rik Noyce (5394) 04:25:30
938. Gary Vasquez (5399) 04:25:35
939. Raul Hernandez (5407) 04:25:39
940. Michael Markarian (5414) 04:25:43
941. Val Mina (5415) 04:25:43
942. Douglas Wagoner (5420) 04:25:47
943. Howard Dowdell (5462) 04:26:11
944. Bret Nelson (5463) 04:26:11
945. Phillips Park (5467) 04:26:16
946. Mario Nieto (5474) 04:26:21
947. Victor Camey Chonay (5475) 04:26:23
948. Mark Romo (5482) 04:26:27
949. Henry Reyes (5483) 04:26:28
950. John Mc Clennon (5500) 04:26:40
951. Kirk Mueller (5502) 04:26:41
952. Silvestre Ramirez (5515) 04:26:53
953. Thomas Tallarino (5518) 04:26:57
954. Michael Schiepke (5531) 04:27:09
955. Mark Mercer (5536) 04:27:10
956. Cameron Hum (5543) 04:27:13
957. Bruce Worrilow (5548) 04:27:19
958. Leo Lopez (5549) 04:27:19
959. Yasutomo Yamanoi (5552) 04:27:20
960. Rodolfo Estrada (5587) 04:27:40
961. Martin Meza (5610) 04:27:55
962. Ikuo Kizaki (5615) 04:27:57
963. Richard Hawk (5618) 04:28:00
964. Kevin Rice (5623) 04:28:02
965. Genaro Legorreta (5625) 04:28:02
966. Joel Lenz (5630) 04:28:05
967. Armand Gastelo (5634) 04:28:06
968. Frank Chicu (5647) 04:28:17
969. Ray Diggs (5659) 04:28:26
970. Thomas Donham (5664) 04:28:29
971. Hugo Martin (5667) 04:28:32
972. Ben Gutierrez (5688) 04:28:44
973. Mario Baez (5692) 04:28:48
974. Rafael Lizardo (5697) 04:28:51
975. Brett Selph (5701) 04:28:54
976. Walt Wolf (5707) 04:28:58
977. Andy Skane (5736) 04:29:15
978. Clark Poulsen (5741) 04:29:18
979. Ruma Povlsen (5743) 04:29:18
980. Toshiya Tanaka (5753) 04:29:27
981. Jose Alfredo Castro (5775) 04:29:39
982. Thorlough Carter (5777) 04:29:40
983. Roman Kepczyk (5786) 04:29:49
984. Ramiro Quezada (5792) 04:29:53
985. Mark Nockels (5794) 04:29:54
986. Jeff Knight (5799) 04:30:01
987. John Hughes (5805) 04:30:04
988. Paul Calderon (5806) 04:30:06
989. Greg Middleton (5808) 04:30:07
990. James Gilbert (5820) 04:30:17
991. Marco Gonzales (5824) 04:30:21
992. Lazaro Morales (5829) 04:30:25
993. Ian Osborne (5837) 04:30:28
994. William Bloomer (5838) 04:30:28
995. Russell Jones (5851) 04:30:33
996. Roger Cuevas (5865) 04:30:39
997. Robert Farrell (5867) 04:30:40
998. Vic Vizcarra (5871) 04:30:41
999. Isaias Pedroza (5872) 04:30:41
1000. James Wu (5874) 04:30:42
1001. Ken McClusky (5882) 04:30:45
1002. Terry Curella (5884) 04:30:48
1003. Sheila McCann (5887) 04:30:50
1004. David Gilbert (5893) 04:30:55
1005. Nelson Trans (5894) 04:30:56
1006. John Grimm (5909) 04:31:06
1007. Edward Resetar (5910) 04:31:06
1008. Ray Adamyk (5913) 04:31:07
1009. Nono Ajemian (5914) 04:31:08
1010. Pierre Gruson (5923) 04:31:15
1011. Luis Fong (5927) 04:31:21
1012. Mike Vandemortel (5928) 04:31:22
1013. Nick Slater (5936) 04:31:26
1014. Mark Tanzer (5946) 04:31:30
1015. Ray Masumoto (5953) 04:31:38
1016. Eric Rosa (5958) 04:31:41
1017. Chris Budny (5961) 04:31:43
1018. Steve Maedel (5965) 04:31:45
1019. Roy Ituralde (5970) 04:31:48
1020. Michael Yuzon (5983) 04:31:59
1021. Miguel Lopez (5986) 04:32:01
1022. Paul Corey (6002) 04:32:18
1023. Guy Kibbe (6008) 04:32:21
1024. Ian Hoad (6012) 04:32:23
1025. Louie Galvan (6013) 04:32:23
1026. Jose Hurtado (6022) 04:32:30
1027. Daryl Elizalde (6027) 04:32:35
1028. David Lake (6040) 04:32:46
1029. Jay Brasel (6041) 04:32:46
1030. Henry Santos (6048) 04:32:49
1031. David Costenbader (6054) 04:32:54
1032. Robert Gutierrez (6086) 04:33:14
1033. Darryl Wells (6095) 04:33:21
1034. Steven Lotto (6098) 04:33:22
1035. Anthony Barrios (6102) 04:33:27
1036. Robert Yan (6104) 04:33:27
1037. Raymond Reyes (6109) 04:33:30
1038. Elias Garcia (6111) 04:33:31
1039. George Albanes (6117) 04:33:34
1040. Thomas Cunningham (6118) 04:33:35
1041. Paul Rodriguez (6129) 04:33:43
1042. Michael Dando (6141) 04:33:53
1043. Jose Dino (6154) 04:34:05
1044. Victor Espinoza (6166) 04:34:10
1045. Robert Grace (6185) 04:34:24
1046. Nayyer Bilal (6193) 04:34:27
1047. Jay Lenner (6205) 04:34:36
1048. Jose Torres (6212) 04:34:41
1049. Larry Chacon (6221) 04:34:45
1050. Chris Measures (6252) 04:35:07
1051. Kevin Garrity (6256) 04:35:11
1052. Fon Wong (6266) 04:35:17
1053. Jim Lofthus (6269) 04:35:19
1054. Michael Lash (6274) 04:35:21
1055. Jim Howley (6277) 04:35:23
1056. Larry Johnson (6293) 04:35:34
1057. Nay-Wei Soong (6302) 04:35:39
1058. James Gallivan (6303) 04:35:40
1059. Joseph Wells (6329) 04:35:54
1060. Heinrich Ackermann (6334) 04:35:56
1061. Ernesto Alvarez (6345) 04:36:07
1062. William Mar (6349) 04:36:09
1063. Noe Reyes (6350) 04:36:09
1064. Darrel Guilbeau (6354) 04:36:11
1065. Andy Northrup (6362) 04:36:16
1066. Christopher Marsh (6368) 04:36:19
1067. Dan Kelley (6380) 04:36:24
1068. Stefan Kindler (6381) 04:36:25
1069. Michael Bryce (6391) 04:36:28
1070. Ray Montoya (6398) 04:36:32
1071. Tarcis Verfaillie (6400) 04:36:33
1072. Brett Wood (6403) 04:36:35
1073. Glenn Guzman (6405) 04:36:36
1074. Nick Palma (6416) 04:36:41
1075. B Rowe (6417) 04:36:41
1076. John Peterson (6434) 04:36:58
1077. Nick Bazarevitsch (6442) 04:37:06
1078. Louis Mo (6443) 04:37:07
1079. Gary Niebergall (6459) 04:37:22
1080. Stan Bailey (6465) 04:37:25
1081. James Neyna (6470) 04:37:27
1082. Dennis Cadavona (6474) 04:37:29
1083. William Thompson (6479) 04:37:31
1084. Erik Orre (6480) 04:37:32
1085. Ernest Lohman (6481) 04:37:32
1086. Froylan Vasquez (6490) 04:37:38
1087. Joe Desantis (6495) 04:37:40
1088. Mario Vazquez (6514) 04:37:50
1089. Michael Wilson (6524) 04:37:58
1090. Alan Fields (6527) 04:38:00
1091. Horacio Montes (6531) 04:38:03
1092. Marshall Rea (6543) 04:38:10
1093. Charles Martinez (6545) 04:38:11
1094. Kelly Hayes (6546) 04:38:11
1095. Paul Stewart (6554) 04:38:15
1096. Stephen Ornellas (6570) 04:38:25
1097. Pat Marsh (6584) 04:38:35
1098. Mark Burns (6599) 04:38:42
1099. Hagop Alexanian (6605) 04:38:46
1100. Martin Solis (6617) 04:38:54
1101. Carlos Cortes (6619) 04:38:54
1102. Luis Sandoval (6623) 04:38:57
1103. Clyde Fischer (6629) 04:38:59
1104. Carlos Lopez (6630) 04:38:59
1105. Ernesto Galvez (6650) 04:39:14
1106. David Parks (6656) 04:39:24
1107. Russell Beebe (6669) 04:39:34
1108. Paul Krewski (6671) 04:39:36
1109. William Jones (6679) 04:39:40
1110. David Saenz (6682) 04:39:42
1111. Jason Song (6700) 04:39:51
1112. Mike Ezzedine (6717) 04:40:05
1113. Italo Malerba (6720) 04:40:10
1114. Felipe Gonzalez (6723) 04:40:13
1115. Phillip Anderson (6728) 04:40:19
1116. James McDevitt (6730) 04:40:20
1117. Aki Hashimoto (6741) 04:40:30
1118. Wilfredo Martinez (6746) 04:40:34
1119. Ruben Mejorado (6747) 04:40:34
1120. Armando Garcia (6752) 04:40:37
1121. Florentino Bacaoan (6771) 04:40:57
1122. Christopher Leone (6782) 04:41:04
1123. David Zebny (6787) 04:41:06
1124. David Duggan (6788) 04:41:06
1125. Steve Zamora (6802) 04:41:17
1126. John Boken (6806) 04:41:22
1127. Thomas Rasmussen (6807) 04:41:22
1128. Joel Rodgers (6833) 04:41:44
1129. Mancin Taylor (6834) 04:41:44
1130. Gary Richardson (6836) 04:41:45
1131. Kevin Phillips (6842) 04:41:49
1132. Alfredo Ayala (6853) 04:41:56
1133. Sam Daye (6855) 04:41:57
1134. Richard Gaines (6857) 04:41:58
1135. Nelson Recinos (6858) 04:41:59
1136. Ken Arimura (6861) 04:42:02
1137. Jeff Estopellan (6862) 04:42:03
1138. Jose Padilla (6868) 04:42:06
1139. Jeff West (6881) 04:42:20
1140. Blair Taylor (6893) 04:42:30
1141. Kenneth Maddox (6895) 04:42:31
1142. Pastor Vicente (6916) 04:42:48
1143. Jose Salazar (6921) 04:42:49
1144. Edward Schemine (6930) 04:42:57
1145. Connie Denver III (6931) 04:42:57
1146. Keith Goffney (6933) 04:42:59
1147. Cruz Torres (6936) 04:43:01
1148. Wayne Hrushka (6940) 04:43:03
1149. Bradley Carlson (6953) 04:43:08
1150. Steven Bain (6954) 04:43:09
1151. Justin Beckett (6970) 04:43:21
1152. Cecil Cox (6972) 04:43:22
1153. Jaime Morales (6976) 04:43:23
1154. Jack O'Neil (6997) 04:43:36
1155. Jack Corrigan (7003) 04:43:39
1156. Robert Hoopengarner (7009) 04:43:41
1157. J D Lowes (7017) 04:43:49
1158. Thurman Hines (7019) 04:43:52
1159. Paolo Tombesi (7025) 04:43:54
1160. Ethan Brown (7027) 04:43:55
1161. Jeffrey Plesser (7032) 04:43:58
1162. Stephen Shoemaker (7041) 04:44:03
1163. Kenichi Nakagawa (7045) 04:44:06
1164. Steve Smith (7049) 04:44:13
1165. Adulio Ochoa (7055) 04:44:17
1166. Matrin Dominguez (7068) 04:44:27
1167. Richard Palm (7075) 04:44:34
1168. Randy Cassel (7076) 04:44:35
1169. Gregory Fitzpatrick (7078) 04:44:36
1170. Richard Glover (7083) 04:44:43
1171. Brian Bradburn (7090) 04:44:50
1172. Daryl Rodriguez (7093) 04:44:51
1173. Heberto Morales (7094) 04:44:51
1174. Randy Ponder (7098) 04:44:53
1175. Christopher Barham (7100) 04:44:54
1176. Jeffrey Peters (7101) 04:44:54
1177. Koichi Takeda (7103) 04:44:55
1178. Jose Moran (7108) 04:44:59
1179. Nisan Kececioglu (7110) 04:45:00
1180. Charles Foster (7123) 04:45:08
1181. David Pfaff (7132) 04:45:14
1182. Peted Ellis (7156) 04:45:39
1183. Doanh Nguyen (7158) 04:45:39
1184. Daniel Healy (7160) 04:45:40
1185. Steven Oblen (7172) 04:45:45
1186. Jim Colocho (7173) 04:45:46
1187. Rogelio Espinosa Jr (7182) 04:45:55
1188. Richard Andrade (7185) 04:45:57
1189. Stanley Ito (7193) 04:46:02
1190. Ray Mosack (7196) 04:46:05
1191. Ruben Valencia (7203) 04:46:09
1192. Bradford Hanson (7206) 04:46:11
1193. Felix Cruz (7212) 04:46:13
1194. Julian Estrada-Arechiga (7214) 04:46:16
1195. Satomi Eiki (7228) 04:46:28
1196. David Olivas (7235) 04:46:32
1197. Steve Corona (7239) 04:46:34
1198. Peter Star (7251) 04:46:43
1199. Eric Lauer (7281) 04:47:00
1200. David Pyle (7285) 04:47:03
1201. Avel Flores (7289) 04:47:07
1202. Max Yoshikawa (7291) 04:47:09
1203. Thomas Wada (7300) 04:47:15
1204. Yuzuru Naruse (7303) 04:47:17
1205. Sanjay Kulkarni (7306) 04:47:18
1206. Lance Ebarb (7308) 04:47:19
1207. Mark Dix (7312) 04:47:24
1208. Carlos Balarezo (7317) 04:47:26
1209. John Michel (7324) 04:47:29
1210. Ramiro Cantu Jr (7328) 04:47:32
1211. Michael Williams (7329) 04:47:32
1212. Daniel Torres (7368) 04:48:03
1213. Manuel Duarte (7372) 04:48:05
1214. Alex Ortega (7374) 04:48:08
1215. Jon Lamori (7376) 04:48:10
1216. Jonell Del Carpio (7392) 04:48:16
1217. Pablo Aceves (7396) 04:48:18
1218. Tomoyuki Ishikawa (7398) 04:48:20
1219. Kevin Chapin (7403) 04:48:24
1220. Masahiko Kojima (7417) 04:48:33
1221. Daniel Lyons (7425) 04:48:40
1222. Alan Piotrowski (7446) 04:48:54
1223. Eldon Forcey (7454) 04:48:58
1224. Timothy Leiterman (7492) 04:49:21
1225. Edward Doogan (7499) 04:49:23
1226. Doe Albarran (7500) 04:49:24
1227. Paul Pitzner (7502) 04:49:24
1228. Hal Meltzer (7504) 04:49:27
1229. Robert Ferguson (7513) 04:49:31
1230. Jene St Pierre (7515) 04:49:32
1231. Vabor Bartolo (7522) 04:49:35
1232. Mohamad Merher (7538) 04:49:50
1233. Fidel Castillo (7559) 04:50:04
1234. Matthew Morris (7561) 04:50:06
1235. John Espinosa (7565) 04:50:10
1236. Evan Mecham (7577) 04:50:19
1237. Jose Luis Salazar (7580) 04:50:21
1238. Floren Domingo (7582) 04:50:23
1239. Brent Hoffmann (7586) 04:50:26
1240. Nelson Lopez (7618) 04:50:50
1241. Bob Jolicoeur (7619) 04:50:51
1242. Terry Halberg (7623) 04:50:55
1243. Jose Hernandez (7625) 04:50:56
1244. John Holloway (7650) 04:51:19
1245. Jaime Ortiz (7667) 04:51:32
1246. Palle Weber (7668) 04:51:35
1247. Victor Miller (7674) 04:51:39
1248. David Pace (7692) 04:51:49
1249. Thomas Tebbs (7696) 04:51:54
1250. Iso Moreno (7709) 04:52:05
1251. Jeff Turner (7716) 04:52:08
1252. Raul Velasco (7720) 04:52:13
1253. Jon Coyle (7721) 04:52:13
1254. David Sinegal (7726) 04:52:17
1255. Young Lim (7740) 04:52:30
1256. Adam Carreon (7767) 04:52:51
1257. Daniel Garcia (7788) 04:53:04
1258. Ricky Bennett (7790) 04:53:08
1259. John Murray (7813) 04:53:25
1260. Patrick Traylor (7820) 04:53:30
1261. Gary Farrell (7823) 04:53:30
1262. Jon Stachelrodt (7824) 04:53:31
1263. Ed Reynolds (7848) 04:53:47
1264. Frank Pantoja (7855) 04:53:52
1265. Jose Nillasenor (7860) 04:53:54
1266. Dan Statler (7893) 04:54:17
1267. Scott Thomas (7902) 04:54:22
1268. Ron Walker (7915) 04:54:28
1269. Timothy Ray (7925) 04:54:32
1270. Rey Reyes (7944) 04:54:40
1271. Miguel Guzman (7955) 04:54:45
1272. Adrian Rodriguez (7960) 04:54:47

1273. Gabriel Muniz (7972) 04:54:53
1274. Ray Salcedo (7980) 04:55:07
1275. Paul Miller (7995) 04:55:19
1276. Robert Blume (8019) 04:55:40
1277. Edward Herbclock (8022) 04:55:43
1278. Rich Story (8037) 04:55:51
1279. Steven Peinetti (8042) 04:55:54
1280. John Nishimoto (8055) 04:56:07
1281. Chuck Tapia (8057) 04:56:09
1282. Greg Palmer (8060) 04:56:10
1283. Masamichi Takeda (8064) 04:56:13
1284. Sylvester Robles (8079) 04:56:25
1285. Andy McCormick (8092) 04:56:33
1286. Martin Sanchez (8107) 04:56:44
1287. Martin Corona (8121) 04:56:56
1288. Vicente Valencia (8124) 04:56:59
1289. Wenefrido Ugalde (8133) 04:57:07
1290. John Delgado (8140) 04:57:12
1291. Robert Hayes (8142) 04:57:14
1292. Rodrigo Iglesias (8144) 04:57:15
1293. Jeffrey Dadow (8160) 04:57:26
1294. Martin Rubio (8163) 04:57:27
1295. Jim Ochoa (8170) 04:57:34
1296. Kozo Iwasaki (8182) 04:57:40
1297. Salvador Ventura (8188) 04:57:48
1298. David Ireland (8198) 04:57:53
1299. Brad Cole (8204) 04:57:57
1300. Anthony Arinillo (8216) 04:58:02
1301. Howard Cohen (8226) 04:58:08
1302. Robert Miller (8258) 04:58:26
1303. Paul Musico (8263) 04:58:29
1304. Ken Brougher (8264) 04:58:30
1305. Sergio Rulli (8268) 04:58:32
1306. Micheal Butts (8279) 04:58:43
1307. Richard Giffen (8316) 04:59:02
1308. Frank Zakravsky (8319) 04:59:04
1309. Jeff Caldwell (8328) 04:59:10
1310. Joseph English (8329) 04:59:11
1311. Rich Randal (8339) 04:59:16
1312. Alberto Arturro Aguirre (8344) 04:59:19
1313. James Morrissey (8369) 04:59:38
1314. Art Tiscareno (8371) 04:59:38
1315. Michael Speziale (8383) 04:59:47
1316. Hosendo Corona (8384) 04:59:47
1317. David Heiland (8388) 04:59:49
1318. Steven Tollefsrud (8390) 04:59:49
1319. John Wilson (8395) 04:59:57
1320. Dale Hershey (8397) 05:00:00
1321. Glenn Rodriguez (8407) 05:00:13
1322. Ric Saenz (8411) 05:00:16
1323. Richard Hayatian (8413) 05:00:17
1324. David Marshall (8418) 05:00:21
1325. Joseph Bailey (8423) 05:00:26
1326. Richard Hew (8436) 05:00:43
1327. James Huff (8443) 05:00:52
1328. Daniel Sacadana (8446) 05:00:53
1329. Alvin McKean (8450) 05:00:57
1330. Dwight Carwell (8455) 05:01:00
1331. Michael Steele (8456) 05:01:01
1332. Luis Monteagudo Jr (8471) 05:01:10
1333. David Castillo (8473) 05:01:12
1334. Steven Reynolds (8475) 05:01:13
1335. Jim Tappan (8482) 05:01:20
1336. Chris Rommelmann (8487) 05:01:23
1337. Francisco Pineda (8498) 05:01:29
1338. Richard Rozinskas (8506) 05:01:34
1339. Phillip Dominguez (8510) 05:01:39
1340. Sergio Alvarez (8517) 05:01:42
1341. Greg Vander Kooy (8556) 05:02:11
1342. Anthony Noblett (8558) 05:02:12
1343. Michael Beauchemin (8569) 05:02:20
1344. Richard Beloz (8573) 05:02:23
1345. Phuong Nguyen (8582) 05:02:29
1346. Joel Villanova (8586) 05:02:41
1347. Carlos Medina (8600) 05:02:58
1348. Daniel Cota (8607) 05:03:05
1349. Tony Manghelli (8627) 05:03:18
1350. Celso Mendoza (8629) 05:03:21
1351. Paul Mansonhing (8635) 05:03:23
1352. Alejandro Gonzales (8645) 05:03:36
1353. Martin Langston (8654) 05:03:46
1354. Henry Wai Lee (8695) 05:04:18
1355. Thomas Cali (8701) 05:04:19
1356. Peter Costa (8705) 05:04:20
1357. Diogba Gbye (8714) 05:04:30
1358. Edwin Elineema (8728) 05:04:45
1359. Daniel Gomes (8739) 05:04:57
1360. Stephen Wott (8746) 05:05:09
1361. Christopher Cribbs (8756) 05:05:20
1362. Frank Garcia (8767) 05:05:30
1363. Juan Castillo (8772) 05:05:33
1364. Phillip Santillian (8782) 05:05:45
1365. Ron Rissler (8786) 05:05:47
1366. Blake Suzuki (8799) 05:06:00
1367. Bill Sauser (8811) 05:06:15
1368. Tony Velasquez (8832) 05:06:34
1369. Daniel Monzon (8834) 05:06:35
1370. Yan Dukhovny (8864) 05:07:09
1371. Arthur Varela (8873) 05:07:14
1372. Richard Garcia (8879) 05:07:26
1373. Terry Johns (8882) 05:07:31
1374. Lindsey Bowden (8894) 05:07:43
1375. Robert Steele (8900) 05:07:47
1376. Javier Mariscal (8913) 05:07:58
1377. Tom Rosso (8914) 05:07:59
1378. Robert Shubin (8938) 05:08:24
1379. John Dalton (8942) 05:08:28
1380. Val Avina (8963) 05:08:39
1381. Donald Ward (8969) 05:08:42
1382. John Wandro (8970) 05:08:42
1383. Bart Miles (8973) 05:08:43
1384. David Strand (8981) 05:08:52
1385. George McQuistion (8983) 05:08:58
1386. Jesse Reyes (8990) 05:09:03
1387. Victor Morgan (9000) 05:09:07
1388. Gerald Wright (9008) 05:09:12
1389. Ralph Quesada (9021) 05:09:24
1390. Rick Garrison (9023) 05:09:25
1391. Nicholas Smedley (9035) 05:09:39
1392. Robert Klein (9051) 05:09:50
1393. Jose Gonzalez-Chew (9059) 05:09:57
1394. James Mann (9097) 05:10:18
1395. Michael Struckhoff (9107) 05:10:22
1396. Oscar Gonzalez (9127) 05:10:39
1397. Paul Trapani (9136) 05:10:47
1398. Richard Clark (9152) 05:11:01
1399. Noriyuki Yokoyama (9168) 05:11:26
1400. Mike Kurami (9174) 05:11:31
1401. Michael Brown (9186) 05:11:38
1402. Mario Alvarado Martinez (9198) 05:11:46
1403. Javier Becerra (9201) 05:11:48
1404. Stuart Geter (9210) 05:11:56
1405. Gilbert Hernandez (9213) 05:11:59
1406. Michael Friedl (9210) 05:12:11
1407. Katsunori Iwama (9225) 05:12:17
1408. Eduardo Galvan (9250) 05:12:40
1409. Michael Ramsdale (9257) 05:12:49
1410. Gilbert Avalos (9264) 05:12:54
1411. James Wilson (9269) 05:13:01
1412. Johnny Yoon (9279) 05:13:10
1413. Fidel Mendoza (9280) 05:13:11
1414. Thomas Traylor (9283) 05:13:13
1415. Jimmy Kwan (9290) 05:13:17
1416. George Garcia (9296) 05:13:23
1417. Jason Frye (9298) 05:13:25
1418. Mark Mosher (9301) 05:13:26
1419. Eric Jauregui (9322) 05:13:36
1420. Jeffrey Liss (9330) 05:13:40
1421. Jose Ramos (9331) 05:13:41
1422. John Tene (9333) 05:13:41
1423. Bruce Roggoss (9342) 05:13:48
1424. Alan Partch (9344) 05:13:52
1425. Erwin Gee (9349) 05:13:54
1426. Manuel Duarte (9353) 05:13:55
1427. Ronald Galbraith (9358) 05:14:00
1428. Joseph Miller (9363) 05:14:00
1429. Dennis Breiner (9365) 05:14:07
1430. Scott Mcmaster (9371) 05:14:09
1431. Craig Miranda (9380) 05:14:20
1432. Paul Bonin (9396) 05:14:38
1433. Sixto Navartete Jr (9398) 05:14:39
1434. John Kim (9402) 05:14:44
1435. Neal Cook (9404) 05:14:46
1436. Hipolito Serrano (9415) 05:15:00
1437. Edwin Quintanilla (9434) 05:15:23
1438. Gregory Albanese (9439) 05:15:29
1439. Santiago Mercado (9449) 05:15:44
1440. Frederick Howard (9457) 05:15:53
1441. Robert Morgan (9473) 05:16:08
1442. Ross Lawrence (9491) 05:16:23
1443. Eric Sasano (9492) 05:16:24
1444. Gonzo Tiscareno (9494) 05:16:27
1445. Lance Goulet (9495) 05:16:27
1446. Guillermo Sesma (9503) 05:16:34
1447. Robert Skands (9505) 05:16:35
1448. Howard Martinez (9509) 05:16:36
1449. Christopher Reilly (9530) 05:17:00
1450. Manuel Castaneda (9565) 05:17:21
1451. Mike Hayden (9567) 05:17:23
1452. Jun Yoneyama (9576) 05:17:29
1453. Ron Nagaoka (9586) 05:17:39
1454. Manuel Alvarez (9604) 05:17:57
1455. Nick Maugeri (9616) 05:18:14
1456. Aldo Cos (9619) 05:18:17
1457. Jose Leon (9620) 05:18:18
1458. Jeff Arbuckle (9622) 05:18:20
1459. David Keating (9633) 05:18:29
1460. William Mitchell (9641) 05:18:34
1461. Lin-Den Green (9651) 05:18:40
1462. Anthony Castro (9654) 05:18:44
1463. Nathan Lavire (9660) 05:18:50
1464. Andres Marton (9667) 05:18:58
1465. Carlos Qinones (9670) 05:19:00
1466. Ray Andrzejewski (9683) 05:19:09
1467. Victor Martin (9701) 05:19:25
1468. Matthew McLeese (9702) 05:19:26
1469. Timothy Yip (9731) 05:20:08
1470. Prem Kumar (9733) 05:20:09
1471. Robert Revita Jr (9743) 05:20:20
1472. David Garcia (9756) 05:20:31
1473. Maurice Hall (9757) 05:20:31
1474. Julio Thompson (9766) 05:20:37
1475. Liam Carroll (9776) 05:20:44
1476. Mario Velasquez (9782) 05:20:49
1477. David Rivera (9811) 05:21:12
1478. Jeffrey Francisco (9812) 05:21:12
1479. Mark Baklarz (9819) 05:21:19
1480. Louis Quevedo (9820) 05:21:20
1481. Peter Maldonado (9821) 05:21:21
1482. Timothy Chessani (9834) 05:21:38
1483. Ricardo Amarilla (9846) 05:21:47
1484. Eugene Luster (9848) 05:21:47
1485. Michael Wintz (9865) 05:21:58
1486. David Yoffe (9871) 05:22:03
1487. Andy Walter (9887) 05:22:15
1488. Robert Lawson (9901) 05:22:32
1489. Dan Grassman (9927) 05:23:01
1490. Daryl Mulligan (9950) 05:23:28
1491. David Price (9952) 05:23:30
1492. Michael Murray (9959) 05:23:36
1493. Gus Vargas (9968) 05:23:46
1494. Paul Shomer (9986) 05:24:04
1495. Bill Gray (9989) 05:24:06
1496. Dermot Cooper (9993) 05:24:10
1497. Richard Montoya (9998) 05:24:14
1498. Randy Barnett (10008) 05:24:28
1499. Mark Koszeghy (10012) 05:24:30
1500. Charles Walker (10013) 05:24:31
1501. Joey Otero (10029) 05:24:56
1502. Daniel Sosa (10030) 05:24:56
1503. James Blau (10032) 05:24:58
1504. Pierre Sycip (10033) 05:25:00
1505. Ariel Drachenberg (10035) 05:25:01
1506. Christopher Costantino (10044) 05:25:11
1507. Michael Elias (10046) 05:25:15
1508. John Booth (10055) 05:25:30
1509. Juan Robles (10068) 05:25:40
1510. Akifumi Yamamoto (10079) 05:25:46
1511. Waldo Banks Jr (10081) 05:25:47
1512. Kevin Russ (10091) 05:25:55
1513. Francisco Valladares (10120) 05:26:28
1514. George Castro (10123) 05:26:32
1515. Vinson Lee (10135) 05:26:43
1516. Fidel Villegas (10138) 05:26:48
1517. Pablo Castillo (10148) 05:26:57
1518. Julio Acosta (10155) 05:27:07
1519. Carlos Castillo (10165) 05:27:15
1520. Carlos Gonzalez (10169) 05:27:20
1521. Guillermo Barillas (10182) 05:27:29
1522. Manuel Felix (10200) 05:27:45
1523. Guillermo Cruz (10205) 05:27:48
1524. John Bergstresser (10206) 05:27:49
1525. Francisco Munoz (10221) 05:28:01
1526. Jonathan Taylor (10239) 05:28:16
1527. Jose Marquez (10285) 05:29:00
1528. Albert Madrid (10294) 05:29:10
1529. Carlos Hernandez (10338) 05:29:52
1530. Julio Mendez (10342) 05:29:55
1531. Timothy O'Crowley (10344) 05:29:56
1532. Brant Bily (10346) 05:29:58
1533. Reynaldo Herrera (10363) 05:30:17
1534. Eric Buxton (10388) 05:30:37
1535. Allen Gervais Jr (10410) 05:31:01
1536. Gary Kwan (10414) 05:31:06
1537. Daniel Friedenthal (10416) 05:31:08
1538. Michael Brown (10427) 05:31:18
1539. Glenn Loria (10438) 05:31:27
1540. Jimmy White (10439) 05:31:27
1541. Angel Medina (10467) 05:31:49
1542. Jeff Johnson (10471) 05:31:50
1543. Edgar Ramirez (10490) 05:32:08
1544. Rafael Alzua (10518) 05:32:45
1545. Arthur Fong (10530) 05:32:53
1546. Rob Wood (10542) 05:33:03
1547. John Carter (10548) 05:33:09
1548. John Wernet (10552) 05:33:13
1549. Yuzo Motosugi (10568) 05:33:28
1550. Glenn Thompson (10571) 05:33:28
1551. David Dixon (10581) 05:33:40
1552. Colin Milner (10582) 05:33:41
1553. Michel Larcheveque (10605) 05:33:54
1554. Lorenzo Zavala (10610) 05:33:57
1555. Steven Howard (10618) 05:34:04
1556. Hugo Jauregui (10627) 05:34:08
1557. James Valinoti (10632) 05:34:17
1558. Ken Ashman (10637) 05:34:25
1559. Carlos Gutierrez (10647) 05:34:33
1560. Bryan Ohira (10649) 05:34:36
1561. Constantino Alva (10653) 05:34:39
1562. Omar Serrato (10656) 05:34:41
1563. Manuel Morales (10662) 05:34:43
1564. Markel Siremore (10673) 05:34:57
1565. Martin Medina (10689) 05:35:10
1566. Luis Rodriguez (10691) 05:35:11
1567. Ezequiel Lopez (10696) 05:35:21
1568. David Munoz (10700) 05:35:23
1569. Chi Chung Tong (10706) 05:35:26
1570. James Carstensen (10720) 05:35:39
1571. Bill Perucca (10730) 05:35:49
1572. Michael Scott (10753) 05:36:13
1573. Alejandro Fernandez (10757) 05:36:18
1574. John Klutke (10782) 05:36:47
1575. David Won (10818) 05:37:24
1576. Kenzo Minamiguchi (10827) 05:37:33
1577. Fabian Grandoli (10830) 05:37:35
1578. John Judy (10831) 05:37:36
1579. Ed Mueller (10833) 05:37:38
1580. Ramon Cordero (10845) 05:37:56
1581. Rick Drew (10855) 05:38:07
1582. David Patron (10856) 05:38:08
1583. Alfonso Herrera (10859) 05:38:10
1584. Carlos Reyna (10861) 05:38:12
1585. Douglas Blasdell (10870) 05:38:33
1586. Koichiro Kawano (10904) 05:39:13
1587. Troy Malonzo (10926) 05:39:48
1588. Paul Furie (10940) 05:40:05
1589. Hoan Luu (10952) 05:40:20
1590. William Hardesty (10975) 05:40:49
1591. Julian Gater (10977) 05:41:02
1592. Sean Laughlin (10986) 05:41:11
1593. Thomas Brown (10987) 05:41:13
1594. Enrique Guerra (11034) 05:42:04
1595. Michael Adams (11059) 05:42:20
1596. Steven Lucero (11064) 05:42:26
1597. David Collins (11080) 05:42:41
1598. Carlos Galvez (11083) 05:42:42
1599. Mark Yin (11095) 05:42:55
1600. Stefan Ogrodzinski (11123) 05:43:28
1601. Yasushi Watanabe (11129) 05:43:33
1602. Scott Halsema (11142) 05:43:40
1603. Steven Schwartz (11147) 05:43:51
1604. James Jaeger (11165) 05:44:12
1605. Marcos Alvarez (11168) 05:44:13
1606. Mark Jones (11175) 05:44:15
1607. Andrew Duncan (11190) 05:44:22
1608. Dilip Budhrani (11205) 05:44:33
1609. Carlos Araujo (11207) 05:44:34
1610. Edward Hernandez (11211) 05:44:36
1611. Joe Rowser (11219) 05:44:41
1612. Thaddeus Bui (11220) 05:44:42
1613. Larry Smith (11239) 05:45:02
1614. Michael Cruz (11241) 05:45:05
1615. Hector Rodriguez (11325) 05:46:42
1616. Manuel Cortez (11332) 05:46:51
1617. Miguel Vasquez (11334) 05:46:53
1618. Berton Banta (11345) 05:47:11
1619. Hideki Nara (11348) 05:47:19
1620. David Paul (11357) 05:47:30
1621. Bill Amejka (11360) 05:47:36
1622. Atsushi Kajioka (11400) 05:48:59
1623. Sam Assad (11414) 05:49:08
1624. Francisco Sandoval (11421) 05:49:18
1625. Steve Koehler (11427) 05:49:24
1626. Thomas Watson (11436) 05:49:32
1627. Brian Shapiro (11440) 05:49:35
1628. Albert Gee (11452) 05:49:44
1629. Bernardo Cabreros (11488) 05:50:19
1630. Sergio Ruiz (11501) 05:50:28
1631. Robert Pattison (11516) 05:50:36
1632. James Drew (11534) 05:50:56
1633. Sreesha Rao (11566) 05:51:47
1634. Greg Willins (11580) 05:52:10
1635. Michael Savage (11584) 05:52:11
1636. Lawrence Blackmon (11591) 05:52:17
1637. Byron Aldana (11608) 05:52:40
1638. Eric Williams (11609) 05:52:42
1639. Julian Manalo (11613) 05:52:48
1640. Julian Vega (11619) 05:52:58
1641. Bryan Johnson (11630) 05:53:00
1642. Jose Sanchez (11633) 05:53:01
1643. Ray Jalili (11638) 05:53:09
1644. Wing-Hung Ki (11642) 05:53:13
1645. Mikeal Hamilton (11682) 05:53:53
1646. Damon Simmons (11684) 05:53:53
1647. Armando Salomon (11689) 05:53:58
1648. Jose Nieves (11692) 05:54:01
1649. Chikara Kurosaki (11721) 05:54:49
1650. Bert Obregon (11722) 05:54:50
1651. Shant Chobanian (11724) 05:54:54
1652. Victorio Gutierrez (11727) 05:55:00
1653. David Mc Lean (11747) 05:55:21
1654. Ahmed Dawlatly (11749) 05:55:22
1655. Efrem Gallegos (11758) 05:55:34
1656. Richard Rosen (11764) 05:55:42
1657. John Mitio (11767) 05:55:46
1658. Thomas Maclas (11772) 05:55:51
1659. Patrick Tam (11781) 05:56:01
1660. Ray Nulod (11796) 05:56:30
1661. Rick Fung (11813) 05:56:53
1662. Tom Vasquez (11822) 05:57:07
1663. Rich Lynn (11829) 05:57:17
1664. Shinya Toyoda (11845) 05:57:42
1665. Michael Larkin (11852) 05:57:55
1666. Paul Tomlin (11853) 05:57:57
1667. Theodore Booker (11854) 05:57:58
1668. Pablo Gonzalez (11859) 05:58:03
1669. Marcelino Perez Jr (11869) 05:58:14
1670. Satoshi Suzuki (11870) 05:58:17
1671. Brian Beziat (11886) 05:58:27
1672. Robert Bennett (11889) 05:58:32
1673. Glen Johnson (11890) 05:58:32
1674. Rod Damer (11921) 05:59:20
1675. Steven Tisser (11928) 05:59:24
1676. Michael Ume (11943) 05:59:45
1677. Joel Kobayashi (11957) 05:59:57
1678. George Natiudad (11962) 06:00:12
1679. Andy Soemardi (11963) 06:00:13
1680. Christopher Brockel (11966) 06:00:14
1681. Damon Wing (11969) 06:00:17
1682. Pete Soriano (11973) 06:00:26
1683. Art Negrete (11986) 06:00:51
1684. Robert Tancinco (12007) 06:01:23
1685. Ricky Doanle (12020) 06:01:49
1686. Oscar Jimenez (12031) 06:02:02
1687. Robert Ramos (12052) 06:02:34
1688. Steve Tung (12055) 06:02:41
1689. Robert Scott (12076) 06:03:21
1690. Dave Norton (12095) 06:03:51
1691. James Young (12106) 06:04:18
1692. Charles Beeson (12123) 06:04:40
1693. Alvaro Amador (12131) 06:04:44
1694. Martin Perez (12136) 06:04:49
1695. Ray Dyer (12157) 06:05:22
1696. Carlos Cuffman (12162) 06:05:28
1697. Victor Kodama (12163) 06:05:30
1698. Peter Au (12166) 06:05:32
1699. Stephen Lew (12182) 06:05:58
1700. Stephen Lam (12183) 06:06:05
1701. Mark Groth (12188) 06:06:12
1702. Rene Hernandez (12197) 06:06:24
1703. Mori Hiroki (12211) 06:07:01
1704. Alfredo Gonzalez (12239) 06:07:50
1705. Denver Locke (12245) 06:07:59
1706. Cory Van Gelder (12249) 06:08:05
1707. Drew Cannon (12252) 06:08:09
1708. Mario Agno (12269) 06:08:36
1709. Kevin Neighbors (12283) 06:08:50
1710. Carlos Villarreal (12288) 06:08:53
1711. Daniel Arlt (12314) 06:09:25
1712. Eddy Vargas (12317) 06:09:29
1713. Joseph Ramirez (12328) 06:09:49
1714. Hemraj Nair (12341) 06:10:05
1715. Kenneth Garland (12350) 06:10:31
1716. William Stahl (12355) 06:10:33
1717. Frank Valdez (12370) 06:11:03
1718. Jeff Holliday (12373) 06:11:06
1719. Tim Pearce (12381) 06:11:18
1720. Mauricio Ramirez (12385) 06:11:22
1721. Larry Hess (12391) 06:11:31
1722. Brett Diaz (12393) 06:11:35
1723. Jose Yamanoha (12402) 06:11:48
1724. Raffi Garabed (12427) 06:12:34
1725. Gary Getler (12497) 06:14:18
1726. Alejandro Cruz (12498) 06:14:21
1727. Paul Jones (12517) 06:14:52
1728. Steve Ford (12527) 06:15:11
1729. Kenji Kawahigashi (12544) 06:15:28
1730. Gerald Doswell (12547) 06:15:36
1731. Thomas Harris (12554) 06:15:41
1732. Christopher Avila (12561) 06:15:55
1733. Juan Sil (12566) 06:15:58
1734. Michael Arnold (12584) 06:16:35
1735. Barry Preston (12590) 06:16:44
1736. Paul Wims Jr (12593) 06:16:49
1737. Mario Haidar (12626) 06:17:38
1738. Kenneth Sayers (12640) 06:18:17
1739. Adam Pitt (12642) 06:18:18
1740. Steve Lopez (12643) 06:18:19
1741. Richard Park (12651) 06:18:31
1742. Arthur Batucal (12657) 06:18:48
1743. Michael Newhouse (12673) 06:19:21
1744. Yoshio Shigenobu (12674) 06:19:22
1745. Hajime Tokushiku (12680) 06:19:35
1746. Frank Moncado (12685) 06:19:42
1747. Duke Shibata (12725) 06:20:56
1748. Edward Milhomme (12767) 06:21:56
1749. Edward Blunnie (12769) 06:21:58
1750. Gregorio Morales (12772) 06:22:01
1751. Marshall Vandermey (12784) 06:22:20
1752. Koji Wakayoshi (12850) 06:24:03
1753. Hideo Tsubaki (12911) 06:26:11
1754. Leslie Kelly (12940) 06:26:49
1755. Richard Mercado Jr (12941) 06:26:51
1756. Miguel Flores (12993) 06:28:30
1757. Thomas Wu (13011) 06:28:49
1758. Minoru Fujita (13015) 06:29:06
1759. Mike Swindell (13046) 06:30:09
1760. Frank Byrne (13052) 06:30:27
1761. Maurice Moreno (13055) 06:30:37
1762. Michael Bridges (13057) 06:30:43
1763. John Lockler (13064) 06:30:48
1764. Seiji Hara (13067) 06:30:55
1765. Marvin James Barruga (13093) 06:31:34
1766. Hector Gomez (13098) 06:31:48
1767. George Gutierrez (13103) 06:31:57
1768. Douglas Bowden (13121) 06:32:30
1769. Miguel Licea (13125) 06:32:32
1770. Scott Zechiel (13139) 06:32:45
1771. Adolfo Garcia (13175) 06:33:36
1772. Raul Zavala (13189) 06:34:10
1773. Brian Bakke (13193) 06:34:13
1774. Willy Munguia (13225) 06:35:05
1775. Andrew Gibson (13229) 06:35:11
1776. David Descargar (13259) 06:36:05
1777. Hideo Takeuchi (13278) 06:36:32
1778. Andrew Fisher (13291) 06:37:07
1779. Selby Jessup (13294) 06:37:08
1780. Ricci Barnes (13297) 06:37:28
1781. Ryuta Sasahara (13298) 06:37:28
1782. Harrison Thomas (13324) 06:38:28
1783. Murray Pleasant (13340) 06:39:01
1784. Don Nunes (13374) 06:40:06
1785. Johnny Cuto (13379) 06:40:26
1786. Marvin Hora (13401) 06:41:10
1787. Ramin Hatami (13404) 06:41:18
1788. Michael McCarron (13418) 06:41:49
1789. Michael Tolchard (13427) 06:42:06
1790. John Li (13429) 06:42:08
1791. Sergio Sanchez (13448) 06:42:41
1792. Kazuya Bamba (13459) 06:43:01
1793. Shuji Matsuda (13489) 06:44:19
1794. Daryle Boyd (13506) 06:45:08
1795. Juan Muniz (13524) 06:45:52
1796. Kenneth Ng (13525) 06:45:53
1797. J Brown (13537) 06:46:13
1798. William Witcher (13573) 06:47:29
1799. Will Koegler (13603) 06:48:22
1800. Henry Villafana (13649) 06:49:59
1801. Jose Razon (13652) 06:50:01
1802. Seki Hidekazu (13658) 06:50:05
1803. Kenneth Martinez (13687) 06:50:39
1804. Glenn Calfee (13716) 06:51:46
1805. Hiroshi Morie (13723) 06:51:52
1806. Gerardo Delgado (13772) 06:54:33
1807. Jim Watt (13781) 06:54:56
1808. Victor Venegas-Collins (13790) 06:55:05
1809. Brian Alt (13804) 06:55:26
1810. Frank Barcelo (13821) 06:55:52
1811. Leopoldo Valdes (13824) 06:55:56
1812. David Morrison (13829) 06:56:02
1813. Toshio Odaka (13838) 06:56:33
1814. Michael Waterman (13848) 06:56:49
1815. Franklin Magarro (13853) 06:56:59
1816. Harmon Kong (13854) 06:57:00
1817. David Ramos (13857) 06:57:01
1818. Jason Hanakeawe (13882) 06:57:51
1819. Jeffrey Anderson (13904) 06:58:31
1820. Julian Ely III (13930) 06:59:04
1821. Roberta Munoz (13932) 06:59:05
1822. Tae Ahn (13935) 06:59:08
1823. David Cooper (13937) 06:59:09
1824. Sid Truong (13941) 06:59:25
1825. Todd Zeller (13988) 07:01:01
1826. Paul Scire Jr (13994) 07:01:03
1827. Davinder Bhalla (14002) 07:01:18
1828. John Ruiz (14049) 07:03:13
1829. Mike Graeber (14087) 07:05:04
1830. Gilbert Serrano (14126) 07:07:59
1831. Terence O'Bryant (14129) 07:08:15
1832. Victor Mansour (14135) 07:08:28
1833. Gustavo Ochoa (14141) 07:08:35
1834. Robert Alcantara (14161) 07:10:41
1835. Charles Richardson (14211) 07:13:04
1836. Rick Rodabaugh (14249) 07:15:26
1837. Charles Tierney (14254) 07:15:36
1838. Yavuz Sap (14257) 07:15:37
1839. Anthony Barkley (14258) 07:15:38
1840. Hiro Hirata (14289) 07:17:22
1841. Harold Arano (14292) 07:17:28
1842. Victor Varela (14329) 07:20:07
1843. Frank Alani (14354) 07:21:39
1844. Ed Young (14388) 07:23:55
1845. Jimmy Young (14389) 07:23:56
1846. Shigetoshi Namoto (14396) 07:24:36
1847. Brad Rhodes (14446) 07:29:03
1848. Ishmael Obeso (14472) 07:30:51
1849. Troy Kelley (14476) 07:31:21
1850. John Thietje (14495) 07:33:33
1851. Takeshi Oya (14502) 07:34:12
1852. Dan Adler (14525) 07:35:52
1853. Derrick Mitchell (14540) 07:36:46
1854. Randall Hong (14575) 07:39:11
1855. Arnel Orejana (14595) 07:40:39
1856. Peter Gonzalez (14597) 07:40:56
1857. Greg Patterson (14610) 07:41:43
1858. Gerardo Villalobos (14653) 07:42:22
1859. Alonzo Rivera (14668) 07:47:45
1860. Guy Takahashi (14683) 07:49:17
1861. Victor Gonzalez (14711) 07:51:45
1862. Brian Miller (14769) 07:56:11
1863. Alfredo Neyra (14782) 07:57:39
1864. Daniel Kim (14813) 08:01:35
1865. Ron Arceneaux (14887) 08:13:49
1866. Sergio Altina (14953) 08:22:20
1867. Andy Dayani (14959) 08:23:41
1868. Ray Trejo (15009) 08:33:32
1869. Hanny Munoz (15026) 08:36:29
1870. Chun Shong Chiao (15051) 08:46:23
1871. Victor Valdez (15079) 08:55:21
1872. Steven Stover (15110) 09:14:58
1873. Dino Shorte (15120) 09:20:30
1874. Mark Madsen (15141) 00:13:45
1875. Daniel Draper (15145) 00:40:02

WOMEN 30 TO 34

1. Anna Rybicka (29) 02:32:59
2. Kirsi Rauta (56) 02:41:46
3. Olia Kosolapova (71) 02:44:49
4. Keena Carstensen (267) 03:02:16
5. Jill Horne (312) 03:04:23
6. Leticia Macias (317) 03:04:43
7. Gilda Mendez De Moran (321) 03:04:58
8. Holly Nybo (336) 03:05:46
9. Griselda Estrada Esquivel (428) 03:09:23
10. Elida Ortiz (668) 03:17:19
11. Anna-Maria Howard (681) 03:17:33
12. Vickie Ford (729) 03:19:10
13. Martha Gandy (908) 03:23:27
14. Lari Nusinov (1019) 03:25:57
15. Louise Menashe (1083) 03:27:22
16. Carla Bressler (1157) 03:28:44
17. Carrie Sova (1170) 03:28:58
18. Araceli Aguilar (1223) 03:29:46
19. Leticia Melgoza (1245) 03:30:18
20. Tommie Moreau (1314) 03:31:36
21. Kelly Zirbes (1367) 03:32:37
22. Nancy Nunn (1373) 03:32:45
23. Shelly Bancroft (1377) 03:32:48
24. Brenda Villanueva (1464) 03:34:49
25. Brenda Corona (1503) 03:35:29
26. Liz Broakway (1511) 03:35:35
27. Tamara Dawn Hew (1513) 03:35:38
28. Caroline Heron (1548) 03:36:15
29. Yolanda Lopez (1594) 03:37:06
30. Judy Oman (1629) 03:37:50
31. Cathi Remington (1640) 03:37:56

32. Martha Solis Torres (1690) 03:38:48
33. Julie Chamberlain (1718) 03:39:17
34. Sheri Pogue (1724) 03:39:24
35. Debbie Simon (1788) 03:40:26
36. Maria Louise Papadeas (1876) 03:41:41
37. Pamela Rubly (1877) 03:41:42
38. Ronni Ross (1889) 03:41:48
39. Virginia Vargas (1906) 03:42:03
40. Gayle Spicer (1908) 03:42:04
41. Liane Monaco (1936) 03:42:40
42. Terie West (1949) 03:43:03
43. Ann Marie Castro (1958) 03:43:09
44. Sue Runyon (1974) 03:43:27
45. Maria Lemuz (2001) 03:43:55
46. Eva Castellon (2071) 03:44:45
47. Donna Short (2083) 03:44:57
48. Tracy Hild (2120) 03:45:21
49. Kyomi Paz (2160) 03:46:01
50. Lori Stuckers (2181) 03:46:22
51. Vicki Nichols (2191) 03:46:30
52. Mary Jones (2192) 03:46:32
53. Carrie Beckstrom (2212) 03:46:55
54. Wanda Johnson (2218) 03:46:59
55. Susan Howard (2220) 03:47:00
56. Jamy Myatt (2299) 03:48:07
57. Dianne Jones (2337) 03:48:36
58. Maria Calvert (2356) 03:48:50
59. Kim Harrington (2390) 03:49:17
60. Virginia Andrade (2403) 03:49:23
61. Linda McFadden (2413) 03:49:35
62. Kathy Pickell (2425) 03:49:44
63. Charlotte Helmkamp (2450) 03:50:06
64. Lara Riscol (2464) 03:50:19
65. Lupe Mora (2512) 03:50:56
66. Kimberly Abbott (2536) 03:51:17
67. Margi Stroh (2628) 03:52:32
68. Monika Marbacher (2630) 03:52:34
69. Michelle Natalier (2665) 03:52:58
70. Karen Fazio (2680) 03:53:10
71. Janet Westergaard (2799) 03:54:35
72. Margaret Cooper (2803) 03:54:37
73. Teri Corpuz (2828) 03:54:53
74. Lora Zagnoli (2906) 03:55:49
75. Ana Alex (2917) 03:55:57
76. Kath Weigel (2924) 03:55:59
77. Leslie Gershman (2944) 03:56:13
78. Melissa Rossin (2947) 03:56:16
79. Carolyn Coradeschi (2955) 03:56:20
80. Karen Hickey (2983) 03:56:45
81. Diane Ver Steeg (3092) 03:57:46
82. Sheila Roth (3094) 03:57:46
83. Terri Foreman (3148) 03:58:25
84. Jeanine Deherrera (3174) 03:58:42
85. Carol Gordon (3223) 03:59:20
86. Terri Buzzard (3229) 03:59:22
87. Hiromi Suzuki (3231) 03:59:24
88. Ashley Dodge (3290) 03:59:57
89. Lianne Kimball (3303) 04:00:03
90. Anna Maria LeVeaux-Washington (3335) 04:00:26
91. Pilar Silva (3345) 04:00:33
92. Joanna Dehen (3416) 04:01:29
93. Karen Vankirk (3432) 04:01:41
94. Donna Archuleta (3458) 04:02:05
95. Wendy Sandler (3491) 04:02:34
96. Valerie Leatherwood (3501) 04:02:41
97. Pam Lanzaratta (3527) 04:03:05
98. Marguerite Fahy (3582) 04:03:56
99. Colleen Shea (3616) 04:04:20
100. Jocelyn Saidenberg (3662) 04:04:47
101. Carla Kiefer (3679) 04:04:59
102. Barbara Gilbert (3690) 04:05:06
103. Dolly Sanders (3728) 04:05:38
104. Peggy Newcomer (3744) 04:05:53
105. Linda Morash (3781) 04:06:23
106. Linda Haymes (3783) 04:06:26
107. Eva De Porcel (3785) 04:06:27
108. Leslie Ablaza (3793) 04:06:31
109. Patricia Gutierrez (3798) 04:06:35
110. Barbara Brace (3817) 04:06:48
111. Susan Larsen (3819) 04:06:50
112. Maureen McGrath (3830) 04:06:58
113. Roberta Murar (3834) 04:07:00
114. Georgia Gallaher (3855) 04:07:10
115. Maria Palmer (3858) 04:07:15
116. Denise Icaza (3863) 04:07:18
117. Sonia Gonzalez (3876) 04:07:30
118. Carol Koontz (3881) 04:07:33
119. Lisa Green (3899) 04:07:44
120. Gayle Whittemore (3949) 04:08:23
121. Joan Yoshioka (3952) 04:08:24
122. Tracy Reusch (3973) 04:08:44
123. Erika Cronshagen (3989) 04:08:58
124. Veronica Montoya (4000) 04:09:06
125. Diana Graham (4014) 04:09:16
126. Stephanie O'Neill (4028) 04:09:25
127. Cat Doran (4032) 04:09:29
128. Brenda Reynolds (4069) 04:10:01
129. Ronal Ellison (4104) 04:10:30
130. Tammy Kizer (4116) 04:10:39
131. Shari Handy (4117) 04:10:39
132. Donna Nadajewski (4123) 04:10:44
133. Linda Warner (4139) 04:10:54
134. Rubi Morales Henriquez (4179) 04:11:17
135. Atsuko Yamamoto (4282) 04:12:42
136. Diana Fried (4283) 04:12:43
137. Deborah Finn (4291) 04:12:51
138. Priscilla Rosen (4296) 04:12:55
139. Masami Fukuhara (4299) 04:12:58
140. Susan Chamberlain (4319) 04:13:09
141. Shannon Griefer (4341) 04:13:26
142. Leslie Rehak (4346) 04:13:31
143. Diana Rush (4379) 04:13:57
144. Kathryn Stroupe (4402) 04:14:14
145. Theresa Haley (4405) 04:14:18
146. Julie Anderson (4421) 04:14:24
147. Yvonne Kunstenaar (4466) 04:14:47
148. Susan Griego (4490) 04:15:00
149. Meganne Kanatani (4503) 04:15:11
150. Michelle Harmony (4523) 04:15:30
151. Julia Lockwood (4553) 04:15:43
152. Marylou Green (4561) 04:15:48
153. Maggie Avila (4564) 04:15:49
154. Crystal Richmond (4572) 04:15:53
155. Kim Masoner (4580) 04:16:01
156. Robin Sehenreich (4600) 04:16:12
157. Kimberly Klein (4629) 04:16:31
158. Kathryn Adelman (4639) 04:16:37
159. Mary Jo Braun (4686) 04:17:16
160. Linda Meadows (4709) 04:17:34
161. Naima Genitempo (4807) 04:18:41
162. Maureen Bakey (4810) 04:18:42
163. Sheri Chessani (4812) 04:18:43
164. Linda Destefano (4859) 04:19:09
165. Trina Long (4876) 04:19:18
166. Cheryl Ingram (4878) 04:19:18
167. Janet Hatch (4882) 04:19:22
168. Alison Wrigley (4924) 04:19:51
169. Michelle Crawford (4951) 04:20:12
170. Caroline Baron (4956) 04:20:16
171. Iris Ziegler (4976) 04:20:36
172. Yun Lee (4987) 04:20:44
173. Susan Wassermann (5028) 04:21:23
174. Laura Baker (5037) 04:21:31
175. Melinda Vallens (5048) 04:21:38
176. Annie Daniels (5049) 04:21:39
177. Rosa Contreras (5059) 04:21:43
178. Tracy Puckett (5077) 04:21:52
179. Catherine Shott (5136) 04:22:25
180. Vicky Kay (5140) 04:22:31
181. Lynn Renken (5157) 04:22:42
182. Sandy Burchett (5209) 04:23:17
183. Benita Shaw (5214) 04:23:19
184. Ann Eckels (5231) 04:23:34
185. Sally Martin (5239) 04:23:38
186. Mary Yee (5278) 04:24:18
187. Deidre Weber (5283) 04:24:23
188. Kay Kostlan (5296) 04:24:31
189. Rosina Szele (5342) 04:25:02
190. Michele Bayer (5381) 04:25:23
191. Cindy Boeldt (5412) 04:25:41
192. Dawn Resnick (5466) 04:26:14
193. Stephanie Mailman (5469) 04:26:18
194. Annmarie Grossman (5476) 04:26:24
195. Tiana Boyman (5478) 04:26:26
196. Pamela Shapir (5485) 04:26:29
197. Kimberly Siegel (5497) 04:26:39
198. Kimberly Nolan (5541) 04:27:13
199. Janean Cook (5560) 04:27:24
200. Liz Sims (5565) 04:27:28
201. Vickie House (5570) 04:27:31
202. Dianne Caruth (5572) 04:27:31
203. Kari Verjil (5581) 04:27:35
204. Kimberly Richardson-Harris (5603) 04:27:51
205. Barbara Galbraith (5637) 04:28:10
206. Deborah Gorman (5665) 04:28:30
207. Lisa Pate (5696) 04:28:50
208. Susan Peck (5702) 04:28:55
209. Jamie Meszkat (5713) 04:29:02
210. Angela Parrott-Deatsch (5734) 04:29:15
211. Kristina Millhorn (5760) 04:29:31
212. Heidi Tavernetti (5762) 04:29:33
213. Lisa Huntoon (5766) 04:29:34
214. Sheila Crofts (5770) 04:29:37
215. Katherine Ellis (5779) 04:29:42
216. Martha Gomez (5787) 04:29:50
217. Maria Smith (5793) 04:29:54
218. Leslie Oliran (5800) 04:30:01
219. Jacqueline Ryan (5821) 04:30:17
220. Vanessa Vasquez (5827) 04:30:23
221. Elisa Verduzco (5866) 04:30:39
222. Jane Shielly (5892) 04:30:55
223. Jenny McMahon (5915) 04:31:09
224. Cindy Plumlee (5947) 04:31:30
225. Sally Majidian (5972) 04:31:51
226. Janiece Greer (5991) 04:32:05
227. Andi Leibsohn (6035) 04:32:44
228. Michelle Boutet (6047) 04:32:49
229. Elizabeth Allman (6083) 04:33:13
230. Alicia Denley (6092) 04:33:19
231. Grace Hickey (6107) 04:33:29
232. Darlene Piltingsrud (6115) 04:33:34
233. Karen Potwora (6143) 04:33:54
234. Beth Vito (6148) 04:33:58
235. Jeanne Billhartz (6178) 04:34:19
236. Leona Vlassis (6184) 04:34:23
237. Lori Sage (6188) 04:34:25
238. Lisa Diaz (6211) 04:34:40
239. Jennifer Kirkgaard (6231) 04:34:51
240. Susan Waddy (6289) 04:35:28
241. Datsy Cunas (6325) 04:35:52
242. Melinda Gaffney (6369) 04:36:20
243. Maureen Clarke (6388) 04:36:27
244. Michele Hartwick (6399) 04:36:33
245. Carmen Knibbs (6415) 04:36:40
246. Jacqueline Leigh (6455) 04:37:20
247. Suzy Curtis (6505) 04:37:45
248. Michaela De Vos (6506) 04:37:46
249. Rene Martinez (6519) 04:37:53
250. Germaine Ward (6534) 04:38:05
251. Terry Herrera (6540) 04:38:08
252. Lynda Arnold (6603) 04:38:45
253. Sharon Martin (6606) 04:38:47
254. Gretchen Humbert (6614) 04:38:52
255. Lynne Smith (6633) 04:39:03
256. Heidi Solderholm (6684) 04:39:43
257. Jennifer Doerflinger (6698) 04:39:50
258. Paige Oden (6769) 04:40:56
259. Karen Kalil (6781) 04:41:04
260. Melody Hainline (6795) 04:41:10
261. Kathy McKay (6837) 04:41:46
262. Lynne Wahl (6873) 04:42:09
263. Chang Lee (6877) 04:42:13
264. Holly Middlekauff (6955) 04:43:09
265. Leslie York (6957) 04:43:14
266. Ramona Carl (6986) 04:43:29
267. Nomi Renella (7044) 04:44:05
268. Mary Maxwell (7054) 04:44:17
269. Elaine Lopez (7074) 04:44:34
270. Helen Valdez (7079) 04:44:36
271. Iselda Valdez (7102) 04:44:54
272. Grace Devault (7107) 04:44:57
273. Miguel Rodriguez (7122) 04:45:06
274. Teri Quinones (7139) 04:45:19
275. Jamie Wood (7180) 04:45:52
276. Dena Decker (7219) 04:46:20
277. Michele Zeolla (7253) 04:46:44
278. Maria Newkirk (7256) 04:46:45
279. Cynthia Geskes (7264) 04:46:52
280. Silvia Perez (7271) 04:46:56
281. Lisa Brinegar (7293) 04:47:10
282. TC Proctor (7297) 04:47:12
283. Mary Mullenhoff (7337) 04:47:38
284. Lisa Wilson (7366) 04:48:01
285. Mine Budiman (7418) 04:48:35
286. Sheri Crowe (7430) 04:48:44
287. Leslie Bringolf (7470) 04:49:08
288. Ana Portillo (7509) 04:49:29
289. Suzanne Tara (7518) 04:49:33
290. Izumi Maki (7530) 04:49:43
291. Krisanne Elsner (7535) 04:49:48
292. Arlette Godges (7597) 04:50:36
293. Elizabeth Janson (7603) 04:50:42
294. Lynda Anderson (7628) 04:50:58
295. Susan Potter (7656) 04:51:23
296. Claudine Campion (7675) 04:51:39
297. Heidi Grahn (7711) 04:52:06
298. Dina Vanpelt (7738) 04:52:28
299. Pamela Haber (7746) 04:52:36
300. Laura Lowe (7758) 04:52:43
301. Kimberly Bertram (7766) 04:52:51
302. Kellee Gilbert (7776) 04:52:57
303. Laurie Wexler (7781) 04:52:59
304. Maria Mares (7798) 04:53:15
305. Stephanie Kovac (7814) 04:53:26
306. Keri Medina (7819) 04:53:29
307. Vanessa Johnson (7889) 04:54:14
308. Ann McFadden (7909) 04:54:24
309. Gema Santos (7919) 04:54:30
310. Joyce Kaehler (7924) 04:54:32
311. Kathy Moore (7926) 04:54:33
312. Otlia Vera (7961) 04:54:47
313. Eileen Michaels (7998) 04:55:21
314. Marilyn Cooper (8002) 04:55:27
315. Gail Gordon (8032) 04:55:49
316. Josie Garcia (8054) 04:56:06
317. Debra Tennen (8080) 04:56:26
318. Dori Dunn (8089) 04:56:33
319. Lynette Decker (8112) 04:56:46
320. Annette Krogh (8114) 04:56:46
321. Dulce Alcala (8118) 04:56:50
322. Maia Sorensen (8122) 04:56:56
323. Pauline Nzeribe (8129) 04:57:03
324. Marlene Gadinis (8153) 04:57:21
325. Patricia Greenberg (8174) 04:57:37
326. Kathleen Busfield (8232) 04:58:14
327. Deborah Louchheim (8235) 04:58:14
328. Katy Lyden (8241) 04:58:16
329. Bianca Mora (8244) 04:58:17
330. Martha Sutton (8254) 04:58:25
331. Lisa Underkoffler (8262) 04:58:29
332. Katrina Moiso (8275) 04:58:41
333. Tracy Lehr (8302) 04:58:54
334. Deana Delgado (8317) 04:59:02
335. Sueling Cho (8321) 04:59:05
336. Mary Caldwell (8327) 04:59:09
337. Lilia Fuentes (8347) 04:59:25
338. Kelly Enright (8349) 04:59:27
339. Hilary Cohen (8358) 04:59:33
340. Jeannette Painovich (8359) 04:59:33
341. Mary Kite (8360) 04:59:35
342. Robin Devereux (8367) 04:59:38
343. Kelly Majdick (8376) 04:59:41
344. Susan Abeloe (8385) 04:59:48
345. Lauren Powell (8386) 04:59:49
346. Carlynn Hedrick (8399) 05:00:01
347. Lissette Habelmann (8458) 05:01:02
348. Nancy Rommelmann (8486) 05:01:23
349. Maria Martinez (8508) 05:01:35
350. Laura Hogan (8520) 05:01:43
351. Linda Hoover (8530) 05:01:48
352. Diana Yao (8550) 05:02:06
353. Valerie Van Galder (8576) 05:02:25
354. Elizabeth Avina (8587) 05:02:41
355. Terri Baker (8597) 05:02:51
356. Stacibelle Baker (8598) 05:02:54
357. Kimberly O'Neill (8615) 05:03:09
358. Yuriko Sugawara (8642) 05:03:32
359. Cathy Braughton-Bazant (8655) 05:03:47
360. Jennifer McNinch (8675) 05:04:00
361. Jeanette Lutton (8676) 05:04:00
362. Janet Townsen (8689) 05:04:11
363. Gissela Dorantes (8698) 05:04:18
364. Terri Vega (8702) 05:04:20
365. Lucila Gonzalez (8730) 05:04:47
366. Olivia Rosas (8735) 05:04:51
367. Debra Walker (8755) 05:05:18
368. Susan Naber (8757) 05:05:21
369. Cassie Hobbs (8758) 05:05:22
370. Kimberly Brown (8763) 05:05:26
371. Joann Ornelas (8779) 05:05:38
372. Romnia Drever-Harper (8800) 05:06:02
373. Lynette Lalonde (8809) 05:06:14
374. Freda Yoshioka (8816) 05:06:22
375. Marinella Navas (8823) 05:06:25
376. Linda Sharpe (8830) 05:06:33
377. Elvia Torres (8839) 05:06:39
378. Bridgette Driver (8853) 05:06:59
379. Kathleen Crain (8859) 05:07:04
380. Ana Gonzalez (8860) 05:07:05
381. Lucy Rivera (8868) 05:07:10
382. Tammy Gatti (8872) 05:07:13
383. Lisa Duran (8875) 05:07:15
384. Cheryl Thomas (8920) 05:08:05
385. Lynn Stephens-Preiss (8925) 05:08:07
386. Heather Hartley (8935) 05:08:16
387. Christina Allen (8941) 05:08:28
388. Joanna Brody (8965) 05:08:40
389. Guadalupe Buenrostro (8968) 05:08:42
390. Susan Niestemski (8971) 05:08:42
391. Nancy Albert (8974) 05:08:43
392. Joann Flavin (8988) 05:09:02
393. Beth Peterson (9077) 05:10:09
394. Deanie Caffey (9084) 05:10:13
395. Silvia Ariniello (9096) 05:10:17
396. Etsuko Bost (9142) 05:10:54
397. Dawn Ashimine (9175) 05:11:33
398. Jennifer Holden (9176) 05:11:33
399. Kathy Parker (9191) 05:11:40
400. Donna Volpicella (9195) 05:11:45
401. Sarah Hanlon (9218) 05:12:11
402. Julie Francisco (9220) 05:12:12
403. Mayra De La Torre (9255) 05:12:48
404. Juanesta Holmes (9262) 05:12:53
405. Laura Risser (9271) 05:13:03
406. Dalyce Barnett (9319) 05:13:35
407. Patricia Fleeger (9334) 05:13:42
408. Endo Shino (9337) 05:13:46
409. Julie Barbo-Garcia (9382) 05:14:22
410. Jo Barbo (9383) 05:14:23
411. Blanca Munoz (9393) 05:14:30
412. Julie Conlon (9399) 05:14:40
413. Bonnie Shuster (9428) 05:15:18
414. Debra Broberg (9459) 05:15:55
415. Lauren Hollenbeck (9476) 05:16:12
416. Deb Field (9480) 05:16:16
417. Sandie Kobrine (9483) 05:16:17
418. Eileen Decker (9484) 05:16:18
419. Jackie Jank (9524) 05:16:48
420. Yvonne Keller (9557) 05:17:13
421. Stella Castro (9648) 05:18:39
422. Maria Leon (9664) 05:18:56
423. Rachelle Nesgoda (9688) 05:19:14
424. Mayumi Iizuka (9695) 05:19:20
425. Kay Lyn Byrne (9716) 05:19:45
426. Karen Romero-Flores (9717) 05:19:45
427. Gail Wetmore (9727) 05:20:02
428. Sansanee McGee (9755) 05:20:30
429. Tina Gallman (9773) 05:20:42
430. Marci Moran (9833) 05:21:38
431. Sherise MacGregor (9845) 05:21:46
432. Melody Rooney (9913) 05:22:48
433. Donna Thomas (9918) 05:22:53
434. Akiko Kunimoto (9928) 05:23:03
435. Nicole Hawkins (9930) 05:23:08
436. Sabine Schellscheidt (9937) 05:23:18
437. Tsukumi Fujita (9948) 05:23:26
438. S DeAnn Dickens (9978) 05:23:56
439. Melissa Zipnick (9981) 05:24:01
440. Sue Belgin (9987) 05:24:05
441. Francine Spada (10060) 05:25:35
442. Maggie Esbenshade (10067) 05:25:38
443. Akiko Yoshida (10077) 05:25:46
444. Nancie Havinoviski (10096) 05:26:02
445. Tammy Brown (10113) 05:26:17
446. Sarah Santos (10176) 05:27:24
447. Pat Krauss-Fitoa (10197) 05:27:42
448. Sally Arroyo (10233) 05:28:09
449. Laura Wolff (10276) 05:28:53
450. Jane Limm (10306) 05:29:15
451. Pam Plivelich (10313) 05:29:18
452. Jodi Okun (10315) 05:29:19
453. Melinda Orozco (10328) 05:29:40
454. Jane Diaz (10348) 05:29:59
455. Suzanne Fortman (10359) 05:30:14
456. Kristine Peterka (10371) 05:30:23
457. Mariaelena Bradshaw (10398) 05:30:44
458. Diana Estrada (10441) 05:31:28
459. Lori Lynn Everett (10479) 05:31:56
460. Cindy Boeldt (10485) 05:32:02
461. Kashmira Vijaiyan (10505) 05:32:23
462. Joanna Chen (10544) 05:33:04
463. Monita Abernathy (10585) 05:33:41
464. Rebeca Martinez (10594) 05:33:47
465. Malia Weinmann (10600) 05:33:51
466. Evelia Torres (10609) 05:33:56
467. Tiffanie Vo (10620) 05:34:05
468. Marri Collom (10702) 05:35:25
469. Ilyce Bolotin (10751) 05:36:13
470. Rosa Trenado (10763) 05:36:27
471. Terry Mendez (10772) 05:36:36
472. Julie Sanchez (10773) 05:36:37
473. Michele Lewallen (10776) 05:36:39
474. Kirsten Gray (10821) 05:37:27
475. Lori Henry (10847) 05:37:58
476. Lisa Morton (10854) 05:38:06
477. Suzanne Wilson (10877) 05:38:47
478. Linda Atkinson (10887) 05:38:52
479. Ivonne Paez (10893) 05:38:55
480. Patricia Suarez (10901) 05:39:12
481. Trinidad Nunez (10913) 05:39:24
482. Janet O'Bryan (10972) 05:40:46
483. Vicke Marz (11005) 05:41:33
484. Robin Wilcox-Murray (11016) 05:41:44
485. Julie Davis (11042) 05:42:10
486. Amy Keenan (11049) 05:42:18
487. Kimberly Kelley (11071) 05:42:33
488. Debra Keyzers (11073) 05:42:35
489. Cindy Burt (11074) 05:42:35
490. Nancy Ramirez (11077) 05:42:38
491. Rena Johnson (11094) 05:42:54
492. Judy Lujan (11140) 05:43:54
493. Susan Resetar (11183) 05:44:20
494. Linda Olson (11192) 05:44:24
495. Kelly McMahon (11214) 05:44:37
496. Ann Anderson (11223) 05:44:47
497. Karen Slusarski (11238) 05:45:01
498. Maria Hurtado (11281) 05:45:55
499. Carmen Ochoa (11327) 05:46:48
500. Ginger Smith (11343) 05:47:08
501. Julie Weitz (11359) 05:47:33
502. Bronda Everett (11365) 05:47:45
503. Kimberly Tatera (11379) 05:48:17
504. Elizabeth Diaz (11396) 05:48:53
505. Keiko Shibata (11405) 05:49:01
506. Robin Meleney (11413) 05:49:08
507. Lisa Long (11453) 05:49:45
508. Beth Whisenand (11461) 05:49:50
509. Sherri Harrison (11468) 05:49:59
510. Audrey Romero (11486) 05:50:15
511. Teresa Buenviaje (11550) 05:51:23
512. Lake Alicia (11625) 05:52:59
513. Mildred Marca (11644) 05:53:15
514. Trang Pham (11645) 05:53:15
515. Emmeline Lane (11652) 05:53:22
516. Hilary Fischer (11677) 05:53:49
517. Josie Gallegos (11683) 05:53:53
518. Sonia Vega (11707) 05:54:31
519. Pamela Green (11713) 05:54:36
520. Rita Fuentes (11714) 05:54:37
521. Cecile Najera (11748) 05:55:21
522. Janis Fodran (11771) 05:55:50
523. Carmen Mardany (11786) 05:56:13
524. Haruko Ibe (11797) 05:56:34
525. Patricia Filous-Hidalgo (11802) 05:56:43
526. Karen Wright (11825) 05:57:11
527. Jill Hickey (11841) 05:57:35
528. Peggy Munroe (11899) 05:58:40
529. Cyndya Kolasz (11903) 05:58:45
530. Kim White (11904) 05:58:48
531. Linda Drew (11911) 05:58:54
532. Irene Miranker (11914) 05:58:55
533. Margarita Mejia (11917) 05:58:59
534. Eunice Kim (11940) 05:59:41
535. Sheri Hill (11948) 05:59:53
536. Margaret Fujitaki (11952) 05:59:56
537. Heidi Graham (11980) 06:00:31
538. Jennifer Russell (11995) 06:01:03
539. Olivia Jimenez (12030) 06:02:01
540. Julie Hernandez (12044) 06:02:21
541. Sandra D'amato (12047) 06:02:24
542. Beckie Fisher (12060) 06:02:46
543. Leticia Hernandez (12070) 06:03:07
544. Maria Gonzalez (12086) 06:03:41
545. Rosa Jimenez (12087) 06:03:42
546. Terry Norton (12094) 06:03:50
547. Karen Heller (12140) 06:04:59
548. Leaen Nelson (12228) 06:07:24
549. Christina Eyssallenne (12229) 06:07:26
550. Alex Avalos (12262) 06:08:21
551. Mary Carmen Guzman (12297) 06:09:01
552. Cindy Mason (12301) 06:09:06
553. Joy Lewis (12319) 06:09:37
554. Silvia Navarro (12331) 06:09:51
555. Ellen Granado (12349) 06:10:22
556. Nobuko Peterson (12374) 06:11:06
557. Leticia Ruben (12378) 06:11:15
558. Lori Ann Nishimura (12451) 06:13:09
559. Irma Rodriguez (12470) 06:13:38
560. Mirna Acosta (12485) 06:14:00
561. Linette Banks (12516) 06:14:51
562. Cheryl Stone (12520) 06:14:55
563. Rochell Newton (12535) 06:15:18
564. Kari Kahal (12538) 06:15:25
565. Rosa Avila (12560) 06:15:54
566. Julie Gerstner (12563) 06:15:56
567. Emalee Baptiste (12608) 06:16:59
568. Rebekah Parker (12620) 06:17:30
569. Sayumi Maruyama (12632) 06:17:57
570. Julie Dewitts (12647) 06:18:26
571. Robin Williams (12652) 06:18:32
572. Marcia Osborne (12659) 06:18:54
573. Maria Gonzalez (12677) 06:19:31
574. Rosemary Dade (12686) 06:19:44
575. Birgit Velasquez (12704) 06:20:13
576. Nan Budge (12710) 06:20:26
577. Maria Zamarripa (12720) 06:20:40
578. Janelle Howe (12730) 06:21:14
579. Mary Nieman (12752) 06:21:37
580. Brandye Smith (12757) 06:21:46
581. Tamara Williams (12761) 06:21:52
582. Lily Furlong (12765) 06:21:54
583. Linda Cohen (12782) 06:22:14
584. Alma Cervantes (12802) 06:22:50
585. Diane Medina (12829) 06:23:39
586. Beverly Coughlin (12875) 06:24:53
587. Colette Taylor (12887) 06:25:26
588. Julie Kang-Kim (12894) 06:25:40
589. Harue Marsden (12906) 06:25:55
590. Elizabeth Allen (12939) 06:26:48
591. Cassandra Pham (12955) 06:27:35
592. Jacqueline Ash (12956) 06:27:36
593. Madelaine Gavel (12957) 06:27:37
594. Patricia Savage (12959) 06:27:40
595. Ollie Breckenridge (12985) 06:28:09
596. Julie Haupert (13023) 06:29:17
597. Cathie Wurth (13024) 06:29:20
598. Jodi Jenson (13032) 06:29:40
599. Susan Brunasso (13038) 06:30:02
600. Cynthia Frandsen (13074) 06:31:06
601. Koren Paalman (13087) 06:31:31
602. Tracy Thrower (13123) 06:32:31
603. Gigi Gelenian (13155) 06:33:00
604. Hrair Messerlian (13156) 06:33:00
605. Annette Revel (13174) 06:33:35
606. Patricia Gibson (13228) 06:35:10
607. Susan Connelly (13260) 06:36:06
608. Lisa Carter (13261) 06:36:06
609. Diane Porcella (13265) 06:36:12
610. Catherine Nicklin (13270) 06:36:20
611. Debra Fisher (13292) 06:37:07
612. Estelle Langis (13309) 06:37:52
613. Debra Jones (13310) 06:37:52
614. Elaine Gallegos-Garcia (13347) 06:39:07
615. Hilary Grey (13352) 06:39:16
616. Julie Tuttle (13360) 06:39:32
617. Staci Choate (13397) 06:40:58
618. Karen Humphrey (13400) 06:41:04
619. Merry Goodman (13415) 06:41:31
620. Sarah Allen (13421) 06:41:55
621. Michelle Keyser (13432) 06:42:11
622. Irma McCleary (13439) 06:42:19
623. Martha Laurn (13462) 06:43:19
624. Tamara Hanna (13482) 06:44:09
625. Kinette Cager (13483) 06:44:09
626. Alma Corona (13520) 06:45:40
627. Bridgette Cheeks (13531) 06:46:00
628. Annette Cuomo (13554) 06:46:40
629. Janet Dyer (13585) 06:47:48
630. Nora Constantino (13593) 06:48:08
631. Rebecca Constantino (13594) 06:48:09
632. Ruth Artz (13596) 06:48:10
633. Maychen Tham (13600) 06:48:19
634. Martha Sandoval (13611) 06:48:33
635. Maryellen Westerberg (13637) 06:49:35
636. Debbie Tellez (13640) 06:49:43
637. Michelle Del Guercio (13669) 06:50:27
638. Maria Jimenez (13683) 06:50:36
639. Gina Johnson (13696) 06:50:55
640. Christina Marquez-Miles (13719) 06:51:47
641. Beverly Wiles (13728) 06:52:05
642. Diana Turk (13734) 06:52:28
643. Debbie Callis (13766) 06:54:22
644. Ashley Kwan (13768) 06:54:24
645. Jennifer Brown (13815) 06:55:47
646. Sherri Miller-Hunter (13820) 06:55:52
647. Veda Barcelo (13822) 06:55:53
648. Rikako Takei (13830) 06:56:02
649. Karen Biedebach (13844) 06:56:44
650. Thelma Jackson (13859) 06:57:07
651. Stephanie Vassallo (13890) 06:58:03
652. Shirley Narimatsu (13915) 06:58:44
653. Beth Steinberg (13922) 06:58:56
654. Jolene Hruska (13926) 06:59:00
655. Barbara Lodge (13928) 06:59:03
656. Crystal Smith (13962) 07:00:23
657. Setsugan Ryu (13966) 07:00:31
658. Sherry Craig (13989) 07:01:01
659. Carol Archambeault (13990) 07:01:02
660. Asun Floresca (14017) 07:01:59
661. Arnita Watson (14088) 07:05:13
662. Toni Chassman (14097) 07:06:17
663. Irma Payan (14099) 07:06:19
664. Antonia Soriano (14108) 07:06:46
665. Misty Griffin (14143) 07:08:50
666. Rosie Cedeno (14155) 07:10:10
667. Guadalupe Ruiz (14169) 07:10:54
668. Shirley Boujikian (14198) 07:12:39

669. Jackie Rauda (14227) 07:14:34
670. Laura Chan (14243) 07:14:57
671. Ina Bridges (14287) 07:17:01
672. Lejeune Seary (14293) 07:17:28
673. Cynthia Coa (14323) 07:19:37
674. Melissa Mitchell (14336) 07:20:27
675. Shana Hazard (14378) 07:23:00
676. Monique Mooney (14381) 07:23:03
677. Gwyndollyn Morasko (14403) 07:25:01
678. Denise Rico (14408) 07:26:05
679. Michelle Tyler (14413) 07:26:13
680. Linda Schoen (14422) 07:26:50
681. Cammie Strong (14433) 07:27:38
682. Cheryl Traylor (14434) 07:27:38
683. Nichelle Briley (14451) 07:29:43
684. Sheila Forte (14462) 07:30:21
685. Val Worrell (14463) 07:30:29
686. Annette Stewart (14464) 07:30:31
687. Joanne McClellan (14510) 07:35:02
688. Patricia Muratori (14528) 07:36:03
689. Kim Heggenberger (14534) 07:36:16
690. Shamara Velasco (14563) 07:38:34
691. Jill Robinson (14617) 07:42:46
692. Yumiko Oishi (14672) 07:48:16
693. Ghlisa Au (14678) 07:48:37
694. Jill Langley (14716) 07:52:15
695. Lynne Mac Vean (14720) 07:52:26
696. Valerie Wilson (14745) 07:54:42
697. Sonia Woodhouse (14751) 07:55:03
698. Marina Armendariz (14755) 07:55:13
699. Leticia Mandujano (14761) 07:55:42
700. Donna Leffall (14767) 07:56:07
701. Jackie Brown (14783) 07:58:26
702. Susan Miller (14787) 07:59:24
703. Cynthia Lopez (14797) 08:00:37
704. Shawna Allen (14800) 08:00:49
705. Mary Elaine Palacio (14811) 08:01:31
706. Kevy Rousseau (14828) 08:02:32
707. Valerie Nguyen (14860) 08:08:51
708. Beth Monroe (14862) 08:09:39
709. Joyce Finch (14872) 08:11:11
710. Laura Grewer (14882) 08:12:32
711. Alejandra Gomez (14901) 08:16:31
712. Brigette Millhouse (14921) 08:18:51
713. Lillian Valadez-Rodela (14926) 08:19:24
714. Norma Perez Sanford (14932) 08:20:09
715. Fran Haiem (14970) 08:26:39
716. Maryellen Basurto (14982) 08:28:40
717. Wanda Davis (14983) 08:28:41
718. Monica Chan (14987) 08:28:51
719. Dana Lundquist (14999) 08:31:57
720. Karen Shepard-Grimes (15004) 08:33:06
721. Barbara Wood (15006) 08:33:11
722. Suzanne Sumner (15008) 08:33:30
723. Amelia Saiz (15019) 08:35:34
724. Deborah Thompson (15058) 08:48:51
725. Talat Ashtar (15070) 08:53:30
726. Teresa Rueff (15082) 08:56:03
727. Susan Edra (15090) 08:59:00
728. Roxanne Airhart (15111) 09:14:50
729. Jacqueline Gipson (15121) 09:26:30
730. Jacqueline Anderson (15124) 09:28:35
731. Luticia Pedroza (15139) 09:38:37
732. Diana Konnelly (15140) 09:40:10
733. Cynthia Baker (15143) 09:45:58
734. Francine Sena (15151) 09:52:00
735. Treci Bonfils (15154) 09:53:04

MEN 35 TO 39

1. Martin Pitayo (3) 02:12:49
2. Redge Heislitz (18) 02:29:04
3. Pete Kaplan (37) 02:36:21
4. Stephen Wright (38) 02:36:24
5. Harry Johnson III (40) 02:37:02
6. Rigoberto Vega (42) 02:37:43
7. Manny Nunes (46) 02:39:38
8. Armando Lopez (73) 02:45:12
9. Antonio Gamez Cornelio (75) 02:45:35
10. Leobardo Flores (88) 02:47:52
11. Joe Steinman (92) 02:49:20
12. Rodrigo Casas (93) 02:49:23
13. James Wright (106) 02:51:16
14. Masaru Tamura (107) 02:51:27
15. David South (114) 02:52:11
16. Marco Tulio Lopez Lopez (120) 02:52:29
17. James Brennan (125) 02:52:41
18. Jeff Snyder (129) 02:52:54
19. Al Ross (131) 02:53:01
20. Christopher Woolley (139) 02:53:44
21. Bruce Wilson (151) 02:54:40
22. Mark Grams (154) 02:55:01
23. Kie Soohoo (161) 02:55:42
24. David Hernandez (168) 02:56:21
25. Al Val Verde (169) 02:56:24
26. Ronald Valkenburg (173) 02:56:39
27. Casimiro Eliserio (174) 02:56:40
28. Dario Boror Chiroy (177) 02:56:50
29. Keith Daniels (180) 02:57:03
30. Chris Pappas (184) 02:57:15
31. Brad Knoernschild (186) 02:57:19
32. Jesus Juarez (192) 02:57:39
33. Stephen Diciurcio (201) 02:58:17
34. Larry Eckles (204) 02:58:24
35. Tim Cary (205) 02:58:25
36. Angel Castillo (206) 02:58:31
37. Bill Kee (211) 02:58:47
38. Samuel Cortez (212) 02:58:55
39. John Araujo (215) 02:59:17
40. Jose Mendez Martinez (216) 02:59:19
41. J Ernesto Ramos (223) 02:59:34
42. Jeffrey Welker (225) 02:59:37
43. Robert Haro (231) 02:59:59
44. Danny Westergaard (233) 03:00:02
45. Israel Escobar (236) 03:00:34
46. Carter Nakashima (244) 03:00:52
47. Jesus Gallegos (249) 03:01:01
48. Joe Peterson (256) 03:01:31
49. Larry Lee (258) 03:01:38
50. Peter Remme (268) 03:02:19
51. Robert Fitzgerald (269) 03:02:23
52. Fernando Ferhan Tarango (274) 03:02:35
53. Doug Sims (279) 03:02:53
54. Luis Trujillo (281) 03:02:58
55. Ron Wald (300) 03:03:41
56. Julio Jaramillo (302) 03:03:49
57. Carl Maravilla (313) 03:04:29
58. Salvador Macias (314) 03:04:31
59. Steve Haas (327) 03:05:15
60. Carlos Perez (329) 03:05:29
61. Abraham Meza (331) 03:06:35
62. Troy Belme (332) 03:05:36
63. Bob Veazie (339) 03:05:55
64. Steven Yee (347) 03:06:16
65. Harold Fleeger (349) 03:06:24
66. Mark Gerrie (356) 03:06:46
67. Omar De Leon (362) 03:07:03
68. Wolfgang Resch (364) 03:07:13
69. Bruce Lander (369) 03:07:21
70. Miko Delgado (373) 03:07:28
71. Jose Reyes (376) 03:07:33
72. Don Tanaka (377) 03:07:34
73. Frank Benson (378) 03:07:39
74. Albert Portillo (380) 03:07:43
75. Billy Prentice (383) 03:07:46
76. Frank Tai (394) 03:08:12
77. Peter Kim (395) 03:08:14
78. Roger Furman (397) 03:08:14
79. Cresencio Sanchez (398) 03:08:15
80. Kenneth Chism (406) 03:08:31
81. Gonzalo Samaniego (408) 03:08:38
82. Eric Marx (409) 03:08:39
83. Derek Spinney (415) 03:08:53
84. Juan Hernandez (417) 03:08:55
85. Fred Dubbelt (419) 03:09:03
86. Guillermo Reyes Elias (421) 03:09:11
87. Steven Reed (422) 03:09:12
88. Daniel Carothers (424) 03:09:13
89. Edwin Kitchen (425) 03:09:16
90. Don Buck (429) 03:09:24
91. Paul Suprono Jr (440) 03:09:42
92. James Van Patten (442) 03:09:44
93. Chuck Teixeira (444) 03:09:45
94. Felix Herwawdez (448) 03:09:53
95. Keith Matter (449) 03:09:55
96. Rodrigo Espinoza Torres (451) 03:09:59
97. Michael Kennedy (452) 03:09:59
98. James Park (457) 03:10:08
99. Johnny Estrada (459) 03:10:17
100. Todd Jones (475) 03:11:05
101. Remy Fajardo (494) 03:11:56
102. David Reifsnyder (500) 03:12:11
103. Manny Bautista (507) 03:12:20
104. Scott Imhoff (511) 03:12:31
105. Robert Gonzalez (516) 03:12:42
106. Adan Gonzalez Mejia (517) 03:12:46
107. Lauro Ruiz (527) 03:13:05
108. Vicente Rivera (533) 03:13:16
109. Ramon Arroyo (535) 03:13:18
110. Manuel Reed (538) 03:13:27
111. John Mcdaniel (543) 03:13:33
112. Eduardo Luna (549) 03:13:42
113. Benito Salgado (550) 03:13:44
114. Bill Dougher (551) 03:13:45
115. Joseph Morales (554) 03:13:47
116. Jimmy Granados (555) 03:13:48
117. Keith Harnden (560) 03:13:53
118. Rick Waterman (570) 03:14:12
119. Felix Castillo (576) 03:14:22
120. Abel Contreras (578) 03:14:26
121. Ric Munoz (582) 03:14:31
122. Manuel Jimenez (585) 03:14:40
123. Guillermo Letechipia (586) 03:14:40
124. Anthony Grady (592) 03:14:48
125. Gregor Robin (595) 03:14:54
126. Jorge Herrera (596) 03:14:59
127. Mark Hershey (604) 03:15:16
128. Juan Silva (605) 03:15:19
129. Myles Helm (606) 03:15:24
130. Jaime Rincon (612) 03:15:36
131. Philip Frazier (617) 03:15:48
132. Mike Stephens (619) 03:15:57
133. Kazuki Watanabe (622) 03:16:03
134. Jeffery Vannini (623) 03:16:04
135. Jorge Corona Hernandez (625) 03:16:11
136. Javier Esteban (628) 03:16:15
137. Stephen Hudgens (633) 03:16:22
138. Ed Bickley (634) 03:16:28
139. Robert Page (636) 03:16:33
140. Rich Weast (646) 03:16:47
141. Ed Corpuz (653) 03:16:54
142. Carl Garbus (662) 03:17:09
143. Nol Burger (667) 03:17:19
144. Joaquin Salazar (674) 03:17:23
145. Sergio Ramos (678) 03:17:26
146. Lou Bernal (680) 03:17:28
147. Gumercindo Boche Saban (686) 03:17:43
148. James Copp (689) 03:17:52
149. Hakim Belaidi (696) 03:18:04
150. Juan Cruz (703) 03:18:17
151. Vidal Gutierrez (706) 03:18:22
152. Seiichi Yoshizawa (711) 03:18:33
153. Ross Donoghue (717) 03:18:44
154. Ruben Banuelos Acuna (726) 03:19:03
155. Daniel Wleten (727) 03:19:06
156. Brian Copeland (731) 03:19:13
157. Pete Kirkham (737) 03:19:22
158. Eduardo Morales (745) 03:19:28
159. William Isaac (747) 03:19:33
160. Shigy Suzuki (754) 03:19:45
161. Christopher Robbins (756) 03:19:46
162. Armando Jimenez Ochoa (758) 03:19:49
163. Duke Alexander (759) 03:19:52
164. Sean McDermott (763) 03:19:50
165. Bruce Deeter (768) 03:20:08
166. Jim Blanck (771) 03:20:12
167. Doug Malcolm (772) 03:20:13
168. Tim Hickok (784) 03:20:31
169. Pascual Martinez (787) 03:20:37
170. Jesse Perez (793) 03:20:45
171. Mark Kajiwara (795) 03:20:54
172. Rick Nelson (797) 03:21:00
173. Thomas Hewko (798) 03:21:01
174. Steven Watanabe (799) 03:21:01
175. David Van Houten (806) 03:21:17
176. William Salem Jr (816) 03:21:29
177. Jaime Mora Gonzalez (820) 03:21:31
178. Raymond Bermudes (826) 03:21:41
179. John Lengacher (839) 03:22:00
180. Jose Martinez (841) 03:22:01
181. Kevin Cimarusti (851) 03:22:16
182. Duane Mc Dowell (852) 03:22:16
183. Dale Ahlstrom (855) 03:22:21
184. Larry Meyers (856) 03:22:22
185. David Granado (860) 03:22:26
186. Carl Kravitz (864) 03:22:29
187. Roberto Fierro (865) 03:22:31
188. Les Mazon (869) 03:22:35
189. Javier Lopez (870) 03:22:39
190. Rob Hogan (877) 03:22:45
191. Don Newman (886) 03:22:57
192. Kelly Skeels (894) 03:23:10
193. Frank Shapiro (899) 03:23:17
194. Jim Slepski (913) 03:23:36
195. Joseph Tholt (915) 03:23:38
196. Michael Bergan (916) 03:23:39
197. Gary Rodgers (934) 03:24:00
198. Dan Takahashi (941) 03:24:07
199. Jaime Lopez (943) 03:24:11
200. Carlos Ruiz (946) 03:24:18
201. Roland Lang (954) 03:24:25
202. Leonel Palomino (957) 03:24:30
203. Paul Lee (958) 03:24:32
204. Michael Barge (964) 03:24:34
205. Scott Smith (984) 03:25:07
206. Abel Ramos (994) 03:25:19
207. August Hoffman (998) 03:25:26
208. Sam Aviles Eduardo (1003) 03:25:33
209. George Morales (1005) 03:25:36
210. Leo Corral (1008) 03:25:39
211. Robert Dubois (1018) 03:25:57
212. Yossi Alter (1026) 03:26:07
213. Jesus Alfaro (1038) 03:26:21
214. Rick Loyola (1040) 03:26:25
215. Enrique Sigala (1043) 03:26:33
216. Brian Kunibe (1053) 03:26:44
217. Carlos Ortiz (1061) 03:27:00
218. William Gordon III (1066) 03:27:07
219. John Piccini (1069) 03:27:08
220. Patrick Burge (1074) 03:27:15
221. Chris Borg (1087) 03:27:28
222. David De Lap (1092) 03:27:32
223. Jose Ocampo (1102) 03:27:39
224. Alan Mahanes (1106) 03:27:41
225. Istvan Cselenyak (1108) 03:27:45
226. David Tarango (1112) 03:27:52
227. Alejandro Herrera (1113) 03:27:52
228. Joe Terrones (1116) 03:27:54
229. Emmanuel Fritsch (1117) 03:27:55
230. Joseph Bugbee (1122) 03:28:03
231. Victor Rodriguez (1132) 03:28:11
232. Willie Roland (1136) 03:28:16
233. Royce Bunag (1145) 03:28:23
234. Ruben Ballesteros (1160) 03:28:46
235. Peter Von Kleist (1163) 03:28:49
236. Brent Moon (1167) 03:28:53
237. Larry Gassan (1100) 03:28:56
238. Chris Hogsberg (1178) 03:29:05
239. Celso Olivares Osorio (1188) 03:29:17
240. Anaslacio Salgado (1193) 03:29:21
241. Eliborio Chavez (1198) 03:29:26
242. Miguel Aguilera (1206) 03:29:35
243. Cody Koopmann (1207) 03:29:35
244. Marc Hertle (1212) 03:29:37
245. Edward Jimenez (1216) 03:29:40
246. Jeffery Clarke (1227) 03:29:53
247. Gary Gray (1228) 03:29:55
248. Fitzgerald Lee (1233) 03:30:00
249. Mark Erickson (1239) 03:30:11
250. Randy Bernhagen (1241) 03:30:15
251. Eric Wenner (1247) 03:30:21
252. Clemente Imperiali (1250) 03:30:23
253. Jose Escalante (1257) 03:30:31
254. Mark Penn (1260) 03:30:32
255. Paul Prochaska (1264) 03:30:40
256. Edward Reyes (1267) 03:30:49
257. John Mizenko (1288) 03:31:09
258. Fred Mathis (1291) 03:31:17
259. Jerry Skoglund (1292) 03:31:17
260. Dieter Hirch (1293) 03:31:17
261. William Fulbrook (1294) 03:31:20
262. Jaime Aznar (1306) 03:31:28
263. Willie Moore (1318) 03:31:39
264. Richard Swartz (1341) 03:32:05
265. Robert Chavez (1354) 03:32:19
266. Arturo Molina (1360) 03:32:24
267. Daniel Moreno (1362) 03:32:28
268. Rafael Gomez (1363) 03:32:28
269. David Fetah (1365) 03:32:32
270. Clayton Moore (1366) 03:32:33
271. Dana Joanou (1369) 03:32:40
272. Angel Toxtle (1376) 03:32:47
273. Phillip Wright (1380) 03:32:50
274. Angel Lucero (1382) 03:32:52
275. Jesus Renteria (1383) 03:32:53
276. Dennis Perkins (1386) 03:32:57
277. Robert Harris (1388) 03:33:01
278. Xavier Grossemy (1390) 03:33:02
279. Horacio Martinez (1397) 03:33:07
280. Scott Ryder (1402) 03:33:21
281. Ramon Gonzales (1408) 03:33:27
282. John Dohle (1411) 03:33:36
283. Robin Dickinson (1416) 03:33:46
284. Steven McGlawn (1419) 03:33:47
285. Robert Porter (1422) 03:33:54
286. Michael Pappas (1423) 03:33:55
287. Alfredo Torres (1425) 03:33:58
288. James Yannotta (1428) 03:34:02
289. Paul Ronney (1433) 03:34:04
290. Wolfgang Hoffmann (1440) 03:34:09
291. Nelson Hendry (1443) 03:34:13
292. Mark Kerper (1448) 03:34:30
293. Joe Struzinsky (1457) 03:34:46
294. Rosenod Zamora (1466) 03:34:50
295. Craig Yamauchi (1475) 03:35:00
296. Panfilo Bray (1477) 03:35:01
297. Thomas Linde (1493) 03:35:15
298. Robert Barraza (1494) 03:35:15
299. Robert Smith (1495) 03:35:16
300. Manuel Jarvis (1501) 03:35:25
301. Joel Adler (1504) 03:35:32
302. Chris Thomas (1508) 03:35:34
303. David Wilson (1521) 03:35:46
304. Art Folsom (1523) 03:35:47
305. Douglas Chabot (1546) 03:36:13
306. Jac Rombouts (1550) 03:36:17
307. Luis Novoa (1553) 03:36:19
308. Mike Kukuchka (1557) 03:36:27
309. Eduardo Hernandez (1567) 03:36:40
310. Joe Valdespino Jr (1572) 03:36:44
311. Stephen Thompson (1576) 03:36:47
312. Yoshio Minato (1577) 03:36:47
313. Mark Conover (1579) 03:36:53
314. David Campbell (1591) 03:37:02
315. Freddie Washington (1592) 03:37:02
316. Kevin Keenan (1593) 03:37:05
317. Gary Burroughs (1596) 03:37:07
318. Dezi Reszneky (1597) 03:37:08
319. Gary Citron (1602) 03:37:14
320. Rick Sherrill (1603) 03:37:15
321. Dave Durflinger (1604) 03:37:16
322. Charles Buttitta (1610) 03:37:21
323. Porfirio Ayala (1613) 03:37:23
324. Ruben Solorio (1622) 03:37:40
325. Yvon Greer (1632) 03:37:53
326. Pedro Ozuna (1639) 03:37:56
327. Jeff Ryder (1643) 03:38:01
328. Forrest Appleton (1645) 03:38:03
329. Dan Simpson (1658) 03:38:14
330. Dwight Des Lauriers (1675) 03:38:35
331. Michael Wiederich (1678) 03:38:40
332. Marlon Feiger (1679) 03:38:40
333. George Estrada (1685) 03:38:44
334. Ely Fernandez (1707) 03:39:08
335. Felipe Garcia (1708) 03:39:08
336. Jon Sarver (1712) 03:39:10
337. Greg May (1717) 03:39:14
338. Andrew Davenport (1722) 03:39:22
339. Luis Leon (1725) 03:39:26
340. Christopher Murphy (1734) 03:39:36
341. Michael Hinton (1752) 03:39:54
342. James Fitzgerald (1771) 03:40:16
343. Tim Wakefield (1774) 03:40:19
344. Hung Nguyen (1784) 03:40:24
345. Carlos Barrio (1793) 03:40:34
346. Laurence Wagner (1796) 03:40:36
347. Warren Kirschner (1815) 03:40:54
348. Alton Davis (1822) 03:41:01
349. Dan Johnson (1831) 03:41:05
350. Kerry Skochin (1833) 03:41:06
351. Daniel Falk (1839) 03:41:12
352. Michael Lindheim (1841) 03:41:15
353. Angelo Stewart (1849) 03:41:18
354. Bruce Bornhurst (1851) 03:41:21
355. Ric Alviso (1853) 03:41:21
356. Robert Bloom (1855) 03:41:22
357. Fernando Zarate (1861) 03:41:27
358. John Ochoa (1864) 03:41:30
359. Robert Zeisler (1875) 03:41:40
360. Mark Sweo (1883) 03:41:44
361. Dar Warmke (1890) 03:41:49
362. Kevin Steele (1894) 03:41:54
363. Kirk Boylston (1896) 03:41:55
364. Jose Rivera (1900) 03:41:57
365. Gregory Ambrose (1913) 03:42:15
366. Ernest Chavez (1914) 03:42:15
367. Jacob Reinbolt (1923) 03:42:21
368. Marc Shapiro (1932) 03:42:33
369. Francisco Bustamante (1940) 03:42:48
370. Scott Suhr (1955) 03:43:08
371. Ronn Powell (1957) 03:43:09
372. Blake Kelly (1959) 03:43:10
373. John Barry (1968) 03:43:18
374. Eduard Gruber (1978) 03:43:30
375. Tim McDonough (1982) 03:43:32
376. Steven Imgrund (1988) 03:43:38
377. Rosalio Figueroa (1996) 03:43:49
378. Rodolfo Madriz (1997) 03:43:50
379. Robert Mendoza (1998) 03:43:51
380. Fidel Santacruz (2000) 03:43:54
381. Kenny Kappen (2003) 03:43:55
382. Rudy Perez (2006) 03:43:58
383. Mariano Lopez (2015) 03:44:03
384. Gary Bowers (2023) 03:44:09
385. Jim Shaw (2027) 03:44:14
386. Glenn Horiuchi (2028) 03:44:14
387. Gregory Iorio (2045) 03:44:25
388. Timothy Barnett (2046) 03:44:25
389. Jose Vargas (2052) 03:44:33
390. Jesse Machado (2055) 03:44:34
391. Stephan Cohn (2056) 03:44:35
392. Edwin Lucie (2088) 03:45:00
393. Joseph Drabinski (2090) 03:45:00
394. John Rogers (2093) 03:45:02
395. Sangman Lee (2094) 03:45:03
396. Jim Allan (2097) 03:45:07
397. William Jensen (2098) 03:45:08
398. Mark Vanleer (2099) 03:45:09
399. Robert Mills (2105) 03:45:14
400. Daniel Levin (2116) 03:45:20
401. Chris Ackerman (2117) 03:45:20
402. Lionel Adams (2133) 03:45:39
403. William Fritzsche (2135) 03:45:41
404. Reginald Thornton (2150) 03:45:53
405. Jose Hernandez (2164) 03:46:04
406. Patrick Metivier (2165) 03:46:09
407. Scott Sullivan (2166) 03:46:09
408. Cliff Jewell (2182) 03:46:22
409. Kenneth Marschall (2189) 03:46:28
410. Mitch Turley (2202) 03:46:47
411. Gustavo Ceja (2209) 03:46:53
412. Esteban Can (2238) 03:47:16
413. Eric Pacheco (2242) 03:47:21
414. Michael Smith (2245) 03:47:23
415. Ron Moser (2246) 03:47:23
416. Bill Ralph (2250) 03:47:27
417. Bruce Murray (2254) 03:47:30
418. John Vallett (2260) 03:47:35
419. Bruce Walton (2264) 03:47:39
420. David Fox (2273) 03:47:44
421. Peter Eschenburg (2275) 03:47:45
422. Christian Lytle (2278) 03:47:49
423. Jack Villegas (2281) 03:47:52
424. Bil Bothwell (2285) 03:47:56
425. Gerald Goblirsch (2294) 03:48:02
426. Micheal Flowers (2295) 03:48:03
427. Thomas Malone (2301) 03:48:08
428. Andrew Sutcliffe (2303) 03:48:09
429. Thomas Brown (2304) 03:48:10
430. Rocky Stenico (2305) 03:48:11
431. John Chin (2307) 03:48:12
432. Greg Newberry (2312) 03:48:14
433. Claudio Gomez (2313) 03:48:16
434. Dennis Vorndran (2315) 03:48:17
435. W Michael Brown (2334) 03:48:34
436. Hugo Martinez (2339) 03:48:36
437. Armando Martos (2362) 03:48:58
438. Benjamin Gonzalez Sr (2367) 03:49:02
439. Mark Bailey (2371) 03:49:05
440. Alfonso Ramirez (2377) 03:49:08
441. Sean Oconnor (2391) 03:49:18
442. Hugo Alberto Alvarado Pieado (2411) 03:49:33
443. Peter Lyon (2419) 03:49:41
444. Bob Dewitt (2421) 03:49:41
445. James Lue (2423) 03:49:42
446. Genaro De La Torre (2429) 03:49:40
447. Timothy Petersen (2434) 03:49:52
448. Jose Chavez (2442) 03:50:00
449. Benjamin Gaetos (2443) 03:50:00
450. Fernando Espiritusanto (2449) 03:50:05
451. Tim Harrington (2451) 03:50:06
452. Ernesto Ixcoy (2454) 03:50:09
453. Otto Galindo (2456) 03:50:10
454. Brett Carver (2468) 03:50:23
455. Sergio Fausto (2487) 03:50:36
456. Kenneth Horii (2494) 03:50:40
457. Carl Tang (2514) 03:50:58
458. Anthony Gasbarre (2516) 03:50:59
459. Paul Jerome (2527) 03:51:08
460. Jose Ramirez (2532) 03:51:14
461. Jacinto Quezada (2533) 03:51:15
462. Jeff Bell (2544) 03:51:26
463. Carlos Arellanes (2546) 03:51:27
464. Alexander McMahon (2554) 03:51:30
465. Haruo Matsuoka (2558) 03:51:36
466. Tony Wehbe (2571) 03:51:44
467. Steven Garcia (2573) 03:51:48
468. Francisco Castro (2598) 03:52:09
469. Rick West (2601) 03:52:12
470. Frank Barbosa (2606) 03:52:17
471. Juan Perez (2608) 03:52:17
472. Philip Kent (2610) 03:52:19
473. Frank Buono (2614) 03:52:22
474. Dan Desmui (2621) 03:52:27
475. Samuel Schreiber (2622) 03:52:28
476. Jose Alfredo Cornejo Rodriguez (2623) 03:52:29
477. Scott Dempster (2629) 03:52:34
478. Gary Lalley Jr (2644) 03:52:45
479. Christian Markey III (2647) 03:52:46
480. Nelson Jovel-Aviles (2650) 03:52:47
481. Edward Sifuentes (2655) 03:52:49
482. Jerry Mesa (2662) 03:52:55
483. Rick Ellison (2669) 03:53:00
484. Howard Lucas (2670) 03:53:01
485. Hilario Cisneros (2681) 03:53:11
486. Hector Sanchez (2682) 03:53:13
487. Jeffrey Ratliff (2687) 03:53:16
488. Patrick Richardson (2704) 03:53:26
489. Pedro Hernandez (2715) 03:53:38
490. Carlos Hassey (2716) 03:53:39
491. Michael Stonebraker (2717) 03:53:39
492. Jerry Becker (2719) 03:53:40
493. Jaime Marroquin (2741) 03:53:55
494. Guy De Burgh (2743) 03:53:57
495. Kevin Daly (2747) 03:54:01
496. Eric Lemke (2758) 03:54:12
497. Rodney Williams (2766) 03:54:15
498. Balazs Denes (2770) 03:54:18
499. Wayne Hyde (2775) 03:54:24
500. Fidel Martinez (2786) 03:54:26
501. Miguel Negrete (2791) 03:54:30
502. Robert Austin (2795) 03:54:32
503. Sergio Varela (2814) 03:54:45
504. Youn Han (2818) 03:54:47
505. Cameron Cosgrove (2824) 03:54:51
506. David Perez (2826) 03:54:52
507. James Yanoschik (2835) 03:54:59
508. Jonathan Eisen (2847) 03:55:10
509. Dennis Hall (2850) 03:55:12
510. Marl Herschthal (2858) 03:55:18
511. Gilberto Espinoza (2860) 03:55:19
512. John Stefanchik (2882) 03:55:29
513. Michael Cullen (2894) 03:55:36
514. Robert Ruiz (2900) 03:55:45
515. Jean-Claude Camoin (2904) 03:55:48
516. Gregory Loveland (2908) 03:55:52
517. Jaimes Lopez (2909) 03:55:53
518. Noe Cruz Rivera (2913) 03:55:55
519. Dana Eubanks (2916) 03:55:56
520. Dima Khodko (2918) 03:55:57
521. Mark Delanghe (2932) 03:56:07
522. Jose Tovar Montanez (2934) 03:56:08
523. Walter Tletski (2951) 03:56:18
524. Rudy Garcia (2954) 03:56:20
525. John Chambers (2958) 03:56:23
526. Harvey Beiglo (2960) 03:56:24
527. Gabriel Desrosiers (2978) 03:56:39
528. Juan Baello (2979) 03:56:40
529. Jeffrey Lichtenstein (2980) 03:56:40
530. Larry Riese (2986) 03:56:45
531. Daniel Clark (2988) 03:56:46
532. Lee Rosen (2987) 03:56:47
533. David Kerr (3000) 03:56:49
534. Henry Provencher (3001) 03:56:49
535. John Kacura (3025) 03:57:01
536. Renne Gardner (3039) 03:57:08
537. Roger Hart (3049) 03:57:16
538. Alberto Serrano Sotolo (3054) 03:57:19
539. Rick Gould (3055) 03:57:20
540. Eamon Sherlock (3058) 03:57:22
541. Tony Donagrechia (3067) 03:57:29
542. Paul Flores (3078) 03:57:37
543. Mark Hays (3087) 03:57:44
544. David Leo (3093) 03:57:46
545. Gary Grewer (3098) 03:57:49
546. Toyokazu Naito (3103) 03:57:52
547. David Emmons (3104) 03:57:53
548. Douglas Edwards (3107) 03:57:54
549. Esteban Cedeno (3122) 03:58:04
550. Michael Washlake (3123) 03:58:05
551. Melchor Lopez (3126) 03:58:06
552. Julian Sands (3134) 03:58:15
553. Yonan Benjamin (3144) 03:58:22
554. Alan Calnan (3145) 03:58:23
555. Wayne Diamond (3150) 03:58:26
556. Lou Amendola (3154) 03:58:29
557. Thom Bobadilla (3157) 03:58:32
558. Jeremy Johnson (3158) 03:58:33
559. Randy Dunn (3167) 03:58:37
560. Barry Leonard (3169) 03:58:38
561. Francisco Lopez Hernandez (3173) 03:58:42
562. Julio Mendizabal (3176) 03:58:44
563. Scott Gerbasi (3179) 03:58:46
564. Paul Eickhoff (3184) 03:58:51
565. Rich Parker (3197) 03:58:58
566. David Orbach (3200) 03:59:00
567. Ian Christenberry (3206) 03:59:04

568. Brian Jorgensen (3217) 03:59:12
569. Michael Hurst (3222) 03:59:18
570. George Vogel (3226) 03:59:20
571. Charles Maes (3239) 03:59:28
572. Mark Kelly (3257) 03:59:42
573. Lars Schneider (3262) 03:59:44
574. John Hazlett (3267) 03:59:46
575. Guillermo Lopez (3275) 03:59:51
576. William Vaughn (3278) 03:59:51
577. John Carr (3279) 03:59:52
578. Robert Herrera (3281) 03:59:52
579. Isidro Rodriguez (3283) 03:59:53
580. Spencer Meggs (3293) 03:59:58
581. Michael Taylor (3305) 04:00:04
582. Dan Marino (3308) 04:00:06
583. Alberto Blen (3309) 04:00:06
584. Thomas Eads (3311) 04:00:07
585. Ronald Lem (3321) 04:00:16
586. Tiburcio Godoy (3332) 04:00:22
587. Russell Cheetham Jr (3338) 04:00:27
588. Thomas Niekamp (3356) 04:00:43
589. Jose Amparo Garcia (3357) 04:00:44
590. Peter Measures (3359) 04:00:48
591. Wayne Hirao (3361) 04:00:50
592. Keith Mordoff (3373) 04:00:59
593. James Desimio (3388) 04:01:09
594. Mark Mayer (3401) 04:01:16
595. Tim Torres (3406) 04:01:20
596. Julian Miranda (3408) 04:01:21
597. Patrick Hutchings (3417) 04:01:30
598. Dale Willey (3420) 04:01:31
599. Chris Borgeson (3427) 04:01:37
600. Matt Mulder (3441) 04:01:48
601. Scott Mitchell (3443) 04:01:54
602. Silverio Rivas (3449) 04:01:57
603. Francisco Pedraza (3451) 04:01:58
604. Merlin Tripp (3452) 04:01:59
605. Stephen Masoner (3453) 04:02:00
606. Tripop Thongkam (3480) 04:02:21
607. Thomas Mc Watters III (3485) 04:02:25
608. Aris Corkos (3486) 04:02:26
609. Gabriel Villafana (3489) 04:02:32
610. Gil Alaniz (3498) 04:02:39
611. Ronald Powell (3509) 04:02:50
612. Luis Alatorre (3513) 04:02:53
613. Bob Perkins (3517) 04:02:55
614. Niguel Saldana (3524) 04:03:02
615. Felipe Delgado (3526) 04:03:04
616. Brian Fitzgerald (3531) 04:03:07
617. Johnnie Cooper (3551) 04:03:28
618. Jerome Berkovich (3561) 04:03:36
619. Carl Henry (3562) 04:03:36
620. Fernando Arriola (3572) 04:03:46
621. Neal Flyer (3579) 04:03:55
622. Jesus Velazquez (3591) 04:04:05
623. Neil Groom (3608) 04:04:15
624. William Caldwell (3611) 04:04:18
625. Hisanori Makisako (3624) 04:04:25
626. Ronald Exley (3628) 04:04:28
627. Phillip Page (3633) 04:04:31
628. Julia Pineda (3638) 04:04:33
629. Rafael Mejia (3640) 04:04:33
630. Denis Dempsey (3643) 04:04:34
631. Jose Santana (3648) 04:04:39
632. Jessie Pilgrim (3650) 04:04:40
633. Fred Martinez (3655) 04:04:44
634. Thomas Horth (3656) 04:04:45
635. Sergio Silva (3666) 04:04:50
636. Paul Schubert (3672) 04:04:53
637. Mikel Cancio (3674) 04:04:57
638. Robert Smith (3682) 04:04:59
639. Kevin Stratton (3687) 04:05:04
640. Timothy Callen (3696) 04:05:09
641. Willie Reed (3703) 04:05:13
642. Timothy Denardo (3706) 04:05:19
643. Charles Gaylor (3710) 04:05:24
644. Luis Santillan (3722) 04:05:33
645. Jay Whitehead (3725) 04:05:34
646. Tom Kagy (3757) 04:06:03
647. David Schrimmer (3762) 04:06:05
648. Robin Turner (3771) 04:06:12
649. Blake Sova (3780) 04:06:22
650. Mike Casdenada (3805) 04:06:41
651. Matthew Richards (3806) 04:06:42
652. Tim Quinn (3807) 04:06:42
653. Kurt Harms (3811) 04:06:44
654. Juan Romero (3813) 04:06:45
655. Alfred Pascual (3820) 04:06:51
656. Santos Diaz (3826) 04:06:56
657. Michael Corsello (3831) 04:06:58
658. Robert Lieban Jr (3837) 04:07:02
659. Bill Gerber (3840) 04:07:03
660. Baltazar Castillo (3851) 04:07:08
661. Allen Aleksa (3862) 04:07:18
662. Robert Fleming (3866) 04:07:21
663. Alvin Martinez (3870) 04:07:24
664. William Mathews (3877) 04:07:31
665. Ian Hockin (3880) 04:07:32
666. Raymond Hazlett (3882) 04:07:34
667. Robert Phillips (3888) 04:07:37
668. Chris Rushing (3898) 04:07:44
669. Steven Gold (3900) 04:07:45
670. Dennis Kato (3903) 04:07:46
671. John Calhoun (3912) 04:07:53
672. Felix Figueroa (3913) 04:07:55
673. James Murphy (3914) 04:07:56
674. Ralph Ayala (3917) 04:07:59
675. John Gebhardt (3918) 04:08:02
676. Roger Lewis (3925) 04:08:10
677. Michael Jones (3927) 04:08:11
678. Michael Clayton (3931) 04:08:14
679. Andy Obrecki (3935) 04:08:15
680. Gary Bacio (3939) 04:08:17
681. Ossie Crenshaw (3944) 04:08:21
682. Bart Lanni (3956) 04:08:26
683. Kevin Brown (3965) 04:08:39
684. Gustavo Del Cid (3971) 04:08:44
685. Brad Hatten (3975) 04:08:46
686. Denis Peper (3980) 04:08:49
687. Juan Arriaga (4003) 04:09:08
688. William Porter (4006) 04:09:12
689. Sean Stephens (4021) 04:09:22
690. Marco Villanuveva (4040) 04:09:37
691. Paul Stenson (4042) 04:09:39
692. Carlos Segura (4057) 04:09:53
693. James Brandt (4060) 04:09:54
694. Keith Reynolds (4067) 04:10:00
695. Shawn Murray (4076) 04:10:08
696. Kun Kim (4087) 04:10:15
697. Ken Williams (4113) 04:10:36
698. Manny Guzman (4114) 04:10:36
699. Greg Hinton (4122) 04:10:44
700. David Escobedo (4125) 04:10:47
701. William Townsend (4127) 04:10:48
702. Kenneth Hunt (4145) 04:10:56
703. Joe Morgan (4161) 04:11:04
704. Michael Hampson (4165) 04:11:07
705. Gary Greenfield (4168) 04:11:10
706. Mark Wilde (4185) 04:11:24
707. Scott Sarran (4192) 04:11:31
708. Oscar Flores (4194) 04:11:33
709. Paul Sproviero (4206) 04:11:41
710. Brian Hopp (4212) 04:11:50
711. Jose Martin Garcia (4216) 04:11:54
712. Ernesto Carlos (4226) 04:12:00
713. Kevin Quail (4228) 04:12:01
714. Anthony Terrazas (4252) 04:12:20
715. Tony Griffin (4259) 04:12:25
716. Jorry Bonello (4260) 04:12:26
717. Larry Kelly (4273) 04:12:35
718. Claudio Patino (4278) 04:12:41
719. Stan Jackson (4286) 04:12:44
720. Jose Leon (4287) 04:12:44
721. Daniel Murphy (4292) 04:12:53
722. Jose Roberto Burgos (4298) 04:12:57
723. Kurt Voelker (4300) 04:12:58
724. Jack Hanna (4303) 04:12:59
725. Kary Harris (4309) 04:13:05
726. Robert Varela (4318) 04:13:09
727. Albert Medrano (4323) 04:13:11
728. Jon Tice (4325) 04:13:13
729. Andrew Horan (4326) 04:13:14
730. Kevin Byrne (4328) 04:13:15
731. Jose Gonzalez (4330) 04:13:20
732. Marc Rizzo (4334) 04:13:21
733. Soren Eilertsen (4337) 04:13:23
734. David Nuno (4340) 04:13:25
735. Peter Somogyi (4345) 04:13:29
736. Thomas Erikson (4353) 04:13:40
737. Chuck Fieland (4354) 04:13:42
738. James Picker (4359) 04:13:45
739. Jim Hoover (4368) 04:13:53
740. Winston Winterink (4374) 04:13:55
741. Kevin McAndrews (4392) 04:14:05
742. Marshall Avila (4396) 04:14:08
743. Brian Rodgers (4404) 04:14:16
744. Mel Mecham (4406) 04:14:18
745. Jose Navarrete (4411) 04:14:21
746. David Gallardo (4419) 04:14:23
747. Mo Saprour (4425) 04:14:27
748. Rafael Vega (4429) 04:14:29
749. James Lynch (4441) 04:14:36
750. Martin Barbeau (4443) 04:14:37
751. Andrew Cazares (4450) 04:14:40
752. James Keiger (4459) 04:14:44
753. Carl Walsh (4461) 04:14:47
754. Alvaro Morales (4465) 04:14:47
755. Telesforo Hernandez (4468) 04:14:48
756. John Blauert (4476) 04:14:52
757. Ralph Perez (4482) 04:14:55
758. Bob Larue (4483) 04:14:55
759. Glenn McFadden (4494) 04:15:02
760. David Strandberg (4498) 04:15:06
761. Ken Hodnett (4508) 04:15:17
762. Dennis Smith (4509) 04:15:18
763. Pete Hilling (4511) 04:15:19
764. Dan Couse (4513) 04:15:20
765. Sharky Neff (4526) 04:15:30
766. William Russell (4527) 04:15:31
767. Curtiss Briggs (4528) 04:15:32
768. Christopher Conlon (4541) 04:15:35
769. German Vilar (4545) 04:15:39
770. Eleazar Khacom (4554) 04:15:44
771. Henry Smith (4555) 04:15:45
772. Jonathan Schor (4576) 04:15:59
773. Peter Thumm (4581) 04:16:01
774. Takashi Mezaki (4590) 04:16:05
775. Raul Banuelos (4615) 04:16:25
776. Mark Manning (4622) 04:16:28
777. William Costello (4624) 04:16:29
778. Alan Stern (4631) 04:16:32
779. Zia Jamali (4632) 04:16:32
780. Terry Blair (4633) 04:16:33
781. Oracio Crisanto (4634) 04:16:34
782. Jonathan Gordon (4638) 04:16:37
783. William Hutton (4646) 04:16:42
784. Jan Regnstrom (4648) 04:16:43
785. Jusus Castillo (4670) 04:17:03
786. Chris Carlson (4692) 04:17:22
787. Stephan Matsuda (4707) 04:17:31
788. Arthur Miller (4715) 04:17:39
789. Gary Askland (4717) 04:17:41
790. Salvador Gallegos (4727) 04:17:51
791. Kang Wang (4728) 04:17:51
792. Jose Vasquez (4734) 04:17:54
793. Larry Lean (4746) 04:18:01
794. Paul Bartasavich (4747) 04:18:02
795. Allan Hollingsworth (4759) 04:18:10
796. Derek King (4769) 04:18:19
797. Aron Yanagi (4772) 04:18:20
798. Russ Bishop (4781) 04:18:24
799. Eric Sarksians (4786) 04:18:29
800. Rafael Velazco (4790) 04:18:31
801. Mike Solis (4791) 04:18:31
802. Virgil Freeman (4795) 04:18:32
803. David Weintraub (4806) 04:18:40
804. Craig Gleason (4820) 04:18:48
805. Henry Guerrero (4821) 04:18:48
806. Martin Hermann (4832) 04:18:54
807. John Herr (4841) 04:18:58
808. James Schmitz (4842) 04:18:58
809. Peter Biffar (4851) 04:19:03
810. Thomas Ward (4880) 04:19:20
811. Taurino Torres (4881) 04:19:21
812. Keith Hippely (4889) 04:19:28
813. Stan Kiefer (4890) 04:19:29
814. Roger Caballero (4895) 04:19:33
815. Martin Ramirez (4898) 04:19:35
816. Sunder Nambiar (4900) 04:19:36
817. Luis Garcia (4906) 04:19:40
818. Jonathan Ash (4908) 04:19:41
819. Raymond Graham (4911) 04:19:42
820. Maxio Soto (4932) 04:19:58
821. Jon Dredd (4933) 04:19:58
822. Alon Nuni (4937) 04:20:01
823. Diego Galvan (4938) 04:20:02
824. Scot Thacker (4948) 04:20:08
825. Jaoquin Galan (4963) 04:20:25
826. Gregory Koellner (4978) 04:20:37
827. Robert Chen (4982) 04:20:40
828. Jeff Phillips (4988) 04:20:44
829. Roland Ekstrand (4989) 04:20:47
830. Rick Aleman (4991) 04:20:53
831. Kyle Matsuda (4997) 04:20:57
832. Brian Kirk (5000) 04:21:00
833. Yasuo Asako (5008) 04:21:12
834. Richard Williamson (5014) 04:21:17
835. Michael Cofsky (5017) 04:21:18
836. Brian McMahon (5025) 04:21:22
837. Hamid Rostamian (5055) 04:21:41
838. Raymond Bustos (5061) 04:21:44
839. Paul Manfrini (5062) 04:21:45
840. Getahun Mewosha (5065) 04:21:47
841. Rick Manovkian (5067) 04:21:48
842. Alfred Abril (5070) 04:21:50
843. Mark Parkstone (5073) 04:21:51
844. Jose Barragan (5083) 04:21:54
845. Jonathan Seltzer (5089) 04:21:50
846. James Kersey (5100) 04:22:03
847. Reginald Bruhn (5138) 04:22:29
848. Russell Peck (5143) 04:22:32
849. Manuel Rocha (5150) 04:22:37
850. John Prendergast (5160) 04:22:45
851. Lloyd Ito (5166) 04:22:49
852. Robert Kidwell (5178) 04:22:57
853. Don Shundo (5186) 04:23:03
854. Gilbert Polanco (5188) 04:23:06
855. Jefferson Sa (5190) 04:23:07
856. Miguel Cardena Mazvn (5198) 04:23:12
857. Dylan Stark (5200) 04:23:13
858. Joseph Reed (5207) 04:23:17
859. Orlando Aristizabal (5210) 04:23:18
860. Robert Begin (5211) 04:23:18
861. Rick Kissler (5222) 04:23:28
862. Victor Razo (5227) 04:23:30
863. Peter Bentley (5235) 04:23:36
864. Filippo Favazza (5238) 04:23:38
865. Bruce Thomson (5261) 04:24:06
866. Kevin Moe (5267) 04:24:09
867. Michael Parks (5276) 04:24:16
868. Cheng-Pao Li (5301) 04:24:32
869. Thomas Rodke (5302) 04:24:33
870. Mark Fino (5303) 04:24:33
871. Michael Wright (5306) 04:24:34
872. David Escalona (5320) 04:24:43
873. Enrique Sandoval (5333) 04:24:55
874. Andrew Septimus (5334) 04:24:55
875. Hiroshi Tokashiki (5338) 04:24:59
876. Juan Tax (5339) 04:25:00
877. Michael Sabo (5346) 04:25:05
878. Edward De La Torre (5356) 04:25:13
879. William Westafer (5358) 04:25:14
880. Anthony Elias (5364) 04:25:16
881. Wojtek Lesiak (5365) 04:25:16
882. Ernie Luna (5367) 04:25:17
883. Jose Arambula (5372) 04:25:20
884. Stephen Gadinis (5378) 04:25:22
885. Nils Sundberg (5383) 04:25:25
886. Gerard Dalziek (5388) 04:25:27
887. Carlos Arellano (5396) 04:25:31
888. Brian Hamblin (5402) 04:25:37
889. Jose Coreas (5416) 04:25:44
890. Mark Krueger (5429) 04:25:51
891. Raul Canchola (5431) 04:25:53
892. Quincy Martin (5436) 04:25:56
893. Mark MacFarlane (5439) 04:25:58
894. Brian Lacy (5449) 04:26:03
895. J Aguilar (5450) 04:26:03
896. John Amendola (5454) 04:26:04
897. Gary Ortega (5459) 04:26:09
898. David Lowe (5460) 04:26:10
899. Talee Garcia (5472) 04:26:20
900. Scott Lear (5479) 04:26:26
901. Bryan Allen (5493) 04:26:36
902. Gusztav Varga (5507) 04:26:48
903. Charles Spiekermann (5520) 04:26:57
904. Nagayuki Ebata (5526) 04:27:03
905. Sean Oconnor (5528) 04:27:06
906. Alberto Marquez (5533) 04:27:09
907. Marty Bordato (5545) 04:27:16
908. Thomas Reimann (5551) 04:27:20
909. Mariano Guarneros (5557) 04:27:22
910. Andrew Hernandez (5559) 04:27:23
911. Ronald Hill (5563) 04:27:26
912. Joseph Vega (5574) 04:27:32
913. Nicolas Aguirre (5593) 04:27:43
914. Slip Taylor (5605) 04:27:53
915. Stephan Poulter (5609) 04:27:54
916. Mike Miyamoto (5632) 04:28:06
917. Dave Petit (5642) 04:28:14
918. Julian Santillan (5650) 04:28:18
919. Richard Agata (5653) 04:28:21
920. David Johnson (5654) 04:28:22
921. Fernando Hernandez (5656) 04:28:23
922. Raymond Solis (5663) 04:28:29
923. Wayne Matsumura (5683) 04:28:40
924. Mark Santoro (5687) 04:28:43
925. Mark Shephard (5689) 04:28:44
926. Sam Makkar (5690) 04:28:46
927. DeWayne Starnes (5711) 04:29:01
928. Dean Taker (5726) 04:29:06
929. Laurentino Zarate (5739) 04:29:17
930. Abel Santana (5755) 04:29:28
931. Glenn Gibson (5765) 04:29:34
932. Jose Magallanes (5773) 04:29:39
933. Varant Vartabedian (5778) 04:29:41
934. Chris Dahms (5802) 04:30:02
935. Joseph Carrillo (5810) 04:30:09
936. Marty Godwin (5831) 04:30:26
937. John Felton (5832) 04:30:26
938. Garry Smith (5834) 04:30:27
939. Joel Millikin (5836) 04:30:27
940. Louis Totoro (5840) 04:30:29
941. Thomas Hartmann (5841) 04:30:29
942. Scott Seward (5846) 04:30:32
943. Ron Badua (5855) 04:30:34
944. Darryl Ketchens (5856) 04:30:35
945. Tony Gammariello (5864) 04:30:38
946. Carl Brown (5868) 04:30:40
947. Steve Johnson (5895) 04:30:57
948. Farhad Mousavipour (5901) 04:31:02
949. Raul Benavidez (5907) 04:31:05
950. Rick Wallace (5926) 04:31:18
951. Sal Gorrocino (5931) 04:31:24
952. Dave Blank (5935) 04:31:25
953. Michael Long (5963) 04:31:45
954. Juan Garduno Martinez (5966) 04:31:47
955. Carlos Alfaro (5968) 04:31:47
956. Terry Profitt (5971) 04:31:51
957. Samuel Larkin (5977) 04:31:55
958. Danny Roman (5978) 04:31:56
959. Ron Nee (5979) 04:31:57
960. Danny Demercado (5981) 04:31:58
961. Gerald Rivas (5990) 04:32:04
962. Terry Alexanfer (6000) 04:32:15
963. Mike Pendergrass (6018) 04:32:27
964. Jesus Garcia (6019) 04:32:27
965. Tony Tan (6023) 04:32:31
966. Yoichi Takaku (6031) 04:32:43
967. Steve Montgomery (6038) 04:32:45
968. Valerio Valdez (6042) 04:32:46
969. Sergio Garcia (6043) 04:32:47
970. Uve Sillat (6045) 04:32:47
971. Hiroshi Kijima (6062) 04:33:01
972. Samir Shahin (6067) 04:33:02
973. Joseph Kazzi (6073) 04:33:05
974. Frank Spasaro (6085) 04:33:14
975. Steve Jefferson (6093) 04:33:20
976. Steve Wells (6094) 04:33:20
977. Randy Lawrence (6122) 04:33:39
978. Rick Beardsley (6123) 04:33:40
979. Lenny Gisbert (6130) 04:33:43
980. Paul Hadden (6133) 04:33:46
981. Cipriano Meza (6138) 04:33:50
982. Shep Bentley (6156) 04:34:06
983. Bradford Couture (6157) 04:34:07
984. Ray Brown (6159) 04:34:08
985. Francisco Rivera (6173) 04:34:14
986. Dan Sheriff (6186) 04:34:24
987. Ramon Donato (6200) 04:34:31
988. Manuel Ramirez (6210) 04:34:39
989. Marcos Cedillo Jr (6220) 04:34:44
990. Chas Schreiber (6226) 04:34:47
991. Kevin Davidson (6257) 04:35:12
992. Carl Molina (6271) 04:35:20
993. John Bain (6272) 04:35:20
994. Tim Maimone (6273) 04:35:21
995. Michael Lynch III (6294) 04:35:35
996. Paul Watkins (6301) 04:35:37
997. Anthony Hudson (6308) 04:35:42
998. Brian Bartholomew (6309) 04:35:42
999. Dan Robles (6315) 04:35:46
1000. Ron Schlager (6318) 04:35:49
1001. Steven Lee (6320) 04:35:50
1002. Rod Kelley (6322) 04:35:51
1003. Stan Nakaso (6328) 04:35:53
1004. Roberto Vera (6332) 04:35:55
1005. Ken Franklin (6335) 04:35:56
1006. Mario Alberto Tovar (6358) 04:36:14
1007. Frank Archibeque (6370) 04:36:21
1008. Nelson Ildefonso (6382) 04:36:25
1009. Michael Delbuono (6396) 04:36:31
1010. Donald Rose (6410) 04:36:39
1011. Raymond Lawson (6418) 04:36:41
1012. Joseph Lee (6420) 04:36:45
1013. Abraham Gonzalez (6423) 04:36:46
1014. Fernando Moran (6427) 04:36:52
1015. Mark Bellack (6449) 04:37:14
1016. Eduardo Angel (6457) 04:37:21
1017. Ralph Norwood III (6478) 04:37:31
1018. Huitzi Urbina (6484) 04:37:34
1019. Craig Johnson (6486) 04:37:35
1020. Michael Bowman (6487) 04:37:36
1021. Luis Loesa (6503) 04:37:44
1022. Joe Pinedo (6522) 04:37:55
1023. Jeff Hindman (6523) 04:37:56
1024. Jorge Menendez (6526) 04:37:59
1025. Mike Schwartz (6530) 04:38:02
1026. Gomez Jose Caltillo (6532) 04:38:04
1027. Bill Ryburn (6536) 04:38:06
1028. Ray Drlik (6552) 04:30:14
1029. Douglas Stewart (6558) 04:38:16
1030. Bradley Winters (6563) 04:38:19
1031. Thomas Gonzales (6569) 04:38:25
1032. Alberto Olvera Resendiz (6575) 04:38:30
1033. Frank Jilek III (6582) 04:38:33
1034. Mark Lacher (6593) 04:38:40
1035. Yatendra Solanki (6607) 04:38:48
1036. Alfred Gonzales (6646) 04:39:12
1037. Jack Dorsey (6654) 04:39:21
1038. Rob Duron (6655) 04:39:22
1039. Michael Winchester (6657) 04:39:25
1040. Robert Wolcott (6659) 04:39:26
1041. Bradly Hamby (6663) 04:39:29
1042. Behrouz Khodnegah (6678) 04:39:40
1043. David Walper (6680) 04:39:41
1044. Durrell Nelson Jr (6686) 04:39:44
1045. Michael Israelsky (6691) 04:39:46
1046. Leroy Gibson (6692) 04:39:47
1047. Francisco Cruz (6694) 04:39:48
1048. Michael Trenkle (6704) 04:39:56
1049. Kim Wong (6706) 04:39:59
1050. Ivan Ulloa (6718) 04:40:08
1051. Luis Garcia (6725) 04:40:17
1052. John Perry (6731) 04:40:20
1053. Tim Chilton (6740) 04:40:27
1054. Miguel Castanera (6742) 04:40:33
1055. Nick Sherr (6748) 04:40:35
1056. Juan Dominguez (6750) 04:40:36
1057. Jorge Velasco (6785) 04:41:05
1058. Daniel Bryce (6789) 04:41:06
1059. Harry Redinger (6796) 04:41:11
1060. Ruben Mejia (6797) 04:41:11
1061. Ernesto Ortiz (6800) 04:41:15
1062. Faust Grijalva (6815) 04:41:30
1063. Jaime Rivera (6839) 04:41:48
1064. Craig Leurfeld (6844) 04:41:50
1065. David Lasky (6848) 04:41:54
1066. Jeffry Manasse (6849) 04:41:54
1067. Jose Friaz (6852) 04:41:56
1068. Tomoyuki Miyoshi (6859) 04:42:00
1069. John Peretz (6878) 04:42:15
1070. Douglas Murray (6879) 04:42:17
1071. Dan Romero (6883) 04:42:24
1072. Barry Sandridge (6886) 04:42:26
1073. Brian Matthews (6914) 04:42:47
1074. Jose Sandoval (6926) 04:42:54
1075. Michael Willey (6939) 04:43:03
1076. Sean Spaulding (6952) 04:43:08
1077. Jude Schreiner (6967) 04:43:20
1078. Charles Fong (6978) 04:43:23
1079. Angel Augulo (6981) 04:43:27
1080. John Burke (6982) 04:43:28
1081. Patrick MacAuley (6999) 04:43:37
1082. Bobby Castillo (7010) 04:43:41
1083. Scott Appleton (7037) 04:44:01
1084. Wil Lafayette (7048) 04:44:10
1085. Mitchell Polon (7053) 04:44:16
1086. Joel Ruiz (7060) 04:44:20
1087. Wilfredo Cruz Rivas (7069) 04:44:27
1088. Jay Shih (7080) 04:44:37
1089. Troy Tran (7099) 04:44:54
1090. Brian Warpack (7104) 04:44:56
1091. James Rosenthal (7109) 04:45:00
1092. Phillip Bland (7116) 04:45:03
1093. Darryl Edwards (7121) 04:45:05
1094. Dave Mullins (7127) 04:45:11
1095. Mark Hansen (7135) 04:45:15
1096. Stuart Barrett (7138) 04:45:18
1097. Dan Whitten (7159) 04:45:40
1098. Wayne Klein (7166) 04:45:42
1099. Efren Miranda (7176) 04:45:49
1100. Stephen Olear (7191) 04:46:00
1101. David De Vault (7199) 04:46:07
1102. Marcus Meakin (7216) 04:46:18
1103. Chris Basom (7220) 04:46:21
1104. Andy Rea (7231) 04:46:30
1105. Tony La Bruno (7236) 04:46:32
1106. Larry Herschler (7242) 04:46:35
1107. Kory Kelley (7250) 04:46:43
1108. Kevin Rodgers (7252) 04:46:43
1109. Kevin Hopp (7255) 04:46:45
1110. Scott Barnes (7261) 04:46:49
1111. Timothy Simpson (7265) 04:46:53
1112. Manuel Medina (7268) 04:46:55
1113. David Hoffman (7276) 04:46:58
1114. Ed Dea (7301) 04:47:15
1115. Raymond Flowers (7305) 04:47:18
1116. Thomas Philo (7311) 04:47:23
1117. Stephen Walsh (7313) 04:47:24
1118. Robert Jenks (7316) 04:47:25
1119. Dan Baker (7334) 04:47:35
1120. Jeffrey Listenbee (7336) 04:47:38
1121. Duane Marshall (7344) 04:47:43
1122. Fermin Lopez (7345) 04:47:43
1123. Erol Ceran (7350) 04:47:46
1124. John Hearn (7351) 04:47:47
1125. Hector Gonzalez (7357) 04:47:55
1126. Peter Bennett (7363) 04:47:59
1127. Scott Porter (7369) 04:48:03
1128. Jon Marshall Muncy (7419) 04:48:35
1129. Paul Cannavan (7424) 04:48:39
1130. Cecil Fowler (7427) 04:48:42
1131. Timothy Anast (7447) 04:48:55
1132. Scott Homuth (7450) 04:48:57
1133. Manuel Herman Sagastume (7456) 04:49:01
1134. Dan McFeeley (7463) 04:49:04
1135. David Barulich (7475) 04:49:11
1136. Tim Swett (7479) 04:49:13
1137. Daniel Kinder (7497) 04:49:23
1138. James Orange (7503) 04:49:26
1139. Jesse Vega (7519) 04:49:34
1140. Jeff Roberts (7524) 04:49:36
1141. Gordon Thiele (7539) 04:49:51
1142. Richard Yamashita (7544) 04:49:53
1143. Luis Velazquez III (7545) 04:49:53
1144. Robert Holmes (7551) 04:49:59
1145. William Grey Mc Laren (7558) 04:50:02
1146. David Koster (7566) 04:50:12
1147. Roy Hernandez (7571) 04:50:15
1148. Richard Sherrell (7585) 04:50:25
1149. Art Ramos (7589) 04:50:31
1150. Roger Stephens (7592) 04:50:33
1151. Steve Hernandez (7604) 04:50:42
1152. Rob Stevens (7621) 04:50:53
1153. Frank Vizcarra (7624) 04:50:56
1154. Tony Acosta (7627) 04:50:57
1155. Phillip Fernandez (7630) 04:50:59
1156. Jeffrey Hunter (7642) 04:51:07
1157. Sal Molina (7647) 04:51:13
1158. Gilbert Arangure (7651) 04:51:21
1159. Guillermo Alcantara (7665) 04:51:32
1160. Takeshi Takeuchi (7680) 04:51:40
1161. Kazumi Nakano (7683) 04:51:40
1162. George Stevens (7686) 04:51:42
1163. Jeffrey Allen (7689) 04:51:46
1164. Rolando Cisne (7690) 04:51:46
1165. Isaias Romo (7691) 04:51:48
1166. Paul Steen (7695) 04:51:53
1167. Wes Bermeister (7700) 04:51:59
1168. Salvatore Rallo (7701) 04:51:59
1169. Richard Marias (7707) 04:52:04
1170. Luis Melendrez (7723) 04:52:15
1171. Gary Gaston (7733) 04:52:25
1172. Frank Dikken (7736) 04:52:27
1173. Acejanoro Rosella (7751) 04:52:40
1174. Kenneth Miles (7753) 04:52:41
1175. Rod Stolk (7761) 04:52:46
1176. Jose Escobedo (7768) 04:52:52
1177. Timothy Stanton (7773) 04:52:54
1178. Dan Finklea (7784) 04:53:01
1179. Paul Flores (7801) 04:53:16
1180. Jay Jahanmir (7810) 04:53:24
1181. Bill Morris (7821) 04:53:30
1182. Fred Dengler (7828) 04:53:33
1183. Richard Crater (7835) 04:53:37
1184. Stephen Belsito (7841) 04:53:41
1185. Eric Olsson (7850) 04:53:48
1186. Miguelito Sanchez (7866) 04:53:58
1187. Daniel Leff (7871) 04:54:02
1188. Joe Velasquez (7873) 04:54:04
1189. Prosper Godonoo (7881) 04:54:08
1190. Ted Liston (7898) 04:54:19
1191. Frank Aguilar (7908) 04:54:24
1192. William Bellows (7913) 04:54:27
1193. Christopher Hohensinner (7921) 04:54:31
1194. Mike Wapner (7935) 04:54:35
1195. Fred Magana (7951) 04:54:45
1196. Andy White (7954) 04:54:45
1197. Tom Duran (7991) 04:55:15
1198. Jesus Suarez (8014) 04:55:35
1199. Richard Carpenter Jr (8043) 04:55:55
1200. Helmet Roth (8048) 04:56:00
1201. Randy Martens (8068) 04:56:16
1202. James Barden (8087) 04:56:32
1203. Kevin Mcgrade (8094) 04:56:34
1204. Mario Medrano (8100) 04:56:40

1205. Jerry Rollison (8104) 04:56:42
1206. Randal Ziglar (8117) 04:56:48
1207. Gabriel Quijano (8141) 04:57:13
1208. Robert Arrieta (8154) 04:57:22
1209. Ernie Sparks (8162) 04:57:26
1210. Gary Kasper (8177) 04:57:38
1211. Arthur Picon (8183) 04:57:41
1212. Timothy Kirchoff (8196) 04:57:52
1213. Melvin Olds (8207) 04:57:59
1214. Bobby Sierra (8214) 04:58:01
1215. Jerry Wilder (8234) 04:58:14
1216. Avila Kahey (8239) 04:58:15
1217. Christopher Kraskin (8242) 04:58:16
1218. Arie Carmelli (8272) 04:58:35
1219. Clinton Juhl (8273) 04:58:35
1220. Ramasamy Marayanan (8276) 04:58:41
1221. David Frahm (8278) 04:58:43
1222. Kevin Rodgers (8311) 04:58:57
1223. Thomas Szabo (8314) 04:59:01
1224. Mikey Wineman (8315) 04:59:02
1225. Peter Jones (8323) 04:59:07
1226. Dana Leung (8335) 04:59:14
1227. Enrique Rosales Valles (8337) 04:59:15
1228. Rogelia Gonzalez (8346) 04:59:24
1229. Wayne Watanabe (8353) 04:59:29
1230. Michael Schuenemeyer (8363) 04:59:36
1231. Noray Papazoglu (8366) 04:59:37
1232. Henry Johns (8370) 04:59:38
1233. Richard Villa (8396) 04:59:58
1234. Bradley Routh (8410) 05:00:16
1235. Domino Speca (8429) 05:00:33
1236. Jim Witt II (8431) 05:00:37
1237. Tim Ledbetter (8432) 05:00:39
1238. Eliot Roberts (8448) 05:00:55
1239. Victor Del Aguila (8464) 05:01:06
1240. Jose Ponce (8478) 05:01:16
1241. Michael Gutierrez (8479) 05:01:18
1242. William Baker (8501) 05:01:32
1243. Charles Pomeroy (8522) 05:01:44
1244. Joe Reyes (8523) 05:01:44
1245. Richard Gari (8525) 05:01:45
1246. Jesse Morales (8529) 05:01:48
1247. Gary Seto (8536) 05:01:54
1248. Mark Davis (8537) 05:01:55
1249. Jahan Jomehri (8546) 05:02:04
1250. Jae Yi (8551) 05:02:08
1251. Paul Sanden (8554) 05:02:10
1252. Thomas Tomsic (8561) 05:02:15
1253. Joseph Grandt (8564) 05:02:17
1254. Alberto Salinas (8566) 05:02:19
1255. Wayne Espy (8601) 05:03:00
1256. James Doss (8602) 05:03:02
1257. Rufino Leal (8617) 05:03:11
1258. John Prude (8620) 05:03:13
1259. Calvin Shatto (8624) 05:03:14
1260. Bill Franco (8630) 05:03:21
1261. Eugene Anton (8636) 05:03:28
1262. Robert Kresowski (8651) 05:03:45
1263. Felipe Aguirre (8678) 05:04:01
1264. Gregory Rivera (8693) 05:04:17
1265. Jose Reyna (8696) 05:04:18
1266. Angel Carrillo (8718) 05:04:33
1267. Jose Esquivel (8726) 05:04:43
1268. Tuan Tran (8737) 05:04:53
1269. Robert Garcia (8743) 05:05:04
1270. Roger Neyrey (8750) 05:05:14
1271. Patrick Condon (8752) 05:05:15
1272. Al Alvarez (8778) 05:05:38
1273. James Kendall (8781) 05:05:43
1274. Jose Arias (8787) 05:05:48
1275. Jerry Talcott (8788) 05:05:50
1276. Richard Azofeifa (8789) 05:05:51
1277. Michael Harris (8791) 05:05:53
1278. Paul Hilliard (8797) 05:05:57
1279. John Rossato (8803) 05:06:05
1280. Daniel Bleich (8822) 05:06:25
1281. Gabino Gallardo (8824) 05:06:27
1282. Travis Heflin (8826) 05:06:29
1283. Scott Tommey (8828) 05:06:32
1284. Dan Chapel (8835) 05:06:36
1285. John Gross (8836) 05:06:37
1286. Eddie Robertson (8837) 05:06:37
1287. Guillermo Ramirez (8840) 05:06:42
1288. Guy Ghiader (8847) 05:06:55
1289. Bill Mason (8866) 05:07:10
1290. John Livermont (8881) 05:07:31
1291. John Mosqueda (8884) 05:07:33
1292. Phil Larson (8891) 05:07:39
1293. Anatolio Cruz (8904) 05:07:51
1294. Wayne Howard (8907) 05:07:53
1295. Trevor Wainwright (8910) 05:07:56
1296. Steve Davis (8911) 05:07:56
1297. John McMullen (8931) 05:08:12
1298. Hideaki Kato (8944) 05:08:29
1299. Shane Kindel (8949) 05:08:32
1300. Fernando Guzma Zavala (8950) 05:08:32
1301. Jose Iniguez (8953) 05:08:35
1302. Vicente Martinez (8961) 05:08:39
1303. Gerald Taylor (8994) 05:09:06
1304. John Barnett (9009) 05:09:13
1305. Craig Wilson (9020) 05:09:22
1306. Joseph Asbury (9024) 05:09:26
1307. Ananillias Becerra (9030) 05:09:30
1308. Derric Morris (9034) 05:09:37
1309. Jose Mejia Esquerra (9039) 05:09:43
1310. Ivan Zetina (9044) 05:09:45
1311. Nedyalko Ivanov (9057) 05:09:55
1312. Luis Salem (9062) 05:09:58
1313. Changiz Parchini (9069) 05:10:01
1314. Ray Beaty (9073) 05:10:04
1315. Rick Politte (9085) 05:10:13
1316. James Bentley (9095) 05:10:17
1317. Paul Samaniego (9104) 05:10:21
1318. Shugo Kanai (9117) 05:10:26
1319. Donald Whitted (9129) 05:10:40
1320. George Padgett (9132) 05:10:44
1321. Peter Wong (9135) 05:10:47
1322. Jose Cadenas (9144) 05:10:55
1323. Ronnie Villanueva (9161) 05:11:14
1324. Victor De La Loza (9178) 05:11:34
1325. Paul Alderson (9193) 05:11:43
1326. Hoshang Dubash (9203) 05:11:50
1327. Robin Villa (9246) 05:12:36
1328. Keith Lovendosky (9247) 05:12:36
1329. Ed Martin (9248) 05:12:38
1330. Greg Davis (9254) 05:12:48
1331. John Miller (9273) 05:13:05
1332. Javier Razo (9284) 05:13:15
1333. Bill Bates (9289) 05:13:16
1334. Steve Moehlman (9302) 05:13:27
1335. Tony Romero (9318) 05:13:34
1336. Robert Wilkinson (9332) 05:13:41
1337. Thomas Jackson Jr (9343) 05:13:51
1338. Felipe Plascencia (9350) 05:13:54
1339. Miguel Enriquez (9367) 05:14:08
1340. Steven Serrano (9369) 05:14:09
1341. Yukio Onizuka (9378) 05:14:19
1342. John Bell (9395) 05:14:36
1343. Anderson Connor (9410) 05:14:55
1344. Shinji Kokubo (9433) 05:15:22
1345. Robert Basile (9450) 05:15:45
1346. Roland Beverly (9455) 05:15:52
1347. Ebie Zahabian (9458) 05:15:54
1348. Will Leader (9462) 05:15:57
1349. Bob Campbell (9471) 05:16:07
1350. Roy Ramirez (9474) 05:16:09
1351. Victor Jones (9475) 05:16:10
1352. Michael Berger (9496) 05:16:28
1353. Jesus Trojo (9513) 05:16:39
1354. Joe Cosio (9517) 05:16:42
1355. Tom Finlayson (9539) 05:17:03
1356. Joseph Connolly (9556) 05:17:12
1357. John Clinnin (9575) 05:17:20
1358. Buford Thompson (9583) 05:17:04
1359. Richard Meza (9591) 05:17:44
1360. Sergio Suarez (9607) 05:17:58
1361. Richard Trevett (9632) 05:18:29
1362. Jimmy Vasquez (9668) 05:18:58
1363. Michael Wirges (9689) 05:19:14
1364. David Weissman (9693) 05:19:18
1365. Hitoshi Takakura (9699) 05:19:24
1366. Eric Spears (9709) 05:19:34
1367. Rob Hager (9713) 05:19:44
1368. Gustavo Gubel (9718) 05:19:46
1369. Thomas Young (9719) 05:19:47
1370. Robert Siew (9724) 05:19:54
1371. George Harros (9736) 05:20:12
1372. Michael Yoo (9759) 05:20:32
1373. Kevin Seeker (9764) 05:20:36
1374. Jeff Watson (9770) 05:20:39
1375. Terry Eckenwiler (9778) 05:20:46
1376. Hidenori Ito (9787) 05:20:51
1377. Phillip Charles (9798) 05:21:01
1378. Josslyn Gordon (9806) 05:21:08
1379. Daniel Masuda (9815) 05:21:16
1380. Lee Ruttenberg (9822) 05:21:26
1381. Salah Assaf (9829) 05:21:36
1382. Ted Vasquez (9836) 05:21:39
1383. Robert Carreon (9838) 05:21:40
1384. Roberto Becerra (9850) 05:21:47
1385. James Housel (9851) 05:21:48
1386. Kirk Clyatt (9853) 05:21:48
1387. Sidney Torres (9876) 05:22:07
1388. Manuel Giron (9877) 05:22:09
1389. Jesus Andrade (9882) 05:22:12
1390. Michael Lee (9898) 05:22:27
1391. Louie Nevarez (9906) 05:22:39
1392. Thomas Maimone II (9909) 05:22:44
1393. David Smith (9920) 05:22:53
1394. Victoriano Meza (9929) 05:23:04
1395. Armando Urena (9941) 05:23:21
1396. George Moore (9943) 05:23:23
1397. William Euler (9947) 05:23:25
1398. Larry Lofton (9954) 05:23:32
1399. Alberto Rosario (9961) 05:23:40
1400. John Moreno (9984) 05:24:03
1401. Bruce Johnson (9997) 05:24:13
1402. Clay Harmon (10001) 05:24:22
1403. Glenn Buskirk (10007) 05:24:28
1404. William Beene (10009) 05:24:28
1405. Koyan Smith (10018) 05:24:42
1406. Scott Lawrence (10024) 05:24:49
1407. Gerardo Padilla (10027) 05:24:52
1408. Dan Johnson (10034) 05:25:00
1409. Vargas Cayetano Santanero (10049) 05:25:17
1410. Dale Burns (10057) 05:25:32
1411. Ken Curtis (10076) 05:25:46
1412. Saul Alvarado (10080) 05:25:47
1413. Thom Kerr (10088) 05:25:52
1414. Stephen Hampar (10107) 05:26:12
1415. Brent Shapiro (10108) 05:26:13
1416. Hayma Washington (10139) 05:26:48
1417. Robert Sundlie (10161) 05:27:12
1418. Raymond Campbell (10198) 05:27:44
1419. James Buchanan (10209) 05:27:50
1420. Edward Resto (10227) 05:28:08
1421. Randy Thiele (10247) 05:28:36
1422. John Wieland (10248) 05:28:36
1423. Eric Finnila (10249) 05:28:37
1424. Luule Medrano (10266) 05:28:48
1425. Andre Obirek (10272) 05:28:51
1426. Ali Pouraghabagher (10273) 05:28:52
1427. Henry Nierodzik (10290) 05:29:02
1428. Douglas Hibbard (10296) 05:29:12
1429. Marvin Reece (10304) 05:29:15
1430. Randall Austin (10307) 05:29:15
1431. Albert Ortiz (10308) 05:29:16
1432. Hexbext Diaz (10311) 05:29:16
1433. David Hernandez (10317) 05:29:21
1434. Les Avila (10324) 05:29:32
1435. Joseph Ramirez (10325) 05:29:33
1436. William Skelly (10331) 05:29:47
1437. Richard Beltran (10341) 05:29:54
1438. Phillip Cohen (10351) 05:30:07
1439. Jeffrey Kozminske (10375) 05:30:26
1440. Allan Jackson (10401) 05:30:47
1441. Hung Nguyen (10402) 05:30:47
1442. Stanley Scates (10408) 05:30:58
1443. John Drew (10411) 05:31:04
1444. Vincint Buenrosto (10431) 05:31:23
1445. Kenneth Kirk (10452) 05:31:36
1446. Art Tinajero (10457) 05:31:40
1447. Joe Vilaubi (10458) 05:31:41
1448. Henry Angsiy (10460) 05:31:43
1449. Fred Chaidez (10476) 05:31:52
1450. Gil Alzona (10489) 05:32:07
1451. Clifton Hibbert (10492) 05:32:10
1452. Kao-Shen Wang (10495) 05:32:13
1453. Anthony Ward (10515) 05:32:40
1454. Rashid Razavi (10517) 05:32:44
1455. Harvey Wade (10532) 05:32:54
1456. Stephen Breen (10535) 05:32:55
1457. Barry Deutsch (10539) 05:32:56
1458. Daniel Holmes (10540) 05:32:57
1459. Anton Saucedo (10549) 05:33:11
1460. Pat Pepatphong (10558) 05:33:24
1461. Nasir Jeevanjee (10567) 05:33:27
1462. Gregory Dubose (10574) 05:33:31
1463. Homar Maravilla (10576) 05:33:34
1464. Richard Burd (10577) 05:33:35
1465. Hiroshi Hagiwara (10586) 05:33:42
1466. Will Saylor (10589) 05:33:42
1467. Marlon McGee (10592) 05:33:45
1468. Paul Aguirre (10593) 05:33:46
1469. Jorge Paulin (10601) 05:33:52
1470. Henry Yanez (10619) 05:34:05
1471. Koichi Suzuki (10626) 05:34:07
1472. Carlos Zubyk (10636) 05:34:24
1473. Phillip Pineda (10638) 05:34:25
1474. Henry Glowa (10643) 05:34:30
1475. Jeff Windhorst (10650) 05:34:37
1476. Jeffrey Landon (10666) 05:34:45
1477. Chris Dukes (10674) 05:34:58
1478. Gil Rocco (10710) 05:35:28
1479. Son Nguyen (10739) 05:35:56
1480. Eusebio Lopez (10745) 05:36:09
1481. Donald Tillman (10780) 05:36:41
1482. Stevan Dumas (10787) 05:36:50
1483. Kevin McClenton (10790) 05:36:53
1484. Syd Taylor (10794) 05:37:00
1485. J J Apetrior (10799) 05:37:04
1486. Santiago Sifuentes (10813) 05:37:19
1487. David Rowley (10819) 05:37:25
1488. Miro Lhotsky (10837) 05:37:43
1489. Edmund Gomez (10858) 05:38:10
1490. Jeffrey Hallman (10879) 05:38:48
1491. Sal Sanchez (10908) 05:39:19
1492. Kayed Khalil (10921) 05:39:44
1493. Samuel Bailey (10928) 05:39:49
1494. Timothy Fair (10935) 05:39:56
1495. Roland Mamea (10939) 05:40:05
1496. John Williamson (10947) 05:40:13
1497. Joe Gonsalves (10950) 05:40:16
1498. Edmundo Lemus (10957) 05:40:25
1499. Ronald Ratlief (10976) 05:40:56
1500. Fernando Ayala (10994) 05:41:20
1501. Marcel Van Someren (10996) 05:41:26
1502. Daniel McCoy (11006) 05:41:34
1503. Peter Cayan (11008) 05:41:35
1504. Andrew Romero (11015) 05:41:43
1505. Daniel Kemp (11032) 05:42:01
1506. Rocco Grimaldi (11058) 05:42:20
1507. Joe Nino (11066) 05:42:27
1508. Oscar Ramos (11076) 05:42:38
1509. David Tuche (11082) 05:42:42
1510. Juan Urista (11084) 05:42:42
1511. Bill Holderby (11087) 05:42:45
1512. Ronald Pyle (11103) 05:43:03
1513. Jaime Aguirre (11108) 05:43:06
1514. Arthur Yaskin (11118) 05:43:19
1515. Adrian Garcia (11122) 05:43:27
1516. Gilbert McKenzie (11124) 05:43:30
1517. Arthur Otsuka (11139) 05:43:42
1518. William Chan (11150) 05:43:58
1519. Raul Melara (11152) 05:44:00
1520. Samuel Almonte (11162) 05:44:08
1521. Lee Wilson (11176) 05:44:15
1522. Carlos Lopez (11178) 05:44:16
1523. Lance McCall (11182) 05:44:19
1524. Steve Herfert (11209) 05:44:35
1525. Johnathon Wilson (11212) 05:44:37
1526. Jim Craven (11215) 05:44:38
1527. Kenn Beal (11217) 05:44:38
1528. Marc Zavala (11228) 05:44:52
1529. Jeff Jansen (11234) 05:44:56
1530. David Mace (11235) 05:44:57
1531. Maxie Jones (11240) 05:45:04
1532. German Castellanos (11244) 05:45:10
1533. Blaine Blackstone (11247) 05:45:13
1534. Jesus Johnson (11254) 05:45:22
1535. Eddie Zubyk (11263) 05:45:31
1536. Hiroshi Nakajima (11204) 05:45:33
1537. John Clayton (11272) 05:45:45
1538. Hirotsugu Hongo (11275) 05:45:47
1539. Willard Lewallen (11278) 05:45:52
1540. Rick Nawrocki (11282) 05:45:55
1541. Gus Jimenez (11293) 05:46:06
1542. Will Youngling (11324) 05:46:41
1543. Patrick De La Torre (11330) 05:46:51
1544. David Thompson (11344) 05:47:09
1545. Dale McCree (11377) 05:48:14
1546. Enrique De La Paz (11384) 05:48:26
1547. Tony Fernandes (11412) 05:49:07
1548. Alberto Santiago (11422) 05:49:18
1549. Marco Polanco (11444) 05:49:40
1550. Michael Bare (11469) 05:50:00
1551. Ronald Takasugi (11475) 05:50:05
1552. Ronald Ushijima (11481) 05:50:12
1553. Robert Warsaw (11495) 05:50:26
1554. Thomas Trimbach (11504) 05:50:30
1555. Pete Antunez (11507) 05:50:31
1556. Darrell Reed (11515) 05:50:36
1557. Ramon Valenzuela (11545) 05:51:11
1558. Yoshihiro Matsumoto (11546) 05:51:11
1559. Stephen Beverly (11552) 05:51:26
1560. Carlos Smith (11563) 05:51:41
1561. Louis Ramirez (11593) 05:52:18
1562. Wayne Winstead (11594) 05:52:19
1563. Eric Espinoza (11617) 05:52:58
1564. Rick Restifo (11622) 05:52:59
1565. David Dominguez (11623) 05:52:59
1566. Earl Battey (11629) 05:53:00
1567. Daniel Freeman (11673) 05:53:44
1568. Javier Salas (11678) 05:53:51
1569. Jim Thomas (11685) 05:53:54
1570. Roy Buranday (11695) 05:54:07
1571. Manuel Caldera (11741) 05:55:16
1572. Geronimo Young (11742) 05:55:17
1573. David Eichinger (11745) 05:55:19
1574. Katsuhiko Kimura (11803) 05:56:43
1575. Farzam Afshar (11820) 05:57:00
1576. Benjamin Boyd (11827) 05:57:15
1577. Jim Gardemann (11830) 05:57:17
1578. Gary Brigandi (11842) 05:57:36
1579. John Clegg (11855) 05:58:00
1580. Rene Durant (11858) 05:58:02
1581. Karl White (11916) 05:58:57
1582. Jose Mendoza (11918) 05:59:02
1583. Rick Miali (11923) 05:59:21
1584. Virgil County (11931) 05:59:28
1585. Lester Sakuma (11967) 06:00:17
1586. Brian Sakuma (11968) 06:00:17
1587. Rob Slingsby (11971) 06:00:18
1588. Anthony Cruz (11981) 06:00:32
1589. Steve Davis (12028) 06:01:59
1590. Fernando Barraza (12029) 06:02:01
1591. Luis Suarez (12036) 06:02:13
1592. John Vidovich (12068) 06:03:04
1593. Brian MacFarland (12075) 06:03:17
1594. Juan Reyes (12089) 06:03:45
1595. Stanislav Sestak (12092) 06:03:46
1596. Alberto Robles (12114) 06:04:35
1597. Harry Shabazian (12129) 06:04:43
1598. Doug Ashley (12135) 06:04:48
1599. Shigenao Kumakura (12137) 06:04:51
1600. Eduljee Chikhliwala (12144) 06:05:03
1601. Robert Hahnlein (12154) 06:05:19
1602. Michael Garcia (12159) 06:05:24
1603. Nelson Daza (12161) 06:05:26
1604. Mark Cain (12169) 06:05:34
1605. Hal Harmsen (12170) 06:05:36
1606. Ant Lampareki (12176) 06:05:47
1607. Adele Cortinas (12179) 06:05:50
1608. Michael Gonzalez (12210) 06:06:59
1609. J Whitney Halloran (12241) 06:07:53
1610. Michael Robinson (12246) 06:08:01
1611. Miko Gutierrez (12290) 06:08:55
1612. Gerald Randolph (12296) 06:09:01
1613. Adrian Canizales (12306) 06:09:11
1614. Alvin Jackson (12326) 06:09:47
1615. John Eberts (12335) 06:09:58
1616. Jessie Dominguez (12338) 06:10:00
1617. Sal Trapani (12360) 06:10:53
1618. Lance Emi (12377) 06:11:12
1619. Costas Synolakis (12380) 06:11:17
1620. Ranjit Patel (12398) 06:11:42
1621. Shinzi Kubo (12415) 06:12:08
1622. Julian Szlamka (12419) 06:12:15
1623. Abel Alvarado (12422) 06:12:20
1624. Juan Alvarado (12428) 06:12:37
1625. Roberto Ochoa (12438) 06:12:47
1626. Armand Ramos (12439) 06:12:47
1627. Paul Rifino (12440) 06:12:50
1628. Michael Prokupuk (12448) 06:13:05
1629. Kevin Meehan (12460) 06:13:25
1630. Seyed Fattahy (12461) 06:13:29
1631. Franco Royna (12463) 06:13:31
1632. Francisco Lemus (12465) 06:13:32
1633. Clarence Pasley (12489) 06:14:03
1634. Doug Cummings (12507) 06:14:34
1635. Nigel Garraway (12518) 06:14:52
1636. Javier Barrera (12525) 06:15:09
1637. Gregory Newton (12536) 06:15:19
1638. Maurice Lathouwers (12539) 06:15:25
1639. Hirano Jun (12541) 06:15:26
1640. Shigeru Takeuchi (12575) 06:16:17
1641. Vincent Yamada (12588) 06:16:42
1642. Angel Cisneros (12591) 06:16:44
1643. Dennis Winegarner (12594) 06:16:49
1644. Yrej Taslakian (12613) 06:17:15
1645. Jerome Trost (12636) 06:18:15
1646. Donald Hunter (12644) 06:18:20
1647. Onyelukachukwu Ajufoh (12665) 06:19:07
1648. Gerald Laird (12669) 06:19:14
1649. Tom Peters (12687) 06:19:45
1650. Dimas Iglesias (12690) 06:19:47
1651. Juan Bohorquez (12693) 06:19:56
1652. Ian Budge (12711) 06:20:28
1653. Mitsutoshi Kawauchi (12714) 06:20:31
1654. Oscar Flores (12716) 06:20:36
1655. Jake Jaime (12723) 06:20:51
1656. Naoki Takehara (12759) 06:21:50
1657. Rudy Hernandez (12775) 06:22:04
1658. Gregory Molden (12778) 06:22:07
1659. Mark Foster (12793) 06:22:41
1660. Nick Pinedo (12815) 06:23:23
1661. Hector Garcia (12830) 06:23:39
1662. Frank Zubiate (12839) 06:23:49
1663. Michael Yarbrough (12880) 06:25:10
1664. Stuart Kaplan (12920) 06:26:25
1665. Matt Murphy (12960) 06:27:41
1666. Nick Barson (12973) 06:27:57
1667. Joe Fowler (13007) 06:28:47
1668. Paul Konenkamp (13009) 06:28:48
1669. Gerald Kimble (13013) 06:29:01
1670. Jose Hernandez (13020) 06:29:15
1671. George Gradias (13044) 06:30:08
1672. Evan Warshawsky (13061) 06:30:44
1673. Eugene Ricasa (13077) 06:31:15
1674. James Winstead (13116) 06:32:22
1675. Richard Acosta (13136) 06:32:42
1676. Jon Graves (13142) 06:32:46
1677. Jim Graves (13145) 06:32:47
1678. Hilario Rivera (13154) 06:32:59
1679. Mauro Flores (13172) 06:33:32
1680. Fidel Cupino (13185) 06:34:00
1681. Maurice White (13239) 06:35:29
1682. John Meyer (13240) 06:35:31
1683. Eddie Aldaco (13246) 06:35:42
1684. Don Bush (13252) 06:35:52
1685. Richard Gatewood (13264) 06:36:07
1686. Harry Sager III (13305) 06:37:33
1687. Ron Barrios (13321) 06:38:23
1688. Kevin Joseph McCarthy (13359) 06:39:31
1689. Sam Demerjian (13372) 06:39:58
1690. Gilbert Estrada (13385) 06:40:35
1691. Salvador Cortez (13390) 06:40:46
1692. Mark Kujiraoka (13402) 06:41:17
1693. James Wolker II (13407) 06:41:22
1694. David Riding (13412) 06:41:26
1695. Thomas Ouimet (13433) 06:42:14
1696. Robert Ayala (13460) 06:43:04
1697. Alton Nakama (13471) 06:43:41
1698. Brian Foss (13516) 06:45:21
1699. Jeffrey Lewis (13556) 06:46:49
1700. Daniel Ontell (13564) 06:46:57
1701. Michael Cooper (13565) 06:46:58
1702. William Iriart (13566) 06:47:00
1703. Steve Mendez (13569) 06:47:03
1704. George Lomax (13581) 06:47:33
1705. Frank Carpenter (13588) 06:47:50
1706. Charles Liskey (13654) 06:50:02
1707. Pete Hernandez (13662) 06:50:08
1708. Presley Burroughs (13675) 06:50:30
1709. Laura Chaides (13682) 06:50:35
1710. James Garcia (13710) 06:51:30
1711. Dana Marshall (13721) 06:51:50
1712. Lawrence Varblow (13725) 06:51:56
1713. Tom Tellez (13739) 06:52:42
1714. Jose Auelat (13746) 06:53:12
1715. Shao-I Hu (13755) 06:53:40
1716. Robert Duitoman (13894) 06:58:17
1717. Robert Barry (13903) 06:58:20
1718. Steven Lodge (13929) 06:59:03
1719. Mikihiro Ohkita (13965) 07:00:28
1720. Wendell McClenton (13993) 07:01:03
1721. Mitchell Garber (14001) 07:01:13
1722. Richard Sunn (14004) 07:01:24
1723. Arnold Goldman (14032) 07:02:31
1724. Ronald Brock (14033) 07:02:32
1725. Christopher Lazalde (14051) 07:03:19
1726. Adrian Ricard (14062) 07:03:59
1727. John Lee Jr (14075) 07:04:43
1728. Harold Vollkommer (14081) 07:04:57
1729. Rick Baca (14089) 07:05:17
1730. Max Hernandez (14091) 07:05:37
1731. Lonnie Banks Jr (14144) 07:09:01
1732. Ron Finch (14145) 07:09:04
1733. Gerardo Morales (14148) 07:09:10
1734. Hector Salazar (14180) 07:11:41
1735. Ismael Diaz (14238) 07:14:43
1736. Steven Lawrence (14251) 07:15:31
1737. Dana Jackson (14261) 07:15:43
1738. Dwayne Edwards (14269) 07:16:03
1739. Calvin Sakaniwa (14285) 07:16:59
1740. Albert Rodela (14313) 07:19:03
1741. Steven Hazard (14379) 07:23:01
1742. Arthur Meier (14420) 07:26:47
1743. K Douglas Weaver (14436) 07:28:05
1744. David Bullock (14483) 07:32:41
1745. Richard Haines (14536) 07:36:24
1746. Elena Shaw (14587) 07:40:02
1747. Garry Galvan (14591) 07:40:27
1748. David Callahan (14592) 07:40:33
1749. Carlos Haro (14613) 07:42:13
1750. Glenda Morrison (14631) 07:44:16
1751. Panfilo Mata (14651) 07:46:03
1752. Marcelino Tinajero Jr (14688) 07:49:38
1753. Rick Torrez (14700) 07:50:54
1754. William Jones Jr (14746) 07:54:46
1755. Donald Miller (14770) 07:56:12
1756. Jesse Renteria (14784) 07:58:29
1757. Brian Hammock (14824) 08:02:30
1758. Anthony Givhan (14826) 08:02:31
1759. Douglas Canyon Jr (14846) 08:05:03
1760. Hesham Ellmossallamy (14854) 08:07:25
1761. Louis Escarcega (14858) 08:08:23
1762. Kevin Kelly (14864) 08:10:00
1763. Stephen Walsh (14945) 08:21:18
1764. James Corralejo (14952) 08:22:20
1765. Steven Yasutake (14964) 08:25:17
1766. David Mark (14986) 08:28:49
1767. Joe Ruiz (15018) 08:35:16
1768. Robert Fox (15035) 08:39:24
1769. Jay Jackson (15038) 08:42:44
1770. George Jaquez (15043) 08:45:30
1771. Gilbert Juarez (15049) 08:46:01
1772. Rich Chavez (15109) 09:11:25
1773. Aaron Alvarado (15114) 09:16:09
1774. Greg Hawkins (15122) 09:26:30
1775. Aleck Papanicolopoulos (15163) 10:05:48

WOMEN 35 TO 39

1. Lyobov Klochko (30) 02:33:31
2. Judy Mercon (165) 02:55:57
3. Nancy Abrahams (724) 03:19:01
4. Erendira McCormick (878) 03:22:46
5. Heidi Tisovic (974) 03:24:51
6. Tere Wierson (1050) 03:26:40
7. Debra Matthews (1201) 03:29:29
8. Sherril Clark (1214) 03:29:40
9. Elizabeth Kelly (1231) 03:29:59
10. Patricia Peck (1202) 03:30:58
11. Marie Romero (1313) 03:31:36
12. Kathy Yamazawa (1364) 03:32:31
13. Kathryn Gushue (1410) 03:33:31
14. Sue Osborn (1498) 03:35:20
15. Sarah Zivich (1556) 03:36:21
16. Marilyn Salinger (1647) 03:38:06
17. Cary Craig (1650) 03:38:09
18. Estela Huerta (1654) 03:38:11
19. Julie Lock (1692) 03:38:50
20. Sally Baker (1760) 03:40:05
21. Linda Hood (1778) 03:40:20
22. Denise Sprague (1785) 03:40:24
23. Laurie Singer (1820) 03:40:57
24. Josita Bear (1899) 03:41:57
25. Christina Tuggle (2008) 03:43:59
26. Maureen Erbe (2019) 03:44:06
27. Barbara Lewis (2036) 03:44:20
28. Tracy Hurd (2108) 03:45:16
29. Elizabeth Saenz (2109) 03:45:17
30. Christine Fotis (2124) 03:45:28
31. Alice Yu (2200) 03:46:45
32. Andrea Ricketts (2286) 03:47:59
33. Jacinta Derian (2375) 03:49:07
34. Teresa Neill (2424) 03:49:43
35. Janet Collinge (2436) 03:49:54
36. Maureen Meyer (2445) 03:50:02
37. Lori Thomas (2467) 03:50:23
38. Julie Hiromatsu (2489) 03:50:37
39. Sharon Spray (2578) 03:51:50
40. Carol Milki (2635) 03:52:41
41. Margaret Jones (2643) 03:52:45
42. Shona Drunagel (2683) 03:53:14
43. Charlene Cameron (2702) 03:53:25
44. Irene Leonard (2732) 03:53:48
45. Debbie Wells (2738) 03:53:53
46. Glenda Wong (2796) 03:54:32
47. Karen O'Connell (2877) 03:55:28
48. Juoy Fierro (2879) 03:55:28
49. Patricia Korn (2935) 03:56:09
50. Kathy White (2972) 03:56:36
51. Bonnie Chun (2976) 03:56:37
52. Barbara Gales (2992) 03:56:47
53. Melissa Foster (3004) 03:56:51
54. Patricia Galvez (3028) 03:57:02
55. Davine Lieberman (3064) 03:57:27
56. Alida Mascitelli (3083) 03:57:41
57. Laurie Ward (3110) 03:57:55
58. Sandy Amendola (3153) 03:58:28
59. Rosanne Mayer (3175) 03:58:43
60. Patricia Alexander (3243) 03:59:32
61. Lupe Najera (3258) 03:59:43
62. Odile Grossemy (3324) 04:00:17
63. Donna Silveria (3370) 04:00:56

64. Ellen Drucker (3375) 04:01:00
65. Mary Perrot (3376) 04:01:01
66. Helen Cashman (3391) 04:01:11
67. Lupe Labourdett (3442) 04:01:60
68. Olivia Guzzi (3487) 04:02:28
69. Adriana Dena (3497) 04:02:38
70. Patricia Perez (3542) 04:03:22
71. Elizabeth Venturina (3544) 04:03:23
72. Rita Flagler (3546) 04:03:25
73. Karen Wiersum (3626) 04:04:27
74. Becky Peterson (3642) 04:04:34
75. Giovanna Aguilera (3681) 04:04:59
76. Mary Jost (3776) 04:06:17
77. Jill Misko (3818) 04:06:49
78. Tricia Silas (3853) 04:07:09
79. Sharon Barkdull (3943) 04:08:21
80. Cherron Smith (3948) 04:08:22
81. Lisa Smithline (3950) 04:08:23
82. Maureen Zimmer (4017) 04:09:19
83. Anne Curran (4084) 04:10:14
84. Yen Darcy (4144) 04:10:56
85. Keri Netzel (4151) 04:10:59
86. Rosa Arevalo] (4239) 04:12:10
87. Brigitte Buisson (4241) 04:12:12
88. Lorine Wright (4351) 04:13:37
89. Cynthia Shiba (4361) 04:13:48
90. Debbra Zockoll (4364) 04:13:51
91. Brenda Graff (4366) 04:13:51
92. Susan Reimers (4370) 04:13:54
93. Barbara Fitzpatrick (4416) 04:14:22
94. Marie Beard (4431) 04:14:31
95. Lesley Pougnet (4469) 04:14:48
96. Carmel Shields (4512) 04:15:20
97. Nancy Goglia (4606) 04:16:20
98. Randy Cohen (4649) 04:16:43
99. Betty Bowen (4660) 04:16:56
100. Ellen Engelke (4668) 04:17:02
101. Carol Reeb (4684) 04:17:15
102. Angel Dominguez (4689) 04:17:18
103. Maureen Coleman (4743) 04:17:58
104. Monica Hoops (4777) 04:18:22
105. Linda Hoffman (4798) 04:18:37
106. Carmen Sanchez (4811) 04:18:43
107. Joan Callahan (4813) 04:18:43
108. Anne Kahl (4838) 04:18:57
109. Dawn Upchurch (4846) 04:19:00
110. Lupe Zisman (4857) 04:19:07
111. Deborah Estrin (4901) 04:19:37
112. Patricia Colin (4925) 04:19:52
113. Nancy Mangham (4970) 04:20:31
114. Susan Lester (5007) 04:21:11
115. Sonia Santacruz (5054) 04:21:40
116. Yolanda Bishop (5056) 04:21:42
117. Jaynie Cherkasky (5066) 04:21:47
118. Yolanda Stinchcomb (5112) 04:22:08
119. Becky Navarro (5129) 04:22:21
120. Charlene Mitchell (5139) 04:22:30
121. Betty Romeo (5142) 04:22:31
122. Laurie Weyman (5217) 04:23:21
123. Margaret Moran-Tejada (5221) 04:23:27
124. Nancy Driver (5241) 04:23:39
125. Maria Beltran (5255) 04:23:55
126. Margie McGrath (5260) 04:24:03
127. Susan Ledrew (5281) 04:24:21
128. Sandy Downing (5318) 04:24:42
129. Francine Halamicek (5348) 04:25:08
130. Kathleen Graves (5387) 04:25:26
131. Lynette Milakovich (5409) 04:25:40
132. Laurel Sgro (5423) 04:25:49
133. Tracy Vasquez (5473) 04:26:21
134. Lisa Olshansky (5487) 04:26:30
135. Kathy Kirchner (5498) 04:26:39
136. Karin Whiteley (5506) 04:26:47
137. Mary Slayton (5511) 04:26:51
138. Donna Loftus (5537) 04:27:11
139. Deborah Ferguson (5547) 04:27:18
140. Eriko Yamanoi (5554) 04:27:21
141. Cindy Lawson (5590) 04:27:41
142. Susan Achuff (5620) 04:28:00
143. Cynthia Cramer (5622) 04:28:01
144. Jean Pasco (5648) 04:28:17
145. Alice Joan Valdez (5655) 04:28:22
146. Charmanie Najee (5658) 04:28:24
147. Teresa Evers (5660) 04:28:26
148. Barbara Alba (5669) 04:28:33
149. Jody Maxwell (5681) 04:28:39
150. Luann Campo (5691) 04:28:48
151. Debbie Raygoza-Wells (5709) 04:29:00
152. Margaret Bryant (5735) 04:29:15
153. Diane Melvin (5812) 04:30:10
154. Laura Lee Rasmussen (5847) 04:30:32
155. Domitilia Dos Santos (5852) 04:30:33
156. Michelle Robertson (5886) 04:30:49
157. Christina Ciatti (5918) 04:31:12
158. Rosa Marin (5933) 04:31:25
159. Deborah Arnesen (5939) 04:31:27
160. Denise Beck (5993) 04:32:06
161. Dianne Siegel (5994) 04:32:07
162. Veronique Longmire (6015) 04:32:26
163. Marsha Wagner (6029) 04:32:37
164. Yolanda Parra (6069) 04:33:03
165. Suzanna Hubbard (6090) 04:33:18
166. Laura Kantorowski (6110) 04:33:30
167. Robyn Kranian (6262) 04:35:15
168. April MacNair (6278) 04:35:24
169. Kwang An (6298) 04:35:36
170. Greta Stanford (6324) 04:35:52
171. Fong-Chiao Gant (6344) 04:36:06
172. Julie Espinosa (6353) 04:36:11
173. Miriam Tomboc (6371) 04:36:21
174. Sheila Wells (6375) 04:36:23
175. Carolyn McGrady (6393) 04:36:30
176. Toni Brackins (6409) 04:36:38
177. Marie Willson (6444) 04:37:08
178. Amy Goriesky (6445) 04:37:10
179. Sharon Springer (6513) 04:37:48
180. Jeannie Palermo (6521) 04:37:55
181. Susie Lasoya (6571) 04:38:25
182. Carol Lang (6596) 04:38:41
183. Janet Van Etten (6637) 04:39:08
184. Jennifer Hamby (6661) 04:39:28
185. Ann Phillips (6665) 04:39:31
186. Catherine Cranford (6708) 04:40:00
187. Anne Hanna-Kunkle (6709) 04:40:01
188. Juanella Pereyra (6729) 04:40:19
189. Dianne Haskins (6765) 04:40:50
190. Sally Sladics (6817) 04:41:32
191. Lawrnne France (6843) 04:41:50
192. Lisa Zecchini (6867) 04:42:05
193. Jean Ditolla (6918) 04:42:48
194. Joannes Ferguson (6979) 04:43:24
195. Karen Gaines (7005) 04:43:39
196. Linda Flinn (7007) 04:43:40
197. Debra McPheeters (7033) 04:43:58
198. Deborah Scott (7039) 04:44:02
199. Shannon Miller (7040) 04:44:02
200. Peggy Falconett (7051) 04:44:15
201. Clair Coon (7084) 04:44:43
202. Ana Hernandez (7095) 04:44:52
203. Theresa Quilico (7125) 04:45:11
204. Adriana Covell (7141) 04:45:21
205. Jeanne Singleton (7147) 04:45:30
206. Egzine Richardson (7171) 04:45:44
207. Nancy Jones (7194) 04:46:04
208. Nalini Sri-Kumar (7209) 04:46:12
209. Camille Corona (7237) 04:46:32
210. Toni McDonald (7266) 04:46:54
211. Sara Santillan (7286) 04:47:06
212. Roxanne Marquez (7288) 04:47:07
213. Carma Poindexter (7304) 04:47:17
214. Judy Carter (7326) 04:47:31
215. Lucy Bravo (7360) 04:47:58
216. Mary Forgione (7415) 04:48:31
217. Elaine Bingham (7438) 04:48:49
218. Linda Regalado (7473) 04:49:09
219. Ellen Anderson (7482) 04:49:15
220. Carole Neary (7488) 04:49:20
221. Sue Leone (7491) 04:49:21
222. Eileen Larkins (7494) 04:49:22
223. Deborah Gobins (7534) 04:49:47
224. Rita Valdez (7575) 04:50:18
225. Amanda Anthony (7587) 04:50:29
226. Julie Griffith (7605) 04:50:43
227. Michele Waltler (7626) 04:50:57
228. Deb Burgess (7671) 04:51:37
229. Leslie Stepan (7737) 04:52:28
230. Darlene Valle (7743) 04:52:32
231. Margit Ahlin (7754) 04:52:41
232. Carri Nordin (7764) 04:52:50
233. Lori Wolff (7794) 04:53:12
234. Rochelle Martel (7826) 04:53:32
235. Nancy Tominaga (7832) 04:53:35
236. Sarah Brown (7887) 04:54:11
237. Rachel Kroncke (7932) 04:54:34
238. Sylvia Cumplido (7939) 04:54:37
239. Celia Domingue-Pettus (7950) 04:54:44
240. Teresa Eggen-Ramos (8007) 04:55:30
241. Patricia King (8041) 04:55:54
242. Jennifer Tam (8075) 04:56:21
243. Carla Seegraves (8126) 04:57:01
244. Lisa Sinoway (8137) 04:57:11
245. Frances Lopez (8139) 04:57:12
246. Laura Martinez (8169) 04:57:34
247. Nancy McCleary (8171) 04:57:35
248. Patricia Salazar (8251) 04:58:20
249. Felicia Young (8284) 04:58:46
250. Mary Casperson (8296) 04:58:52
251. Caty Van Houten (8305) 04:58:55
252. MaryAnn Hobert (8365) 04:59:37
253. Teresa Angeles (8368) 04:59:38
254. Cynthia Utilla (8372) 04:59:39
255. Saundra Sparks (8382) 04:59:46
256. Cheryl Klopper (8393) 04:59:56
257. Lisa Smith (8467) 05:01:07
258. Sigrid Stevens (8489) 05:01:24
259. Wendy Eberle (8532) 05:01:50
260. Karin Drexler (8539) 05:01:58
261. Brenda Jacobs (8568) 05:02:19
262. Carole Caddick (8583) 05:02:32
263. Susan McDermott (8592) 05:02:46
264. Gail Hale (8609) 05:03:07
265. Donna Washington (8652) 05:03:45
266. Denise Whitson (8783) 05:05:46
267. Tara Taylor (8812) 05:06:15
268. Judith Hernandez (8819) 05:06:23
269. Maggie Elliston-Belker (8833) 05:06:34
270. Debbie Pietreface (8843) 05:06:49
271. Elaine Qualy (8846) 05:06:54
272. Paula Potter (8856) 05:06:59
273. Juliana Peregretti (8870) 05:07:11
274. Lindsey O'Sullivan (8871) 05:07:12
275. Desiree Forshay (8958) 05:08:37
276. Debra Vaughan (8985) 05:08:59
277. Carol Walter (8986) 05:08:59
278. Cheryl Patterson (8995) 05:09:06
279. Kimberly Prange (9011) 05:09:14
280. Cindy Newman (9037) 05:09:42
281. Patricia Viramontes (9108) 05:10:23
282. Cynthia Dillon (9123) 05:10:30
283. Lisa De La Loza (9179) 05:11:34
284. Victoria Innis (9204) 05:11:52
285. Gayle Collier (9214) 05:12:03
286. Marsha Slough (9277) 05:13:08
287. Valerie Mosher (9300) 05:13:26
288. April Jackson (9354) 05:13:55
289. Virginia Requa (9391) 05:14:28
290. Gerri Clarke (9419) 05:15:09
291. Mary Cowherd (9443) 05:15:34
292. Patricia Ryan (9465) 05:15:59
293. Sue Harris (9487) 05:16:19
294. Tina Uhrich (9500) 05:16:31
295. Lois Rhee (9519) 05:16:44
296. Karole Holland (9526) 05:16:50
297. Susan Lucibello (9536) 05:17:00
298. Rhonda Dale Patton (9546) 05:17:07
299. Nancy Pyo (9553) 05:17:10
300. Lyn Rauls (9577) 05:17:30
301. Donna Campbell (9625) 05:18:25
302. Alicia Becks (9674) 05:19:01
303. Diane Hartunian (9704) 05:19:27
304. Donna Thompson (9738) 05:20:13
305. Sharon Zamora (9750) 05:20:26
306. Anita Jackson (9765) 05:20:37
307. Cathy Uchida (9784) 05:20:49
308. Gail Pinkham-Hancock (9835) 05:21:38
309. Susana Mata (9849) 05:21:47
310. Joni Yung (9864) 05:21:58
311. Anne Driscoll (9894) 05:22:24
312. Anne Ryan (9903) 05:22:35
313. Brenda Battey (9907) 05:22:42
314. Patricia Williams (9915) 05:22:49
315. Deana Haffner (10003) 05:24:26
316. Linda Murray (10023) 05:24:48
317. Donna Helm (10045) 05:25:14
318. Nancy Perong (10106) 05:26:12
319. Milagros Baello (10110) 05:26:13
320. Kathy McAdam (10129) 05:26:37
321. Anita Jaime (10134) 05:26:41
322. Marcia Salazar (10164) 05:27:15
323. Candace Buchanan (10207) 05:27:49
324. Cheri Henneberque (10283) 05:28:59
325. Linda McDonald (10312) 05:29:17
326. Maria Riach (10318) 05:29:22
327. Donna Zabala (10329) 05:29:41
328. Debra Gose (10332) 05:29:47
329. Lori Gentry (10358) 05:30:12
330. Sally Huskins (10381) 05:30:31
331. Vikki Grounds (10396) 05:30:41
332. Marlyn Tivera-Garcia (10406) 05:30:51
333. Rosalinda Mireles (10420) 05:31:10
334. Laura Warren (10445) 05:31:29
335. Yukiko Kagawa (10478) 05:31:54
336. Mary Dignan (10486) 05:32:03
337. Barbara Lizarraga (10512) 05:32:37
338. Ellen Gordon (10521) 05:32:49
339. Laura Hobgood (10556) 05:33:23
340. Diane Kirschner (10584) 05:33:41
341. Leslie Nuccitelli (10611) 05:33:57
342. Consuelo Alonzo (10614) 05:34:02
343. Cheryl Dubell (10659) 05:34:42
344. Sylvia Furlan (10678) 05:35:01
345. Lindsay Hitchcock (10684) 05:35:03
346. Debra Hartin (10703) 05:35:25
347. Maricruz Arellano (10725) 05:35:44
348. Yolanda Abril (10742) 05:36:04
349. Mary Roberson (10748) 05:36:12
350. Julie Juarez (10754) 05:36:14
351. Carrie Kaspian (10781) 05:36:46
352. Rochelle Tracey (10800) 05:37:05
353. Michelle Martinez (10869) 05:38:32
354. Patricia Prokuski Barber (10871) 05:38:34
355. Lorraine Ramirez-Ortiz (10880) 05:38:48
356. Luz Medina (10881) 05:38:48
357. Rita Coronado (10882) 05:38:48
358. Barbara Berger (10894) 05:38:56
359. Debbie Martin (10965) 05:40:35
360. Shirin Nazarian (10971) 05:40:46
361. Judith McKenzie (11023) 05:41:50
362. Toby Bachenheimer (11046) 05:42:14
363. Pamela Delaney (11054) 05:42:19
364. Christy Garan (11056) 05:42:20
365. Caroline Shahin (11062) 05:42:25
366. Lori Meyer (11085) 05:42:43
367. Antonia Routt (11113) 05:43:13
368. Teresa Squires (11119) 05:43:22
369. Laura Brugger (11131) 05:43:35
370. Marianne Saralegui (11160) 05:44:07
371. Michelle Jaeger (11164) 05:44:11
372. Herminia Zamudio (11185) 05:44:20
373. Linda Leone (11191) 05:44:23
374. Denice Lanuti (11193) 05:44:25
375. June Harris (11201) 05:44:31
376. Liz Herbert (11213) 05:44:37
377. Sharron Lanier (11218) 05:44:40
378. Rita McCain (11231) 05:44:54
379. Renee Tey (11248) 05:45:15
380. Pamela Jackson (11256) 05:45:26
381. Wanda Katinszky (11269) 05:45:38
382. Lauma Jurkevics (11273) 05:45:46
383. Sheri Okamoto (11274) 05:45:46
384. Maria Lopez (11291) 05:46:02
385. Deborah Parckys (11296) 05:46:11
386. Brenda Sampson (11319) 05:46:40
387. Kate O'Connor (11322) 05:46:40
388. Brooke Ward (11358) 05:47:31
389. Sandra Barcelo (11390) 05:48:38
390. Joyce Bolton (11429) 05:49:29
391. Dureen Hughes (11531) 05:50:54
392. Kelly Calderon (11535) 05:50:57
393. Dianne Howes (11578) 05:52:09
394. Peaches Olson (11588) 05:52:15
395. Robin Patel (11592) 05:52:18
396. Teresa Hutson (11612) 05:52:48
397. Maggi Jefferson (11698) 05:54:18
398. Dianna Hull (11700) 05:54:19
399. Sharon Schutt Wormington (11709) 05:54:35
400. Amy Yee (11716) 05:54:43
401. Susan Iizuka (11861) 05:58:07
402. Debra Michel (11867) 05:58:13
403. Sharon Collins (11872) 05:58:21
404. Susan Beezley (11888) 05:58:31
405. Maria Sanchez (11892) 05:58:32
406. Carolyn Fine (11909) 05:58:54
407. Hilu Bloch (11932) 05:59:29
408. Rosa Kusiak (11949) 05:59:54
409. Debbie Rutledge (12012) 06:01:36
410. Denise Collins (12013) 06:01:38
411. Sue Crouse (12059) 06:02:46
412. Sydney Hutchings (12064) 06:02:55
413. Susan Slater (12080) 06:03:30
414. Emma Goldsmith (12096) 06:03:51
415. Rossana Perez (12104) 06:04:16
416. Linda Parrott (12109) 06:04:29
417. Denise Barreras (12132) 06:04:44
418. Julia Brown (12141) 06:05:00
419. Dee Cogliati (12150) 06:05:13
420. Patricia Alcaraz (12171) 06:05:39
421. Norma Taylor (12201) 06:06:37
422. Amy Sullivan (12214) 06:07:07
423. Ana Ramirez (12232) 06:07:40
424. Yong Kim (12234) 06:07:41
425. Laurie Baylis (12255) 06:08:17
426. Rokio Hardin (12266) 06:08:26
427. Judy Nahan (12279) 06:08:47
428. Dollie Smith (12280) 06:08:48
429. Lori Kritzer (12293) 06:08:59
430. Pamela Jimenez (12295) 06:09:00
431. Lynette Miles (12312) 06:09:20
432. Debbie De Witt (12333) 06:09:55
433. Alicia Spracklin (12343) 06:10:11
434. Jil Jensen-Winters (12344) 06:10:11
435. April Adams (12346) 06:10:13
436. Vanessa Lewis (12376) 06:11:10
437. Linda Ratlief (12382) 06:11:19
438. Leticia Ponzariani (12383) 06:11:20
439. Naoko Sato (12390) 06:11:29
440. Linda Miller (12399) 06:11:47
441. K C Marelich (12433) 06:12:43
442. Lisa Lanton (12450) 06:13:08
443. Silvia Vazquez Zavala (12454) 06:13:11
444. Linda Turner (12474) 06:13:47
445. Angela Cisneros (12492) 06:14:12
446. Theresa Hernamdez (12508) 06:14:34
447. Tess Rude (12513) 06:14:47
448. Raquel Sandi (12530) 06:15:14
449. Mary Hopkins (12545) 06:15:29
450. Carmen Mancera (12571) 06:16:11
451. Tonya Johnson (12573) 06:16:15
452. Gail Horton (12585) 06:16:39
453. Sue Coleman (12589) 06:16:43
454. Kathy Johnson (12664) 06:19:06
455. Susan Daley (12682) 06:19:39
456. Vilma Iglesias (12691) 06:19:47
457. Lori Morris (12701) 06:20:10
458. Ruth Gunn (12708) 06:20:23
459. Carmen Lopez (12758) 06:21:48
460. Kathleen Murphy (12760) 06:21:51
461. Cyndee Foscue (12787) 06:22:30
462. Ann Feinstein (12824) 06:23:35
463. Falcon Bawolski (12840) 06:23:50
464. Cathryn Burbidge (12844) 06:23:54
465. Lita Villicana (12849) 06:24:02
466. Siony Griffith (12857) 06:24:14
467. Graciela Rebalcaba (12891) 06:25:36
468. Holly Durkin (12904) 06:25:53
469. Linda Reynolds (12905) 06:25:53
470. Lori Braithwaite (12917) 06:26:17
471. Julie Rico (12946) 06:27:02
472. Sylvia Guerrero (12964) 06:27:47
473. Debra Rodriguez (12965) 06:27:48
474. Lama Khayr (12971) 06:27:56
475. Patty Barson (12972) 06:27:56
476. Cynthia Scanlin (12987) 06:28:11
477. Stacy Fowler (13006) 06:28:47
478. Karen Foster (13036) 06:30:00
479. Zadie Cannon-Shorts (13043) 06:30:08
480. Debbie Karaman (13051) 06:30:26
481. Nancy Parsons (13065) 06:30:51
482. Katherine Pelayo (13095) 06:31:41
483. Isabel Caldwell (13117) 06:32:23
484. Helen Ayala-Wardell (13131) 06:32:37
485. Ann Ransom-Denardo (13148) 06:32:52
486. Cynthia Pearson (13167) 06:33:18
487. Charmayne Caulfield (13171) 06:33:27
488. Marina Castillo (13184) 06:33:59
489. Lilli Gorence (13204) 06:34:34
490. Maria Robles (13205) 06:34:34
491. Susan Dahms (13215) 06:34:48
492. Anita Wright-Edior (13226) 06:35:06
493. Maria Najera (13234) 06:35:20
494. Olvera Dominguez (13236) 06:35:23
495. Rosalia Descargar (13258) 06:36:05
496. Debbie Solano (13275) 06:36:26
497. Catherine Cobb (13296) 06:37:25
498. Linda Navarro (13301) 06:37:31
499. Karla Pergande (13329) 06:38:38
500. Karen Suveg (13332) 06:38:39
501. Blanche Watson (13338) 06:38:59
502. Julie Okuda (13339) 06:39:01
503. Jill Lederer (13355) 06:39:26
504. Judith Strutz (13356) 06:39:27
505. Gloria Romo (13394) 06:40:48
506. Lora Avery (13409) 06:41:24
507. Cindy Blitz (13417) 06:41:48
508. Jade Hudson (13422) 06:41:56
509. Lourdes Narvaez (13452) 06:42:52
510. Alma Morales (13477) 06:43:57
511. Jill Triplett (13481) 06:44:08
512. Mary Anne Khan (13486) 06:44:15
513. Robin Autio (13487) 06:44:18
514. Pamela Johnson (13511) 06:45:17
515. Catalina Esparza (13514) 06:45:19
516. Andrea Diamond (13522) 06:45:49
517. Lucy Garcia (13530) 06:45:59
518. Michelle Jones (13539) 06:46:17
519. Ellen Henderson (13540) 06:46:17
520. Jo Ann Mendez (13553) 06:46:40
521. Dale Hudson (13557) 06:46:49
522. Josefina Martinez (13579) 06:47:32
523. Raquel Sandoval (13610) 06:48:33
524. Jane-Frances Mburu (13648) 06:49:59
525. Velma O'Grady (13664) 06:50:15
526. J T Rapport (13670) 06:50:27
527. Trudy Dumont (13672) 06:50:28
528. Linda Waterman (13708) 06:51:28
529. Phyllis Juan (13709) 06:51:30
530. Hilda Flores (13714) 06:51:36
531. Carolyn Perkins (13718) 06:51:47
532. Lolita Wee (13735) 06:52:33
533. Deborah Lewis (13767) 06:54:23
534. Denise Vidato (13777) 06:54:46
535. Linda Flores (13793) 06:55:09
536. A Lucille Allen (13831) 06:56:10
537. Evangelina Muniz (13846) 06:56:45
538. Trisha Tempo (13849) 06:56:51
539. Carmen Attwood (13907) 06:58:37
540. Joan Berry (13918) 06:58:51
541. Wanda Savage (13919) 06:58:54
542. Claire Wilcock (13921) 06:58:55
543. Kaye Henley (13924) 06:58:59
544. Nancy Jackson (13925) 06:58:59
545. Elsa Thatcher (13933) 06:59:07
546. Cynthia Jackson (13947) 06:59:47
547. Lori Saller (13986) 07:00:59
548. Cheryl Brown (14005) 07:01:35
549. Sharon Tanikawa (14009) 07:01:46
550. Ly Nn Hiduera (14012) 07:01:51
551. Virginia Menjares (14021) 07:02:07
552. Sheree Cogan (14025) 07:02:10
553. Silvia Murp (14042) 07:02:48
554. Sherril D'espyne (14048) 07:03:09
555. Denise Robert (14093) 07:05:42
556. Fayde Barron Kirkwood (14140) 07:08:35
557. Carla Arthur (14158) 07:10:26
558. Laura Thomas (14175) 07:11:10
559. Kim Chatelain (14191) 07:12:17
560. Kathy Weiss (14192) 07:12:18
561. Linda Wallace (14196) 07:12:38
562. Nancy Conway (14199) 07:12:39
563. Lisa Obershaw (14217) 07:13:40
564. Debera Manoogian (14226) 07:14:33
565. Joanne Ford (14240) 07:14:51
566. Cathy Loy (14241) 07:14:51
567. Sandi Ross (14244) 07:14:57
568. Juanita Banks (14248) 07:15:25
569. Mary Richartz (14252) 07:15:34
570. Corinne Tanon-Freeman (14256) 07:15:37
571. Clara Kamunde (14262) 07:15:47
572. She' She' Yancy (14273) 07:16:17
573. Paula McMurtray (14286) 07:17:00
574. Danette Williams (14288) 07:17:13
575. Belinda Zepeda (14300) 07:18:05
576. Deby Nguyen (14330) 07:20:11
577. Felicia Gonzalez (14350) 07:21:24
578. Lilly Mettler (14363) 07:22:12
579. Venetya Evans (14364) 07:22:34
580. Patricia Douglas (14367) 07:22:35
581. Mary Burke (14390) 07:24:04
582. Karyn Kimble (14417) 07:26:34
583. Patricia Cueva (14431) 07:27:35
584. Pauline Nishida (14443) 07:28:57
585. Sabrina Nichols (14489) 07:33:11
586. Leslie Baer-Brown (14497) 07:33:36
587. Luzselenia Carrillo (14509) 07:35:01
588. Christine Fentress (14512) 07:35:10
589. Brenda Sanchez (14516) 07:35:19
590. Barb Westek (14542) 07:36:53
591. Martha Capetillo (14555) 07:37:26
592. Linda Silva (14568) 07:38:47
593. Angela Battaglia (14570) 07:38:53
594. Cath Macwillie (14596) 07:40:55
595. Gayle Corn (14629) 07:43:59
596. Kim Marshall (14632) 07:44:23
597. Cheryl Vergo (14664) 07:47:31
598. Sheryl Brenneman (14709) 07:51:42
599. Ruth Laity (14721) 07:52:27
600. Cynthia Williams (14727) 07:53:08
601. Judith Biggs (14730) 07:53:13
602. Ethel Davidson (14732) 07:53:32
603. Dee Mellor (14737) 07:53:59
604. Janet Singleton (14740) 07:54:19
605. Kim Ryan (14749) 07:54:57
606. Lisa Pferdner (14754) 07:55:04
607. Kathy Christensen (14777) 07:56:48
608. Jennifer Johnson (14789) 07:59:37
609. Pamela Heist (14791) 07:59:55
610. Danita Guerrero (14803) 08:00:58
611. Lois Shivers (14818) 08:01:44
612. Martha Sanchez (14837) 08:03:27
613. Dolores Martinez (14888) 08:14:31
614. Jean Thornhill (14894) 08:14:54
615. Charlotte Hagos (14898) 08:15:34
616. Ivania Pineda (14900) 08:16:23
617. Bertaa Enriquez (14923) 08:19:05
618. Lori Roberts (14927) 08:19:32
619. Nancy Corralejo (14951) 08:21:56
620. Rejoice Anthony (14971) 08:26:44
621. Karen Schmauss (14984) 08:28:42
622. Jing Mark (14985) 08:28:44
623. Karen Atkinson (14990) 08:30:12
624. Novaline Smith (14995) 08:31:28
625. Carmelita Holmes (14996) 08:31:28
626. Masako Miwa (15037) 08:41:48
627. Lillian Clagett (15052) 08:46:29
628. Glenda Cook (15055) 08:48:31
629. Mary Fisher (15071) 08:53:35
630. Theresa Valdez (15076) 08:55:20
631. Alison Fairchild (15081) 08:55:24
632. Judy Yiu (15087) 08:57:51
633. Myra Nakata (15088) 08:57:55
634. Andrew Rodarte (15115) 09:18:09
635. Destra Heagy (15123) 09:26:30
636. Juanita Parker (15142) 09:45:58
637. Melissa Fulton (15152) 09:52:56
638. Jill Sibler (15153) 09:53:00

MEN 40 TO 44

1. Ronald Coleman (52) 02:41:18
2. Dana Gemme (57) 02:42:05
3. Lucio Arriaga (90) 02:48:35
4. Rae Clark (95) 02:49:51
5. Scott Taylor (97) 02:50:05
6. Leonard Aguilar (100) 02:50:23
7. Jose Gomez (104) 02:50:52
8. Thomas Hall (110) 02:51:44
9. Mendoza Adalberto (111) 02:51:56
10. Glen Nakano (113) 02:52:05
11. Sal Arellano (115) 02:52:13
12. Eugenio Campuzano Villalobos (132) 02:53:20
13. Fred Pichay (135) 02:53:30
14. Mateo Xo Rax (136) 02:53:32
15. Manuel Diaz (141) 02:53:49
16. Arturo Radillo (145) 02:54:02
17. Fernando Montes Chavez (150) 02:54:32
18. Felix Ramos (171) 02:56:30
19. Jose Aponte (172) 02:56:35
20. Gerald Valdez (187) 02:57:20
21. Mike Gangwer (193) 02:57:41
22. Kris Ohlenkamp (194) 02:57:45
23. Bertrand Groussin (199) 02:58:08
24. Patrick Bonneton (202) 02:58:20
25. Phil Donnelly (218) 02:59:26
26. Christopher Johnson (224) 02:59:35
27. Aristeo Galvan (227) 02:59:52
28. Craig Davidson (238) 03:00:35
29. Bill Kissell (241) 03:00:37
30. Stephen Harris (243) 03:00:41
31. Myron Oakes (250) 03:01:04
32. Akira Yamaguchi (251) 03:01:06
33. Daniel Goff (265) 03:02:14
34. Abel Ibarra (295) 03:03:32
35. George Arellano (303) 03:03:54
36. Scott Weir (306) 03:04:05
37. Ismael Lopez (307) 03:04:09
38. Samuel Gardner Jr (309) 03:04:18
39. Jim Stuebe (320) 03:04:57
40. Art Juarez (322) 03:05:08
41. John McLeish Jr (333) 03:05:37
42. Saul Reyes (343) 03:06:09
43. Mauricio Martinez (344) 03:06:12
44. James Stepan (387) 03:07:56
45. Robert Lopez (393) 03:08:09
46. Charles Swenson (396) 03:08:14
47. Perry Petschar (401) 03:08:21
48. Greg Klein (402) 03:08:21
49. Romell Hamlin (405) 03:08:23
50. Phillip Snyder (416) 03:08:54
51. John Contreraz (426) 03:09:21
52. Roy Morigaki (461) 03:10:20
53. Christian Lhotte (462) 03:10:21
54. Paul Brooks (463) 03:10:28
55. Nicolas Hernandez (476) 03:11:05
56. Samuel Gourley (477) 03:11:07
57. Frank Rice (478) 03:11:08
58. Thom Narita (483) 03:11:15
59. Kyle McNeil (492) 03:11:39

60. Sean Kelly (493) ... 03:11:47
61. Leo Arellanes (496) ... 03:12:02
62. Oscar Yancor (499) ... 03:12:09
63. Han Schindeler (508) ... 03:12:22
64. Ernesto Pena (524) ... 03:12:59
65. August Calabrese (525) ... 03:13:00
66. Michael Duran (530) ... 03:13:11
67. Herbert Fragosa (531) ... 03:13:14
68. James Reno (537) ... 03:13:22
69. Bruce Guter (542) ... 03:13:33
70. Hugo De Leon (556) ... 03:13:48
71. Wayne Petersen (558) ... 03:13:50
72. Fred Guerra (564) ... 03:14:02
73. Trevor Baylor (569) ... 03:14:10
74. Roger Jensen (574) ... 03:14:20
75. John Sigler (599) ... 03:15:07
76. Miguel Covarrubias (607) ... 03:15:25
77. John Bozung (608) ... 03:15:25
78. Robert Rose (613) ... 03:15:37
79. Jim Everett (616) ... 03:15:47
80. Raumond Deschenes (629) ... 03:16:18
81. Robert Williams (638) ... 03:16:39
82. David Edgar (641) ... 03:16:44
83. John Burwasser (655) ... 03:16:57
84. Alain Ardiet (657) ... 03:17:01
85. Murray Greenberg (659) ... 03:17:05
86. Claude Gorlier (660) ... 03:17:06
87. Lyle Teske (664) ... 03:17:14
88. Jose Antonio Gomez Cortes (671) ... 03:17:21
89. Thomas Celio (673) ... 03:17:22
90. Herb Ortiz (677) ... 03:17:25
91. Charles Gibbons (679) ... 03:17:27
92. Raul Santana (685) ... 03:17:40
93. Arturo Salcedo Sanchez (692) ... 03:17:55
94. Dan Graham (697) ... 03:18:05
95. Thomas Ziola (698) ... 03:18:09
96. Patric Jordan (700) ... 03:18:12
97. Joseph Juarez (709) ... 03:18:30
98. Felipe Echeverria (713) ... 03:18:41
99. Rick Delanty (719) ... 03:18:51
100. Stan Gertler (742) ... 03:19:25
101. Brian Taylor (744) ... 03:19:27
102. Francesco Siqueiros (760) ... 03:19:53
103. James Thomas (767) ... 03:20:04
104. Francisco Rubio (778) ... 03:20:23
105. David Madrigal (779) ... 03:20:24
106. Mike Pierceall (782) ... 03:20:28
107. Primo Hermosillo (796) ... 03:20:56
108. Rufino Mazariegos (800) ... 03:21:08
109. Marcelino Arellano (808) ... 03:21:20
110. Anthony Valenzuela (815) ... 03:21:28
111. Paul Estey (843) ... 03:22:05
112. Gary Lewis (857) ... 03:22:22
113. Tom Power (862) ... 03:22:27
114. Jorge Ramirez (881) ... 03:22:48
115. Jose Lepe (902) ... 03:23:20
116. Raymond Bryan (910) ... 03:23:31
117. Hugo Montenegro (923) ... 03:23:46
118. Juan Cano (924) ... 03:23:47
119. Patrick Roarty (931) ... 03:23:57
120. Clay Shaw (935) ... 03:24:01
121. Jim McVay (937) ... 03:24:04
122. Stanley Reyes Jr (940) ... 03:24:06
123. Gordon Niva (942) ... 03:24:09
124. Rich Endo (975) ... 03:24:53
125. Steve Bustillos (977) ... 03:24:55
126. Ted Stull (983) ... 03:25:06
127. Jerry Montanez (985) ... 03:25:08
128. Robert Contreras (1000) ... 03:25:29
129. Alfredo Garcia Jr (1011) ... 03:25:40
130. Bob Shupper (1014) ... 03:25:45
131. Mark Enany (1021) ... 03:26:00
132. Lorenzo Chavez (1025) ... 03:26:05
133. Carl Peternell (1027) ... 03:26:09
134. Stephan Edwards (1028) ... 03:26:10
135. Frank Tasnadi (1030) ... 03:26:11
136. Hector Sanchez (1047) ... 03:26:39
137. Jerome Roberts (1054) ... 03:26:44
138. William Wesselink (1055) ... 03:26:48
139. Curt Dahlberg (1064) ... 03:27:04
140. Rich Johnson (1077) ... 03:27:17
141. Jerry Kyle (1080) ... 03:27:20
142. Steven Schnaars (1084) ... 03:27:23
143. Brian Draper (1085) ... 03:27:24
144. Leo Sitton (1095) ... 03:27:33
145. Daniel Soto (1100) ... 03:27:37
146. David Frankenthal (1123) ... 03:28:03
147. Robin Ross (1128) ... 03:28:06
148. Willie Guevara (1130) ... 03:28:10
149. Ignacio Rivera (1140) ... 03:28:19
150. Andrew Altman (1147) ... 03:28:25
151. Martin Wildgoose (1152) ... 03:28:31
152. Alfred Martinez (1159) ... 03:28:45
153. Leigh Murphy (1180) ... 03:29:07
154. Michael Howson (1187) ... 03:29:17
155. Christopher Whitman (1199) ... 03:29:27
156. Stephen Marques (1202) ... 03:29:30
157. David Stull (1205) ... 03:29:35
158. Frank Hofmann (1209) ... 03:29:36
159. Lou Camargo (1221) ... 03:29:45
160. Pedro Rios (1226) ... 03:29:52
161. Mark Russak (1243) ... 03:30:17
162. Tim Reynolds (1248) ... 03:30:21
163. Carlos Cabral (1249) ... 03:30:22
164. Dave Jacob (1252) ... 03:30:25
165. Jafar Monazzam (1274) ... 03:30:55
166. Miguel Carranza (1276) ... 03:30:56
167. Rich Mendoza (1283) ... 03:30:59
168. Jerry Davila (1287) ... 03:31:09
169. Ian Parker (1297) ... 03:31:22
170. Craig Mead (1300) ... 03:31:25
171. Loren Meier (1312) ... 03:31:35
172. Rafael Farias (1323) ... 03:31:41
173. Angel Villacis (1331) ... 03:31:51
174. Lawrence Liang (1338) ... 03:31:58
175. Andrei Slezak (1352) ... 03:32:17
176. Daniel Hutchinson (1358) ... 03:32:22
177. Chuck Lytle (1379) ... 03:32:50
178. Roberto Valerin Ugalde (1413) ... 03:33:41
179. Rodger Low (1417) ... 03:33:46
180. Sanuel Alvarado (1430) ... 03:34:03
181. Stephen Musser (1431) ... 03:34:04
182. Armando Hernandez (1437) ... 03:34:06
183. Ray Tomlinson (1438) ... 03:34:07
184. Steve Doering (1446) ... 03:34:25
185. Paul Schuster (1447) ... 03:34:28
186. Jan Pedersen (1452) ... 03:34:34
187. John Roulstone (1453) ... 03:34:36
188. Lawrence Sheridan (1454) ... 03:34:38
189. John Hanc (1472) ... 03:34:55
190. Bill Higgins (1481) ... 03:35:03
191. John Torres (1483) ... 03:35:05
192. Patrick Healy (1497) ... 03:35:19
193. Jeff Slepski (1499) ... 03:35:20
194. Ignacio Rivera (1500) ... 03:35:22
195. Eugene Jackson (1502) ... 03:35:25
196. John Comenac (1531) ... 03:35:54
197. Jack Horvath (1539) ... 03:36:02
198. Ron Quintia (1540) ... 03:36:04
199. Charles Coleman (1543) ... 03:36:09
200. J Darrell Lindgren (1544) ... 03:36:11
201. Rene Arana (1552) ... 03:36:18
202. Carlos Castaneda (1555) ... 03:36:21
203. Jim Rowell (1585) ... 03:36:57
204. Brian Koshman (1587) ... 03:36:59
205. John Stoessel (1606) ... 03:37:17
206. Saturnino Hernandez (1611) ... 03:37:21
207. Carl Lindberg (1617) ... 03:37:27
208. Jose Franco Morales (1620) ... 03:37:33
209. Mike McNees (1623) ... 03:37:41
210. Andre Untiedt (1630) ... 03:37:51
211. Larry Bone (1631) ... 03:37:51
212. Masahiko Fujita (1642) ... 03:37:59
213. Frank Ganaden (1606) ... 03:38:53
214. Tom Boggess (1706) ... 03:39:05
215. David Legendre (1709) ... 03:39:09
216. Douglas Kays (1710) ... 03:39:09
217. Kirk Daley (1713) ... 03:39:10
218. Michael Gonzales (1723) ... 03:39:22
219. Jerry Brown (1730) ... 03:39:33
220. John Catanese (1741) ... 03:39:42
221. Ronnie Winston (1742) ... 03:39:43
222. Helios Palafox (1751) ... 03:39:53
223. Mark Craig (1755) ... 03:39:59
224. Bob Lewis (1763) ... 03:40:09
225. Barry Dancher (1770) ... 03:40:15
226. Michael Dupuy (1773) ... 03:40:18
227. Mark Hickerson (1776) ... 03:40:20
228. Kevin McGrath (1786) ... 03:40:25
229. Roberto De Alba Guzman (1794) ... 03:40:34
230. Stephen Kelly (1797) ... 03:40:37
231. Chris Stecko (1798) ... 03:40:38
232. Georga Wallace (1816) ... 03:40:55
233. John Caldwell (1832) ... 03:41:05
234. Gary Nelson (1838) ... 03:41:10
235. Vincent Montenegro (1841) ... 03:41:14
236. John Battan (1854) ... 03:41:21
237. David Perry (1867) ... 03:41:32
238. Jim Stevens (1874) ... 03:41:38
239. Charles Perry (1879) ... 03:41:43
240. Doug Wilde (1895) ... 03:41:54
241. Stephen Fisher (1897) ... 03:41:56
242. Jorge Silva-Risso (1898) ... 03:41:56
243. Brian Faulkner (1907) ... 03:42:03
244. Arthur Cabral (1909) ... 03:42:06
245. Steve Goo (1910) ... 03:42:08
246. Art Orcutt (1917) ... 03:42:17
247. Raul Gutierrez (1920) ... 03:42:19
248. Rich Valdez (1941) ... 03:42:50
249. Alexander Ward (1950) ... 03:43:04
250. David Waldman (1952) ... 03:43:05
251. Art Armas (1962) ... 03:43:12
252. Stephen Powers (1995) ... 03:43:48
253. David Kappen (1999) ... 03:43:54
254. Jay Buckley (2017) ... 03:44:04
255. Greg Kimura (2018) ... 03:44:05
256. Robert Wallen (2020) ... 03:44:07
257. Rick Graf (2025) ... 03:44:12
258. Brent Ledrew (2026) ... 03:44:13
259. Junichi Takao (2029) ... 03:44:15
260. Hossein Djabbari (2037) ... 03:44:21
261. Abel Sedillo Jr (2038) ... 03:44:21
262. Ninrood Aguilar (2064) ... 03:44:41
263. Brian Ferguson (2065) ... 03:44:42
264. Eduardo Cruz (2084) ... 03:44:58
265. Randy Green (2085) ... 03:44:59
266. Fred Morales (2095) ... 03:45:03
267. James O'Connor (2106) ... 03:45:14
268. Lynn Whitney (2110) ... 03:45:17
269. Ricky San Julian (2112) ... 03:45:19
270. Tommy Carrillo (2119) ... 03:45:20
271. Carl Costanzo (2126) ... 03:45:29
272. John Riley (2128) ... 03:45:34
273. Joseph Gonzaque (2143) ... 03:45:49
274. Fred Ellstrom (2153) ... 03:45:55
275. John Baron (2154) ... 03:45:55
276. Ray Callen (2174) ... 03:46:14
277. Scott Minium (2184) ... 03:46:24
278. Ed Franco (2201) ... 03:46:46
279. Michael Orlando (2208) ... 03:46:52
280. Mario Tamayo (2223) ... 03:47:04
281. Michael Carbuto (2225) ... 03:47:05
282. Rodney Weaver (2228) ... 03:47:09
283. Joe O'Sullivan (2231) ... 03:47.12
284. Steve Woods (2237) ... 03:47:15
285. Jon Mahoney (2239) ... 03:47:17
286. Ricardo Zapien (2244) ... 03:47:22
287. Askar Sheibani (2251) ... 03:47:28
288. Marc Garner (2256) ... 03:47:31
289. John Dominguez (2261) ... 03:47:37
290. Richard Schubert (2262) ... 03:47:38
291. Barney McCrea (2266) ... 03:47:41
292. Steve Cole (2268) ... 03:47:42
293. Charles Hsu (2272) ... 03:47:44
294. Jim Uren (2277) ... 03:47:48
295. Robert Brereton (2289) ... 03:48:00
296. Michael Young (2296) ... 03:48:03
297. Tom Chaplin (2308) ... 03:48:13
298. Kim Stocksdale (2317) ... 03:48:18
299. Scott Annis (2326) ... 03:48:30
300. Harold Perry (2330) ... 03:48:31
301. Jose Vargas (2347) ... 03:48:40
302. Rogelio Alvarado (2348) ... 03:48:40
303. Francisco Alcantara (2349) ... 03:48:42
304. Adonis De Jesus (2361) ... 03:48:56
305. German Ugaz (2363) ... 03:48:59
306. Felipe Reynoso (2372) ... 03:49:06
307. Istvan Gelley (2373) ... 03:49:06
308. Stuart Clark (2382) ... 03:49:09
309. Dan Armand (2383) ... 03:49:10
310. Hector Rubio (2389) ... 03:49:17
311. Richard Oppenheim (2392) ... 03:49:18
312. Dave Bolt (2404) ... 03:49:24
313. Angel Montez (2405) ... 03:49:27
314. Jay Anderson (2461) ... 03:50:16
315. Dwight Elliott (2466) ... 03:50:21
316. Yoshinori Nishigakiuchi (2470) ... 03:50:24
317. Juan Lopez (2471) ... 03:50:24
318. Jeffrey Trevena (2479) ... 03:50:28
319. Fred Tsutsi (2481) ... 03:50:29
320. Hisao Homma (2484) ... 03:50:34
321. Larry Silverstein (2529) ... 03:51:09
322. Thomas Garvin (2534) ... 03:51:16
323. Ernst-Peter Vallerius (2538) ... 03:51:19
324. Ted Springer II (2541) ... 03:51:24
325. Jack Gibbons (2552) ... 03:51:29
326. Daniel Williams (2555) ... 03:51:33
327. Dan Kridelbaugh (2559) ... 03:51:36
328. Hernando Osuna Capaceta (2560) ... 03:51:37
329. Harold Steen (2570) ... 03:51:42
330. Ernesto Murillo (2580) ... 03:51:52
331. Major Wayne Keen (2584) ... 03:51:55
332. Josiah Chu (2587) ... 03:51:57
333. Jorge Jarrin (2592) ... 03:52:00
334. Jess Molina (2600) ... 03:52:12
335. Mark Foster (2602) ... 03:52:12
336. Lawrence Delgado (2615) ... 03:52:22
337. Philippe Martin (2616) ... 03:52:22
338. Loic Moisan (2620) ... 03:52:25
339. John Medina (2627) ... 03:52:31
340. Javier Cazares Gonzalez (2633) ... 03:52:37
341. William Currie (2636) ... 03:52:42
342. Steven Weber (2652) ... 03:52:48
343. Robert Rodriguez (2657) ... 03:52:51
344. Jeffrey Arehart (2659) ... 03:52:53
345. P Jackson (2672) ... 03:53:02
346. Vincent Campbell (2675) ... 03:53:07
347. Lawrence Wagman (2679) ... 03:53:10
348. George Golden (2693) ... 03:53:19
349. Michael Fludd (2696) ... 03:53:21
350. George Salazar Rojas (2723) ... 03:53:42
351. Ralph Tuttle (2725) ... 03:53:44
352. Alfonso Najera (2733) ... 03:53:49
353. Thomas Tilton (2739) ... 03:53:54
354. Raymond Willard (2740) ... 03:53:54
355. Arnold Ross (2745) ... 03:54:00
356. John Hunter (2748) ... 03:54:03
357. Gary Zicker (2750) ... 03:54:08
358. Joseluis Zepeda (2755) ... 03:54:09
359. Stan Broadfoot (2757) ... 03:54:11
360. Christopher Staudle (2760) ... 03:54:13
361. Daniel Vereker (2761) ... 03:54:14
362. Louis Diaz (2774) ... 03:54:23
363. Philip James (2776) ... 03:54:24
364. Michael Monks (2779) ... 03:54:24
365. Pete Amico (2789) ... 03:54:29
366. Van Ryujin (2798) ... 03:54:34
367. Gonzalo Galvez (2802) ... 03:54:35
368. Arturo Lopez (2807) ... 03:54:40
369. Francisco Fabian (2817) ... 03:54:46
370. Bill Chaffin (2831) ... 03:54:55
371. Rene Covarrubias (2844) ... 03:55:06
372. Alfredo Gonzalez (2868) ... 03:55:25
373. Peter Bond (2870) ... 03:55:26
374. Craig Landsverk (2872) ... 03:55:26
375. Ronald Johnson (2880) ... 03:55:28
376. Severino Hernandez Sanchez (2895) ... 03:55:37
377. Sal Morano (2927) ... 03:56:00
378. Michael Whelan (2928) ... 03:56:01
379. Bill Olsen (2948) ... 03:56:16
380. John Wilshire (2962) ... 03:56:28
381. Randy Ligh (2964) ... 03:56:29
382. Maximo Torres (2967) ... 03:56:33
383. Joel Greene (2981) ... 03:56:42
384. Stephen James (2987) ... 03:56:46
385. John Armstrong (3007) ... 03:56:52
386. Santiago Ramos (3009) ... 03:56:53
387. Dennis Ingram (3011) ... 03:56:54
388. John Dwyer (3018) ... 03:56:59
389. James Myers (3024) ... 03:57:01
390. William Brooks (3029) ... 03:57:02
391. Irv Rey (3030) ... 03:57:02
392. Lee Widerynski (3031) ... 03:57:03
393. Daniel Trudeau (3048) ... 03:57:15
394. Michael Mestas (3052) ... 03:57:18
395. Steve Henrich (3056) ... 03:57:20
396. Danny Nunez (3063) ... 03:57:25
397. Milton Real (3065) ... 03:57:28
398. Sherman Lambert (3076) ... 03:57:33
399. Fabian Carrillo (3081) ... 03:57:39
400. Stephan Madrid (3082) ... 03:57:41
401. Carl Pantoja (3096) ... 03:57:48
402. Roberto Beta Granillo (3099) ... 03:57:49
403. Dana Kreger (3106) ... 03:57:54
404. Reynaldo Sanchez (3117) ... 03:57:59
405. Carlos Lopez (3125) ... 03:58:06
406. Jeff Roberts (3151) ... 03:58:27
407. Ralph Chavez (3168) ... 03:58:37
408. Henry Barcikowski (3172) ... 03:58:40
409. Tom Henley (3178) ... 03:58:45
410. Art Farias (3183) ... 03:58:50
411. Robert Morris (3185) ... 03:58:51
412. Paul Craig (3186) ... 03:58:52
413. Jacques Beser (3189) ... 03:58:53
414. Steven Jackson (3191) ... 03:58:54
415. Sal Castaneda (3194) ... 03:58:56
416. Alexander De Oliveira (3209) ... 03:59:06
417. Kirk Mader (3211) ... 03:59:07
418. Klaus Von Schwanebach (3213) ... 03:59:08
419. Mike Baron (3248) ... 03:59:37
420. Michael Holt (3255) ... 03:59:42
421. Rick Gutman (3256) ... 03:59:42
422. Dennis Matsumoto (3264) ... 03:59:45
423. Terry Collier (3284) ... 03:59:54
424. Jim Baril (3288) ... 03:59:55
425. Mike Rodriguez (3297) ... 04:00:00
426. Danny Yamazaki (3320) ... 04:00:15
427. Bruce Hudson (3326) ... 04:00:18
428. Victor Jimenez (3333) ... 04:00:23
429. Paul Smith (3347) ... 04:00:34
430. Gilbert Hill (3348) ... 04:00:35
431. Steve Mairel (3350) ... 04:00:38
432. Ben Dunn (3360) ... 04:00:48
433. Elias Garcia (3372) ... 04:00:58
434. Mike McGill (3377) ... 04:01:01
435. Neal Shindel (3383) ... 04:01:03
436. Edwin Fernandez (3394) ... 04:01:13
437. Donald Vulich (3399) ... 04:01:15
438. Walter Burenin (3400) ... 04:01:15
439. Eric Verschraegen (3418) ... 04:01:30
440. Jose Garcia (3433) ... 04:01:42
441. Henry Polanco (3439) ... 04:01:47
442. Stephen Wakely (3450) ... 04:01:57
443. Randy Douglas (3464) ... 04:02:11
444. Gregory Hickey (3473) ... 04:02:17
445. Francois Gouin (3481) ... 04:02:22
446. Eduardo Zuniga (3482) ... 04:02:23
447. Eric Lesser (3503) ... 04:02:45
448. Mike Nadalsky (3508) ... 04:02:49
449. Tim Macrorie (3510) ... 04:02:50
450. M.G. Gonzalez (3529) ... 04:03:06
451. Jaime Sanchez (3534) ... 04:03:09
452. Mark Levander (3545) ... 04:03:25
453. Louis Herran (3547) ... 04:03:25
454. Scott Musselman (3555) ... 04:03:32
455. Chad Fenwick (3563) ... 04:03:37
456. Jesus Fabrera (3567) ... 04:03:40
457. Paul Martos (3602) ... 04:04:13
458. Charles Orlowski (3609) ... 04:04:15
459. John Herlihy (3637) ... 04:04:32
460. Jose Munoz (3644) ... 04:04:35
461. Jorge Gasparri (3646) ... 04:04:37
462. Alan Ho (3652) ... 04:04:41
463. Sassan Guilani (3658) ... 04:04:45
464. Steve Amgwert (3663) ... 04:04:47
465. Gabriel Murillo (3664) ... 04:04:47
466. Gary Pilgrim (3671) ... 04:04:53
467. Michael Smith (3677) ... 04:04:58
468. Scott Mc Conaughey (3699) ... 04:05:10
469. Santiago Cintas (3719) ... 04:05:32
470. Jesus Chavez (3733) ... 04:05:45
471. Rainer Thieme (3734) ... 04:05:46
472. Daniel Callahan (3739) ... 04:05:50
473. Luis Jubany (3740) ... 04:05:50
474. Howard Cahn (3765) ... 04:06:08
475. Robert Ferguson (3770) ... 04:06:12
476. Michael Gilman (3779) ... 04:06:22
477. Ted Troseth (3782) ... 04:06:24
478. Craig Lagese (3786) ... 04:06:27
479. Claude Nicolet (3792) ... 04:06:30
480. Vic Tomono (3796) ... 04:06:33
481. Bruce Bopp (3800) ... 04:06:36
482. Dana Farnsworth (3804) ... 04:06:40
483. Robert Morten (3812) ... 04:06:45
484. Richard Hernandez (3822) ... 04:06:52
485. David Heaslip (3845) ... 04:07:05
486. Tom Vasquez (3846) ... 04:07:05
487. George Thompson (3867) ... 04:07:22
488. Laurie Loon (3878) ... 04:07:31
489. Carlos Celiz (3887) ... 04:07:37
490. James Gann (3897) ... 04:07:43
491. Fred Jepson (3930) ... 04:08:13
492. Thomas Delafosse (3954) ... 04:08:25
493. Craig Snapp (3955) ... 04:08:25
494. John Hartley (3959) ... 04:08:29
495. Ruben Sierra (3999) ... 04:09:05
496. Richard Humphrys (4002) ... 04:09:08
497. Anthony Prince (4008) ... 04:09:13
498. Richard Cirillo (4024) ... 04:09:23
499. Kevin Culliton (4041) ... 04:09:38
500. Peter Dowhan (4048) ... 04:09:46
501. Robert Morris (4052) ... 04:09:48
502. Luis Lopez (4058) ... 04:09:53
503. Gilbert Martinez (4088) ... 04:10:15
504. Frank Read (4093) ... 04:10:16
505. Joseph Davis (4101) ... 04:10:28
506. Ascanio Perez (4120) ... 04:10:41
507. John Graham (4134) ... 04:10:51
508. Walter Takakuwa (4135) ... 04:10:51
509. Willy Mora (4138) ... 04:10:53
510. Glenn Beach (4141) ... 04:10:55
511. Gary Mangham (4148) ... 04:10:57
512. Randy Torr (4160) ... 04:11:04
513. Peter Peluszkewycz (4172) ... 04:11:12
514. Mark Gavin (4176) ... 04:11:16
515. Uzi Kraus (4180) ... 04:11:19
516. John Savchik (4197) ... 04:11:36
517. John Marquez (4199) ... 04:11:38
518. Jose Amaral (4207) ... 04:11:41
519. Dennis Smith (4213) ... 04:11:50
520. Jorge Talamante (4214) ... 04:11:52
521. James Ransom (4218) ... 04:11:56
522. Sohrab Milanian (4227) ... 04:12:00
523. Thomas Shoup (4253) ... 04:12:20
524. David Dempsey (4267) ... 04:12:29
525. Treneir Woodland (4274) ... 04:12:35
526. Dan Wood (4277) ... 04:12:38
527. Steve Kupsak (4289) ... 04:12:48
528. Santiago Muro (4301) ... 04:12:58
529. Felipe Avalos (4320) ... 04:13:10
530. Larry Albert (4355) ... 04:13:43
531. Dennis Carmona (4357) ... 04:13:44
532. Michael Talbot (4358) ... 04:13:44
533. Luis Mendez (4381) ... 04:14:00
534. Terry Andrues (4387) ... 04:14:03
535. Ralph Whittington (4393) ... 04:14:06
536. Michael Kadrmas (4400) ... 04:14:11
537. Hisatoshi Matsumura (4410) ... 04:14:20
538. Onorio Delarosa (4433) ... 04:14:31
539. Greg Murphy (4492) ... 04:15:01
540. Jerry Silhan (4496) ... 04:15:04
541. Rayment Neale (4497) ... 04:15:05
542. Douglas Kaylor (4499) ... 04:15:07
543. Doug Alderman (4506) ... 04:15:16
544. Michael Volk (4548) ... 04:15:41
545. Randall Merchant (4550) ... 04:15:41
546. Lawrence Malinowski (4558) ... 04:15:46
547. Allen Gilbert (4559) ... 04:15:47
548. Edward Klestinec (4566) ... 04:15:51
549. Sherwin Forde (4579) ... 04:16:00
550. Guillermo Guerrero (4582) ... 04:16:01
551. Daniel Bertheaud (4588) ... 04:16:04
552. Masuhiro Yamashita (4592) ... 04:16:06
553. Paul Whitehouse (4593) ... 04:16:07
554. Michael Hoodman (4604) ... 04:16:19
555. Terasilpa Sirivedin (4626) ... 04:16:29
556. Donald Lieu (4636) ... 04:16:35
557. Frank Pichardo (4642) ... 04:16:39
558. Jack Hahn (4654) ... 04:16:51
559. Clarence Gardner (4659) ... 04:16:55
560. David Macmillan (4675) ... 04:17:08
561. Orson Jordan (4678) ... 04:17:10
562. Glenn Nordlow (4679) ... 04:17:11
563. Gary Smith (4685) ... 04:17:15
564. Paul McDonald (4705) ... 04:17:30
565. Tim Stirens (4737) ... 04:17:55
566. John Novak (4741) ... 04:17:57
567. Tony Wang (4771) ... 04:18:20
568. Rick Schwartz (4789) ... 04:18:31
569. Dave Vint (4802) ... 04:18:39
570. Siergot Sully (4845) ... 04:18:59
571. Patricio O'brien (4852) ... 04:19:00
572. Shintaro Shiomi (4854) ... 04:19:05
573. Steven Stoecklein (4858) ... 04:19:09
574. Carlos Torres (4890) ... 04:19:34
575. Chalor Jaroensook (4913) ... 04:19:43
576. Rolf Knuth (4914) ... 04:19:44
577. George Lara (4915) ... 04:19:45
578. Wayne Valdez (4916) ... 04:19:46
579. Sostenes Garcia V (4928) ... 04:19:55
580. Mark Konenkamp (4931) ... 04:19:56
581. Tim Fairbanks (4941) ... 04:20:04
582. Edward Fredrick (4950) ... 04:20:11
583. Gary Turner (4967) ... 04:20:29
584. Baegun Park (4977) ... 04:20:36
585. James Woody (4980) ... 04:20:38
586. Saul Negrete (4984) ... 04:20:42
587. Robert Mancillas (5004) ... 04:21:04
588. Gardner Bartlett (5005) ... 04:21:05
589. Jorge Castro (5009) ... 04:21:13
590. Klaus Verhelst (5019) ... 04:21:18
591. James Zarrillo (5026) ... 04:21:22
592. Al Fischer (5035) ... 04:21:30
593. Dov Klempner (5038) ... 04:21:31
594. Hamlet Manouchehri (5040) ... 04:21:34
595. Samuel Gardea (5045) ... 04:21:37
596. Mario Del Haro (5057) ... 04:21:42
597. Alan Cherkasky (5064) ... 04:21:46
598. Mark Justice (5080) ... 04:21:53
599. David Chiodo (5113) ... 04:22:09
600. Yuen Wong (5123) ... 04:22:17
601. Edward Rodriguez (5126) ... 04:22:18
602. Mario Razo (5128) ... 04:22:20
603. Ronald Pollack (5130) ... 04:22:22
604. Fred Perez (5137) ... 04:22:26
605. Randall Villareal (5141) ... 04:22:31
606. Benjamin Garcia (5144) ... 04:22:33
607. Daniel Witt (5153) ... 04:22:38
608. James Burns (5154) ... 04:22:39
609. Charles McCaw (5185) ... 04:23:02
610. Fred Dean (5192) ... 04:23:08
611. Michael Cunningham (5194) ... 04:23:10
612. John Erickson (5196) ... 04:23:11
613. James Lavally (5199) ... 04:23:13
614. David Sanders (5208) ... 04:23:17
615. Ben Bar (5228) ... 04:23:30
616. Jose Guzman (5237) ... 04:23:37
617. Michael Tracas (5249) ... 04:23:50
618. John Peterson (5258) ... 04:24:02
619. Frank Contreraz (5265) ... 04:24:09
620. John Schaefer (5266) ... 04:24:09
621. Sergio Rodriguez (5268) ... 04:24:09
622. Mahmoud Redja (5284) ... 04:24:23
623. Taiji Shimizu (5288) ... 04:24:27
624. Martin White (5290) ... 04:24:27
625. Carlos De La Cruz (5291) ... 04:24:28
626. Jim Taylor (5292) ... 04:24:28
627. Dennis Kelley (5305) ... 04:24:34
628. Jose Urbina (5307) ... 04:24:35
629. Ralf Wichmann (5313) ... 04:24:38
630. Gleason Poolaw (5317) ... 04:24:41
631. Allen Nickols (5319) ... 04:24:43
632. Thomas Weber (5326) ... 04:24:52
633. Ralph Cinque (5328) ... 04:24:54
634. Bruce Bocking (5331) ... 04:24:55
635. Mike Moutes (5344) ... 04:25:03
636. Brian Coleman (5350) ... 04:25:09
637. Robert Deeds (5352) ... 04:25:10
638. Jose Luis Anda Sr (5355) ... 04:25:12
639. David Klumph (5363) ... 04:25:15
640. Rafael Montes (5371) ... 04:25:19
641. Ed Le Mus Jr (5385) ... 04:25:25
642. Steven Ogata (5390) ... 04:25:27
643. David Claudon (5404) ... 04:25:38
644. Gerardo Rodriguez (5440) ... 04:25:58
645. Richard Glimp (5464) ... 04:26:12
646. Eleazar Chavez (5486) ... 04:26:30
647. Al Raubitschek (5495) ... 04:26:37
648. Fabian Falconett (5499) ... 04:26:40
649. Enrique Flores (5503) ... 04:26:42
650. Sal Flamenco (5504) ... 04:26:43
651. Dave Dean (5510) ... 04:26:51
652. Jesus Montes (5512) ... 04:26:52
653. Carlos Pineda (5513) ... 04:26:52
654. Carlos Trujillo (5522) ... 04:27:00
655. Kerry Zemp (5527) ... 04:27:05
656. Brian Kendrick (5538) ... 04:27:11
657. Robert Hamm (5539) ... 04:27:12
658. Ming Quon (5562) ... 04:27:25
659. Pedro Bolanos (5567) ... 04:27:30
660. William Cannon (5569) ... 04:27:31
661. David Duran (5577) ... 04:27:33
662. Charles Lindsey (5589) ... 04:27:40
663. Lope Castro (5595) ... 04:27:44
664. Mark Connaughton (5597) ... 04:27:47
665. Steven Burres (5601) ... 04:27:48
666. Donald Ralph (5606) ... 04:27:54
667. Michael Cleary (5616) ... 04:27:57
668. Tony Brizzolara (5617) ... 04:27:58
669. Jim Muth (5693) ... 04:28:48
670. Richard Walton (5712) ... 04:29:01
671. Guy Adams (5714) ... 04:29:02
672. Michael Heagy (5719) ... 04:29:04
673. Jason Pleis (5724) ... 04:29:05
674. Yves Vercellis (5731) ... 04:29:12
675. Miguelangel Rodriguez-Silva (5732) ... 04:29:12
676. Timothy Blied (5742) ... 04:29:18
677. Gerald Sandoval (5746) ... 04:29:19
678. Anthony Alarid (5751) ... 04:29:25
679. Jesse Mellor (5756) ... 04:29:29
680. Thomas Motter (5768) ... 04:29:36
681. Dale Benson (5769) ... 04:29:37
682. Salvador Lopez (5772) ... 04:29:38
683. Steve Chase (5774) ... 04:29:39
684. Michael Thompson (5784) ... 04:29:47
685. Gary Forte (5789) ... 04:29:51
686. Herbert Cobb (5797) ... 04:29:59
687. David Gleason (5798) ... 04:30:00
688. Don Richkas (5816) ... 04:30:14
689. Don Lassig (5825) ... 04:30:21
690. George Rosas (5835) ... 04:30:27
691. John Pancake (5843) ... 04:30:30
692. Barry Standley (5845) ... 04:30:32
693. Frank Poturica (5860) ... 04:30:36
694. Michael Reidy (5861) ... 04:30:36
695. Jose Son Moralez (5873) ... 04:30:42
696. Jose Meza (5878) ... 04:30:43

697. John Sharkey (5883) ... 04:30:48
698. Stephen Shoop (5898) ... 04:30:58
699. Ray O'Dell (5899) ... 04:31:02
700. Leslie Caldera (5920) ... 04:31:10
701. Milt Sheetz (5921) ... 04:31:14
702. David Romo (5922) ... 04:31:15
703. Richard Jamison (5929) ... 04:31:22
704. Denny Dick (5952) ... 04:31:34
705. Jimmy Toy (5954) ... 04:31:38
706. Yoshio Dupree (5960) ... 04:31:42
707. Mark Huckenpahler (5964) ... 04:31:45
708. James Gries (5967) ... 04:31:47
709. Jim Breithaupt (5992) ... 04:32:05
710. Stephen Kraynick (5999) ... 04:32:14
711. Rick Strobaugh (6006) ... 04:32:20
712. Leonard Lumas (6014) ... 04:32:25
713. Richard Fuentes (6017) ... 04:32:26
714. Art Rodriguez (6026) ... 04:32:35
715. Richard Wong (6053) ... 04:32:53
716. Bruce Miller (6056) ... 04:32:55
717. Steve Robinson (6059) ... 04:32:58
718. Cesar Delaguila (6061) ... 04:33:00
719. David Styler (6072) ... 04:33:04
720. Melrose Larry Green (6076) ... 04:33:08
721. Paul Masi (6078) ... 04:33:11
722. Joe Lesniak (6079) ... 04:33:11
723. Ed Ortega (6080) ... 04:33:12
724. Flavio Aguilera (6081) ... 04:33:12
725. Stevenson Payne (6100) ... 04:33:25
726. Frederick Ashley (6103) ... 04:33:27
727. Daniel DeWitt (6112) ... 04:33:32
728. Tim Ceperley (6116) ... 04:33:34
729. Kazuyuki Matsuya (6128) ... 04:33:42
730. Fred Kuester (6150) ... 04:34:03
731. Manuel Emo Valenzuela De La Cruz (6151) 04:34:03
732. William Colangelo (6164) ... 04:34:09
733. Jon McGraw (6172) ... 04:34:12
734. Alfred Mendoza (6181) ... 04:34:22
735. John Krolicki (6196) ... 04:34:29
736. Jose Romero (6198) ... 04:34:30
737. Mikio Nagato (6207) ... 04:34:38
738. Alex Stencel (6215) ... 04:34:42
739. Jerrold Takechi (6225) ... 04:34:46
740. Phil Vazquez (6235) ... 04:34:56
741. Stephen Johnson (6236) ... 04:34:56
742. Bob Reilly (6237) ... 04:34:56
743. Patrick Tomada (6238) ... 04:34:57
744. Steve Watkins (6241) ... 04:34:59
745. Hugo Espino (6243) ... 04:35:00
746. Manuel Suarez (6250) ... 04:35:06
747. Victor Gomez (6251) ... 04:35:07
748. Jim Villa (6253) ... 04:35:08
749. Gary Gibeaut (6267) ... 04:35:17
750. Ted Deery (6270) ... 04:35:19
751. Victor De Silva (6280) ... 04:35:25
752. Nabor Barba (6281) ... 04:35:25
753. Kenji Tajii (6288) ... 04:35:28
754. Tsosie Beach (6291) ... 04:35:32
755. Alexander Aranda (6295) ... 04:35:35
756. Ken Kreider (6297) ... 04:35:36
757. Thom Spadaro (6313) ... 04:35:45
758. Suguru Tangi (6327) ... 04:35:52
759. Andres Gonzalez (6352) ... 04:36:10
760. Dan Hart (6364) ... 04:36:16
761. Antonio Sanchez (6372) ... 04:36:21
762. Timothy Corcoran (6373) ... 04:36:22
763. Conrad Salinas (6376) ... 04:36:23
764. Ken Shapiro (6384) ... 04:36:25
765. Royger Hobson (6397) ... 04:36:31
766. Wilfredo Espinueva (6419) ... 04:36:42
767. Dan Wallman (6425) ... 04:36:49
768. Stephen Livingston (6429) ... 04:36:53
769. Philip Palacio (6437) ... 04:37:04
770. Dennis Marsella (6441) ... 04:37:06
771. Duane Evans (6461) ... 04:37:23
772. Richard Murphy (6462) ... 04:37:23
773. Steven Olivas (6463) ... 04:37:24
774. Don Creley (6488) ... 04:37:37
775. Brian Gillespie (6498) ... 04:37:41
776. Jeff Duce (6516) ... 04:37:51
777. James Snipes (6520) ... 04:37:54
778. Dale Snowberger (6529) ... 04:38:01
779. Thomas Romaneck (6535) ... 04:38:06
780. Howard Wilf (6559) ... 04:38:16
781. Paul Friedman (6562) ... 04:38:17
782. Sheldon Draimin (6565) ... 04:38:21
783. Gary Braun (6573) ... 04:38:28
784. Kirk Jones (6586) ... 04:38:36
785. Daniel Rupp (6602) ... 04:38:43
786. Michael Rivas (6608) ... 04:38:48
787. Edward Arnold (6609) ... 04:38:48
788. Noel Poole (6610) ... 04:38:50
789. George Troia (6613) ... 04:38:52
790. Don Barton (6626) ... 04:38:58
791. Lawrence Crittenton (6647) ... 04:39:12
792. Ramiro Gomez (6648) ... 04:39:13
793. Wayne Hasch (6652) ... 04:39:19
794. Don Karl (6677) ... 04:39:40
795. Len Carlson (6688) ... 04:39:45
796. Steve Clark (6689) ... 04:39:45
797. Rudy Acuna (6693) ... 04:39:47
798. James Vita (6703) ... 04:39:55
799. Robert Harrison (6733) ... 04:40:21
800. Vincent Schodolski (6739) ... 04:40:26
801. German Duran (6761) ... 04:40:46
802. Arturo Gonzalez Gonzalez (6762) ... 04:40:47
803. Jay Burdick (6763) ... 04:40:48
804. James Wolff (6767) ... 04:40:55
805. Rudy Wagner (6770) ... 04:40:57
806. Jorge Lange (6778) ... 04:41:02
807. Jose D'Jesus Lopez (6808) ... 04:41:23
808. Mac Webb (6811) ... 04:41:27
809. Ernesto Garcia (6819) ... 04:41:34
810. Mariano Garcia (6821) ... 04:41:34
811. Jorge Lizama (6823) ... 04:41:36
812. Edgar Perez (6825) ... 04:41:37
813. Mitchell Sperling (6829) ... 04:41:40
814. Alfonzo Gonzalez (6854) ... 04:41:57
815. Jose Jimenez (6880) ... 04:42:18
816. David Pinuelas (6889) ... 04:42:27
817. Kurt Rasmussen (6898) ... 04:42:34
818. Dino Valadez (6907) ... 04:42:43
819. George Villanueva (6915) ... 04:42:47
820. Thomas Govreau (6917) ... 04:42:48
821. Ron Kahn (6927) ... 04:42:54
822. Jeffrey Grant (6934) ... 04:43:00
823. Michael Lewis (6946) ... 04:43:05
824. Edberto Macaraeg (6959) ... 04:43:16
825. Thomas Johnson (6965) ... 04:43:19
826. Jose Navarrete (6980) ... 04:43:25
827. Delbert Baker (6990) ... 04:43:31
828. Hector Ayala (7020) ... 04:43:52
829. Gary Born (7046) ... 04:44:07
830. Edwin Rios (7059) ... 04:44:19
831. Dave Hamilton (7091) ... 04:44:50
832. Donald Pusateri (7096) ... 04:44:52
833. Nick Palacio (7112) ... 04:45:01
834. Aniceto Hernando Jr (7118) ... 04:45:03
835. Kenneth Blackwood (7129) ... 04:45:12
836. Mark Detwiler (7133) ... 04:45:14
837. George Franco (7136) ... 04:45:16
838. John Ralles (7144) ... 04:45:22
839. Terrence Smith (7145) ... 04:45:26
840. Emeterio Hernandez (7152) ... 04:45:37
841. Harvey Myron Jr (7153) ... 04:45:37
842. Robert Rife (7155) ... 04:45:38
843. Dennis Besselman (7163) ... 04:45:41
844. Stanley Ricketts (7170) ... 04:45:44
845. Paul Fitzpatrick (7179) ... 04:45:51
846. Felix Salazar (7184) ... 04:45:57
847. Tony Aquaro (7198) ... 04:46:07
848. Majid Naficy (7202) ... 04:46:09
849. Danny Bowman (7217) ... 04:46:18
850. David Hunzicker (7226) ... 04:46:26
851. Yasunori Nakayama (7229) ... 04:46:28
852. Gary Boyles (7246) ... 04:46:37
853. Stephen Pake (7254) ... 04:46:44
854. Edmund Wong (7274) ... 04:46:57
855. Darwin Schwochow (7277) ... 04:46:58
856. Fred Garcia (7294) ... 04:47:11
857. Kenneth Kohler (7295) ... 04:47:12
858. David Swafford (7315) ... 04:47:24
859. John Rodgers (7322) ... 04:47:28
860. Edward Galan (7325) ... 04:47:30
861. Jack Allen (7339) ... 04:47:38
862. Fernando Quintero (7354) ... 04:47:51
863. Ernest Newman III (7365) ... 04:48:01
864. Jim Hines (7371) ... 04:48:05
865. Sam Tinsley (7375) ... 04:48:08
866. Jerry Salazar (7386) ... 04:48:13
867. Charles Donaghho (7387) ... 04:48:13
868. Leon Hutton (7393) ... 04:48:17
869. Getachew Tamrat (7416) ... 04:48:32
870. Edward Kenney (7431) ... 04:48:45
871. Phil Cataldi (7435) ... 04:48:47
872. Denis Alvarez (7442) ... 04:48:51
873. George Kozonis (7460) ... 04:49:03
874. Miguel Gonzalez (7466) ... 04:49:06
875. Satoshi Suzuki (7476) ... 04:49:12
876. James McEwan (7498) ... 04:49:23
877. Jose Lopez (7506) ... 04:49:27
878. Peter Renteria (7537) ... 04:49:49
879. Richard Cohen (7541) ... 04:49:51
880. Michael Calvert (7546) ... 04:49:54
881. Arthur Mercado (7550) ... 04:49:58
882. Jesus Padilla (7555) ... 04:50:01
883. Ken Yamagata (7556) ... 04:50:01
884. William Mclalau (7557) ... 04:50:01
885. Edward Berumen (7567) ... 04:50:13
886. Andy Medina (7578) ... 04:50:20
887. James Wilson (7591) ... 04:50:33
888. Art Grimmitt Jr (7611) ... 04:50:46
889. Jose Barron (7633) ... 04:51:00
890. Don Mardie (7636) ... 04:51:02
891. Bernnie Gonzalez (7637) ... 04:51:03
892. Ray Croil (7638) ... 04:51:04
893. Carole Taub (7639) ... 04:51:05
894. Timothy Williams (7640) ... 04:51:05
895. Horst Fahr (7643) ... 04:51:07
896. Greg Loaney (7649) ... 04:51:19
897. Lynn Breegle (7669) ... 04:51:36
898. Frank Dipolito (7670) ... 04:51:36
899. Ralph Siu (7676) ... 04:51:39
900. Paul Bodsworth (7681) ... 04:51:40
901. John Krick (7688) ... 04:51:45
902. Felix Oseguera (7708) ... 04:52:05
903. Steven Miller (7715) ... 04:52:08
904. Ira Barksdale Jr (7725) ... 04:52:16
905. Rudy Mayer (7739) ... 04:52:29
906. Gordon St Mary (7742) ... 04:52:31
907. Dennis Moore (7747) ... 04:52:36
908. Jesus Sousa (7755) ... 04:52:42
909. Yolanda Sanchez (7759) ... 04:52:43
910. Gary Condon (7765) ... 04:52:50
911. Lee Leverette (7777) ... 04:52:58
912. Rhett McKenzie (7780) ... 04:52:58
913. Emil Hogen (7787) ... 04:53:03
914. Walter Stewart (7789) ... 04:53:06
915. Bob Turner (7804) ... 04:53:18
916. Marcel Bonafe (7805) ... 04:53:18
917. Stuart Lowry (7808) ... 04:53:20
918. Gordon Rose (7818) ... 04:53:28
919. Robert Ulander (7827) ... 04:53:33
920. Wayne Carnahan (7829) ... 04:53:33
921. Hugh Kelly (7830) ... 04:53:34
922. Kenneth Lacy (7840) ... 04:53:39
923. Ralph Nunez (7842) ... 04:53:41
924. Ricardo Alfaro (7849) ... 04:53:48
925. Ralph Perez (7857) ... 04:53:53
926. Patrick West (7859) ... 04:53:54
927. Michael Saldana (7878) ... 04:54:07
928. Stephen Desoto (7879) ... 04:54:07
929. Frank Kase (7882) ... 04:54:08
930. Carlos Rivera (7885) ... 04:54:10
931. Sakae Uematsu (7897) ... 04:54:18
932. Michael Borio (7907) ... 04:54:24
933. Jess Villa (7911) ... 04:54:26
934. William Lee (7914) ... 04:54:28
935. Joseph Hegna (7918) ... 04:54:30
936. Ray Valdepena Jr (7930) ... 04:54:34
937. Joe Gonzales Jr (7931) ... 04:54:34
938. Lonnell Johns (7936) ... 04:54:35
939. Frank Molles (7952) ... 04:54:45
940. Ronald Sanceda (7963) ... 04:54:48
941. Mohamed Asal (7970) ... 04:54:51
942. Chris Lewis (7976) ... 04:55:04
943. Mark Nagayama (7985) ... 04:55:10
944. Jose Castaneda (7987) ... 04:55:10
945. Angel Monroy (8000) ... 04:55:25
946. Mara Batungbacal (8034) ... 04:55:50
947. Ernest Jones (8038) ... 04:55:52
948. Gary Inouye (8044) ... 04:55:56
949. Robert Lucas (8069) ... 04:56:17
950. Robert Buehler (8070) ... 04:56:17
951. Mark McInerney (8072) ... 04:56:18
952. Frank Poynton (8077) ... 04:56:23
953. Rigoberto Contreras (8081) ... 04:56:28
954. Conley Peyton (8085) ... 04:56:30
955. Bruce Polidori (8086) ... 04:56:31
956. Jimmy Fullerton (8091) ... 04:56:33
957. Benny Shadwick (8093) ... 04:56:34
958. Stephen Stenson (8105) ... 04:56:43
959. Patrick Hennessey (8113) ... 04:56:46
960. Regan Seegraves (8127) ... 04:57:01
961. Armin Del Rosario (8128) ... 04:57:02
962. William Andress (8173) ... 04:57:36
963. Timothy Wrighton (8186) ... 04:57:47
964. Sanford Erickson (8189) ... 04:57:48
965. Christopher Jenkins (8192) ... 04:57:49
966. Bob Holguin (8199) ... 04:57:54
967. Alejandro Olavarria (8206) ... 04:57:59
968. Brendan Lee (8213) ... 04:58:01
969. Alfred Kurzawski (8221) ... 04:58:06
970. James Lee (8224) ... 04:58:07
971. David Kirchner (8233) ... 04:58:14
972. Kenneth Terry (8236) ... 04:58:14
973. Gary Bain (8240) ... 04:58:15
974. John Grue (8245) ... 04:58:18
975. David Beltran (8249) ... 04:58:19
976. Purcell Twisdale (8253) ... 04:58:24
977. Rory Randall (8274) ... 04:58:38
978. Robert McKeown (8277) ... 04:58:42
979. Robert Zaragoza (8288) ... 04:58:49
980. Calvin Hom (8293) ... 04:58:50
981. Salvador Medina Jr (8304) ... 04:58:55
982. Antonio Frayre (8322) ... 04:59:06
983. John Dodrill (8333) ... 04:59:13
984. Ed Kahle (8334) ... 04:59:13
985. John Bauer (8345) ... 04:59:20
986. Frank Sangiorgi (8357) ... 04:59:31
987. Ed Fonda (8377) ... 04:59:41
988. Stephen Jennings (8408) ... 05:00:14
989. John Link (8420) ... 05:00:22
990. Raymond Smitke (8424) ... 05:00:28
991. Didacus French (8426) ... 05:00:31
992. Terry LaPorte (8427) ... 05:00:31
993. Richard Deslauriers (8428) ... 05:00:32
994. Andrew Mitchell (8430) ... 05:00:34
995. Morgan Behr (8440) ... 05:00:48
996. Ruben Contreras (8444) ... 05:00:52
997. Edmond Noll (8453) ... 05:00:59
998. Juan Jose Jimenez (8459) ... 05:01:03
999. David Smith (8465) ... 05:01:07
1000. J Dennis Lewis (8466) ... 05:01:07
1001. Robert Howard (8468) ... 05:01:08
1002. Kenneth Marangell (8472) ... 05:01:11
1003. Moises Torres (8481) ... 05:01:20
1004. Jesus Castaneda (8485) ... 05:01:22
1005. Bob Mitchell (8491) ... 05:01:26
1006. Rafael Martinez (8493) ... 05:01:27
1007. Richard Dominguez (8526) ... 05:01:46
1008. Yves Hepperle (8538) ... 05:01:56
1009. Gerald Robinson (8545) ... 05:02:03
1010. Anthony Ashmore (8548) ... 05:02:05
1011. Ted Thomas (8549) ... 05:02:05
1012. Howard Kieffer (8553) ... 05:02:09
1013. Arthur Csillag (8563) ... 05:02:16
1014. John Ong (8580) ... 05:02:28
1015. Kenji Chikaraishi (8585) ... 05:02:41
1016. John Park (8589) ... 05:02:43
1017. D Dean Benforado (8599) ... 05:02:58
1018. Rafael Echeverria (8637) ... 05:03:28
1019. Seth Verbel (8641) ... 05:03:31
1020. Justin Yim (8650) ... 05:03:44
1021. David De Pinto (8666) ... 05:03:56
1022. Gary Abraham (8672) ... 05:03:59
1023. Neal Newstat (8679) ... 05:04:02
1024. Chuck Ogier (8684) ... 05:04:07
1025. Dagomar Ordonez (8697) ... 05:04:18
1026. Mark Navarro (8699) ... 05:04:19
1027. Arturo Lozano (8700) ... 05:04:19
1028. James Forsen (8710) ... 05:04:27
1029. David Malone (8724) ... 05:04:41
1030. Luis Achig (8761) ... 05:05:23
1031. William Baughman (8770) ... 05:05:32
1032. Oscar Vargas (8793) ... 05:05:56
1033. John Gilligan (8831) ... 05:06:34
1034. Dan Almanza (8838) ... 05:06:37
1035. Larry Reese (8841) ... 05:06:45
1036. Joseph Pannone (8849) ... 05:06:56
1037. John Wilson (8850) ... 05:06:57
1038. David Castenholz (8854) ... 05:06:59
1039. Patrick Holbert (8878) ... 05:07:23
1040. Michael Happe (8889) ... 05:07:36
1041. Don Russell (8896) ... 05:07:45
1042. Jim Bettini (8906) ... 05:07:52
1043. Enrique Villanueva Aguilar (8939) ... 05:08:25
1044. Henry Rogers (8946) ... 05:08:29
1045. Paul Haviland (8952) ... 05:08:33
1046. Daniel Hibbard (8962) ... 05:08:39
1047. Jose Colmenares (9012) ... 05:09:14
1048. Candido Viloria (9015) ... 05:09:18
1049. Carlos Amaral (9026) ... 05:09:27
1050. Rene Taylor (9072) ... 05:10:03
1051. Elmo Johnson (9081) ... 05:10:12
1052. Gary Tickel (9098) ... 05:10:18
1053. Alberto Rosas (9101) ... 05:10:19
1054. Frank Viramontes (9110) ... 05:10:23
1055. Ed Diaz (9118) ... 05:10:27
1056. Roland Carrillo (9130) ... 05:10:41
1057. Joseph Hardin (9137) ... 05:10:48
1058. Hugo Hernandez (9155) ... 05:11:04
1059. Ernie Negrete (9160) ... 05:11:12
1060. Benny Rios Jr (9164) ... 05:11:21
1061. Al Franco (9187) ... 05:11:38
1062. Larry Anderson (9196) ... 05:11:45
1063. Jeremy Perkins (9199) ... 05:11:46
1064. Steve Sohm (9205) ... 05:11:53
1065. Jack Glowen (9211) ... 05:11:57
1066. Robert Valenzuela (9215) ... 05:12:04
1067. Conrad Dawson (9217) ... 05:12:11
1068. John Kim (9222) ... 05:12:13
1069. John Jaskulsky (9223) ... 05:12:15
1070. Gary Dumlao (9238) ... 05:12:29
1071. Glen Stilo (9252) ... 05:12:43
1072. Alex Wallace (9260) ... 05:12:51
1073. Rafael Santiago (9293) ... 05:13:19
1074. Tom Blanchfield (9297) ... 05:13:25
1075. Robert Ross (9305) ... 05:13:29
1076. Gustavo Pineda (9311) ... 05:13:31
1077. Patrick Michael (9325) ... 05:13:38
1078. Rahim Ranjkesh (9351) ... 05:13:55
1079. Saeed Sammii-Zafarghandi (9352) ... 05:13:55
1080. Roger Cook (9397) ... 05:14:38
1081. Bruce Breeden (9400) ... 05:14:41
1082. Eduardo Jerezano (9407) ... 05:14:50
1083. Chi Mui (9416) ... 05:15:06
1084. Michael Guillot (9421) ... 05:15:11
1085. Lionel Villanueva Jr (9426) ... 05:15:16
1086. Don Baird (9430) ... 05:15:18
1087. Guillermo Rangel (9440) ... 05:15:29
1088. Kevin O'Reilly (9441) ... 05:15:30
1089. Dennis Smallcomb (9444) ... 05:15:34
1090. David Brindeiro (9447) ... 05:15:39
1091. Bob Zark (9448) ... 05:15:41
1092. Jeff Field (9481) ... 05:16:16
1093. Michael Vanni (9493) ... 05:16:26
1094. Edward Thompson (9498) ... 05:16:30
1095. Paul Matsukawa (9512) ... 05:16:38
1096. Art Ruiz (9516) ... 05:16:41
1097. Richard Olmeda (9518) ... 05:16:43
1098. Vincent Lucibello (9537) ... 05:17:02
1099. Georges Heinis (9548) ... 05:17:09
1100. Cedric Van De Walle (9549) ... 05:17:09
1101. Richard Vogel (9551) ... 05:17:10
1102. Walter Morris (9588) ... 05:17:41
1103. Emilio USI (9590) ... 05:17:43
1104. Vasilios Rellos (9594) ... 05:17:48
1105. Tim Fitzhugh (9601) ... 05:17:54
1106. James Jespersen-Wheat (9603) ... 05:17:55
1107. Jorge Fernandez (9638) ... 05:18:32
1108. Joseph Peden (9644) ... 05:18:37
1109. Bibiano Ramos (9645) ... 05:18:38
1110. Zaw Hla (9655) ... 05:18:45
1111. Bob Morris (9658) ... 05:18:48
1112. Dave Flores (9661) ... 05:18:52
1113. Jack Putnam (9665) ... 05:18:56
1114. Ruben Aguirre (9684) ... 05:19:10
1115. Robert Vanlighten (9694) ... 05:19:20
1116. Charlie Basham (9696) ... 05:19:21
1117. Rob Kay (9720) ... 05:19:47
1118. Frank Corona (9722) ... 05:19:48
1119. Jaime Arteaga (9729) ... 05:20:06
1120. Ed Nava (9734) ... 05:20:11
1121. Frank Bacus (9740) ... 05:20:17
1122. William Lopez (9741) ... 05:20:17
1123. Guillermo Arguelles (9745) ... 05:20:21
1124. Ron Holloway (9749) ... 05:20:25
1125. Ronald Hancock Sr (9751) ... 05:20:26
1126. Ronald Hatakeyama (9758) ... 05:20:31
1127. Mark Borenstein (9763) ... 05:20:36
1128. Bruce Chippindale (9786) ... 05:20:50
1129. Steven Haber (9799) ... 05:21:02
1130. Albert Chung (9803) ... 05:21:06
1131. Mitchell Morgenstern (9830) ... 05:21:37
1132. Charles Pearlman (9879) ... 05:22:10
1133. Michael Butcher (9881) ... 05:22:11
1134. Michael Massengale (9891) ... 05:22:18
1135. Kevin Hiland (9910) ... 05:22:44
1136. Miguel Trujillo (9914) ... 05:22:49
1137. Dennis Blanks (9916) ... 05:22:50
1138. Michael La Grassa (9917) ... 05:22:50
1139. Miguel Balcaceres (9921) ... 05:22:54
1140. Joseph Soliz (9951) ... 05:23:29
1141. Mike Campbell (9973) ... 05:23:53
1142. Ray Williams (9975) ... 05:23:54
1143. Mark Gaston (9977) ... 05:23:56
1144. Steven Friedrich (10002) ... 05:24:25
1145. Luis Castro (10006) ... 05:24:27
1146. Robert Dawson (10014) ... 05:24:31
1147. Steve Woods (10020) ... 05:24:44
1148. Ken Deppe (10041) ... 05:25:05
1149. Rudy Aranda (10050) ... 05:25:18
1150. Dick Orciuch (10052) ... 05:25:22
1151. James Lundy (10061) ... 05:25:35
1152. Benjamin Bailey (10083) ... 05:25:48
1153. Jesse Saenz (10084) ... 05:25:49
1154. Scott Baxter (10094) ... 05:26:00
1155. Rob Camargo (10100) ... 05:26:06
1156. Ed Vega (10111) ... 05:26:16
1157. Paul Copeskey (10121) ... 05:26:29
1158. Gary Fulton (10126) ... 05:26:35
1159. Enrique Alba (10136) ... 05:26:45
1160. Jesse Gonzalez (10159) ... 05:27:10
1161. Patrick Cannon (10171) ... 05:27:22
1162. Lawrence Quezada (10187) ... 05:27:31
1163. Mario Ruiz (10188) ... 05:27:32
1164. Elder Harveu (10210) ... 05:27:52
1165. Joseph Byrnes (10240) ... 05:28:18
1166. Jim Walker (10241) ... 05:28:20
1167. Jeff Coleman (10250) ... 05:28:37
1168. Rob McNair (10252) ... 05:28:38
1169. Nigel Wright (10257) ... 05:28:44
1170. Stephen Auth (10269) ... 05:28:49
1171. Alan Spencer (10282) ... 05:28:59
1172. Robert Galbraith (10293) ... 05:29:09
1173. Jose Acosta (10295) ... 05:29:11
1174. Scott Cejda (10297) ... 05:29:12
1175. Juan Cuadra (10319) ... 05:29:23
1176. Chris Sato (10335) ... 05:29:50
1177. Michael McGivney (10356) ... 05:30:10
1178. Curtis Martin (10364) ... 05:30:17
1179. Daniel Mindrum (10387) ... 05:30:36
1180. David Sofranko (10394) ... 05:30:39
1181. Mercedes Parodi (10397) ... 05:30:42
1182. Chris Cochran (10399) ... 05:30:45
1183. Reginald Alberts (10413) ... 05:31:05
1184. Alvin Maxwell (10419) ... 05:31:09
1185. Merwin Rasmussen (10462) ... 05:31:46
1186. Mark Sambrano (10466) ... 05:31:48
1187. Wayne Fairchild (10511) ... 05:32:36
1188. Stephen Wolla (10514) ... 05:32:40
1189. James Thompson (10534) ... 05:32:55
1190. Brian Smith (10583) ... 05:33:41
1191. Robert Recker (10587) ... 05:33:42
1192. Rick Blakely (10590) ... 05:33:43
1193. David Amenda (10595) ... 05:33:47
1194. Kenneth Babamoto (10604) ... 05:33:53
1195. Alfredo Crespo (10607) ... 05:33:55
1196. Allen Binner (10630) ... 05:34:15
1197. Kevin Armstrong (10641) ... 05:34:28
1198. Wes Keusder (10651) ... 05:34:38
1199. Richard Jacks (10657) ... 05:34:42
1200. Juan Gutierrez (10663) ... 05:34:44
1201. Frank Cole (10665) ... 05:34:44
1202. Robert Mitchell (10668) ... 05:34:46
1203. Dan Michael (10669) ... 05:34:47
1204. Mark Burley (10676) ... 05:35:00
1205. Masakatsu Sakashita (10685) ... 05:35:05
1206. Larry Ahlstrom (10692) ... 05:35:15
1207. Daniel Sever (10727) ... 05:35:48
1208. William Jones (10752) ... 05:36:13
1209. Sanford Jossen (10755) ... 05:36:15
1210. Rick Odland (10814) ... 05:37:20
1211. Hamid Barang (10835) ... 05:37:40
1212. Roger Zelaya (10838) ... 05:37:44
1213. Roger Lemasters (10841) ... 05:37:50
1214. Fernando Coronado (10875) ... 05:38:42
1215. Daniel Roman (10896) ... 05:38:59
1216. Mark Zelig (10902) ... 05:39:13
1217. Charles Wills (10915) ... 05:39:33
1218. Abel Herndon (10916) ... 05:39:33
1219. Larry Silver (10933) ... 05:39:54
1220. Carlos De La Cerda (10948) ... 05:40:14
1221. Pete Wysocki (10958) ... 05:40:26
1222. Sol Wroclawsky (10973) ... 05:40:46
1223. Everett Clark (10980) ... 05:41:06
1224. Vicente Pascua Jr (10993) ... 05:41:17
1225. Pedro Cabrera (11007) ... 05:41:34
1226. David Alley (11012) ... 05:41:42
1227. Francisco Caballeros (11024) ... 05:41:53
1228. Eugene Pietrini (11029) ... 05:41:58
1229. Louis Montes (11050) ... 05:42:18
1230. Terry Collins (11051) ... 05:42:18
1231. John McCarthy (11067) ... 05:42:28
1232. Rene Edelos Monteros (11070) ... 05:42:32
1233. David Dickinson (11101) ... 05:43:02
1234. Michael Huang (11126) ... 05:43:31
1235. Sean Slwani (11134) ... 05:43:37
1236. Jorge Negrete (11144) ... 05:43:50
1237. Toshiyuki Kuritani (11194) ... 05:44:26
1238. Greg Ervin (11202) ... 05:44:31
1239. Jose Araujo (11216) ... 05:44:38
1240. Hiroshi Koyama (11222) ... 05:44:45
1241. Joe Moore (11230) ... 05:44:54
1242. Tom Hughes (11233) ... 05:44:56
1243. Shigeo Nagayama (11237) ... 05:44:59
1244. Gary Goldberg (11249) ... 05:45:16
1245. Mitchell Alberi (11255) ... 05:45:25
1246. Robert Chacon (11258) ... 05:45:27
1247. Leroy Mersnall (11260) ... 05:45:28
1248. Reggie Tucker (11285) ... 05:46:00
1249. Jonathan Chin (11287) ... 05:46:00
1250. Gary Johnson (11342) ... 05:47:07
1251. Gregory Oconnor (11375) ... 05:48:09
1252. Dwight Moore (11380) ... 05:48:18
1253. James Doyle (11385) ... 05:48:28
1254. Gerald Morris (11406) ... 05:49:02
1255. Benjamin Esparza (11420) ... 05:49:18
1256. Robert Martino (11454) ... 05:49:47
1257. Lamont Williams (11456) ... 05:49:47
1258. John Weisickle (11467) ... 05:49:54
1259. Valentine Mares (11487) ... 05:50:18
1260. Ernie Valdez (11489) ... 05:50:20
1261. Manuel Garcia (11491) ... 05:50:24
1262. Harris Warsaw (11496) ... 05:50:26
1263. Frank Nainoa (11497) ... 05:50:27
1264. Roger Egans Jr (11512) ... 05:50:35
1265. Luis Gallardo (11521) ... 05:50:41
1266. Dougg Healy (11527) ... 05:50:52
1267. Dennis Junker (11556) ... 05:51:32
1268. Joe McGreggor (11577) ... 05:52:09
1269. Clint Seal (11587) ... 05:52:14
1270. Ken McLain (11599) ... 05:52:22
1271. James Anderson (11634) ... 05:53:03
1272. Daniel Gonzalez (11647) ... 05:53:18
1273. Ruben Mejia (11651) ... 05:53:21
1274. Richard McKernan (11687) ... 05:53:56
1275. Mark Juarez (11690) ... 05:53:59
1276. Kenichi Iteya (11715) ... 05:54:42
1277. Stan Yee (11717) ... 05:54:43
1278. Brad Malamud (11718) ... 05:54:43
1279. Ed Estrada (11729) ... 05:55:01
1280. Les Hill (11740) ... 05:55:14
1281. James Cimino (11756) ... 05:55:30
1282. Leslie Chaplin (11775) ... 05:55:57
1283. Edward Valdez (11782) ... 05:56:03
1284. Carlos Orosco (11799) ... 05:56:37
1285. Thomas Cingire (11824) ... 05:57:10
1286. Dennis McGonagle (11833) ... 05:57:23
1287. Peter Thompson (11834) ... 05:57:24
1288. Tatsumi Tomimori (11843) ... 05:57:38
1289. Thomas Church (11846) ... 05:57:43
1290. Michael Snellings (11849) ... 05:57:50
1291. Ray Sieverling (11851) ... 05:57:53
1292. Mark Ozaki (11860) ... 05:58:06
1293. Thomas Loffarelli (11863) ... 05:58:08
1294. Roger Pureur (11874) ... 05:58:23
1295. Alvin Wero (11880) ... 05:58:25
1296. Manuel Hernandez (11887) ... 05:58:29
1297. William Jemison (11891) ... 05:58:32
1298. Kaveh Soodjani (11894) ... 05:58:34
1299. Kenneth Letterman (11905) ... 05:58:50
1300. Jim Given (11915) ... 05:58:55
1301. William Dance (11937) ... 05:59:39
1302. Tony Trebino (11970) ... 06:00:18
1303. Frank Rodriguez (11982) ... 06:00:32
1304. Yervand Tokuzyan (11994) ... 06:01:00
1305. Jose Esparza (12039) ... 06:02:18
1306. Joseph Villegas (12041) ... 06:02:19
1307. Marcelino Roman Jr (12056) ... 06:02:42
1308. Frederick Cooley (12071) ... 06:03:09
1309. Randolph Windom (12074) ... 06:03:12
1310. Steve Schindler (12081) ... 06:03:30
1311. Bruce Burch (12098) ... 06:04:00
1312. Rob Espinoza (12103) ... 06:04:16
1313. Tai Chung (12110) ... 06:04:29
1314. Bill Crosgrune (12111) ... 06:04:30
1315. John Alipio (12117) ... 06:04:37
1316. Manuel Perez (12121) ... 06:04:40
1317. Yoichi Muroya (12127) ... 06:04:43
1318. Dan Trejo (12151) ... 06:05:14
1319. Newgene Rawls (12158) ... 06:05:23
1320. Humberto Delacruz (12174) ... 06:05:41
1321. Joel Marks (12185) ... 06:06:02
1322. Michael Depascal (12204) ... 06:06:43
1323. Jerry Parz (12218) ... 06:07:15
1324. Terrance Davis (12224) ... 06:07:20
1325. Clyde Middleton (12226) ... 06:07:21
1326. John Wasson (12233) ... 06:07:41
1327. Rubin Herrera (12238) ... 06:07:49
1328. Joseph Watson (12242) ... 06:07:54
1329. Anthony Miles (12243) ... 06:07:57
1330. Hector Hernandez (12298) ... 06:09:02
1331. Patrick Kelly (12316) ... 06:09:26
1332. Mark Hodnick (12320) ... 06:09:38
1333. Scott Krentel (12327) ... 06:09:48

1334. Kazushige Nishimura (12347) 06:10:15
1335. Erasmo Hernandez (12359) 06:10:50
1336. Gus Dominguez (12366) 06:11:01
1337. Javier Duque (12388) 06:11:24
1338. Luis Gutierrez (12403) 06:11:51
1339. David Prentler (12443) 06:12:56
1340. Martin Valinsky (12464) 06:13:32
1341. Efren Ramos (12537) 06:15:24
1342. Victor Diaz (12565) 06:15:58
1343. Jose Madera (12583) 06:16:32
1344. Earl McKinley (12615) 06:17:18
1345. Ian Lyons (12623) 06:17:37
1346. Partho Mandal (12625) 06:17:37
1347. Steven Davis (12631) 06:17:56
1348. Carlos Lopez (12635) 06:18:14
1349. Spasoje Neskovic (12639) 06:18:17
1350. Leonids Jurkevics (12672) 06:19:17
1351. Luis Meza (12684) 06:19:41
1352. John Leamon (12705) 06:20:16
1353. John Allen (12707) 06:20:22
1354. Larry Dardick (12731) 06:21:17
1355. George Feher (12732) 06:21:19
1356. John Casato (12743) 06:21:34
1357. Dennis Dobberpuhl (12746) 06:21:35
1358. Enriquez Castanceda (12749) 06:21:36
1359. Art Heirshberg (12756) 06:21:46
1360. Terry Sheehan (12762) 06:21:53
1361. Lambert Olaes (12763) 06:21:53
1362. Richard Beauregard (12848) 06:24:00
1363. Chris Hieatt (12854) 06:24:09
1364. Peter Ashworth (12889) 06:25:29
1365. John Hendrix (12902) 06:25:51
1366. Rickey Ivie (12927) 06:26:33
1367. Manny Briseno (12938) 06:26:47
1368. Jeffry Pollard (12943) 06:26:58
1369. Robert Lozano (12947) 06:27:02
1370. Larry Hagan (12969) 06:27:51
1371. Manual Barragan Sr (12978) 06:28:02
1372. David Farber (12990) 06:28:21
1373. Wade Austin (12997) 06:28:34
1374. Michael McClellan (12998) 06:28:35
1375. Alvaro Paramo (13030) 06:30:03
1376. Steve Madoff (13047) 06:30:10
1377. Daniel Segura (13048) 06:30:23
1378. Daniel Davidson (13049) 06:30:23
1379. Ganesan Naicker (13107) 06:32:00
1380. Mohammad Khaki (13191) 06:34:11
1381. Mitch Viturino (13220) 06:34:54
1382. Abraham Valladares (13242) 06:35:37
1383. Gary Acosta (13243) 06:35:38
1384. Jim Franchino (13312) 06:37:58
1385. William Potts (13325) 06:38:29
1386. Yasunobu Uehara (13358) 06:39:30
1387. Ikuta Koji (13426) 06:42:05
1388. Shelton Sanders (13445) 06:42:36
1389. Sam Reynolds Jr (13455) 06:42:58
1390. Ernest Leon (13457) 06:42:59
1391. Nigel Philcox (13501) 06:44:54
1392. Rubert Alvarez Jr (13521) 06:45:42
1393. Hector Torres (13580) 06:46:54
1394. Pavel Knizek (13602) 06:48:21
1395. Angelo Martinez (13624) 06:49:02
1396. Jimmie Cueva (13625) 06:49:03
1397. Edward Mundy (13712) 06:51:35
1398. Francisco Muniles (13750) 06:53:21
1399. Guy White (13774) 06:54:38
1400. Joel Kirscher (13794) 06:55:10
1401. Burtis Buchanan (13807) 06:55:30
1402. Armen Ross (13809) 06:55:36
1403. Frank Head (13810) 06:55:42
1404. Willie Williams (13840) 06:56:38
1405. David Rodican (13858) 06:57:04
1406. Anthony Ketentse (13870) 06:57:21
1407. Pedro Rincan (13931) 06:59:04
1408. Roberto Rebalcaba (13938) 06:59:13
1409. Sanlokh Singh (13943) 06:59:33
1410. Richard Carpenter Jr (13983) 07:00:53
1411. Craig Lawrence (13985) 07:00:55
1412. John Thomas (13995) 07:01:06
1413. Zach Millon (14020) 07:02:03
1414. Eddie Pepatphongse (14076) 07:04:50
1415. Waymond Lee (14113) 07:07:01
1416. Mike Antich (14115) 07:07:05
1417. Manuel Hernandez (14116) 07:07:18
1418. Steve Underwood (14131) 07:08:15
1419. Abelardo Rodriguez (14168) 07:10:49
1420. Steve Stackhouse (14170) 07:10:55
1421. Randy Saks (14197) 07:12:38
1422. Randy Senn (14209) 07:13:03
1423. Bernard Stadler (14216) 07:13:34
1424. Rod Ratzlaff (14229) 07:14:37
1425. George Moran (14247) 07:15:16
1426. Dave Sherwin (14281) 07:16:42
1427. Allan Wagner (14296) 07:17:42
1428. Cesar Martinez (14314) 07:19:09
1429. Jon Montoya (14317) 07:19:14
1430. John Whitman (14327) 07:19:54
1431. Sheryl Ali (14331) 07:20:15
1432. Kevin Sheu (14332) 07:20:20
1433. Andy Mahindru (14343) 07:20:48
1434. Edward Mooney (14380) 07:23:02
1435. Angel Rodriguez (14395) 07:24:30
1436. Billy Corrigan (14412) 07:26:13
1437. Kiyoshi Suzuki (14440) 07:28:40
1438. Daniel Montano (14441) 07:28:44
1439. Mike Gray (14486) 07:32:54
1440. Jose Cortes (14496) 07:33:35
1441. David Nunez (14503) 07:34:15
1442. Robert Dickson (14556) 07:37:42
1443. Alberto Velasco (14564) 07:38:36
1444. Nicholas Galvan (14590) 07:40:27
1445. Hari Hanumantha (14633) 07:44:30
1446. N Prasad (14634) 07:44:31
1447. Marc Steinberg (14652) 07:46:11
1448. Manly Hyde (14662) 07:47:16
1449. James Kennedy (14663) 07:47:20
1450. Taihei Takahashi (14698) 07:50:50
1451. Roderick Williams Sr (14702) 07:51:04
1452. Steve Wilson (14708) 07:51:42
1453. Larry Finnan (14738) 07:54:02
1454. Robert Smith (14752) 07:55:04
1455. Ricardo Barbosa (14795) 08:00:05
1456. Scott Adishian (14810) 08:01:29
1457. Ralph Rayburn (15000) 08:32:11
1458. Samuel Kato (15001) 08:32:16
1459. Judith Besse (15013) 08:34:42
1460. Carl Banks (15039) 08:43:59
1461. Bernard Ojeda Sr (15075) 08:55:16
1462. Kook Dean (15086) 08:57:48
1463. Charles Kobrin (15117) 09:21:05
1464. Charley De La Pena (15159) 10:01:38

WOMEN 40 TO 44

1. Alfreda Iglehart (540) 03:13:29
2. Leslie King (773) 03:20:14
3. Cecilia Ramos (1004) 03:25:34
4. Leda Whitmer (1063) 03:27:01
5. Victoria Devita (1175) 03:29:01
6. Liz Sponagle (1261) 03:30:33
7. Candelaria Clark (1324) 03:31:43
8. Dale Libeau (1434) 03:34:04
9. Cecilia Laue (1545) 03:36:13
10. Gail Schnaars (1575) 03:36:45
11. Harriet Braverman (1634) 03:37:54
12. Belinda Connor (1648) 03:38:06
13. Micki Welch (1812) 03:40:53
14. Denise Pilnak (1814) 03:40:54
15. Victoria Eyre (1893) 03:41:52
16. Nancy Barfield (1903) 03:42:01
17. June Gessner (1963) 03:43:13
18. Mellie Gillman (2101) 03:45:11
19. Elena Sherman (2163) 03:46:03
20. Bagley Linda (2211) 03:46:55
21. Arlone Fichman (2226) 03:47:06
22. Carolyn Gill (2249) 03:47:27
23. Christina Zeidel (2355) 03:48:49
24. Denise Hobbs (2379) 03:49:08
25. Kyoko Shimanuki (2400) 03:49:22
26. Janis Bembry (2437) 03:49:54
27. Ellen Stern (2480) 03:50:28
28. Nancy Crocini (2513) 03:50:58
29. Joanne Bebruyn (2661) 03:52:54
30. Suke Gumpel (2864) 03:55:23
31. Dorothy Jamieson (2941) 03:56:11
32. Patty Burt (2960) 03:56:25
33. Debra Schrotz (3008) 03:56:52
34. Barbara Kalmbach (3013) 03:56:56
35. Cullene Murphy (3155) 03:58:29
36. Debra Kenneybrew (3195) 03:58:56
37. Sharlyn Ziprick (3299) 04:00:01
38. Rose Ehman (3431) 04:01:41
39. Arzenia Redcross (3459) 04:02:06
40. Jill Oleary (3516) 04:02:55
41. Joann Weltsch (3583) 04:03:56
42. Maggie Anderson (3623) 04:04:25
43. Marilyn Sheriff (3988) 04:08:58
44. Jan Diederich (4004) 04:09:08
45. Shelly Bowen (4046) 04:09:40
46. Dianne Lum (4096) 04:10:21
47. Joan Osder (4119) 04:10:41
48. Robin Hale (4166) 04:11:08
49. Maria Wilks (4169) 04:11:11
50. Ruth Lopez (4205) 04:11:40
51. Susan Lahr (4224) 04:11:59
52. Karen Thomas (4236) 04:12:07
53. Pamela Albert (4249) 04:12:17
54. Louise Erickson (4314) 04:13:07
55. Blanca Leticia Chavez (4413) 04:14:21
56. Jennie Cole (4430) 04:14:30
57. Jackie Hester (4444) 04:14:37
58. Liz Hodges (4488) 04:14:59
59. Bobbie Provencher (4502) 04:15:10
60. Cyndi Goldbers (4531) 04:15:33
61. Carla Peterson (4584) 04:16:02
62. Pat Whipple-Fox (4616) 04:16:26
63. Luz Esquivel (4645) 04:16:41
64. Dana Nemer (4647) 04:16:42
65. Sharon Lotesto (4650) 04:16:43
66. Kathleen Farrelly (4683) 04:17:14
67. Cori Leone (4713) 04:17:38
68. Julie Johnson (4748) 04:18:02
69. Becky Wecksler (4770) 04:18:19
70. Virginia Hunt (4785) 04:18:29
71. Sandra Alvarado (4861) 04:19:10
72. Nancy Shura (4864) 04:19:12
73. Patricia Tessier (4899) 04:19:36
74. Denise Kelly (4935) 04:19:59
75. Victoria Lewin (4945) 04:20:06
76. Roxanne Natale (4960) 04:20:22
77. Patty Mann (4979) 04:20:37
78. Melanie Warner (5018) 04:21:18
79. Betsy Sochor (5042) 04:21:35
80. Jennifer Rose (5052) 04:21:40
81. Meg Perry (5117) 04:22:12
82. Margaret Stearns (5175) 04:22:55
83. Debra Tyler (5216) 04:23:20
84. Shannon Monahan (5275) 04:24:15
85. Margie Hynes (5321) 04:24:44
86. Sunny Blende (5341) 04:25:02
87. Cathy Wilson (5375) 04:25:21
88. Joan Langston (5386) 04:25:26
89. Linnea Burnette (5422) 04:25:49
90. Laura Perloff (5426) 04:25:50
91. Tish Power (5433) 04:25:54
92. Carla Tulchin (5437) 04:25:57
93. Debora Sue O'Brien (5441) 04:25:59
94. Yuen-Tching Tchen (5451) 04:26:03
95. Suzanne McNeil (5452) 04:26:04
96. Gina Michel (5491) 04:26:33
97. Shirley Smith (5494) 04:26:37
98. Yuriko Sano (5594) 04:27:44
99. Nancy Nebeker (5599) 04:27:48
100. Sook-Cha Villanueva (5626) 04:28:03
101. Lynda Arterbery (5646) 04:28:16
102. Lorraine Norton (5651) 04:28:19
103. Deborah Westbay (5703) 04:28:52
104. Kathy Turner (5723) 04:29:05
105. Karen Orosco (5804) 04:30:04
106. Etsuko Iteya (5911) 04:31:07
107. Sandi Mulliner (5924) 04:31:16
108. Terry Heintz (6091) 04:33:19
109. Amina Maricar (6121) 04:33:38
110. Dora Haikel (0147) 04:33:56
111. Mina Mendeza (6177) 04:34:19
112. Stephanie Mapelli (6182) 04:34:23
113. Susan Gibson (6202) 04:34:33
114. Mimi Brophy (6290) 04:35:29
115. Rena Chastan (6304) 04:35:40
116. Karen Blagmon (6342) 04:36:05
117. Holly Barnes (6360) 04:36:14
118. Susan Sheldon (6392) 04:36:29
119. Susie Sakai (6413) 04:36:39
120. Pamela Deery (6485) 04:37:34
121. Cheryl Cohen (6537) 04:38:07
122. Suellen Estell (6541) 04:38:08
123. Evelyn Vance (6667) 04:39:33
124. Angie Nevarez (6707) 04:40:00
125. Ruth Nelson (6713) 04:40:03
126. Elaine Carey (6738) 04:40:25
127. Kristin Leaf-James (6756) 04:40:40
128. Maria Paiz-Tilton (6799) 04:41:13
129. Grethe Nielsen (6809) 04:41:24
130. Priscilla Mason (6810) 04:41:26
131. Pamela Nagami (6897) 04:42:33
132. Pamela Hosmer (6942) 04:43:03
133. Catherine Talley (6964) 04:43:18
134. Maureen Cudahy (6993) 04:43:33
135. Arleen Delgado (7018) 04:43:51
136. Sharon Hughes (7035) 04:43:59
137. Jean Fogarty (7082) 04:44:40
138. Susan Brambila (7087) 04:44:47
139. Janis Balda (7120) 04:45:05
140. Cassandra Killon (7140) 04:45:20
141. Linda Alexander (7148) 04:45:31
142. Nina Reyer (7195) 04:46:04
143. Laura Castaneda (7222) 04:46:13
144. Kath Nunez (7238) 04:46:33
145. Carleen Kreider (7240) 04:46:34
146. Jenny Paling (7282) 04:47:00
147. Annie Young (7314) 04:47:24
148. Eva Mendez (7378) 04:48:10
149. Leah Boyle (7437) 04:48:49
150. Robin McGuire (7481) 04:49:14
151. Mary Van Orden (7493) 04:49:22
152. Carolyn McEwan (7496) 04:49:23
153. Eveline Auvinet (7511) 04:49:30
154. Linda Francis (7517) 04:49:33
155. Wendy Bracamonte (7548) 04:49:56
156. Debra Bruno (7560) 04:50:05
157. Patty Mehlberg (7594) 04:50:34
158. Nasrin Farokhipour (7615) 04:50:48
159. Donna Sommars (7645) 04:51:10
160. Rachel Tavarez (7655) 04:51:23
161. Patricia Nieto (7658) 04:51:26
162. Cindra Stolk (7698) 04:51:56
163. Jody Isenberg (7702) 04:51:59
164. Harriet Turney (7770) 04:52:52
165. Suzanne Vanamberg (7853) 04:53:51
166. Laurie Piccolotti (7862) 04:53:56
167. Kris Simpson Murphy (7899) 04:54:20
168. Leslie McVae (7900) 04:54:21
169. Lynn Schermerhorn (7905) 04:54:23
170. Debra Hinz (7934) 04:54:35
171. Rosalyn Ongale (7938) 04:54:36
172. Jan Glavan (7948) 04:54:43
173. Lorraine Miller (7966) 04:54:49
174. Rebecca Nieva (7984) 04:55:09
175. Claudia Levine (8052) 04:56:05
176. Maria Avina (8098) 04:56:38
177. Marsha Wickett (8103) 04:56:42
178. Abigail Gourley (8136) 04:57:09
179. Elsa Barnes (8150) 04:57:18
180. Julie Ward (8156) 04:57:24
181. Susan Myers (8159) 04:57:25
182. Glenda Sweils (8161) 04:57:26
183. Carol Morton (8176) 04:57:38
184. Nena Cordova-Gandara (8179) 04:57:39
185. Marian Cristobal (8187) 04:57:47
186. Vicki Marmorstein (8230) 04:58:13
187. Terry Gilman (8238) 04:58:15
188. Linda Trudeau (8257) 04:58:26
189. Sue Yoshino (8283) 04:58:45
190. Beatriz McCarten (8308) 04:58:56
191. Debralee Howard (8309) 04:58:57
192. Phebe Sauceda (8375) 04:59:41
193. Salley Mann (8409) 05:00:15
194. Azam Azaditabar (8425) 05:00:30
195. Jayne Haggar (8451) 05:00:57
196. Sharon Demarah-Bowen (8477) 05:01:14
197. Jeanne Swanson (8512) 05:01:40
198. Maria Medrano (8544) 05:02:01
199. Sandra Reynolds (8552) 05:02:09
200. Sylvia Edgar (8579) 05:02:28
201. Jodi Galvin (8581) 05:02:29
202. Debra Burke-Goltz (8596) 05:02:51
203. Bernadette King (8634) 05:03:23
204. Nancy Dewald (8644) 05:03:34
205. Louise Yeilding (8648) 05:03:41
206. Michelle Weitz (8720) 05:04:39
207. Beatrice Luna (8774) 05:05:34
208. Thomalee Olsen (8777) 05:05:35
209. Nicole Lhotte (8807) 05:06:08
210. Diane Cano (8862) 05:07:08
211. Sarah Butler (8877) 05:07:18
212. Katherine Coates (8886) 05:07:33
213. Diane Knight (8929) 05:08:12
214. Michele Wantink (8954) 05:08:35
215. Kathy Bittle (8975) 05:08:44
216. Vilma Mejia (8993) 05:09:06
217. Marilee Cosgrove (9005) 05:09:09
218. Anne Greatbatch (9013) 05:09:16
219. Martine Cardin-Allen (9046) 05:09:46
220. Joyce Menta (9055) 05:09:54
221. Karen Embree (9091) 05:10:16
222. Andrea Yee (9106) 05:10:22
223. Tani Leung (9177) 05:11:34
224. May Du Bois (9197) 05:11:46
225. Freeda Latimore (9244) 05:12:33
226. Vicki Bates (9286) 05:13:15
227. Alever Jones (9303) 05:13:27
228. Barbara Kudsk (9328) 05:13:39
229. Mariana Schaffer (9345) 05:13:52
230. Karen Ruiz (9387) 05:14:26
231. Maureen Stratton (9423) 05:15:12
232. Pam Medhurst (9442) 05:15:33
233. Delise Lucas (9470) 05:16:06
234. Fahamisha Butler (9541) 05:17:03
235. Lourdes Navarette (9544) 05:17:05
236. Sherri Ferraro (9561) 05:17:19
237. Victoria Del Hard (9568) 05:17:23
238. Jo Lavey (9581) 05:17:33
239. Diane Marie Fitzhugh (9602) 05:17:54
240. Soraya Behnam (9657) 05:18:48
241. Nancy Peterson (9672) 05:19:01
242. Michelle Deleu (9677) 05:19:05
243. Deborah Tomaw (9732) 05:20:08
244. Colleen Baquet (9742) 05:20:19
245. Palmira Malone (9748) 05:20:23
246. Lisa Licavoli (9760) 05:20:32
247. Eileen Anderson (9792) 05:20:56
248. Sandi Mellin (9809) 05:21:11
249. Jenenne Macklin (9823) 05:21:26
250. Julie Claydon (9859) 05:21:54
251. Debbie Nicholls (9897) 05:22:26
252. Teresa Luna (9899) 05:22:28
253. Marie Washington (9912) 05:22:46
254. Deborah McDonald (9962) 05:23:41
255. Jpy Shiraishi (9967) 05:23:44
256. Claudia Newsom (9971) 05:23:48
257. Debby Dufresne (10040) 05:25:03
258. Carol Hunt (10074) 05:25:44
259. Nancy Kerr (10087) 05:25:50
260. Sharon Diaz (10095) 05:26:00
261. Nancy Gertler (10103) 05:26:09
262. Evon Douglas (10122) 05:26:31
263. Aura Barillaas (10130) 05:26:37
264. Maria Solorzano (10145) 05:26:54
265. Cindy Gillis (10156) 05:27:08
266. Olivia Koehl (10193) 05:27:37
267. Deborah Andrews (10212) 05:27:55
268. Pamela Manning (10231) 05:28:09
269. Anne Bothwell (10277) 05:28:54
270. Renee Lowry (10303) 05:29:14
271. Julia Cory (10321) 05:29:25
272. Mary Mailander-Cain (10366) 05:30:18
273. Gail Alberts (10412) 05:31:05
274. Nancy Rosenfelt (10421) 05:31:10
275. Carol Steffen (10426) 05:31:18
276. Lauren Preston (10443) 05:31:29
277. Barbara Rollins (10451) 05:31:35
278. Yitka Krofta (10494) 05:32:07
279. Mary Romo (10496) 05:32:14
280. Karen Schulte (10536) 05:32:55
281. Sarah Press (10537) 05:32:56
282. Mary Jo Watkins (10588) 05:33:42
283. Luisa Hernandez (10602) 05:33:52
284. Stephanie Gorvin (10603) 05:33:53
285. Theresa Von Hutten (10631) 05:34:16
286. Juanita Thompson (10645) 05:34:31
287. Merilyn Smith (10675) 05:34:59
288. Frances Solomon (10712) 05:35:28
289. Adela De La Torre (10734) 05:35:53
290. Adrienne Davis (10738) 05:35:56
291. Alison Dreael (10777) 05:36:39
292. Lori Smith (10804) 05:37:07
293. Rhonda Bergen (10812) 05:37:18
294. Maureen Schumacher (10820) 05:37:26
295. Nancy O'Brien (10857) 05:38:09
296. Jennie Zelig (10903) 05:39:13
297. Kathleen Drummy (10910) 05:39:20
298. Bonnie Stauch (10922) 05:39:45
299. Linda Orozcomartisko (10946) 05:40:13
300. Marie Macrorie (11025) 05:41:54
301. Sunny Castellon (11068) 05:42:29
302. Gloria Harrell (11075) 05:42:36
303. Shirley Kyles (11090) 05:42:52
304. Cheryllyn Lineberry (11098) 05:42:57
305. Joyce Bustos (11125) 05:43:30
306. Mariaelena Lucero (11135) 05:43:38
307. Linda Dinneny (11159) 05:44:06
308. Ruth Grenier (11177) 05:44:15
309. Rebecca Hoskins (11268) 05:45:37
310. Julie Salazar (11270) 05:45:39
311. Julie Landgard (11284) 05:45:58
312. Sonia Quezada (11286) 05:46:00
313. Brenda Johnson (11328) 05:46:48
314. Tina Booher (11340) 05:47:05
315. Rosemary Esparza (11363) 05:47:44
316. Shirley Cooper (11408) 05:49:06
317. Linda Lee (11419) 05:49:15
318. Michele Dea (11425) 05:49:21
319. Jan Fields (11433) 05:49:31
320. Sylvia Toste-Rodgers (11465) 05:49:53
321. Piedad Burmaz (11505) 05:50:30
322. Susan Slesinger (11544) 05:51:11
323. Mikki Siegel (11595) 05:52:20
324. Kenna Villanueva (11610) 05:52:43
325. Ruth Cope (11649) 05:53:19
326. Edwina Holguin (11650) 05:53:20
327. Judy Harman (11654) 05:53:23
328. Kathy Jaffe (11656) 05:53:24
329. Kris Ballinger (11657) 05:53:26
330. Toni Caylor (11676) 05:53:47
331. Gladys Vargas (11686) 05:53:55
332. Sue Berkman (11697) 05:54:10
333. Bonnie Ikemura (11699) 05:54:19
334. Gale Jamison (11706) 05:54:30
335. Kathy Miller (11710) 05:54:35
336. Cathie Slaughter (11725) 05:54:58
337. Robin Dilley (11731) 05:55:05
338. Mary Allport (11753) 05:55:25
339. Gail Rosenbaum (11800) 05:56:40
340. Harriet Cooks (11839) 05:57:30
341. Christina Davis (11847) 05:57:45
342. Sally Martinez (11864) 05:58:09
343. Wendy Gilmore (11893) 05:58:33
344. Emy Alona (11908) 05:58:51
345. Chris Hitchcock (11955) 05:59:57
346. Gina Greene-Cullins (12027) 06:01:57
347. Lorraine Cisneros (12034) 06:02:09
348. Deborah McMahon (12038) 06:02:18
349. Paula Gonzales (12054) 06:02:39
350. Cynthia Cohen (12077) 06:03:22
351. Lorie Bonis (12084) 06:03:37
352. Bhagwati Patel (12088) 06:03:44
353. Sherry Burrell (12130) 06:04:44
354. Cheryl Fox (12167) 06:05:32
355. Lady Esther Herrera (12203) 06:00:42
356. Jennifer Porter (12207) 06:06:53
357. Carol Ganci (12216) 06:07:10
358. Lena Ballesteros (12227) 06:07:22
359. Velvie Simpson (12235) 06:07:43
360. Millie Holmes (12257) 06:08:19
361. Yehudit Coutin (12261) 06:08:20
362. Nadine Skutnik (12300) 06:09:04
363. Lisa Harris (12302) 06:09:07
364. Drucie Riley (12332) 06:09:54
365. Snuwdie Bankhead (12351) 06:10:32
366. Elaine Gbur (12363) 06:10:59
367. Bebe Reynolds (12364) 06:11:00
368. Barbara Britton (12369) 06:11:03
369. Rachel Huber (12397) 06:11:38
370. Hilary Krawczyk (12421) 06:12:17
371. Christel Pareigis (12434) 06:12:44
372. Diane Shamhart (12445) 06:13:02
373. Maria Jaquez (12456) 06:13:17
374. Terri Ward (12457) 06:13:18
375. Lorraine Fleischmann (12467) 06:13:36
376. Karen Tanabe (12468) 06:13:36
377. Cynthia Huerta (12476) 06:13:48
378. Debbie Eubanks (12499) 06:14:08
379. Pamela Gelfand (12501) 06:14:22
380. Diane Tyler (12512) 06:14:43
381. Laurie Burpee (12581) 06:16:31
382. Yoletto Rios (12582) 06:16:32
383. Michal Bracha (12598) 06:16:52
384. Gerry O'Brien (12604) 06:19:59
385. Muriel Schonbachler (12722) 06:20:43
386. Mabel Taylor (12728) 06:21:10
387. Trinidad Ortega (12737) 06:21:27
388. Roberta Casato (12744) 06:21:34
389. Ann Dobberpuhl (12745) 06:21:35
390. Libby Manuelito (12768) 06:21:57
391. Norma Fragoso (12771) 06:22:00
392. Leonora Barron (12786) 06:22:29
393. Karen Ziskin (12794) 06:22:43
394. Cecilia Medellin (12809) 06:23:06
395. Maria Amaya (12813) 06:23:18
396. Sondra Budwig (12845) 06:23:54
397. Sue Mullins (12853) 06:24:09
398. Dharmaseeli Moses (12872) 06:24:49
399. Gail Campbell (12881) 06:25:12
400. Gail Goulet (12884) 06:25:23
401. Lillianmarie Munoz (12893) 06:25:40
402. Cath Fox (12908) 06:26:00
403. Dianne Godbout (12932) 06:26:36
404. Geri Burrows (12977) 06:28:01
405. Cecilia Orozco (13017) 06:29:08
406. Karen Willand (13029) 06:29:30
407. Diana Nunez (13033) 06:29:47
408. Mary Chandler (13083) 06:31:20
409. Judy Remland (13092) 06:31:33
410. Marta Sotelo (13153) 06:32:59
411. Judith Doll (13159) 06:33:05
412. Nayna Patel (13162) 06:33:06
413. Lunda Lightsy (13173) 06:33:35
414. Rosario Salazar (13176) 06:33:39
415. Terry Willard (13179) 06:33:50
416. Roseann Pulido (13207) 06:34:38
417. Patricia McKeever (13222) 06:34:57
418. Patricia Brenton (13232) 06:35:15
419. Hain Sullivan (13248) 06:35:45
420. Anne Gibeaut (13249) 06:35:46
421. Deborah Augborne-Allen (13263) 06:36:07
422. Libby Miranda (13315) 06:38:05
423. Paula Aliewine (13337) 06:38:55
424. Anne Looman (13363) 06:39:38
425. Sue Burchfiel (13377) 06:40:24
426. Bhuvana Viswanathan (13378) 06:40:25
427. Dilcia Sealey (13384) 06:40:34
428. Jeanne Hancock (13398) 06:40:58
429. Maggie O'Donnell (13399) 06:41:01
430. Estee Anderson (13414) 06:41:27
431. Jennifer Marple (13438) 06:42:16
432. Yolanda Pena-Duggan (13440) 06:42:21
433. Martha Hetzler (13493) 06:44:38
434. Betty Miller (13541) 06:46:18
435. Rene Brice (13542) 06:46:19
436. Eva Cup Choy (13551) 06:46:35
437. Ryoko Inada (13555) 06:46:43
438. Eva MacFarland (13572) 06:47:15
439. Venessa Carson (13586) 06:47:49
440. Flo Hinckley (13612) 06:48:34
441. Andy Washington (13617) 06:48:53
442. Katherine Liskey (13653) 06:50:02
443. Linda Davis (13657) 06:50:05
444. Carol Nylander (13661) 06:50:07
445. Yvonne Thompson (13665) 06:50:18
446. Libby Manuelito (13666) 06:50:22
447. Diana Velasquez (13676) 06:50:32
448. Susanne Sager (13711) 06:51:34
449. Cherie Province (13748) 06:53:13
450. Peggy Becker (13775) 06:54:42
451. Rosa Cervantes (13782) 06:54:57
452. Marta Lovasz (13795) 06:55:11
453. Marion Meitz (13813) 06:55:47
454. Jane Melville (13814) 06:55:47
455. Aida Hernandez (13817) 06:55:51
456. Gwendolyn Broaden (13861) 06:57:12
457. Linda Kepler (13862) 06:57:13
458. Carolyn Payne (13889) 06:58:02
459. Linda Embry (13892) 06:58:12
460. Mary Bradley (13914) 06:58:44
461. Stephanie Winfrey Caffarella (13939) 06:59:17
462. Costeina Hall-Daniels (13961) 07:00:18
463. Stephanie Lawrence (13977) 07:00:45
464. Barbara Wolff (13979) 07:00:47
465. Cathy Lawrence (13984) 07:00:55
466. Christel Quinn (14000) 07:01:10
467. Pamela Moore (14024) 07:02:10
468. Janet Mundy (14040) 07:02:41
469. Judy Knutson (14054) 07:03:24
470. Shirley Bates (14059) 07:03:47
471. Hazel Giyman (14086) 07:05:01
472. Bernice Hernandez (14120) 07:07:22
473. Margaret Hix (14123) 07:07:27
474. Valerie Cannon (14139) 07:08:33
475. Bertha Alatricto (14142) 07:08:50
476. Sonia Barksdale (14151) 07:09:35
477. Beverly Pasok (14156) 07:10:11
478. Caroline Vannorman (14184) 07:11:54
479. Diane Hight (14189) 07:12:10
480. Charis Forney (14200) 07:12:48
481. Masayo Miyake (14253) 07:15:34
482. Cecelia Gambrell (14267) 07:16:02
483. Gladys Vedol (14309) 07:18:57
484. Christine Simmons (14311) 07:18:58
485. Marianne Hinsberger (14319) 07:19:16
486. Nelly Canar (14334) 07:20:22
487. Roslyn Thomas (14337) 07:20:27
488. Johanna Wightman (14340) 07:20:46
489. Holly Holyk (14349) 07:21:13
490. Carolyn Graves (14387) 07:23:54
491. Michelle Martin (14391) 07:24:04
492. Evangeline Tumaliuan (14400) 07:24:49
493. Barbara Jilek (14423) 07:26:50
494. Rosemarie Lippman (14424) 07:26:50
495. Viola Murray (14439) 07:28:32
496. Lilian Sanchez Cordoba (14444) 07:28:59
497. Elsy Huete (14447) 07:29:26
498. Joan Dallis (14461) 07:30:21
499. K. Dancy Moore (14465) 07:30:31
500. Marsha Hawkins (14466) 07:30:32
501. Thuy Vu (14478) 07:31:39
502. Patsy Taylor (14482) 07:32:36
503. Margie Corona (14537) 07:36:26

504. Deena Altman (14544) 07:37:02
505. Margarita Whitehead (14561) 07:38:31
506. Barbara Fowler (14562) 07:38:33
507. Maureen Hessler (14580) 07:40:02
508. Mary Paradice (14588) 07:40:06
509. Karen Galvan (14589) 07:40:27
510. Margit Rubins (14606) 07:41:36
511. Ruby Moten (14611) 07:41:54
512. Margaret Hoebink (14614) 07:42:17
513. Janet Savage (14636) 07:44:52
514. Janice Jones (14655) 07:46:37
515. Mary Jane Lundin (14661) 07:47:16
516. Lavonne Johnson (14666) 07:47:33
517. Miriam Simmons (14674) 07:48:20
518. Gloria Pimentel (14701) 07:50:55
519. Carole Knight (14703) 07:51:05
520. Rebecca Escobar (14707) 07:51:38
521. Kristin Hamilton (14710) 07:51:43
522. Madeline Mozee (14712) 07:51:45
523. Deborah Dailey (14724) 07:52:30
524. Margaretha Cash (14729) 07:53:08
525. Fran Weber (14735) 07:53:51
526. Ellen Roth (14756) 07:55:28
527. Karin West (14757) 07:55:32
528. Ofelia Garcia (14764) 07:56:00
529. Norma Zelaya (14768) 07:56:07
530. Susan Whitehead (14771) 07:56:22
531. Ester Bailey (14778) 07:56:48
532. Teresa Anaya (14793) 07:59:56
533. Tina Hummel (14798) 08:00:38
534. Stanette Kennebrew (14815) 08:01:36
535. Elizabeth Bower (14822) 08:02:10
536. Valerie Johnson (14839) 08:03:29
537. Alicia Alcalder-Atkinson (14842) 08:03:49
538. Marcia Wade (14845) 08:04:58
539. Hilda Magaleno (14847) 08:05:17
540. Acexis Rhines Watson (14851) 08:06:46
541. Irma Llamosa (14868) 08:10:35
542. Melody Buchanan (14874) 08:11:15
543. Rosemarie Koscielny (14893) 08:14:53
544. Vickie Casino (14906) 08:16:50
545. Jennifer Cole (14912) 08:17:30
546. Ellen Bork (14913) 08:17:36
547. Wendy Nassiri (14917) 08:18:27
548. Tonie Valdez (14928) 08:19:32
549. Sandy Harbin (14930) 08:19:54
550. Charlesetta Jones (14939) 08:20:32
551. B J Atwood (14940) 08:21:03
552. Marla Jackson (14965) 08:25:22
553. Marianne Powell (14969) 08:26:18
554. Kathleen Maher (14972) 08:26:47
555. Nancy Perry (14974) 08:28:05
556. Wilma Almaraz (14977) 08:28:29
557. Gisele Lowy (14979) 08:28:38
558. Desiree Amos (14993) 08:30:42
559. Stephanie Banks (15022) 08:36:08
560. Ilania Frazier (15028) 08:36:32
561. Gail Chapman (15047) 08:45:52
562. Susan Clark (15059) 08:49:19
563. Vilas Pandya (15083) 08:56:45
564. Carole Klamfoth (15089) 08:57:57
565. Joycel Lundy (15103) 09:09:20
566. Vivian Tanamachi (15107) 09:11:00
567. Aura Meng (15149) 09:48:40
568. Mary Youngblood (15167) 10:07:13

MEN 45 TO 49

1. John Bednarski (39) 02:36:40
2. Randy Winn (41) 02:37:02
3. Klaus Pester (49) 02:40:47
4. Jussi Hamalainen (60) 02:42:54
5. Carlos Ruiz (61) 02:43:00
6. Dennis Bock (64) 02:43:37
7. Baldomero Bernudez Garcia (77) 02:45:42
8. Michael Andrade (133) 02:53:20
9. Humberto Carrasco (164) 02:55:56
10. Matt Jordan (170) 02:56:28
11. Frank Bressendorf (182) 02:57:07
12. Faustino Campos (189) 02:57:28
13. Ray Parker (214) 02:59:04
14. Charly Sanchez (255) 03:01:25
15. Moretti Giuseppe (262) 03:02:05
16. Jean Pierre Daumy (290) 03:03:14
17. Carlos Banderas (316) 03:04:40
18. Paul Garnett (323) 03:05:10
19. Donald Ocana (324) 03:05:12
20. Joe Murillo (335) 03:05:42
21. Dennis Huffman (341) 03:05:57
22. Patrick Kalen (342) 03:06:07
23. William McNelly (353) 03:06:33
24. Estanislao Rodriguez (355) 03:06:46
25. Anthony Servio (357) 03:06:47
26. Camilo Gregorio (381) 03:07:44
27. Joseph Kaplan (386) 03:07:54
28. Mickey Dopalo (389) 03:07:57
29. Maurilio Amezcua (391) 03:08:07
30. Richard Holly (400) 03:08:20
31. Carlos Saturno (411) 03:08:45
32. Larry Owens (420) 03:09:08
33. Alphonzo Jackson (435) 03:09:34
34. Bill Steiner (438) 03:09:39
35. Jack Boyster (454) 03:10:01
36. Glenn Morigaki (460) 03:10:20
37. Lou Briones (464) 03:10:34
38. Alan Saunders (466) 03:10:38
39. Alan Thompson (473) 03:10:59
40. Michael Smith (485) 03:11:18
41. Terry Cammack (495) 03:12:00
42. Vicente Romero (498) 03:12:08
43. Don McLean (504) 03:12:17
44. Hazziz Ali (514) 03:12:39
45. Edson Sanches (526) 03:13:02
46. Arie Dagon (534) 03:13:18
47. Edward Hunt (539) 03:13:27
48. Alan White (541) 03:13:30
49. John Helm (546) 03:13:38
50. Hans Horder (568) 03:14:08
51. Joseph Banach (583) 03:14:35
52. Jeff Bristow (588) 03:14:42
53. James Rucker (590) 03:14:43
54. Douglas Brooms (593) 03:14:50
55. Arturo Castro (601) 03:15:12
56. Bill Ernst (610) 03:15:32
57. Jeffrey Mintz (631) 03:16:21
58. Arturo Ramirez (651) 03:16:52
59. Carlos Martinez (687) 03:17:44
60. Bill Sampson (693) 03:17:59
61. Daniel Martin (707) 03:18:27
62. Richard Massa (736) 03:19:20
63. Patrick Harlan (765) 03:20:03
64. Raul Nava Ramos (774) 03:20:14
65. Hiroshi Moriyasu (781) 03:20:27
66. Micheal Griffith (802) 03:21:11
67. Ian Sebastian (817) 03:21:29
68. Robert Traller (821) 03:21:33
69. Cliff Housego (823) 03:21:39
70. Gary Patrick (830) 03:21:43
71. Gustavo Gonzalez (836) 03:21:58
72. Joseph Rizza (871) 03:22:40
73. Walter Bodan (873) 03:22:42
74. Yose Lopez (901) 03:23:19
75. Paul Bishop (911) 03:23:34
76. Gunnar Thowsen (912) 03:23:34
77. Horacio Sanchez (918) 03:23:40
78. Kent De Pew (927) 03:23:50
79. Frederick Hanhauser (929) 03:23:55
80. Graham Rose (938) 03:24:04
81. Georges Barrere (945) 03:24:17
82. Philip Beauchamp (947) 03:24:19
83. Barry Rittberg (951) 03:24:23
84. David Book (962) 03:24:33
85. Steve Farrah (970) 03:24:47
86. Rick Andrews (988) 03:25:11
87. Leroy Anderson (990) 03:25:14
88. Pedro Rodriguez (997) 03:25:24
89. Richard Schaefer (1007) 03:25:39
90. Paul Semnacher (1039) 03:26:23
91. Paul Kleinmann (1045) 03:26:36
92. Allan Milliken (1046) 03:26:38
93. Jose Paez (1056) 03:26:50
94. Kenneth Sako (1058) 03:26:54
95. Saul Serrano (1059) 03:26:55
96. Gabriel Ramirez (1060) 03:26:57
97. Ramon Quirarte (1075) 03:27:16
98. Vincent McMillen (1081) 03:27:21
99. Lou Urzua (1094) 03:27:33
100. Gilberto Amillano (1097) 03:27:36
101. Stephen Stroud (1105) 03:27:41
102. Robert Adjemian (1111) 03:27:51
103. Doug Kinn (1125) 03:28:05
104. Gil Meachum (1126) 03:28:05
105. August Simien Jr (1138) 03:28:16
106. Paul Liming (1153) 03:28:32
107. Charles Paz (1164) 03:28:50
108. Jerry Kisling (1204) 03:29:34
109. Perry Garth (1211) 03:29:37
110. Jesse Hernandez (1236) 03:30:08
111. Dominique Pena (1240) 03:30:13
112. Eulalio Mendez (1253) 03:30:26
113. Donald Bettencourt (1262) 03:30:35
114. Jim Pool (1268) 03:30:50
115. Hiroshi Kimura (1279) 03:30:57
116. Porfirio Castro (1295) 03:31:20
117. Gustavo Valenzuela (1296) 03:31:21
118. Joseph Harvey (1307) 03:31:29
119. Frankie Dowey (1309) 03:31:30
120. Alan Woodruff (1316) 03:31:37
121. Mario Gaitan (1319) 03:31:39
122. Ralph Semprevio (1320) 03:31:39
123. Carlos Alaniz (1326) 03:31:45
124. Rick Auerbach (1342) 03:32:06
125. Michel Baudry (1346) 03:32:10
126. John Lester (1361) 03:32:27
127. Joseph Lyvers (1368) 03:32:39
128. Rob Russell (1381) 03:32:51
129. Brent Delameter (1398) 03:33:09
130. William Surridge (1409) 03:33:30
131. Edward Barraza (1427) 03:34:02
132. Robert Williams (1429) 03:34:03
133. Paul Allen (1436) 03:34:05
134. Jim Rivas (1444) 03:34:14
135. Steve Kohler (1445) 03:34:15
136. Hendrik Van Der Hoven (1470) 03:34:52
137. Scot Hunter (1490) 03:35:12
138. Moo Lim (1533) 03:35:56
139. Alfonso Ramirez (1537) 03:36:01
140. Leon Figueroa (1547) 03:36:14
141. John Mah (1551) 03:36:17
142. John Cochra (1565) 03:36:38
143. Carl Galloway (1568) 03:36:41
144. Daniel Mergil (1571) 03:36:43
145. Don Echols (1612) 03:37:22
146. John Scribner (1633) 03:37:54
147. Rich Morales (1635) 03:37:54
148. Rick Kalinowski (1636) 03:37:55
149. Maurice King (1641) 03:37:59
150. Paul Woods (1644) 03:38:02
151. Gary Hiltunen (1651) 03:38:09
152. Daniel Pillasch (1666) 03:38:19
153. Caru Das (1684) 03:38:44
154. Alex Jones (1693) 03:38:51
155. Bryan Hayward (1701) 03:39:00
156. Kozo Yamada (1702) 03:39:02
157. Francisco Rosito (1721) 03:39:21
158. Jean Pierre Auvinet (1732) 03:39:35
159. Timothy Lynch (1735) 03:39:37
160. Reid Nathan (1738) 03:39:40
161. Fritz Jaeger (1747) 03:39:48
162. Wilfrido Hernandez (1750) 03:39:53
163. Joseph Gilroy (1753) 03:39:54
164. Albert Allen (1754) 03:39:55
165. Jose Hernandez (1766) 03:40:12
166. Gary Barker (1782) 03:40:23
167. Arturo Garcia (1805) 03:40:43
168. Bill Babbitt (1808) 03:40:49
169. Lloyd Fukuda (1810) 03:40:52
170. Ramon Garcia (1811) 03:40:52
171. Ruben Gomez (1829) 03:41:04
172. Patrick McGovern (1840) 03:41:13
173. Abel Umogbai (1857) 03:41:23
174. Lloyd Miller (1859) 03:41:26
175. Mick Hemp (1865) 03:41:31
176. Joe Armstrong (1884) 03:41:45
177. Michael Powles (1885) 03:41:46
178. Dan Orr (1888) 03:41:48
179. David Gerald Syms (1916) 03:42:16
180. Ernest Molina (1938) 03:42:44
181. Roger Richards (1942) 03:42:51
182. James Brueggemann (1948) 03:43:02
183. John Poidevin (1951) 03:43:05
184. Gary Campbell (1953) 03:43:07
185. Linden Wise (1983) 03:43:33
186. Wim Sijen (2024) 03:44:11
187. Jonathan Steele (2041) 03:44:23
188. Ron Negrete (2048) 03:44:29
189. Russell Patrick (2070) 03:44:44
190. Bohuslav Barlow (2078) 03:44:53
191. Douglas Shannon (2086) 03:44:59
192. William Lovelace (2089) 03:45:00
193. John Butcher (2102) 03:45:12
194. Philippe Greard (2136) 03:45:43
195. John Lee (2148) 03:45:52
196. Jack Conrad (2155) 03:45:56
197. Michael Fejes (2157) 03:45:57
198. Raymond Gossett (2162) 03:46:03
199. Juan Castaneda (2168) 03:46:09
200. Mitch Lansdell (2170) 03:46:11
201. Sergio Lazaro (2175) 03:46:14
202. Thomas Trujillo (2180) 03:46:21
203. George Miyazato (2194) 03:46:33
204. Grant Lawless (2195) 03:46:35
205. Werner Duerst (2197) 03:46:42
206. Jacob De Koeyer (2205) 03:46:52
207. Victor Cabrera (2210) 03:46:54
208. Joseph Costa (2219) 03:46:59
209. Hermann Poehling (2224) 03:47:04
210. Richard Picheny (2240) 03:47:18
211. Michael Spiro (2267) 03:47:42
212. Jorge Cordon (2274) 03:47:45
213. Al Perez (2311) 03:48:14
214. Lev Stachkevitch (2321) 03:40:22
215. Mel Hutchison (2341) 03:48:37
216. Carl Zika (2342) 03:48:37
217. Bert Estrada (2344) 03:48:38
218. Michael McQuerrey (2376) 03:49:07
219. Robert Staley (2388) 03:49:16
220. Wayne Landis (2412) 03:49:34
221. Bernardo Rodriguez (2441) 03:49:57
222. Philip Coupland (2452) 03:50:07
223. Hoo Chung (2469) 03:50:23
224. John Frisch (2485) 03:50:35
225. Jack Murphy (2522) 03:51:03
226. Richard Haas (2528) 03:51:08
227. Paul Evraire (2535) 03:51:17
228. Juan Cueva (2549) 03:51:28
229. Raymond Tiberg (2553) 03:51:29
230. Christian Hardy (2581) 03:51:52
231. Doug Crimmel (2583) 03:51:55
232. Michael Guasti (2591) 03:51:59
233. Larry Ward (2594) 03:52:04
234. Grady Buck (2607) 03:52:17
235. Jose De Alba (2611) 03:52:20
236. Lars Clutterham (2634) 03:52:37
237. Rafael Zamora (2646) 03:52:46
238. Rene Carmona (2649) 03:52:47
239. George Harker III (2653) 03:52:48
240. Robert O'neill (2668) 03:53:00
241. Cortland Stark (2677) 03:53:09
242. Dana White (2692) 03:53:19
243. Santiago Ramos (2701) 03:53:25
244. Dave Dobrow (2724) 03:53:43
245. Wally Oakes (2735) 03:53:51
246. Guy Bolduc (2736) 03:53:51
247. Edward Kies (2746) 03:54:01
248. Okutani Yoshinori (2753) 03:54:09
249. Bob Vlloa (2756) 03:54:10
250. John Peterson (2784) 03:54:26
251. Howard Loeb (2800) 03:54:35
252. Francisco Sanabria (2809) 03:54:42
253. Peter Durham (2820) 03:54:47
254. Clayton Behm (2827) 03:54:52
255. Manuel Garcia (2829) 03:54:54
256. Richard Hargis (2837) 03:55:02
257. John Kay (2838) 03:55:03
258. John Barcellona (2845) 03:55:08
259. Michael Donish (2848) 03:55:11
260. Louis Cammarota (2849) 03:55:12
261. John Fernandez (2854) 03:55:14
262. Tom Kilgore (2856) 03:55:15
263. Charles Didinger (2859) 03:55:18
264. Salvador Lara Salvador (2871) 03:55:26
265. Stevem Teays (2873) 03:55:27
266. Auggie Gomez (2874) 03:55:27
267. Bruce Mauldin (2878) 03:55:28
268. Victor Levoit (2881) 03:55:29
269. Steven Evans (2885) 03:55:31
270. Wayne Wightman (2899) 03:55:44
271. Joe Orozco (2901) 03:55:45
272. Stanley Joffe (2910) 03:55:54
273. Steve Notaro (2914) 03:55:55
274. Rohn Walker (2933) 03:56:07
275. Bill Trapp (2940) 03:56:11
276. Pete Noftz (2949) 03:56:17
277. Raymond Ybarra (2953) 03:56:20
278. Tom Harvey (2965) 03:56:29
279. Andrew Quinn (2984) 03:56:45
280. Joe Valdez (2985) 03:56:45
281. Mark Krenzien (2994) 03:56:47
282. Denis Abrams (2995) 03:56:47
283. Jun Potts (2998) 03:56:48
284. Miguel Ovando (3003) 03:56:50
285. Larry Fambrough (3027) 03:57:02
286. Grant Williams (3033) 03:57:03
287. Federico De Alba Guzman (3034) 03:57:04
288. Camerino Resendiz (3036) 03:57:06
289. David Keeling (3046) 03:57:13
290. Ken Hill (3062) 03:57:25
291. David Munoz (3070) 03:57:30
292. Ibra Morales (3079) 03:57:37
293. Phil Richards (3095) 03:57:47
294. Daniel Noonan (3100) 03:57:50
295. Harrison Long (3112) 03:57:56
296. Jerry O'Donnell (3114) 03:57:57
297. Robert Hernandez (3131) 03:58:11
298. Richard O'Neil (3140) 03:58:20
299. Ron Brusca (3159) 03:58:33
300. Bill Yanez (3163) 03:58:35
301. Jack Spaulding (3164) 03:58:36
302. Jonah Johnson (3171) 03:58:40
303. Stephen Weed (3188) 03:58:52
304. John Randolph Backman (3199) 03:59:00
305. Ronald Eichler (3203) 03:59:03
306. Gregory Brown (3207) 03:59:04
307. Mario Franco Jr (3224) 03:59:20
308. Robert Korechoff (3227) 03:59:20
309. L Jeff Butzlaff (3233) 03:59:26
310. Carlos Prieto (3250) 03:59:38
311. Kimio Naito (3274) 03:59:50
312. Steve Watts (3277) 03:59:51
313. Peter Fiamengo (3286) 03:59:54
314. Silvestre Cortez (3287) 03:59:54
315. Edward Grageda (3312) 04:00:08
316. David Brink (3337) 04:00:27
317. Richard Forrester (3354) 04:00:42
318. Rick Salas (3358) 04:00:46
319. Jean Flemion (3368) 04:00:55
320. Steve Frank (3374) 04:01:00
321. James Geary (3379) 04:01:02
322. Karl Sauer (3385) 04:01:05
323. Gordon Wang (3386) 04:01:06
324. Dan Klausen (3387) 04:01:08
325. Harry Bash (3390) 04:01:10
326. Stephen Cohen (3435) 04:01:42
327. Jeffrey White (3484) 04:02:24
328. Thomas Duval (3499) 04:02:39
329. Barry Van Patten (3528) 04:03:05
330. Francisco Arevald (3536) 04:03:12
331. Thomas Husman (3541) 04:03:21
332. Ronald Nixon (3543) 04:03:23
333. Peter Specker (3548) 04:03:25
334. David Eisenhart (3569) 04:03:42
335. Kendall Wagner (3570) 04:03:42
336. David Love (3580) 04:03:55
337. Richard Gaines (3587) 04:04:01
338. Paul Howard (3588) 04:04:02
339. Bill Sigafoos (3593) 04:04:08
340. Dan Carroll (3595) 04:04:10
341. Peter Aguirre (3597) 04:04:10
342. Francisco Hernandez Sanchez (3606) 04:04:14
343. Timothy Knappen (3610) 04:04:15
344. Eduardo Merida (3618) 04:04:21
345. Richard Campanella (3631) 04:04:30
346. Craig Vaughan (3635) 04:04:32
347. Lynn Carlington (3639) 04:04:33
348. Todd Hoover (3654) 04:04:43
349. Michael Albanese (3669) 04:04:52
350. Ruben Rosales (3673) 04:04:54
351. Jerry Bonds (3685) 04:05:02
352. Mark Giebel (3691) 04:05:07
353. Tom Gawley (3697) 04:05:10
354. Ward Nyhus (3702) 04:05:12
355. Michael Marcus (3708) 04:05:20
356. Gary Mann (3730) 04:05:39
357. Hechtor Venegas Vazquez (3748) 04:05:55
358. Christopher McComb (3750) 04:05:57
359. David Giannotti (3772) 04:06:13
360. Richard Fearn (3778) 04:06:21
361. Henry Gracia Jr (3787) 04:06:28
362. Linsey Ewell (3789) 04:06:29
363. Francis Haton (3803) 04:06:40
364. Paul Piplani (3810) 04:06:43
365. Martin Brody (3814) 04:06:46
366. Fred Whitson (3825) 04:06:56
367. Robert Kawamoto (3827) 04:06:57
368. Jay Madhure (3832) 04:06:59
369. Steve Suto (3844) 04:07:05
370. George Durr (3847) 04:07:06
371. Frank Rugani (3865) 04:07:20
372. Jeff Ter Keurst (3871) 04:07:27
373. Tim Mason (3874) 04:07:29
374. Mike Jamieson (3883) 04:07:34
375. Gar Wilson (3894) 04:07:40
376. Joe Banda (3923) 04:08:08
377. Eric Richter (3926) 04:08:10
378. Paul Myers (3932) 04:08:15
379. Michael Penkert (3951) 04:08:23
380. Kyung Chiang (3953) 04:08:24
381. Andrew Gomez (3961) 04:08:30
382. Tom Jackman (3963) 04:08:34
383. Pascual Barcena (3968) 04:08:41
384. Christopher Smith (3972) 04:08:44
385. Paul Sullivan (3992) 04:09:00
386. Bill Diederich (4005) 04:09:09
387. Luis Espinosa (4010) 04:09:13
388. Stephen Parker (4011) 04:09:14
389. Herman Avilez (4012) 04:09:15
390. Ned Albright (4020) 04:09:21
391. Hector Menchaca (4025) 04:09:23
392. William Lyons (4026) 04:09:24
393. Robert McDaniel (4039) 04:09:36
394. Jerry Lebowitz (4054) 04:09:49
395. Gary Davis (4056) 04:09:52
396. Randall Jost (4063) 04:09:57
397. Steve Fichter (4080) 04:10:10
398. Ron Cakurai (4094) 04:10:17
399. Craig Chambers (4108) 04:10:33
400. Jose Perez (4143) 04:10:56
401. Michael Hernandez (4146) 04:10:57
402. Bob Merzoian Jr (4171) 04:11:12
403. Balaji Keshava (4173) 04:11:13
404. Sean Riley (4191) 04:11:30
405. Norman Kerr (4200) 04:11:38
406. Willie Spinoza (4211) 04:11:50
407. Alan Romansky (4221) 04:11:58
408. Phillip Thomason (4232) 04:12:04
409. Michael Estelle (4234) 04:12:05
410. Lud Cibelli (4240) 04:12:12
411. Bill Harrington (4244) 04:12:14
412. Christopher Nicoletti (4256) 04:12:23
413. Richard Hammervold (4288) 04:12:47
414. David Steinberger (4293) 04:12:53
415. John Pratt (4297) 04:12:55
416. Tomas Fierro (4331) 04:13:20
417. Neil Macey (4335) 04:13:21
418. Fernando Vizcarra (4382) 04:14:00
419. Kenneth Berry (4384) 04:14:01
420. David Follett (4390) 04:14:04
421. Joseph Scaggs (4414) 04:14:21
422. Jay Smith (4424) 04:14:26
423. Jacob Wolstein (4427) 04:14:28
424. Giovanni Tromba (4437) 04:14:34
425. Jim Hilger (4446) 04:14:38
426. Walter Savage (4455) 04:14:43
427. Ernest Lareau (4461) 04:14:45
428. Michael Winter (4473) 04:14:50
429. Walt Walters (4474) 04:14:51
430. Ulysses Abeita (4481) 04:14:54
431. Brian Considine (4486) 04:14:58
432. Thomas Kesterson (4493) 04:15:02
433. Bob Demay (4507) 04:15:16
434. Joseph Franko (4535) 04:15:34
435. Martin Graham (4556) 04:15:45
436. Chuck Henderson (4575) 04:15:58
437. Michael Turon (4591) 04:16:06
438. Larry Satler (4595) 04:16:09
439. James Coburn (4599) 04:16:12
440. Stuart Cannold (4608) 04:16:20
441. Michael Spatola (4651) 04:16:44
442. Andres Perez (4652) 04:16:49
443. Gary Navin (4664) 04:16:58
444. Michael Fry (4687) 04:17:17
445. Karoly Buzasi (4691) 04:17:21
446. Paul Hernandez (4706) 04:17:31
447. David Johnson (4712) 04:17:37
448. Randall Reece (4716) 04:17:40
449. Steve Crane (4718) 04:17:42
450. Heriberto Contreras (4723) 04:17:49
451. William Carter (4732) 04:17:53
452. Jose Gudino (4749) 04:18:03
453. Ken Klein (4768) 04:18:14
454. Howard Clark (4776) 04:18:22
455. Everett Wilson (4792) 04:18:31
456. Andy Alvidrez (4797) 04:18:36
457. Dean King (4803) 04:18:39
458. Clennon Taylor (4817) 04:18:45
459. Thomas Swain (4822) 04:18:49
460. Alfonso Garibay (4830) 04:18:53
461. Jim Kelso (4844) 04:18:59
462. Lester Powell (4850) 04:19:02
463. Michael Jones (4870) 04:19:15
464. Robocop Del Campo (4891) 04:19:29
465. Jeffrey Smith (4909) 04:19:41
466. Ismael Herrera (4926) 04:19:53
467. Carlos Thornton (4927) 04:19:55
468. Robert Montelongo (4934) 04:19:59
469. Darrell Voth (4940) 04:20:03
470. Thomas Kelley (4942) 04:20:04
471. Randall Ziglar (4943) 04:20:05
472. Fernando Pacheco Urcadiz (4952) 04:20:14
473. Humberto Morales (4971) 04:20:33
474. Antonio Jorge Rosales Ramires (4999) 04:20:59
475. George Kaliope (5003) 04:21:03
476. Don Anderson (5029) 04:21:24
477. Gregory Ewertz (5031) 04:21:26
478. Ron Grusd (5034) 04:21:30
479. David Dixon (5041) 04:21:34
480. Paul Gore (5047) 04:21:38
481. Fred Salter (5071) 04:21:51
482. David Berry (5072) 04:21:51
483. Manuel Vasquez (5087) 04:21:56
484. Lloyd Sweet (5098) 04:22:03
485. Richard Slack (5106) 04:22:07
486. Joe Salinas (5124) 04:22:18
487. John Reid (5170) 04:22:53
488. Russell Linderman (5173) 04:22:55
489. Larry Inadomi (5174) 04:22:55
490. Donald Farrar (5201) 04:23:13
491. Daniel Castanaza (5200) 04:23:16
492. Takao Saiki (5226) 04:23:29
493. Steve Hudson (5251) 04:23:51
494. Takashi Suto (5259) 04:24:03
495. Jim Heller (5272) 04:24:12
496. Pedro Vazquez (5285) 04:24:25
497. Richard Jeffries (5295) 04:24:30
498. Alberto Bobadilla (5314) 04:24:39
499. Alex Nevgloski (5322) 04:24:48
500. Hugo Paiagonia (5327) 04:24:53
501. Salvador Monroy (5345) 04:25:04
502. James Watt McCormick (5370) 04:25:18
503. Hector Gonzalez (5373) 04:25:20
504. Bill Edmonds (5377) 04:25:22
505. David Villanueva (5380) 04:25:23
506. William Boswell (5391) 04:25:28
507. Steve Peterson (5401) 04:25:37
508. James Mikkelson (5417) 04:25:44
509. David Nesmith (5430) 04:25:52
510. Arthur Barela (5432) 04:25:53
511. Tim Matthieson (5458) 04:26:08
512. Eleazar Flores (5481) 04:26:27
513. James Grimes (5490) 04:26:33
514. Carlos Martinez (5516) 04:26:56
515. James PON (5517) 04:26:56
516. Dale Jackson (5535) 04:27:10
517. Robert Novell (5540) 04:27:12
518. Dale Beldin (5550) 04:27:20
519. Ed Christopher (5558) 04:27:23
520. Philip Fuchs (5571) 04:27:31
521. Gonzalo Melgoza (5573) 04:27:32
522. Raul Perez (5583) 04:27:39
523. Rob Gandin (5588) 04:27:40
524. John Ortega (5602) 04:27:48
525. Steve Shaffer (5614) 04:27:57
526. Jose Ramirez (5621) 04:28:01
527. Mark O'Reilly (5624) 04:28:02
528. Moise Hendeles (5636) 04:28:10
529. Frank Piermarini (5645) 04:28:14
530. Steven Nadler (5662) 04:28:28
531. Ronald Stinchcomb (5670) 04:28:33
532. Jaime Villa (5672) 04:28:35
533. Mark Sperling (5695) 04:28:49
534. Andrew Gillespie (5698) 04:28:51
535. Jesus Roman (5700) 04:28:53
536. Thomas Wilson (5705) 04:28:57
537. Alfonso Barragan (5706) 04:28:58
538. John Adame (5728) 04:29:07
539. Peter Frey (5748) 04:29:21
540. Jerry Coffey (5749) 04:29:23
541. Bob Turrietta (5750) 04:29:24
542. Manny Torrez (5785) 04:29:48
543. Henry Espinoza (5788) 04:29:51
544. Robert Murcott (5795) 04:29:56
545. Ryoji Inoda (5815) 04:30:14
546. Marco Mejia (5849) 04:30:33
547. Gary Brugman (5850) 04:30:33
548. Armand Miranda (5857) 04:30:35
549. Donald Hutchinson (5885) 04:30:49
550. Joe Chacon (5890) 04:30:53
551. Bruce Gietzen (5896) 04:30:57
552. Nicholas Such (5906) 04:31:05
553. Kennith Thompson (5945) 04:31:29
554. James Bixler (5959) 04:31:42
555. Paul Bonds (5995) 04:32:08
556. Vladimir Lange (5998) 04:32:13
557. Richard Guerrero (6024) 04:32:31
558. Rick Morsch (6064) 04:33:01
559. Ron Felix (6065) 04:33:02
560. Roberto Ruvalcaba (6084) 04:33:14
561. Don Ploeser (6096) 04:33:21
562. Larry Reeves (6105) 04:33:28
563. David Saine (6108) 04:33:29
564. Bruce Sutherland (6124) 04:33:40
565. Richard Radkay (6126) 04:33:41
566. Martin Ramos (6139) 04:33:50
567. Dale Koelling (6144) 04:33:54
568. Mitsuo Mori (6152) 04:34:04
569. Yafet Tekle (6160) 04:34:09

570. Gary McMillen (6162) 04:34:09
571. Stan Maddison (6165) 04:34:09
572. Donald Morse (6170) 04:34:11
573. Calvin Lau (6171) 04:34:11
574. Thomas Phillips (6180) 04:34:21
575. David Escoto (6187) 04:34:25
576. Charles Pollick (6199) 04:34:31
577. Robert Fambrini (6208) 04:34:39
578. Ray Menzies (6234) 04:34:54
579. Brian Silver (6249) 04:35:05
580. Winston Alt (6254) 04:35:09
581. Jim Baumann (6264) 04:35:16
582. Jan Schulte (6265) 04:35:17
583. Louw Jacobs (6275) 04:35:22
584. Robert Hildebrandt (6305) 04:35:40
585. Daniel Louradour (6307) 04:35:41
586. David Pedroza (6316) 04:35:47
587. Richard Brenner (6317) 04:35:48
588. Frederick Merkin (6323) 04:35:51
589. Manuel Romero (6326) 04:35:52
590. Tomohisa Nago (6330) 04:35:54
591. Joseph Krogstad (6337) 04:35:57
592. Paul Lapierre (6338) 04:35:57
593. James Babcock (6343) 04:36:06
594. Feliciano Hernandez Cantor (6347) 04:36:08
595. Wesley Steele (6348) 04:36:09
596. K Lance Tyler (6363) 04:36:16
597. Paul Kelly (6383) 04:36:25
598. Carl Franklin (6414) 04:36:40
599. Waheed Balogun (6422) 04:36:46
600. Jim Love (6424) 04:36:47
601. Andrew Walko (6438) 04:37:05
602. Donald Choi (6448) 04:37:14
603. Jose Navarro (6450) 04:37:15
604. Ken Miyamoto (6466) 04:37:26
605. Gary Naragon (6493) 04:37:39
606. Steven Patrick (6499) 04:37:42
607. Lawrence Diggs (6501) 04:37:43
608. Denny Fryman (6517) 04:37:51
609. Duane Litz (6518) 04:37:53
610. Kraig Marton (6539) 04:38:07
611. Anibal Cabral (6561) 04:38:17
612. Ignak Mazadiego (6585) 04:38:36
613. Mauro Cicchini (6591) 04:38:40
614. Sergio De La Cruz (6592) 04:38:40
615. Donald Hardy (6594) 04:38:41
616. Anthony Dean (6597) 04:38:42
617. Richard Stoecklein (6601) 04:38:42
618. Richard Popper (6622) 04:38:57
619. Peter Kappelos (6624) 04:38:57
620. James Varga (6627) 04:38:58
621. Simon Silbertasch (6632) 04:39:00
622. David Salzman (6638) 04:39:08
623. Robert Peterson (6640) 04:39:10
624. David Padberg (6653) 04:39:20
625. Timothy Butler (6675) 04:39:38
626. William Turk (6676) 04:39:39
627. Apolinar Pimentel (6695) 04:39:49
628. Joe Cordova (6702) 04:39:53
629. Sergio Cedillo (6710) 04:40:01
630. James Kowalski (6716) 04:40:05
631. Fred Yeilding (6719) 04:40:09
632. John Shipman (6722) 04:40:11
633. Jose Lopez Hernandez (6727) 04:40:18
634. Stephen Sakamoto (6734) 04:40:21
635. James Gutzwiller (6735) 04:40:22
636. Michael Beekman (6736) 04:40:23
637. Allen Munro (6784) 04:41:05
638. David Grice (6786) 04:41:05
639. Charles Gorentein (6792) 04:41:09
640. Garydean Jones (6820) 04:41:34
641. Steven Ito (6828) 04:41:38
642. Pete Martinez (6869) 04:42:07
643. Greg Kidman (6871) 04:42:07
644. Amer Omar (6876) 04:42:13
645. Yotin Sadjatumwadee (6888) 04:42:26
646. Roger Sutton (6892) 04:42:30
647. Thomas Farley (6902) 04:42:38
648. Armando Lamb (6913) 04:42:47
649. Manuel Gonzalez (6935) 04:43:00
650. Robert Ollins (6947) 04:43:06
651. Miguel Gonzalez (6983) 04:43:28
652. Ronald Crittendon (6991) 04:43:31
653. Jesse Trevino (6992) 04:43:31
654. Reggie Rigamat (7016) 04:43:44
655. Steve Read (7021) 04:43:53
656. James Lace (7024) 04:43:54
657. Natverlal Patel (7028) 04:43:56
658. Dan Scuri (7030) 04:43:57
659. Desi Rhoden (7031) 04:43:58
660. Jose Vidauri (7050) 04:44:14
661. Michael Raneses (7065) 04:44:23
662. Vincenzo Benevento Jr (7066) 04:44:23
663. Martin Swanson (7072) 04:44:31
664. Jack Daley (7089) 04:44:48
665. Jose Chanez (7105) 04:44:56
666. David Hill (7106) 04:44:56
667. Barry Lederman (7115) 04:45:02
668. Joseph Tomei (7119) 04:45:04
669. Stephen Denison (7142) 04:45:21
670. Rene Herard (7146) 04:45:30
671. Kazuyuki Yoshida (7164) 04:45:41
672. Samuel Cann Jr (7168) 04:45:42
673. Jim Crutchfield (7183) 04:45:56
674. Joe Miyamoto (7205) 04:46:10
675. Kent Petersen (7215) 04:46:17
676. Leonardo Torras (7227) 04:46:27
677. Richard Clausman (7232) 04:46:31
678. Steve Zeppegno (7241) 04:46:35
679. Robert Beck (7244) 04:46:36
680. Lee Mallory (7257) 04:46:45
681. Matthew Leung (7273) 04:46:57
682. Albin Watson (7290) 04:47:09
683. Jose Montoya (7318) 04:47:27
684. Ron Silvis (7330) 04:47:32
685. Jay Burbank (7335) 04:47:37
686. James Rodriguez (7353) 04:47:51
687. Ted Raychek (7373) 04:48:07
688. Paul Karasik (7395) 04:48:17
689. Se Kim (7420) 04:48:36
690. Ant Salazar (7426) 04:48:40
691. Edward Mann (7428) 04:48:44
692. Denis Stokes (7433) 04:48:46
693. Joseph Borda (7452) 04:48:58
694. Bhanu Patel (7453) 04:48:58
695. Gregory Willis (7458) 04:49:02
696. Bruce MacDonald (7464) 04:49:05
697. John Smith (7467) 04:49:07
698. Mitch Golant (7525) 04:49:37
699. James Miller (7547) 04:49:56
700. David Thompson (7549) 04:49:58
701. Stephen Riley (7570) 04:50:15
702. Steve Zukmann (7584) 04:50:25
703. Fred Rosenfelt (7593) 04:50:33
704. Donald Cyphers (7595) 04:50:35
705. Chester Mitchell (7609) 04:50:45
706. Harry Thad Morris (7635) 04:51:01
707. David Clunn (7650) 04:51:27
708. James Caver (7664) 04:51:32
709. Venkataraman Sambasivan (7666) 04:51:32
710. Gray Ellrodt (7693) 04:51:50
711. Marty Nash (7694) 04:51:52
712. Steven Simons (7697) 04:51:54
713. Manuel Fernandez (7705) 04:52:01
714. George Atilano (7719) 04:52:12
715. Paul Skok (7722) 04:52:14
716. Bruce Cholakian (7731) 04:52:23
717. Stu Van Bibber (7732) 04:52:24
718. Lawrence Lavenberg (7734) 04:52:26
719. Joseph Kendall (7752) 04:52:41
720. Roberto Escobar (7774) 04:52:56
721. Michael Morrow (7786) 04:53:03
722. John Rademacher (7803) 04:53:17
723. Herb Eisenberg (7800) 04:53:21
724. Peter Kinman (7816) 04:53:27
725. Devadas Moses (7822) 04:53:30
726. Peter Suttichanond (7839) 04:53:39
727. Michael Gombar (7854) 04:53:51
728. Joseph Wiger (7868) 04:53:59
729. Francis Akahoshi (7870) 04:54:01
730. Ken Lowlor (7875) 04:54:05
731. Rick Hodges (7877) 04:54:06
732. Wade Laquire (7884) 04:54:09
733. Wayne Schirner (7892) 04:54:16
734. Kunio Hayashi (7896) 04:54:18
735. Benny Anderson (7916) 04:54:29
736. John Moskal Jr (7923) 04:54:32
737. Robert Westphaln (7941) 04:54:39
738. Deepak Bondade (7962) 04:54:48
739. Jon Challgren (7964) 04:54:48
740. James Ford Sr (7981) 04:55:08
741. John Odell (7996) 04:55:20
742. Robert Kniceley (8001) 04:55:25
743. Edward Colburn (8003) 04:55:27
744. Bob Morris (8011) 04:55:34
745. Steven Scully (8012) 04:55:34
746. Steven Pettit (8015) 04:55:35
747. Doyle Hubbell (8016) 04:55:36
748. Vince Regala (8021) 04:55:42
749. Orville Ware (8024) 04:55:44
750. Rick Brosca (8025) 04:55:45
751. Dana Carmody (8031) 04:55:48
752. Eli Montoya (8045) 04:55:58
753. Peter Carlson (8046) 04:55:59
754. Dale Nelson (8063) 04:56:12
755. Bud Lacy (8065) 04:56:14
756. Ralph Bailey (8066) 04:56:15
757. R K Chetty (8067) 04:56:16
758. Ignacio Gonzalez (8083) 04:56:29
759. David King (8131) 04:57:04
760. Joe Wegener (8149) 04:57:18
761. Allan Knight (8165) 04:57:28
762. Joe Lickteig (8175) 04:57:37
763. David Stuyvenberg (8180) 04:57:39
764. Don Anderson (8190) 04:57:48
765. Ruben Cardona (8201) 04:57:56
766. Modesto Augilar (8202) 04:57:56
767. James Bryce (8205) 04:57:58
768. Stephen De La Rosa (8212) 04:58:01
769. Dennis Wong (8228) 04:58:09
770. Jones Low (8229) 04:58:12
771. Perry Morse (8256) 04:58:25
772. Douglas Wright (8267) 04:58:31
773. Roger Palmer (8287) 04:58:48
774. Lou Ramirez (8362) 04:59:36
775. Jackson Sleet (8374) 04:59:43
776. David Harris (8398) 05:00:01
777. Jack Nelson (8405) 05:00:10
778. Harold Staples (8421) 05:00:22
779. Jim Dunleavy (8441) 05:00:51
780. Dennis Koci (8461) 05:01:04
781. Salvador Sandoval (8474) 05:01:13
782. Raul Flores (8497) 05:01:28
783. William Hinz (8500) 05:01:32
784. Bruce Campopiano (8518) 05:01:43
785. Marshall Castillo (8519) 05:01:43
786. John McGann (8557) 05:02:11
787. Carlos Encinas (8562) 05:02:15
788. Ik Son (8590) 05:02:44
789. Chris Ellie (8591) 05:02:44
790. Juan Gordo (8632) 05:03:22
791. Victor Avila (8639) 05:03:31
792. Sam Utley (8660) 05:03:50
793. Joe Gallagher (8661) 05:03:53
794. John Nann (8664) 05:03:53
795. John Fleming (8674) 05:04:00
796. Tom Townsen (8690) 05:04:12
797. Jerry Sydow (8703) 05:04:20
798. Harvey Alperin (8706) 05:04:21
799. Jerry Woods (8709) 05:04:25
800. Robert Larry Evans (8727) 05:04:44
801. Jesse Corpus Sr (8749) 05:05:13
802. Carlos Mansille (8753) 05:05:16
803. Ken Hirth (8766) 05:05:29
804. John Jocz (8769) 05:05:32
805. Laurence Mercer (8771) 05:05:33
806. Joel Lobel (8775) 05:05:35
807. Dave Price (8806) 05:06:07
808. Frank PON (8813) 05:06:16
809. Clifford Olson (8842) 05:06:49
810. Rod Torres (8845) 05:06:54
811. Raymond Bell Jr (8895) 05:07:44
812. Vicente Garhoa (8905) 05:07:51
813. Ron Guerrer (8916) 05:08:01
814. Paul Mundry (8918) 05:08:03
815. Glenn Higaki (8921) 05:08:06
816. Robert Gillis (8922) 05:08:07
817. Gary Buehm (8933) 05:08:13
818. Murray Teitell (8959) 05:08:38
819. Shiro Kageyama (8978) 05:08:47
820. John Patterson (8997) 05:09:06
821. Leslie Bennett (9004) 05:09:09
822. Steve Schleier (9007) 05:09:11
823. Vicente Villegas (9010) 05:09:13
824. Mike Lopertido (9017) 05:09:21
825. Michael Johnston (9018) 05:09:21
826. Lawrence Meyer (9042) 05:09:44
827. Dave Butler (9048) 05:09:47
828. John West (9064) 05:09:59
829. Jerry Bragg (9070) 05:10:01
830. Roger Myers (9088) 05:10:14
831. Ronald Robinson (9115) 05:10:26
832. Brian Muldoon (9120) 05:10:28
833. Bill Deom (9133) 05:10:45
834. Mike Bayer (9141) 05:10:54
835. Matthew Pope (9143) 05:10:54
836. Vince Ellescas (9150) 05:11:00
837. Miguel Iturbe (9171) 05:11:28
838. Edmund Wong (9184) 05:11:38
839. Richard Greenig (9192) 05:11:42
840. Darryl Munson (9207) 05:11:54
841. Wendall Hubbard (9237) 05:12:28
842. Fermin Rivas (9258) 05:12:49
843. Jeffrey Bettinger (9288) 05:13:16
844. Kimm Richardson (9292) 05:13:18
845. Guadalupe Alba (9299) 05:13:26
846. Sooren Karayan (9316) 05:13:33
847. Vazgen Aghajani (9324) 05:13:38
848. Richard Ruddock (9327) 05:13:39
849. Samuel Villanueva (9329) 05:13:40
850. Leonel Aquino (9338) 05:13:47
851. John Bradford (9360) 05:14:02
852. Miguel Cruz (9374) 05:14:15
853. Marty Bowin (9376) 05:14:17
854. Jeffrey Urband (9411) 05:14:56
855. Rafael Garay (9445) 05:15:35
856. Paul Seto (9464) 05:15:59
857. Richard Serocki (9466) 05:16:00
858. John Boyd (9478) 05:16:14
859. Tadashi Nagayama (9489) 05:16:21
860. Robert Soliz (9527) 05:16:52
861. Orlando Rivas (9543) 05:17:04
862. Rodney Owens (9552) 05:17:10
863. Craig Cummings (9566) 05:17:22
864. Paul Anderson (9587) 05:17:40
865. Tetsuo Sakai (9589) 05:17:42
866. Fred Kingdon (9608) 05:18:01
867. Greg Campbell (9614) 05:18:09
868. Ernesto Miranda (9630) 05:18:28
869. Shigenobu Okada (9634) 05:18:30
870. Edward Schuppe (9646) 05:18:38
871. Jose Luis Gutierrez (9662) 05:18:53
872. Michael Teixeira (9669) 05:18:59
873. Lonnie Harris (9676) 05:19:04
874. Greg Duran (9686) 05:19:13
875. Carlos Argueta (9687) 05:19:14
876. George Quashie (9711) 05:19:37
877. Michael Clark (9761) 05:20:35
878. Randy Chin Yee (9762) 05:20:35
879. John Brown (9777) 05:20:45
880. Rohitkumar Vasa (9793) 05:20:56
881. Thomas Whitley (9797) 05:20:58
882. Jeffrey Leites (9828) 05:21:35
883. Peter Means (9841) 05:21:42
884. Dale Fuller (9855) 05:21:52
885. Moxy De Mira (9867) 05:22:02
886. Paul White (9872) 05:22:03
887. Hector Murataya (9902) 05:22:34
888. Victor Bhatt (9957) 05:23:34
889. Richard Brys (9958) 05:23:34
890. Masao Mitsui (9960) 05:23:39
891. John Mitchell (9963) 05:23:42
892. Noah Rollins (9965) 05:23:42
893. Paul Parr (9980) 05:24:01
894. Efren Arias (9988) 05:24:05
895. Gary Spradlin (9991) 05:24:07
896. Bruce Jones (9999) 05:24:14
897. William Watson (10005) 05:24:27
898. William Everson (10017) 05:24:37
899. Phil Barrett (10019) 05:24:43
900. George Baker III (10022) 05:24:47
901. Luis Alver (10025) 05:24:51
902. John Rand (10043) 05:25:10
903. Vincent Dulcich (10047) 05:25:16
904. Michio Komatsu (10051) 05:25:21
905. Johnnie Smith (10056) 05:25:31
906. Burke Painter (10063) 05:25:36
907. Bill Tom (10093) 05:25:57
908. Gary Wagoner (10099) 05:26:06
909. Jeffrey Weber (10118) 05:26:24
910. Tokio Shigeishi (10124) 05:26:33
911. Ron Morgan (10133) 05:26:39
912. George Nieva (10168) 05:27:20
913. Kazutoshi Hori (10175) 05:27:24
914. Jeffrey Gershoff (10192) 05:27:36
915. Veera Tangsakula (10195) 05:27:37
916. Jim McLaughlin (10199) 05:27:45
917. Justo Rivera (10202) 05:27:46
918. Sherwin Boucher (10204) 05:27:47
919. Roger Peter (10214) 05:27:57
920. Robert Lee (10225) 05:28:05
921. Chuck O'Shea (10230) 05:28:09
922. Werner Rose (10238) 05:28:34
923. Leo Hernandez (10253) 05:28:38
924. Lawrence Yates (10262) 05:28:46
925. John Melville (10275) 05:28:53
926. Cecil Redmond (10302) 05:29:14
927. Michael Fandal (10309) 05:29:16
928. Larry Dozier (10323) 05:29:30
929. Frank Cazares (10326) 05:29:33
930. Salvador Flemate (10330) 05:29:45
931. David Schroer (10337) 05:29:52
932. Edward Salmon (10354) 05:30:08
933. Scott Cline (10379) 05:30:30
934. John Janisch (10385) 05:30:35
935. Charles Page (10391) 05:30:38
936. Umesh Dip (10395) 05:30:39
937. Bill Hicks (10404) 05:30:49
938. Kip Kerlin (10423) 05:31:12
939. Robert Oshita (10430) 05:31:21
940. David Segura (10437) 05:31:26
941. Jong Kim (10446) 05:31:30
942. Leo Cotter (10463) 05:31:47
943. Lorenzo Gonzalez (10564) 05:33:26
944. Robert Madison (10569) 05:33:28
945. Albert Vaughn (10570) 05:33:28
946. Raj Vasan (10591) 05:33:43
947. Frank Cooper II (10599) 05:33:50
948. Hank Smith (10617) 05:34:04
949. Bob Hillard (10629) 05:34:08
950. Walter Sanchez (10634) 05:34:23
951. Jim Stickler (10682) 05:35:02
952. Sun Lee (10683) 05:35:03
953. John Santiago (10686) 05:35:06
954. Joe Fox (10705) 05:35:26
955. Paul Garcia Jr (10718) 05:35:38
956. Satoshi Yamazaki (10722) 05:35:40
957. Ronnie Lee (10731) 05:35:50
958. Anthony Dipasquale (10741) 05:36:03
959. Fernando Tapia (10743) 05:36:05
960. Michael Pfeifer (10744) 05:36:07
961. Jay Martinez (10771) 05:36:36
962. Jerry Williams (10779) 05:36:40
963. Javier Rodriguez (10789) 05:36:52
964. Michael Gill (10792) 05:36:56
965. Eladio Mendoza (10832) 05:37:37
966. Craig Moisio (10836) 05:37:42
967. Van Hutchins (10849) 05:37:59
968. Alfred Munguia (10863) 05:38:14
969. Glenn Palmer (10885) 05:38:50
970. James Larson (10895) 05:38:57
971. Michael Wang (10932) 05:39:53
972. James Montgomery (10953) 05:40:22
973. Richard Embry (10964) 05:40:35
974. Abol Badani (10970) 05:40:45
975. Stuart Sachs (10981) 05:41:07
976. Chuok Narcho (11002) 05:41:30
977. Michael Whitehead (11010) 05:41:39
978. Dennis Roberson (11019) 05:41:46
979. Ken Sandford (11043) 05:42:12
980. Michael Goldman (11060) 05:42:23
981. Young Park (11086) 05:42:44
982. Jeff Steinberger (11089) 05:42:49
983. Michael Arteaga (11091) 05:42:52
984. Greg Goltz (11111) 05:43:11
985. Richard Jean (11127) 05:43:31
986. Earl Vinson (11128) 05:43:32
987. William Alban (11136) 05:43:39
988. Harvey Cogen (11145) 05:43:50
989. Kinji Takei (11146) 05:43:50
990. David Uwins (11187) 05:44:21
991. Arturo Ortiz (11196) 05:44:28
992. Ray Nakatani (11204) 05:44:33
993. Raymond Cule (11206) 05:44:34
994. Ralph Riccatelli (11251) 05:45:18
995. T C Hou (11259) 05:45:27
996. Marlin Owen (11261) 05:45:28
997. Stuart Caudillo (11262) 05:45:29
998. David Burciaga (11271) 05:45:39
999. Ruben Jauregui (11303) 05:46:18
1000. Paul Martinez (11304) 05:46:19
1001. Mark Levinson (11305) 05:46:21
1002. Chuck Harget (11307) 05:46:23
1003. Keiji Watanabe (11308) 05:46:24
1004. Jasper Ayala (11309) 05:46:27
1005. Nimrod Mabaquiao (11333) 05:46:52
1006. Richard Ackley (11361) 05:47:37
1007. Jaime Ludmir (11364) 05:47:44
1008. John Rusling (11372) 05:47:58
1009. Frank Fernandez (11374) 05:48:03
1010. David Rodrigues (11378) 05:48:15
1011. Monte Khoshnevisan (11381) 05:48:20
1012. Alex Lopez (11392) 05:48:50
1013. Richard Elliott (11401) 05:48:59
1014. Peter Scheibenreif (11426) 05:49:22
1015. Mike Gardner (11428) 05:49:28
1016. Stephen Fraser (11434) 05:49:31
1017. Pete Coffin (11437) 05:49:33
1018. Reid Smith (11438) 05:49:34
1019. Stephen Doyle (11450) 05:49:44
1020. Douglas Kinzle (11457) 05:49:48
1021. Max Kord (11471) 05:50:03
1022. Dennis Johns (11479) 05:50:10
1023. Franklin Moreno (11482) 05:50:12
1024. Jesse Mota (11503) 05:50:30
1025. Ronald Ribstein (11528) 05:50:53
1026. Howard Einberg (11529) 05:50:53
1027. Michael Gissing (11530) 05:50:54
1028. Ernest Rivera (11553) 05:51:28
1029. Seishiro Shioda (11567) 05:51:51
1030. Kenneth Williams (11572) 05:52:07
1031. Lonnie Morgan (11581) 05:52:10
1032. Richard Gurman (11586) 05:52:13
1033. Ronald Schlaifer (11632) 05:53:01
1034. Ernie Stucki (11639) 05:53:09
1035. Bruce Harman (11655) 05:53:24
1036. Harold Babb (11660) 05:53:30
1037. Frederick Garcia (11672) 05:53:42
1038. Telmo Acevedo (11694) 05:54:04
1039. Dominique Lecoq (11704) 05:54:29
1040. Dervin Collims (11708) 05:54:34
1041. Jose Britto (11739) 05:55:14
1042. Gerald Emery (11746) 05:55:20
1043. Thurman Robinson (11755) 05:55:29
1044. Rand Anderson (11761) 05:55:40
1045. Robert Simmons (11769) 05:55:48
1046. Russell Yamanaka (11777) 05:55:59
1047. Richard Snyder (11804) 05:56:44
1048. Gene Hernandez (11819) 05:56:59
1049. Dale Alojipan (11848) 05:57:47
1050. Romeo Montemayor (11868) 05:58:13
1051. Ben Park (11885) 05:58:27
1052. James Yazzie (11895) 05:58:36
1053. James Grivich (11902) 05:58:45
1054. Christopher Chadwick (11979) 06:00:30
1055. Ernie Mercado (11984) 06:00:38
1056. Payakapan Polrath (11985) 06:00:41
1057. Don Dotulong (11996) 06:01:03
1058. Andres Cervantes (11998) 06:01:05
1059. Earnest Joyce (12010) 06:01:31
1060. Dennis Gray (12045) 06:02:22
1061. Jim Presley (12062) 06:02:50
1062. Geoff Dutton (12063) 06:02:52
1063. Henry Kubo (12085) 06:03:39
1064. Francisco Luistro Jr (12116) 06:04:36
1065. Richard Kimmel (12174) 06:04:41
1066. Ryan Scott (12128) 06:04:43
1067. Ray Abeyta (12149) 06:05:12
1068. Jack Berger (12156) 06:05:21
1069. J D Boswell (12190) 06:06:14
1070. Jose Torres (12198) 06:06:26
1071. John Alexander (12213) 06:07:05
1072. George Garcia (12244) 06:07:58
1073. Michael Murphy (12274) 06:08:41
1074. Joel Potts (12291) 06:08:57
1075. David King (12318) 06:09:35
1076. Frank Sabato (12329) 06:09:50
1077. Ernesto Trinidad (12337) 06:10:00
1078. Michael Yoomans (12348) 06:10:20
1079. Eric Joseph (12372) 06:11:05
1080. Lee Williams (12408) 06:11:55
1081. Bruce Cuyle (12475) 06:13:47
1082. Anthony Marquez (12503) 06:14:24
1083. John Thvedt (12510) 06:14:41
1084. Fulogio Mamaril (12542) 06:15:27
1085. Gary Jones (12582) 06:15:55
1086. Don Estes (12596) 06:16:50
1087. John Graham (12611) 06:17:03
1088. Tom Givens (12612) 06:17:03
1089. Raymond Haymon (12638) 06:18:16
1090. John Lara (12648) 06:18:27
1091. William Christofferson (12650) 06:18:30
1092. Joe Blancas (12653) 06:18:33
1093. Robert Gonzaga (12661) 06:18:56
1094. Steven Maline (12662) 06:19:03
1095. William Parker (12675) 06:19:25
1096. Rene Lopez (12692) 06:19:52
1097. Pedro Vasquez (12706) 06:20:19
1098. Stephen Sommers (12719) 06:20:39
1099. Buenaventura Cube Jr (12764) 06:21:53
1100. Dom Braswell (12777) 06:22:06
1101. William Caloudes (12781) 06:22:14
1102. Willie Martinez (12803) 06:22:50
1103. Calvin Newman (12828) 06:23:39
1104. Art Salter (12837) 06:23:48
1105. Suvie John David (12851) 06:24:07
1106. Harry Griffith (12858) 06:24:16
1107. Ashok Shah (12865) 06:24:22
1108. Frank Glavan (12869) 06:24:41
1109. John Rozenbergs (12873) 06:24:50
1110. Marcus Cisneros (12883) 06:25:22
1111. Santiago Barberena (12888) 06:25:27
1112. Dean Bisterfeldt (12909) 06:26:01
1113. Jorge Gegea (12919) 06:26:23
1114. Archie Salary (12936) 06:26:46
1115. Carlos Montiel (12951) 06:27:24
1116. Alex Buys (12979) 06:28:03
1117. Danny Winne (13022) 06:29:17
1118. Robert Heredia (13027) 06:29:28
1119. Ashok Patel (13069) 06:31:01
1120. Ashok Kumar (13071) 06:31:04
1121. Douglas Gangwer (13073) 06:31:05
1122. Bill Sturges (13084) 06:31:20
1123. Harald Azuma (13088) 06:31:31
1124. Aristotales Elkaddoum (13101) 06:31:51
1125. Phillip Kirkpatrick (13134) 06:32:42
1126. Bob Seijas (13147) 06:32:49
1127. John Doll (13160) 06:33:05
1128. Herbert Belt (13177) 06:33:43
1129. Ross Lewis Jr (13210) 06:34:42
1130. Billie Moore (13214) 06:34:47
1131. David Martinez Jr (13223) 06:35:00
1132. Skip Deal (13231) 06:35:13
1133. Sam Zorrilla (13256) 06:36:00
1134. Glen Seto (13257) 06:36:05
1135. Edgar Bertumen (13272) 06:36:21
1136. Jorge Rodriguez (13303) 06:37:33
1137. Steve Villa (13317) 06:38:16
1138. Johnnie Jameson (13334) 06:38:48
1139. Iristeal Thomas (13336) 06:38:52
1140. William Blanco (13365) 06:39:42
1141. Dan Elias (13373) 06:40:02
1142. Cagle Moore (13444) 06:42:33
1143. Christopher Forte (13475) 06:43:51
1144. Daniel McKenzie (13498) 06:44:53
1145. John Cosgrove (13508) 06:45:14
1146. Clifford Mosby (13517) 06:45:24
1147. Lawrence Piper (13529) 06:45:56
1148. Calvin Jones (13590) 06:47:51
1149. Ronaldo Geronimo (13621) 06:48:57
1150. Bruce Rapport (13671) 06:50:27
1151. Tomas Espinoza (13689) 06:50:43
1152. Gene Pukite (13694) 06:50:53
1153. Jack Wear (13778) 06:54:48
1154. Louis Velazquez (13812) 06:55:46
1155. Al Plotkine (13823) 06:55:55
1156. Anthony Di Bari (13863) 06:57:14
1157. Santiago Griego (13906) 06:58:34
1158. Thomas Sitter (14028) 07:02:17
1159. John Avvampato (14060) 07:03:55
1160. Ronald Jauch (14090) 07:05:23
1161. James Corbett (14103) 07:06:32
1162. Ray Curry III (14136) 07:08:28
1163. Samuel Jackson (14201) 07:12:52
1164. John Durham (14218) 07:13:43
1165. Godofredo Astudillo (14233) 07:14:39
1166. Steve Keene (14237) 07:14:42
1167. Richard Vasquez (14250) 07:15:29
1168. Somio Miyazaki (14290) 07:17:25
1169. Howard Stark (14304) 07:18:26
1170. Geoff Gillie (14342) 07:20:47
1171. Tom Van Vliet (14347) 07:21:11
1172. Lee Schroder (14355) 07:21:40
1173. Franklin Blumer (14359) 07:21:58
1174. Irvin Henry Jr (14401) 07:24:50
1175. Theodore Westerhold (14442) 07:28:54
1176. Charles Carson (14470) 07:30:40
1177. Jesus Acosta (14473) 07:31:05
1178. Donald Hubus (14488) 07:33:06
1179. Ray Griffin (14498) 07:33:38
1180. Richard Sokolowski (14526) 07:35:52
1181. Jim Hazard Jr (14541) 07:36:52
1182. Percy Pleasant (14547) 07:37:04
1183. David Noguchi (14626) 07:43:13
1184. Ronald Simmons (14675) 07:48:21
1185. Vic Gutierrez (14679) 07:48:40
1186. Robert Aleria (14690) 07:49:51
1187. Gene Avila (14691) 07:49:52
1188. John Slowe (14693) 07:49:56
1189. Michael Brunelle (14760) 07:55:40
1190. Charles Williams Sr (14785) 07:58:39
1191. Doug Thompson (14801) 08:00:56
1192. Cesar Montes (14856) 08:07:56
1193. Jesus Hernandez (14861) 08:09:03
1194. David McKeever (14878) 08:11:44
1195. Ciro Ferreira (14899) 08:16:20
1196. Godofredo Astudillo (14907) 08:16:51
1197. Alex Manzano (14910) 08:17:14
1198. George Ruiz (14929) 08:19:43
1199. Larry Barbeaux (14937) 08:20:28
1200. Hugh Lawrence (14942) 08:21:06
1201. Warren Atwood (14944) 08:21:14
1202. Rafael Martinez (14955) 08:22:34
1203. Danny Churchill (14992) 08:30:31
1204. Richard Anderson (15003) 08:32:49
1205. Michael Dingman (15010) 08:34:12
1206. Kenneth Besse (15014) 08:34:44

1207. Bradford McAllen (15091) 08:59:51

WOMEN 45 TO 49

1. Kathleen Slinger (1076) 03:27:16
2. Julie Lister (1099) 03:27:37
3. Gloria McCoy (1418) 03:33:47
4. Mary Campbell (1614) 03:37:23
5. Marygail Brauner (1670) 03:38:27
6. Ruth Higley (1767) 03:40:13
7. Chantal Haton (1862) 03:41:28
8. Lee Denham (2011) 03:44:02
9. Cathy Caballero (2104) 03:45:13
10. Patricia Bates (2444) 03:50:01
11. Randy Pollock (2561) 03:51:37
12. Sharon Shorer (2577) 03:51:49
13. Marilyn Howard (2780) 03:54:25
14. Wendy Lusby (2787) 03:54:27
15. Estella Elizondo (2833) 03:54:58
16. Valerie Henning (2974) 03:56:36
17. Verna Evans (3037) 03:57:07
18. Catherine Kaspersky (3059) 03:57:22
19. Barbara Vantighem (3105) 03:57:53
20. Judy Boehme (3381) 04:01:02
21. Kathy Sweo (3393) 04:01:13
22. Nelida Arnez (3483) 04:02:24
23. Belinda Holguin (3500) 04:02:40
24. Sandra Israel (3523) 04:03:02
25. Rosalia Mireles (3891) 04:07:39
26. Linda Silver (3905) 04:07:47
27. Janice Garcia-Diaz (4243) 04:12:13
28. Martha Darby (4304) 04:13:01
29. Rose Okumoto (4342) 04:13:27
30. Adell Williams (4380) 04:13:59
31. Stephanie Ebia (4484) 04:14:56
32. Sharlene Cadwallader (4534) 04:15:34
33. Sheila Jackson (4539) 04:15:35
34. Barbara Reukema (4571) 04:15:53
35. Sue Reinhardt (4583) 04:16:02
36. Eiko Petty (4586) 04:16:03
37. Renee Russell (4614) 04:16:25
38. Dorothy Sparks (4618) 04:16:27
39. Gloria Rivas (4751) 04:18:03
40. Susan Guenard (4796) 04:18:34
41. Irma Hutton (4866) 04:19:13
42. Harriet Shapiro (4902) 04:19:38
43. Maryann Anderson (4949) 04:20:10
44. Gila Schneider (4973) 04:20:34
45. Penelope O'Donnell (5156) 04:22:42
46. Elizabeth Priedkalns (5158) 04:22:43
47. Carole Goldberg-Ambrose (5179) 04:22:57
48. Carolyn Slade (5180) 04:22:58
49. Sandra Tripp (5324) 04:24:49
50. Sharyn Slick (5340) 04:25:00
51. Karen Lessman (5374) 04:25:20
52. Verene Baglin (5400) 04:25:36
53. Ellen Pearlman (5424) 04:25:50
54. Ellen Reinstein (5425) 04:25:50
55. Joan Miller (5427) 04:25:51
56. Elaine Heilig (5477) 04:26:26
57. Sandy Cammack (5480) 04:26:26
58. Frankie Gragg (5530) 04:27:08
59. Kathleen O'Hare (5608) 04:27:54
60. Anita Greenberg (5677) 04:28:37
61. Ana Maria Cain (5733) 04:29:14
62. Judith Morton (5819) 04:30:17
63. Alicia Alvarez De Sainz (5839) 04:30:28
64. Elizabeth Bell (5908) 04:31:06
65. Marie McCoy (5974) 04:31:53
66. Susan Jones (6001) 04:32:16
67. Ellyn Flaherty (6021) 04:32:29
68. Shirley Lester (6028) 04:32:37
69. Patricia Swan (6087) 04:33:15
70. Cathy Abrams (6119) 04:33:36
71. Peggy Liebelt (6149) 04:34:00
72. Cathi Hofstetter (6175) 04:34:15
73. Diane Buckman (6189) 04:34:25
74. Margaret Butterworth (6365) 04:36:17
75. Molly Montgomery (6378) 04:36:24
76. Linda Siqueiros (6451) 04:37:16
77. Cipriana Rolando (6538) 04:38:07
78. Rosa Turcios (6581) 04:38:33
79. Kathleen Chan (6587) 04:38:38
80. Shaie-Mei Temple (6604) 04:38:45
81. Linda Whiting (6649) 04:39:13
82. Lisa Felder (6721) 04:40:10
83. Marvis Friesen (6754) 04:40:39
84. Miguel Perez (6758) 04:40:41
85. Maggie Ennis (6783) 04:41:04
86. Bertha Marineo (6804) 04:41:21
87. Diane Ito (6827) 04:41:38
88. Pam Smart (6830) 04:41:40
89. Susy Wagner (6850) 04:41:54
90. Norma Severloh (6909) 04:42:46
91. Sylvia Baldino (6975) 04:43:23
92. Karen Melford (6987) 04:43:29
93. Kathy Blattner (7137) 04:45:17
94. Maria Payne (7377) 04:48:10
95. Dale Roseberry (7389) 04:48:14
96. Theresa Riley (7401) 04:48:23
97. Natalia De Los Santos (7402) 04:48:24
98. Barbara Whitsitt (7471) 04:49:09
99. Susan Kuntz (7483) 04:49:15
100. Sue Lemaire (7569) 04:50:14
101. Adele Williams (7572) 04:50:16
102. Bonnie Ades (7634) 04:51:01
103. Linda Hiltunen (7663) 04:51:31
104. Joycie Yee (7730) 04:52:21
105. Doreen Bhatt (7748) 04:52:37
106. Jane Granskog (7756) 04:52:43
107. Kathleen Morrow (7783) 04:53:01
108. Char Abeyta (7792) 04:53:11
109. Jessica Dunning (7800) 04:53:16
110. Heather Hodges (7817) 04:53:27
111. Linda Arborn (7965) 04:54:49
112. Jane Tomlinson (7988) 04:55:11
113. Eileen Cohen (8006) 04:55:29
114. Peggy Johnson (8009) 04:55:31
115. Marcia Zacharias (8029) 04:55:48
116. Elizabeth Russell (8047) 04:56:00
117. Denise Jones (8090) 04:56:33
118. Marie Ocafrain (8099) 04:56:39
119. Joan Schulte (8152) 04:57:20
120. Margaret Pinuelas (8285) 04:58:47
121. Sharlene Wills (8303) 04:58:55
122. Rosemarie Rieger (8306) 04:58:56
123. Alexandria Phillips (8318) 04:59:03
124. Diane Lich (8350) 04:59:27
125. Sandi Askew (8400) 05:00:04
126. Donna Willinson (8513) 05:01:40
127. Cassadra Johnson (8570) 05:02:20
128. Klara Zysman (8606) 05:03:04
129. Ana Buylding (8821) 05:06:24
130. Johnnie De'laney (8861) 05:07:08
131. Dara Fairchild (8883) 05:07:32
132. Nixia Johnson (8934) 05:08:13
133. Tonee Bertalan (8976) 05:08:44
134. Hilda Garcia-Parra (9054) 05:09:52
135. Kathy Edmonds (9149) 05:11:00
136. Darla Hochhalter (9159) 05:11:10
137. Tonya Mauldin (9173) 05:11:30
138. Iris Bellson (9188) 05:11:39
139. Paula Zizzi (9216) 05:12:06
140. Linda Patterson (9227) 05:12:19
141. Pamela Roberts (9236) 05:12:27
142. Lynda Lariosa (9245) 05:12:36
143. Kareen Fulce (9274) 05:13:05
144. Ruth Bettinger (9287) 05:13:15
145. Carol Belcher (9304) 05:13:28
146. Guadalupe Angeles (9314) 05:13:32
147. Silvia Rodriguez (9438) 05:15:27
148. Deborah Talbott (9454) 05:15:51
149. Rosalinde Reece (9463) 05:15:58
150. Barbara Allan (9486) 05:16:19
151. Nancy Deloge (9520) 05:16:45
152. Martina Travis-Blount (9522) 05:16:46
153. Barbara Dixon (9615) 05:18:11
154. Artis Fleming (9627) 05:18:26
155. Cyndy Burgess (9691) 05:19:15
156. Jean Connor (9697) 05:19:23
157. Susan James (9698) 05:19:23
158. Naomi Hornstock (9723) 05:19:51
159. Bonnie Wright (9827) 05:21:33
160. Sandra Donaldson (9889) 05:22:18
161. Sally Nicholson (9935) 05:23:17
162. Rosario Rivera (9955) 05:23:33
163. Erlinda Cooper (10037) 05:25:02
164. Lynn James (10086) 05:25:50
165. Barbara Allen (10102) 05:26:08
166. Robyn Varho (10167) 05:27:18
167. Susan Klutnick (10190) 05:27:34
168. Joyce Williams (10347) 05:29:58
169. Katy Stewart (10382) 05:30:32
170. Irma Lopez (10417) 05:31:08
171. Rebecca Deitrich (10433) 05:31:24
172. Sylvia Ramos (10435) 05:31:26
173. Jan Bleiweiss (10468) 05:31:49
174. Carol Slavik (10469) 05:31:49
175. Judy Wolfe (10497) 05:32:15
176. Sharon Moseley (10498) 05:32:16
177. Judy Munzig (10499) 05:32:17
178. Dora Mesa (10516) 05:32:42
179. Dorothy Rodgers (10523) 05:32:51
180. Barbara Suto (10541) 05:33:01
181. Amy Allen (10561) 05:33:26
182. Marsha Martin (10671) 05:34:54
183. Kathleen Bryan (10677) 05:35:00
184. Margie Sabo (10695) 05:35:20
185. Rose Fox (10704) 05:35:25
186. Martha Munoz (10719) 05:35:38
187. Gloria Marin (10732) 05:35:52
188. Connie Lopez (10746) 05:36:10
189. Susan Kahn (10756) 05:36:18
190. Anneda Dahlstrom (10783) 05:36:47
191. Carolyn McGrath (10807) 05:37:11
192. Lilia Vaudreuil (10809) 05:37:13
193. Letitia Nahaku (10810) 05:37:14
194. Lynette Creasy (10824) 05:37:30
195. Jan Nikaido (10929) 05:39:50
196. Leslie Derbish (10945) 05:40:12
197. Tressie Woods (10982) 05:41:07
198. Esmeralda Fucci (11036) 05:42:06
199. Edvernor Burney (11072) 05:42:34
200. Cristine Trapp (11096) 05:42:56
201. Kathy Tardy-Vallernaud (11104) 05:43:04
202. Lynn Hybbert (11109) 05:43:07
203. Dorothy Allen (11140) 05:43:43
204. Linda Pincombe (11195) 05:44:27
205. Trish Hittinger (11250) 05:45:17
206. Angie McCaffery (11312) 05:46:34
207. Marilyn Hoch (11318) 05:46:39
208. Joyce Jacobs (11349) 05:47:19
209. Betty Gomez (11402) 05:49:00
210. Susan Meisinger (11446) 05:49:42
211. Margie Cherry (11520) 05:50:41
212. Sarah Hromish (11526) 05:50:48
213. Jeanne Robertson (11548) 05:51:18
214. Katie Azouz (11551) 05:51:24
215. Susan Cherritt-Nave (11554) 05:51:30
216. Mary Foley (11559) 05:51:38
217. Dianne Young (11768) 05:55:46
218. Tawney Anderson (11774) 05:55:55
219. Jeffree Kundrat (11879) 05:58:25
220. Maura Potillo (11884) 05:58:27
221. Cookie Avvampato (11925) 05:59:23
222. Velma Blue (11929) 05:59:24
223. Uta Robinson (11934) 05:59:32
224. Ann Frisch (11942) 05:59:45
225. Donna Brown (11954) 05:59:56
226. Barbara Felts (11958) 05:59:59
227. Eileen Doyle (11965) 06:00:14
228. Nancy Lindner (11976) 06:00:28
229. Esther Crump (11977) 06:00:28
230. Vivian Watts (12009) 06:01:28
231. Bev Byran (12015) 06:01:42
232. Jeanine Johnson-Caloudes (12018) 06:01:45
233. Laura Blackwell (12019) 06:01:45
234. Soussan Arfaania (12026) 06:01:54
235. Carmalita Bernardo (12069) 06:03:07
236. Maribel Martinez (12072) 06:03:10
237. Gloria Lockhart (12112) 06:04:30
238. Nancy Romero (12118) 06:04:37
239. Irene Realyvasquez (12165) 06:05:31
240. Linda Peace (12178) 06:05:50
241. Corinne Romero (12181) 06:05:55
242. Linda Blackburn (12194) 06:06:20
243. Mary Hirsch (12219) 06:07:18
244. Caroll Hesseltine (12237) 06:07:47
245. Rosemary Guerrero (12258) 06:08:19
246. Valerie Keller (12272) 06:08:39
247. Fran Rushie (12281) 06:08:48
248. Miranda Ullrich (12303) 06:09:08
249. Iris Stein (12330) 06:09:50
250. Blanche Harris (12367) 06:11:01
251. Terri Mitchell (12410) 06:11:56
252. Sheila Gremse (12432) 06:12:41
253. Blanca Prentler (12442) 06:12:54
254. Susan Baker (12477) 06:13:48
255. Diana Kreinbring (12480) 06:13:56
256. Carol Jones (12496) 06:14:16
257. Diane Mindrum (12524) 06:15:09
258. Janice McIntyre (12531) 06:15:16
259. Jean Chromoy (12579) 06:16:29
260. Karen Smith (12602) 06:16:55
261. Linda Farrell (12618) 06:17:23
262. Ofelia Martinez (12633) 06:18:04
263. Elba Edwards (12709) 06:20:24
264. Meg Yacawych (12715) 06:20:32
265. Linda Sellaro (12729) 06:21:13
266. Charlotte Prather (12740) 06:21:31
267. Wilma Hopkins (12751) 06:21:37
268. Tarinee Jareonsok (12755) 06:21:44
269. Elena Godby (12779) 06:22:08
270. Donna Goodman (12788) 06:22:32
271. Sharron Robinson (12812) 06:23:18
272. Janice Johnson (12816) 06:23:24
273. Robbie Single (12818) 06:23:25
274. Anita Newman (12843) 06:23:53
275. Anne Savy (12876) 06:24:55
276. Geri Putman (12898) 06:25:48
277. Joyce Thurber (12899) 06:25:48
278. Eleanor Monroe (12910) 06:26:02
279. Olga Zamora (12937) 06:26:46
280. Suzanne Vertin (12942) 06:26:54
281. Elsa Seipp (12962) 06:27:46
282. Annette Jeffries (12983) 06:28:06
283. Barbara Hubbard (13000) 06:28:36
284. Ma Mullins (13016) 06:29:07
285. Vicki Cabot (13025) 06:29:21
286. Juri Williams (13059) 06:30:43
287. Susan Courtney (13072) 06:31:05
288. Habiba Herbert (13082) 06:31:20
289. Sherry Slaughter (13090) 06:31:32
290. Linda Haines (13124) 06:32:31
291. Virginia Dakin (13161) 06:33:06
292. Gloria Britton (13165) 06:33:17
293. Catherine Rives (13170) 06:33:25
294. Stefan Deal (13198) 06:34:27
295. Judy Trimble (13202) 06:34:33
296. Elizabeth Van Voorhis (13209) 06:34:39
297. Carol Hubbard (13233) 06:35:19
298. Deanne Simmons (13247) 06:35:44
299. Pamela Jimenez (13253) 06:35:56
300. Suzanne Schweitzer (13271) 06:36:21
301. Gloria Ewers (13273) 06:36:22
302. Susan Hoffman (13274) 06:36:25
303. Jan Schirmer (13282) 06:36:46
304. Helen Sundling (13289) 06:37:03
305. Jacquelyn Major (13328) 06:38:36
306. Nancy Tye (13354) 06:39:25
307. Alice Alvarez (13376) 06:40:18
308. Dawn Ajax (13381) 06:40:26
309. Gwen Hampton (13396) 06:40:57
310. Irene Farber (13474) 06:43:51
311. Tina Van Meeteren (13491) 06:44:27
312. Kathy Moscarello (13494) 06:44:39
313. Janice Newbold (13502) 06:44:55
314. Juanita Mayer (13509) 06:45:17
315. Gwen Stokes (13510) 06:45:17
316. Nettie Houston (13515) 06:45:20
317. Arlene Marquardt (13533) 06:46:08
318. Judy Myers (13552) 06:46:36
319. Alice Loo (13609) 06:48:32
320. Umilta Wolfe (13613) 06:48:36
321. Bertha Austria (13618) 06:48:53
322. Bev Burns (13619) 06:48:54
323. Carol Jackson (13631) 06:49:19
324. Alberta Vander Wal (13634) 06:49:24
325. Betsy Jentz (13636) 06:49:28
326. Maria Fernandez (13644) 06:49:54
327. Sheila Anthony (13655) 06:50:03
328. Deborah Agata (13656) 06:50:04
329. Carol Johnson (13684) 06:50:38
330. Erma Bludso (13690) 06:50:45
331. Cynthia Desrochers (13726) 06:52:01
332. Linda Lindsey (13733) 06:52:21
333. Marli Crane (13738) 06:52:41
334. Bettye Thomas (13751) 06:53:22
335. Rachel Hernandez (13756) 06:53:49
336. Allera Lenoir (13784) 06:54:59
337. Georgia Pettis (13786) 06:55:03
338. Monica Lewis (13797) 06:55:14
339. Joyce Klein (13805) 06:55:28
340. Susan Zavala (13808) 06:55:33
341. Elaine Maxwell (13811) 06:55:45
342. Niru Patel (13818) 06:55:51
343. Kathleen Cureton (13837) 06:56:28
344. Doris Bufford (13842) 06:56:43
345. Jocelyn Woodson (13873) 06:57:28
346. Terry Lawton (13875) 06:57:31
347. Kathleen Bryant (13895) 06:58:17
348. Cecilia Canales (13896) 06:58:18
349. Ollie Webb (13897) 06:58:19
350. Betti Madsen (13899) 06:58:20
351. Theresa Coleman (13940) 06:59:20
352. Pramila Patel (13976) 07:00:44
353. Carolyn Smith (13980) 07:00:50
354. Helen Nielsen (13996) 07:01:07
355. Diane McElroy (14008) 07:01:37
356. Dana Perryman (14010) 07:01:50
357. Joyce Potter (14011) 07:01:50
358. Mazel Bordenave (14013) 07:01:53
359. Linda Thiel (14029) 07:02:21
360. Cathy Karr (14035) 07:02:37
361. Stella Reina (14041) 07:02:43
362. Barbara Benoit (14044) 07:03:00
363. Jenny Marroquin (14045) 07:03:05
364. Angela Moten (14052) 07:03:21
365. Novetta Williams (14070) 07:04:21
366. Lorena Martinez (14073) 07:04:41
367. Terrilyn Salter (14077) 07:04:52
368. Enriqueta Montenegro (14100) 07:06:20
369. Shirley Creviston (14119) 07:07:22
370. Patricia Hughes (14124) 07:07:28
371. Lynn Williams (14127) 07:08:02
372. Carol Wolff (14152) 07:09:38
373. Cristie Clifford (14154) 07:10:00
374. Abigail Duran (14159) 07:10:33
375. Karen Mason (14160) 07:10:36
376. Veronica Mann (14162) 07:10:43
377. Hana Shahin (14177) 07:11:12
378. Sarah Price (14183) 07:11:46
379. Karin Keene (14236) 07:14:41
380. Pauline Field (14271) 07:16:15
381. Ellen Meyers (14272) 07:16:15
382. Joann Miraglia (14283) 07:16:47
383. Joyce Abelson (14291) 07:17:26
384. Gwen Fishbeck (14297) 07:17:53
385. Najuma Shurn (14301) 07:18:06
386. Djenaba Awolana (14302) 07:18:07
387. Carmen Estrada (14303) 07:18:14
388. Maureen Boyd (14310) 07:18:57
389. Tina Mayoral (14315) 07:19:11
390. Manuela Baldwin-Ings (14322) 07:19:35
391. Yvonne Thomas (14325) 07:19:41
392. Kris Wolf (14335) 07:20:27
393. Barb Bonesteele (14338) 07:20:35
394. Carole Gillie (14341) 07:20:47
395. Cheryl Holyk (14348) 07:21:12
396. Beatrice Houston (14351) 07:21:26
397. Lilian Geronimo (14361) 07:22:06
398. Ellen Cope (14368) 07:22:36
399. Myrelean Moore (14373) 07:22:45
400. Charlene Limenih (14399) 07:24:48
401. Lyndia Theel (14405) 07:25:11
402. Barbara Federoff (14410) 07:26:10
403. Geneve Ceniceros (14425) 07:26:51
404. Yvonne Mooney (14430) 07:27:28
405. Char Guevara (14454) 07:29:46
406. Linda Bonifiglio (14458) 07:30:15
407. Justine Quinones (14459) 07:30:17
408. Erni Bridges (14501) 07:34:08
409. Maryann Samarin (14535) 07:36:16
410. Corrie Brunner (14549) 07:37:08
411. Fern Salka (14557) 07:38:08
412. Susan Beadle (14558) 07:38:20
413. Yolanda Sokolowski (14567) 07:38:42
414. Jacqueline Gordon (14577) 07:39:31
415. Rebecca Roeder (14608) 07:41:38
416. Mary Nava (14622) 07:42:54
417. Mary Noguchi (14625) 07:43:12
418. Santana Manasrangsz (14628) 07:43:56
419. Deneice Cotton (14637) 07:44:57
420. Chris Weis (14650) 07:46:02
421. Ida Alcantar (14657) 07:46:40
422. Renae Randle (14658) 07:46:47
423. Malvenia Lewis (14665) 07:47:32
424. Bernard Davis (14667) 07:47:38
425. Ms Tigerwoman (14677) 07:48:37
426. Evi Roberson (14713) 07:51:55
427. Felicia Coye (14728) 07:53:08
428. Lavella Narcho (14734) 07:53:49
429. Janice Martin (14748) 07:54:54
430. Sarah Berger (14775) 07:56:47
431. Tracy Stark (14776) 07:56:47
432. Lin Cohoat (14790) 07:59:41
433. Lorraine Grey (14804) 08:01:05
434. Jean Guelpa (14823) 08:02:30
435. Marva Mills (14830) 08:02:44
436. Vicki Iritano (14833) 08:03:14
437. Yvonne Payne (14834) 08:03:18
438. Rosemary Regalbuto (14840) 08:03:36
439. Rhodora Sino-Cruz (14844) 08:04:51
440. Peggy Amenta (14850) 08:06:36
441. Annis Collins (14859) 08:08:48
442. Martha Treadway (14867) 08:10:29
443. Elnora Beltran (14869) 08:11:03
444. Virginia Moore (14873) 08:11:14
445. Lorain Oritz (14896) 08:15:09
446. Zoreh Salamatian (14897) 08:15:16
447. Ruffy Manzano (14911) 08:17:25
448. Susan McManus (14935) 08:20:27
449. Laura Schwedhelm (14936) 08:20:27
450. Carol Bautista (14956) 08:23:04
451. Loretta Holt (14957) 08:23:09
452. Mary Ledonne (14958) 08:23:30
453. Danuta Gross (14960) 08:23:41
454. Helen Cecchi (14961) 08:24:15
455. Rita Gadwa (15031) 08:36:50
456. Maggie Leduc (15032) 08:36:50
457. Betty Phillips (15034) 08:37:57
458. Sue Goss (15040) 08:44:27
459. Kathy Sengir (15046) 08:45:46
460. Darlene Arch (15061) 08:49:32
461. Christine Turner (15066) 08:51:44
462. Christine Haughey (15067) 08:52:15
463. Carla Jennings (15097) 09:01:46
464. Rosemarie Hull (15113) 09:15:05
465. Louise Kotchkowski (15137) 09:36:38
466. Jo Ann Culberson (15146) 09:48:02
467. Virginia Driggins (15164) 10:05:48
468. Lupe Santelices (15171) 10:11:11

MEN 50 TO 54

1. Wayne Mitchell (167) 02:56:15
2. Abel Martinez (221) 02:59:33
3. Pancera Primo (261) 03:02:05
4. Mike Sanchez (283) 03:03:01
5. Patrick Wickens (308) 03:04:11
6. Peter Scott (310) 03:04:20
7. Robert Aby (458) 03:10:09
8. Lou Pals (502) 03:12:15
9. Roy Gardner (506) 03:12:19
10. Jesse Rascow (545) 03:13:37
11. Tom Glenn (589) 03:14:43
12. Yoshinobu Minowa (597) 03:15:02
13. Heriberto Landa (632) 03:16:22
14. Lynn Borland (670) 03:17:21
15. Michael Payne (694) 03:17:59
16. Joe Fox (695) 03:18:00
17. Bernhard Teicher (705) 03:18:19
18. Florenzio Vargas Jr (715) 03:18:43
19. Masahiro Noma (735) 03:19:19
20. Norm Bornstein (752) 03:19:42
21. Russell Schuh (762) 03:19:55
22. Mauro Rodriguez (766) 03:20:04
23. Richard James (803) 03:21:16
24. Chris Carlson (833) 03:21:45
25. Ron Allin (847) 03:22:12
26. Freddie Perez (854) 03:22:20
27. Michael Lovell (866) 03:22:31
28. Jose Ruiz Rodas (876) 03:22:44
29. Carlos Solomon Ramirez Godimez (898) 03:23:15
30. Alexandre Nichchouk (903) 03:23:21
31. Donald Schultz (956) 03:24:27
32. Carlos Lopez-Graves (1006) 03:25:36
33. Ken Reimer (1015) 03:25:47
34. Salvador Torres (1022) 03:26:02
35. Richard Kirschner (1049) 03:26:39
36. Rod Chalmers (1051) 03:26:43
37. Don Weir (1052) 03:26:43
38. Silvino Valdez (1091) 03:27:31
39. James Furnish (1104) 03:27:40
40. Denis Trafecanty (1121) 03:28:01
41. Gene Drabinski (1137) 03:28:16
42. Fred Mascorro (1143) 03:28:22
43. Guillermo Ortiz (1155) 03:28:38
44. Bernard Davis (1161) 03:28:48
45. Steve Waltner (1174) 03:29:00
46. Dave Sek (1190) 03:29:19
47. Michael McLaughlin (1194) 03:29:22
48. Jean-Pierre Theveny (1197) 03:29:24
49. Clark Bunton (1200) 03:29:28
50. Donald Caldwell (1229) 03:29:55
51. Isao Suzuki (1244) 03:30:17
52. Edward Loh (1255) 03:30:29
53. Jorge Lopez (1290) 03:31:14
54. Alfredo Estrada (1321) 03:31:40
55. Mo Jourdang (1329) 03:31:49
56. Phil Govert (1356) 03:32:20
57. Paul Scibetta (1378) 03:32:50
58. Kent Padovich (1391) 03:33:02
59. Katsuo Okubo (1394) 03:33:06
60. Joseph Wojcik (1395) 03:33:06
61. Ken Beger (1424) 03:33:56
62. Manouch Lankarani (1432) 03:34:04
63. Frank Rapallo Jr (1465) 03:34:50
64. Robert Oliva (1485) 03:35:07
65. Liam Fenelon (1491) 03:35:13
66. Jim Romero (1538) 03:36:01
67. Cuauhtemoc Paredes (1564) 03:36:37
68. Daniel Henderson III (1625) 03:37:44
69. Dorsh Sanders (1653) 03:38:11
70. Rene Diaz (1743) 03:39:44
71. Michael Bossard (1748) 03:39:51
72. Michael Paul (1764) 03:40:11
73. Walter Reeves (1772) 03:40:18
74. Jerry Wothe (1783) 03:40:24
75. Doug Wells (1787) 03:40:25
76. Big Foot Wells (1824) 03:41:03
77. Bill Halsworth (1856) 03:41:22
78. Robert King (1858) 03:41:23
79. Anthony Teske (1860) 03:41:27
80. Albert Martinez (1868) 03:41:33
81. Raymond Eastwood (1892) 03:41:52
82. William Thiede (1979) 03:43:30
83. Robert Goldstein (2005) 03:43:56
84. Dieter Kleinmann (2047) 03:44:26
85. John Haltom (2058) 03:44:36
86. Vincent Webber (2059) 03:44:37
87. John Ganahl (2074) 03:44:47
88. Michael Roberts (2076) 03:44:51
89. Jim McIntosh (2077) 03:44:52
90. David Rios (2079) 03:44:54
91. Ross Contreras (2080) 03:44:55
92. Edward Barvick (2091) 03:45:00
93. Don Gillman (2103) 03:45:12
94. Paul Cunniff (2111) 03:45:18
95. Raoof Saleem (2158) 03:45:58
96. Rigo Contreras (2198) 03:46:43
97. Donald Holly (2206) 03:46:52
98. Len Hunt (2243) 03:47:21
99. William Gerdes III (2263) 03:47:38
100. Mike Vasquez (2280) 03:47:51
101. Warren Karib (2284) 03:47:55
102. Nicolas Perez (2309) 03:48:13
103. Richard Schott (2318) 03:48:18
104. Roger Renou (2329) 03:48:31
105. Steve Dequer (2331) 03:48:32
106. Kenneth Hart (2395) 03:49:20
107. Alejandro Morales (2409) 03:49:32
108. Thomas Sutton (2447) 03:50:03
109. Richard Everett (2457) 03:50:12
110. Charles Yoo (2491) 03:50:38
111. Chuck Jones (2518) 03:51:01
112. Milton Rensink (2519) 03:51:01
113. John Roper (2530) 03:51:11
114. Rodrigo Estrada (2537) 03:51:17
115. Harry Mckoy (2542) 03:51:25
116. James Davis (2545) 03:51:27
117. Gary Goldman (2631) 03:52:36
118. Jerone Walker (2651) 03:52:47
119. Rick Brush (2726) 03:53:44
120. Ralph Bliquez (2731) 03:53:48
121. George Arita (2765) 03:54:14
122. Nicolas Romero (2771) 03:54:19
123. Larry Gorden (2801) 03:54:35
124. William McLain (2830) 03:54:54
125. James Stotler (2842) 03:55:05
126. Willie Lewis (2857) 03:55:17
127. Gilbert Soto (2862) 03:55:21
128. Dennis Keating (2866) 03:55:24
129. Carlos Castillo (2869) 03:55:26
130. Shapour Mobasser (2886) 03:55:31
131. James Cornelison (2930) 03:56:05
132. Thomas Hodges (2939) 03:56:10
133. Brownell Payne (2950) 03:56:18
134. Robert Alvarez (2996) 03:56:47
135. Koichi Fujita (3020) 03:57:00
136. Jerome Culliver (3042) 03:57:09
137. Alford Claiborne (3045) 03:57:12
138. John Taussig (3061) 03:57:24
139. Sumio Takahashi (3073) 03:57:31
140. Marcos Benavides Bonilla (3084) 03:57:42
141. Phillip Shattuck (3111) 03:57:55
142. Gary Roberts (3177) 03:58:44
143. Joseph Hesse (3190) 03:58:53
144. John Olsen (3219) 03:59:14
145. Jerry Shea (3220) 03:59:15
146. Ronald Cooperman (3240) 03:59:29
147. Robert Schmidt (3263) 03:59:44
148. Thomas Lakin (3294) 03:59:58
149. Mario Gerla (3340) 04:00:30
150. Manuel Portillo (3403) 04:01:18
151. Robert Good (3422) 04:01:33
152. Wayne Phillips (3425) 04:01:34
153. Thomas Edwards (3447) 04:01:56
154. Suresh Iyengar (3468) 04:02:13
155. Hermann Haastrup (3478) 04:02:19
156. Roderick Leonard (3525) 04:03:03
157. James Bryant (3530) 04:03:07
158. Jasper Sharp Jr (3533) 04:03:09
159. Lincoln Spurgeon (3552) 04:03:29
160. Lawrence Orbin (3559) 04:03:35
161. Mario Duarte (3585) 04:03:59
162. Frank Hernandez (3668) 04:04:51

163. Russell Cheney (3689) 04:05:05
164. Daniel Cobos (3701) 04:05:12
165. Achilles Sangster (3717) 04:05:31
166. Panfild Velazquez (3723) 04:05:33
167. Clay Dunning (3746) 04:05:54
168. Antonio Esteban Navarro (3758) 04:06:03
169. Wesley Vincent (3766) 04:06:09
170. Guillermo Campbell (3768) 04:06:10
171. Ralph Kaye (3773) 04:06:13
172. Kenneth Sherman (3777) 04:06:20
173. Marvin Houck (3790) 04:06:29
174. Dick Cole (3802) 04:06:37
175. Ben Caro (3821) 04:06:51
176. Lionell Greenberg (3829) 04:06:58
177. Dennis Faust (3839) 04:07:03
178. Ed Andrade (3895) 04:07:40
179. Richard Mathias (3922) 04:08:08
180. William Osheroff (3938) 04:08:17
181. Ricardo Chapa (3941) 04:08:18
182. Richard Rioux (3942) 04:08:19
183. Mike Stone (3957) 04:08:27
184. Vince Agura (3983) 04:08:52
185. Richard Buchness (3994) 04:09:02
186. Donald Harrington (4019) 04:09:21
187. Neal Dempsey III (4035) 04:09:31
188. Dieter Ratsch (4051) 04:09:47
189. Henry Davis (4105) 04:10:31
190. Gerald Smith (4115) 04:10:37
191. Javier Aranda (4126) 04:10:47
192. Gerardo Vindas (4128) 04:10:48
193. Dana Young (4163) 04:11:05
194. Wigberto Veluz (4167) 04:11:09
195. Alan Shapiro (4201) 04:11:38
196. Neil Goodman (4208) 04:11:44
197. Lee Colburn (4210) 04:11:49
198. Dan Turberville (4220) 04:11:57
199. John Clark (4225) 04:12:00
200. Charles Cherry (4233) 04:12:04
201. Les Martisko (4238) 04:12:10
202. Ronald Bucy (4265) 04:12:28
203. Winston Richards (4266) 04:12:28
204. Pete Gonzalez (4284) 04:12:43
205. Dave Kretchman (4307) 04:13:03
206. Shiv Shankar (4352) 04:13:40
207. Joseph Wilson (4383) 04:14:01
208. Alan Mackey (4386) 04:14:02
209. John Carey (4394) 04:14:06
210. Jerome Mittman (4399) 04:14:09
211. Klaus-Dieter Krasel (4422) 04:14:25
212. Philip Baily (4432) 04:14:31
213. Laszlo Buliczka (4449) 04:14:40
214. James Becker (4520) 04:15:29
215. Frank Lee (4522) 04:15:29
216. Mario Avila (4529) 04:15:32
217. David Sork (4540) 04:15:35
218. Pete Cerda (4577) 04:15:59
219. Bernhard Schoentag (4598) 04:16:10
220. Ritchie Scott (4602) 04:16:16
221. Sergio Garcia (4605) 04:16:19
222. Dwight Tackett (4617) 04:16:26
223. John Bramlet (4625) 04:16:29
224. John Edwards (4630) 04:16:31
225. Gary Miller (4636) 04:16:34
226. Roger Parsons (4650) 04:16:53
227. Gerald Wong (4661) 04:16:56
228. Charlie Gonzales (4690) 04:17:19
229. Robert Weiner (4704) 04:17:30
230. Alex Meade (4708) 04:17:32
231. Joseph Zednik (4735) 04:17:54
232. Steven Chudos (4740) 04:17:57
233. Kenneth Blum (4744) 04:17:58
234. Douglas Partridge (4750) 04:18:03
235. Chuck Church (4760) 04:18:10
236. Richard Clark (4762) 04:18:12
237. Isao Narikawa (4766) 04:18:13
238. Mitchell Schwary (4773) 04:18:20
239. Lee Evans (4779) 04:18:24
240. Khalil Sheibani (4816) 04:18:44
241. Jean Pierre Von Kanel (4828) 04:18:52
242. Joseph Cordero Jr (4835) 04:18:56
243. Wendell Keith (4847) 04:19:00
244. Michael Groener (4867) 04:19:14
245. Michael McCaffery (4869) 04:19:15
246. J Love (4894) 04:19:31
247. Rex Page (4922) 04:19:50
248. Mitsugi Shinohara (4930) 04:19:56
249. Leo Rutten (4936) 04:20:00
250. Luis De La Cruz Murillo (4966) 04:20:27
251. Martin Epstein (4998) 04:20:59
252. John Schroder (5006) 04:21:07
253. Mike Johnstone (5011) 04:21:14
254. David Winsor (5016) 04:21:17
255. Robert Sidenfaden (5023) 04:21:20
256. Jerry Robinson (5044) 04:21:37
257. William Haber (5063) 04:21:45
258. Stephen Marpet (5068) 04:21:49
259. Mike Buis (5076) 04:21:52
260. James McGann (5101) 04:22:04
261. Donald Stewart (5135) 04:22:25
262. Robert Mulcahy (5149) 04:22:37
263. Ronald Johnson (5165) 04:22:49
264. John Nevins (5177) 04:22:56
265. Enrique Valenzuela Becerra (5187) 04:23:05
266. Kenneth Heinly (5230) 04:23:33
267. James Simpson (5315) 04:24:40
268. William Hallmark (5343) 04:25:03
269. David Abelson (5351) 04:25:09
270. Henry Del Rey Jr (5395) 04:25:31
271. Gaylon Rodin (5411) 04:25:41
272. Robert Joseph (5421) 04:25:48
273. Bruce Jaffe (5428) 04:25:51
274. Guillermo Campos (5465) 04:26:13
275. Jim Schultz (5501) 04:26:40
276. Albert Hutter (5523) 04:27:00
277. Art Lenke (5553) 04:27:20
278. Frank Flores (5555) 04:27:22
279. George Good (5561) 04:27:25
280. David Gastel (5576) 04:27:32
281. Steven Charnow (5578) 04:27:34
282. Gary Munson (5584) 04:27:39
283. Theodore Bankhead (5586) 04:27:39
284. Isaac Nunn Jr (5596) 04:27:47
285. Ed De La Ossa (5619) 04:28:00
286. Barry Hamilton (5628) 04:28:04
287. David Hoth (5644) 04:28:14
288. Thomas Davis (5699) 04:28:52
289. Robert Keller (5716) 04:29:03
290. Gene Gramzow (5717) 04:29:03
291. George Crespo (6754) 04:29:28
292. Charles Malmgren (5757) 04:29:30
293. Jose Michel (5783) 04:29:46
294. John Pierce (5823) 04:30:19
295. Ward Rusling (5875) 04:30:42
296. Ronald Vinje (5876) 04:30:42
297. Joe Bautista (5877) 04:30:43
298. Mack Ray Hernandez (5888) 04:30:51
299. Eugene Regala (5903) 04:31:03
300. Frank Hotchkiss (5912) 04:31:07
301. Rigoberto Cervantes (5932) 04:31:24
302. David Gothard (5943) 04:31:28
303. Roger Amey (5969) 04:31:48
304. Richard Franco (5982) 04:31:58
305. Peter Parsons (5997) 04:32:10
306. Cliff Rodrigues (6020) 04:32:29
307. John Rivera (6060) 04:32:59
308. William Woolson (6063) 04:33:01
309. Brian Smith (6068) 04:33:03
310. David Wirtschafter (6070) 04:33:03
311. Ken Orphey (6082) 04:33:13
312. Charles Koppany (6120) 04:33:37
313. Raymond Votaw (6179) 04:34:20
314. Genaro Ayam-Lau (6183) 04:34:23
315. Raymond Rodriguez (6218) 04:34:43
316. Daniel Taverne (6227) 04:34:49
317. Ronald Polacsek (6229) 04:34:50
318. Dean Kroeker (6244) 04:35:01
319. Lars Johnsson (6248) 04:35:05
320. Lonny Lazaro (6282) 04:35:25
321. Rito Cervantes (6283) 04:35:25
322. John Williams (6292) 04:35:34
323. James Bender (6306) 04:35:41
324. Alan Higa (6340) 04:36:02
325. Alfred Solano (6341) 04:36:04
326. Guy Wilks (6357) 04:36:12
327. Jerry Weyer (6395) 04:36:30
328. Ben Hernandez (6401) 04:36:34
329. Lou Colletta (6435) 04:37:00
330. Warren Mullisen (6452) 04:37:18
331. Rodolfo Castellanos (6453) 04:37:19
332. Jay Hoffman (6469) 04:37:27
333. Michael Torres (6496) 04:37:40
334. Nick Graham (6547) 04:38:12
335. Marshall Fisher (6556) 04:38:15
336. Dennis Walsh (6595) 04:38:41
337. Derek Pereira (6651) 04:39:18
338. Walter De Cuir Jr (6658) 04:39:26
339. Ward Wright (6670) 04:39:35
340. Richard Oginz (6672) 04:39:37
341. Salvador Rosas (6696) 04:39:50
342. Bob Rodgers (6715) 04:40:04
343. Rubben Arteaga (6749) 04:40:35
344. Allan Johns (6790) 04:41:07
345. Matthew Sharp (6801) 04:41:15
346. Larry Hilton (6816) 04:41:31
347. Walt Rush (6838) 04:41:47
348. Floyd Andersen (6847) 04:41:53
349. Bill Green (6851) 04:41:55
350. Richard Main (6874) 04:42:11
351. Ken Kochakji (6887) 04:42:26
352. Gary Kunkler (6941) 04:43:03
353. Arch Bryant (6943) 04:43:04
354. Michael Nissman (6956) 04:43:09
355. Andre Baldino (6977) 04:43:23
356. Bruce Gaines (7006) 04:43:40
357. Daniel Hernandez (7008) 04:43:40
358. Michael Passmore (7058) 04:44:18
359. Charles Bennett (7071) 04:44:31
360. Douglas Olson (7077) 04:44:35
361. Chester Graine III (7086) 04:44:47
362. Luis Garcia (7151) 04:45:36
363. Marvin Mayes (7154) 04:45:38
364. Charles Alvord (7174) 04:45:46
365. Terry Rhodes (7175) 04:45:47
366. Bill Demoss (7211) 04:46:13
367. Edd Stevens (7263) 04:46:52
368. Barry Sylvester (7278) 04:46:59
369. William Russell (7296) 04:47:12
370. Gordon Gross (7327) 04:47:31
371. Jim Davis (7364) 04:48:00
372. Larry Monteilh (7385) 04:48:12
373. Carlos De La Rivera (7408) 04:48:27
374. Leonard Riccio (7412) 04:48:29
375. Javier Narvaez (7423) 04:48:39
376. Tomas Jacobo (7429) 04:48:44
377. Ronald Badie (7449) 04:48:56
378. Wilfrido Garcia (7455) 04:49:00
379. Adolf Rothleitner (7465) 04:49:06
380. Robert Kuntz (7484) 04:49:16
381. Ralph Hollis (7579) 04:50:20
382. Ronald Norsell (7588) 04:50:30
383. Cipriano Gomez-Delgadillo (7607) 04:50:43
384. Gary Shusett (7614) 04:50:48
385. John Dee Sanders (7646) 04:51:12
386. David Solomon (7664) 04:51:22
387. Leslie Schwartz (7678) 04:51:40
388. Michael Carlston (7699) 04:51:58
389. Jose Seanez (7749) 04:52:39
390. Charles Beck (7760) 04:52:44
391. John Sussman (7763) 04:52:49
392. Bob Braunhardt (7785) 04:53:03
393. Robert Hanneman (7831) 04:53:35
394. Willie Rupert (7843) 04:53:42
395. Bill Van Berckelaer (7864) 04:53:57
396. Joseph Hinds (7867) 04:53:58
397. Jurgen Ankenbrand (7901) 04:54:21
398. Oscar Olivo (7906) 04:54:24
399. Ken Carlson (7910) 04:54:25
400. Charles Garcia (7929) 04:54:33
401. Jerry Rican (7943) 04:54:39
402. Bruce Jackson (7971) 04:54:52
403. Timothy Norland (7978) 04:55:08
404. Wolfgang Scheele (7986) 04:55:10
405. Jim Reese (7993) 04:55:10
406. Peter Becker (8023) 04:55:44
407. Hans Marciniak (8020) 04:55:46
408. Stephen Teele (8030) 04:55:40
409. Franklin Gillespie (8050) 04:56:04
410. James Burns (8053) 04:56:06
411. Rafael Figueroa (8082) 04:56:28
412. Michael Claydon (8095) 04:56:35
413. Michael Lee (8135) 04:57:07
414. Barry Kunz (8168) 04:57:33
415. Rodney Rosso (8197) 04:57:53
416. Joe Pate (8218) 04:58:03
417. Donald Artis (8222) 04:58:06
418. Larshelby Dantzler (8223) 04:58:07
419. Ray Perez (8231) 04:58:13
420. Vinod Patwardhan (8255) 04:58:25
421. Jon Shelgren (8261) 04:58:28
422. David Landsberg (8271) 04:58:34
423. Jon Kranzler (8281) 04:58:44
424. Otto Rieger (8298) 04:58:53
425. Ernst Weiss (8301) 04:58:54
426. Peter Geltner (8307) 04:58:56
427. Laurence Chafe (8320) 04:59:04
428. Michael Hadley (8340) 04:59:17
429. Stephen Norton (8355) 04:59:30
430. Smiley Apodaca (8379) 04:59:42
431. John Petrie (8387) 04:59:49
432. Don Muhsin (8406) 05:00:11
433. Larry Buccat (8447) 05:00:53
434. Joe Tassone (8483) 05:01:21
435. Ignacio Banuelos (8496) 05:01:28
436. Pete Garcia (8502) 05:01:33
437. Jose Torres (8509) 05:01:37
438. Juris Priedkans (8516) 05:01:42
439. Art Takahara (8611) 05:03:08
440. Alan Culver (8614) 05:03:09
441. Joshua Lim (8662) 05:03:53
442. Alvin Moore (8665) 05:03:55
443. Lee Simmons (8671) 05:03:58
444. Robert Kane (8680) 05:04:04
445. Paul St Onge (8681) 05:04:06
446. Anthony Lopez (8716) 05:04:31
447. Charles Adams (8721) 05:04:39
448. Harold Liu (8723) 05:04:41
449. Peter Chan (8732) 05:04:48
450. Roberto Escarzaga (8742) 05:05:01
451. Juventino Luna (8762) 05:05:25
452. Irving Hoffman (8785) 05:05:47
453. Stephen Lord (8792) 05:05:55
454. Myron Vaughan (8795) 05:05:57
455. John Roper (8802) 05:06:05
456. Bill Thurman (8814) 05:06:19
457. William Nealy (8820) 05:06:24
458. Javier Bobadilla (8858) 05:07:03
459. Randolph Spalding (8876) 05:07:15
460. Paul Kim (8898) 05:07:46
461. Roger Fischer (8899) 05:07:46
462. Ernest Limon (8902) 05:07:49
463. Robert Baker (8980) 05:08:48
464. Rudi Volti (9001) 05:09:08
465. Howard Ward (9025) 05:09:26
466. Joseph Kinyone (9028) 05:09:29
467. Pasquale Pirri (9047) 05:09:47
468. Hironobu Fukuzawa (9052) 05:09:51
469. Vernon Pitsker (9066) 05:09:59
470. Yong Yim (9086) 05:10:13
471. Raul Nicolaides (9090) 05:10:15
472. Abel Martinez (9124) 05:10:30
473. Roger Enriquez (9147) 05:10:58
474. Robert McMahon (9148) 05:10:59
475. Dave Elkins (9158) 05:11:10
476. Ben Sorebreni (9180) 05:11:34
477. Michael Gorsen (9183) 05:11:37
478. Gary Manildi (9189) 05:11:39
479. Paul Liebman (9243) 05:12:33
480. Tsunemitsu Shinjo (9270) 05:13:01
481. Alan Smith (9282) 05:13:12
482. Lynn Pletcher (9285) 05:13:15
483. Buddy Patane (9310) 05:13:30
484. Jon Bechtel (9313) 05:13:32
485. Paul Brestyanszky (9320) 05:13:35
486. Gregorio Lopez (9362) 05:14:05
487. Jay Davis (9368) 05:14:08
488. Hajime Aoyagi (9386) 05:14:25
489. Horace Rodriuez (9389) 05:14:27
490. Joe Kalajkovic (9403) 05:14:45
491. Julio Ojinaga (9408) 05:14:51
492. Richard Leher (9409) 05:14:53
493. Robert Gay (9429) 05:15:18
494. Ned Lazaro (9452) 05:15:49
495. Pete Ganulin (9469) 05:16:03
496. Ed Roesch (9511) 05:16:38
497. Jacques Meyer (9521) 05:16:46
498. Jorge Gutierrez (9580) 05:17:32
499. Salvador Almanza (9598) 05:17:50
500. James Galyen (9617) 05:18:15
501. Barry Bender (9629) 05:18:27
502. Mario Miranda (9631) 05:18:28
503. Juvencio Gonzalez (9650) 05:18:40
504. Craig Moore (9673) 05:19:01
505. Thomas Alexander (9690) 05:19:15
506. Jose Nebrida (9712) 05:19:41
507. Willie Carter (9721) 05:19:48
508. Masayoshi Kagita (9726) 05:20:02
509. Armando Soto (9788) 05:20:51
510. Richard Masada (9826) 05:21:32
511. John Houghtaling (9832) 05:21:37
512. Robert Burdick (9842) 05:21:42
513. Paul Nightingale (9844) 05:21:45
514. Stanley Bass (9866) 05:22:00
515. Arnold Schwartz (9868) 05:22:02
516. Anthony Sylvester (9900) 05:22:31
517. Shuntaro Noda (9904) 05:22:37
518. Frank Spicciati (9905) 05:22:38
519. Low Dong (9932) 05:23:12
520. Robert Ortiz (9996) 05:24:13
521. James Ward (10042) 05:25:09
522. Leigh Myers (10075) 05:25:45
523. Kim Marvel (10090) 05:25:54
524. Michael Borrett (10104) 05:26:10
525. Dick Kotzbauer (10105) 05:26:10
526. Richard Caruvana (10112) 05:26:17
527. Robert Chisholm (10143) 05:26:53
528. Tom Hanggie (10151) 05:27:03
529. Sig Olsen (10154) 05:27:05
530. Ronald Wakasa (10183) 05:27:29
531. Eike Hohenadl (10232) 05:28:09
532. Don Gillis (10255) 05:28:39
533. Howard McGee (10263) 05:28:47
534. Joe Justo (10265) 05:28:48
535. Daryl Nelson (10286) 05:29:01
536. Jorge Cardenas (10298) 05:29:13
537. Albert Gaskin (10322) 05:29:27
538. Ivan Brandler (10345) 05:29:57
539. Richard Engle (10377) 05:30:28
540. Roger McMurtry (10383) 05:30:33
541. Ralph Cripe (10400) 05:30:46
542. Robert Miller (10409) 05:31:00
543. Larry White (10424) 05:31:12
544. Bob Richmond (10461) 05:31:45
545. Peter Digre (10475) 05:31:51
546. James Pilgrim (10520) 05:32:47
547. Richard Viramontes (10522) 05:32:50
548. Denny Rea (10531) 05:32:54
549. Chuck Wert (10538) 05:32:56
550. Gibert Martin (10546) 05:33:05
551. William Landrey (10553) 05:33:14
552. Robert Ditchey (10554) 05:33:21
553. Don Feinstein (10555) 05:33:23
554. Robert Anderson (10565) 05:33:27
555. David Mills (10572) 05:33:29
556. Ted Ferguson (10580) 05:33:39
557. Jim Hendricks (10606) 05:33:54
558. Michael Thompson (10646) 05:34:32
559. Manuel De Anda (10652) 05:34:39
560. Tom Harned (10699) 05:35:22
561. James Henderson (10709) 05:35:27
562. Ken Resseger (10713) 05:35:29
563. Bernard Lamoureux (10750) 05:36:12
564. Foster Stringfield (10770) 05:36:36
565. Stanley Hoffman (10774) 05:36:37
566. Norman Isaacs (10801) 05:37:05
567. Joseph Gil (10808) 05:37:12
568. David McIntire (10844) 05:37:55
569. Morris Kelly Sr (10848) 05:37:58
570. Jerry Strinden (10850) 05:38:02
571. Eugene Storey (10865) 05:38:16
572. George Hubbard (10883) 05:38:49
573. Robert Lind (10886) 05:38:51
574. Richard Ringwald (10899) 05:39:10
575. Robert Scales (10911) 05:39:22
576. Tak Nikaido (10930) 05:39:50
577. Ferdinando Mendiola (10931) 05:39:50
578. Alvaro Garcia (10951) 05:40:19
579. Jay Williams (10969) 05:40:42
580. Simon Goss Sr (11017) 05:41:45
581. Adalberto Ramirez (11026) 05:41:55
582. Joe Kees (11028) 05:41:57
583. Roland Bynum (11035) 05:42:06
584. Reid Pressley (11063) 05:42:26
585. John Rice (11107) 05:43:06
586. Darwin Bayerkohler (11184) 05:44:20
587. Ken Kerner (11232) 05:44:55
588. Jacques Le Floch (11290) 05:46:01
589. Stanley Slaven (11299) 05:46:15
590. Dave Evangelisti (11306) 05:46:22
591. Daniel Rosado (11310) 05:46:30
592. Roger Suban (11311) 05:46:32
593. Garry Huston (11323) 05:46:41
594. Charles Bearcomesout (11326) 05:46:46
595. Johnny Aisk (11335) 05:46:55
596. Frank Targhetta (11354) 05:47:23
597. Fidel San Juan (11366) 05:47:47
598. Pradip Choksi (11370) 05:47:52
599. Bert Johnson (11387) 05:48:33
600. Jauier Zuniga (11397) 05:48:55
601. Calvin Pettit (11403) 05:49:01
602. Edward Don (11423) 05:49:19
603. Eugene Gritton (11431) 05:49:30
604. Brad Gilson (11442) 05:49:38
605. William Giragos (11455) 05:49:47
606. Cory Rodgers (11466) 05:49:54
607. Wayne Taylor (11484) 05:50:14
608. Dale Turnley (11485) 05:50:14
609. Jim Miles (11494) 05:50:25
610. Carmen Marmo (11513) 05:50:35
611. John-Norman Tuck (11514) 05:50:36
612. Martin Rosenbaum (11532) 05:50:55
613. Harlan Clark (11542) 05:51:07
614. Barry Heifitz (11555) 05:51:31
615. Benjamin Penaloza (11589) 05:52:15
616. Armando Berriz (11616) 05:52:54
617. Peter Dorn (11636) 05:53:06
618. Norman Ward (11648) 05:53:18
619. Thomas Armor (11662) 05:53:35
620. Marvin Harrell (11664) 05:53:37
621. Jesse Metoyer (11667) 05:53:39
622. Fred Ashley (11679) 05:53:51
623. Darius Rahbar (11723) 05:54:51
624. Mike Starr (11733) 05:55:06
625. Randall Yamanaka (11778) 05:56:00
626. Pichit Boonbumrungsub (11798) 05:56:36
627. Mel Tyler (11810) 05:56:49
628. Bud Jansen (11831) 05:57:18
629. Clay Felts (11959) 06:00:02
630. Bill Witt (11974) 06:00:26
631. John Olivas (11993) 06:01:00
632. Robert Norberg (11999) 06:01:07
633. Bhupendra Patel (12001) 06:01:11
634. Garland Tennell (12008) 06:01:26
635. Bernard Barton (12050) 06:02:32
636. James Evans (12153) 06:05:18
637. Gene Overmyer (12199) 06:06:27
638. Thomas Ritchie (12248) 06:08:04
639. Gordon Hopkins (12251) 06:08:09
640. Torkil Hammer (12254) 06:08:16
641. Gerry Gudani (12294) 06:09:00
642. Thor Ericson (12315) 06:09:26
643. Henry Lopez (12354) 06:10:33
644. Jack McLain (12411) 06:12:03
645. Larry Arreola (12430) 06:12:39
646. Jesus Alvarado (12435) 06:12:44
647. Alejandro Martinez (12546) 06:15:33
648. Henry Bernard (12548) 06:15:37
649. Philip Rosen (12549) 06:15:37
650. David Bourne (12572) 06:16:14
651. Larry Irwin (12595) 06:16:49
652. John Swanson (12614) 06:17:16
653. Bob Roberts (12655) 06:18:39
654. Robert Eddy (12678) 06:19:33
655. Nadir Hussain (12699) 06:20:09
656. Cleavon Govan (12735) 06:21:25
657. Manuel Medina (12747) 06:21:35
658. Itdhipol Rumpagaporn (12754) 06:21:44
659. Don Hughes (12780) 06:22:13
660. Dale Synnes (12798) 06:22:46
661. Steve Courtney (12820) 06:23:26
662. Thomas Dorosky (12832) 06:23:44
663. Ken Parlee (12863) 06:24:20
664. Samuel Smith (12868) 06:24:40
665. Alan Wolfe (12890) 06:25:30
666. Robert Cardenas (12918) 06:26:22
667. Skip Lindeman (13008) 06:28:48
668. Rose Banko (13018) 06:29:08
669. Jon Greene (13019) 06:29:10
670. Renate Kierdorf (13042) 06:30:06
671. Joe Spieler (13054) 06:30:28
672. Rasheed Stith (13070) 06:31:01
673. William Givan (13105) 06:31:59
674. Louis Hill (13127) 06:32:36
675. Peter Boonisar (13152) 06:32:59
676. Howard Packer (13267) 06:36:15
677. Weldon Bennett (13277) 06:36:30
678. Sandy English (13286) 06:37:02
679. Richard Lewis (13299) 06:37:29
680. William Whiteside (13302) 06:37:31
681. Rogello Whyte (13316) 06:38:07
682. George Sanchez (13320) 06:38:22
683. Donald Lipschitz (13387) 06:40:41
684. Gary Lendennie (13406) 06:41:21
685. Pete Fonseca (13473) 06:43:50
686. James Davis (13504) 06:45:03
687. Dick Hirsch (13527) 06:45:54
688. David Kahn (13536) 06:46:13
689. Roy Schroeder (13545) 06:46:22
690. Jose Fernandez (13574) 06:47:29
691. Linwood Bracey (13598) 06:48:14
692. Richard Dominguez (13620) 06:48:57
693. Joseph Abe (13639) 06:49:40
694. William Horan (13641) 06:49:48
695. John Chlebnik (13646) 06:49:58
696. John Baca (13692) 06:50:49
697. Peter Salcido (13701) 06:51:03
698. Praful Patel (13791) 06:55:07
699. David Herrera (13799) 06:55:14
700. Ken Czisny (13885) 06:57:55
701. Ernesto Sanchez (13913) 06:58:43
702. Ralph Esparza (13936) 06:59:08
703. Ron Peery (13969) 07:00:32
704. David Nowaczyk Sr (13981) 07:00:52
705. Richard Eckfield (13997) 07:01:08
706. Perry Ross (14003) 07:01:20
707. Eddie Davis (14016) 07:01:57
708. Ronald Offenstein (14019) 07:02:02
709. Tony Gilham (14022) 07:02:09
710. Frederick Richardson (14053) 07:03:29
711. Kris Viswanathan (14065) 07:04:07
712. Gerard Amenta (14092) 07:05:40
713. Ronald Steffen (14117) 07:07:19
714. Bill Weber (14118) 07:07:21
715. Joseph Wick (14125) 07:07:49
716. Barry Robinson (14134) 07:08:24
717. Michael Epstein (14163) 07:10:44
718. Bob Ryan (14213) 07:13:18
719. O Tekin (14259) 07:15:38
720. Frank Ward (14265) 07:15:52
721. Daniel Osborn (14268) 07:16:03
722. Doug Campbell (14278) 07:16:35
723. Robert Falcone (14339) 07:20:37
724. Arturo Guevara (14414) 07:26:19
725. Ken Huthmaker (14426) 07:26:51
726. Dinshaw Fanibanda (14656) 07:46:38
727. Ronald Minami (14681) 07:48:50
728. Bob Dobson (14686) 07:49:35
729. Daniel Richardson (14832) 08:03:08
730. Sharad Patel (14916) 08:18:19
731. David Perkins (14920) 08:18:49
732. Bernard Johnson (14938) 08:20:29
733. Lloyd White (14943) 08:21:13
734. Doug Russell (14981) 08:28:39
735. Pete Salsido (15068) 08:52:22
736. Richard Carscallen (15084) 08:57:01
737. Gerald Hull (15112) 09:15:05
738. Bernard Harkin (15129) 09:30:16
739. Robert Sommers (15132) 09:31:09
740. Brian Scoggins (15135) 09:36:04
741. Andrew Romero (15136) 09:36:08
742. Ildefonso Sino-Cruz (15158) 09:58:33

WOMEN 50 TO 54

1. Patricia Brumbalow (963) 03:24:34
2. Karen Haycraft (1456) 03:34:45
3. Karen Helms (1842) 03:41:14
4. Barbara Buckman (1931) 03:42:31
5. Sally Herrera (2013) 03:44:02
6. Bonnie Robinson (2144) 03:45:50
7. Diane Eastman (2188) 03:46:26
8. Vivian Reinirainen (2394) 03:49:19
9. Ann Tack (2448) 03:50:02
10. Alicemarie Stotler (2839) 03:55:03
11. Teresa Lee (3006) 03:56:51
12. Portia Cornell (3023) 03:57:01
13. Rio Rugg (3215) 03:59:10
14. Judy Kewley (3282) 03:59:53
15. Carp; Edwards (3346) 04:00:34
16. Alnita Dunn (3596) 04:04:10
17. Leona Watson (4375) 04:13:56
18. Christine Rothleitner (4420) 04:14:23
19. Joyce Winter (4471) 04:14:40
20. Dottie Pachot (4672) 04:17:04
21. Gertraud Bornhoff (4862) 04:19:11
22. Carol Jones (4872) 04:19:15
23. Marie Stevenson (5114) 04:22:09
24. Donna Segarra (5134) 04:22:25
25. Susan Hudson (5252) 04:23:52
26. Judith Fisher (5413) 04:25:42
27. Susan Alexander (5842) 04:30:29
28. Meryl Powles (5900) 04:31:02
29. Helga Achterfeldt (6074) 04:33:07
30. Ridgely Montros Keeley (6127) 04:33:41
31. Ilsebill Wolte (6131) 04:33:44
32. Cookie Petrie (6145) 04:33:55
33. Betty Kroeker (6242) 04:35:00
34. Erlinda Sullivan (6339) 04:36:00
35. Atsuko Nanbu (6426) 04:36:49
36. Ann Taylor (6533) 04:38:04
37. Mickey Lester (6568) 04:38:24
38. Sandra Coshi (6576) 04:38:31
39. Kennis Clark (6683) 04:39:43
40. Madeleine Tarnay (6903) 04:42:40
41. Marilyn Walker (6910) 04:42:46
42. Venette Hill (7012) 04:43:42
43. Martha Fuentes (7201) 04:46:09
44. Joyce Spoehr (7298) 04:47:13
45. Ana Schwartz (7474) 04:49:10
46. Richie Berlin (7523) 04:49:35
47. Tricia Strope (7772) 04:52:53
48. Marylym Jowes (7947) 04:54:42
49. Wendy Tucker (8294) 04:58:51
50. Jane Cutting (8449) 05:00:56
51. Rebecca Thyne (8524) 05:01:45
52. Elke Barauskas (8572) 05:02:23
53. Aida Dimaranan (8605) 05:03:04
54. Patricia Houser (8667) 05:03:56

55. Karin Moody (8722) .05:04:40
56. Gay Roper (8804) .05:06:06
57. Keiko Takaoka (9003) .05:09:08
58. Carol Rice (9056) .05:09:54
59. Mieko Nakamula (9060) .05:09:57
60. Ana Martinez (9153) .05:11:01
61. Rosanna Devemark (9221) .05:12:12
62. Anita Lopez (9267) .05:12:56
63. Rosemary Bean (9306) .05:13:29
64. Pat Meyers (9321) .05:13:36
65. Lily Okumura (9340) .05:13:48
66. Christina Cole (9424) .05:15:13
67. Sylvia Bresnik (9432) .05:15:22
68. Diana Sargenti (9467) .05:16:01
69. Faye Goldin (9497) .05:16:29
70. Patricia Roesch (9510) .05:16:37
71. Cathy Fickes (9572) .05:17:26
72. Mary Eller (9596) .05:17:49
73. Marian Janss (9682) .05:19:08
74. Melba Reyes (9804) .05:21:07
75. Barbara Moore (9856) .05:21:52
76. Joyce White (9862) .05:21:55
77. Brigitte Hoelper (9942) .05:23:23
78. Mardi Briggs (9985) .05:24:04
79. Sharon Kerson (10127) .05:26:35
80. Glenda Taylor (10185) .05:27:30
81. Ellen Snead (10191) .05:27:35
82. Glenda Morgan (10236) .05:28:12
83. Susan Hamusek (10244) .05:28:33
84. Marsha Singer (10258) .05:28:44
85. Masako Higuchi (10280) .05:28:55
86. Cindy Nelson (10287) .05:29:01
87. Donna Canales (10349) .05:29:59
88. Marcia Bunnell (10373) .05:30:25
89. Lynne Anderson (10422) .05:31:11
90. Esther Segura (10436) .05:31:26
91. Ann Marie Carbin (10459) .05:31:42
92. Nadine Krebs (10507) .05:32:25
93. Leean Bitterolf (10510) .05:32:35
94. Geri Pilgrim (10519) .05:32:46
95. Jackie Morgan (10615) .05:34:03
96. Karin Konieczny (10670) .05:34:53
97. Joan Harned (10698) .05:35:22
98. Lilia Brandon (10834) .05:37:39
99. Johnnie Ybarra (10867) .05:38:18
100. Darnell Owens (10888) .05:38:52
101. Theresa Daugherty (10890) .05:38:54
102. Lydia Lewis (10917) .05:39:35
103. Randi Decious (10919) .05:39:40
104. Marjorie Sam (10938) .05:40:01
105. Donnette Meek (10949) .05:40:15
106. Lenore Young (11027) .05:41:57
107. Hazel Bond (11048) .05:42:17
108. Darlene Galindo (11099) .05:42:58
109. Roberta Rodin (11100) .05:42:58
110. Sylvia Williams (11116) .05:43:16
111. Marcia Shankle (11132) .05:43:36
112. Patsy Morgan (11180) .05:44:17
113. Kathleen Kelley (11186) .05:44:21
114. Patricia Lightle (11188) .05:44:21
115. Gail Jones (11199) .05:44:30
116. Carole Cathcart (11226) .05:44:51
117. Gwen Gritton (11430) .05:49:29
118. Sally Canaan (11435) .05:49:31
119. Ruby Eason (11502) .05:50:30
120. Sue Mellado (11517) .05:50:38
121. Patricia Addis (11518) .05:50:38
122. Ruth Dixon (11537) .05:50:59
123. Dorothy Kirkland (11549) .05:51:22
124. Diane Arasim (11558) .05:51:38
125. Shannon Lyons (11571) .05:52:05
126. Towi Schwartz (11590) .05:52:16
127. June Wilcox (11621) .05:52:59
128. Michele Schaeffer (11624) .05:52:59
129. Alberta Franklin (11712) .05:54:36
130. Jennifer Short (11773) .05:55:52
131. Anna Balarezo (11881) .05:58:25
132. Rosalie Birk (11924) .05:59:23
133. Penni Dobkin (11951) .05:59:55
134. Jan Busby (12011) .06:01:33
135. Marga Hanks (12021) .06:01:50
136. Ellen Currie (12023) .06:01:53
137. Mary Hawkins (12033) .06:02:04
138. Mary Carr (12090) .06:03:45
139. Faye Billinger (12091) .06:03:46
140. Mary Morigaki (12100) .06:04:05
141. Ruth Ziony (12107) .06:04:23
142. Arlene Stewart (12187) .06:06:08
143. Peggy Stephens (12206) .06:06:52
144. Christine Noutsios (12260) .06:08:19
145. Karma Leeds (12285) .06:08:51
146. Mary Alvo (12308) .06:09:14
147. Carolyn Sripathy (12323) .06:09:44
148. Carol Kirkbride (12361) .06:10:55
149. Sara Gilmore (12441) .06:12:52
150. Darlene Holaway (12453) .06:13:10
151. Martha Watson (12482) .06:13:57
152. Susan Bruce (12505) .06:14:32
153. Maryjane McMaster (12568) .06:16:01
154. Joyce Seneski (12577) .06:16:23
155. Avery Johnson McGhee (12630) .06:17:52
156. Sarah Jones (12637) .06:18:15
157. Yvonne Romero (12663) .06:19:04
158. Vera Brown-Curtis (12721) .06:20:42
159. Charlotte Lesser (12795) .06:22:45
160. Christina Briles (12796) .06:22:45
161. Joy Hampton (12861) .06:24:17
162. Toni Brown (12864) .06:24:21
163. Betty Nasir (12871) .06:24:45
164. Barbara Lilly (12892) .06:25:40
165. Shanthi Rao (12925) .06:26:31
166. Kathleen Forgione (12945) .06:27:01
167. Joscelyn Pierce (12948) .06:27:14
168. Bonnie Curtis (12953) .06:27:31
169. Joyce Breslin (12961) .06:27:42
170. Elena Guisa (12963) .06:27:46
171. Sandy Kobrine (13034) .06:29:55
172. Jacqueline Palmenberg (13035) .06:29:57
173. Betty Lou Tom (13050) .06:30:24
174. Sharon Geltner (13062) .06:30:44
175. Mae Fuchino (13080) .06:31:17
176. Evelyn Beckman (13158) .06:33:03
177. Paula Fairchild (13181) .06:33:51
178. Marie Robinson (13194) .06:34:15
179. Carol Yamaguchi (13203) .06:34:34
180. Margaret Jubb (13216) .06:34:48
181. Maureen Lokken (13217) .06:34:50
182. Sandy Merrell (13250) .06:35:51
183. Ana Maria Martinez (13279) .06:36:33
184. Beverly D'angelo (13346) .06:39:07
185. Ginny Lendennie (13364) .06:39:41
186. Maria Ruiz (13369) .06:39:51
187. Jyotsna Patel (13403) .06:41:17
188. Maureen Black (13405) .06:41:19
189. Karin James (13449) .06:42:43
190. Nina Hirsch (13526) .06:45:54
191. Nancy Moore (13543) .06:46:20
192. Sherry Ashby (13561) .06:46:54
193. Connie Bullock (13563) .06:46:55
194. Rosemary Selberg (13597) .06:48:11
195. W Manyweather (13630) .06:49:17
196. Earnestine Carbins (13635) .06:49:25
197. Carmen Fenoy (13686) .06:50:38
198. Lynda Jarreau (13700) .06:51:03
199. Linda Hubbard (13705) .06:51:22
200. Jenifer O'Brien (13720) .06:51:49
201. Terry Tyndall (13724) .06:51:55
202. Jeane Hallin (13758) .06:53:56
203. Elnous Lewis (13763) .06:54:05
204. Marsha Lewin (13776) .06:54:46
205. Brigid Makiri (13780) .06:54:49
206. Lillian Johnson (13785) .06:54:59
207. Mary Long (13825) .06:55:57
208. Yvonne Gelbman (13847) .06:56:48
209. Inez Moreno (13865) .06:57:17
210. Margaret Moorehead (13872) .06:57:23
211. Suzie Gabri (13876) .06:57:31
212. Cassie Walsh (13898) .06:58:20
213. Deann Eckenwiler (13910) .06:58:40
214. Lilie Shelton (13917) .06:58:49
215. Andrea Ardley (13944) .06:59:37
216. Maryellen Tracy (13951) .06:59:55
217. Anna Hamada (13963) .07:00:25
218. Lorenza Day (14043) .07:02:59
219. Suzanne Denslow (14067) .07:04:10
220. Athalene Brown (14071) .07:04:24
221. Rebecca Dominguez (14128) .07:08:11
222. Kim Fella (14130) .07:08:15
223. Lynn Stevens (14149) .07:09:14
224. ,Ary Celano (14164) .07:10:44
225. Mary Rushie (14178) .07:11:13
226. Frances Nahas (14185) .07:11:57
227. Connie Cedillos (14190) .07:12:13
228. Odell McCormick (14206) .07:12:57
229. Claudine Mitchell (14207) .07:13:01
230. Julie Thompson (14239) .07:14:48
231. Karen Anderson (14245) .07:14:58
232. Janice Ericson (14295) .07:17:38
233. Ana Pichardo-Campos (14298) .07:17:55
234. Billie Bradford (14308) .07:18:41
235. Gloria Turley (14321) .07:19:35
236. Jo Burkhardt (14344) .07:20:57
237. Irene Crayton (14352) .07:21:26
238. Robin Collins (14362) .07:22:11
239. Callie Jones (14369) .07:22:36
240. Helen Citrano (14394) .07:24:28
241. Martha Hyde (14390) .07:24:38
242. Arleen Schneider (14406) .07:25:18
243. Jobie Forte (14418) .07:26:44
244. Carole Dickey (14438) .07:28:31
245. Dorothy Thielges (14455) .07:29:59
246. Peggy Carson (14471) .07:30:41
247. Rita Howard (14485) .07:32:52
248. Faye Elman (14490) .07:33:11
249. Gwen Ward (14500) .07:34:08
250. Janet Slaney (14504) .07:34:22
251. Olie McClellan (14511) .07:35:02
252. Carol Martinez (14551) .07:37:11
253. Polly Profitt (14559) .07:38:20
254. Rosalina Grisco (14579) .07:39:37
255. Jeanne Jean (14580) .07:39:38
256. Elizabeth Hickelton (14600) .07:41:01
257. Marie Kashmer-Stiebing (14602) .07:41:10
258. Marleny Morales (14604) .07:41:29
259. Margo Nikoloric (14609) .07:41:40
260. Robin Benard (14620) .07:42:48
261. Etsuko Yoshioka (14621) .07:42:49
262. Alexina McCallum (14643) .07:45:21
263. Kay Slack (14648) .07:45:48
264. Jeanne Finnegan (14659) .07:47:09
265. Eileen Packer (14739) .07:54:16
266. Ligia Ardon (14772) .07:56:35
267. Veronica Hammock (14825) .08:02:31
268. Mary Sean Hodges (14831) .08:03:02
269. Indira Patel (14870) .08:11:05
270. Angie Felshaw (14895) .08:14:57
271. Kathleen Jones (14919) .08:18:46
272. Jeanne Jones (14922) .08:18:54
273. Pat Parsons (14934) .08:20:20
274. Kathleen Shreves (14946) .08:21:20
275. Sara Angulo (14988) .08:29:05
276. Antoinette Uthoff (14989) .08:30:09
277. Eva Sutton (15002) .08:32:46
278. Martha Chumney (15005) .08:33:11
279. Kieran Vaughan (15024) .08:36:25
280. Christine Vaughan (15025) .08:36:27
281. Jan Foshee (15030) .08:36:48
282. Pam Flynn (15057) .08:48:44
283. Elizabeth Aitken (15072) .08:53:39
284. Lynne Carscallen (15085) .08:57:06
285. Betty Thain (15092) .08:59:51
286. Colleen Cox (15116) .09:20:35
287. Patricia Harkin (15130) .09:30:16
288. Hanaa Alwardi (15148) .09:48:40

MEN 55 TO 59

1. Carlos Vallel (128) .02:52:48
2. J R Short (142) .02:53:53
3. Paul Redoble (162) .02:55:45
4. James Kim (200) .02:58:12
5. Ron Navarrette (237) .03:00:34
6. John Corralz (325) .03:05:13
7. Charlie Gail (441) .03:09:43
8. Albert Mercado (665) .03:17:16
9. Julio Mendez (755) .03:19:46
10. Raymond Maranda (882) .03:22:49
11. Johann Vetter (961) .03:24:33
12. Ted Alarcon (1086) .03:27:25
13. Rafael Alvarez (1304) .03:31:27
14. Arnie Way (1343) .03:32:07
15. Claude Bruni (1344) .03:32:08
16. Robertp Vargus (1405) .03:33:25
17. Alton Willoughby (1415) .03:33:45
18. Charles Haycraft (1449) .03:34:31
19. Juri Tint (1474) .03:34:56
20. Frank Russo (1480) .03:35:03
21. John Murphy (1562) .03:36:34
22. Clarence Hunter Jr (1563) .03:36:36
23. David Rusher (1584) .03:36:57
24. Kermit Cadrette (1600) .03:37:13
25. Michael Woods (1656) .03:38:12
26. Ron Kobrine (1682) .03:38:42
27. Peter Biche (1697) .03:38:54
28. Leroy Kim (1731) .03:39:33
29. Ken Sparkman (1762) .03:40:06
30. Larry Dervin (1777) .03:40:20
31. Robert Ploos (1809) .03:40:50
32. Methee Yingyuad (1830) .03:41:05
33. Igal Silber (1870) .03:41:34
34. Juvenal Herrera (1919) .03:42:18
35. Bill Ekman (1984) .03:43:33
36. Jean Pierre Capdeville (2033) .03:44:18
37. Dick Lemen (2159) .03:45:59
38. Rogelio Lara Becerbil (2161) .03:46:02
39. Renier Lander (2190) .03:46:28
40. Allen Langdale (2213) .03:46:56
41. Mae Palm (2222) .03:47:03
42. Hiroshi Hasegawa (2230) .03:47:11
43. Enrique Garcia (2387) .03:49:15
44. Richard Hopkins (2520) .03:51:02
45. Norbert Hoffman (2585) .03:51:56
46. William Kim (2707) .03:53:28
47. Alex Turner (2709) .03:53:29
48. Andrew Kotulski (2718) .03:53:39
49. John Marshall (2728) .03:53:45
50. Ernie Thury (2729) .03:53:48
51. Timothy Connors (2769) .03:54:18
52. Stephen Howard (2782) .03:54:25
53. Roberto Flores (2790) .03:54:29
54. Jim Dudley (2816) .03:54:45
55. Ricardo Elizondo (2890) .03:55:32
56. Angel Nunes (2892) .03:55:34
57. Tom Brown (2946) .03:56:14
58. Robert Scuderi (2973) .03:56:36
59. Bernie Castillo Jr (3097) .03:57:48
60. James Woloszyn (3115) .03:57:58
61. Ernest Edo (3141) .03:58:21
62. Raul Estrada (3166) .03:58:36
63. Youngman Cho (3202) .03:59:02
64. John Williams (3204) .03:59:03
65. Isaac Cuevas (3253) .03:59:39
66. Francisco Gallegos (3260) .03:59:44
67. Mas Yamaguchi (3261) .03:59:44
68. Bob Schwarz (3329) .04:00:19
69. Nysan Zysman (3344) .04:00:33
70. Conn Donohoe (3363) .04:00:53
71. Vincent Di Franco (3405) .04:01:19
72. John Michaels (3424) .04:01:34
73. Harry Matsui (3462) .04:02:07
74. Willard Krick (3467) .04:02:12
75. Kan Jew (3577) .04:03:54
76. Francisco Navarrete (3598) .04:04:10
77. Gerd Barda (3619) .04:04:22
78. Philip Porretta (3647) .04:04:37
79. William Mackey (3651) .04:04:40
80. Oscar Chavez (3660) .04:04:46
81. Leo Marquez (3695) .04:05:09
82. James Walker (3704) .04:05:14
83. Bob Fredericks (3712) .04:05:26
84. Kuniyoshi Takenobe (3742) .04:05:52
85. Robert Bernard (3915) .04:07:56
86. George Moncada (4050) .04:09:47
87. Inocencio Balderas (4073) .04:10:05
88. Jim Kelly (4077) .04:10:09
89. Randy Hood (4079) .04:10:09
90. Tom Garcia (4082) .04:10:12
91. R Thurston (4152) .04:11:01
92. Stanley Horn (4219) .04:11:56
93. Stephan Specht (4223) .04:11:59
94. Ron Aubert (4246) .04:12:15
95. Ed Arasim (4257) .04:12:23
96. Rolf Hoelper (4344) .04:13:28
97. Guillermo Lopez (4378) .04:13:57
98. Cy Baumann (4385) .04:14:01
99. Richard Wootton (4428) .04:14:28
100. Peter Mireles (4485) .04:14:56
101. Panfilo Rivera (4619) .04:16:27
102. James Ludgood (4674) .04:17:07
103. Melvin Miles (4677) .04:17:09
104. Larry Mazur (4695) .04:17:26
105. William O'Brien (4726) .04:17:50
106. Gary Hunziker (4738) .04:17:56
107. Byron McIntosh (4778) .04:18:23
108. James Barnum (4879) .04:19:20
109. Tom Carroll (4886) .04:19:25
110. Richard Dishman (4910) .04:19:41
111. Ted Fisher (4994) .04:20:55
112. Bob Mano (5021) .04:21:19
113. Paul Freidin (5027) .04:21:22
114. Susumu Niimi (5108) .04:22:07
115. Bob Norton (5110) .04:22:08
116. Walter Clarke III (5147) .04:22:36
117. Van Kasper (5184) .04:23:02
118. Federico Novoa (5232) .04:23:34
119. Ted Hill (5234) .04:23:35
120. John Miller (5257) .04:24:02
121. Lawrence Coats (5300) .04:24:32
122. Peter Noce (5304) .04:24:33
123. Emile Bareng (5369) .04:25:18
124. David Wilbur (5398) .04:25:34
125. Jan Stenstrom (5445) .04:26:00
126. William Traub (5447) .04:26:01
127. Guy Huffaker (5457) .04:26:05
128. Martin Sigal (5492) .04:26:34
129. Robert Blakemore (5505) .04:26:46
130. James Heinselman (5600) .04:27:48
131. Efraim Navarrete (5604) .04:27:52
132. Joe Iseri (5613) .04:27:57
133. Louie Martinez (5684) .04:28:40
134. Curtis Selph (5745) .04:29:19
135. Antonio Luisoni (5801) .04.30.02
136. John Rous (5813) .04:30:11
137. Larry Cobb (5853) .04:30:34
138. Michael Franzblau (6033) .04:32:43
139. Martin O'Loghlen (6034) .04:32:44
140. Claude Hill (6089) .04:33:17
141. Chuck Miranda (6135) .04:33:47
142. Robert Kimmell (6310) .04:35:42
143. Jochen Schroeder (6333) .04:35:56
144. Thomas Rohrer (6385) .04:36:26
145. Edward Canavan (6387) .04:36:26
146. William Jacoby (6502) .04:37:44
147. Tomeji Tsukada (6544) .04:38:10
148. Abel Jimenez (6549) .04:38:13
149. Eugene DeFronzo (6564) .04:38:20
150. Carlos Vega (6574) .04:38:29
151. Edward Lujan (6621) .04:38:56
152. Harlan Robinson (6634) .04:39:04
153. David Bockelman (6712) .04:40:02
154. Charles Bridges (6760) .04:40:44
155. Ken Boyd (6824) .04:41:37
156. Bill Smith (6845) .04:41:51
157. Raul Chavez (6885) .04:42:25
158. Leo Rein (6900) .04:42:35
159. Gerald Mitchell (6901) .04:42:37
160. Roger Adams (6904) .04:42:40
161. Geza Bottlik (6925) .04:42:52
162. Alden Chase (6938) .04:43:02
163. Anderson Durley (6968) .04:43:20
164. Larry Thomason (6985) .04:43:28
165. Don Uchiyama (6995) .04:43:34
166. Richard Moreno (7011) .04:43:42
167. Wayne Schenck (7013) .04:43:43
168. Jerome Uhrig (7070) .04:44:28
169. Ernie Morales (7088) .04:44:48
170. Arturo Dominguez (7117) .04:45:03
171. Fred Romani (7143) .04:45:21
172. Patrick Farrell (7189) .04:45:58
173. Stephen Lee (7230) .04:46:29
174. Dan Marotte (7245) .04:46:37
175. John Woolley (7331) .04:47:33
176. Andrew Hudson Jr (7332) .04:47:33
177. Bill Leeka (7340) .04:47:39
178. Francisco Ramos (7341) .04:47:40
179. John Mahon (7342) .04:47:41
180. Ray Abrams (7399) .04:48:22
181. Conan Mooney (7400) .04:48:23
182. Gary Yanagi (7459) .04:49:02
183. Alan Ragland (7461) .04:49:03
184. Victor Morales (7477) .04:49:12
185. Joseph Abella (7485) .04:49:19
186. James Borza Sr (7563) .04:50:08
187. Juri Kalviste (7576) .04:50:19
188. Dony Joaquin (7610) .04:50:45
189. Donald Erickson (7613) .04:50:46
190. Joseph Raymond (7622) .04:50:55
191. Shozo Hirano (7672) .04:51:38
192. Gordon Meyers (7757) .04:52:43
193. Georges Gross (7762) .04:52:48
194. Doug Shields (7861) .04:53:54
195. Bart Mata (7872) .04:54:02
196. Lawrence Friedman (7903) .04:54:22
197. Roger Edelson (7949) .04:54:44
198. David Marchetti (8020) .04:55:40
199. Leslie Enloe (8059) .04:56:10
200. Tachi Kiuchi (8071) .04:56:18
201. Paul Norton (8101) .04:56:41
202. John De Santis (8110) .04:56:45
203. Arnold Bertram (8119) .04:56:51
204. Lowell Hardison (8132) .04:57:04
205. Patrick Happekotte (8172) .04:57:35
206. Russell Sidles (8193) .04:57:50
207. Nathan Katz (8290) .04:58:50
208. Chuck Wolfe (8348) .04:59:26
209. Tom Boris (8356) .04:59:31
210. Joseph Alex (8373) .04:59:39
211. Harry Schwochert (8414) .05:00:17
212. Daniel Cohen (8442) .05:00:51
213. Rick Bingham (8462) .05:01:05
214. Roger Stromsta (8528) .05:01:48
215. Jesus Contreras (8531) .05:01:49
216. Norman Haines (8533) .05:01:50
217. David Gracia (8575) .05:02:24
218. William Sides (8612) .05:03:08
219. Willard Thompson (8653) .05:03:46
220. Jimmie Bible (8668) .05:03:56
221. Cal Farnham (8704) .05:04:20
222. Don Marshall (8715) .05:04:31
223. Jerry Margolin (8725) .05:04:42
224. Jim Brewer (8801) .05:06:03
225. George Ketterl (8810) .05:06:14
226. Ben Butler (8817) .05:06:22
227. Dewaine Breeden (8852) .05:06:58
228. Sydney Stevens (8892) .05:07:40
229. Larry Anners (8909) .05:07:56
230. Jim Allen (8943) .05:08:28
231. Arthur Schaefer (8948) .05:08:31
232. Thomas Stewart (8984) .05:08:58
233. Ben Jackson (9029) .05:09:30
234. Donn Conner (9033) .05:09:32
235. Rick Gonzalez (9040) .05:09:43
236. Joseph Alaniz (9043) .05:09:45
237. Joe Cox (9053) .05:09:51
238. Bill Coomber (9063) .05:09:58
239. Luis Pingarron (9163) .05:11:20
240. Jiro Watanabe (9235) .05:12:26
241. Joe Fong Cheng (9256) .05:12:49
242. Fredric Hermann (9261) .05:12:52
243. Thomas Markert (9266) .05:12:55
244. Bruce Bailey (9412) .05:14:57
245. Patrick Morris (9436) .05:15:24
246. Joe Hidalgo (9528) .05:16:56
247. R. Filon (9533) .05:17:00
248. Gary Hirn (9547) .05:17:09
249. Lennie Brown (9573) .05:17:26
250. Antonio Huizar (9592) .05:17:46
251. Frank Genco (9595) .05:17:48
252. Ted Richer (9597) .05:17:49
253. Don Hogue (9600) .05:17:51
254. Alan Bunnage (9768) .05:20:39
255. George Reitz (9769) .05:20:39
256. Dilip Bhatt (9794) .05:20:56
257. Larry King (9814) .05:21:16
258. Leland Jolicoeur (9847) .05:21:47
259. Milton Hall (9869) .05:22:03
260. Roy Abendroth (9875) .05:22:07
261. John Heavens (9919) .05:22:53
262. Rodney Akiyama (9922) .05:22:54
263. Pedro Salmeron (9982) .05:24:01
264. Paul Reilly (10000) .05:24:17
265. Paul Weber (10004) .05:24:26
266. James Foster (10031) .05:24:57
267. Bob Alexander (10071) .05:25:41
268. Yasuhiro Hagihara (10072) .05:25:41
269. William Peplow (10082) .05:25:48
270. Joel Sussman (10114) .05:26:17
271. Harry Thurston (10172) .05:27:23
272. Jack Blair (10186) .05:27:31
273. Michael Godfrey (10201) .05:27:46
274. Andy Tomenchuk (10245) .05:28:33
275. Nemi Imperio (10261) .05:28:46
276. Robert Morgan (10305) .05:29:15
277. Wayne Gose (10334) .05:29:49
278. Roger Shortall (10370) .05:30:20
279. Ray Cervantes Sr (10378) .05:30:29
280. Al Minturn (10384) .05:30:34
281. Mutsuo Mori (10386) .05:30:36
282. Marty Spoto (10429) .05:31:19
283. Goran Ryden (10470) .05:31:50
284. Bill Isaac (10482) .05:31:59
285. John Miller (10550) .05:33:12
286. Benny Langley (10573) .05:33:30
287. Terence Comiskey (10579) .05:33:38
288. Lee Willard (10633) .05:34:22
289. Fred Butler (10733) .05:35:52
290. Robert Wolfe (10765) .05:36:33
291. Celso Chetrancolo (10775) .05:36:38
292. Bobby Vincent (10788) .05:36:51
293. John Lee (10796) .05:37:02
294. Larry Welch (10803) .05:37:06
295. Jon McIntosh (10868) .05:38:30
296. Steve McLean (10925) .05:39:47
297. Robert Closson (10974) .05:40:47
298. John Hill Sr (11102) .05:43:03
299. Harry Yonemura (11137) .05:43:40
300. James Lee (11198) .05:44:29
301. Thomas Marnon (11221) .05:44:43
302. Danh Quach (11245) .05:45:11
303. Jay Foonberg (11297) .05:46:13
304. Yat Wong (11314) .05:46:35
305. Wayne Wirth (11376) .05:48:13
306. Raymond Young (11399) .05:48:58
307. Frank Kostas (11464) .05:49:53
308. Jerome Coyazo (11499) .05:50:28
309. Jacinto Rhines (11641) .05:53:12
310. Keith McPeek (11661) .05:53:31
311. John Walsh (11663) .05:53:37
312. William Doenges (11760) .05:55:36
313. J R Saldivar (11779) .05:56:00
314. Wayne Young (11906) .05:58:51
315. Leo Sam (11907) .05:58:51
316. Ben Blakley (11933) .05:59:30
317. Melvin Turner (11945) .05:59:48
318. Arthur Decker (12003) .06:01:16
319. James Elcock (12004) .06:01:21
320. Phuc Huy Truong (12006) .06:01:22
321. Antonio Valencia (12035) .06:02:13
322. Jack Henry (12066) .06:03:00
323. Stevan Scheff (12147) .06:05:11
324. Hassan Attalla (12164) .06:05:30
325. Charles Braun (12205) .06:06:47
326. Gary Cooper (12250) .06:08:08
327. Thomas Baughman (12265) .06:08:25
328. Donald Cochrane (12334) .06:09:57
329. John Gregory (12357) .06:10:46
330. Richard Wise (12420) .06:12:16
331. Richard Jones (12511) .06:14:42
332. Paul Wims (12592) .06:16:48
333. Phillip Minor (12603) .06:16:55
334. Rafique Khan (12700) .06:20:09
335. Douglas Greene (12718) .06:20:38
336. William Gincig (12770) .06:21:59
337. Joseph Kofsky (12773) .06:22:02
338. Oliver Reinertson (12800) .06:22:49
339. Bobby Avery (12808) .06:23:04
340. Max Curameng (12823) .06:23:33
341. Vicente Ynclino (12825) .06:23:37
342. Thomas Keesee (12930) .06:26:35
343. Lawrence Leon (13026) .06:29:27
344. Cyril Tanin (13113) .06:32:11
345. Bob Rissolo (13133) .06:32:38
346. James Smith (13141) .06:32:45
347. James Graves (13143) .06:32:46
348. Michael Shrubsole (13180) .06:33:50
349. Bill Williams (13221) .06:34:57
350. Lorenzo Mills (13311) .06:37:53
351. Joanne Otte (13353) .06:39:23
352. Donald Roy (13408) .06:41:23
353. Myra Grandison (13428) .06:42:07
354. Ronald Ankrom (13436) .06:42:15
355. Karl Tiedemann (13642) .06:49:52
356. Edward Walencewicz (13678) .06:50:34
357. Barry Schneider (13681) .06:50:35
358. Neil Dobbin (13691) .06:50:48
359. Thomas Ivers (13715) .06:51:37
360. Bani Vasquez (13841) .06:56:42
361. George Clark (13855) .06:57:00
362. Herbie Inglove (13893) .06:58:14
363. Cal Gleaton (13908) .06:58:39
364. Jack Eckenwiler (13911) .06:58:42
365. Norman Cravens (13991) .07:01:02
366. Richard Klutts (14030) .07:02:21
367. Tom James (14031) .07:02:31
368. Milton Johnson (14080) .07:04:57
369. Terrance Miller (14221) .07:13:58
370. John Mayoral (14316) .07:19:11
371. Ted Lengel (14623) .07:42:56
372. Cesar Quinones (14723) .07:52:29
373. Roy Mainero (14819) .08:01:54
374. Joseph Seneski (14866) .08:10:19
375. Kanu Patel (14871) .08:11:06
376. Charlle Allen (14931) .08:19:57
377. Joe Teran (14963) .08:24:53
378. Sukeyoshi Nagakura (14966) .08:26:07
379. John Stearns (15172) .10:40:00

WOMEN 55 TO 59

1. Mary Baker (1154) .03:28:37
2. Suzanne Murphy (1616) .03:37:26
3. Carrie Jean Napier (2785) .03:54:26
4. Laura Pinkney (2963) .03:56:28
5. Barbara Valastro (3051) .03:57:17
6. Joanne Barker (3316) .04:00:13
7. Nena Gebhardt (3504) .04:02:45
8. Elaine Murphy (3684) .04:05:01
9. Marilyn Clark (4075) .04:10:06
10. Kayo Yoneta (5218) .04:23:21
11. Maureen McColligan (6058) .04:32:57
12. Isabelle Rose (6300) .04:35:37
13. Mary Dugan (6408) .04:36:38
14. Katsuko Uema (7441) .04:48:50
15. Mary Hack (7775) .04:52:56
16. Yvette Tauzin (8155) .04:57:23
17. Catherine Kaeller (8330) .04:59:11
18. Joan Rowe (8747) .05:05:11

19. Karen Mallow (9122) 05:10:29
20. Emiko Watanabe (9234) 05:12:26
21. Sandra Gitmed (9356) 05:13:57
22. Christa Sidles (9559) 05:17:14
23. Erica Hersh (10166) 05:27:17
24. Mina Brown (10368) 05:30:19
25. Leora Mudge (10374) 05:30:25
26. Nelda Stuck (10449) 05:31:34
27. Leona Davis (10453) 05:31:37
28. Simone King (10766) 05:36:34
29. Sam Wildman (10811) 05:37:15
30. June Kizu (10815) 05:37:21
31. Joyce Madison (10825) 05:37:31
32. Mamie Strawn (10826) 05:37:32
33. Donna Arbuckle (11112) 05:43:11
34. Patricia Stoll (11200) 05:44:30
35. Phyllis Goldstein (11276) 05:45:49
36. Vikki Richardson (11331) 05:46:51
37. Jean Sarno (11490) 05:50:21
38. Dorothy Strand (11522) 05:50:45
39. Feliza Perez (11691) 05:54:00
40. Vivienne Wynne (12037) 06:02:14
41. Marcia Wolfe (12067) 06:03:00
42. Judith Miller (12148) 06:05:11
43. Evelyn Tapia (12236) 06:07:45
44. Virginia Lespron (12500) 06:14:22
45. Nancy Crowley (12506) 06:14:33
46. Sandra Wise (12528) 06:15:12
47. Judy Casar (12667) 06:19:11
48. Ursula Marti (12681) 06:19:38
49. Sonia Scheideman (12726) 06:20:57
50. Marion Klein (12822) 06:23:30
51. Ruth Milner (12882) 06:25:18
52. Mildred Harrison (12885) 06:25:24
53. Dinah Martin (12913) 06:26:13
54. Mary Jane Helton (12921) 06:26:27
55. Julie Taylor (12922) 06:26:28
56. Rose O'brien (12944) 06:27:00
57. Virginia Tracy (12958) 06:27:38
58. Sallye Steele (13140) 06:32:45
59. Beth Whitaker (13262) 06:36:06
60. Jeannine White (13283) 06:36:50
61. Mary Simmons (13288) 06:37:02
62. Susan Steele (13326) 06:38:30
63. Ruth Carter (13331) 06:38:39
64. Jeri Richmond (13437) 06:42:16
65. Marilyn Katzmark (13532) 06:46:05
66. Carmen Watkins (13546) 06:46:23
67. Norma Zernik (13608) 06:48:31
68. Susan Klenner (13713) 06:51:25
69. Amelia Turney (13702) 06:54:05
70. Martha Marca (13789) 06:55:05
71. Anne Kall (13816) 06:55:49
72. Ruth Nelson (13826) 06:55:58
73. Frances Washington (13916) 06:58:44
74. Donna Saller (13987) 07:00:59
75. Carlotta Cravens (13992) 07:01:02
76. Beverly Sidrow (14074) 07:04:42
77. Jean Williams (14078) 07:04:53
78. Estherly Colton (14004) 07:04:58
79. Vivian Baldo (14101) 07:06:25
80. Marge Shearer (14107) 07:06:45
81. Naomi Bruce (14138) 07:08:33
82. Peggy Manis (14153) 07:09:59
83. Sandy Messerman (14172) 07:11:08
84. Shirley Hiebert (14179) 07:11:18
85. Octavia Miles (14102) 07:11:46
86. Ellen Wright (14214) 07:13:26
87. Maureen Stehle (14219) 07:13:44
88. Olive Reed (14306) 07:18:34
89. Ann Alexander (14318) 07:19:16
90. Mary Laffey (14370) 07:22:36
91. Beverlyn Hardy (14453) 07:29:46
92. Sharene Greene (14456) 07:30:00
93. Sharon Dellamarie (14475) 07:31:12
94. Kelly Ann Hubert (14513) 07:35:10
95. Ruby Brown (14529) 07:36:05
96. Maryjane Delgado (14560) 07:38:30
97. Tessa Gaetos (14569) 07:38:49
98. Darlene Fischer (14618) 07:42:46
99. Mary Steen (14624) 07:43:11
100. Mini Monk-Jackson (14649) 07:45:51
101. Amada Briseno (14671) 07:48:03
102. Joann Hulkower (14676) 07:48:22
103. Susan Rogers (14685) 07:49:35
104. Joan Souza (14695) 07:50:01
105. Lynn Kessler (14705) 07:51:35
106. Fumiko Cable (14763) 07:55:51
107. Sharlene Goodman (14786) 07:59:13
108. Marianne Heidecke (14855) 08:07:27
109. Alice McGrew (14865) 08:10:03
110. Marie Fleming (14880) 08:12:29
111. Patricia Engel (14883) 08:12:42
112. Rita Castaneda (14889) 08:14:47
113. Amy Ibarra (14890) 08:14:47
114. Elena Gallarza (14954) 08:22:21
115. Oni Adunni (14968) 08:26:12
116. Rosina Becerra (14998) 08:31:50
117. Carmel Silva (15007) 08:33:29
118. Margaret Barringer (15017) 08:35:02
119. Mary Campos (15044) 08:45:36

MEN 60 TO 64

1. Epifanio Morales Tellez (146) 02:54:05
2. Hiroshi Ogata (280) 03:02:56
3. John Murphy (469) 03:10:47
4. Alfonso Castillo (510) 03:12:29
5. Wayne Fong (914) 03:23:38
6. Ben Bernal (969) 03:24:46
7. Steve Pinkney (1090) 03:27:30
8. Donald Boyd (1131) 03:28:11
9. Thomas Kramer (1218) 03:29:42
10. Fausto Vettore (1219) 03:29:44
11. Frank Ferrone (1478) 03:35:02
12. Vic Gainer (1598) 03:37:09
13. Fred Vega (1911) 03:42:12
14. Carlos Ruiz (2031) 03:44:16
15. Rex May (2137) 03:45:43
16. Hugh Mc Minigal (2156) 03:45:56
17. Colby Churchman (2292) 03:48:01
18. Irvin Williams (2488) 03:50:36
19. Karl Hering (2496) 03:50:43
20. Louis Simms Jr (2574) 03:51:48
21. John Rudberg (2613) 03:52:21
22. Burt Elliott (2671) 03:53:02
23. Aldo Mora (2694) 03:53:19
24. Preben Poulsen (3012) 03:56:56
25. Charley Penrose (3060) 03:57:23
26. Vladimir Babichev (3142) 03:58:21
27. Werner Buchholz (3196) 03:58:58
28. Steve Mager (3230) 03:59:23
29. Paul Straub (3296) 03:59:59
30. Jim Willis (3415) 04:01:29
31. Rafael Guerrero (3429) 04:01:39
32. John Anderson (3446) 04:01:55
33. Jose Segura (3496) 04:02:37
34. Milton Strief (3538) 04:03:14
35. Ed Donchey (3735) 04:05:47
36. Franz Schmon (3794) 04:06:32
37. Stan Lisiewicz (3838) 04:07:02
38. Robert Maytag (4034) 04:09:31
39. Jim Schnitzler (4132) 04:10:50
40. Juan Salazar (4147) 04:10:57
41. James Shrader (4237) 04:12:08
42. Michael McSkane (4637) 04:16:36
43. Jack Eberly (4697) 04:17:27
44. Edgardo Villalobos (4722) 04:17:48
45. Edward Burman (4763) 04:18:12
46. Norman Ablett (4780) 04:18:24
47. Willie Gilmore (4848) 04:19:01
48. Mel Kindel (4920) 04:19:49
49. Marv Cabelli (4947) 04:20:07
50. Frank Quinn (5069) 04:21:49
51. Bill Steinauer (5171) 04:22:53
52. Maurice Tauzin (5202) 04:23:14
53. Dick Olson (5287) 04:24:28
54. Roger Staebler (5598) 04:27:47
55. Salvador Vega (5611) 04:27:56
56. Robert Burdick (5633) 04:28:06
57. Federico Castro (5676) 04:28:37
58. Michael Moore (5718) 04:29:03
59. John Zablocki (5881) 04:30:45
60. Jim Scarborough (5942) 04:31:28
61. Bobby Francis (5955) 04:31:38
62. Bing Tuthill (5956) 04:31:39
63. Norman Cohen (6003) 04:32:19
64. Lee Dycus (6158) 04:34:08
65. Don Valentine (6224) 04:34:46
66. John Perez (6346) 04:36:07
67. George Butt (6411) 04:36:39
68. Joe Carrillo (6464) 04:37:25
69. Ed Larson (6664) 04:39:30
70. Harold Vance (6668) 04:39:33
71. Horst Sprung (6674) 04:39:38
72. Ignacio Valenzuela (6701) 04:39:52
73. Aloysius Casey (6711) 04:40:02
74. Masatoshi Anma (6777) 04:41:02
75. Miguel Chinea (6791) 04:41:08
76. John Smart (6832) 04:41:42
77. Victor Camarillo (6863) 04:42:04
78. Charles Cabasag (6891) 04:42:29
79. Bill Syverson (6908) 04:42:45
80. Edward Salkin (7022) 04:43:53
81. Richard Van Demark (7029) 04:43:56
82. Larry Beck (7067) 04:44:23
83. Jim Bassler (7085) 04:44:44
84. Stephen Bland (7114) 04:45:02
85. Cesar Gabonia (7178) 04:45:50
86. Ahmed Abdul-Bari (7225) 04:46:26
87. Frank Biehl (7249) 04:46:42
88. Sam Gee (7349) 04:47:46
89. Fred Schneider (7380) 04:48:11
90. Ken Okada (7457) 04:49:02
91. William Price (7495) 04:49:22
92. Lyle Deem (7531) 04:49:45
93. Al Remolino (7600) 04:50:39
94. Emilio Chavez (7612) 04:50:46
95. Hans Walter (7644) 04:51:08
96. Merrill Francis (7652) 04:51:22
97. Howard Leupp (7729) 04:52:19
98. Robert Miller (7795) 04:53:13
99. Jose Cruz Duras (7802) 04:53:17
100. Carlos Cordoba (7811) 04:53:24
101. Dick Windishar (7904) 04:54:23
102. John Valenzuela (7928) 04:54:33
103. Feliciano Olmos (7997) 04:55:20
104. Jack Goldfarb (8033) 04:55:49
105. Ta Nguyen (8040) 04:55:52
106. Richard Cerecedes (8088) 04:56:33
107. Cecil Schoolcraft (8111) 04:56:46
108. Harold Stanley (8248) 04:58:19
109. James Buchanan (8297) 04:58:53
110. Nathan Cass (8351) 04:59:29
111. T C Chung (8394) 04:59:56
112. Donald Fuller (8452) 05:00:58
113. Masato Takahashi (8476) 05:01:13
114. Ron McDaniel (8480) 05:01:18
115. Rafael Valdivia (8594) 05:02:47
116. Whitney Wilson (8603) 05:03:03
117. Nat Landau (8623) 05:03:14
118. David Hoffman (8738) 05:04:55
119. George Bender (8744) 05:05:06
120. James Garren (8867) 05:07:10
121. Russ Graham (8890) 05:07:38
122. Jerry Gullick (8926) 05:08:08
123. Ralph Arceri (8940) 05:08:25
124. Juan Burgos (9049) 05:09:48
125. Muhamed Najmi (9145) 05:10:56
126. Jim Smith (9154) 05:11:02
127. Manny Garcia (9228) 05:12:20
128. Phil Fetchko (9373) 05:14:11
129. Charles Arnold (9385) 05:14:25
130. Hyung Pak (9437) 05:15:26
131. Leoncio Gabriel (9461) 05:15:57
132. Kaoru Higuchi (9508) 05:16:36
133. Stanley Peacock (9515) 05:16:40
134. John Strand (9538) 05:17:03
135. Dumas Tambunan (9574) 05:17:27
136. Jack Heindl (9639) 05:18:33
137. Gus Cardenas (9656) 05:18:46
138. David Sowers (9675) 05:19:02
139. George Spellman (9715) 05:19:44
140. John Chappel (9780) 05:20:47
141. Richard Small (9895) 05:22:24
142. Danny Castellanos (9923) 05:22:55
143. Ignacio Mariscal (9928) 05:22:59
144. Jack Riley (9933) 05:23:14
145. Wade Richmond (9966) 05:23:42
146. Robert Rauch (9976) 05:23:54
147. Cornelius Lino (10174) 05:27:24
148. Matahiko Ide (10343) 05:29:55
149. Peter Anderson (10355) 05:30:09
150. Frank Ota (10365) 05:30:18
151. Philip Shapiro (10418) 05:31:08
152. Gary Jystad (10447) 05:31:33
153. Tony Talbot (10562) 05:33:26
154. Charles Phillips (10578) 05:33:36
155. Rich Metcalfe (10596) 05:33:48
156. John Wells (10621) 05:34:06
157. Paul Whitmarsh (10654) 05:34:40
158. James McMath (10672) 05:34:56
159. Robert Prochaska (10711) 05:35:28
160. William Stevens (10736) 05:35:54
161. Frank Pitts (10740) 05:36:00
162. Ping Chen (10785) 05:36:49
163. Ray Hair (10872) 05:38:36
164. Janis Straubergs (10906) 05:39:16
165. Manuel Nava (10954) 05:40:23
166. Richard Dowling (10983) 05:41:07
167. James Munson (11022) 05:41:50
168. Jaime Martinez (11079) 05:42:41
169. William Phillips (11093) 05:42:54
170. Joseph Juliano (11117) 05:43:17
171. Jacques Souadjian (11143) 05:43:48
172. Bruce Arden (11148) 05:43:52
173. David Padilla (11163) 05:44:11
174. Bert Grigsby (11242) 05:45:07
175. Hoang Pham (11243) 05:45:08
176. Jimmy Tanaka (11277) 05:45:51
177. Carlos Flores (11283) 05:45:56
178. Richard Lem (11292) 05:46:04
179. Bernard Franklin (11295) 05:46:09
180. James Balderas (11398) 05:48:56
181. A Sitaraman (11409) 05:49:06
182. Donald Lang (11462) 05:49:50
183. Boyd Clampitt (11463) 05:49:52
184. Elias Mancilla (11500) 05:50:28
185. Sudyong Toprasert (11568) 05:51:57
186. Johnny Nixon (11600) 05:52:23
187. Dick Moore (11626) 05:53:00
188. Raymond Derek (11751) 05:55:22
189. Ed Saldivar (11780) 05:56:01
190. Ralph Luna (11795) 05:56:30
191. Donald Brody (11857) 05:58:02
192. Henry Lou (11898) 05:58:40
193. Milton Jones (11920) 05:59:15
194. John Barnett (11935) 05:59:32
195. John Davis (11990) 06:00:53
196. Claude Moore (12143) 06:05:02
197. Federico Ocon (12271) 06:08:37
198. Robert Watkins (12384) 06:11:21
199. Richard Simons (12455) 06:13:13
200. Franklyn Venable (12473) 06:13:45
201. Frank Ferren (12478) 06:13:52
202. Sherman Don (12504) 06:14:24
203. Clyde Gonzales (12668) 06:19:12
204. David Hirscher (12831) 06:23:41
205. Ronald Carter (12842) 06:23:51
206. Carleton Brown (12916) 06:26:16
207. Joe Green (12952) 06:27:29
208. Daniel Alvarez (12996) 06:28:33
209. Harry Flynn (13010) 06:28:48
210. Larry Lake (13114) 06:32:13
211. Manuel Cadena (13182) 06:33:51
212. Dee Sedgwick (13208) 06:34:39
213. Lew Winters (13237) 06:35:24
214. Shigeo Sumida (13285) 06:36:02
215. Ted Henry (13322) 06:38:26
216. Mickey Pardo (13370) 06:39:54
217. Rodrick Wallace (13424) 06:42:01
218. Jim Walling (13425) 06:42:01
219. Robert Bils (13442) 06:42:32
220. Foster Myers (13453) 06:42:53
221. Jaris Thomas (13499) 06:44:53
222. Barney Harvey Jr (13587) 06:47:49
223. Walter Brackelmanns (13702) 06:51:06
224. John Squiroo Sr (13704) 06:51:21
225. Ellsworth Wiltz (13757) 06:53:53
226. Grant Cotter (13952) 06:59:56
227. Charles Colton (14069) 07:04:18
228. Brian Drew (14111) 07:07:00
229. Robert Martinez (14132) 07:08:22
230. Sid Rosenblatt (14174) 07:11:10
231. Larry Walker (14193) 07:12:26
232. Richard Wright (14215) 07:13:34
233. Hilario Diaz Jr (14326) 07:19:50
234. Brent Gillis (14340) 07:21:11
235. Luther Jose (14427) 07:26:58
236. Edward Deto (14440) 07:29:28
237. Paul Slaney (14505) 07:34:30
238. Jerry Cotter (14532) 07:36:15
239. Bill White (14853) 08:07:12
240. Walter De Rothn'e Jr (14886) 08:13:21
241. Larry Sherwin (14915) 08:17:39
242. Robert Greeson (15093) 08:59:51

WOMEN 60 TO 64

1. Wen-Shi Yu (2521) 03:51:03
2. Madonna Buder (4281) 04:12:42
3. Fujiko Yamada (4563) 04:15:49
4. Patricia De Vita (6697) 04:39:50
5. Bobbi Pollock (7564) 04:50:08
6. Lilly Viveros (7596) 04:50:35
7. Gertrud Tokloth (8018) 04:55:37
8. Maria Balke (9121) 05:10:28
9. Sheila Miller (9224) 05:12:16
10. Lillian Kirschenbaum (9870) 05:22:03
11. Vici Dehaan (10533) 05:32:54
12. Gudrun Naschak (10701) 05:35:23
13. Elaine Herfert (10726) 05:35:46
14. Lily Dovalina (11316) 05:46:37
15. Aurora Perez (11338) 05:46:58
16. Charlotte Schroeder (11900) 05:58:43
17. Gillian Murdoch (11989) 06:00:52
18. Winifred Tuck (11992) 06:00:58
19. Juana Vance (12057) 06:02:43
20. Willa Porter (12102) 06:04:13
21. Mae Smith (12202) 06:06:40
22. Liza Clinch (12576) 06:16:20
23. Freda Churchman (12597) 06:16:51
24. Anka Patrick (12622) 06:17:36
25. Judith Valles (12683) 06:19:40
26. Elsie Staats (12703) 06:20:12
27. Barbara Green (12835) 06:23:47
28. Beverly Benson (12923) 06:26:28
29. Emily Hernandez (12931) 06:26:35
30. Cappy Jackson (13002) 06:28:39
31. Marjorie West (13012) 06:29:00
32. Maureen Licht (13058) 06:30:43
33. Mary Speights (13183) 06:33:52
34. Marlene Zamberlin (13190) 06:34:11
35. Jeanie Lewis (13206) 06:34:35
36. May Musenga (13224) 06:35:02
37. Audrey Hebert (13287) 06:37:02
38. Nancy Kraft (13351) 06:39:13
39. Shirley Kerr (13423) 06:41:58
40. Kathleen Callaway (13463) 06:43:19
41. Rachel Sandoval (13643) 06:49:53
42. Betty Pagenkopf (13706) 06:51:24
43. Frances Maynard (13731) 06:52:19
44. Marlene Kalish (13806) 06:55:29
45. Ivory Weatherall (13828) 06:56:00
46. Maryann Smith (13860) 06:57:08
47. Jeanie Weil (14072) 07:04:40
48. Eva Morales (14085) 07:05:00
49. Lela Williams (14157) 07:10:17
50. Arlene Rosenblatt (14173) 07:11:09
51. Mary Noble (14224) 07:14:09
52. Frances Seary (14294) 07:17:37
53. Lucille Edwards (14365) 07:22:35
54. Ann Cotter (14531) 07:36:14
55. Ernestine Popplewell (14552) 07:37:17
56. Gloria Sluwe (14694) 07:49:56
57. Patti Hodge (14725) 07:52:31
58. Constance Pierson (14994) 08:30:46
59. Frances Richartz (15010) 08:45:42
60. Carmen Garcia (15054) 08:47:40
61. Regina Schneider (15066) 08:51:50
62. Parsomsee Ruenprom (15077) 08:55:21

MEN 65 TO 69

1. Richard Roodberg (676) 03:17:24
2. Patrick Devine (776) 03:20:16
3. Richard Lamermayer (2043) 03:44:24
4. Eugene Young (2751) 03:54:08
5. Raymond Wright (2819) 03:54:47
6. Curtis Brownfield (3016) 03:56:58
7. Edwin Travers (3129) 03:58:08
8. Robert Waldron (4544) 04:15:38
9. Alan Carlisle (4720) 04:17:47
10. Rao Paladugu (4814) 04:18:44
11. Luis Perez (4863) 04:19:12
12. Luis Marroquin (4883) 04:19:22
13. Don Kirkman (4981) 04:20:30
14. Edgar Driver (5243) 04:23:41
15. Patrick Mulvihill (5854) 04:30:34
16. Hugh McHugh (6137) 04:33:48
17. Hugh McHugh (6255) 04:35:10
18. Thomas Daniel (6489) 04:37:37
19. Jack Rohde-Moe (6497) 04:37:40
20. Dan Sheeran (6555) 04:38:15
21. Leonard Romero (6600) 04:38:42
22. Roque Torres (6699) 04:39:51
23. Daniel Mejia (6969) 04:43:21
24. Joseph Tanski (7223) 04:46:24
25. Robert De Vita (7404) 04:48:24
26. Tatsuya Fujita (7507) 04:49:28
27. John Smets (7573) 04:50:17
28. Gene Doss (7880) 04:54:08
29. Walter San Martin (7933) 04:54:34
30. Ignacio Romero (7942) 04:54:39
31. Bob Goldman (7992) 04:55:16
32. Robert Davis (8166) 04:57:29
33. Sal Chaidez (8184) 04:57:43
34. Jerry Guritzky (8220) 04:58:06
35. Francis Petracek (8246) 04:58:18
36. Frank Chen (8289) 04:58:49
37. Roberto McAfee (8625) 05:03:16
38. Del King (8643) 05:03:32
39. Ira Smith (8688) 05:04:10
40. George Nakai (8707) 05:04:21
41. Allen Bergman (8827) 05:06:30
42. Arthur Zussman (8991) 05:09:04
43. David Harrah (9111) 05:10:24
44. Reuben Strope (9138) 05:10:49
45. Lono Tyson (9151) 05:11:00
46. Robert Soderholm (9169) 05:11:27
47. Reinhold Ullrich (9259) 05:12:50
48. Jerry Kirschenbaum (9624) 05:18:23
49. Henry Terusa (9628) 05:18:26
50. Heitaro Shimomura (9663) 05:18:53
51. Mark Kruse (9886) 05:22:15
52. Harry Anderson (9908) 05:22:42
53. Sir Orville Bingley 3RD (9956) 05:23:33
54. Richard Rhodes (10152) 05:27:05
55. Robert Dubarr (10274) 05:28:52
56. Edward Rasky (10352) 05:30:08
57. Larry Cobb (10393) 05:30:38
58. John Carbin (10487) 05:32:04
59. Jorge Albrecht (10501) 05:32:19
60. Manny Leon (10661) 05:34:43
61. George Hanna (10918) 05:39:35
62. Richard Mead (11001) 05:41:29
63. Thomas Dolan (11236) 05:44:58
64. Alvin Goldstein (11257) 05:45:26
65. Everett West (11646) 05:53:16
66. Takao Ushiyama (11711) 05:54:36
67. Morton Kanter (11791) 05:56:27
68. Saul Meyer (11835) 05:57:25
69. Richard High (12032) 06:02:04
70. Jeff Allan (12180) 06:05:51
71. Ventura Ybarra (12264) 06:08:23
72. Duane Ewers (12309) 06:09:16
73. Jongsung Kim (12356) 06:10:37
74. Esteban Castillo (12431) 06:12:40
75. Florencio Lazalde (12523) 06:15:08
76. George Timchenko (12543) 06:15:27
77. Norb Schlei (12619) 06:17:28
78. Robert Herrera (12774) 06:22:03
79. Sam Emer (12967) 06:27:50
80. Mort Rimer (13021) 06:29:16
81. William Lockwood (13276) 06:36:28
82. Abraham Lakshin (13578) 06:47:31
83. Donald La Venture (13912) 06:58:42
84. Jerry Kaufman (14034) 07:02:36
85. Peter Sasaki (14047) 07:03:08
86. Luis Pagan (14055) 07:03:39
87. Flavio Bisignano (14083) 07:04:58
88. Don Fuller (14106) 07:06:39
89. Rudi Nathalang (14195) 07:12:36
90. Leslie Longshore Jr (14266) 07:15:54
91. Melvin Dallis (14460) 07:30:20
92. Sam Ranshaw (14479) 07:31:39
93. Leonard Zalewski (14635) 07:44:48
94. Mercedes Quinones (14647) 07:45:48
95. Robert Casey (14738) 07:53:52
96. Thomas Anaya (14794) 07:59:58
97. Edward Roman (14796) 08:00:28
98. David Rappoport (14848) 08:05:31
99. Fred Crippen (14863) 08:09:55
100. Ural Ruenprom (15074) 08:54:54

WOMEN 65 TO 69

1. Anna Hollenberg (4653) 04:16:51
2. Antoinette Hill (5484) 04:26:29
3. Linda Lakshin (7287) 04:47:06
4. Mary Ehrlich (7662) 04:51:31
5. Lillian Miller (8151) 04:57:19
6. Barbara Innes (10716) 05:35:32
7. Betty Robinson (11946) 05:59:50
8. Jane Totten (12186) 06:06:05
9. Inez Phillips (12702) 06:20:10
10. Guadalupe Castaneda (12750) 06:21:36
11. Lenore Rebeschini (12886) 06:25:24
12. Trudy Pietrolungo (13037) 06:30:01
13. Virginia Skinner (13327) 06:38:33
14. Esther Hill (13484) 06:44:09
15. Marylou Rooney (13534) 06:46:09
16. Mary Hanna (13628) 06:49:12
17. Lorraine Boyd (13920) 06:58:55
18. Fay Champion (14202) 07:12:52
19. Marie Horowitz (14733) 07:53:48
20. Rita Cobb (14750) 07:55:02
21. Sue Crowell (15042) 08:44:45

MEN 70 TO 74

1. Fred Nagelschmidt (2252) 03:47:28
2. Raymond Penkert (2478) 03:50:28
3. Milton Bassett (5075) 04:21:52
4. Manuel Lara (5985) 04:32:00
5. William Norris (7620) 04:50:51
6. Alonzo Monk (8312) 04:59:00
7. Salvador Avila (8638) 05:03:30
8. Daniel Lujan (8865) 05:07:10
9. Rudy De Leon (9706) 05:19:30
10. Paul Shearer (9810) 05:21:11
11. Kino Metzler (10723) 05:35:40
12. Arthur Bednersh (11294) 05:46:08
13. James Conrad (11317) 05:46:38
14. Benjamin McDonnell (11393) 05:48:51
15. Milton Headley (11541) 05:51:06
16. Eldred Arthur (12277) 06:08:45
17. Philip Smart (12449) 06:13:07
18. Abe Stein (12607) 06:16:58
19. Charles Baldridge (12696) 06:20:05
20. Jaime Del Rosario (12833) 06:23:45
21. Ross Adey (12986) 06:28:10
22. Hart Yoshioka (13150) 06:32:55
23. Robert Albin (13313) 06:38:02
24. Alvin Levenson (13410) 06:41:25
25. Eliot Shimer (13743) 06:52:47
26. John Orliski (14307) 07:18:36
27. Vidal Pedro (14328) 07:19:59
28. Kenneth Davidson (14407) 07:25:59
29. Albert Pugliese (14419) 07:26:45
30. Frank Campbell (14607) 07:41:38

WOMEN 70 TO 74

1. Evelyn Riel (9242) 05:12:32
2. Hortense Tarango (10320) 05:29:24
3. Po Adams (10389) 05:30:37
4. Dorothy Lineberry (11097) 05:42:57
5. Beatrice Baldridge (12791) 06:22:36
6. Gladys Mathes (13485) 06:44:10
7. Catherine Scott (13505) 06:45:07
8. Grace Davidson (13956) 07:00:10
9. Ruth McIntyre (14554) 07:37:18
10. Hope Rosenfeld (15147) 09:48:40
11. Margaret Duarte (15155) 09:53:11

MEN 75 TO 79

1. John Rodriquez (11047) 05:42:17
2. Harry Warshawsky (13060) 06:30:44
3. Felix Saldumbide (13909) 06:58:40
4. Francisco Raul-Rivera (13942) 06:59:32
5. Fred Brooks (13975) 07:00:43
6. Edward Campbell (14392) 07:24:07
7. J Walter Cobb (15053) 08:46:53
8. Andy Wolf Collins (15062) 08:49:51

WOMEN 75 TO 79

1. Sarah London (11765) 05:55:43
2. Priscilla Libby (14773) 07:56:09

MEN 80 TO 90

1. Ernest Van Leeuwen (10866) 05:38:17
2. George Feinstein (11585) 05:52:13
3. John Moen Sr (11671) 05:53:42
4. Al Clark (13686) 06:50:38
5. Vincent Malizia (14018) 07:02:02
6. Tautalalaititi Suluga (14487) 07:32:56
7. William Kuester (14991) 08:30:16

WOMEN 80 TO 98

1. Mavis Lindgren (14697) 07:50:21

WHEELCHAIR RESULTS

1. Paul R. Wiggins, Long Beach 1:36:06
2. Thomas F. Sellers, Ormond Beach,FL 1:40:11
3. Claude Issorat, Guadeloupe 1:41:22
4. Craig Blanchette, Cheney,WA 1:41:23
5. Jeff Adams, Canada 1:46:39
6. David Holding, Great Britain 1:46:40
7. Eric J. Kaiser, Santa Barbara 1:48:08
8. Jean-Marc Berset, Switzerland 1:49:05
9. Gorge Z. Luna, Santa Fe Spring 1:49:24
10. Scott R. Parson, Santa Barbara 1:49:27
11. Mustapha Badid, Austin,TX 1:49:31
12. Heinz Frei, Switzerland 1:51:32
13. Tony Nogueira, Glen Ridge,NJ 1:51:47
14. Jean Driscoll, Champaign,IL 1:52:51
15. David Bailey, Vista 1:53:50
16. Rich M. Wagner, Columbus,OH 1:55:42
17. Carlos Moleda, Fountain Hills,AZ 1:56:12
18. Chad R. Guzman, La Quinta 1:56:16
19. Huber Garcia, Miami,FL 1:56:21
20. Jack McKenna, Great Britain 1:57:14
21. Michel Juteau, Canada 1:57:22
22. Jose Zarragoicochea, Los Angeles 1:59:13
23. Wayne S. Phillips, Canada 1:59:56
24. Louise A. Sauvage, Australia 2:00:48
25. Deanna M. Sodoma, Carlsbad 2:00:49
26. Christopher Waddell, Vail,CO 2:01:51
27. James J. Lilly, Summit Argo,IL 2:03:50
28. Ann C. Walters, Champaign,IL 2:04:03
29. Joe Hamilton, Los Angeles 2:04:06
30. Max Weber, Germany 2:06:10
31. JOHN DOE, ...2:06:11
32. Chantal Petitclerc, Canada 2:09:07
33. Robert F. Nichol, Sharon,MA 2:09:12
34. Scott A. Musser, Bellefontaine,OH 2:09:28
35. Tanni Grey, Great Britain 2:10:47
36. Christoph Etzlstorfer, Austria 2:14:46
37. Bradley M. Ramage, Richmond,VA 2:14:51
38. Luke Gingras, Canada 2:15:16
39. Chris Mogensen, Simi Valley 2:15:34
40. Don Caron, West Hills 2:15:35
41. Brent Mc Mahon, Atlanta,GA 2:16:16
42. John C. Brewer, Salt Lake City,UT 2:18:24
43. Oliver Bedow, Germany 2:19:03
44. Bart D. Bardwell, Stewartville,MN 2:21:16
45. Fred A. Tomkins, Montclair 2:21:18
46. Rose Hill, Great Britain 2:23:47
47. Unidentified 2:24:04
48. Ricardo Castaneda, South Gate 2:24:44
49. Dean Bergeron, Canada 2:25:49
50. Clayton R. Gerein, Canada 2:27:09
51. Mark Cline, Lee's Summit, MO 2:27:19
52. Lily Anggreny, Germany 2:34:06
53. Scot Hollenbeck, Champaign, IL 2:36:42
54. Robert Thornton, Camarillo 2:37:00
55. Hector Jimenez, Venice 2:38:43
56. Sergio Calderon, Los Angeles 2:41:00
57. Mario Medina Pena, Mexico 2:41:49
58. Jon Franks, Venice 2:49:59
59. John H. Wiley, San Gabriel 2:59:10
60. Mary H. Thompson, San Diego 3:00:29
61. Marco Rodriguez, Guatemala 3:05:50
62. Stephen Beck, Fullerton 3:25:21
63. Richard P. Radford, El Segundo 3:46:07
64. Gilberto Alvaez, Los Angeles 3:52:14
65. Aldo Aldana, Los Angeles 3:57:25
66. Alejandro Lopez, Los Angeles 4:03:43
67. Gary Ware, Inglewood 4:57:34
68. Peter L. Lassen, Los Angeles 5:04:29

RACEWALKER RESULTS

1. Enrique Camarena, North Hollywood 4.10.40
2. Mark W. Ericson, Yuma,AZ 4:18:12
3. Christoph Dreher, Glendale 4:23:28
4. Brenda Mac Isaac, Costa Mesa 4:41:17
5. John W. Loeschhorn, Irvine 4:43:05
6. Charles A. Cutting, Loma Linda 4:48:09
7. Arvid Rolle, Cypress 4:52:49
8. Bill Neder, Los Angeles 5:01:06
9. Mel Schultz, Aliso Viejo 5:03:26
10. Dave Thorpe, Solana Beach 5:04:20
11. James S. De Paola, Hacienda Heights 5:04:24
12. James H. Long, Garden Grove 5:07:26
13. Robert F. Mimm, Willingboro,NJ 5:12:57
14. Laura G. Urish, Thousand Oaks 5:14:12
15. Dianne Dalbey, Torrance 5:15:22
16. Brierly F. Reybine, San Francisco 5:16:28
17. Cathy L. Chung, Phoenix,AZ 5:24:36
18. Robbie Sturms, Inglewood 5:24:58
19. James N. Fisher, Mill Valley 5:26:07
20. Gaila Myers, Camarillo 5:27:20
21. Mike K. Uema, Lompoc 5:29:08
22. Sheila L. Galinsky, Camarillo 5:29:57
23. Janos Damnavits, Los Angeles 5:31:04
24. Cheryl A. Davis, Camarillo 5:32:22
25. Stephen L. Collins, Pomona 5:32:24
26. Sharon Davidson, Camarillo 5:32:24
27. Greg Antonio, Cerritos 5:34:41
28. Elizabeth A. Stark, Upland 5:35:28
29. Larry F. Bazinet, Ramona 5:36:03
30. Shoshana W. Murphy, Thousand Oaks ...5:36:04
31. Joel R. Hubler, Mesa,AZ 5:37:10
32. Gloria Hrellanes, Montclair 5:37:21
33. Steve Arellanes, Montclair 5:37:23
34. Richard C. Lenhart, Torrance 5:37:55
35. Micheal D. Higginbotham, San Diego 5:39:20
36. Gilbert Dominguez, Los Angeles 5:39:26
37. Peter H. Doggett, Long Beach 5:40:19
38. Unidentified 5:42:11
39. Ernest C. Clark Jr, Los Angeles 5:43:55
40. Sylvia R. Ortiz, Whittier 5:44:12
41. Moses Dennis, Los Angeles 5:45:03
42. Rafael V. Porter, Inglewood 5:46:14
43. Michael J. Bayne, San Gabriel 5:48:28
44. Dona M. Perry, Camarillo 5:53:15
45. Anthony R. Farinella, El Monte 5:53:16
46. Jacinto Mogena, Lincroft,NJ 5:53:56
47. Suzy M. Reynolds, Atascadero 5:54:26
48. Joann P. Bally, Redondo Beach 5:54:26
49. Calvary M. McGrath, Rancho Cucamonga .5:57:33
50. Dixie L. James, San Rafael 5:58:23
51. Sandra L. Heidtman, Torrance 5:59:37
52. Dotti A. Muxlow, Burnsville,MN 5:60:00
53. Mary A. Chambers, Sioux Falls,SD 5:60:02
54. Linda K. Burri Tjaden, Sioux Falls,SD 5:60:02
55. Victor Macias, Los Angeles 6:02:41
56. Linda W. Burnham, San Diego 6:09:12
57. Marcos Honnes, Los Angeles 6:09:19
58. Kathlyn A. Pierce, Acton 6:11:57
59. Jan M. Joseph, Highland 6:11:57
60. Debbi C. Fullington, Sunland 6:11:58
61. Richard Moskun, Los Angeles 6:12:38
62. Jerri Lamb, Los Angeles 6:12:38
63. Elias Arellano, Los Angeles 6:13:48
64. Karl F. Twyman, Port Hueneme 6:16:57
65. Joe A. Mapalo, Bloomington 6:17:17
66. Judith A. Mapalo, Bloomington 6:17:18
67. Jon Borset, San Francisco 6:17:45
68. Noni Fimbres, Whittier 6:21:47
69. Michael Marin, Los Angeles 6:24:19
70. Joan C. Pledger, Glendale 6:25:20
71. Eloise Donnell, Los Angeles 6:25:21
72. Homa Ferdowsi, Redondo Beach 6:26:27
73. Robert A. Edison, Moorpark 6:26:37
74. Robin A. Clark, Camarillo 6:26:55
75. Sergio Sazo, Los Angeles 6:29:56
76. Arlene Lovejoy-Bluem, Los Angeles 6:31:11
77. Kristina Rolle, Cypress 6:32:08
78. John Radich, Monrovia 6:32:30
79. Dick W. Guttman, Connersville,IN 6:34:04
80. John S. Witt, Honolulu,HI 6:35:55
81. Kathi A. Salinas, Rancho Cucamonga 6:42:29
82. Edward A. Waukazo, Hemet 6:42:38
83. Lucky Sawamura, Los Angeles 6:42:58
84. Pamela L. Coker, San Diego 6:43:07
85. Catherine Bluem, Los Angeles 6:44:37
86. Wendelyn A. Young, Los Angeles 6:44:38
87. Margarita Persico, Westlake Village 6:46:09
88. Michelle R. Houston, Azusa 6:47:31
89. Judith Brown, Los Angeles 6:51:52
90. Stephen C. Lipira, Los Angeles 6:54:00
91. Carol Asuncion, Los Angeles 6:54:43
92. Kim D. Anderson, Agoura Hills 6:56:40
93. Clifford Renfro, Los Angeles 6:59:28
94. Trudie M. Abraham, Los Angeles 6:60:12
95. John R. Merriam, Santa Monica 7:02:37
96. Patricia E. Clemence, Independence,MO .7:05:28
97. Shirley L. Rude, Claremont 7:05:33
98. Russell Cataldo, Los Angeles 7:06:00
99. Anton G. Cataldo, Burbank 7:06:00
100. Midge Renfro, Los Angeles 7:07:45
101. Adam Liebreich-Johnsen, Los Angeles ..7:08:11
102. George Johnsen, Los Angeles 7:08:17
103. Roy E. Tanaka, Cerritos 7:11:15
104. Rebecca Honnes, Los Angeles 7:11:36
105. Ramon Macias, Los Angeles 7:11:36
106. Deborah J. Gal, Los Angeles 7:11:41
107. Maria Hernandez, Los Angeles 7:12:53
108. Heather Brown, Los Angeles 7:14:12
109. Mary F. Wormsbecker, Big Bear Lake ...7:17:58
110. Linda L. Hauxhurst, Lake Forest 7:17:58
111. Jeannette Sabogal, Los Angeles 7:26:42
112. Lidia Sanchez, Culver City 7:33:36
113. Theresa Diaz, Los Angeles 7:33:37
114. Ashok S. Rao, Glendale 7:35:26
115. Sheryl L. Welsh, Glendora 7:42:33
116. Deidre Manzo, Los Angeles 7:45:15
117. Fabian R. Wesson, Los Angeles 7:49:34
118. Jenny L. Ash, Los Angeles 7:49:34
119. Jenny M. Caguimbal, Manhattan Beach .7:49:35
120. Reva M. Wallace, Compton 7:55:01
121. Cathleen Trapani, Simi Valley 7:60:50
122. Noemi Marin, Los Angeles 8:01:29
123. Toby Marin, Los Angeles 8:01:29
124. Roberta L. Hines, Long Beach 8:03:54
125. Bill Greenlee, Culver City 8:11:18
126. Siamak Afshar, West Covina 8:11:30
127. Omar Gonzalez, Los Angeles 8:25:39
128. Lazar Burnley, Los Angeles 9:23:41
129. Jolacerav Burnley, Los Angeles 9:23:41

ACKNOWLEDGEMENTS

The editor is grateful for permission to excerpt material from 10 years of marathon coverage by the following writers for the Los Angeles Times: Sports—Elliott Almond, Chris Baker, Julie Cart, Jerry Crowe, Mike Downey, Mal Florence, Jim Hodges, Jeff Meyers, Jim Murray, Scott Ostler, Mike Penner, Bill Plaschke, Steve Springer, Elliott Teaford. News—Laurie Becklund, Russell Chandler, David Colker, Cathleen Decker, Andrew S. Doctoroff, David Ferrell, Larry Gordon, Scott Harris, Steve Harvey, Dianne Klein, Frederick M. Muir, Lisa Respers, Stephanie Simon, Sheryl Stolberg, Ginger Thompson, Wendy Witherspoon. Features—Paul Dean, David Larsen, Gary Libman, Dick Roraback.

Members of the Los Angeles Times Syndicate staff providing support for this project were: Permissions—Lupe Salazar, Jacquie Araujo, Francine Della-Catena. Production and Operations—Harry Yip, Conchita Cox, Yvonne Hill, Ray Recendez, Adam McGaughey. Promotion—Cathy Irvine, Susan Gross.

At Los Angeles Marathon headquarters, technical and research assistance was provided by Lee Barr, Joe Blackstone, Autumn Burke, Keli Butler, Terra Hannah, Edye Hill, Jane Jones, Edna Milner, Lisa Rosenfield, Reggie Stanley and Joyce Snyder.

The Department of Special Collections at University Research Library, UCLA, assisted in obtaining photographs.

Principal research and interviews by Diana Fox.

PHOTO CREDITS

Foreword—Page 4: LAM.

Introduction—Page 5: Marathon Foto. Page 6: Marathon Foto. Page 7: LAM. Page 8: Marathon Foto. Page 9: S. Dawson (left); Marathon Foto (right).

Part I: The Anniversary—Page 10: Iris Schneider, L.A. Times. Page 12: Lori Shepler, L.A. Times (left); Carol Cheetham, L.A. Times (all others). Page 13: Al Seib, L.A. Times. Page 14: Marathon Foto. Page 16: Iris Schneider, L.A. Times. Page 17: Iris Schneider, L.A. Times.

Part II: A Civic Festival—Page 19: LAM. Page 20: Lori Shepler, L.A. Times. Page 22: LAM (left). Page 22-23: Ellen Jaskol, L.A. Times. Page 23: LAM (right). Page 24: Tim DeFrisco, All-Sport USA (right center); LAM (all others). Page 25: Mathiesen (two in center); LAM (upper right). Page 26: Lori Shepler, L.A. Times. Page 28: Muscolino, Fuji Photo (left); LAM (all others). Page 29: Muscolino, Fuji Photo (left); Marathon Foto (right). Page 30: Thomas Kelsey, L.A. Times (left); LAM (upper right); Mathiesen (lower right.). Page 31: J. Mitel, Fuji Photo (Asner); Marathon Foto (Jarreau); D. Laird, Fuji Photo (Lewis); J. Mitel, Fuji Photo (Joyner-Kersee); LAM (all others). Page 32: Howard L. Bingham. Page 33: Theodora Litsios, L.A. Times (left); LAM (right). Page 34: Howard L. Bingham (left); Marathon Foto (right). Page 35: LAM. Page 36-37: Mark Harris. Page 38: D. Gifford, Fuji Photo.

Part III: The Runners—Page 41: Marathon Foto. Page 42: Mark Harris (lower left); LAM (all others). Page 43: Howard L. Bingham. Page 44: Marathon Foto (left); LAM (right). Page 45: Steve Dykes, L.A. Times. Page 46: LAM. Page 47: D. Gifford, Fuji Photo (left); Marathon Foto (cen-

ter). Page 48: J. Argon. Page 49: Mathiesen. Page 51: Lori Shepler, L.A. Times. Page 52: J. Argon, Fuji Photo (top); J. Mitel, Fuji Photo (bottom left); D. Gifford, (bottom right). Page 53: Mark Harris. Page 54: PPS. Page 56: Marathon Foto. Page 57: Gary Friedman, L.A. Times. Page 58: Lori Shepler, L.A. Times. Page 59: D. Gifford, Fuji Photo. Page 60: Steve Dykes, L.A. Times. Page 61: Howard L. Bingham (upper left); Dawson, Fuji Photo (upper right); J. Mitel, Fuji Photo (next to upper right); LAM (all others). Page 62: Marathon Foto. Page 65: Muscolino, Fuji Photo. Page 66: Paul Lester. Page 67: Howard L. Bingham (top); Foster and Kleiser (bottom). Page 68: Silver Photography. Page 69: Tom LaBonge (upper left); LAM (lower left); Todd Bigelow, L.A. Times (upper right). Page 70: Ricardo DeAratanha, L.A. Times. Page 71: PPS (left); Francine Orr, L.A. Times (center); D. Gifford (right). Page 72: LAM. Page 73: LAM (top); Marathon Foto (center); PPS (right). Page 74: Marathon Foto. Page 75: LAM. Page 76: LAM. Page 77: Muscolino, Fuji Photo (top); LAM (all others). Page 78: LAM (left); Marathon Foto (right). Page 79: LAM. Page 80: Irfan Khan, L.A. Times (left); Thomas Kelsey, L.A. Times (center); LAM (right). Page 81: LAM (left); R. Newnan (right). Page 82: Howard L. Bingham. Page 83: Iris Schneider, L.A. Times. Page 84: Mel Melcon, L.A. Times. Page 85: LAM (upper left); Gary Friedman, L.A. Times (lower right). Page 86: LAM. Page 87: Budd Symes. Page 88: J. Argon, Fuji Photo (lower left); LAM (all others). Page 89: LAM. Page 90: Robert Durell, L.A. Times. Page 91: PPS. Page 92: Mark Harris (left); LAM (right). Page 93: LAM (left); D. Gifford, Fuji Photo (right). Page 94: Mark Harris.

Part IV: The Race—Page 96: LAM. Page 98: Jim Loedding. Page 99: Thomas Kelsey, L.A. Times. Page 100: Steve Dykes, L.A. Times. Page 101: LAM. Page 102: Thomas Kelsey, L.A.

Times. Page 103: LAM. Page 104: Joe Kennedy, L.A. Times. Page 105: LAM. Page 106: Con Keyes, L.A. Times. Page 107: LAM. Page 108: Howard L. Bingham. Page 109: LAM. Page 110-111 (left to right): Marathon Foto; Mathiesen, Fuji Photo; Mark Harris; Con Keyes, L.A. Times; Thomas Kelsey, L.A. Times. Page 112: Lori Shepler, L.A. Times. Page 113: Gary Friedman, L.A. Times (top); Thomas Kelsey, L.A. Times (bottom). Page 114: Lori Shepler, L.A. Times. Page 115: LAM. Page 116: Cuffari, Fuji Photo. Page 117: LAM. Page 118: Mel Melcon, L.A. Times. Page 119: Gary Friedman, L.A. Times. Page 120: Carol Cheetham, L.A. Times. Page 121: Gary Friedman, L.A. Times. Page 123: LAM (top); Lawrence Ho, L.A. Times (bottom). Page 124: Lawrence Ho, L.A. Times. Page 125: Lawrence Ho, L.A. Times (left); Lori Shepler, L.A. Times (center and right). Page 126: Lori Shepler, L.A. Times. Page 127: Francine Orr, L.A. Times. Page 128: Francine Orr, L.A. Times. Page 129: Iris Schneider, L.A. Times. Page 130: Patrick Downs, L.A. Times. Page 131: Marathon Foto (top); LAM (all others). Page 132: Marathon Foto. Page 133: J. Mitel, Fuji Photo (top left); LAM (top right); Steve Dykes, L.A. Times (bottom).

Part V: The Numbers—Page 168: Con Keyes, L.A. Times.

Key:
LAM = photo provided by L.A. Marathon.
PPS = photo provided by subject.

Traffic cop keeps autos at bay while (from left) Rod Dixon, Gary Tuttle, Gidamas Shahanga and Rafael Zepeda make their way through an intersection in first L.A. Marathon.